MW01016728

CLYMER®

SUZUKI

VOLUSIA/BOULEVARD C50 • 2001-2011

The publishers of the world's finest mechanical how-to manuals

CLYMER®

P.O. Box 12901, Overland Park, Kansas 66282-2901

FIRST EDITION
First Printing December, 2006

SECOND EDITION
First Printing June, 2009

THIRD EDITION
First Printing May, 2012

Printed in U.S.A.

CLYMER and colophon are registered trademarks of Penton Business Media, Inc.

ISBN-10: 1-59969-546-4

ISBN-13: 978-1-59969-546-4

Library of Congress: 2012937682

AUTHOR: Mike Morlan.

TECHNICAL PHOTOGRAPHY: Mike Morlan.

TECHNICAL ILLUSTRATIONS: Mitzi McCarthy.

WIRING DIAGRAMS: Bob Meyer and Rick Arens.

EDITOR: Steve Thomas and James Grooms.

PRODUCTION: Holly Messinger.

TOOLS AND EQUIPMENT: K & L Supply Co. at www.klsupply.com.

COVER: Mark Clifford Photography at www.markclifford.com.

CLYMER®

Publisher Ron Rogers

EDITORIAL

Editorial Director
James Grooms

Editor
Steven Thomas

Associate Editor
Rick Arens

Authors
Ed Scott
Ron Wright
Michael Morlan
George Parise
Jay Bogart

Illustrators
Bob Meyer
Steve Amos
Errol McCarthy
Mitzi McCarthy

SALES

Sales Manager–Marine/I&T
Jay Lipton

Sales Manager–Powersport
Matt Tusken

CUSTOMER SERVICE

Customer Service Manager
Terri Cannon

Customer Service Representatives
Dinah Bunnell
Suzanne Johnson
April LeBlond
Sherry Rudkin

PRODUCTION

Director of Production
Dylan Goodwin

Production Manager
Greg Araujo

Senior Production Editors
Darin Watson
Adriane Wineinger

Production Editor
Ashley Bally

Associate Production Editor
Samantha Collins

P.O. Box 12901, Overland Park, KS 66282-2901 • 800-262-1954 • 913-967-1719

More information available at *clymer.com*

CONTENTS

QUICK REFERENCE DATA

MOTORCYCLE INFORMATION

MODEL:_____ YEAR:_____

VIN NUMBER:_____

ENGINE SERIAL NUMBER:_____

CARBURETOR/THROTTLE BODY SERIAL NUMBER OR I.D. MARK:_____

TIRE SPECIFICATIONS

Item	Front	Rear
Tire type	Tube	Tube
Size	130/90-16M/C (67H)	170/80-15M/C (77H)
Minimum tread depth	1.6 mm (0.06 in.)	2.0 mm (0.08 in.)
Inflation pressure (cold)*		
Touring models	225 kPa (33 psi)	225 kPa (33 psi)
All other models		
Solo	200 kPa (29 psi)	250 kPa (36 psi)
Rider and passenger	200 kPa (29 psi)	250 kPa (36 psi)

*Tire inflation pressure for original equipment tires. Aftermarket tires may require different inflation pressure. The use of tires other than those specified by the manufacturer may affect handling.

RECOMMENDED LUBRICANTS AND FLUIDS

Brake fluid	DOT 4
Engine coolant	
Type	Ethylene glycol-based containing corrosion inhibitors for aluminum radiators
Ratio	50:50 distilled water and antifreeze
Capacity*	1.5 L (1.6 qt.)
Engine oil	
Classification	API SF/SG or SH/SJ with JASO MA
Viscosity	SAE 10W40
	(continued)

RECOMMENDED LUBRICANTS AND FLUIDS (continued)

Engine oil (continued)	
Capacity	
Oil change only	3.0 L (3.2 qt.)
Oil and filter change	3.4 L (3.6 qt.)
When engine completely dry	3.7 L (3.9 qt.)
Final drive oil	
Type	SAE 90, GL-5 hypoid
Capacity	200-220 ml (6.8-7.4 oz.)
Fork oil	
Viscosity	Suzuki SS-08 (#10) fork oil or equivalent
Capacity per leg	412 ml (13.9 oz.)
Fuel	
Type	Unleaded
Octane	
U.S. and Canada models	87 [(R + M)/2 method] or research octane of 91 or higher
Non-U.S. and Canada models	91
Fuel tank capacity*	
2001-2004 models	17.0 L (4.5 gal.)
2005-on models	15.5 L (4.1 gal)

*Includes reserve tank

MAINTENANCE AND TUNE-UP SPECIFICATIONS

Battery	
Type	FTX12-BS Maintenance free (sealed)
Capacity	12 volt 10 amp hour
Brake pedal	
Free play	20-30 mm (0.8-1.2 in)
Height	75-85 mm (3.0-3.3 in.)
Clutch lever free play	10-15 mm (0.4-0.6 in.)
Compression pressure (at sea level)	
Standard	1300-1700 kPa (188.5-246.5 psi)
Service limit	1100 kPa (159.5 psi)
Maximum difference between cylinders	200 kPa (28 psi)
Engine oil pressure (hot)	350-650 kPa (51-94 psi) at 3000 rpm
Fast idle TP sensor voltage differential	
2005-on models	0.064-0.096 volts
Fast idle speed	2100 rpm
Idle speed	1000-1200 rpm
Ignition timing	5° BTDC at 1100 rpm
Radiator cap release pressure	95-125 kPa (13.8-18.1 psi)
Spark plug	
Standard plug	
2009-on California, UK, Europe, and Australia models	NGK DR7EA, ND X22ESUR-u
All other models	NGK DPR7EA-9, ND X22EPR-U9
Colder plug	
2009-on California, UK, Europe, and Australia models	NGK DR8EA, ND X24ESR-U
All other models	NGK DPR8EA-9, NDX24EPR-U9

(Continued)

MAINTENANCE AND TUNE-UP SPECIFICATIONS (continued)

Spark plug gap	
2009-on California, UK, Europe, and Australia models	0.6-0.7 mm (0.024-0.028 in.)
All other models	0.8-0.9 mm (0.031-0.035 in.)
Throttle cable free play	2.0-4.0 mm (0.08-0.16 in.)
Valve clearance (cold)	
Intake	0.08-0.13 mm (0.003-0.005 in.)
Exhaust	0.17-0.22 mm (0.007-0.009 in.)
Wheel runout (front and rear)	
Axial	2.0 mm (0.08 in.)
Radial	2.0 mm (0.08 in.)

MAINTENANCE AND TUNE-UP TORQUE SPECIFICATIONS

Item	N•m	in.-lb.	ft.-lb.
Cylinder head cover cap bolt			
(2009-on models)	25	–	18
Engine oil drain plug			
2001-2008 models	23	–	17
2009-on models	21	–	15
Final drive oil drain plug	23	–	17
Fork cap bolt	45	–	33
Fork lower clamp bolts	33	–	24
Front axle	65	–	48
Front axle pinch bolts	33	–	24
Main oil gallery plug	18	159	–
Pivot lever mounting bolt	78	–	58
Pivot link (both ends)	78	–	58
Rear axle nut	65	–	48
Shock absorber mounting bolts	50	–	37
Spark plug			
2009-on California, UK, Europe and Australia models	11	97	-
All other models	18	–	13
Swing arm			
Right pivot locknut	100	–	74
Left pivot bolt	100	–	74
Right pivot bolt	9.5	84	–

CHAPTER ONE

GENERAL INFORMATION

This detailed and comprehensive manual covers the Suzuki Volusia/Boulevard C50 models from 2001-2011.

Procedures and specifications *unique* to the 2009-2011 models are covered in the Supplement at the end of this manual.

The text provides complete information on maintenance, tune-up, repair and overhaul. Hundreds of photographs and illustrations guide the reader through every job. All procedures, tables and figures are designed for the reader who may be working on the motorcycle for the first time.

MANUAL ORGANIZATION

All dimensions and capacities are expressed in metric and U.S. standard units of measurement.

Specifications, when applicable, are listed in the tables at the end of each chapter.

Each chapter is thumb-tabbed for easy reference. Main headings within the chapter are listed in the table of contents and the index.

This chapter provides general information on shop safety, tool use, service fundamentals and shop supplies. **Tables 1-8** at the end of the chapter include general motorcycle and shop information.

Chapter Two provides methods for quick and accurate diagnosis of problems. Troubleshooting procedures present typical symptoms and logical methods to pinpoint and repair the problem.

Chapter Three explains all routine maintenance necessary to keep the motorcycle running well. Chapter Three also includes recommended tune-up

procedures, eliminating the need to constantly consult the chapters on the various assemblies.

Subsequent chapters describe specific systems such as the engine, transmission, clutch, drive system, fuel and exhaust systems, suspension and brakes. Each procedure is discussed in step-by-step form.

WARNINGS, CAUTIONS AND NOTES

The terms WARNING, CAUTION and NOTE have specific meanings in this manual.

A WARNING emphasizes areas where injury or even death could result from negligence. Mechanical damage may also occur. WARNINGS *are to be taken seriously.*

A CAUTION emphasizes areas where equipment damage could result. Disregarding a CAUTION could cause permanent mechanical damage, though injury is unlikely.

A NOTE provides additional information to make a step or procedure easier or clearer. Disregarding a NOTE could cause inconvenience, but would not cause equipment damage or personal injury.

SAFETY

Professional mechanics can work for years and never sustain a serious injury or mishap. Follow these guidelines and practice common sense to safely service the motorcycle.

1. Do not operate the motorcycle in an enclosed area. The exhaust gasses contain carbon monoxide, an odor-

less, colorless, and tasteless poisonous gas. Carbon monoxide levels build quickly in small enclosed areas and can cause unconsciousness and death in a short time. Make sure the work area is properly ventilated or operate the motorcycle outside.

2. *Never* use gasoline or any extremely flammable liquid to clean parts. Refer to *Handling Gasoline Safely* and *Cleaning Parts* in this chapter.

3. *Never* smoke or use a torch in the vicinity of flammable liquids, such as gasoline or cleaning solvent.

4. If welding or brazing on the motorcycle, remove the fuel tank, carburetor or fuel injection components and shocks to a safe distance at least 15 m (50 ft.) away.

5. Use the correct type and size tools to avoid damaging fasteners.

6. Keep tools clean and in good condition. Replace or repair worn or damaged equipment.

7. When loosening a tight fastener, be guided by what would happen if the tool slips.

8. When replacing fasteners, make sure the new fasteners are the same size and strength as the original ones.

9. Keep the work area clean and organized.

10. Wear eye protection *any* time eye safety is in question. This includes procedures involving drilling, grinding, hammering, compressed air and chemicals.

11. Wear the correct clothing for the job. Tie up or cover long hair so it can not get caught in moving equipment.

12. Do not carry sharp tools in clothing pockets.

13. Always have an approved fire extinguisher available. Make sure it is rated for gasoline (Class B) and electrical (Class C) fires.

14. Do not use compressed air to clean clothes, the motorcycle or the work area. Debris may be blown into your eyes or skin. *Never* direct compressed air at anyone. Do not allow children to use or play with any compressed air equipment.

15. When using compressed air to dry rotating parts, hold the part so it can not rotate. Do not allow the force of the air to spin the part. The air jet is capable of rotating parts at extreme speed. The part may disintegrate, causing serious injury.

16. Do not inhale the dust created by brake pad and clutch wear. These particles may contain asbestos. In addition, some types of insulating materials and gaskets may contain asbestos. Inhaling asbestos particles is hazardous to health.

17. Never work on the motorcycle while someone is working under it.

18. When placing the motorcycle on a stand, make sure it is secure before walking away.

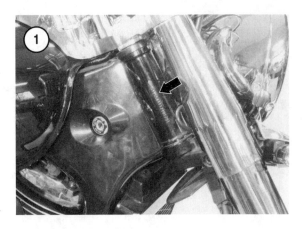

Handling Gasoline Safely

Gasoline is a volatile flammable liquid and is one of the most dangerous items in the shop. Because gasoline is used so often, many people forget it is hazardous. Only use gasoline as fuel for gasoline internal combustion engines. Keep in mind, when working on a motorcycle, gasoline is always present in the fuel tank, fuel line and carburetor or fuel injection system. To avoid a disastrous accident when working around the fuel system, carefully observe the following precautions:

1. *Never* use gasoline to clean parts. See *Cleaning Parts* in this chapter.

2. Wear gloves to prevent skin contact with gasoline. If gasoline comes in contact with your skin, wash thoroughly with soap and water.

3. When working on the fuel system, work outside or in a well-ventilated area.

4. Do not add fuel to the fuel tank or service the fuel system while the motorcycle is near open flames, sparks or where someone is smoking. Gasoline vapor is heavier than air, it collects in low areas and is more easily ignited than liquid gasoline.

5. Allow the engine to cool completely before working on any fuel system component.

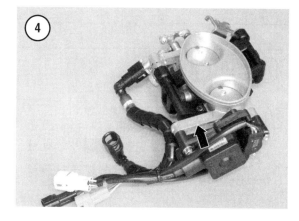

vapor buildup, fire and serious injury, observe each product warning label and note the following:

1. Read and observe the entire product label before using any chemical. Always know what type of chemical is being used and whether it is poisonous and/or flammable.

2. Do not use more than one type of cleaning solvent at a time. If mixing chemicals is called for, measure the proper amounts according to the manufacturer.

3. Work in a well-ventilated area.

4. Wear chemical-resistant gloves.

5. Wear safety glasses.

6. Wear a vapor respirator if the instructions call for it.

7. Wash hands and arms thoroughly after cleaning parts.

8. Keep chemical products away from children and pets.

9. Thoroughly clean all oil, grease and cleaner residue from any part that must be heated.

10. Use a nylon brush when cleaning parts. Metal brushes may cause a spark.

11. When using a parts washer, only use the solvent recommended by the manufacturer. Make sure the parts washer is equipped with a metal lid that will lower in case of fire.

6. When draining the carburetor or fuel injection system, catch the fuel in a plastic container and then pour it into an approved gasoline storage devise.

7. Do not store gasoline in glass containers. If the glass breaks, a serious explosion or fire may occur.

8. Immediately wipe up spilled gasoline with rags. Store the rags in a metal container with a lid until they can be properly disposed of, or place them outside in a safe place for the fuel to evaporate.

9. Do not pour water onto a gasoline fire. Water spreads the fire and makes it more difficult to put out. Use a class B, BC or ABC fire extinguisher to extinguish the fire.

10. Always turn off the engine before refueling. Do not spill fuel onto the engine or exhaust system. Do not overfill the fuel tank. Leave an air space at the top of the tank to allow room for the fuel to expand due to temperature fluctuations.

Cleaning Parts

Cleaning parts is one of the more tedious and difficult service jobs performed in the home garage. There are many types of chemical cleaners and solvents available for shop use. Most are poisonous and extremely flammable. To prevent chemical exposure,

Warning Labels

Most manufacturers attach information and warning labels to the motorcycle. These labels contain instructions that are important to personal safety when operating, servicing, transporting and storing the motorcycle. Refer to the owner's manual for the description and location of labels. Order replacement labels from the manufacturer if they are missing or damaged.

SERIAL NUMBERS

Serial numbers are stamped on various locations on the frame, engine, transmission and fuel system components. Record these numbers in the *Quick Reference Data* section in the front of the book. Have these numbers available when ordering parts.

The frame serial number (VIN number) is stamped on the right side of the steering head (**Figure 1**).

The engine serial number is stamped on a pad on the upper surface of the right crankcase (**Figure 2**).

The carburetor serial number (**Figure 3**) is located on the right side of the carburetor body above the float bowl.

The fuel injection throttle body serial number is located on an upper boss (**Figure 4**).

FASTENERS

WARNING
Do not install fasteners with a strength
classification lower than that originally
installed by the manufacturer. Doing so
may cause equipment failure and/or
damage.

Proper fastener selection and installation is important to ensure that the motorcycle operates as designed and can be serviced efficiently. The choice of original equipment fasteners is not arrived at by chance. Make sure that replacement fasteners meet all the same requirements as the originals.

Threaded Fasteners

Threaded fasteners secure most of the components on the motorcycle. Most are tightened by turning them clockwise (right-hand threads). If the normal rotation of the component being tightened would loosen the fastener, it may have left-hand threads. If a left-hand threaded fastener is used, it is noted in the text.

Two dimensions are required to match the size of the fastener: the number of threads in a given distance and the outside diameter of the threads.

Two systems are currently used to specify threaded fastener dimensions: the U.S. Standard system and the metric system (**Figure 5**). Pay particular attention when working with unidentified fasteners; mismatching thread types can damage threads.

NOTE
To ensure that the fastener threads are
not mismatched or cross-threaded,
start all fasteners by hand. If a fastener
is hard to start or turn, determine the
cause before tightening with a wrench.

The length (L, **Figure 6**), diameter (D) and distance between thread crests (pitch) (T) classify metric screws and bolts. A typical bolt may be identified by the numbers, 8—1.25 × 130. This indicates the bolt has diameter of 8 mm, the distance between thread crests is 1.25 mm and the length is 130 mm. Always measure bolt length as shown in L, **Figure 6** to avoid purchasing replacements of the wrong length.

The numbers located on the top of the fastener (**Figure 6**) indicate the strength of metric screws and bolts. Typically, the higher the number, the stronger the fastener is. Unnumbered fasteners are the weakest.

Many screws, bolts and studs are combined with nuts to secure particular components. To indicate the

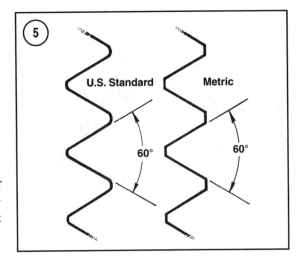

U.S. Standard   Metric
60°   60°

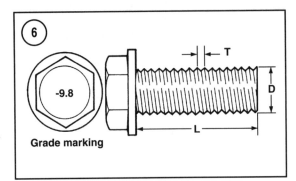

-9.8

Grade marking

T

D

L

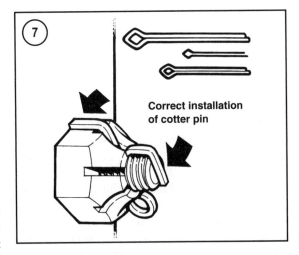

Correct installation
of cotter pin

size of a nut, manufacturers specify the internal diameter and the thread pitch.

The measurement across two flats on a nut or bolt indicates the wrench size.

Torque Specifications

The materials used in the manufacture of the motorcycle may be subjected to uneven stresses if the fasteners of the various subassemblies are not in-

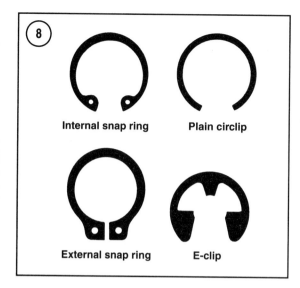

Internal snap ring   Plain circlip

External snap ring   E-clip

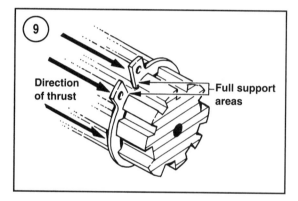

Direction of thrust — Full support areas

tance to vibration. Self-locking fasteners cannot be reused. The material used to form the lock becomes distorted after the initial installation and removal. Discard and replace self-locking fasteners after their removal. Do not replace self-locking fasteners with standard fasteners.

Washers

There are two basic types of washers: flat washers and lockwashers. Flat washers are simple discs with a hole to fit a screw or bolt. Lockwashers are used to prevent a fastener from working loose. Washers can be used as spacers and seals, or to help distribute fastener load and to prevent the fastener from damaging the component.

As with fasteners, when replacing washers make sure the replacement washers are of the same design and quality.

Cotter Pins

A cotter pin is a split metal pin inserted into a hole or slot to prevent a fastener from loosening. In certain applications, such as the rear axle on a motorcycle, the fastener must be secured in this way. For these applications, a cotter pin and castellated (slotted) nut is used.

To use a cotter pin, first make sure the diameter is correct for the hole in the fastener. After correctly tightening the fastener and aligning the holes, insert the cotter pin through the hole and bend the ends over the fastener (**Figure 7**). Unless instructed to do so, never loosen a tightened fastener to align the holes. If the holes do not align, tighten the fastener just enough to achieve alignment.

Cotter pins are available in various diameters and lengths. Measure length from the bottom of the head to the tip of the shortest pin.

Snap Rings and E-clips

Snap rings (**Figure 8**) are circular-shaped metal retaining clips. They are required to secure parts and gears in place on parts such as shafts, pins or rods. External type snap rings are used to retain items on shafts. Internal type snap rings secure parts within housing bores. In some applications, in addition to securing the component(s), snap rings of varying thickness also determine endplay. These are usually called selective snap rings.

Two basic types of snap rings are used: machined and stamped snap rings. Machined snap rings (**Figure 9**) can be installed in either direction, since both

stalled and tightened correctly. Fasteners that are improperly installed or work loose can cause extensive damage. It is essential to use an accurate torque wrench, described in this chapter, with the torque specifications in this manual.

Specifications for torque are provided in Newton-meters (N•m), foot-pounds (ft.-lb.) and inch-pounds (in.-lb.). Refer to **Table 4** for torque recomendations. To use **Table 4**, first determine the size of the fastener as described in *Fasteners* in this chapter. Torque specifications for specific components are at the end of the appropriate chapters. Torque wrenches are covered in the *Tools* section.

Self-Locking Fasteners

Several types of bolts, screws and nuts incorporate a system that creates interference between the two fasteners. Interference is achieved in various ways. The most common types are the nylon insert nut, or a dry adhesive coating on the threads of a bolt.

Self-locking fasteners offer greater holding strength than standard fasteners, which improves their resis-

faces have sharp edges. Stamped snap rings (**Figure 10**) are manufactured with a sharp edge and a round edge. When installing a stamped circlip in a thrust application, install the sharp edge facing away from the part producing the thrust.

E-clips are used when it is not practical to use a circlip. Remove E-clips with a flat blade screwdriver by prying between the shaft and E-clip. To install an E-clip, center it over the shaft groove and push or tap it into place.

Observe the following when installing snap rings:
1. Remove and install snap rings with snap ring pliers. See *Tools* in this chapter.
2. In some applications, it may be necessary to replace snap rings after removing them.
3. Compress or expand snap rings only enough to install them. If overly expanded, they lose their retaining ability.
4. After installing a snap ring, make sure it seats completely.
5. Wear eye protection when removing and installing snap rings.

SHOP SUPPLIES

Lubricants and Fluids

Periodic lubrication helps ensure a long service life for any type of equipment. Using the correct type of lubricant is as important as performing the lubrication service, although in an emergency the wrong type is better than none. The following section describes the types of lubricants most often required. Make sure to follow the manufacturer's recommendations for lubricant types.

Engine oils

Engine oil is classified by two standards: the American Petroleum Institute (API) service classification and the Society of Automotive Engineers (SAE) viscosity rating. This information is on the oil container label. Two letters indicate the API service classification. The number or sequence of numbers and letter (10W-40 for example) is the oil's viscosity rating. The API service classification and the SAE viscosity index are not indications of oil quality.

The service classification indicates that the oil meets specific lubrication standards. The first letter in the classification, *S,* indicates that the oil is for gasoline engines. The second letter indicates the standard the oil satisfies.

When selecting an API classified oil make sure the classification is correct (Chapter Three, **Table 3**) and

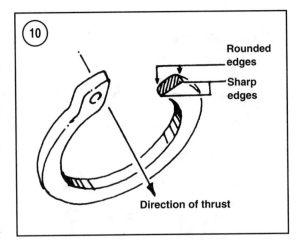

the circular API service label does not indicate the oil as *ENERGY CONSERVING.* This type of oil is not designed for motorcycle applications. Using oil with the incorrect classification can cause engine damage.

In addition to the API classification, some oils carry the Japanese Automobile Standards Organization (JASO) classification for use in motorcycle engines. These motorcycle specific oils (JASO T 903 Standard*)* with the MA (high-friction applications) designation are designed for motorcycle applications.

Viscosity is an indication of the oil's thickness. Thin oils have a lower number while thick oils have a higher number. Engine oils fall into the 5- to 50-weight range for single-grade oils.

Most manufacturers recommend multi-grade oil. These oils perform efficiently across a wide range of operating conditions. Multi-grade oils are identified by a *W* after the first number, which indicates the low-temperature viscosity.

Engine oils are most commonly mineral (petroleum) based; however, synthetic and semi-synthetic types are used more frequently. When selecting engine oil, follow the manufacturer's recommendation for type, classification and viscosity when selecting engine oil.

Greases

Grease is lubricating oil with thickening agents added to it. The National Lubricating Grease Institute (NLGI) grades grease. Grades range from No. 000 to No. 6, with No. 6 being the thickest. Typical multipurpose grease is NLGI No. 2. For specific applications, manufacturers may recommend water-resistant grease or one with an additive such as molybdenum disulfide (MoS^2).

Brake fluid

Brake fluid is the hydraulic fluid used to transmit hydraulic pressure (force) to the wheel brakes. Brake fluid is classified by the Department of Transportation (DOT). This classification, DOT 4 for example, appears on the fluid container.

Each type of brake fluid has its own definite characteristics. Do not intermix different types of brake fluid as this may cause brake system failure. DOT 5 brake fluid is silicone based. DOT 5 is not compatible with other brake fluids or in systems for which it was not designed. Mixing DOT 5 fluid with other fluids may cause brake system failure. When adding brake fluid, *only* use the fluid recommended by the manufacturer. Refer to Chapter Three, **Table 3**.

Brake fluid will damage any plastic, painted or plated surface it contacts. Use extreme care when working with brake fluid and remove any spills immediately with soap and water.

Hydraulic brake systems require clean and moisture free brake fluid. Never reuse brake fluid. Keep containers and reservoirs properly sealed.

> *WARNING*
> *Never put a mineral-based (petroleum) oil into the brake system. Mineral oil will cause rubber parts in the system to swell and break apart, resulting in complete brake failure.*

Coolant

Coolant is a mixture of water and antifreeze used to dissipate engine heat. Ethylene glycol is the most common form of antifreeze used. Check the motorcycle manufacturer's recommendations (Chapter Three, **Table 3**) when selecting antifreeze; most require one specifically designed for use in aluminum engines. These types of antifreeze have additives that inhibit corrosion.

Only mix distilled water with antifreeze. Impurities in tap water may damage internal cooling system passages.

Cleaners, Degreasers and Solvents

Many chemicals are available to remove oil, grease and other residue from the motorcycle. Before using cleaning solvents, consider how they will be used and disposed of, particularly if they are not water-soluble. Local ordinances may require special procedures for the disposal of many types of cleaning chemicals. Refer to *Safety* in this chapter for more information on their use.

Use brake parts cleaner to clean brake system components because contact with petroleum-based products will damage seals. Brake parts cleaner leaves no residue. Use electrical contact cleaner to clean electrical connections and components without leaving any residue. Carburetor cleaner is a powerful solvent used to remove fuel deposits and varnish from fuel system components. Use this cleaner carefully, as it may damage finishes.

Generally, degreasers are strong cleaners used to remove heavy accumulations of grease from engine and frame components.

Most solvents are designed to be used with a parts washing cabinet for individual component cleaning. For safety, use only nonflammable or high flash point solvents.

Gasket Sealant

Sealants are often used with a gasket or seal, or occasionally alone. Follow the manufacturer's recommendation when using sealants. Use extreme care when choosing a sealant different from the type originally recommended. Choose sealants based on their resistance to heat, various fluids and their sealing capabilities.

One of the most common sealants is RTV, or room temperature vulcanizing sealant. This sealant cures at room temperature over a specific time period. This allows the repositioning of components without damaging gaskets.

Moisture in the air causes the RTV sealant to cure. Always install the tube cap as soon as possible after applying RTV sealant. RTV sealant has a limited shelf life and will not cure properly if the shelf life has expired. Keep partial tubes sealed and discard them if they have surpassed the expiration date.

Applying RTV sealant

Clean all old gasket residue from the mating surfaces. Remove all gasket material from blind threaded holes; it can cause inaccurate bolt torque. Spray the mating surfaces with aerosol parts cleaner and then wipe with a lint-free cloth. The area must be clean for the sealant to adhere.

Apply RTV sealant in a continuous bead 2-3 mm (0.08-0.12 in.) thick. Circle all the fastener holes unless otherwise specified. Do not allow any sealant to enter these holes. Assemble and tighten the fasteners to the specified torque within the time frame recommended by the RTV sealant manufacturer.

Gasket Remover

Aerosol gasket remover can help remove stubborn gaskets. This product can speed up the removal process and prevent damage to the mating surface that may be caused by using a scraping tool. Most of these types of products are very caustic. Follow the gasket remover manufacturer's instructions for use.

Threadlocking Compound

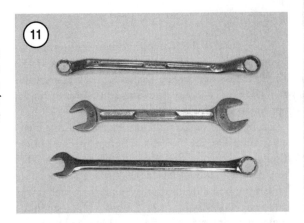

CAUTION
Threadlocking compounds are anaero-
bic and will damage most plastic parts
and surfaces. Use caution when using
these products in area where plastic
components are located.

A threadlocking compound is a fluid applied to the threads of fasteners. After tightening the fastener, the fluid dries and becomes a solid filler between the threads. This makes it difficult for the fastener to work loose from vibration, or heat expansion and contraction. Some threadlocking compounds also provide a seal against fluid leaks.

Before applying threadlocking compound, remove any old compound from both thread areas and clean them with aerosol parts cleaner. Use the compound sparingly. Excess fluid can run into adjoining parts.

Threadlocking compounds are available for different strength, temperature and repair applications.

TOOLS

Most of the procedures in this manual can be carried out with simple hand tools and test equipment familiar to the home mechanic. Always use the correct tools for the job at hand. Keep tools organized and clean. Store them in a tool chest with related tools organized together.

Quality tools are essential. The best are constructed of high-strength alloy steel. These tools are light, easy to use and resistant to wear. Their working surface is devoid of sharp edges and the tool is carefully polished. They have an easy-to-clean finish and are comfortable to use. Quality tools are a good investment.

When purchasing tools to perform the procedures covered in this manual, consider the tool's potential frequency of use. If starting a new tool kit, consider purchasing a basic tool set from a quality tool supplier. These sets are available in many tool combinations and offer substantial savings when compared to individually purchased tools. As work experience

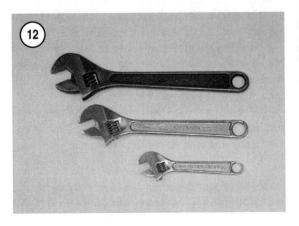

grows and tasks become more complicated, specialized tools can be added.

Some of the procedures in this manual specify special tools. In most cases, the tool is illustrated in use. Well-equipped mechanics may be able to substitute similar tools or fabricate a suitable replacement. However, in some cases, the specialized equipment or expertise may make it impractical for the home mechanic to attempt the procedure. When necessary, such operations are identified in the text with the recommendation to have a dealership or specialist perform the task. It may be less expensive to have a professional perform these jobs, especially when considering the cost of the equipment.

The manufacturer's part number is provided for many of the tools mentioned in this manual. These part numbers are correct at the time of original publication. The publisher cannot guarantee the part number or the tools in this manual will be available in the future.

Screwdrivers

Screwdrivers of various lengths and types are mandatory for the simplest tool kit. The two basic types are the slotted tip (flat blade) and the Phillips tip.

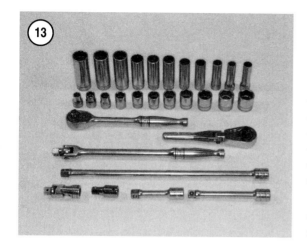

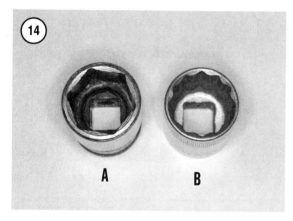

across a wider area at all six edges. For general use, the 12-point works well. It allows the wrench to be removed and reinstalled without moving the handle over such a wide arc.

An open-end wrench is fast and works best in areas with limited access. It contacts the fastener at only two points, and is subject to slipping under heavy force, or if the tool or fastener is worn. A box-end wrench is preferred in most instances, especially when breaking loose and applying the final tightness to a fastener.

The combination wrench has a box-end on one end, and an open-end on the other. This combination makes it a very convenient tool.

Adjustable Wrenches

An adjustable wrench, or Crescent wrench (**Figure 12**), can fit nearly any nut or bolt head that has clear access around its entire perimeter. Adjustable wrenches are best used as a backup wrench to keep a large nut or bolt from turning while the other end is being loosened or tightened with a box-end or socket wrench.

Adjustable wrenches contact the fastener at only two points, which makes them more subject to slipping off the fastener. Because one jaw is adjustable and may loosen, make sure the solid jaw is the one transmitting the force.

Socket Wrenches, Ratchets and Handles

> *WARNING*
> *Do not use hand sockets with air or impact tools, as they may shatter and cause injury. Always wear eye protection when using impact or air tools.*

Sockets that attach to a ratchet handle (**Figure 13**) are available with 6-point (A, **Figure 14**) or 12-point (B) openings and different drive sizes. The drive size indicates the size of the square hole that accepts the ratchet handle. The number stamped on the socket is the size of the work area and must match the fastener head.

As with wrenches, a 6-point socket provides superior holding ability, while a 12-point socket needs to be moved only half as far to reposition it on the fastener.

Sockets are designated for either hand or impact use. Impact sockets are made of thicker material for more durability. Compare the size and wall thickness of a 19-mm hand socket (A, **Figure 15**) and the 19-mm impact socket (B). Use impact sockets when

These are available in sets that often include an assortment of tip sizes and shaft lengths.

As with all tools, use a screwdriver designed for the job. Make sure the size of the tip conforms to the size and shape of the fastener. Use them only for driving screws. Never use a screwdriver for prying or chiseling. Repair or replace worn or damaged screwdrivers. A worn tip may damage the fastener, making it difficult to remove.

Wrenches

Box-end, open-end, and combination wrenches (**Figure 11**) are available in a variety of types and sizes.

The number stamped on the wrench refers to the distance between the work areas. This size must match the size of the fastener head.

The box-end wrench is an excellent tool because it grips the fastener on all sides. This reduces the chance of the tool slipping. The box-end wrench is designed with either a 6- or 12-point opening. For stubborn or damaged fasteners, the 6-point provides superior holding ability by contacting the fastener

using an impact driver or air tools. Use hand sockets with hand-driven attachments.

Various handles are available for sockets. The speed handle is used for fast operation. Flexible ratchet heads in varying lengths allow the socket to be turned with varying force, and at odd angles. Extension bars allow the socket setup to reach difficult areas. The ratchet is the most versatile. It allows the user to install or remove the nut without removing the socket.

Sockets combined with any number of drivers make them undoubtedly the fastest, safest and most convenient tool for fastener removal and installation.

Impact Driver

> *WARNING*
> *Do not use hand sockets with air or impact tools as they may shatter and cause injury. Always wear eye protection when using impact or air tools.*

An impact driver provides extra force for removing fasteners, by converting the impact of a hammer into a turning motion. This makes it possible to remove stubborn fasteners without damaging them. Impact drivers and interchangeable bits (**Figure 16**) are available from most tool suppliers. When using a socket with an impact driver make sure the socket is designed for impact use. Refer to *Socket Wrenches, Ratchets and Handles* in this section.

Allen Wrenches

Allen or setscrew wrenches (**Figure 17**) are used on fasteners with hexagonal recesses in the fastener head. These wrenches are available in L-shaped bar, socket and T-handle types. A metric set is required when working on most motorcycles. Allen bolts are sometimes called socket bolts.

Torque Wrenches

A torque wrench (**Figure 18**) is used with a socket, torque adapter or similar extension to tighten a fastener to a measured torque. Torque wrenches come in several drive sizes (1/4, 3/8, 1/2 and 3/4) and have various methods for reading the torque value. The drive size indicates the size of the square drive that accepts the socket, adapter or extension. Common methods for reading the torque value are the deflecting beam, the dial indicator and the audible click. When choosing a torque wrench, consider the torque range, drive size and accuracy. The torque specifica-

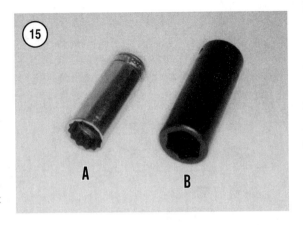

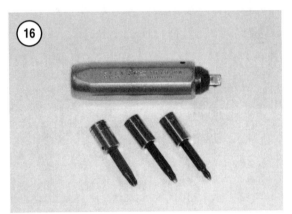

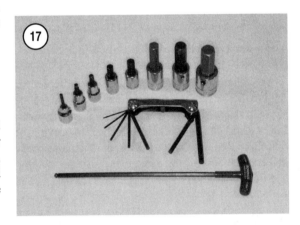

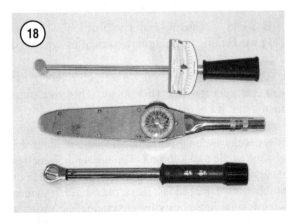

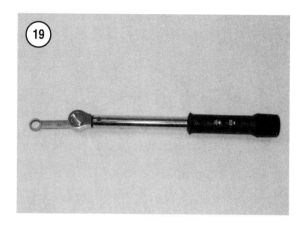

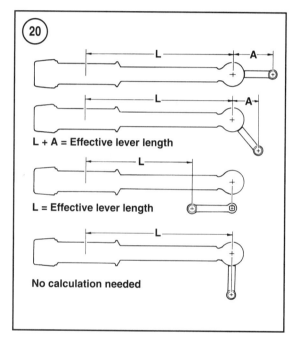

L + A = Effective lever length

L = Effective lever length

No calculation needed

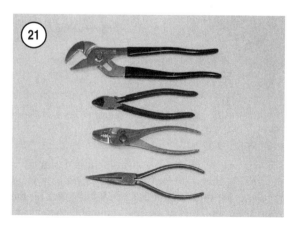

a toolbox. Follow the manufacturer's instructions for their care and calibration.

Torque Adapters

Torque adapters, or extensions, extend or reduce the reach of a torque wrench. The torque adapter shown in **Figure 19** is used to tighten a fastener that cannot be reached due to the size of the torque wrench head, drive, and socket. If a torque adapter changes the effective lever length (**Figure 20**), the torque reading on the wrench will not equal the actual torque applied to the fastener. It is necessary to recalibrate the torque setting on the wrench to compensate for the change of lever length. When a torque adapter is used at a right angle to the drive head, calibration is not required, since the effective length has not changed.

To recalculate a torque reading when using a torque adapter, use the following formula, and refer to **Figure 20**:

$$TW = \frac{TA \times L}{L + A}$$

TW is the torque setting or dial reading on the wrench.

TA is the torque specification and the actual amount of torque that will be applied to the fastener.

A is the amount that the adapter increases (or in some cases reduces) the effective lever length as measured along the centerline of the torque wrench.

L is the lever length of the wrench as measured from the center of the drive to the center of the grip.

The effective length is the sum of L and A.

Example:

TA = 20 ft.-lb.
A = 3 in.
L = 14 in.
$$TW = \frac{20 \times 14}{14 + 3} = \frac{280}{17} = 16.5 \text{ ft. lb.}$$

In this example, the torque wrench would be set to the recalculated torque value (TW = 16.5 ft.-lb.) . When using a beam-type wrench, tighten the fastener until the pointer aligns with 16.5 ft.-lb. In this example, although the torque wrench is pre-set to 16.5 ft.-lb., the actual torque is 20 ft.-lb.

Pliers

Pliers come in a wide range of types and sizes. Pliers are useful for holding, cutting, bending, and crimping. Do not use them to turn fasteners. **Figure 21** and **Figure 22** show several types of useful pliers. Each design has a specialized function.

tions in this manual provide an indication of the range required.

A torque wrench is a precision tool that must be properly cared for to remain accurate. Store torque wrenches in cases or separate padded drawers within

Slip-joint pliers are general-purpose pliers used for gripping and bending. Diagonal cutting pliers are needed to cut wire and can be used to remove cotter pins. Needlenose pliers are used to hold or bend small objects. Locking pliers (**Figure 22**), sometimes called Vise-grips, are used to hold objects very tightly. They have many uses ranging from holding two parts together, to gripping the end of a broken stud. Use caution when using locking pliers, as the sharp jaws will damage the objects they hold.

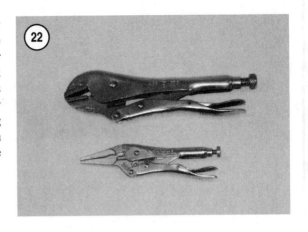

Snap Ring Pliers

> *WARNING*
> *Snap rings can slip and fly off when removing and installing them. Also, the snap ring pliers tips may break. Always wear eye protection when using snap ring pliers.*

Snap ring pliers are specialized pliers with tips that fit into the ends of snap rings to remove and install them.

Snap ring pliers are available with a fixed action (either internal or external) or convertible (one tool works on both internal and external snap rings). They may have fixed tips or interchangeable ones of various sizes and angles. For general use, select a convertible type of pliers with interchangeable tips.

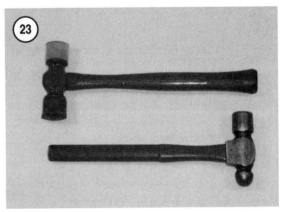

Hammers

Various types of hammers (**Figure 23**) are available to fit a number of applications. A ball-peen hammer is used to strike another tool, such as a punch or chisel. Soft-faced hammers are required when a metal object must be struck without damaging it. *Never* use a metal-faced hammer on engine and suspension components, as damage will occur in most cases.

Always wear eye protection when using hammers. Make sure the hammer face is in good condition and the handle is not cracked. Select the correct hammer for the job and make sure to strike the object squarely. Do not use the handle or the side of the hammer to strike an object.

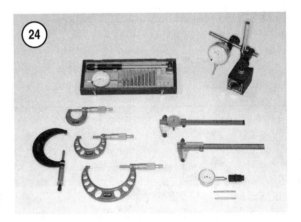

MEASURING TOOLS

The ability to accurately measure components is essential to perform many of the procedures in this manual. Equipment is manufactured to close tolerances, and obtaining consistently accurate measure-

ments is essential to determining which components require replacement or further service.

Each type of measuring instrument is designed to measure a dimension with a certain degree of accuracy and within a certain range. When selecting the measuring tool, make sure it is applicable to the task. Refer to **Figure 24** for a comprehensive measuring set.

As with all tools, measuring tools provide the best results if cared for properly. Improper use can damage the tool and result in inaccurate results. If any measurement is questionable, verify the measure-

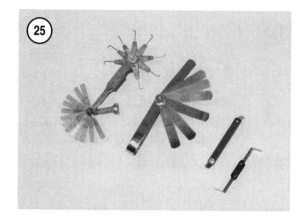

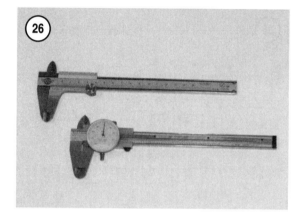

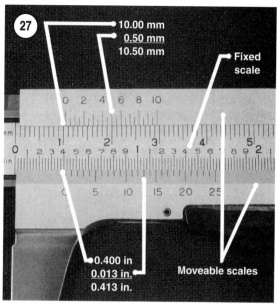

ment using another tool. A standard gauge is usually provided with measuring tools to check accuracy and calibrate the tool if necessary.

Precision measurements can vary according to the experience of the person performing the procedure. Accurate results are only possible if the mechanic possesses a feel for using the tool. Heavy-handed use of measuring tools will produce less accurate results. Hold the tool gently by the fingertips so the point at which the tool contacts the object is easily felt. This feel for the equipment will produce more accurate measurements and reduce the risk of damaging the tool or component. Refer to the following sections for specific measuring tools.

Feeler Gauge

The feeler or thickness gauge (**Figure 25**) is used for measuring the distance between two surfaces.

A feeler gauge set consists of an assortment of steel strips of graduated thickness. Each blade is marked with its thickness. Blades can be of various lengths and angles for different procedures.

A common use for a feeler gauge is to measure valve clearance. Wire (round) type gauges are used to measure spark plug gap.

Calipers

Calipers (**Figure 26**) are excellent tools for obtaining inside, outside and depth measurements. Although not as precise as a micrometer, they allow reasonable precision, typically to within 0.05 mm (0.001 in.). Most calipers have a range up to 150 mm (6 in.).

Calipers are available in dial, vernier or digital versions. Dial calipers have a dial readout that provides convenient reading. Vernier calipers have marked scales that must be compared to determine the measurement. The digital caliper uses a LCD to show the measurement.

Properly maintain the measuring surfaces of the caliper. There must not be any dirt or burrs between the tool and the object being measured. Never force the caliper closed around an object; close the caliper around the highest point so it can be removed with a slight drag. Some calipers require calibration. Always refer to the manufacturer's instructions when using a new or unfamiliar caliper.

To read a vernier caliper refer to **Figure 27**. The fixed scale is marked in 1 mm increments. Ten individual lines on the fixed scale equal 1 cm. The moveable scale is marked in 0.05 mm (hundredth) increments. To obtain a reading, establish the first number by the location of the 0 line on the movable scale in relation to the first line to the left on the fixed scale. In this example, the number is 10 mm. To determine the next number, note which of the lines on the movable scale align with a mark on the fixed scale. A number of lines will seem close, but only one will align exactly. In this case, 0.50 mm is the reading

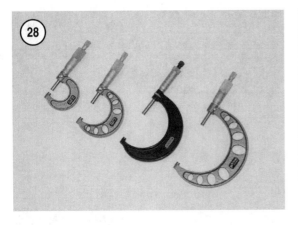

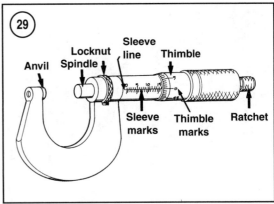

to add to the first number. The result of adding 10 mm and 0.50 mm is a measurement of 10.50 mm.

Micrometers

A micrometer is an instrument designed for linear measurement using the decimal divisions of the inch or meter. While there are many types and styles of micrometers, most of the procedures in this manual call for an outside micrometer. The outside micrometer is used to measure the outside diameter of cylindrical forms and the thickness of materials.

A micrometer's size indicates the minimum and maximum size of a part that it can measure. The usual sizes (**Figure 28**) are 0-25 mm (0-1 in.), 25-50 mm (1-2 in.), 50-75 mm (2-3 in.) and 75-100 mm (3-4 in.).

Micrometers that cover a wider range of measurements are available. These use a large frame with interchangeable anvils of various lengths. This type of micrometer offers a cost savings; however, its overall size may make it less convenient.

Adjustment

Before using a micrometer, check its adjustment as follows.

1. Clean the anvil and spindle faces.

2A. To check a 0-25 mm (0-1 in.) micrometer:
   a. Turn the thimble until the spindle contacts the anvil. If the micrometer has a ratchet stop, use it to ensure that the proper amount of pressure is applied.
   b. If the adjustment is correct, the 0 mark on the thimble will align exactly with the 0 mark on the sleeve line. If the marks do not align, the micrometer is out of adjustment.
   c. Follow the manufacturer's instructions to adjust the micrometer.

2B. To check a micrometer larger than 25 mm (1 in.) use the standard gauge supplied by the manufacturer.

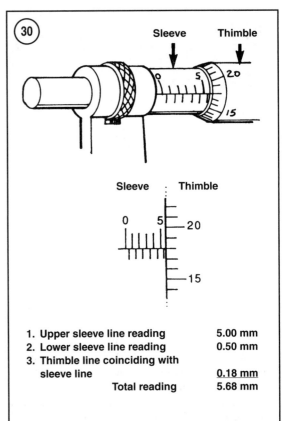

1. Upper sleeve line reading	5.00 mm
2. Lower sleeve line reading	0.50 mm
3. Thimble line coinciding with sleeve line	0.18 mm
Total reading	5.68 mm

A standard gauge is a steel block, disc or rod that is machined to an exact size.
   a. Place the standard gauge between the spindle and anvil, and measure its outside diameter or length. If the micrometer has a ratchet stop, use it to ensure that the proper amount of pressure is applied.
   b. If the adjustment is correct, the 0 mark on the thimble will align exactly with the 0 mark on the sleeve line. If the marks do not align, the micrometer is out of adjustment.
   c. Follow the manufacturer's instructions to adjust the micrometer.

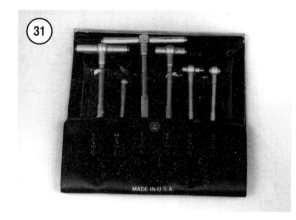

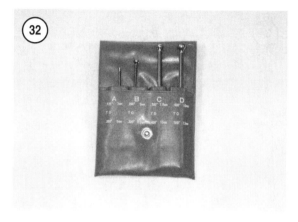

Care

Micrometers are precision instruments. They must be used and maintained with care.

1. Store micrometers in protective cases or separate padded drawers in a toolbox.

2. When in storage, make sure the spindle and anvil faces do not contact each other or another object. If they do, temperature changes and corrosion may damage the contact faces.

3. Do not clean a micrometer with compressed air. Dirt forced into the tool will cause wear.

4. Lubricate micrometers to prevent corrosion.

Reading

When reading a micrometer, numbers are taken from different scales and added together.

For accurate results, properly maintain the measuring surfaces of the micrometer. There can not be any dirt or burrs between the tool and the measured object. Never force the micrometer closed around an object. Close the micrometer around the highest point so it can be removed with a slight drag.

Metric micrometer

The standard metric micrometer (**Figure 29**) is accurate to one one-hundredth of a millimeter (0.01-mm). The sleeve line is graduated in millimeter and half millimeter increments. The marks on the upper half of the sleeve line equal 1.00 mm. Each fifth mark above the sleeve line is identified with a number. The number sequence depends on the size of the micrometer. A 0-25 mm micrometer, for example, will have sleeve marks numbered 0 through 25 in. (5 mm) increments. This numbering sequence continues with larger micrometers. On all metric micrometers, each mark on the lower half of the sleeve equals 0.50 mm.

The tapered end of the thimble has fifty lines marked around it. Each mark equals 0.01 mm. One complete turn of the thimble aligns its 0 mark with the first line on the lower half of the sleeve line or 0.50 mm.

When reading a metric micrometer, add the number of millimeters and half-millimeters on the sleeve line to the number of one one-hundredth millimeters on the thimble. Perform the following steps while referring to **Figure 30**.

1. Read the upper half of the sleeve line and count the number of lines visible. Each upper line equals 1 mm.

2. See if the half-millimeter line is visible on the lower sleeve line. If so, add 0.50 mm to the reading in Step 1.

3. Read the thimble mark that aligns with the sleeve line. Each thimble mark equals 0.01 mm. If a thimble mark does not align exactly with the sleeve line, estimate the amount between the lines. For accurate readings in two-thousandths of a millimeter (0.002 mm), use a metric vernier micrometer.

4. Add the readings from Steps 1-3.

Telescoping and Small Bore Gauges

Use telescoping gauges (**Figure 31**) and small hole gauges (**Figure 32**) to measure bores. Neither gauge has a scale for direct readings. An outside micrometer must be used to determine the reading.

To use a telescoping gauge, select the correct size gauge for the bore. Compress the movable post and carefully insert the gauge into the bore. Carefully move the gauge in the bore to make sure it is centered. Tighten the knurled end of the gauge to hold the movable post in position. Remove the gauge and measure the length of the posts. Telescoping gauges are typically used to measure cylinder bores.

To use a small-bore gauge, select the correct size gauge for the bore. Carefully insert the gauge into the bore. Tighten the knurled end of the gauge to expand the gauge fingers to the limit within the bore. Do not overtighten the gauge, as there is no built-in release. Excessive tightening can damage the bore surface and damage the tool. Remove the gauge and measure the outside dimension (**Figure 33**). Small hole gauges are typically used to measure valve guides.

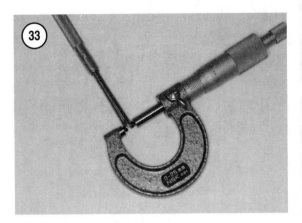

Dial Indicator

A dial indicator (**Figure 34**) is a gauge with a dial face and needle used to measure variations in dimensions and movements. Measuring brake rotor runout is a typical use for a dial indicator.

Dial indicators are available in various ranges and graduations and with three basic types of mounting bases: magnetic, clamp, or screw-in stud.

Cylinder Bore Gauge

A cylinder bore gauge is similar to a dial indicator. The gauge set shown in **Figure 35** consists of a dial indicator, handle, and different length adapters (anvils) to fit the gauge to various bore sizes. The bore gauge is used to measure bore size, taper and out-of-round. When using a bore gauge, follow the manufacturer's instructions.

Compression Gauge

A compression gauge (**Figure 36**) measures combustion chamber (cylinder) pressure, usually in psi or kg/cm^2. The gauge adapter is either inserted or screwed into the spark plug hole to obtain the reading. Disable the engine so it will not start and hold the throttle in the wide-open position when performing a compression test. An engine that does not have adequate compression cannot be properly tuned. See Chapter Three.

Multimeter

A multimeter (**Figure 37**) is an essential tool for electrical system diagnosis. The voltage function indicates the voltage applied or available to various electrical components. The ohmmeter function tests circuits for continuity, or lack of continuity, and measures the resistance of a circuit.

Some manufacturers' specifications for electrical components are based on results using a specific test meter. Results may vary if a meter not recommend by the manufacturer is used. Such requirements are noted when applicable.

Each time an analog ohmmeter is used or if the scale is changed, the ohmmeter must be calibrated.

Digital ohmmeters do not require calibration.

ELECTRICAL SYSTEM FUNDAMENTALS

A thorough study of the many types of electrical systems used in today's motorcycles is beyond the

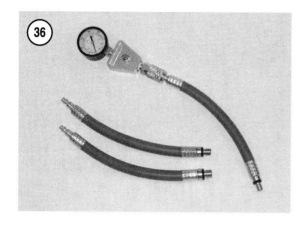

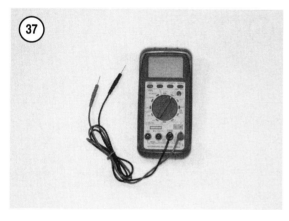

scope of this manual. However, a basic understanding of electrical basics is necessary to perform simple diagnostic tests.

Refer to Chapter Two and Chapter Ten for specific test procedures.

Voltage

Voltage is the electrical potential or pressure in an electrical circuit and is expressed in volts. The more pressure (voltage) in a circuit, the more work that can be performed.

Direct current (DC) voltage means the electricity flows in one direction. All circuits powered by a battery are DC circuits.

Alternating current (AC) means that the electricity flows in one direction momentarily then switches to the opposite direction. Alternator output is an example of AC voltage. This voltage must be changed, or rectified, to direct current to operate in a battery powered system.

Resistance

Resistance is the opposition to the flow of electricity within a circuit or component and is measured in

ohms. Resistance causes a reduction in available current and voltage.

Resistance is measured in a inactive circuit with an ohmmeter. The ohmmeter sends a small amount of current into the circuit and measures how difficult it is to push the current through the circuit.

An ohmmeter, although useful, is not always a good indicator of a circuit's actual ability under operating conditions. This is due to the low voltage (6-9 volts) that the meter uses to test the circuit. The voltage in an ignition coil secondary winding can be several thousand volts. Such high voltage can cause the coil to malfunction, even though it tests acceptable during a resistance test.

Resistance generally increases with temperature. Perform all testing with the component or circuit at room temperature. Resistance tests performed at high temperatures may indicate high resistance readings and result in the unnecessary replacement of a component.

Amperage

Amperage is the unit of measure for the amount of current within a circuit. Current is the actual flow of electricity. The higher the current, the more work that can be performed up to a given point. If the current flow exceeds the circuit or component capacity, the system will be damaged.

SERVICE METHODS

Most of the procedures in this manual are straightforward and can be performed by anyone reasonably competent with tools. However, consider personal capabilities carefully before attempting any operation involving major disassembly of the engine.

1. Front, in this manual, refers to the front of the motorcycle. The front of any component is the end closest to the front of the motorcycle. The left and right sides refer to the position of the parts as viewed by the rider sitting on the seat facing forward.

2. Whenever servicing an engine or suspension component, secure the motorcycle in a safe manner.

3. Tag all similar parts for location and mark all mating parts for position. Record the number and thickness of any shims as they are removed. Identify parts by placing them in sealed and labeled plastic sandwich bags.

4. Tag disconnected wires and connectors with masking tape and a marking pen. Do not rely on memory alone.

5. Protect finished surfaces from physical damage or corrosion. Keep gasoline and other chemicals off painted surfaces.

6. Use penetrating oil on frozen or tight bolts. Avoid using heat where possible. Heat can warp, melt or affect the temper of parts. Heat also damages the finish of paint and plastics.

7. When a part is a press fit or requires a special tool for removal, the information or type of tool is identified in the text. Otherwise, if a part is difficult to remove or install, determine the cause before proceeding.

8. To prevent objects or debris from falling into the engine, cover all openings.

9. Read each procedure thoroughly and compare the illustrations to the actual components before starting the procedure. Perform the procedure in sequence.

10. Recommendations are occasionally made to refer service to a dealership or specialist. In these cases, the work can be performed more economically by the specialist, than by the home mechanic.

11. The term *replace* means to discard a defective part and replace it with a new part. *Overhaul* means to remove, disassemble, inspect, measure, repair and/or replace parts as required to recondition an assembly.

12. Some operations require the use of a hydraulic press. If a press is not available, have these operations performed by a shop equipped with the necessary equipment. Do not use makeshift equipment that may damage the motorcycle.

> *CAUTION*
> *Do not direct high-pressure water at steering bearings, carburetor hoses, wheel bearings, suspension and electrical components. The water will force the grease out of the bearings and possibly damage the seals.*

13. Repairs are much faster and easier if the motorcycle is clean before starting work. Degrease the motorcycle with a commercial degreaser; follow the directions on the container for the best results. Clean all parts with cleaning solvent as they are removed.

14. If special tools are required, have them available before starting the procedure. When special tools are required, they will be described at the beginning of the procedure.

15. Make diagrams of similar-appearing parts. For instance, crankcase bolts are often not the same lengths. Do not rely on memory alone. It is possible that carefully laid out parts will become disturbed, making it difficult to reassemble the components correctly without a diagram.

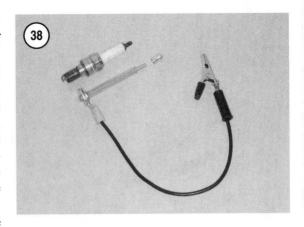

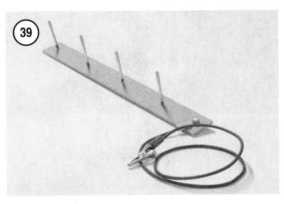

16. Make sure all shims and washers are reinstalled in the same location and position.

17. Whenever rotating parts contact a stationary part, look for a shim or washer.

18. Use new gaskets if there is any doubt about the condition of old ones.

19. If self-locking fasteners are used, replace them with new ones. Do not install standard fasteners in place of self-locking ones.

20. Use grease to hold small parts in place if they tend to fall out during assembly. Do not apply grease to electrical or brake components.

Ignition Grounding

Modern motorcycle ignition systems produce sufficient voltage to damage ignition components if the secondary voltage is not grounded during operation. During normal operation, grounding of the secondary circuit occurs at the spark plug. When performing some tests, such as compression testing, it may be necessary to disconnect the spark plug cap from the spark plug. It is a good practice to ground a disconnected spark plug cap to the engine if the ignition is on, and may be required by some manufacturers to protect the ignition system.

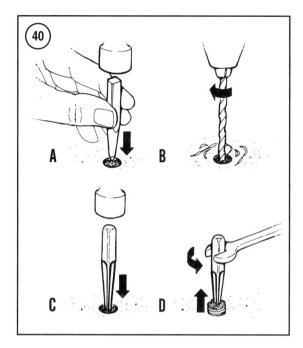

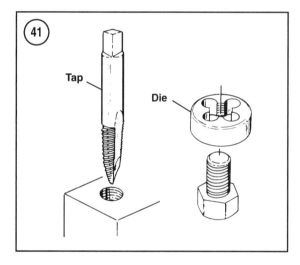

mer. Do not hit it hard enough to cause damage. Re-apply the penetrating oil if necessary.

For frozen screws, apply penetrating oil as described, then insert a screwdriver in the slot and rap the top of the screwdriver with a hammer. This loosens the rust so the screw can be removed in the normal way. If the screw head is too damaged to use this method, grip the head with locking pliers and twist the screw out.

Avoid applying heat unless specifically instructed, as it may melt, warp or remove the temper from parts.

Removing Broken Fasteners

If the head breaks off a screw or bolt, several methods are available for removing the remaining portion. If a large portion of the remainder projects out, try gripping it with locking pliers. If the projecting portion is too small, file it to fit a wrench or cut a slot in it to fit a screwdriver.

If the head breaks off flush, use a screw extractor. To do this, centerpunch the exact center of the remaining portion of the screw or bolt (A, **Figure 40**). Drill a small hole in the screw (B, **Figure 40**) and tap the extractor into the hole (C). Back the screw out with a wrench on the extractor (D, **Figure 40**).

Repairing Damaged Threads

Occasionally, threads are stripped through carelessness or impact damage. Often the threads can be repaired by running a tap (for internal threads on nuts) or die (for external threads on bolts) through the threads (**Figure 41**). To clean or repair spark plug threads, use a spark plug tap.

If an internal thread is damaged, it may be necessary to install a Helicoil or some other type of thread insert. Follow the manufacturer's instructions when installing their insert.

If it is necessary to drill and tap a hole, refer to **Table 7** for metric tap and drill sizes.

A grounding device may be fabricated to route secondary circuit voltage to the engine. **Figure 38** shows a tool that is useful when grounding a single spark plug cap, and **Figure 39** shows a grounding strap that allows the grounding of several spark plug caps. Both tools use a stud or bolt that fits the spark plug connector in the spark plug cap. An alligator clip permits electrical connection to suitable points on the engine.

Removing Frozen Fasteners

If a fastener cannot be removed, several methods may be used to loosen it. First, apply penetrating oil. Apply it liberally and let it penetrate for 10-15 minutes. Rap the fastener several times with a small ham-

Stud Removal/Installation

A stud removal tool (**Figure 42**) is available from most tool suppliers. This tool makes the removal and installation of studs easier. If one is not available, thread two nuts onto the stud and tighten them against each other. Remove the stud by turning the lower nut.

1. Measure the height of the stud above the surface.
2. Thread the stud removal tool onto the stud and tighten it.
3. Remove the stud by turning the stud remover.

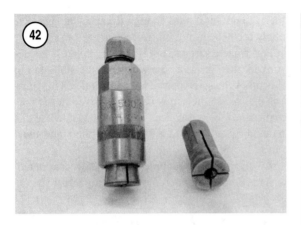

4. Remove any threadlocking compound from the threaded hole. Clean the threads with an aerosol parts cleaner.

5. Install the stud removal tool onto the new stud.

6. Apply threadlocking compound to the threads of the stud.

7. Install the stud and tighten.

8. Install the stud to the height noted in Step 1 or to its torque specification.

9. Remove the stud removal tool or the two nuts.

Removing Hoses

When removing hoses, do not exert excessive force on the hose or fitting. Remove the hose clamp and carefully insert a small screwdriver or pick tool between the fitting and hose. Apply spray lubricant under the hose and carefully twist the hose off the fitting. Clean the fitting of any corrosion or rubber hose material with a wire brush. Clean the inside of the hose thoroughly. Do not use any lubricant when installing the hose (new or old). The lubricant may allow the hose to come off the fitting, even with the clamp secure.

Bearings

Bearings are used in the engine and transmission assembly to reduce power loss, heat and noise resulting from friction. Because bearings are precision parts, they must be maintained with proper lubrication and maintenance. If a bearing is damaged, replace it immediately. When installing a new bearing, take care to prevent damaging it. Bearing replacement procedures are included in the individual chapters where applicable; however, use the following sections as a guideline.

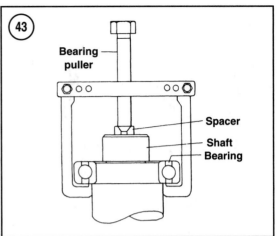

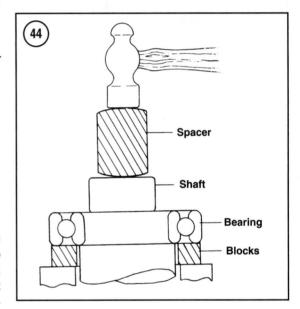

Removal

While bearings are normally removed only when damaged, there may be times when it is necessary to remove a bearing that is in good condition. However, improper bearing removal will damage the bearing and maybe the shaft or case half. Note the following when removing bearings.

1. When using a puller to remove a bearing from a shaft, take care that the shaft is not damaged. Always place a piece of metal between the end of the shaft and the puller screw. In addition, place the puller arms next to the inner bearing race (**Figure 43**).

2. When using a hammer to remove a bearing from a shaft, do not strike the hammer directly against the shaft. Instead, use a brass or aluminum rod between the hammer and shaft (**Figure 44**) and make sure to support both bearing races with wooden blocks as shown.

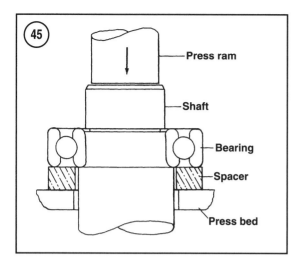

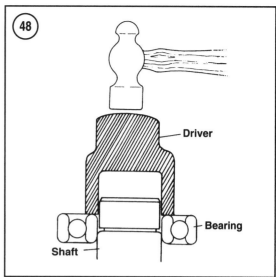

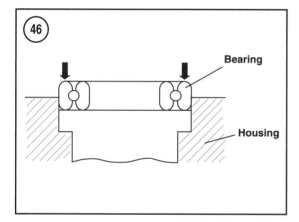

c. The moment the shaft is free of the bearing, it will drop to the floor. Secure or hold the shaft to prevent it from falling.

Installation

NOTE
Unless otherwise specified, install bearings with the manufacturer's mark or number facing outward.

1. When installing a bearing in a housing, apply pressure to the *outer* bearing race (**Figure 46**). When installing a bearing on a shaft, apply pressure to the *inner* bearing race (**Figure 47**).

2. When installing a bearing as described in Step 1, some type of driver is required. Never strike the bearing directly with a hammer or the bearing will be damaged. When installing a bearing, use a piece of pipe or a driver (**Figure 48**) with a diameter that matches the bearing inner race.

3. Step 1 describes how to install a bearing in a case half or over a shaft. However, when installing a bearing over a shaft and into the housing at the same time, a tight fit will be required for both outer and inner bearing races. In this situation, install a spacer underneath the driver tool so that pressure is applied evenly across both races (**Figure 49**). If the outer race is not supported as shown, the balls will push against the outer bearing race and damage it.

Interference Fit

1. Follow this procedure when installing a bearing over a shaft. When a tight fit is required, the bearing inside diameter will be smaller than the shaft. In this

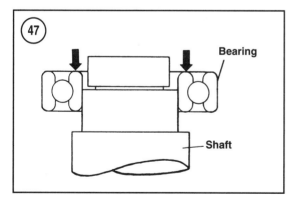

3. The ideal method of bearing removal is with a hydraulic press. Note the following when using a press:

a. Always support the inner and outer bearing races with a suitable size wooden or aluminum ring (**Figure 45**). If only the outer race is supported, pressure applied against the balls and/or the inner race will damage them.

b. Always make sure the press ram (**Figure 45**) aligns with the center of the shaft. If the arm is not centered, it may damage the bearing and/or shaft.

case, driving the bearing on the shaft using normal methods may cause bearing damage. Instead, heat the bearing before installation. Note the following:

a. Secure the shaft so it is ready for bearing installation.

b. Clean all residues from the bearing surface of the shaft. Remove burrs with a file or sandpaper.

c. Fill a suitable pot or beaker with clean mineral oil. Place a thermometer rated above 120° C (248° F) in the oil. Support the thermometer so that it does not rest on the bottom or side of the pot.

d. Remove the bearing from its wrapper and secure it with a piece of heavy wire bent to hold it in the pot. Hang the bearing in the pot so it does not touch the bottom or sides of the pot.

e. Turn the heat on and monitor the thermometer. When the oil temperature rises to approximately 120° C (248° F), remove the bearing from the pot and quickly install it. If necessary, place a socket on the inner bearing race and tap the bearing into place. As the bearing chills, it will tighten on the shaft, so installation must be done quickly. Make sure the bearing is installed completely.

2. Follow this step when installing a bearing in a housing. Bearings are generally installed in a housing with a slight interference fit. Driving the bearing into the housing using normal methods may damage the housing or cause bearing damage. Instead, heat the housing before the bearing is installed. Note the following:

CAUTION
Before heating the housing in this procedure, wash the housing thoroughly with detergent and water. Rinse and rewash the cases as required to remove all traces of oil and other chemical deposits.

CAUTION
Do not heat the housing with a propane or acetylene torch. Never bring a flame into contact with the bearing or housing. The direct heat will destroy the case hardening of the bearing and will likely warp the housing.

a. Heat the housing to approximately 100° C (212° F) in an oven or on a hot plate. An easy way to check that it is the proper temperature is to place tiny drops of water on the housing. If they sizzle and evaporate immediately, the temperature is correct. Heat only one housing at a time.

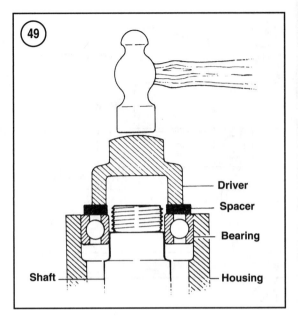

(49)

Driver
Spacer
Bearing
Shaft
Housing

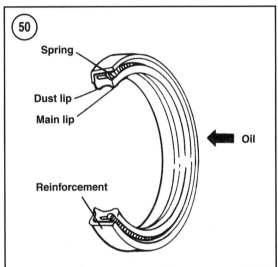

(50)

Spring
Dust lip
Main lip
Oil
Reinforcement

b. Remove the housing from the oven or hot plate, and hold onto the housing with a kitchen potholder, heavy gloves or heavy shop cloth.

NOTE
Remove and install the bearings with a suitable size socket and extension.

c. Hold the housing with the bearing side down and tap the bearing out. Repeat for all bearings in the housing.

d. Before heating the bearing housing, place the new bearing in a freezer if possible. Chilling a bearing slightly reduces its outside diameter while the heated bearing housing assembly is slightly larger due to heat expansion. This will make bearing installation easier.

4. Install seals with a socket placed on the outside of the seal as shown in **Figure 52**. Drive the seal squarely into the housing until it is flush (**Figure 53**). Never install a seal by hitting against the top of the seal with a hammer.

STORAGE

Several months of non-use can cause a general deterioration of the motorcycle. This is especially true in areas of extreme temperature variations. This deterioration can be minimized with careful preparation for storage. A properly stored motorcycle will be much easier to return to service.

Storage Area Selection

When selecting a storage area, consider the following:
1. The storage area must be dry. A heated area is best, but not necessary. It should be insulated to minimize extreme temperature variations.
2. If the building has large window areas, mask them to keep sunlight off the motorcycle.
3. Avoid buildings in industrial areas where corrosive emissions may be present. Avoid areas close to saltwater.
4. Consider the area's risk of fire, theft or vandalism. Check with an insurer regarding motorcycle coverage while in storage.

Preparing the Motorcycle for Storage

The amount of preparation a motorcycle should undergo before storage depends on the expected length of non-use, storage area conditions and personal preference. Consider the following list the minimum requirement:

e. While the housing is still hot, install the new bearing(s) into the housing. Install the bearings by hand, if possible. If necessary, lightly tap the bearing(s) into the housing with a socket placed on the outer bearing race (**Figure 46**). Do not install new bearings by driving on the inner bearing race. Install the bearing(s) until it seats completely.

Seal Replacement

Seals (**Figure 50**) are used to contain oil, water, grease or combustion gasses in a housing or shaft. Improper removal of a seal can damage the housing or shaft. Improper installation of the seal can damage the seal. Note the following:
1. Prying is generally the easiest and most effective method of removing a seal from the housing. However, always place a rag underneath the pry tool (**Figure 51**) to prevent damage to the housing.
2. Pack waterproof grease in the seal lips before the seal is installed.
3. In most cases, install seals with the manufacturer's numbers or marks face out.

1. Wash the motorcycle thoroughly. Make sure all dirt, mud and road debris are removed.

2. Start the engine and allow it to reach operating temperature. Drain the engine oil, and transmission oil, regardless of the riding time since the last service. Fill the engine and transmission with the recommended type of oil.

3. On carbureted models, drain all fuel from the fuel tank, then run the engine until all the fuel is consumed from the lines and carburetor. Drain the fuel from the carburetor as follows:
   a. Remove the fuel tank as described in Chapter Eight and Chapter Nine.
   b. Open the drain screw and thoroughly drain the fuel from the float bowl into a suitable container.
   c. Move the choke knob to the full open position.
   d. Operate the start button and try to start the engine. This will draw out all remaining fuel from the jets.

4. On fuel-injected models, fill the fuel tank with gasoline mixed with fuel stabilizer. Mix the gasoline and fuel stabilizer as directed by the stabilizer manufacturer. Run the engine for a few minutes so the stabilized fuel can enter the fuel injection system.

5. Remove the spark plugs and pour a teaspoon of engine oil into the cylinders. Place a rag over the openings and slowly turn the engine over to distribute the oil. Reinstall the spark plugs.

6. Remove the battery. Store the battery in a cool and dry location.

7. Cover the exhaust and intake openings.

8. Apply a protective substance to the plastic and rubber components, including the tires. Make sure to follow the manufacturer's instructions for each type of product being used.

9. Place the motorcycle on a stand or wooden blocks, so the wheels are off the ground. If this is not possible, place a piece of plywood between the tires and the ground. Inflate the tires to the recommended pressure if the motorcycle can not be elevated.

10. Cover the motorcycle with old bed sheets or something similar. Do not cover it with any plastic material that will trap moisture.

Returning the Motorcycle to Service

The amount of service required when returning a motorcycle to service after storage depends on the length of non-use and storage conditions. In addition to performing the reverse of the above procedure, make sure the brakes, clutch, throttle and engine stop switch work properly before operating the motorcycle. Refer to Chapter Three and evaluate the service intervals to determine which areas require service.

Table 1 MOTORCYCLE DIMENSIONS

Overall length	2510 mm (98.8 in.)
Overall width	985 mm (38.8 in.)
Overall height	1100 mm (43.3 in.)
Wheelbase	1655 mm (65.2 in.)
Seat height	700 mm (27.6 in.)
Ground clearance	140 mm (5.51 in.)
Turning radius	3.0 m (9.8 ft.)

Table 2 MOTORCYCLE WEIGHT

Dry weight	
2001-2004	241 kg (531 lb.)
2005-on	246 kg (542 lb.)
Maximum load capacity	206 kg (454 lb.)

Table 3 FUEL TANK CAPACITY

2001-2004	17.0 liters (4.5 U.S. gal.)
2005-on	15.5 liters (4.1 U.S. gal.)

Table 4 TORQUE RECOMMENDATIONS

Fastener size or type	N•m	in.-lb.	ft.-lb.
5 mm screw	4	35	–
5 mm bolt and nut	5	44	–
6 mm screw	9	80	–
6 mm bolt and nut	10	88	–
6 mm flange bolt (8 mm head, small flange)	9	80	–
6 mm flange bolt (10 mm head) and nut	12	106	–
8 mm bolt and nut	22	–	16
8 mm flange bolt and nut	27	–	20
10 mm bolt and nut	35	–	26
10 mm flange bolt and nut	40	–	30
12 mm bolt and nut	55	–	41

Table 5 CONVERSION FORMULAS

Multiply:	By:	To get the equivalent of:
Length		
Inches	25.4	Millimeter
Inches	2.54	Centimeter
Miles	1.609	Kilometer
Feet	0.3048	Meter
Millimeter	0.03937	Inches
Centimeter	0.3937	Inches
Kilometer	0.6214	Mile
Meter	3.281	Feet
Fluid volume		
U.S. quarts	0.9463	Liters
U.S. gallons	3.785	Liters
U.S. ounces	29.573529	Milliliters
Imperial gallons	4.54609	Liters
Imperial quarts	1.1365	Liters
Liters	0.2641721	U.S. gallons
Liters	1.0566882	U.S. quarts
Liters	33.814023	U.S. ounces
Liters	0.22	Imperial gallons
Liters	0.8799	Imperial quarts
Milliliters	0.033814	U.S. ounces
Milliliters	1.0	Cubic centimeters
Milliliters	0.001	Liters
Torque		
Foot-pounds	1.3558	Newton-meters
Foot-pounds	0.138255	Meters-kilograms
Inch-pounds	0.11299	Newton-meters
Newton-meters	0.7375622	Foot-pounds
Newton-meters	8.8507	Inch-pounds
Meters-kilograms	7.2330139	Foot-pounds
Volume		
Cubic inches	16.387064	Cubic centimeters
Cubic centimeters	0.0610237	Cubic inches
Temperature		
Fahrenheit	(°F – 32) × 0.556	Centigrade
Centigrade	(°C × 1.8) + 32	Fahrenheit
Weight		
Ounces	28.3495	Grams
Pounds	0.4535924	Kilograms
Grams	0.035274	Ounces
Kilograms	2.2046224	Pounds

(continued)

Table 5 CONVERSION FORMULAS (continued)

Multiply:	By:	To get the equivalent of:
Pressure		
Pounds per square inch	0.070307	Kilograms per square centimeter
Kilograms per square centimeter	14.223343	Pounds per square inch
Kilopascals	0.1450	Pounds per square inch
Pounds per square inch	6.895	Kilopascals
Speed		
Miles per hour	1.609344	Kilometers per hour
Kilometers per hour	0.6213712	Miles per hour

Table 6 TECHNICAL ABBREVIATIONS

ABDC	After bottom dead center
ATDC	After top dead center
BBDC	Before bottom dead center
BDC	Bottom dead center
BTDC	Before top dead center
BAS	Bank angle sensor
C	Celsius (centigrade)
cc	Cubic centimeters
cid	Cubic inch displacement
CKP	Crankshaft position sensor
CDI	Capacitor discharge ignition
CMP	Camshaft position sensor
cu. in.	Cubic inches
ECM	Electronic control module
ECT	Engine coolant temperature sensor
EVAP	Evaporative emission system
F	Fahrenheit
ft.	Feet
ft.-lb.	Foot-pounds
gal.	Gallons
GP	Gear position sensor
H/A	High altitude
HO_2	Heated oxygen sensor
IAP	Intake air pressure sensor
IAT	Intake air temperature sensor
hp	Horsepower
in.	Inches
in. Hg	Inches of mercury
in.-lb.	Inch-pounds
I.D.	Inside diameter
kg	Kilograms
kgm	Kilogram meters
km	Kilometer
kPa	Kilopascals
L	Liter
LCD	Liquid crystal display
m	Meter
MAG	Magneto
MAP	Manifold absolute pressure sensor
ml	Milliliter
mm	Millimeter
mm Hg	Millimeters of mercury
N•m	Newton-meter
O.D.	Outside diameter
oz.	Ounces
PAIR	Pulsed seondary air injection
psi	Pounds per square inch
PTO	Power take off
pt.	Pint
qt.	Quart

(continued)

Table 6 TECHNICAL ABBREVIATIONS (continued)

rpm	Revolutions per minute
STP	Secondary throttle position sensor
STVA	Secondary throttle valve actuator
TP	Throttle position sensor

Table 7 METRIC TAP AND DRILL SIZES

Metric size	Drill equivalent	Decimal fraction	Nearest fraction
3 × 0.50	No. 39	0.0995	3/32
3 × 0.60	3/32	0.0937	3/32
4 × 0.70	No. 30	0.1285	1/8
4 × 0.75	1/8	0.125	1/8
5 × 0.80	No. 19	0.166	11/64
5 × 0.90	No. 20	0.161	5/32
6 × 1.00	No. 9	0.196	13/64
7 × 1.00	16/64	0.234	15/64
8 × 1.00	J	0.277	9/32
8 × 1.25	17/64	0.265	17/64
9 × 1.00	5/16	0.3125	5/16
9 × 1.25	5/16	0.3125	5/16
10 × 1.25	11/32	0.3437	11/32
10 × 1.50	R	0.339	11/32
11 × 1.50	3/8	0.375	3/8
12 × 1.50	13/32	0.406	13/32
12 × 1.75	13/32	0.406	13/32

Table 8 METRIC, DECIMAL AND FRACTIONAL EQUIVALENTS

mm	in.	Nearest fraction	mm	in.	Nearest fraction
1	0.0394	1/32	26	1.0236	1 1/32
2	0.0787	3/32	27	1.0630	1 1/16
3	0.1181	1/8	28	1.1024	1 3/32
4	0.1575	5/32	29	1.1417	1 5/32
5	0.1969	3/16	30	1.1811	1 3/16
6	0.2362	1/4	31	1.2205	1 7/32
7	0.2756	9/32	32	1.2598	1 1/4
8	0.3150	5/16	33	1.2992	1 5/16
9	0.3543	11/32	34	1.3386	1 11/32
10	0.3937	13/32	35	1.3780	1 3/8
11	0.4331	7/16	36	1.4173	1 13/32
12	0.4724	15/32	37	1.4567	1 15/32
13	0.5118	1/2	38	1.4961	1 1/2
14	0.5512	9/16	39	1.5354	1 17/32
15	0.5906	19/32	40	1.5748	1 9/16
16	0.6299	5/8	41	1.6142	1 5/8
17	0.6693	21/32	42	1.6535	1 21/32
18	0.7087	23/32	43	1.6929	1 11/16
19	0.7480	3/4	44	1.7323	1 23/32
20	0.7874	25/32	45	1.7717	1 25/32
21	0.8268	13/16	46	1.8110	1 13/16
22	0.8661	7/8	47	1.8504	1 27/32
23	0.9055	29/32	48	1.8898	1 7/8
24	0.9449	15/16	49	1.9291	1 15/16
25	0.9843	31/32	50	1.9685	1 31/32

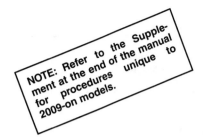
NOTE: Refer to the Supplement at the end of the manual for procedures unique to 2009-on models.

CHAPTER TWO

TROUBLESHOOTING

This chapter covers troubleshooting procedures. Each section provides typical symptoms and logical methods for isolating the cause(s). There may be several ways to solve a problem, but a systematic approach will avoid wasted time and unnecessary parts replacement.

An engine needs three elements to run properly: correct air/fuel mixture, compression and a spark at the right time. If one element is missing, the engine will not run.

Gather as much information as possible to aid in diagnosis. Never assume anything and do not overlook the obvious. Make sure the start switch is in the run position and there is fuel in the tank. Learning to recognize symptoms will make troubleshooting easier. In most cases, specialized test equipment is not needed to determine whether repairs can be performed at home. On the other hand, be realistic and do not start procedures that are beyond the experience and equipment available. If the motorcycle does require the attention of a professional, describe symptoms and conditions accurately and fully. The more information a technician has available, the easier it will be to diagnose the problem.

STARTING THE ENGINE

The following sections describe recommended starting procedures at various ambient temperatures and engine conditions.

CAUTION
Do not operate the starter for more than five seconds at a time. Wait for approximately ten seconds between starting attempts.

Starting System Operation

1. The position of the sidestand will affect engine starting. Note the following:
   a. The engine cannot start when the sidestand is down and the clutch lever released, or the transmission is not in neutral.
   b. The engine can start when the sidestand is down if the clutch lever is pulled in and the transmission is in neutral. The engine will remain running if the clutch lever is released with the transmission in neutral, but stop if the transmission is put in gear with the sidestand down.
   c. The engine can be started when the sidestand is up and the transmission is in neutral or in gear with the clutch lever pulled in.

2. Before starting the engine, shift the transmission into neutral and place the engine stop switch in the run position.

3. Turn the ignition switch on and confirm the following:
   a. The neutral indicator light is on (when the transmission is in neutral).

b. The oil pressure and coolant temperature warning lights should come on.

4. The engine is now ready to start. Refer to the starting procedure that best describes the conditions.

Starting Procedures (2001-2004 Models)

Engine cold

1. Review *Starting System Operation* in this chapter.
2. Turn the ignition switch on.
3. Place the engine stop switch in the run position.

> *CAUTION*
> *On 2001-2004 models, excessive choke use can cause a rich fuel mixture. This condition can wash oil off the pistons and cylinder walls, causing piston and cylinder scuffing.*

4. Pull out the choke knob (**Figure 1**) to the fully on position.

> *CAUTION*
> *The warning lights should go off a few seconds after the engine starts. If a light stays on, turn the engine off and check the relevant item.*

5. Operate the starter button and start the engine. Do not open the throttle or a lean mixture will result and cause hard starting.
6. With the engine running, operate the choke knob as required to keep the engine idle between 1500-2000 rpm.
7. After approximately 30 seconds, push the choke knob (**Figure 1**) to the fully off position. In extremely cold weather it may be necessary to operate the engine with the choke on for a longer period. Operate the engine until the choke can be pushed in to the fully off position and the engine responds to the throttle cleanly.

Warm engine

1. Review *Starting System Operation* in this chapter.
2. Turn the ignition switch on.
3. Place the engine stop switch in the run position.

> *CAUTION*
> *The warning lights should go off a few seconds after the engine starts. If a light stays on, turn the engine off and check the relevant item.*

4. Open the throttle slightly and push the starter button. Do not operate the choke.

Engine flooded

If the engine will not start after a few attempts, and a gasoline smell is present, the engine is probably flooded. To start a flooded engine, proceed as follows:
1. Turn the ignition key switch on.
2. Turn the engine stop switch to the off position.
3. Push in the choke knob (**Figure 1**) to the off position.

> *CAUTION*
> *The warning lights should go off a few seconds after the engine starts. If a light stays on, turn the engine off and check the relevant item.*

4. Open the throttle completely and operate the starter for five seconds.
5. Wait ten seconds, then continue with Step 6.
6. Place the engine stop switch in the run position.
7. Open the throttle slightly and push the starter button to start the engine. Do not use the choke.

Starting Procedures (2005-On Models)

All engine temperatures

1. Review *Starting System Operation* in this chapter.
2. Turn the ignition switch on.
3. Place the engine stop switch in the run position.

> *CAUTION*
> *The warning lights should go off after a few seconds or after the engine starts. If a light stays on, turn the engine off and check the relevant item.*

4. The following indicator lights should turn on when the main switch is on.
   a. The neutral indicator light (when the transmission is in neutral).
   b. Low oil pressure indicator LED.
   c. Coolant temperature LCD.

    d. Fuel level indicator LCD.

    e. The tachometer needle swings to its maximum setting and then returns to zero.

5. Depress the starter button and start the engine. Do not open the throttle when pressing the starter button.

Engine flooded

If the engine will not start and a strong gasoline smell is present, the engine is probably flooded. To start a flooded engine:

1. Turn the engine stop switch off.

2. Open the throttle fully.

> *CAUTION*
> *The warning lights should go off after a few seconds or after the engine starts. If a light stays on, turn the engine off and check the relevant item.*

3. Turn the ignition switch on.

4. The following indicator lights should turn on when the main switch is on.

    a. The neutral indicator light (when the transmission is in neutral).

    b. Low oil pressure indicator LED.

    c. Coolant temperature LCD.

    d. Fuel level indicator LCD.

    e. The tachometer needle swings to its maximum setting and then returns to zero.

5. Operate the starter button for five seconds.

6. Follow the procedure under *All Engine Temperatures*. Note the following:

    a. If the engine starts but idles roughly, vary the throttle position slightly until the engine idles and responds smoothly.

    b. If the engine does not start, turn the ignition switch off and wait approximately ten seconds. Then repeat Steps 1-5. If the engine still will not start, refer to *Engine Will Not Start* in this chapter.

ENGINE WILL NOT START

Identifying the Problem

If the engine does not start, perform the following procedure in sequence. If the engine fails to start after performing these checks, refer to the troubleshooting procedures indicated in the steps.

2005-on models are equipped with an engine management system capable of self-diagnosis. Refer to *Electronic Diagnostic System* in this chapter.

1. Refer to *Starting the Engine* in this chapter to make sure all switches and starting procedures are correct.

2. If the starter does not operate, refer to *Starting System* in this chapter.

3. If the starter operates, and the engine seems flooded, refer to *Starting the Engine* in this chapter. If the engine is not flooded, continue with Step 4.

4. Turn the ignition switch on and check the fuel gauge, if so equipped. If the fuel level low-level light flickers the fuel level in the tank is low. The amount of fuel remaining in the tank when the fuel level light flickers is approximately 1.5 liter (0.4 gallon).

5. If there is sufficient fuel in the fuel tank, remove one of the spark plugs immediately after attempting to start the engine. The spark plug insulator should be wet, indicating that fuel is reaching the engine. If the plug tip is dry, fuel is not reaching the engine. Confirm this condition by checking the other spark plug. A faulty fuel pump or a clogged fuel filter can cause this condition. Refer to *Fuel System* in this chapter. If there is fuel on the spark plug and the engine will not start, the engine may not have adequate spark. Continue with Step 6.

6. Make sure each spark plug cap is securely attached to the spark plug. If the engine does not start, continue with Step 7.

7. Perform the *Spark Test* described in this section. If there is a strong spark, perform Step 8. If there is no spark or if the spark is very weak, refer to *Ignition System* in this chapter.

8. If the fuel and ignition systems are working correctly, perform a leakdown test (this chapter) and compression test (Chapter Three). If the compression is low, refer to *Engine Performance* in this chapter. Check cylinder compression as described in Chapter Three.

Spark Test

Perform a spark test to determine if the ignition system is producing adequate spark. This test can be performed with a spark plug or a spark tester (Motion Pro part No. 08-0122). A spark tester is used as a substitute for the spark plug and allows the spark to be more easily observed between the adjustable air gap. If a spark tester is not available, use a new spark plug.

> *WARNING*
> *Do not hold the spark plugs, tester, wire or connector, or a serious electrical shock may result.*

1. Remove the spark plugs as described in Chapter Three.

2. Connect each spark plug wire and connector to a new spark plug or tester, and touch each spark plug

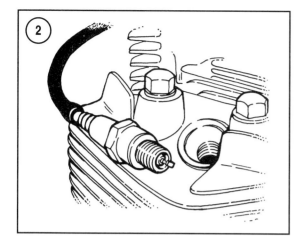

base or tester to a good engine ground (**Figure 2**). Position the spark plugs or tester away from the spark plug holes and so the electrodes are visible.

3. Shift the transmission to neutral, turn the ignition system on and place the engine stop switch in the run position.

4. Operate the starter button to turn the engine over. A fat blue spark must be evident across the spark plug electrodes or between the tester terminals. Repeat for each cylinder.

5. If the spark is good at each spark plug, the ignition system is functioning properly. Check for one or more of the following possible malfunctions:
   a. Faulty fuel system component. Refer to *Fuel System* in this chapter.
   b. Engine damage (low compression).
   c. Engine flooded.

6. If the spark was weak or if there was no spark at one or both plugs, note the following:
   a. If there is no spark on both of the plugs, check for a problem on the input side of the ignition system or the ignitor unit as described in *Ignition System* in this chapter.
   b. If there is no spark at one spark plug only, the spark plug is probably faulty or there is a problem with the spark plug wire or plug cap. Retest with a spark tester, or use a new spark plug. If there is still no spark at that one plug, make sure the spark plug cap is installed correctly.
   c. If there is no spark, the ignition coil is faulty.
   d. Troubleshoot the ignition system as described in this chapter.

7. Install the spark plugs as described in Chapter Three.

Engine is Difficult to Start

1. After attempting to start the engine, remove one of the spark plugs as described in Chapter Three and check for the presence of fuel on the plug tip. Note the following:
   a. If there is no fuel visible on the plug, remove another spark plug. If there is no fuel on this plug, perform Step 2.
   b. If there is fuel on the plug tip, go to Step 4.
   c. If there is an excessive amount of fuel on the plug, check for a clogged or plugged air filter, incorrect choke operation and adjustment (2001-2004 models).

2. Test the fuel pump as described in Chapter Eight or Chapter Nine. Note the following:
   a. If the fuel pump operation is correct, go to Step 3.
   b. If there is fuel flow but the volume is minimal, check for a clogged fuel system.
   c. If the fuel pump operation is faulty, replace the fuel pump and retest the fuel system.

3. Perform the *Spark Test* in this section. Note the following:
   a. If the spark is weak or if there is no spark, go to Step 4.
   b. If the spark is good, go to Step 5.

4. If the spark is weak or if there is no spark, check the following:
   a. Fouled spark plug(s).
   b. Damaged spark plug(s).
   c. Loose or damaged spark plug wire(s).
   d. Loose or damaged spark plug cap(s).
   e. Faulty ignitor unit (2001-2004 models).
   f. Faulty ECM (2005-on models).
   g. Faulty ignition pickup coil (2001-2004 models).
   h. Faulty crankshaft position sensor (2005-on models).
   i. Faulty ignition coil(s).
   j. Faulty engine stop switch.
   k. Faulty ignition switch.
   l. Dirty or loose-fitting terminals.

5. If the engine turns over but does not start, the engine compression may be low. Check for the following possible malfunctions:
   a. Leaking cylinder head gasket.
   b. Valve clearance too tight.
   c. Bent or stuck valve(s).
   d. Incorrect valve timing. Worn cylinders and/or piston rings.

6. If the spark is good, try starting the engine by following normal starting procedures. If the engine starts but then stops, check for the following conditions:
   a. Incorrect choke operation (2001-2004 models).
   b. Leaking or damaged intake duct.
   c. Contaminated fuel.

d. Incorrect ignition timing.

Engine Will Not Crank

If the engine will not turn over, check for one or more of the following possible malfunctions:

1. Blown main fuse.
2. Discharged battery.
3. Defective starter or starter relay switch.
4. Seized piston(s).
5. Seized crankshaft bearings.
6. Broken connecting rod(s).
7. Locked-up transmission or clutch assembly.
8. Defective starter clutch.

ENGINE PERFORMANCE

If the engine runs, but performance is unsatisfactory, refer to the following procedure(s) that best describes the symptom(s).

2005-on models are equipped with an engine management system capable of self-diagnosis. Refer to *Electronic Diagnostic System* in this chapter for identification of malfunctioning components that may cause a performance problem.

The ignition timing is not adjustable. If incorrect ignition timing is suspected as being the cause of a malfunction, check the timing as described in Chapter Three. If the timing is incorrect, a defective ignition system component is indicated. Refer to *Ignition System* in this chapter.

Engine Will Not Idle

1. Clogged air filter element.
2. Poor fuel flow.
3. Incorrect carburetor or throttle body synchronization.
4. Fouled or improperly gapped spark plug(s).
5. Leaking head gasket or vacuum leak.
6. Leaking or damaged intake duct.
7. Low engine compression.
8. Obstructed or defective carburetor (2001-2004 models).
9. Obstructed throttle body or defective fuel injector (2005-on models).
10. Incorrect ignition timing (2001-2004 models), caused by faulty ignitor unit or ignition pickup coil.
11. Incorrect ignition timing (2005-on models), caused by a faulty ECM or crankshaft position sensor.

Poor Overall Performance

1. Place the motorcycle on the centerstand, then spin the rear wheel by hand. If the wheel spins freely, perform Step 2. If the wheel does not spin freely, check for the following conditions:
    a. Dragging rear brake.
    b. Damaged rear axle assembly.
    c. Damaged final drive.
2. Check the clutch adjustment and operation. If the clutch slips, refer to *Clutch* in this chapter.
3. If Step 1 and Step 2 did not locate the problem, test ride the motorcycle and accelerate lightly. If the engine speed increases according to throttle position, perform Step 4. If the engine speed did not increase, check for one or more of the following problems:
    a. Clogged air filter.
    b. Restricted fuel flow.
    c. Clogged or damaged muffler.
4. Check for one or more of the following problems:
    a. Low engine compression.
    b. Worn spark plugs.
    c. Fouled spark plug(s).
    d. Incorrect spark plug heat range.
    e. Incorrect oil level (too high or too low).
    f. Contaminated oil.
    g. Worn or damaged valve train assembly.
    h. Engine overheating. Refer to *Engine Overheating* in this section.
    i. Incorrect ignition timing (2001-2004 models), caused by faulty ignitor unit or ignition pickup coil.
    j. Incorrect ignition timing (2005-on models) caused by a faulty ECM or crankshaft position sensor.
5. If the engine knocks during acceleration or when running at high speed, check for one or more of the following possible malfunctions:
    a. Incorrect type of fuel.
    b. Lean fuel mixture.
    c. Excessive carbon buildup in combustion chamber.
    d. Worn pistons and/or cylinder bores.
    e. Advanced ignition timing (2001-2004 models) caused by a faulty ignitor unit or ignition pickup coil.
    f. Advanced ignition timing (2005-on models) caused by a faulty ECM or crankshaft position sensor.

Poor Idle or Low Speed Performance

1. Check for damaged intake duct and air filter housing hose clamps.

2. Check the fuel system (Chapter Eight or Chapter Nine).

3. Perform the spark test in this section. Note the following:

    a. If the spark is good, go to Step 4.

    b. If the spark is weak, test the ignition system as described in this chapter.

4. Check the ignition timing as described in Chapter Three. Note the following:

    a. If the ignition timing is incorrect, check the ignition system (Chapter Ten).

    b. If the ignition timing is correct, recheck the fuel system.

Poor High Speed Performance

1. Check the fuel system (Chapter Eight or Chapter Nine).

2. Check ignition timing as described in Chapter Three. If ignition timing is incorrect, perform Step 3.

3. If the timing is incorrect, test the following ignition system components as described in Chapter Ten:

    a. Ignition coils.

    b. Ignition pickup coil (2001-2004 models).

    c. Crankshaft position sensor (2005-on models).

    d. Ignitor unit (2001-2004 models).

    e. ECM (2005-on models).

4. Check the valve clearance as described in Chapter Three. Note the following:

    a. If the valve clearance is correct, perform Step 5.

    b. If the clearance is incorrect, readjust the valves.

5. Incorrect valve timing and worn or damaged valve springs can cause poor high-speed performance. If the camshafts were timed just prior to the motorcycle experiencing this type of problem, the cam timing may be incorrect. If the cam timing was not set or changed, and all of the other inspection procedures in this section failed to locate the problem, inspect the camshafts and valve assembly.

Engine Overheating

Cooling system malfunction

1. Low coolant level.

2. Air in cooling system.

3. Clogged radiator, hose or engine coolant passages.

4. Thermostat stuck closed.

5. Worn or damaged radiator cap.

6. Damaged water pump.

7. Damaged fan motor switch.

8. Damaged fan motor.

9. Damaged coolant temperature sensor.

Other causes

1. Incorrect carburetor jet size (2001-2004 models).

2. Improper spark plug heat range.

3. Low oil level.

4. Oil not circulating properly.

5. Valves leaking.

6. Heavy engine carbon deposits in combustion chamber.

7. Dragging brake(s).

8. Clutch slip.

Engine Not Reaching Operating Temperature

1. Thermostat stuck open.

2. Defective fan motor switch.

3. Inaccurate temperature gauge.

4. Defective coolant temperature sensor.

Engine Backfires

1. Incorrect ignition timing due to loose or defective ignition system component.

2. Incorrect carburetor jet size (2001-2004 models).

Engine Misfires During Acceleration

1. Incorrect ignition timing due to loose or defective ignition system component.

2. Incorrect carburetor jet size (2001-2004 models).

ENGINE NOISES

Unusual noises are often the first indication of a developing problem. Investigate any new noises as soon as possible. Something that may be a minor problem, if corrected, could prevent the possibility of more extensive damage.

Use a mechanic's stethoscope or a small section of hose held near the ear (not directly on the ear) with the other end close to the source of the noise to isolate the location. Determining the exact cause of a noise can be difficult. If this is the case, consult with a professional mechanic to determine the cause. Do not disassemble major components until all other possibilities have been eliminated.

Consider the following when troubleshooting engine noises:

1. Knocking or pinging during acceleration is usually caused by using a lower octane fuel than recommended. It may also be caused by poor fuel. Pinging

can also be caused by an incorrect spark plug heat range or carbon build-up in the combustion chamber. Refer to *Spark Plugs* and *Compression Test* in Chapter Three.

2. A slapping or rattling noise at low speed or during acceleration is typically caused by excessive piston-to-cylinder wall clearance (piston slap). Piston slap is easier to detect when the engine is cold and before the pistons have expanded. Once the engine has warmed up, piston expansion reduces piston-to-cylinder clearance.

3. A knocking or rapping during deceleration is usually caused by excessive rod bearing clearance.

4. Persistent knocking and vibration at every crankshaft rotation are usually caused by worn rod or main bearing(s). It can also be caused by broken piston rings or damaged piston pins.

5. A rapid on-off squeal is due to a compression leak around the cylinder head gasket or spark plug(s).

6. In case of valve train noise, check for the following:
   a. Excessive valve clearance.
   b. Worn or damaged camshaft.
   c. Damaged camshaft, camshaft drive chain and guides.
   d. Worn or damaged valve lifter(s).
   e. Damaged valve lifter bore(s).
   f. Valve sticking in guide(s).
   g. Broken valve spring(s).
   h. Low oil pressure.
   i. Clogged cylinder oil hole or oil passage.

Engine Smoke

The color of engine smoke can help diagnose engine problems or operating conditions.

Black smoke

Black smoke is an indication of a rich air/fuel mixture where an excessive amount of fuel is being burned in the combustion chamber. On carbureted models, verify carburetor operation as described in Chapter Eight. Check for a leaking fuel injector(s) or a damaged pressure regulator as described in Chapter Nine.

Blue smoke

Blue smoke indicates that the engine is burning oil in the combustion chamber as it leaks past worn valve stem seals and piston rings. Excessive oil consumption is another indicator of an engine that is burning oil. Perform a compression test (Chapter Three) to isolate the problem.

White smoke or steam

It is normal to see white smoke or steam from the exhaust after first starting the engine in cold weather. This is actually condensed steam formed by the engine during combustion. If the motorcycle is ridden far enough, the water cannot buildup in the crankcase and should not be a problem. Once the engine heats up to normal operating temperature, the water evaporates and exits the engine through the crankcase vent system. However, if the motorcycle is ridden for short trips or repeatedly started and stopped and allowed to cool off without the engine getting warm enough, water will start to collect in the crankcase. With each short run of the engine, more water collects. As this water mixes with the oil in the crankcase, sludge is produced. Water sludge can eventually cause engine damage as it circulates through the lubrication system and blocks off oil passages. Water draining from drain holes in exhaust pipes indicate water buildup.

Large amounts of steam can also be caused by a cracked cylinder head or cylinder block surface that allows antifreeze to leak into the combustion chamber. Perform a coolant pressure test as described in Chapter Eleven.

Low Engine Compression

Problems with the engine top end will affect engine performance and derivability. When the engine is suspect, perform the leakdown test in this chapter and do a compression test as described in Chapter Three. Interpret the results as described in each procedure to troubleshoot the suspect area. An engine can lose compression through the following areas.

1. Valves:
   a. Incorrect valve adjustment.
   b. Incorrect valve timing.
   c. Worn or damaged valve seats (valve and/or cylinder head).
   d. Bent valves.
   e. Weak or broken valve springs.
2. Cylinder head:
   a. Loose spark plug or damaged spark plug hole.
   b. Damaged cylinder head gasket.
   c. Warped or cracked cylinder head.

ENGINE LUBRICATION

An improperly operating engine lubrication system will quickly lead to engine seizure. Check the engine

oil level before each ride, and top off as described in Chapter Three. Oil pump service is in Chapter Five.

High Oil Consumption or Excessive Exhaust Smoke

1. Worn valve guides.
2. Worn or damaged piston rings.

Oil Leaks

1. Clogged air filter housing breather hose.
2. Loose engine parts.
3. Damaged gasket sealing surfaces.

High Oil Pressure

1. Clogged oil filter.
2. Clogged oil passageways.
3. Incorrect type of engine oil.

Low Oil Pressure

1. Low oil level.
2. Defective oil pump.
3. Clogged oil strainer screen.
4. Clogged oil filter.
5. Internal oil leaks.
6. Incorrect type of engine oil.

No Oil Pressure

1. Low oil level.
2. Damaged oil pump drive shaft.
3. Damaged oil pump drive sprocket.
4. Incorrect oil pump installation.
5. Defective oil pump.

Oil Contamination

1. Blown head gasket allowing coolant to leak into the engine.
2. Water contamination.
3. Oil and filter not changed at specified intervals or when operating conditions demand more frequent changes.

OIL PRESSURE TEST

Check the oil pressure after installing a new oil pump, reassembling the engine or when troubleshooting the lubrication system.

To check the oil pressure, an oil pressure gauge hose (Suzuki part No. 09915-74510), gauge attachment (09915-74531) and high pressure meter (09915-77330) are required.

1. Make sure the engine oil level is correct as described in Chapter Three. Add oil if necessary.
2. Start the engine and allow it to reach normal operating temperature. Turn off the engine.
3. Place a drain pan under the main oil gallery plug (**Figure 3**) to catch the oil that drains out during the test.
4. Unscrew and remove the main oil gallery plug from the crankcase.

> *CAUTION*
> *Keep the gauge hose away from the exhaust pipe during this test. If the hose contacts the exhaust pipes, it may melt and spray hot oil onto the hot exhaust pipe, resulting in a fire.*

5. Install the adapter, then install the gauge into the main oil gallery. Make sure the fitting is tight to avoid an oil loss.
6. Start the engine and let it idle. Increase engine speed to 3000 rpm. The oil pressure should be 350-650 kPa (51-94 psi) when the oil temperature is 60° C (140° F).
7. If the oil pressure is lower than specified, check the following:
   a. Low oil level.
   b. Incorrect type of engine oil.
   c. Clogged oil strainer screen.
   d. Clogged oil filter.
   e. Oil leak from oil passageway.
   f. Damaged oil seal(s).
   g. Defective oil pump.
   h. Combination of the above.
8. If the oil pressure is higher than specified check the following:
   a. Incorrect type of engine oil.

b. Clogged oil passageways.

c. Clogged oil filter.

d. Combination of the above.

9. Shut off the engine and remove the test equipment.

10. Install the plug (**Figure 3**) and gasket onto the crankcase. Tighten the plug securely.

11. Check oil level and adjust if necessary. (Chapter Three.)

LEAKDOWN TEST

A leakdown test can locate engine problems from leaking valves, blown head gaskets or broken, worn or stuck piston rings. This test is performed by applying compressed air to the cylinder and then measuring the loss percentage. Use a cylinder leakdown tester (**Figure 4**) and an air compressor to perform this test.

Follow the manufacturer's directions along with the following information when performing a cylinder leak down test.

1. Start and run the engine until it reaches normal operating temperature, then turn off the engine.

2. Open and secure the throttle so it remains in the wide open position.

3. Remove both spark plugs as described in Chapter Three. This makes it easier to turn the engine by hand.

4. Remove the timing inspection plug (A, **Figure 5**).

5. Remove the alternator bolt access plug (B, **Figure 5**).

6. Insert a suitably sized socket through the alternator cover to engage the alternator rotor bolt (**Figure 6**).

NOTE
The alternator rotor has lines marked F or R to indicate top dead center for the front cylinder (F) or rear cylinder (R).

7. Rotate the engine *counterclockwise*, as viewed from the left side of the motorcycle. Rotate the alternator rotor until the *F* or *R* line, depending on the cylinder being tested, aligns with the mark on the timing inspection hole as shown in **Figure 7**. To determine if the piston is on the compression stroke, hold your finger on the spark plug hole of the cylinder being tested to feel for compression.

8. Install the leakdown tester into the spark plug hole. Connect an air compressor to the tester fitting.

NOTE
The engine may turn over when air pressure is applied to the cylinder. To prevent this from happening, shift the transmission into fifth gear.

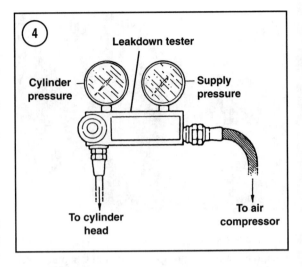

9. Apply compressed air to the leakdown tester. Read the leak rate on the gauge and record the measurement.

10. Listen for air escaping from the engine at the following points.

   a. Air leaking through the exhaust pipe indicates a leaking exhaust valve.

   b. Air leaking through the carburetor indicates a leaking intake valve.

   c. Air leaking through the crankcase breather tube indicates worn piston rings.

   d. Air leaking into the cooling system causes the coolant to bubble in the radiator. If this occurs, check for a damaged cylinder head gasket and/or a warped or cracked cylinder head or cylinder block surface.

11. Repeat Steps 7-10 for the remaining cylinder.

   a. For a new or rebuilt engine, a pressure loss of 0 to 5 percent per cylinder is desirable. A pressure loss of 6 to 14 percent is acceptable and means the engine is in good condition.

   b. If testing a used engine, the critical parameter is not each cylinder's leak rate, but the difference between the cylinders. On a used engine, a dif-

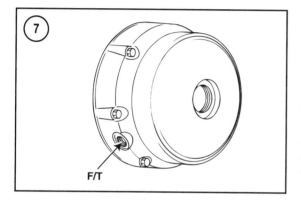

F/T

mechanism can be examined after disassembling the crankcase.

TRANSMISSION

Transmission symptoms are sometimes hard to distinguish from clutch symptoms. Prior to working on the transmission, be sure the clutch and gearshift linkage assemblies are not causing the problem.

Refer to **Figure 10** for possible causes of transmission problems. Refer to Chapter Seven for transmission service procedures.

FUEL SYSTEM
(CARBURETED MODELS)

Do not assume that the carburetors are at fault when the engine does not run properly. While fuel system problems are not uncommon, random adjustments will only compound the problem.

Make sure the ignition system is working properly. Attempt to isolate the problem to the fuel tank, fuel shutoff valve and filter, fuel pump, fuel hoses or the carburetor.

Identifying Carburetor Conditions

Refer to the following conditions to identify whether the engine is running lean or rich.

Rich

1. Fouled spark plugs.
2. Engine misfires and runs rough under load.
3. Excessive exhaust smoke as the throttle is increased.
4. An extreme rich condition results in a choked or dull sound from the exhaust and an inability to clear the exhaust with the throttle held wide open.

Lean

1. Blistered or very white spark plug electrodes.
2. Engine overheats.
3. Slow acceleration, engine power is reduced.
4. Flat spots on acceleration that are similar in feel to when the engine starts to run out of gas.
5. Engine speed fluctuates at full throttle.

Fuel Level System

Proper carburetor operation depends on a constant and correct carburetor fuel level. As fuel is drawn

ference of 10 percent or less between the cylinders is acceptable.

  c. If the pressure loss between cylinders differs by more than 10 percent, the engine is in poor condition and further testing is required.

10. When finished, reinstall the spark plugs as described in Chapter Three and tightly install the timing inspection plug (A, **Figure 5**) and the alternator bolt access plut (B).

CLUTCH

Refer to **Figure 8** for possible clutch malfunction causes. Refer to Chapter Six for clutch service procedures.

Make sure the clutch problem is not due to a faulty clutch cable or actuator before investigating internal causes.

GEARSHIFT LINKAGE

The gearshift linkage assembly connects the gearshift pedal (external shift mechanism) to the shift drum (internal shift mechanism). Refer to **Figure 9** for possible causes of gearshift problems.

The external shift mechanism can be examined after removing the clutch assembly. The internal shift

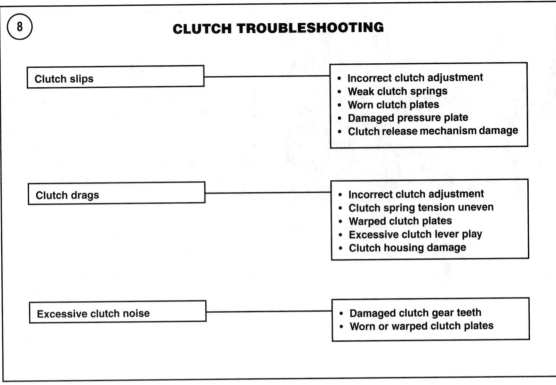

⑧ CLUTCH TROUBLESHOOTING

Clutch slips
- Incorrect clutch adjustment
- Weak clutch springs
- Worn clutch plates
- Damaged pressure plate
- Clutch release mechanism damage

Clutch drags
- Incorrect clutch adjustment
- Clutch spring tension uneven
- Warped clutch plates
- Excessive clutch lever play
- Clutch housing damage

Excessive clutch noise
- Damaged clutch gear teeth
- Worn or warped clutch plates

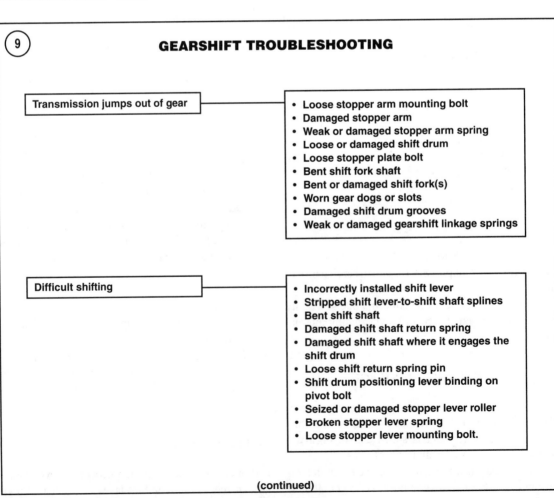

⑨ GEARSHIFT TROUBLESHOOTING

Transmission jumps out of gear
- Loose stopper arm mounting bolt
- Damaged stopper arm
- Weak or damaged stopper arm spring
- Loose or damaged shift drum
- Loose stopper plate bolt
- Bent shift fork shaft
- Bent or damaged shift fork(s)
- Worn gear dogs or slots
- Damaged shift drum grooves
- Weak or damaged gearshift linkage springs

Difficult shifting
- Incorrectly installed shift lever
- Stripped shift lever-to-shift shaft splines
- Bent shift shaft
- Damaged shift shaft return spring
- Damaged shift shaft where it engages the shift drum
- Loose shift return spring pin
- Shift drum positioning lever binding on pivot bolt
- Seized or damaged stopper lever roller
- Broken stopper lever spring
- Loose stopper lever mounting bolt.

(continued)

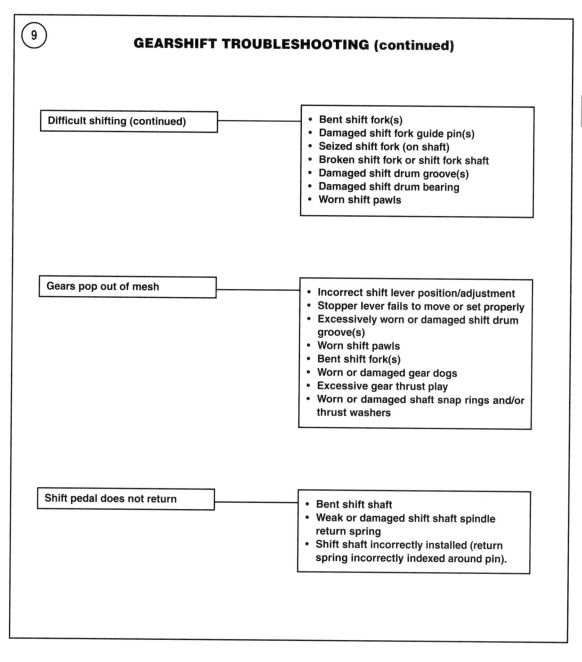

⑨ **GEARSHIFT TROUBLESHOOTING (continued)**

Difficult shifting (continued)
- Bent shift fork(s)
- Damaged shift fork guide pin(s)
- Seized shift fork (on shaft)
- Broken shift fork or shift fork shaft
- Damaged shift drum groove(s)
- Damaged shift drum bearing
- Worn shift pawls

Gears pop out of mesh
- Incorrect shift lever position/adjustment
- Stopper lever fails to move or set properly
- Excessively worn or damaged shift drum groove(s)
- Worn shift pawls
- Bent shift fork(s)
- Worn or damaged gear dogs
- Excessive gear thrust play
- Worn or damaged shaft snap rings and/or thrust washers

Shift pedal does not return
- Bent shift shaft
- Weak or damaged shift shaft spindle return spring
- Shift shaft incorrectly installed (return spring incorrectly indexed around pin).

from the float bowl during engine operation, the float level in the bowl drops. As the float drops, the fuel valve moves away from its seat and allows fuel to flow through the seat into the float bowl. Fuel entering the float bowl will cause the float to rise and push against the fuel valve. When the fuel level reaches a predetermined level, the fuel valve is pushed against the seat to prevent the float bowl from overfilling.

If the fuel valve fails to close, the engine will run too rich, or flood, with fuel. Symptoms of this problem are rough running, excessive black smoke and poor acceleration. This condition will sometimes clear up when the engine is run at wide-open throttle, as the fuel is being drawn into the engine before the

float bowl can overfill. As the engine speed is reduced, however, the rich running condition returns.

Several things can cause fuel overflow. In most instances, it can be as simple as a small piece of dirt trapped between the fuel valve and seat or an incorrect float level.

Starting Enrichment (Choke) System

A cold engine requires a rich mixture to start and run properly. A cable-actuated starting enrichment (choke) lever located on the left side handlebar and the valve on each carburetor are used for cold starting.

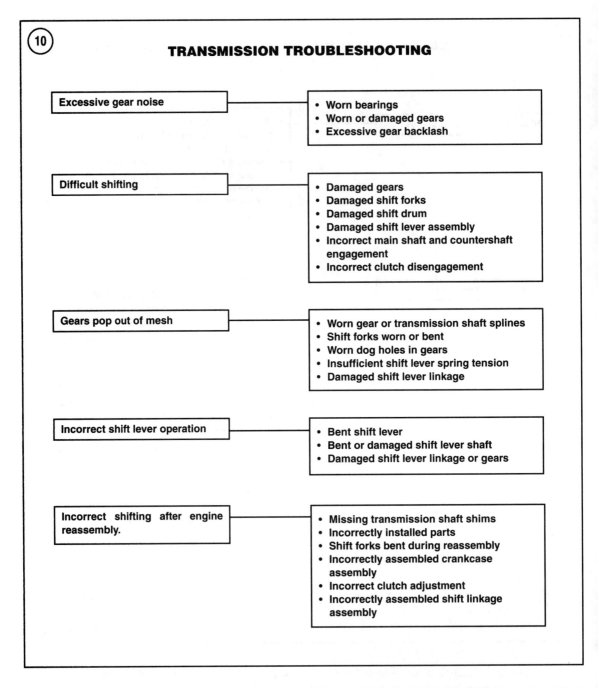

TRANSMISSION TROUBLESHOOTING

Excessive gear noise

- Worn bearings
- Worn or damaged gears
- Excessive gear backlash

Difficult shifting

- Damaged gears
- Damaged shift forks
- Damaged shift drum
- Damaged shift lever assembly
- Incorrect main shaft and countershaft engagement
- Incorrect clutch disengagement

Gears pop out of mesh

- Worn gear or transmission shaft splines
- Shift forks worn or bent
- Worn dog holes in gears
- Insufficient shift lever spring tension
- Damaged shift lever linkage

Incorrect shift lever operation

- Bent shift lever
- Bent or damaged shift lever shaft
- Damaged shift lever linkage or gears

Incorrect shifting after engine reassembly.

- Missing transmission shaft shims
- Incorrectly installed parts
- Shift forks bent during reassembly
- Incorrectly assembled crankcase assembly
- Incorrect clutch adjustment
- Incorrectly assembled shift linkage assembly

If the engine is difficult to start when cold, check the starting enrichment (choke) cable operation. If necessary, lubricate the cable assembly as described in Chapter Three.

ELECTRONIC DIAGNOSTIC SYSTEM

The electronic control module (ECM) includes a self-diagnostic function that monitors electrical components of the ignition and fuel injection systems. Whenever an error is detected, the ECM stores the malfunction and sets a malfunction code. It also turns

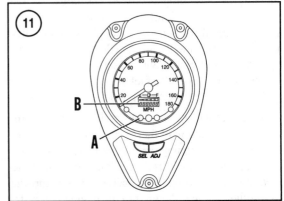

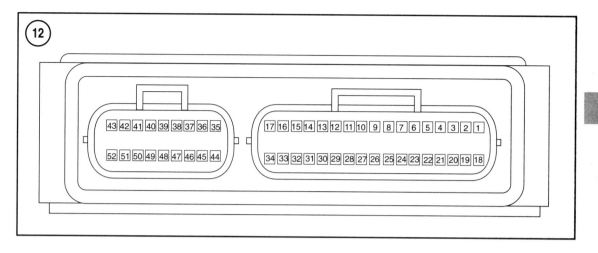

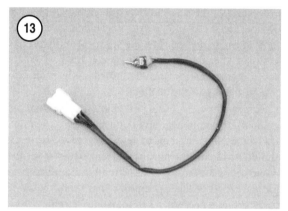

ECM Testing

Fuel injection troubleshooting frequently includes testing the ECM wiring. Some wiring colors are used more than once in the ECM 34-pin and 18-pin connectors. To ensure the correct wire is tested, the test procedures include the wire color and pin location to describe a test point. The number in parentheses after a wiring color refers to the pin location number. Refer to **Figure 12** to determine where that terminal is located in the relevant ECM connector.

If testing indicates that the ECM is faulty, take the motorcycle to a dealership for further testing before purchasing a replacement ECM. If possible, install a known good ECM and confirm that the ECM is the problem.

Malfunction Code Retrieval

When the system is in dealer mode, the meter assembly LCD displays any stored malfunction codes.

A mode select switch (Suzuki part No. 09930-82720) is needed to enter the dealer mode (**Figure 13**).

> *CAUTION*
> *Do not attempt this procedure without the mode select switch. Shorting the terminals in the dealer mode connector could damage the ECM.*

1. Remove the right side cover as described in Chapter Sixteen.

2. Connect the mode select switch to the white dealer mode connector near the upper, rear frame rail (**Figure 14**).

3. Run the engine for four seconds. If the engine will not start, crank the engine for four seconds.

4. After four seconds, turn the mode select switch on. The system enters the dealer mode, and displays a

on the indicator LED (A, **Figure 11**) in the meter assembly and *FI* appears in the odometer portion (B) of the meter display.

Electrical Component Replacement

Most motorcycle dealerships and parts suppliers will not accept the return of any electrical part. Consider any test results carefully before replacing a component that tests only slightly out of specification, especially resistance.

stored malfunction code in the LCD portion of the meter assembly. If more than one code is stored, codes are displayed in numeric order starting with the lowest numbered code.

5. Record any malfunction codes before disconnecting the ECM connectors from the ECM, the ECM ground wire from the harness or engine, or the battery cables or before pulling the main fuse. Any of these actions erases the malfunction code(s) from memory. The malfunction code table (**Figure 15**) lists the malfunction codes and the likely causes.

Fail-Safe Operation

For some malfunction codes, the ECM sets the affected component to a preset value so the motorcycle can still operate. This fail-safe operation allows the motorcycle to still run. Refer to **Figure 16** for the fail-safe actions taken when a particular malfunction code is set. This chart also describes whether the motorcycle can continue to operate once a code has been set or if it can be restarted after the engine has been turned off.

Even if the motorcycle continues to run with a malfunction code stored, troubleshoot the system and eliminate the problem immediately. If the problem cannot be solved, take the motorcycle to a dealership as soon as possible.

Malfunction Code Troubleshooting

Perform the following to troubleshoot a problem with the fuel injection system.

1. Enter the dealer mode as described in *Malfunction Code Retrieval* in this section.

2. Record any displayed malfunction code(s).

3. Refer to the troubleshooting chart (**Figure 17**), and identify the relevant diagnostic flow chart for the malfunction code.

> *NOTE*
> *The diagnostic flow charts refer to various test procedures for the affected components. The removal, adjustment and test procedures for most of the mentioned components are in this chapter. Any exceptions are noted in the flow charts.*

4. Turn to the indicated diagnostic flow chart (**Figures 18-33**). Perform the test procedures in order until the problem is resolved.

5. Once a fault has been corrected, reset the self-diagnostic system as described in this section.

Resetting the Self-diagnostic System

Perform the following to reset the system once a fuel injection system malfunction has been corrected.

1. While in the dealer mode, turn the ignition switch off and then turn it back on.

2. The LCD should display the no fault code: c00.

3. Turn the dealer mode switch to off, and disconnect the switch from the dealer mode connector.

4. Reinstall the right side cover.

ELECTRICAL TESTING

This section describes typical test equipment and how to troubleshoot with them.

Never assume anything and do not overlook the obvious, such as a blown fuse or an electrical connector that has separated. Test the simplest and most obvious items first and try to make tests at easily accessible points on the motorcycle. Make sure to troubleshoot systematically.

Refer to the color wiring diagrams at the end of the manual for component and connector identification. Use the wiring diagrams to determine how the circuit should work by tracing the current paths from the power source through the circuit components to ground. Also check any circuits that share the same fuse, ground or switch. If the other circuits work properly and the shared wiring is good, the cause must be in the wiring used only by the suspect circuit. If all related circuits are faulty at the same time, the probable cause is a poor ground connection or a blown fuse(s).

Preliminary Checks and Precautions

Before starting any electrical troubleshooting, perform the following:

1. Inspect the fuse for the suspected circuit, and replace it if blown. Refer to *Fuses* in Chapter Ten.

2. Inspect the battery (Chapter Three). Make sure it is fully charged and the battery leads are clean and securely attached to the battery terminals.

3. Electrical connectors are often the cause of electrical system problems. Inspect the connectors as follows:

   a. Disconnect each electrical connector in the suspect circuit and make sure there are no bent terminals in the electrical connector. A bent terminal will not connect to its mate, causing an open circuit.

   b. Make sure the terminals are pushed all the way into the connector. If not, carefully push them in with a narrow blade screwdriver.

(15)

MALFUNCTION CODE TABLE

2

Malfunction Code	Related Item	Detected Failure	Probable Cause
c00	No error	-	-
c12	Crankshaft position (CKP) sensor	The ECM has not received a signal from the crankshaft position sensor 3 seconds after it received the start signal.	Faulty crankshaft position sensor, its wiring or connector.
c13 (front cyl.) c17 (rear cyl.)	Intake air pressure (IAP) sensor	The sensor's voltage is outside the range 0.1-4.8 volts.	Faulty intake air pressure sensor, its wiring or connector.
c14	Throttle position (TP) sensor	The sensor's voltage is outside the range 0.1-4.8 volts.	Faulty throttle position sensor, its wiring or connector.
c15	Engine coolant temperature (ECT) sensor	The sensor's voltage is outside the range: 0.1-4.6 volts.	Faulty engine coolant temperature sensor, its wiring or connector.
c21	Intake air temperature (IAT) sensor	The sensor's voltage is outside the range 0.1-4.6 volts.	Faulty intake air temperature sensor, its wiring or connector.
c23	Tip-over (TO) sensor	The sensor's voltage is not within the range of 0.2 – 4.6 volts 2 seconds after the ignition switch has been turned on.	Faulty tip over sensor, its wiring or connector.
c24 (rear cyl.) c25 (front cyl.)	Ignition system malfunction	The ECM does not receive a proper signal from an ignition coil.	Faulty ignition coil, its wiring or connector. Faulty power supply from the battery.
c28	Secondary throttle valve actuator (STVA)	Signal voltage from the ECM is not reaching the actuator, the ECM is not receiving a signal from the actuator, or load voltage is not reaching the actuator motor.	Faulty secondary throttle valve actuator, its wiring or connector.
c29	Secondary throttle position (STP) sensor	The sensor's voltage is outside the range 0.1-4.8 volts.	Faulty secondary throttle position sensor, its wiring or connector.
c31	Gear position (GP) signal	The gear position sensor's voltage is less than 0.6 volts for 3 or more seconds.	Faulty gear position sensor, its wiring, connector or faulty shift cam.
c32 (rear cyl.) c33 (front cyl.)	Fuel injector	The ECM does not receive a proper signal from the fuel injector.	Faulty fuel injector, its wiring or connector. Faulty power supply to the injector.
c41	Fuel pump relay	The ECM does not receive a signal from the fuel pump relay.	Faulty fuel pump relay, wiring or connector. Faulty power source to the fuel pump relay or injectors.

(continued)

(15)

MALFUNCTION CODE TABLE (continued)

Malfunction Code	Related Item	Detected Failure	Probable Cause
c42	Ignition switch signal	The ECM does not receive a signal from ignition switch.	Faulty ignition switch, its wiring or connector.
c44	HO$_2$	No oxygen sensor voltage to ECM. No heater voltage to sensor.	Faulty wiring or connector. No battery voltage to sensor.
c49	PAIR control solenoid valve	The ECM does not receive voltage from PAIR control solenoid valve.	Faulty PAIR solenoid, wiring or connector.

(16)

FAIL-SAFE ACTION

Failed Item	Fail-safe Action	Operation Status
Crankshaft position sensor.	The motorcycle stops.	Engine stops operating; cannot restart.
Intake air pressure sensor.	Intake air pressure is set to 760 mmHg (29.92 in. Hg).	Engine continues operating; can restart.
Throttle position sensor.	Throttle valve is set to its fully open position. Ignition timing is set to a present value	Engine continues operating; can restart.
Engine coolant temperature sensor.	Engine coolant temperature is set to 80° C (176° F).	Engine continues operating; can restart.
Intake air temperature sensor.	Intake air temperature set to 40° C (104° F).	Engine continues operating; can restart.
Ignition signal.	No spark at cylinder.	Cylinder can operate.
Fuel injector.	Fuel cut-off to injector.	Cylinder can operate.
Secondary throttle valve actuator.	Secondary throttle valve is set to the fully closed position.	Engine continues operating; can restart.
Secondary throttle position sensor.	Secondary throttle valve is set to the fully closed position.	Engine continues operating; can restart.
Exhaust control valve actuator	Exhaust control valve set to the fully opened position.	Engine continues operating; can restart.
Gear position signal.	Gear position signal set to fifth gear.	Engine continues operating; can restart.
Heated oxygen sensor.	Air/fuel ratio fixed to normal condition.	Engine continues operating; can restart.
PAIR control solenoid valve.	ECM ceases control of PAIR control solenoid valve.	Engine continues operating; can restart.

⑰	TROUBLESHOOTING CHART

Malfunction Code	Diagnostic Flow Chart
c00	No fault detected
c12	Figure 18
c13	Figure 19
c14	Figure 20
c15	Figure 21
c17	Figure 22
c21	Figure 23
c23	Figure 24
c24 or c25	Figure 25
c28	Figure 26
c29	Figure 27
c31	Figure 28
c32 or c33	Figure 29
c41	Figure 30
c42	Figure 31
c44	Figure 32
c49	Figure 33

2

c. Check the wires where they attach to the terminals for damage.

d. Make sure each terminal is clean and free of corrosion. Clean them, if necessary, and pack the connectors with dielectric grease.

e. Push the connector halves together. Make sure the connectors are fully engaged and locked together.

f. Never pull the wires when disconnecting a connector. Pull only on the connector housing.

4. Never use a self-powered test light on circuits that contain solid-state devices. The solid-state devices may be damaged.

Intermittent Problems

Problems that do not occur all the time can be difficult to isolate during testing. For example, when a problem only occurs when the motorcycle is ridden over rough roads (vibration) or in wet conditions (water penetration). Note the following:

1. Vibration. This is a common problem with loose or damaged electrical connectors.

a. Perform a continuity test as described in the appropriate service procedure or under *Continuity Test* in this section.

b. Lightly pull or wiggle the connectors while repeating the test. Do the same when checking the wiring harness and individual components, especially where the wires enter a housing or connector.

c. A change in meter readings indicates a poor connection. Find and repair the problem or replace the part. Check for wires with cracked or broken insulation.

NOTE
An analog ohmmeter is useful when making this type of test. Slight needle movements are visibly apparent, which indicate a loose connection.

2. Heat. This is a common problem with connectors or joints that have loose or poor connections. As these connections heat up, the connection or joint expands and separates, causing an open circuit. Other

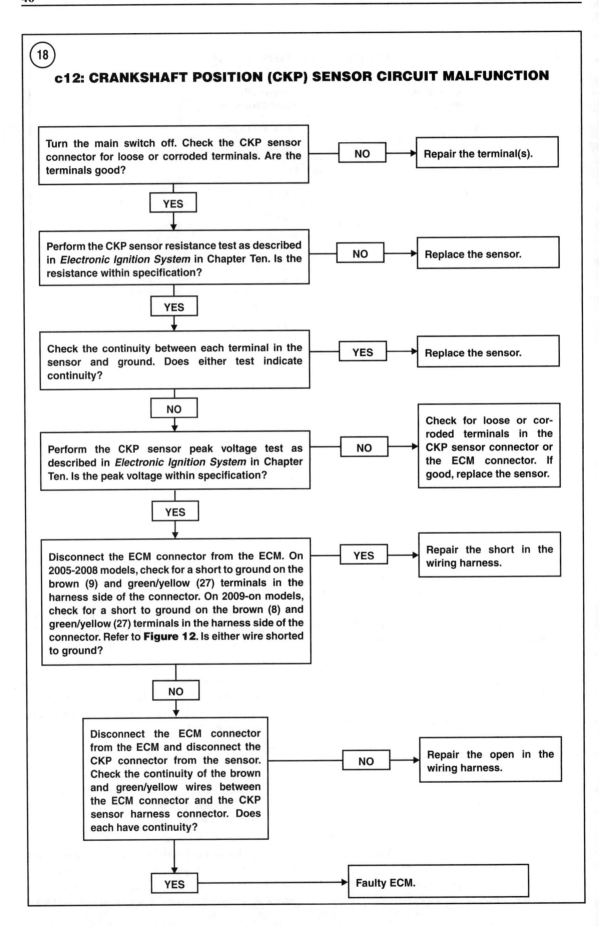

(18)

c12: CRANKSHAFT POSITION (CKP) SENSOR CIRCUIT MALFUNCTION

Turn the main switch off. Check the CKP sensor connector for loose or corroded terminals. Are the terminals good? → NO → Repair the terminal(s).

YES ↓

Perform the CKP sensor resistance test as described in *Electronic Ignition System* in Chapter Ten. Is the resistance within specification? → NO → Replace the sensor.

YES ↓

Check the continuity between each terminal in the sensor and ground. Does either test indicate continuity? → YES → Replace the sensor.

NO ↓

Perform the CKP sensor peak voltage test as described in *Electronic Ignition System* in Chapter Ten. Is the peak voltage within specification? → NO → Check for loose or corroded terminals in the CKP sensor connector or the ECM connector. If good, replace the sensor.

YES ↓

Disconnect the ECM connector from the ECM. On 2005-2008 models, check for a short to ground on the brown (9) and green/yellow (27) terminals in the harness side of the connector. On 2009-on models, check for a short to ground on the brown (8) and green/yellow (27) terminals in the harness side of the connector. Refer to **Figure 12**. Is either wire shorted to ground? → YES → Repair the short in the wiring harness.

NO ↓

Disconnect the ECM connector from the ECM and disconnect the CKP connector from the sensor. Check the continuity of the brown and green/yellow wires between the ECM connector and the CKP sensor harness connector. Does each have continuity? → NO → Repair the open in the wiring harness.

YES → Faulty ECM.

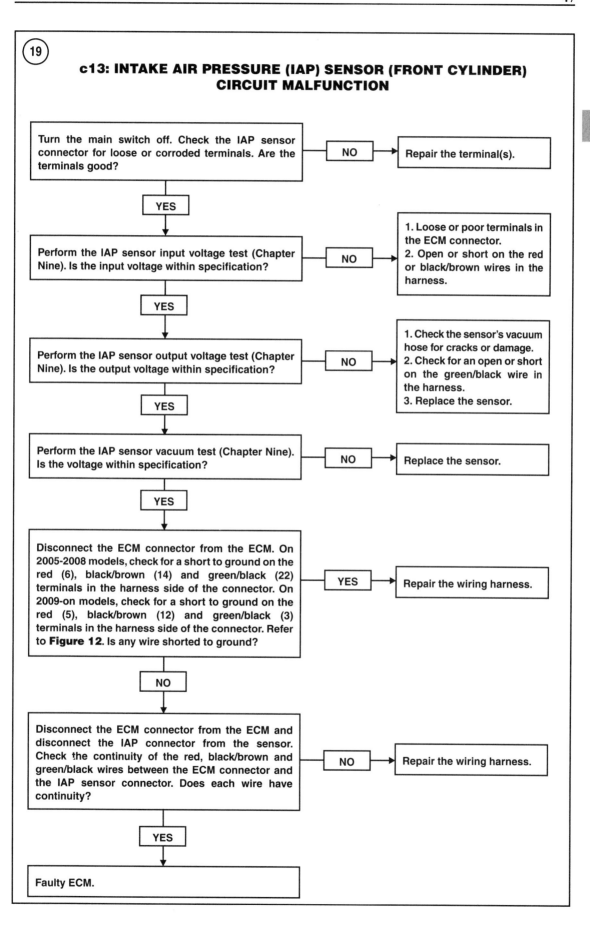

19

c13: INTAKE AIR PRESSURE (IAP) SENSOR (FRONT CYLINDER) CIRCUIT MALFUNCTION

Turn the main switch off. Check the IAP sensor connector for loose or corroded terminals. Are the terminals good? → **NO** → Repair the terminal(s).

↓ **YES**

Perform the IAP sensor input voltage test (Chapter Nine). Is the input voltage within specification? → **NO** →
1. Loose or poor terminals in the ECM connector.
2. Open or short on the red or black/brown wires in the harness.

↓ **YES**

Perform the IAP sensor output voltage test (Chapter Nine). Is the output voltage within specification? → **NO** →
1. Check the sensor's vacuum hose for cracks or damage.
2. Check for an open or short on the green/black wire in the harness.
3. Replace the sensor.

↓ **YES**

Perform the IAP sensor vacuum test (Chapter Nine). Is the voltage within specification? → **NO** → Replace the sensor.

↓ **YES**

Disconnect the ECM connector from the ECM. On 2005-2008 models, check for a short to ground on the red (6), black/brown (14) and green/black (22) terminals in the harness side of the connector. On 2009-on models, check for a short to ground on the red (5), black/brown (12) and green/black (3) terminals in the harness side of the connector. Refer to **Figure 12**. Is any wire shorted to ground? → **YES** → Repair the wiring harness.

↓ **NO**

Disconnect the ECM connector from the ECM and disconnect the IAP connector from the sensor. Check the continuity of the red, black/brown and green/black wires between the ECM connector and the IAP sensor connector. Does each wire have continuity? → **NO** → Repair the wiring harness.

↓ **YES**

Faulty ECM.

2

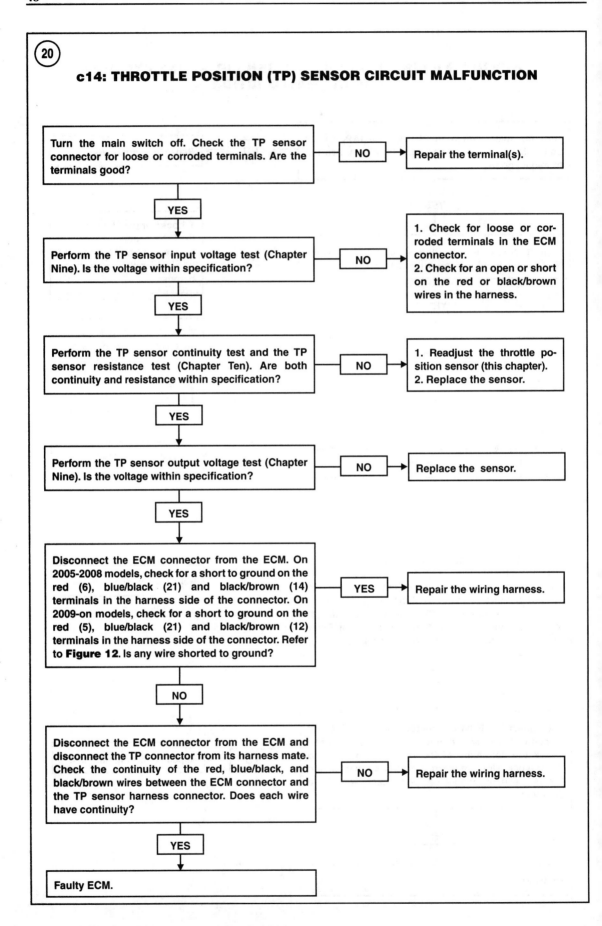

20

c14: THROTTLE POSITION (TP) SENSOR CIRCUIT MALFUNCTION

Turn the main switch off. Check the TP sensor connector for loose or corroded terminals. Are the terminals good? → **NO** → Repair the terminal(s).

↓ **YES**

Perform the TP sensor input voltage test (Chapter Nine). Is the voltage within specification? → **NO** →
1. Check for loose or corroded terminals in the ECM connector.
2. Check for an open or short on the red or black/brown wires in the harness.

↓ **YES**

Perform the TP sensor continuity test and the TP sensor resistance test (Chapter Ten). Are both continuity and resistance within specification? → **NO** →
1. Readjust the throttle position sensor (this chapter).
2. Replace the sensor.

↓ **YES**

Perform the TP sensor output voltage test (Chapter Nine). Is the voltage within specification? → **NO** → Replace the sensor.

↓ **YES**

Disconnect the ECM connector from the ECM. On 2005-2008 models, check for a short to ground on the red (6), blue/black (21) and black/brown (14) terminals in the harness side of the connector. On 2009-on models, check for a short to ground on the red (5), blue/black (21) and black/brown (12) terminals in the harness side of the connector. Refer to **Figure 12**. Is any wire shorted to ground? → **YES** → Repair the wiring harness.

↓ **NO**

Disconnect the ECM connector from the ECM and disconnect the TP connector from its harness mate. Check the continuity of the red, blue/black, and black/brown wires between the ECM connector and the TP sensor harness connector. Does each wire have continuity? → **NO** → Repair the wiring harness.

↓ **YES**

Faulty ECM.

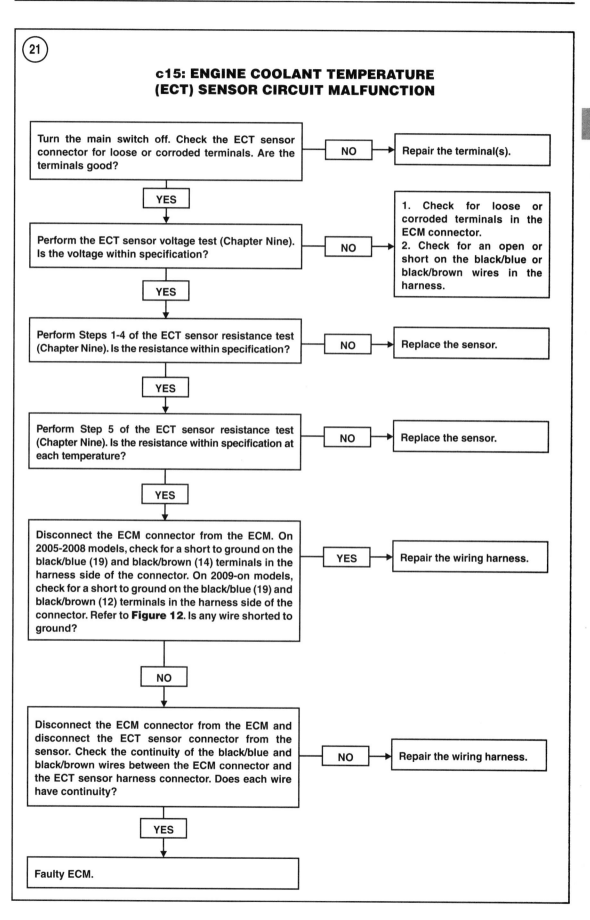

(21)

c15: ENGINE COOLANT TEMPERATURE (ECT) SENSOR CIRCUIT MALFUNCTION

2

Turn the main switch off. Check the ECT sensor connector for loose or corroded terminals. Are the terminals good? → **NO** → Repair the terminal(s).

↓ **YES**

Perform the ECT sensor voltage test (Chapter Nine). Is the voltage within specification? → **NO** → 1. Check for loose or corroded terminals in the ECM connector.
2. Check for an open or short on the black/blue or black/brown wires in the harness.

↓ **YES**

Perform Steps 1-4 of the ECT sensor resistance test (Chapter Nine). Is the resistance within specification? → **NO** → Replace the sensor.

↓ **YES**

Perform Step 5 of the ECT sensor resistance test (Chapter Nine). Is the resistance within specification at each temperature? → **NO** → Replace the sensor.

↓ **YES**

Disconnect the ECM connector from the ECM. On 2005-2008 models, check for a short to ground on the black/blue (19) and black/brown (14) terminals in the harness side of the connector. On 2009-on models, check for a short to ground on the black/blue (19) and black/brown (12) terminals in the harness side of the connector. Refer to **Figure 12**. Is any wire shorted to ground? → **YES** → Repair the wiring harness.

↓ **NO**

Disconnect the ECM connector from the ECM and disconnect the ECT sensor connector from the sensor. Check the continuity of the black/blue and black/brown wires between the ECM connector and the ECT sensor harness connector. Does each wire have continuity? → **NO** → Repair the wiring harness.

↓ **YES**

Faulty ECM.

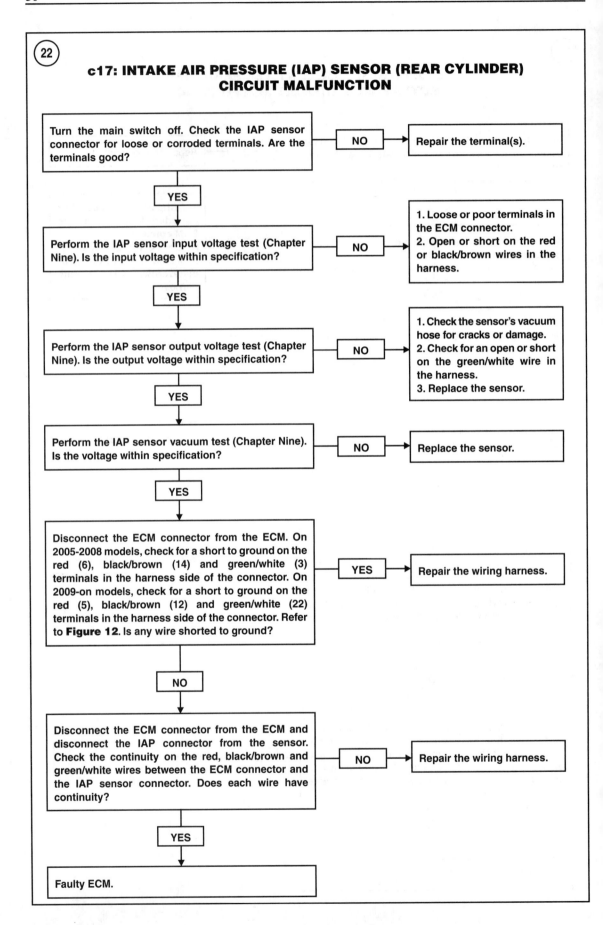

(22)

c17: INTAKE AIR PRESSURE (IAP) SENSOR (REAR CYLINDER) CIRCUIT MALFUNCTION

Turn the main switch off. Check the IAP sensor connector for loose or corroded terminals. Are the terminals good? → **NO** → Repair the terminal(s).

YES

Perform the IAP sensor input voltage test (Chapter Nine). Is the input voltage within specification? → **NO** → 1. Loose or poor terminals in the ECM connector. 2. Open or short on the red or black/brown wires in the harness.

YES

Perform the IAP sensor output voltage test (Chapter Nine). Is the output voltage within specification? → **NO** → 1. Check the sensor's vacuum hose for cracks or damage. 2. Check for an open or short on the green/white wire in the harness. 3. Replace the sensor.

YES

Perform the IAP sensor vacuum test (Chapter Nine). Is the voltage within specification? → **NO** → Replace the sensor.

YES

Disconnect the ECM connector from the ECM. On 2005-2008 models, check for a short to ground on the red (6), black/brown (14) and green/white (3) terminals in the harness side of the connector. On 2009-on models, check for a short to ground on the red (5), black/brown (12) and green/white (22) terminals in the harness side of the connector. Refer to **Figure 12**. Is any wire shorted to ground? → **YES** → Repair the wiring harness.

NO

Disconnect the ECM connector from the ECM and disconnect the IAP connector from the sensor. Check the continuity on the red, black/brown and green/white wires between the ECM connector and the IAP sensor connector. Does each wire have continuity? → **NO** → Repair the wiring harness.

YES

Faulty ECM.

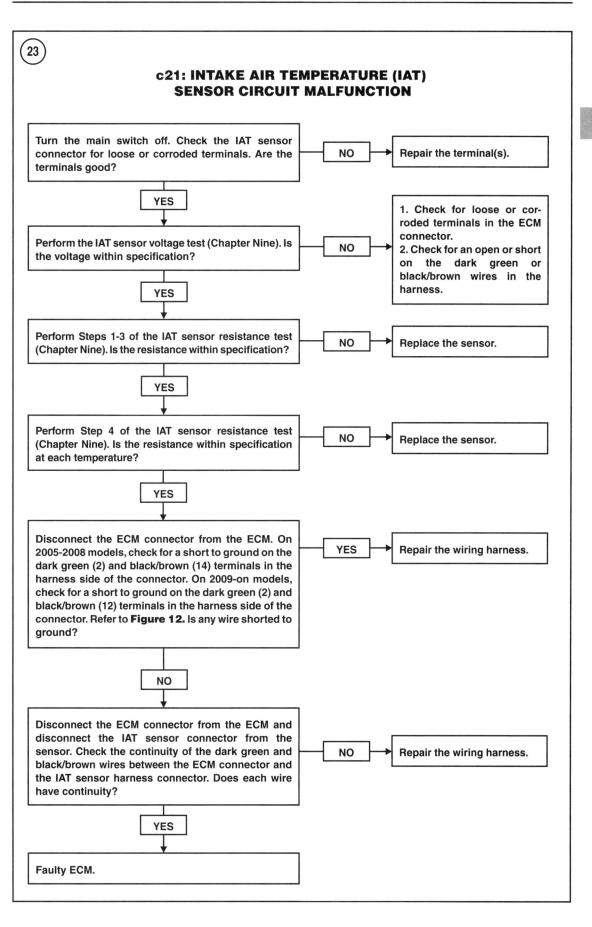

c21: INTAKE AIR TEMPERATURE (IAT) SENSOR CIRCUIT MALFUNCTION

(23)

Turn the main switch off. Check the IAT sensor connector for loose or corroded terminals. Are the terminals good? → **NO** → Repair the terminal(s).

YES ↓

Perform the IAT sensor voltage test (Chapter Nine). Is the voltage within specification? → **NO** → 1. Check for loose or corroded terminals in the ECM connector. 2. Check for an open or short on the dark green or black/brown wires in the harness.

YES ↓

Perform Steps 1-3 of the IAT sensor resistance test (Chapter Nine). Is the resistance within specification? → **NO** → Replace the sensor.

YES ↓

Perform Step 4 of the IAT sensor resistance test (Chapter Nine). Is the resistance within specification at each temperature? → **NO** → Replace the sensor.

YES ↓

Disconnect the ECM connector from the ECM. On 2005-2008 models, check for a short to ground on the dark green (2) and black/brown (14) terminals in the harness side of the connector. On 2009-on models, check for a short to ground on the dark green (2) and black/brown (12) terminals in the harness side of the connector. Refer to **Figure 12.** Is any wire shorted to ground? → **YES** → Repair the wiring harness.

NO ↓

Disconnect the ECM connector from the ECM and disconnect the IAT sensor connector from the sensor. Check the continuity of the dark green and black/brown wires between the ECM connector and the IAT sensor harness connector. Does each wire have continuity? → **NO** → Repair the wiring harness.

YES ↓

Faulty ECM.

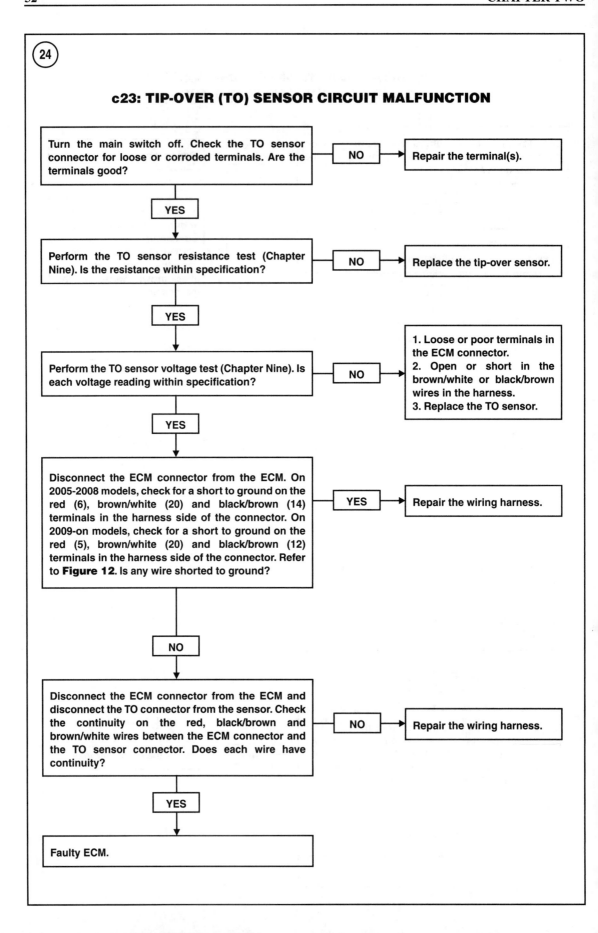

(24)

c23: TIP-OVER (TO) SENSOR CIRCUIT MALFUNCTION

Turn the main switch off. Check the TO sensor connector for loose or corroded terminals. Are the terminals good? → **NO** → Repair the terminal(s).

YES

Perform the TO sensor resistance test (Chapter Nine). Is the resistance within specification? → **NO** → Replace the tip-over sensor.

YES

Perform the TO sensor voltage test (Chapter Nine). Is each voltage reading within specification? → **NO** →
1. Loose or poor terminals in the ECM connector.
2. Open or short in the brown/white or black/brown wires in the harness.
3. Replace the TO sensor.

YES

Disconnect the ECM connector from the ECM. On 2005-2008 models, check for a short to ground on the red (6), brown/white (20) and black/brown (14) terminals in the harness side of the connector. On 2009-on models, check for a short to ground on the red (5), brown/white (20) and black/brown (12) terminals in the harness side of the connector. Refer to **Figure 12**. Is any wire shorted to ground? → **YES** → Repair the wiring harness.

NO

Disconnect the ECM connector from the ECM and disconnect the TO connector from the sensor. Check the continuity on the red, black/brown and brown/white wires between the ECM connector and the TO sensor connector. Does each wire have continuity? → **NO** → Repair the wiring harness.

YES

Faulty ECM.

(25)

c24 or c25: IGNITION SYSTEM MALFUNCTION

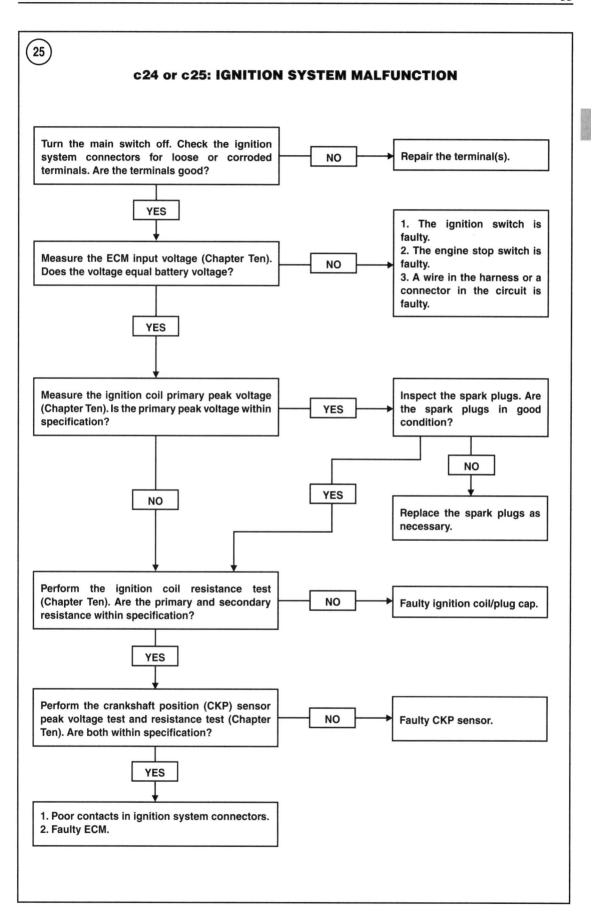

Turn the main switch off. Check the ignition system connectors for loose or corroded terminals. Are the terminals good? — **NO** → Repair the terminal(s).

YES ↓

Measure the ECM input voltage (Chapter Ten). Does the voltage equal battery voltage? — **NO** →
1. The ignition switch is faulty.
2. The engine stop switch is faulty.
3. A wire in the harness or a connector in the circuit is faulty.

YES ↓

Measure the ignition coil primary peak voltage (Chapter Ten). Is the primary peak voltage within specification? — **YES** → Inspect the spark plugs. Are the spark plugs in good condition?

NO — **YES** — **NO**

Replace the spark plugs as necessary.

Perform the ignition coil resistance test (Chapter Ten). Are the primary and secondary resistance within specification? — **NO** → Faulty ignition coil/plug cap.

YES ↓

Perform the crankshaft position (CKP) sensor peak voltage test and resistance test (Chapter Ten). Are both within specification? — **NO** → Faulty CKP sensor.

YES ↓

1. Poor contacts in ignition system connectors.
2. Faulty ECM.

(26)

c28: SECONDARY THROTTLE VALVE
ACTUATOR (STVA) CIRCUIT MALFUNCTION

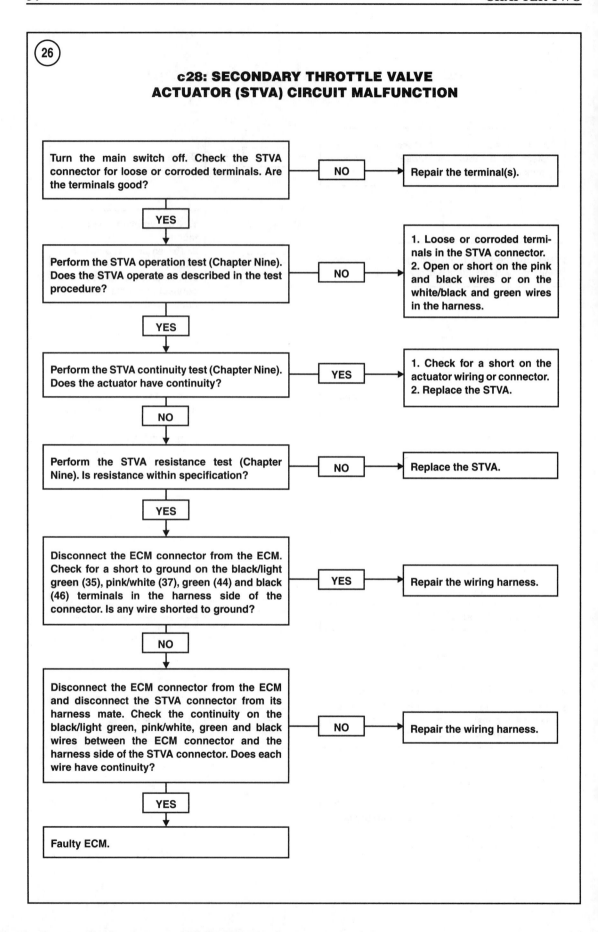

Turn the main switch off. Check the STVA connector for loose or corroded terminals. Are the terminals good? → **NO** → Repair the terminal(s).

↓ **YES**

Perform the STVA operation test (Chapter Nine). Does the STVA operate as described in the test procedure? → **NO** →
1. Loose or corroded terminals in the STVA connector.
2. Open or short on the pink and black wires or on the white/black and green wires in the harness.

↓ **YES**

Perform the STVA continuity test (Chapter Nine). Does the actuator have continuity? → **YES** →
1. Check for a short on the actuator wiring or connector.
2. Replace the STVA.

↓ **NO**

Perform the STVA resistance test (Chapter Nine). Is resistance within specification? → **NO** → Replace the STVA.

↓ **YES**

Disconnect the ECM connector from the ECM. Check for a short to ground on the black/light green (35), pink/white (37), green (44) and black (46) terminals in the harness side of the connector. Is any wire shorted to ground? → **YES** → Repair the wiring harness.

↓ **NO**

Disconnect the ECM connector from the ECM and disconnect the STVA connector from its harness mate. Check the continuity on the black/light green, pink/white, green and black wires between the ECM connector and the harness side of the STVA connector. Does each wire have continuity? → **NO** → Repair the wiring harness.

↓ **YES**

Faulty ECM.

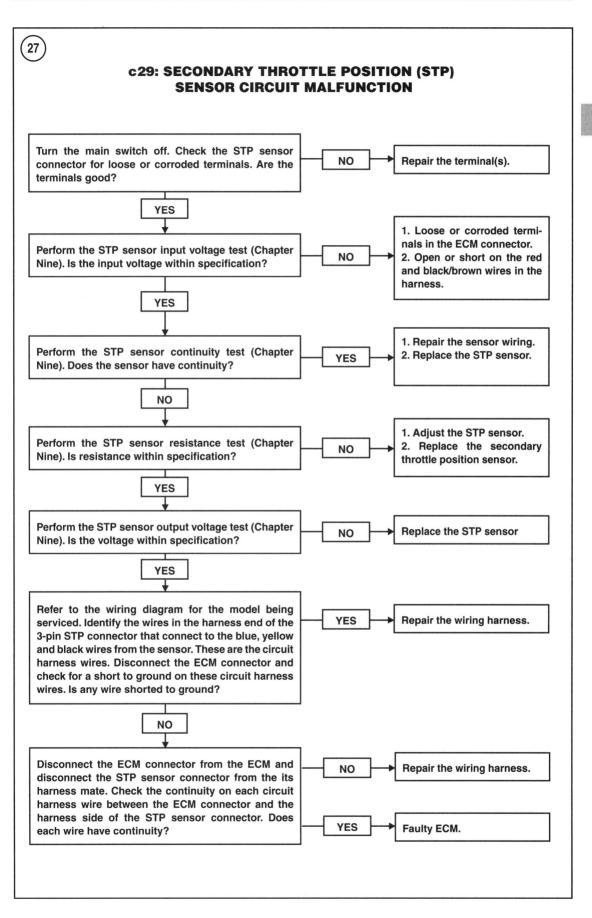

(27)

c29: SECONDARY THROTTLE POSITION (STP) SENSOR CIRCUIT MALFUNCTION

Turn the main switch off. Check the STP sensor connector for loose or corroded terminals. Are the terminals good? — NO → Repair the terminal(s).

YES

Perform the STP sensor input voltage test (Chapter Nine). Is the input voltage within specification? — NO → 1. Loose or corroded terminals in the ECM connector.
2. Open or short on the red and black/brown wires in the harness.

YES

Perform the STP sensor continuity test (Chapter Nine). Does the sensor have continuity? — YES → 1. Repair the sensor wiring.
2. Replace the STP sensor.

NO

Perform the STP sensor resistance test (Chapter Nine). Is resistance within specification? — NO → 1. Adjust the STP sensor.
2. Replace the secondary throttle position sensor.

YES

Perform the STP sensor output voltage test (Chapter Nine). Is the voltage within specification? — NO → Replace the STP sensor

YES

Refer to the wiring diagram for the model being serviced. Identify the wires in the harness end of the 3-pin STP connector that connect to the blue, yellow and black wires from the sensor. These are the circuit harness wires. Disconnect the ECM connector and check for a short to ground on these circuit harness wires. Is any wire shorted to ground? — YES → Repair the wiring harness.

NO

Disconnect the ECM connector from the ECM and disconnect the STP sensor connector from the its harness mate. Check the continuity on each circuit harness wire between the ECM connector and the harness side of the STP sensor connector. Does each wire have continuity? — NO → Repair the wiring harness.

— YES → Faulty ECM.

2

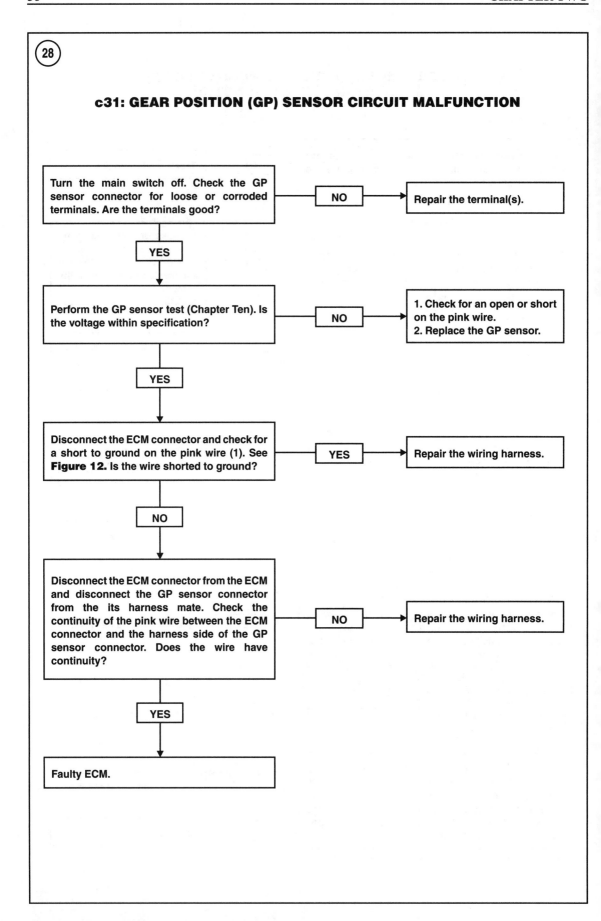

(28)

c31: GEAR POSITION (GP) SENSOR CIRCUIT MALFUNCTION

Turn the main switch off. Check the GP sensor connector for loose or corroded terminals. Are the terminals good? — **NO** → Repair the terminal(s).

YES

Perform the GP sensor test (Chapter Ten). Is the voltage within specification? — **NO** → 1. Check for an open or short on the pink wire.
2. Replace the GP sensor.

YES

Disconnect the ECM connector and check for a short to ground on the pink wire (1). See **Figure 12.** Is the wire shorted to ground? — **YES** → Repair the wiring harness.

NO

Disconnect the ECM connector from the ECM and disconnect the GP sensor connector from the its harness mate. Check the continuity of the pink wire between the ECM connector and the harness side of the GP sensor connector. Does the wire have continuity? — **NO** → Repair the wiring harness.

YES

Faulty ECM.

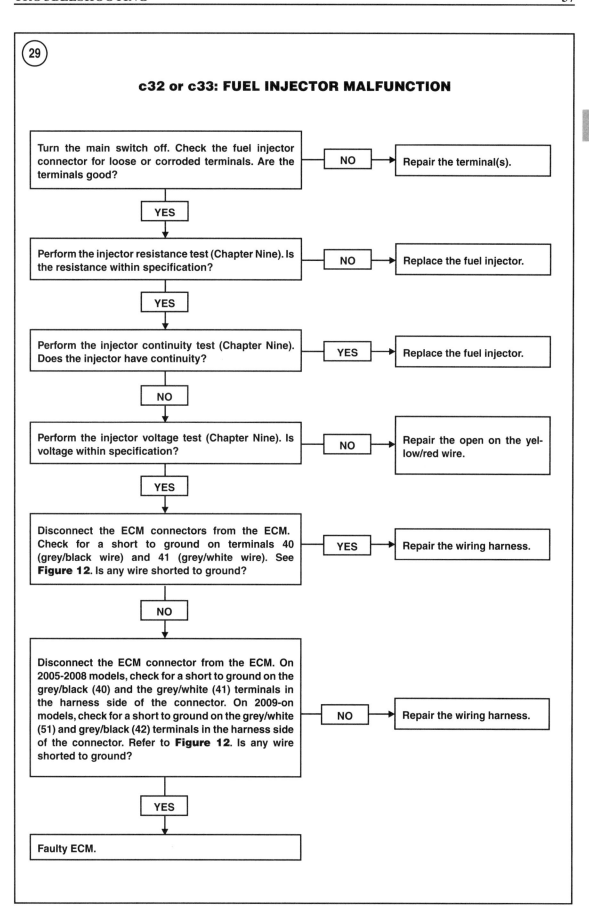

(29)

c32 or c33: FUEL INJECTOR MALFUNCTION

2

Turn the main switch off. Check the fuel injector connector for loose or corroded terminals. Are the terminals good? → **NO** → Repair the terminal(s).

↓ **YES**

Perform the injector resistance test (Chapter Nine). Is the resistance within specification? → **NO** → Replace the fuel injector.

↓ **YES**

Perform the injector continuity test (Chapter Nine). Does the injector have continuity? → **YES** → Replace the fuel injector.

↓ **NO**

Perform the injector voltage test (Chapter Nine). Is voltage within specification? → **NO** → Repair the open on the yellow/red wire.

↓ **YES**

Disconnect the ECM connectors from the ECM. Check for a short to ground on terminals 40 (grey/black wire) and 41 (grey/white wire). See **Figure 12**. Is any wire shorted to ground? → **YES** → Repair the wiring harness.

↓ **NO**

Disconnect the ECM connector from the ECM. On 2005-2008 models, check for a short to ground on the grey/black (40) and the grey/white (41) terminals in the harness side of the connector. On 2009-on models, check for a short to ground on the grey/white (51) and grey/black (42) terminals in the harness side of the connector. Refer to **Figure 12**. Is any wire shorted to ground? → **NO** → Repair the wiring harness.

↓ **YES**

Faulty ECM.

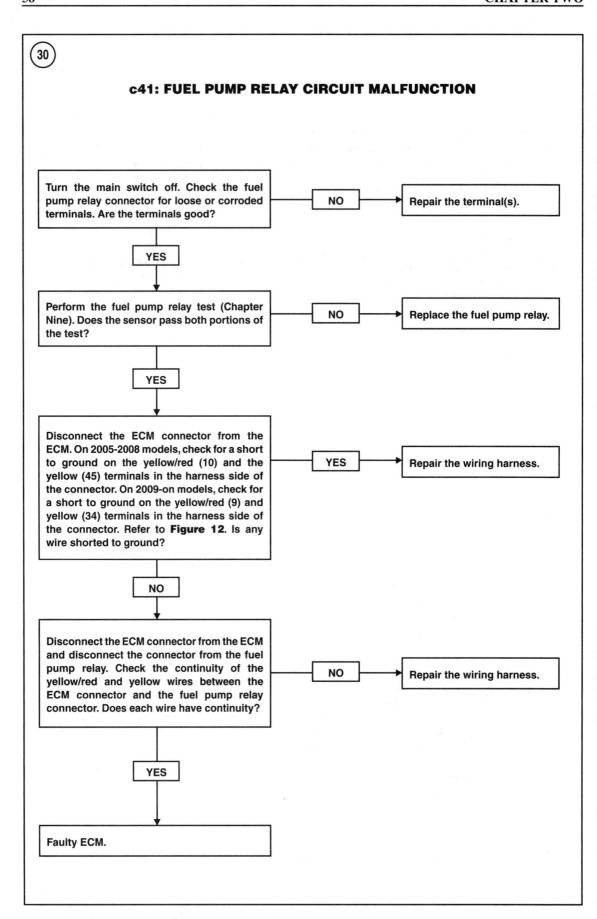

(30)

c41: FUEL PUMP RELAY CIRCUIT MALFUNCTION

Turn the main switch off. Check the fuel pump relay connector for loose or corroded terminals. Are the terminals good? — **NO** → Repair the terminal(s).

YES

Perform the fuel pump relay test (Chapter Nine). Does the sensor pass both portions of the test? — **NO** → Replace the fuel pump relay.

YES

Disconnect the ECM connector from the ECM. On 2005-2008 models, check for a short to ground on the yellow/red (10) and the yellow (45) terminals in the harness side of the connector. On 2009-on models, check for a short to ground on the yellow/red (9) and yellow (34) terminals in the harness side of the connector. Refer to **Figure 12**. Is any wire shorted to ground? — **YES** → Repair the wiring harness.

NO

Disconnect the ECM connector from the ECM and disconnect the connector from the fuel pump relay. Check the continuity of the yellow/red and yellow wires between the ECM connector and the fuel pump relay connector. Does each wire have continuity? — **NO** → Repair the wiring harness.

YES

Faulty ECM.

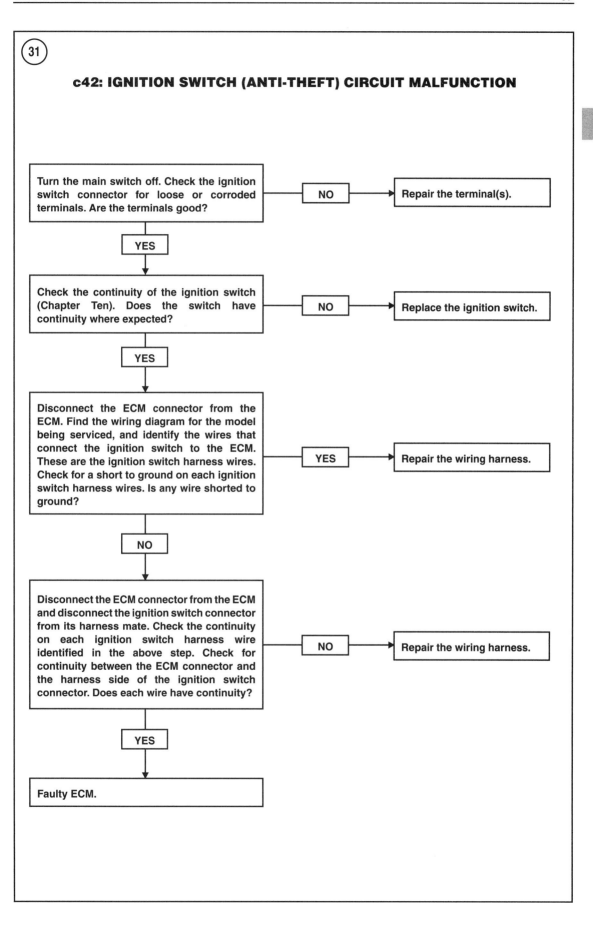

(31)

c42: IGNITION SWITCH (ANTI-THEFT) CIRCUIT MALFUNCTION

Turn the main switch off. Check the ignition switch connector for loose or corroded terminals. Are the terminals good?

NO → Repair the terminal(s).

YES

Check the continuity of the ignition switch (Chapter Ten). Does the switch have continuity where expected?

NO → Replace the ignition switch.

YES

Disconnect the ECM connector from the ECM. Find the wiring diagram for the model being serviced, and identify the wires that connect the ignition switch to the ECM. These are the ignition switch harness wires. Check for a short to ground on each ignition switch harness wires. Is any wire shorted to ground?

YES → Repair the wiring harness.

NO

Disconnect the ECM connector from the ECM and disconnect the ignition switch connector from its harness mate. Check the continuity on each ignition switch harness wire identified in the above step. Check for continuity between the ECM connector and the harness side of the ignition switch connector. Does each wire have continuity?

NO → Repair the wiring harness.

YES

Faulty ECM.

2

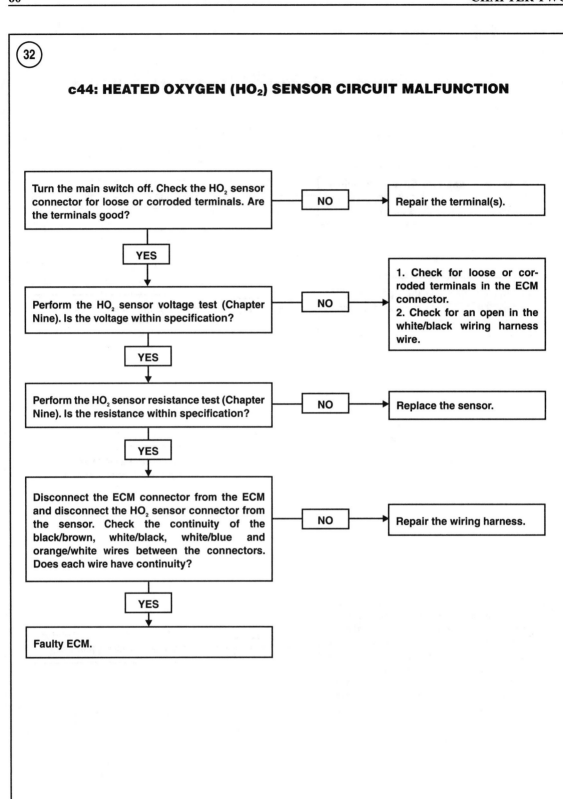

(32)

c44: HEATED OXYGEN (HO₂) SENSOR CIRCUIT MALFUNCTION

Turn the main switch off. Check the HO₂ sensor connector for loose or corroded terminals. Are the terminals good? — **NO** → Repair the terminal(s).

YES

Perform the HO₂ sensor voltage test (Chapter Nine). Is the voltage within specification? — **NO** → 1. Check for loose or corroded terminals in the ECM connector.
2. Check for an open in the white/black wiring harness wire.

YES

Perform the HO₂ sensor resistance test (Chapter Nine). Is the resistance within specification? — **NO** → Replace the sensor.

YES

Disconnect the ECM connector from the ECM and disconnect the HO₂ sensor connector from the sensor. Check the continuity of the black/brown, white/black, white/blue and orange/white wires between the connectors. Does each wire have continuity? — **NO** → Repair the wiring harness.

YES

Faulty ECM.

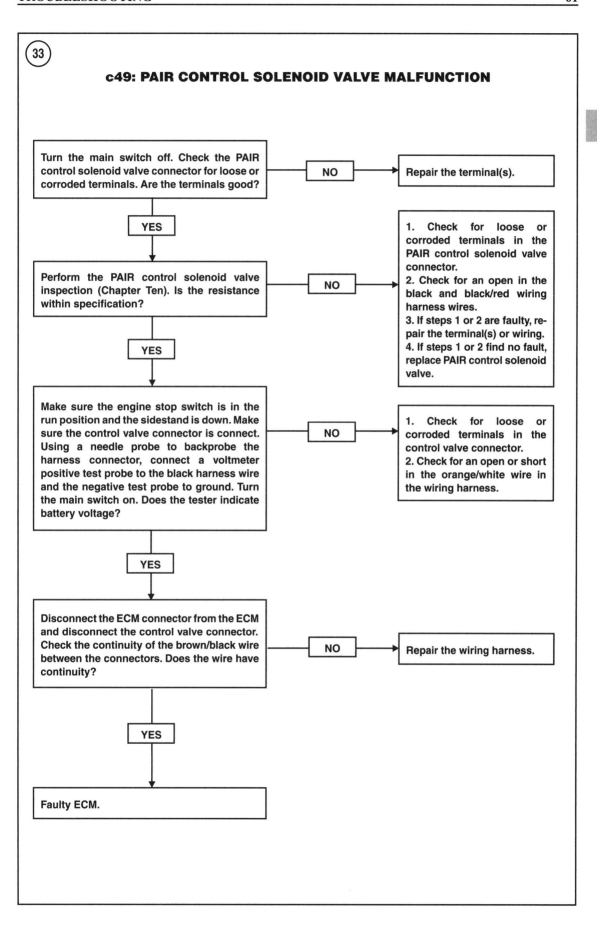

(33)

c49: PAIR CONTROL SOLENOID VALVE MALFUNCTION

2

Turn the main switch off. Check the PAIR control solenoid valve connector for loose or corroded terminals. Are the terminals good?

→ NO → Repair the terminal(s).

YES

Perform the PAIR control solenoid valve inspection (Chapter Ten). Is the resistance within specification?

→ NO →
1. Check for loose or corroded terminals in the PAIR control solenoid valve connector.
2. Check for an open in the black and black/red wiring harness wires.
3. If steps 1 or 2 are faulty, repair the terminal(s) or wiring.
4. If steps 1 or 2 find no fault, replace PAIR control solenoid valve.

YES

Make sure the engine stop switch is in the run position and the sidestand is down. Make sure the control valve connector is connect. Using a needle probe to backprobe the harness connector, connect a voltmeter positive test probe to the black harness wire and the negative test probe to ground. Turn the main switch on. Does the tester indicate battery voltage?

→ NO →
1. Check for loose or corroded terminals in the control valve connector.
2. Check for an open or short in the orange/white wire in the wiring harness.

YES

Disconnect the ECM connector from the ECM and disconnect the control valve connector. Check the continuity of the brown/black wire between the connectors. Does the wire have continuity?

→ NO → Repair the wiring harness.

YES

Faulty ECM.

heat related problems occur when a component starts to fail as it heats up.

   a. Troubleshoot the problem to isolate the circuit.

CAUTION
A heat gun will quickly raise the temperature of the component being tested. Do not apply heat directly to the component or use heat in excess of 60° C (140° F) on any electrical component.

   b. To check a connector, perform a continuity test as described in the appropriate service procedure or under *Continuity Test* in this section. Then repeat the test while heating the connector with a heat gun. If the meter reading was normal (continuity) when the connector was cold, and then fluctuated or read infinity when heat was applied, the connection is bad.

   c. To check a component, allow the engine to cool, and then start and run the engine. Note operational differences when the engine is cold and hot.

   d. If the engine will not start, isolate and remove the suspect component. Test it at room temperature and again after heating it with a heat gun. A change in meter readings indicates a temperature problem.

3. Water. When the problem occurs when riding in wet conditions or in areas with high humidity, start and run the engine in a dry area. Then, with the engine running, spray water onto the suspected component/circuit. Water-related problems often stop after the component heats up and dries.

Test Light or Voltmeter

Use a test light to check for voltage in a circuit. Attach one lead to ground and the other lead to various points along the circuit. It does not make a difference which test lead is attached to ground. The bulb lights when voltage is present.

Use a voltmeter in the same manner as the test light to find out if voltage is present in any given circuit. The voltmeter, unlike the test light, also indicates how much voltage is present at each test point.

Voltage test

Unless otherwise specified, make all voltage tests with the electrical connectors still connected. Insert the test leads into the backside of the connector and make sure the test lead touches the electrical terminal within the connector housing. If the test lead only

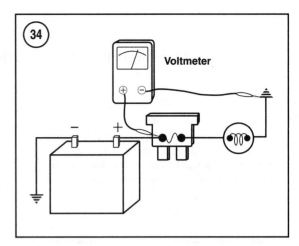

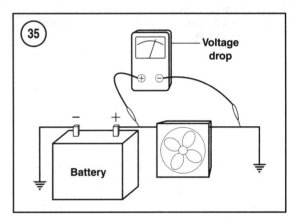

touches the wire insulation, it will cause a false reading.

Always check both sides of the connector because one side may be loose or corroded, thus preventing electrical flow through the connector. This type of test can be performed with a test light or a voltmeter.

1. Attach the voltmeter negative test lead to a confirmed ground location (**Figure 34**). If possible, use the battery ground connection. Make sure the ground is not insulated.

2. Attach the voltmeter positive test lead to the point to be tested.

3. Turn the ignition switch on. If using a test light, the test light will come on if voltage is present. If using a voltmeter, note the voltage reading. The reading should be within 1 volt of battery voltage. If the voltage is less there is a problem in the circuit.

Voltage drop test

The wires, cables, connectors and switches in the electrical circuit are designed to carry current with low resistance. This ensures current can flow through the circuit with a minimum loss of voltage. Voltage drop indicates where there is resistance in a circuit. A

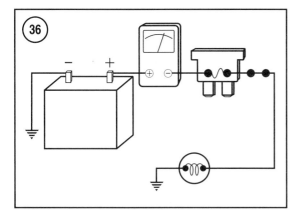

higher-than-normal amount of resistance in a circuit decreases the flow of current and causes the voltage to drop between the source and destination in the circuit.

Because resistance causes voltage to drop, a voltmeter is used to measure voltage drop when current is running through the circuit. If the circuit has no resistance, there is no voltage drop so the voltmeter indicates 0 volts. The greater the resistance in a circuit, the greater the voltage drop reading.

To perform a voltage drop test:

1. Connect the positive meter test lead to the electrical source (where electricity is coming from).

2. Connect the voltmeter negative test lead to the electrical load (where the electricity is going). Refer to **Figure 35**.

3. If necessary, activate the component(s) in the circuit.

4. Read the voltage drop (difference in voltage between the source and destination) on the voltmeter. Note the following:

   a. The voltmeter should indicate 0 volts. If there is a drop of 1 volt or more, there is a problem within the circuit. A voltage drop reading of 12 volts indicates an open in the circuit.

   b. A voltage drop of 1 or more volts indicates that a circuit has excessive resistance.

   c. For example, consider a starting problem where the battery is fully charged but the starter turns over slowly. Voltage drop would be the difference in the voltage at the battery (source) and the voltage at the starter (destination) as the engine is being started (current is flowing through the battery cables). A corroded battery cable would cause a high voltage drop (high resistance) and slow engine cranking.

   d. Common sources of voltage drop are loose or corroded connectors and poor ground connections.

Short test

A test light may also be used.

1. Remove the blown fuse from the fuse panel.

2. Connect the voltmeter across the fuse terminals in the fuse panel. Turn the ignition switch on and check for battery voltage.

3. With the voltmeter attached to the fuse terminals, wiggle the wiring harness relating to the suspect circuit at approximately 15.2 cm (6 in.) intervals. Start next to the fuse panel and work systematically away from the panel. Note the voltmeter reading while progressing along the harness.

4. If the voltmeter reading changes (test light blinks), there is a short-to-ground at that point in the harness.

Ammeter

Use an ammeter to measure the flow of current (amps) in a circuit (**Figure 36**). When *connected in series* in a circuit, the ammeter determines if current is flowing through the circuit and if that current flow is excessive because of a short in the circuit. Current flow is often referred to as current draw. Comparing actual current draw in the circuit or component to current draw specification (if specified by the manufacturer) provides useful diagnostic information.

Self-powered Test Light

A self-powered test light can be constructed from a 12-volt light bulb, a pair of test leads and a 12-volt battery. When the test leads are touched together the light bulb should go on.

Use a self-powered test light as follows:

1. Touch the test leads together to make sure the light bulb goes on. If not, correct the problem.

2. Disconnect the motorcycle's battery or remove the fuse(s) that protects the circuit to be tested. Do not connect a self-powered test light to a circuit that has power applied to it.

3. Select two points within the circuit where there should be continuity.

4. Attach one lead of the test light to each point.

5. If there is continuity, the test light bulb will come on.

6. If there is no continuity, the test light bulb will not come on, indicating an open circuit.

Ohmmeter

CAUTION
To prevent damage to the ohmmeter,
never connect it to a circuit that has

power applied to it. Always disconnect the battery negative lead before using an ohmmeter.

Use an ohmmeter to measure the resistance (in ohms) to current flow in a circuit or component.

Ohmmeters may be analog type (needle scale) or digital type (LCD or LED readout). Both types of ohmmeters have a switch that allows the user to select different ranges of resistance for accurate readings. The analog ohmmeter also has a set-adjust control which is used to zero or calibrate the meter (digital ohmmeters do not require calibration). Refer to the ohmmeter's instructions to determine the correct scale setting.

Use an ohmmeter by connecting its test leads to the circuit or component to be tested. If an analog meter is used, it must be calibrated by touching the test leads together and turning the set-adjust knob until the meter needle reads zero. When the leads are uncrossed, the needle should move to the other end of the scale, indicating infinite resistance.

During a continuity test, a reading of infinite resistance indicates an open in the circuit or component. A reading of zero indicates continuity, that is, there is no measurable resistance in the circuit or component. A measured reading indicates the actual resistance to current flow that is present in that circuit. Even though resistance is present, the circuit has continuity.

Continuity test

Perform a continuity test to determine the integrity of a circuit, wire or component. A circuit has continuity if it forms a complete circuit; that is if there are no opens in either the electrical wires or components within the circuit. A circuit with an open, on the other hand, has no continuity.

This type of test can be performed with a self-powered test light or an ohmmeter. An ohmmeter gives the best results.
1. Disconnect the negative battery cable or disconnect the test circuit/component from its power source.
2. Attach one test lead (test light or ohmmeter) to one end of the part of the circuit to be tested.
3. Attach the other test lead to the other end of the part or the circuit to be tested.
4. The self-powered test light comes on if there is continuity. An ohmmeter reads 0 or low resistance if there is continuity. A reading of infinite resistance indicates no continuity; the circuit is open.
5. If testing a component, note the resistance and compare this to the specification if available.

Short test

An analog ohmmeter or one with an audible continuity indicator works best for short testing. A self-powered test light may also be used.
1. Disconnect the negative battery cable.
2. If necessary, remove the blown fuse from the fuse panel.
3. Connect one test lead of the ohmmeter to the load side (battery side) of the fuse terminal in the fuse panel.
4. Connect the other test lead to a confirmed ground location. Make sure the ground is not insulated. If possible, use the battery ground connection.
5. Wiggle the wiring harness relating to the suspect circuit at approximately 15.2 cm (6 in.) intervals. Watch the ohmmeter while progressing along the harness.
6. If the ohmmeter needle moves or the ohmmeter beeps, there is a short to ground at that point in the harness.

Jumper Wire

Use a jumper wire to bypass a potential problem and isolate it to a particular point in a circuit. If a faulty circuit works properly with a jumper wire installed, an open exists between the two jumped points in the circuit.

To troubleshoot with a jumper wire, first use the wire to determine if the problem is on the ground side or the load side of a device. Test the ground by connecting the wire between the lamp and a good ground. If the lamp comes on, the problem is the connection between the lamp and ground. If the lamp does not come on with the wire installed, the lamp's connection to ground is good, so the problem is between the lamp and the power source.

To isolate the problem, connect the wire between the battery and the lamp. If it comes on, the problem is between these two points. Next, connect the wire between the battery and the fuse side of the switch. If the lamp comes on, the switch is good. By successively moving the wire from one point to another, the problem can be isolated to a particular place in the circuit.

Note the following when using a jumper wire:
1. Make sure the wire gauge (thickness) is the same as that used in the circuit being tested. Smaller gauge wire rapidly overheats and could melt.
2. Make sure the jumper wire has insulated alligator clips. This prevents accidental grounding or possible shock.

3. Install an inline fuse/fuse holder in the jumper wire.

4. A jumper wire is a temporary test measure. Do not leave a jumper wire installed as a permanent solution. This creates a fire hazard.

5. Never use a jumper wire across any load (a component that is connected and turned on). This would cause a direct short and blow the fuse(s).

LIGHTING SYSTEM

If bulbs burn out frequently, the cause may be excessive vibration, loose connections that permit sudden current surges or the installation of the wrong type of bulb. Most light and ignition problems are caused by loose or corroded ground connections. Check these prior to replacing a bulb or electrical component.

CHARGING SYSTEM

The charging system consists of the battery, the alternator and a voltage regulator/rectifier. A 30 amp main fuse protects the circuit.

Alternating current generated by the alternator is rectified to direct current. The voltage regulator maintains the voltage to the battery and additional electrical loads at a constant voltage regardless of variations in engine speed and load.

Test each of the following items and refer to the appropriate chapter if applicable.

1. Make sure the battery is fully charged and the cables are not damaged. Make sure the battery-to-cable connections are clean and secure. Test the battery as described in Chapter Three. If the battery cable polarity is reversed, check for a damaged regulator/rectifier.

2. Make sure all wiring and connections between the battery and alternator are clean, secure and undamaged.

3. Perform the output test as described under *Charging System* in Chapter Ten.

4. Test the voltage regulator/rectifier as described in Chapter Ten.

IGNITION SYSTEM

On 2001-2004 models, an igniter unit powers the ignition system. On 2005-on models the igniter unit is contained in the electronic control module (ECM), which also controls the fuel injection system.

Refer to the troubleshooting procedure in **Figure 37** to isolate an ignition system malfunction. Refer to Chapter Nine and Chapter Ten for specific fuel and electrical system tests and to the wiring diagrams at the end of this book.

For 2005-on models, refer also to the *Electronic Diagnostic System* in this chapter and check for malfunction codes applicable to the ignition system.

STARTING SYSTEM

The starting system consists of the starter, starter gears, starter relay switch, starter switch, ignition switch, engine stop switch, starting system cutoff relay, clutch switch, gear position sensor/neutral switch, sidestand switch, main and auxiliary fuses and battery.

> *CAUTION*
> *Do not operate the starter for more than five seconds at a time. Wait approximately 10 seconds between starting attempts.*

When the starter switch (**Figure 38**) is pressed, it allows current to flow through the starter relay switch coil. This will cause the coil contacts to close, allowing electricity to flow from the battery to the starter motor.

The starter should turn when the starter switch button is depressed and the transmission is in neutral and/or the clutch lever pulled in. If the starter does not operate properly, perform the following preliminary checks.

1. Check the battery to make sure it is fully charged. Inspect the battery cables for loose or damaged connections. (Chapter Three).

2. Inspect the starter cable and ground wire for loose or damaged connections.

3. If the starter does not operate correctly after making these checks, perform the test procedure that best describes the starting malfunction.

Starter Inoperative

1. Check for a blown main fuse or sub-fuse (Chapter Ten). If the fuses are good, continue with Step 2.

2. Check the starter cable for an open circuit or dirty or loose-fitting terminals.

3. Check the starter relay switch connectors for dirty or loose-fitting terminals. Clean and repair as required.

4. Check the starter switch (**Figure 39**) as follows. Turn the ignition switch on and depress the starter switch. When the starter switch is depressed, the starter relay switch should click once.

   a. If the relay clicks, continue with Step 7.

   b. If the relay does not click, go to Step 5.

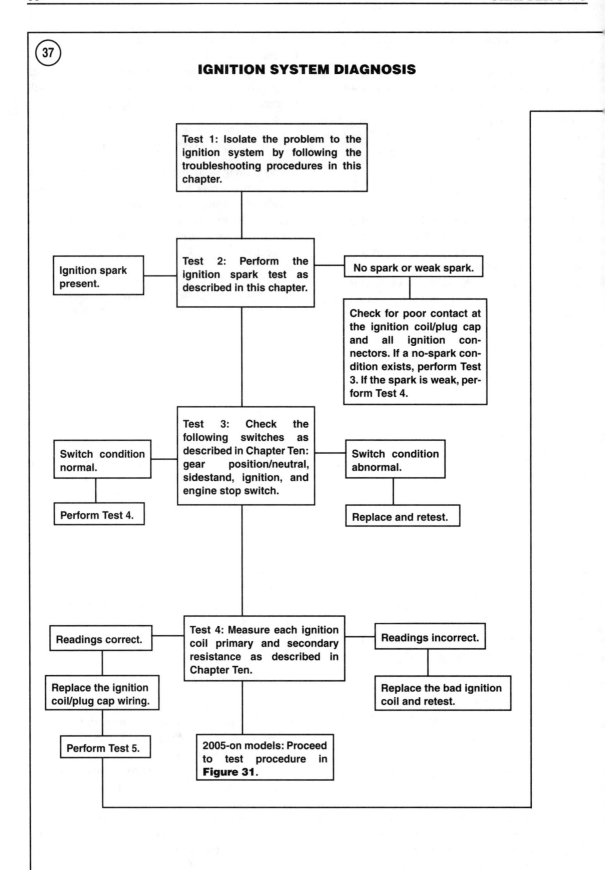

(37)

IGNITION SYSTEM DIAGNOSIS

Test 1: Isolate the problem to the ignition system by following the troubleshooting procedures in this chapter.

Ignition spark present.

Test 2: Perform the ignition spark test as described in this chapter.

No spark or weak spark.

Check for poor contact at the ignition coil/plug cap and all ignition connectors. If a no-spark condition exists, perform Test 3. If the spark is weak, perform Test 4.

Switch condition normal.

Test 3: Check the following switches as described in Chapter Ten: gear position/neutral, sidestand, ignition, and engine stop switch.

Switch condition abnormal.

Perform Test 4.

Replace and retest.

Readings correct.

Test 4: Measure each ignition coil primary and secondary resistance as described in Chapter Ten.

Readings incorrect.

Replace the ignition coil/plug cap wiring.

Replace the bad ignition coil and retest.

Perform Test 5.

2005-on models: Proceed to test procedure in **Figure 31**.

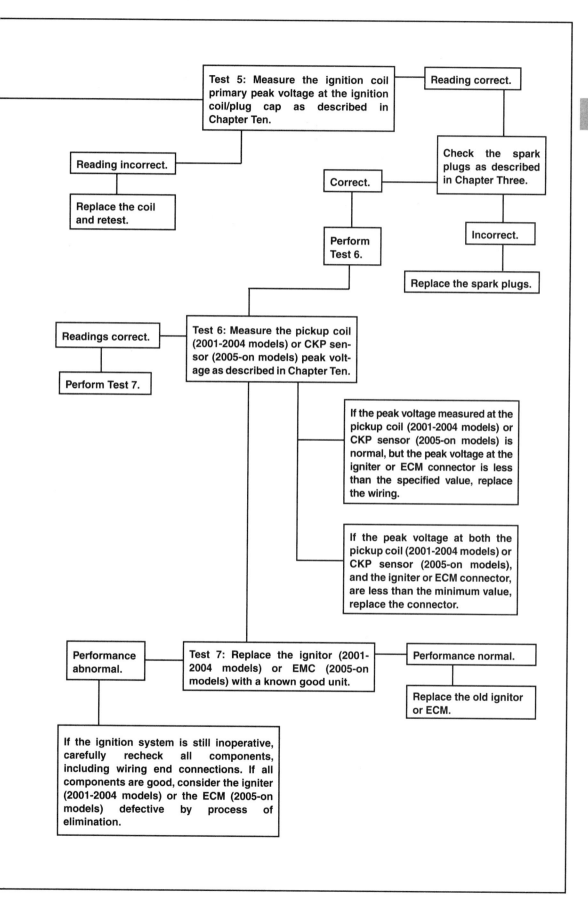

Test 5: Measure the ignition coil primary peak voltage at the ignition coil/plug cap as described in Chapter Ten.

Reading correct.

Reading incorrect.

Check the spark plugs as described in Chapter Three.

Correct.

Replace the coil and retest.

Incorrect.

Perform Test 6.

Replace the spark plugs.

Readings correct.

Test 6: Measure the pickup coil (2001-2004 models) or CKP sensor (2005-on models) peak voltage as described in Chapter Ten.

Perform Test 7.

If the peak voltage measured at the pickup coil (2001-2004 models) or CKP sensor (2005-on models) is normal, but the peak voltage at the igniter or ECM connector is less than the specified value, replace the wiring.

If the peak voltage at both the pickup coil (2001-2004 models) or CKP sensor (2005-on models), and the igniter or ECM connector, are less than the minimum value, replace the connector.

Performance abnormal.

Test 7: Replace the ignitor (2001-2004 models) or EMC (2005-on models) with a known good unit.

Performance normal.

Replace the old ignitor or ECM.

If the ignition system is still inoperative, carefully recheck all components, including wiring end connections. If all components are good, consider the igniter (2001-2004 models) or the ECM (2005-on models) defective by process of elimination.

5. Disconnect the following switches one by one (in the sequence provided) and test them as described in Chapter Ten. If the switch operates correctly, reinstall the switch and test the next one. If the switch does not operate correctly, replace it.

   a. Ignition switch.

   b. Starter switch.

   c. Engine stop switch.

   d. Sidestand switch.

   e. Clutch switch.

   f. Gear position sensor/neutral switch.

6. Inspect the sidestand relay as described in Chapter Ten. Replace the relay if it is defective.

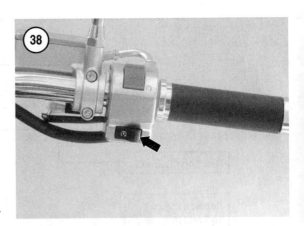

CAUTION
Because of the large amount of current that flows from the battery to the starter in Step 7, use large diameter cables to make the connection.

7. Remove the starter as described in Chapter Ten. Using an auxiliary battery and cables, apply battery voltage directly to the starter. The starter should turn when battery voltage is applied directly.

   a. If the starter did not turn, disassemble and inspect the starter as described in Chapter Ten. Test the starter components and replace worn or damaged parts as required.

   b. If the starter turned, check for loose or damaged starter cables. If the cables are good, check the starter relay as described in Chapter Ten. Replace the starter relay if necessary.

8. Check the starter relay switch (A, **Figure 39**) ground circuit as described in Chapter Ten.

   a. If there is continuity, continue with Step 9.

   b. If there is no continuity reading (high resistance), check for a loose or damaged connector or an open circuit in the wiring harness. If these items are in good condition, test the gear position sensor/neutral switch and sidestand switch as described in Chapter Ten.

   c. Reconnect the starter relay electrical connector (B, **Figure 39**).

9. Check the starter relay voltage as described in Chapter Ten.

   a. If battery voltage is indicated, continue with Step 10.

   b. If there is no battery voltage reading, check for a blown main or sub-fuse (Chapter Ten). If the fuses are good, check for an open circuit in the wiring harness or for dirty or loose-fitting terminals. If the wiring and connectors are in good condition, check for a defective ignition and/or starter switch (Chapter Ten).

10. Perform the starter relay operational check as described in Chapter Ten.

   a. If the starter relay switch is normal, check for dirty or loose-fitting terminals in its connector block.

   b. If the starter relay switch is defective, replace it and retest.

Starter Operates Slowly

If the starter turns slowly and all engine components and systems are normal, perform the following:

1. Test the battery as described in Chapter Three.

2. Check for the following:

   a. Loose or corroded battery terminals.

   b. Loose or corroded battery ground cable.

   c. Loose starter motor cable and ground lead.

3. Remove, disassemble and bench test the starter as described in Chapter Ten.

4. Check the starter for binding during operation. Disassemble the starter and check the armature shafts for bending or damage. Also check the starter clutch as described in Chapter Five.

Starter Operates but Engine Does Not Turn Over

1. If the starter is running backward and the starter was just reassembled, or if the starter motor cables were disconnected and then reconnected to the starter:
   a. The starter is reassembled incorrectly.
   b. The starter cables are incorrectly installed.
2. Check for a damaged starter clutch (Chapter Five).
3. Check for a damaged or faulty starter drive gears (Chapter Five).

Starter Relay Switch Clicks but Engine Does Not Turn

Crankshaft cannot turn because of mechanical failure.

SUSPENSION AND STEERING

Steering is Sluggish

1. Incorrect steering stem adjustment (too tight).
2. Damaged steering head bearings.
3. Tire pressure too low.

Motorcycle Steers to One Side

1. Bent axle.
2. Bent frame.
3. Worn or damaged wheel bearings.
4. Worn or damaged swing arm pivot bearings.
5. Damaged steering head bearings.
6. Bent swing arm.
7. Incorrectly installed wheels.
8. Front and rear wheels are not aligned.
9. Front fork legs positioned unevenly in steering stem.
10. Incorrect drive chain adjustment.

Front Fork Noise

1. Contaminated fork oil.
2. Fork oil level too low.
3. Broken fork spring.
4. Worn front fork bushings.
5. Loose bolts on the suspension.

Rear Shock Absorber Noise

1. Loose shock absorber mounting bolts and nuts.
2. Cracked or broken shock spring.
3. Damaged shock absorber.
4. Loose shock absorber linkage mounting bolts and nuts.
5. Damaged shock absorber linkage.
6. Worn swing arm or shock linkage bearings.

Front Wheel Wobble/Vibration

1. Loose front wheel axle.
2. Loose or damaged wheel bearing(s).
3. Damaged wheel rim(s).
4. Damaged tire(s).
5. Unbalanced tire and wheel assembly.

Hard Suspension (Front Fork)

1. Incorrectly adjusted fork.
2. Excessive tire pressure.
3. Damaged steering head bearings.
4. Incorrect steering head bearing adjustment.
5. Bent fork tubes.
6. Binding slider.
7. Incorrect weight fork oil.
8. Plugged fork oil passage.

Hard Suspension (Rear Shock Absorber)

1. Incorrectly adjusted rear shock.
2. Excessive rear tire pressure.
3. Damaged shock linkage components.
4. Damaged shock absorber bushing(s).
5. Damaged shock absorber bearing.
6. Damaged swing arm pivot bearings.

Soft Suspension (Front Fork)

1. Incorrectly adjusted fork.
2. Insufficient tire pressure.
3. Insufficient fork oil level or fluid capacity.
4. Incorrect fork oil viscosity.
5. Weak or damaged fork springs.

Soft Suspension (Rear Shock Absorber)

1. Incorrectly adjusted rear shock.
2. Insufficient rear tire pressure.
3. Weak or damaged shock absorber spring.
4. Damaged shock absorber.
5. Incorrect shock absorber adjustment.
6. Leaking damper unit.

2

⓵ **40**

BRAKE TROUBLESHOOTING

Brake fluid leaks

- Loose or damaged line fittings
- Worn caliper piston seals
- Scored caliper piston and/or bore
- Loose banjo bolts
- Damaged sealing washers
- Leaking master cylinder diaphragm
- Leaking master cylinder secondary seals
- Cracked master cylinder housing
- Brake fluid level too high
- Loose master cylinder cover

Brake overheating

- Warped brake disc
- Incorrect brake fluid
- Caliper piston and/or brake pads hanging up
- Riding brakes during riding

Brake chatter

- Warped brake disc
- Loose brake disc
- Incorrect caliper alignment
- Loose front axle nut and/or clamps
- Worn wheel bearings
- Damaged front hub
- Restricted brake hydraulic line
- Contaminated brake pads

Brake locking

- Incorrect brake fluid
- Plugged passages in master cylinder
- Incorrect front brake adjustment
- Caliper piston and/or brake pads hanging up
- Warped brake disc

Insufficient brakes

- Air in brake lines
- Worn brake pads
- Low brake fluid level
- Incorrect brake fluid
- Worn brake disc
- Worn caliper piston seals
- Glazed brake pads
- Leaking primary cup seal in master cylinder
- Contaminated brake pads and/or disc

Brake squeal

- Contaminated brake pads and/or disc
- Dust or dirt collected behind brake pads
- Loose parts

BRAKE SYSTEM

Front Disc Brake

Inspect the brakes frequently and repair any problems immediately. The front brake system is a hydraulically actuated disc brake. When replacing or refilling the brake fluid, use only DOT 4 brake fluid from a closed container.

Refer to **Figure 40** for troubleshooting of disc brake problems.

Rear Drum Brake

Inspect the brakes frequently and repair any problem immediately. The rear brake system is a mechanically actuated drum brake.

If the rear drum brake is not working properly, check for one or more of the following conditions:

1. Incorrect rear brake adjustment.
2. Incorrect brake cam lever position.
3. Worn or damaged brake drum.
4. Worn or damaged brake linings.
5. Oil or grease on brake drum or brake lining surfaces.
6. Weak or damaged brake return springs.

2

NOTE: Refer to the Supplement at the end of the manual for procedures unique to 2009-on models.

CHAPTER THREE

LUBRICATION, MAINTENANCE AND TUNE-UP

This chapter covers lubrication, maintenance and tune-up procedures.

Refer to **Table 1** for the recommended maintenance schedule.

Refer to **Tables 2-6** for specifications.

PRE-RIDE CHECK LIST

Perform the following checks before each ride. Each check is described in this chapter. If a component requires service, refer to the appropriate section.

1. Check the engine oil level in the oil inspection window (**Figure 1**) located on the clutch cover. The oil level must be between the upper and lower lines.

WARNING
Do not remove the radiator cap, coolant drain screws or disconnect any coolant hose when the engine and radiator are hot. Scalding fluid and steam will blow out under pressure and cause serious injury.

2. Check the cooling system for leaks and make sure the coolant is between the FULL and LOW marks on the coolant reservoir (**Figure 2**). If the fluid level is below the LOW mark, add coolant to the reservoir until the fluid level is at the FULL mark. Always add coolant to the reservoir, not the radiator.

3. Check the brake fluid level in the front brake master cylinder reservoir (**Figure 3**). Add fluid if necessary.

4. Make sure the final drive oil level is correct as noted in this chapter. Fill with the recommended oil as needed.

5. Turn the handlebar from side to side and check for steering play. Make sure the control cables are properly routed and do not interfere with the handlebar or the handlebar controls.

6. Check the throttle operation. Open the throttle all the way and release it. The throttle should close quickly with no binding or roughness. Repeat this step with the handlebar facing straight ahead and at both full lock positions.

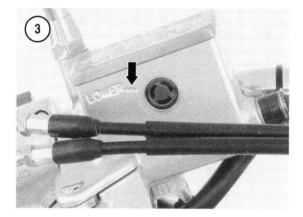

13. Make sure there is sufficient fuel in the fuel tank.
14. Inspect the fuel lines and fittings for wetness.
15. Make sure all lights and the horn operate properly.
16. Check kill switch operation.

MAINTENANCE SCHEDULE

Refer to **Table 1** for a recommended maintenance schedule. If the motorcycle is operated under extreme conditions, perform the appropriate maintenance more frequently.

Most of the services in **Table 1** are described in this chapter. However, some procedures which require more than minor disassembly or adjustment are covered in the appropriate chapter.

TIRES AND WHEELS

Tire Pressure Inspection

Check and adjust tire pressure (**Table 2**) to maintain good handling and to maximize tire life.

Tire Inspection

Inspect the tires for excessive wear, cuts, abrasions, etc. If an object has punctured the tire, mark its location before removing it. This will help locate the hole for repairs. Refer to the tire changing procedure in Chapter Twelve.

Measure the tread depth at the center of the tire (**Figure 4**) using a tread depth gauge or small ruler. Replace the original equipment tires when the tread has worn to the dimensions specified in **Table 2**.

Wheel Inspection

Frequently inspect the wheel spokes (A, **Figure 5**) the rim (B), and the hub. A damaged wheel may affect wheel alignment. Improper wheel alignment can

7. Make sure the clutch and the brake levers operate properly with no binding. Replace damaged levers. Check the lever housings for damage.

8. Inspect the front and rear suspension. Make sure they have a good solid feel with no looseness.

9. Check both wheels and tires for damage.

10. Check tire pressure (**Table 2**).

11. Inspect all fasteners, especially engine, steering and suspension mounting hardware.

12. Check the exhaust system for looseness or damage.

cause severe vibration and result in an unsafe riding condition. Refer to Chapter Twelve for wheel service procedures.

BATTERY

WARNING
Always wear safety glasses while working with a battery. If electrolyte gets into your eyes, call a physician immediately. Force your eyes open and flood them with cool, clean water for approximately 15 minutes and seek medical attention.

Many electrical system troubles can be traced to battery neglect. Periodically clean and inspect the battery. All models are equipped with a maintenance free battery. This is a sealed battery so the electrolyte level cannot be checked.

Some service procedures, and battery removal, require disconnection of the negative battery cable. When removing the battery, disconnect the negative cable first, and then disconnect the positive cable. This minimizes the chance of a tool shorting to ground when disconnecting the battery positive cable.

Removal/Installation

1. Remove the front seat as described in Chapter Sixteen.
2. Remove the bolt and disconnect the negative battery cable (A, **Figure 6**) from the battery terminal.
3. Remove the red protective cap (B, **Figure 6**) from the positive terminal, and disconnect the positive battery cable.
4. Remove the battery.
5. Inspect the cushion pads in the battery compartment for wear or deterioration. Replace if necessary.
6. Position the battery with the negative battery terminal (A, **Figure 6**) on the right side of the frame.
7. Reinstall the battery into the battery compartment in the frame.

CAUTION
Make sure the battery cables are properly connected. The red battery cable must be connected to the positive battery terminal and the black battery cable must be connected to the negative battery terminal. Reversing the polarity will damage the rectifier.

8. Connect the positive battery cable to the battery terminal. Tighten the retaining bolt securely.

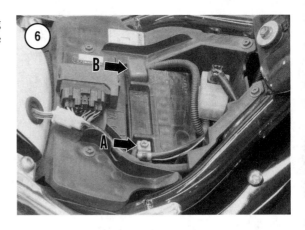

9. Connect the negative battery cable to the battery terminal. Tighten the retaining bolt securely.
10. Coat the battery connections with dielectric grease or petroleum jelly to retard corrosion.
11. Install the red protective cap (B, **Figure 6**) over the positive terminal.
12. Install the front seat as described in Chapter Sixteen.

Inspection and Testing

The battery electrolyte level cannot be serviced. *Never* attempt to remove the sealing bar from the top of the battery. This bar was removed for the initial filling of electrolyte before delivery of the motorcycle, or the installation of a new battery, and is not to be removed thereafter. The battery does not require periodic electrolyte inspection or water refilling.

Even though the battery is a sealed type, protect eyes, skin and clothing in case the battery is cracked and leaking electrolyte. Battery electrolyte is very corrosive and can cause severe chemical burns and permanent injury. If electrolyte spills onto clothing or skin, immediately neutralize the electrolyte with a solution of baking soda and water, and then flush the area with an abundance of clean water.

1. Remove the battery as described in this section. Do not clean the battery while it is mounted in the frame.
2. Place the battery on a stack of newspapers or shop cloths to protect the surface of the workbench.
3. Inspect the battery compartment cushion pads for contamination or damage. Clean with a solution of baking soda and water.
4. Check the entire battery case (A, **Figure 7**) for cracks or other damage. If the battery case is warped, discolored or has a raised top, the battery has overcharged or overheated.
5. Check the battery terminal bolts, spacers and nuts (B, **Figure 7**) for corrosion or damage. Clean parts

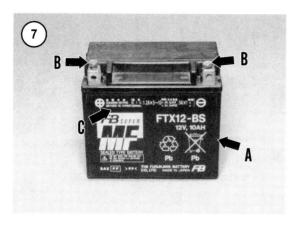

with a solution of baking soda and water. Replace severely corroded or damaged parts.

6. Clean the top of the battery with a stiff bristle brush using a baking soda and water solution.

7. Check the battery cable clamps for corrosion and damage. If corrosion is minor, clean the battery cable clamps with a stiff wire brush. Replace excessively worn or damaged cables.

8. Connect a voltmeter between the battery negative and positive terminals. Note the following:
   a. If the battery voltage is 13 volts (at 20° C [68° F]), or greater, the battery is fully charged.
   b. If the battery voltage is 12.8 volts (at 20° C [68° F]) or less, the battery is undercharged. Recharge it as described in this section.
   c. Once the battery is fully charged, test the charging system as described in Chapter Two.

Charging

WARNING
During charging, highly explosive hydrogen gas is released from the battery. Charge the battery only in a well-ventilated area, away from open flames. Do not allow anyone to smoke in the area. Never check the charge of the bettery by arcing across the terminals. The resulting spark can ignite the hydrogen gas.

If recharging is required on the maintenance free (MF) battery, use a voltmeter and a charger with a built-in ammeter.

If a battery not in use loses its charge within a week after charging, the battery is defective. A good battery self-discharges at a rate of approximately 1 percent each day.

CAUTION
Always disconnect the battery cables from the battery and remove the battery from the motorcycle before connecting

charging equipment. If the cables are left connected, the charger may damage the voltage regulator/rectifier.

1. Remove the battery as described in this section.
2. Set the battery on a stack of newspapers or shop cloths to protect the surface of the workbench.
3. Connect the positive charger lead to the positive battery terminal and the negative charger lead to the negative battery terminal.
4. Set the charger to 12 volts. If the amperage of the charger is variable, select the low setting.

CAUTION
Charging the battery at a rate of greater than 4 amps will damage the battery.

5. The charging time depends on the discharged condition of the battery. Use the suggested charging amperage and length of time charge on the battery label (C, **Figure 7**). Normally, a battery should be charged at a slow charge rate of 1/10th its given capacity.
6. Turn the charger on.
7. After the battery has been charged for the pre-determined time, turn the charger off and disconnect the leads.
8. Wait 30 minutes, and then measure the battery voltage.
   a. If the battery voltage is 13 volts (at 20° C [68° F]), or greater, the battery is fully charged.
   b. If the battery voltage is 12.8 volts (at 20° C [68° F]) or less, the battery is undercharged and requires additional charging time.
9. If the battery remains stable for one hour, the battery is charged.
10. Install the battery as described in this section.

Replacement

NOTE
Most dealerships accept old batteries in trade. Never place a battery in the household trash. It is illegal to place any acid or lead (heavy metal) contents in landfills.

When replacing the original MF battery with one of the same design, make sure the new battery is charged completely before installing it. Failure to do so reduces the life of the battery. Using a new battery without an initial charge will result in a battery never holding more than an 80 percent charge. Charging a new battery after it has been used will not bring its charge to 100 percent. When purchasing a new battery, verify its charge status. If necessary, have the supplier perform the initial or booster charge to bring the battery up to 100 percent charge. A charger specifically designed to charge MF batteries may be necessary.

PERIODIC LUBRICATION

Perform the services in this section at the maintenance intervals in **Table 1**. If the motorcycle is exposed to harder than normal use, perform the services more frequently.

Engine Oil Level Check

Engine oil level is checked with the oil level gauge located on the clutch cover.

1. If the motorcycle has not been run, start the engine and let it warm up approximately 2-3 minutes.
2. Park the motorcycle on the sidestand on level ground.
3. Shut off the engine and let the oil settle for 2-3 minutes.

> *CAUTION*
> *Do not check the oil level with the motorcycle on the sidestand as the oil will flow away from the gauge giving a false reading.*

4. Have an assistant sit on the motorcycle to hold it vertically on level ground.
5. Check the engine oil level in the oil inspection window (**Figure 1**) on the clutch cover. The oil level must be between the upper and lower lines.
6. If the oil level is low, unscrew the oil filler cap (**Figure 8**) from the clutch cover. Add the recommended grade and viscosity of oil (**Table 3**) to correct the level.
7. If the oil level is too high, remove the oil filler cap and draw out the excess oil with a syringe or suitable pump.
8. Inspect the O-ring seal on the oil filler cap. Replace the O-ring if deteriorated or hard.
9. Install the oil filler cap and tighten it securely.
10. Recheck the oil level and adjust if necessary.

Engine Oil and Filter Change

The recommended oil and filter change interval is in **Table 1**. This assumes that the motorcycle is operated in moderate climates. If it is operated under dusty conditions, the oil gets dirty more quickly and should be changed more frequently than recommended.

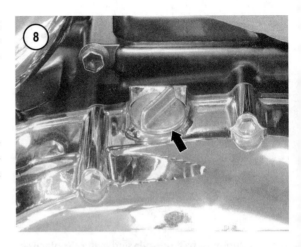

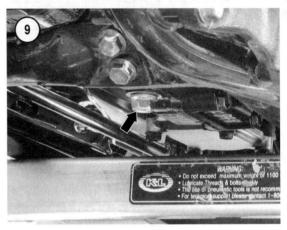

Use only a high-quality detergent motor oil with an API classification of SF or SG. Use SAE 10W-40 weight oil in all models. Use a lighter viscosity oil in cool climates and the heavier viscosity oil in warm climates. Use the same brand of oil at each oil change. Refer to **Table 3** for oil specifications and capacities.

> *NOTE*
> *Never dispose of engine oil in the trash, on the ground, or down the storm drain. Many service stations accept used oil and some waste haulers provide curbside oil collection. Do not combine other fluids with motor oil to be recycled.*

1. Start the engine and let it warm for 2-3 minutes. Shut off the engine.

2. Place the motorcycle on the sidestand on level ground.

3. Place a drain pan under the engine.

4. Remove the oil drain plug (**Figure 9**) and gasket from the bottom of the oil pan.

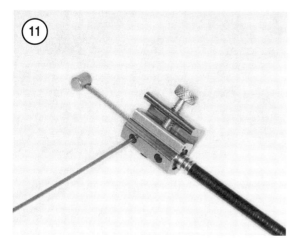

f. Apply a light coat of clean engine oil to the rubber seal on the new oil filter.

g. Install the oil filter onto the threaded fitting on the crankcase.

h. Tighten the filter by hand until the rubber gasket contacts the crankcase surface, and then tighten it an additional two turns.

9. Inspect the oil drain plug gasket for damage. Replace the gasket if necessary.

10. Install the drain plug (**Figure 9**) and gasket. Tighten the oil drain plug to 23 N•m (17 ft.-lb.).

11. Insert a funnel into the oil filler hole and add the quantity of oil specified in **Table 3**.

12. Remove the funnel and screw in the oil filler cap securely.

13. Start the engine and let it idle.

14. Check the oil filter and oil drain plug for leaks. Tighten either if necessary.

15. Turn off the engine and check the engine oil level as described in this section. Adjust the oil level if necessary.

General Lubrication

At the service intervals in **Table 1**, lubricate the brake lever and the clutch lever with engine oil. Lubricate the brake pedal pivot, gearshift lever pivot, and the sidestand pivot and springs with waterproof grease.

5. Loosen the oil filler cap (**Figure 8**). This speeds up the flow of oil.

6. Allow the oil to completely drain.

7. Inspect the condition of the drained oil for contamination. After it has cooled, check for any metal particles or clutch friction disc particles.

8. To replace the oil filter, perform the following:

a. Move the drain pan under the oil filter (**Figure 10**).

b. Install an oil filter wrench onto the oil filter, and turn the filter *counterclockwise* until oil begins to run out. Wait until the oil stops then loosen the filter until it is easy to turn.

c. Remove the oil filter wrench from the end of the filter then completely unscrew and remove the filter. Hold it with the open end facing up.

d. Hold the filter over the drain pan and pour out any remaining oil. Place the old filter in a plastic bag. Discard the old filter properly.

e. Thoroughly clean the filter-to-crankcase surface.

Throttle Control Cable Lubrication

Clean and lubricate the throttle cables at the intervals in **Table 1**, or more frequently if they become stiff or sluggish. In addition, check the cables for kinks and signs of wear and damage or fraying that could cause the cables to fail or stick.

> *CAUTION*
> *When servicing aftermarket cables, follow the cable manufacturer's instructions.*

1. Remove the fuel tank as described in Chapter Eight or Chapter Nine.

2. Disconnect both throttle cables from the right handlebar switch. Refer to *Throttle Cable* in Chapter Eight or Chapter Nine.

3. Attach a cable lubricator (**Figure 11**) to the end of the cable following the manufacturer's instructions.

> *NOTE*
> *Place a shop cloth at the end of the cables to catch the oil as it runs out.*

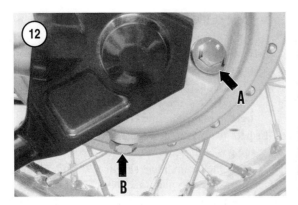

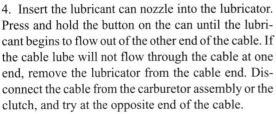

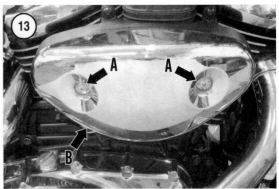

4. Insert the lubricant can nozzle into the lubricator. Press and hold the button on the can until the lubricant begins to flow out of the other end of the cable. If the cable lube will not flow through the cable at one end, remove the lubricator from the cable end. Disconnect the cable from the carburetor assembly or the clutch, and try at the opposite end of the cable.

5. Disconnect the lubricator.

6. Apply a light coat of grease to the cable ends before reconnecting them. Reconnect the cable(s), and adjust them as described in this chapter.

7. Operate the throttle at the handlebar. It should open and close smoothly.

Final Drive Oil Level Check

Check the final drive case oil level when the oil is cool. If the motorcycle has run, allow it to cool down (minimum of 10 minutes), then check the oil level. When checking or changing the final drive oil, do not allow any debris to enter the case opening.

1. Support the motorcycle so it is upright.

2. Wipe the area around the oil filler cap clean and unscrew the filler plug (A, **Figure 12**).

3. The oil level is correct when the oil is up to the lower edge of the filler cap hole. If the oil level is low, add hypoid gear oil until the oil level is correct. Refer to **Table 3** for specified oil viscosity and type.

4. Inspect the O-ring seal on the oil filler plug. Replace if it is deteriorated or hard.

5. Install the oil filler plug and tighten securely.

Final Drive Oil Change

Refer to **Table 1** for the recommended oil change interval.

1. Ride the motorcycle for 15-20 minutes until normal operating temperature is reached.

2. Place the motorcycle on the sidestand.

3. Place a drain pan under the drain plug (B, **Figure 12**).

4. Remove the oil filler plug (A, **Figure 12**) and the drain plug (B).

5. Let the oil drain for at least 15-20 minutes to ensure that the majority of the oil has drained out. Hold the motorcycle upright to drain out any residual oil.

6. Inspect the sealing washer on the drain plug; replace the sealing washer if necessary.

7. Install the drain plug and tighten it to 23 N•m (17 ft.-lb.).

8. Insert a funnel into the oil filler cap hole.

9. Support the motorcycle so it is upright. Add hypoid gear oil until the oil level is correct. Refer to **Table 3** for the specified oil viscosity and type.

10. Install the oil filler plug (A, **Figure 12**) and tighten securely.

11. Test ride the motorcycle and check for oil leaks. Recheck the oil level as described in this section and adjust if necessary.

Swing Arm Bearing Assembly Lubrication

Lubricate the swing arm bearing assemblies whenever they are disassembled. Use a waterproof grease.

The swing arm must be removed and partially disassembled to lubricate the needle bearings and collars. To clean, examine and lubricate the swing arm bearings, remove the swing arm as described in Chapter Fourteen.

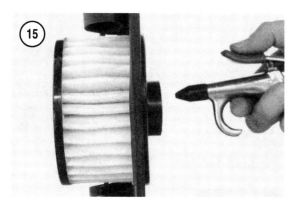

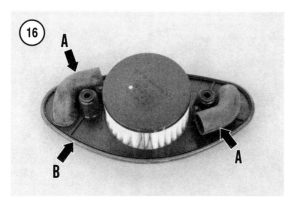

Front Fork Service

Refer to Chapter Thirteen.

Shock Linkage Lubrication

The shock linkage must be removed and partially disassembled to lubricate the needle bearings and collars. Refer to Chapter Fourteen.

Wheel Bearings Inspection

Inspect the wheel bearings whenever the wheel is removed, or if water contamination occurs. Inspect sealed bearings for leaks or damaged seals. Refer to Chapter Twelve.

PERIODIC MAINTENANCE

Air Filter Cleaning

Remove and clean the air filter at the interval in **Table 1**. Replace the element at the recommended interval or if it is damaged or deteriorated.

1. Remove the air box cover retaining bolts (A, **Figure 13**).

2. Remove the air box cover (B, **Figure 13**).

NOTE
The air filter plate assembly may remain in the cover during removal in Step 3.

3. Remove the air filter plate assembly (**Figure 14**).

4. Gently tap the air filter to loosen the trapped dirt and dust.

CAUTION
Do not apply compressed air toward the outside surface of the filter. Air directed at the outside surface forces the dirt and dust into the pores of the element thus restricting air flow.

5. Apply compressed air to the inside surface (**Figure 15**) of the air filter element and remove all loosened dirt and dust.

6. Inspect the filter element. If it is torn or broken in any area, replace the air filter. Do not run the motorcycle with a damaged air filter element.

7. If the air filter is extremely dirty or if there are any holes in the element, wipe out the interior of the air box with a shop rag dampened in cleaning solvent. Remove any debris that may have passed through a broken element.

8. Make sure the air intake tubes (A, **Figure 16**) are in good condition and securely attached to the plate.

9. Inspect the plate gasket (B, **Figure 16**) and replace it if damaged.

10. Install the air filter by reversing the removal procedure.

Air Box Drain Cleaning

1. Place a rag under the drain on the underside of the air box (**Figure 17**). Remove the cap, then drain out any water or debris.

2. Reinstall the drain cap. Make sure it is clamped in place.

Throttle Cable

Inspection

Check the throttle operation at the interval indicated in **Table 1**.

Operate the throttle grip. Check for smooth throttle operation from fully closed to fully open and then back to the fully closed position. The throttle should automatically return to the fully closed position without any hesitation.

Check the throttle cables for damage, wear or deterioration. Make sure the throttle cables are not kinked at any place.

If the throttle does not return to the fully closed position smoothly and if the exterior of the cable sheaths appears to be in good condition, lubricate the throttle cables as described in this chapter. Also apply a light coat of grease to the throttle cable spool at the hand grip.

If cable lubrication does not solve the problem, replace the throttle cables as described in Chapter Eight or Chapter Nine.

Adjustment

> *WARNING*
> *With the engine idling, move the handlebar from side to side. If the idle speed increases during this movement, check the throttle cable routing and adjustment through the frame. Correct any problems immediately. Do **not** ride the motorcycle in this unsafe condition.*

Check the throttle cable free play at the interval indicated in **Table 1**. Specified throttle cable free play is 2.0-4.0 mm (0.08-0.16 in.) as measured on the hand-contact area of the throttle grip.

In time, throttle cable free play increases from cable stretch. This delays throttle response.

Minor adjustments can be made at the throttle grip end of the throttle cables. If proper adjustment cannot be achieved at this location, the cables must be adjusted at the throttle pulley on the carburetor or throttle body assembly.

1. Shift the transmission into neutral.

2. Start the engine and allow it to idle.

3. With the engine at idle speed, slowly twist the throttle to raise engine speed. Note the amount of rotational movement of the throttle grip required to increase engine idle speed. This is the throttle cable free play.

4. If throttle cable free play is not within the specified range, adjust it by performing the following procedure.

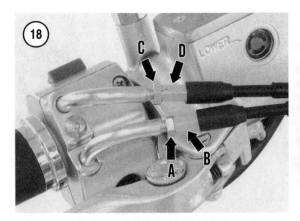

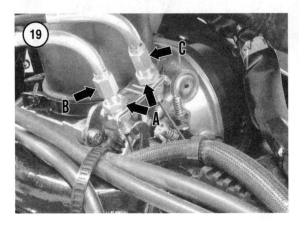

a. Shut off the engine.

b. Loosen the jam nut on the return cable (A, **Figure 18**) and turn the adjuster (B) all the way in.

c. Loosen the jam nut on the pull cable (C, **Figure 18**) and turn the adjuster (D) in either direction until the correct amount of free play is achieved. Hold the pull cable adjuster, then tighten the jam nut securely.

d. Hold the throttle grip in the fully closed position.

e. Slowly turn the adjuster on the return cable (B, **Figure 18**) until there is resistance, then stop. Hold the return cable adjuster (B, **Figure 18**) and tighten the jam nut (A).

5. Restart the engine and repeat Steps 2-4 to make sure the adjustment is correct.

6. If throttle cable free play cannot be properly adjusted with the adjusters at the throttle grip end of the cables, loosen the jam nuts on both cables and turn the adjuster on each cable all the way in toward the throttle housing. Hold the adjuster and tighten the jam nut.

7. Remove the fuel tank as described in Chapter Eight or Chapter Nine.

8. At the throttle cables on the carburetor or throttle body assembly, perform the following:

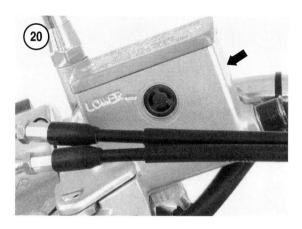

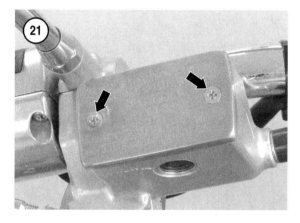

NOTE
*A carburetor is shown in **Figure 19**. Similar cable components are used on fuel-injected models.*

a. Loosen both throttle cable adjuster jam nuts (A, **Figure 19**) on each side of the cable bracket.

b. Rotate each adjuster (B and C, **Figure 19**) so the jam nut and adjuster are against the bracket.

c. Rotate the pull adjuster (C, **Figure 19**) until the correct amount of free play is achieved. Hold the pull cable adjuster, then tighten the jam nuts securely.

d. Hold the throttle grip in the fully closed position.

e. Slowly turn the adjuster on the return cable (B, **Figure 19**) until there is resistance, then stop. Hold the return cable adjuster (B, **Figure 19**) and tighten the jam nuts (A).

9. Recheck the throttle cable free play. If necessary, readjust free play using the adjusters at the throttle grip.

10. If the throttle cable free play cannot be adjusted to specification, the cable(s) is stretched beyond the wear limit and must be replaced. Refer to Chapter Eight or Chapter Nine for this service procedure.

11. Check the throttle cables from grip to carburetor or throttle body. Make sure they are not kinked or chafed. Replace as necessary.

12. Install the fuel tank as described in Chapter Eight or Chapter Nine.

13. Test ride the motorcycle, slowly at first, and make sure the throttle cables are operating correctly. Readjust if necessary.

Brake Fluid Level

WARNING
Use DOT 4 brake fluid from a sealed container. Other types may vaporize and cause brake failure. Always use the same brand of brake fluid. Do not intermix different brands. They may not be compatible. Do not use silicone based (DOT 5) brake fluid. It can cause brake component damage leading to brake system failure.

Check the brake fluid in the front brake master cylinder at the interval in **Table 1**. Also check the brake pads for wear at the same time. Bleeding the system, servicing the brake system components and replacing the brake pads are covered in Chapter Fifteen.

Keep the brake fluid in the reservoir above the LOWER line on the front brake reservoir (**Figure 20**). If necessary, correct the level by adding fresh brake fluid.

CAUTION
Brake fluid will damage most surfaces. Immediately clean up any spilled brake fluid with soapy water. Thoroughly rinse the area with clean water.

1. Position the handlebar so the front master cylinder is in the normal riding position.

2. Clean any dirt from the area around the reservoir cover before removing the cover.

3. Remove the screws (**Figure 21**) securing the reservoir cover. Remove the cover, diaphragm plate and diaphragm.

CAUTION
To control the flow of fluid, punch a small hole into the seal of a new container of brake fluid next to the edge of the pour spout. This helps eliminate fluid spillage while adding fluid to the small reservoir.

4. Refill the master cylinder reservoir, if necessary, to maintain the correct fluid level as indicated on the side of the reservoir.

5. Install the diaphragm, diaphragm plate and cover. Tighten the cover screws securely.

Brake Hose Inspection

Check the brake hoses between the front brake master cylinder and the brake caliper. If there are any leaks, tighten the connections and bleed the brake as described in Chapter Fifteen. If tightening the connection does not stop the leak or if the brake hose is damaged, cracked or chafed, replace the brake hose and bleed the system as described in Chapter Fifteen.

Front Brake Pad Inspection

Inspect the brake pads for wear at the interval in **Table 1**.

On the brake caliper, look at the brake pads where they contact the brake disc and inspect the brake pads for excessive or uneven wear.

> *NOTE*
> *A small inspection mirror may be help-*
> *ful. The wear indicator grooves are vis-*
> *ible on the installed pads. The pads in*
> ***Figure 22*** *were removed for clarity.*

Each brake pad has multiple grooves (**Figure 22**) that serve as wear indicators. If any pad is worn so that any groove is no longer visible, replace both pads as described in Chapter Fifteen.

Brake Fluid Change

To maintain peak braking efficiency, change the brake fluid at the interval in **Table 1**. To change brake fluid, refer to Chapter Fifteen.

Rear Brake Lining Wear Inspection

The rear drum bake is equipped with a brake lining wear indicator. This enables checking the brake lining condition without removing the rear brake assembly for inspection.

1. Apply the rear brake fully.

2. Observe where the line on the brake camshaft (A, **Figure 23**) falls within the embossed wear range indicator (B) on the brake panel.

3. If the line falls within this range the brake lining thickness is within specification and does not require service.

4. If the line falls outside of this range, replace the brake linings.

5. If necessary, replace the rear brake shoes as described in Chapter Fifteen.

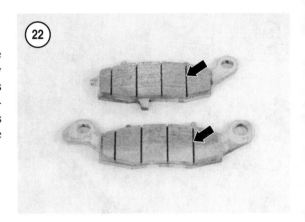

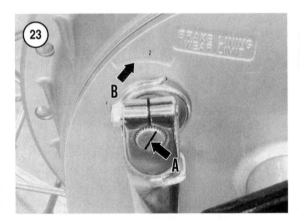

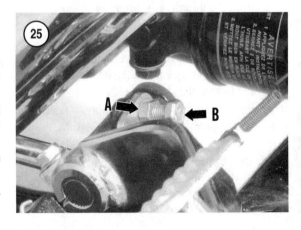

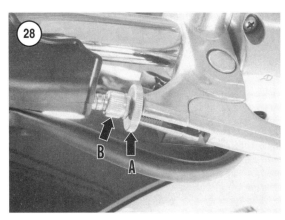

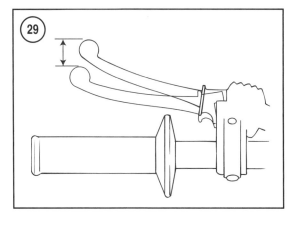

Rear Brake Pedal Height and Free Play Adjustment

Adjust the brake pedal height at the interval in **Table 1**. The pedal height will change as the brake linings wear. The top of the brake pedal should be positioned below the top surface of the footpeg. The distance between the top of the brake pedal and the top of the footpeg (**Figure 24**) should be 75-85 mm (3.0-3.3 in.). The pedal free play should be 20-30 mm (0.8-1.2 in.).

1. Set the brake pedal in the at-rest position.
2. To change height position, loosen the jam nut (A, **Figure 25**) and turn the adjuster bolt (B) in either direction until the brake pedal height equals the specified dimension. Tighten the jam nut securely.
3. To change the free play adjustment, turn the adjuster nut (**Figure 26**) at the end of the brake rod. Turn the nut to obtain the desired pedal free play.

Rear Brake Light Switch Adjustment

1. Turn the ignition switch on.
2. Depress the brake pedal and watch the brake light. The brake light should come on just before feeling pressure at the brake pedal. If necessary, adjust the rear brake light switch as follows:
   a. To adjust the brake light switch, hold the switch body (A, **Figure 27**) and turn the adjusting nut (B). To make the light come on earlier, turn the adjusting nut and move the switch body *up*. Move the switch body *down* to delay the light coming on.
   b. Make sure the brake light comes on when the pedal is depressed and goes off when the pedal is released. Readjust if necessary.
3. Turn the ignition switch off.

Clutch Lever Free Play Adjustment

Adjust the clutch cable at the interval in **Table 1**. For the clutch to fully engage and disengage, there must be free play at the tip of the clutch lever. Specified clutch lever free play is 10-15 mm (0.4-0.6 in.).

For minor adjustments, loosen the jam nut (A, **Figure 28**) and turn the adjuster (B) at the clutch lever until the amount of free play at the end of the clutch lever (**Figure 29**) is within the specified range. Retighten the jam nut.

If the clutch lever free play cannot be adjusted to within specification at the clutch lever, perform the following.
1. Remove the clutch lever boot.

2. Loosen the jam nut (A, **Figure 28**) and turn the adjuster (B) all the way into the clutch lever.

3. Remove the rear engine side cover (**Figure 30**).

4. Remove the clutch release cover (**Figure 31**).

5. Loosen the locknut (A, **Figure 32**) on the clutch release mechanism and turn the adjusting screw (B) two or three turns out.

6. Rotate the jam nuts (**Figure 33**) so there is slack in the clutch cable.

7. Slowly turn in the clutch release adjusting screw (B, **Figure 32**) until resistance is felt.

8. Turn out the clutch release adjusting screw (B, **Figure 32**) 1/4 turn. Hold the position of the screw with a screwdriver and tighten the locknut (A, **Figure 32**).

9. Rotate the jam nuts (**Figure 33**) to obtain the specified clutch lever free play of 10-15 mm (0.4-0.6 in.). Tighten the jam nuts securely.

10. Install the clutch release cover (**Figure 31**).

11. Install the rear engine side cover (**Figure 30**).

12. Tighten the jam nut (A, **Figure 28**).

13. Install the clutch lever boot.

Crankcase Breather Inspection

1. Remove the fuel tank as described in Chapter Eight or Chapter Nine.

2. Inspect the breather hose between its attachment to the intake duct (**Figure 34**) and the rear cylinder head. Replace the hose if cracked or deteriorated. Make sure the hose clamps are in place and tight.

3. Install the fuel tank.

PAIR (Air Supply) System Inspection

The PAIR system introduces fresh air into the exhaust ports to reduce the exhaust emission level.

Refer to the *PAIR (Air Supply) System* in Chapter Eight or Chapter Nine.

Evaporative Emission Control System

California models use an evaporative emissions control system to capture fuel vapors and store them so they will not be released into the atmosphere. The fuel vapors are routed through the charcoal canister, located on the right side of the rear sub-frame. When the engine is started, these stored vapors are drawn from the canister, through the purge control valve and into the carburetor (2001-2004 models) or throttle body (2005-on models). Make sure all evaporative emission control hoses are correctly routed and properly attached. Inspect the hoses and replace any if

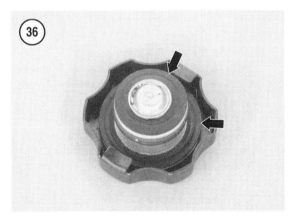

necessary as described in Chapter Eight or Chapter Nine.

NON-SCHEDULED MAINTENANCE

CAUTION
If any fasteners in the following procedures are loose, refer to the appropriate chapter for correct procedures and torque specifications.

Cooling System Inspection

WARNING
Never remove the radiator cap, coolant drain screws or disconnect any hose while the engine and radiator are hot. Scalding fluid and steam can spray out under pressure and cause serious injury.

Once a year, or any time the cooling system requires repeated refilling, check the following items.
1. Remove the fuel tank as described in Chapter Eight or Chapter Nine.
2. With the engine *cold*, remove the radiator cap (**Figure 35**).
3. Check the rubber sealing washers on the radiator cap (**Figure 36**). Replace the cap if the washers show signs of deterioration, cracking or other damage. If the radiator cap is acceptable, perform Step 4.

NOTE
Apply water to the rubber washer in the radiator cap before installing the cap onto the pressure gauge.

4. Pressure test the radiator cap. The radiator cap must be able to hold a pressure of 95-125 kPa (13.8-18.1 psi). Replace the cap if it does not hold pressure or if the relief pressure is too high or too low.
5. Pressure test the radiator and cooling system. If the cooling system will not hold pressure, determine the source of the leak and make the appropriate repairs.

CAUTION
Be careful not to spill coolant on painted, plated or plastic surfaces. It may damage the finish and/or surface. Wash the affected area with soapy water and rinse thoroughly with clean water.

6. With the engine cold, remove the radiator cap and test the specific gravity of the coolant. Use an antifreeze tester following the manufacturer's instruc-

tions. Make sure the mixture is 50 percent antifreeze or corrosion protection will be impaired. Do not use a mixture of 60 percent or greater or the cooling efficiency will be reduced.

7. Check all cooling system hoses and the radiator for damage or deterioration as described in Chapter Eleven.

8. Install the radiator cap. Turn the radiator cap to the first stop. Then push down and turn it until it stops.

Coolant Change

WARNING
Do not dispose of antifreeze by flushing it down a drain or pouring it onto the ground. Place old antifreeze into a suitable container and dispose of it properly. Do not store coolant where it is accessible to children or pets.

WARNING
Do not remove the radiator cap when the engine is hot. The coolant is very hot and under pressure. Severe scalding could result if the coolant comes in contact with your skin.

Use only a high-quality ethylene glycol-based coolant with corrosion inhibitors, formulated for aluminum radiators and engines. Mix the coolant with distilled water at a 50:50 ratio. Coolant capacity is in **Table 3**.

Completely drain and refill the cooling system at the interval listed in **Table 1**.

It is sometimes necessary to drain the coolant from the system to perform a service procedure. If the coolant is in good condition (and not due for replacement), it can be reused if it remains clean. Drain the coolant into a *clean* drain pan and then pour the coolant into a *clean* sealable container and screw on the cap. This coolant can then be reused.

CAUTION
Be careful not to spill coolant on painted, plated or plastic surfaces. It may damage the finish and/or surface. Wash the affected area with soapy water and rinse thoroughly with clean water.

1. Place the motorcycle on level ground on the sidestand.

2. Remove the fuel tank as described in Chapter Eight or Chapter Nine.

3. With the engine *cold*, remove the radiator cap (**Figure 35**).

4. On the left side, place a drain pan under the radiator.

5. Loosen the retaining clamp, then disconnect the lower coolant hose from the radiator (**Figure 37**) and

drain the coolant into the pan. Point the hose downward to be sure all coolant is removed from the hose.

6. Carefully tilt the motorcycle from side to side to drain residual coolant from the cooling system.

NOTE
If the coolant is dirty, flush the system with clean water. Drain out all water from the system.

7. Reconnect the coolant hose to the radiator.

8. Refer to Chapter Eleven and remove the coolant reservoir.

9. Drain the coolant from the coolant reservoir. If necessary, clean the inside of the reservoir with a liquid detergent. Thoroughly rinse it with clean water.

10. Install the coolant reservoir.

11. Place a funnel into the radiator cap opening in the coolant filler neck and refill the radiator and engine.

12. Use a 50:50 mixture of coolant and distilled water. Slowly add the coolant through the radiator filler neck. Add it slowly so it expels as much air as possible from the engine and radiator. Top off the coolant to the bottom of the filler neck. Do not install the radiator cap at this time.

13. Carefully tilt the motorcycle from side to side several times. This helps bleed off trapped air in the cooling system. If necessary, add additional coolant to the system until the coolant level is to the bottom of the filler neck. Do not install the radiator cap at this time.

14. Start the engine and let it run at idle until the engine reaches normal operating temperature. Make sure there are no air bubbles in the coolant and that the coolant level stabilizes at the bottom of the radiator filler neck. Add coolant as needed.

15. Install the radiator cap.

16. Add coolant to the reservoir tank so the coolant level is between the two lines on the tank (**Figure 38**).

17. Test ride the motorcycle and readjust the coolant level in the reservoir tank if necessary.

3

justment will hamper steering. In severe conditions, a loose bearing adjustment can cause loss of control.

1. Support the motorcycle so the front wheel is off the ground.

2. Hold onto the front fork tubes and gently rock the fork assembly back and forth. If there is looseness, adjust the steering head bearings as described in Chapter Thirteen.

Gearshift Pedal Height Adjustment

The gearshift pedal height may be adjusted to accommodate rider preferenceas follows:

1. Loosen the nuts (A, **Figure 39**) on the gearshift rod (B).

2. Rotate the gearshift rod (B, **Figure 39**) as needed to obtain the desired gearshift pedal height.

3. Tighten the nuts (A, **Figure 39**).

Handlebar Inspection

Inspect the handlebar assemblies weekly for any signs of damage. Replace a bent or damaged handlebar. Check the tightness of the holder bolts. Refer to Chapter Thirteen for torque specifications.

Handlebar Grips Inspection

Inspect the handlebar grips for tearing, looseness or excessive wear. Install new grips when required. Use a grip adhesive (ThreeBond Griplock TB1501C, or equivalent) to prevent them from slipping.

Front Suspension Inspection

1. Apply the front brake and pump the front fork up and down vigorously. Check for smooth operation and oil leaks.

2. Refer to Chapter Thirteen and check the following:

   a. Tighten the fork cap bolt (A, **Figure 40**) to 45 N•m (33 ft.-lb.).

   b. Tighten the fork lower clamp bolts (B, **Figure 40**) to 33 N•m (24 ft.-lb.).

   c. On the left side, tighten the front axle (A, **Figure 41**) to 65 N•m (48 ft.-lb.).

   d. Tighten the front axle pinch bolts (B, **Figure 41**) to 33 N•m (24 ft.-lb.).

Exhaust System Inspection

1. Inspect the exhaust system for cracks or dents which could alter performance.

2. Check all exhaust system fasteners and mounting points for loose or damaged parts.

3. Make sure all fasteners are tight. If loose, refer to Chapter Eight or Chapter Nine for torque specifications.

Fuel Line Inspection

WARNING
A damaged or deteriorated fuel line presents a dangerous fire hazard to the rider and the motorcycle if fuel spills onto a hot engine or exhaust pipe.

Inspect the fuel lines from the fuel tank to the carburetor (2001-2004 models) or throttle body (2005-on models) and other remaining hoses. If any hoses are cracked or deteriorated, replace them. Make sure the hose clamps are in place and secure.

Steering Head Inspection

The steering head on all models consists of upper and lower caged ball bearings. A loose bearing ad-

Rear Suspension Inspection

1. Place the motorcycle on level ground on the sidestand.

2. Support the underside of the motorcycle so the rear wheel is off the ground.

3. Push hard on the rear wheel (sideways) to check for side play in the rear swing arm bearings.

4. Refer to Chapter Fourteen and make sure the swing arm pivot bolts are tightened to specification (**Table 6**).

5. Remove the side covers and storage compartment as described in Chapter Sixteen.

6. Refer to Chapter Fourteen and check the following:

   a. Tighten the shock absorber upper (**Figure 42**) and lower (A, **Figure 43**) fasteners to 50 N•m (37 ft.-lb.).

   b. Tighten the shock absorber lever assembly hardware (B, **Figure 43**) to 78 N•m (58 ft.-lb.).

   c. On U.S. and Canada models, make sure the rear axle nut cotter pin (A, **Figure 44**) is in place and the nut (B) is tightened to 65 N•m (48 ft.-lb.).

   d. On models other than U.S. and Canada, make sure the rear axle nut is tightened to 65 N•m (48 ft.-lb.).

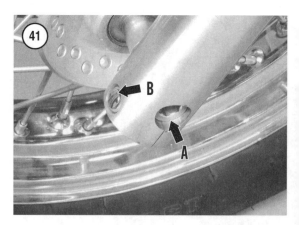

Frame Inspection

Inspect the frame for cracks or damage. Check all areas where welded sections attach to the main frame tubes.

Fastener Inspection

Constant vibration can loosen many of the fasteners on the motorcycle. Refer to the appropriate chapter for torque specifications, and check the tightness of all fasteners, especially those on:

1. Engine mounting hardware.
2. Engine crankcase covers.
3. Handlebar and front fork.
4. Gearshift lever.
5. Brake pedal and lever.
6. Exhaust system.

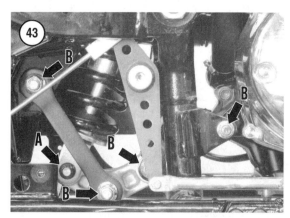

TUNE-UP

Refer to the appropriate section in this chapter when performing the tune-up procedures. Perform these tasks in the following order:

1. Clean or replace the air filter element. Refer to *Periodic Maintenance* in this chapter.
2. Check and adjust the valve clearances (engine must be cold).
3. Perform a compression test.
4. Check or replace the spark plugs.
5. Check and adjust the idle speed.

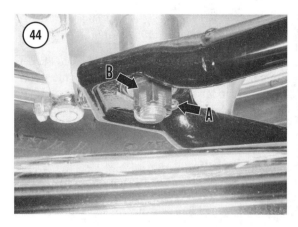

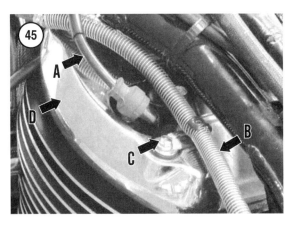

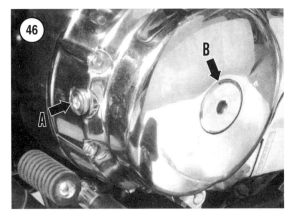

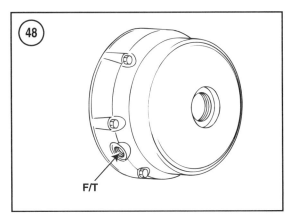

VALVE CLEARANCE

Inspection/Adjustment

The valve clearance is in **Table 4**. The engine must be cold (below 35° C [95° F]) to obtain accurate results. The exhaust valves are located at the front of the cylinder head on the front cylinder and at the rear of the cylinder head on the rear cylinder. The intake valves are located on the opposite side of the cylinder head from the exhaust valves.

The left and right sides refer to the position of the parts as viewed by the rider siting on the seat facing forward.

1. Remove the fuel tank as described in Chapter Eight or Chapter Nine.
2. On the rear cylinder head perform the following:
    a. Detach the spark plug wire (A, **Figure 45**) from the spark plug.
    b. Detach the fuel hose (B, **Figure 45**) from the retaining clamp.
    c. Remove the two retaining bolts (C, **Figure 45**) and remove the cylinder head cover (D).
3. On the front cylinder head repeat the steps in Step 2 (except the fuel hose) to remove the cylinder head cover.
4. Remove both spark plugs as described in this chapter. This makes it easier to turn the engine by hand.
5. Remove the timing hole plug (A, **Figure 46**).
6. Remove the alternator bolt access cover (B, **Figure 46**).
7. Engage a socket to the alternator bolt (**Figure 47**).

> *CAUTION*
> *The camshaft lobes must point away from the rocker arm pad so the pad rests on the camshaft base circle. Clearance dimensions taken with the camshaft in any other position will provide a false reading, resulting in incorrect valve clearance adjustment and possible engine damage.*

> *NOTE*
> *The alternator rotor has lines marked **F** or **R** to indicate top dead center for the front cylinder (F) or rear cylinder (R).*

8A. On the front cylinder, rotate the flywheel counterclockwise, as viewed from the left side of the motorcycle. The piston must be on the compression stroke. Rotate the flywheel until the *F* line is centered in the timing inspection hole as shown in **Figure 48**. If the piston was not on the compression stroke, rotate the flywheel one full turn (360°) until the mark aligns.

8B. On the rear cylinder, rotate the flywheel counter-clockwise, as viewed from the left side of the motorcycle. The piston must be on the compression stroke. Rotate the flywheel until the *R* line is centered on the timing inspection hole as shown in **Figure 49**. If the piston was not on the compression stroke, rotate the flywheel one full turn (360°) until the mark aligns.

9. Remove the rocker covers (**Figure 50**).

10. With the engine in the correct position for the cylinder being checked, measure the valve clearance on the valves.

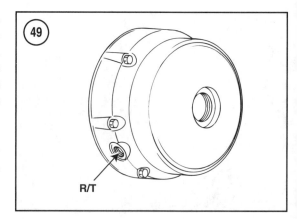

NOTE
When checking the clearance, begin with a feeler gauge of the specified clearance thickness. If this thickness is too large or small, change the gauge thickness until there is a drag on the feeler gauge when it is inserted and withdrawn.

11. Check the clearance by inserting the feeler gauge (A, **Figure 51**) between the valve keeper and the camshaft. When the clearance is correct, there will be a slight resistance on the feeler gauge when it is inserted and withdrawn. Record the clearance dimension. Identify the clearance by cylinder number and by intake or exhaust valve. The clearance dimension is needed if adjustment is necessary.

12. Measure the clearance of all the valves on the cylinder head before beginning the valve adjustment procedure.

13. If the valves require adjustment, perform the following:

    a. Back off the locknut (B, **Figure 51**).

    b. Screw the adjuster (C, **Figure 51**) in or out until there is a slight resistance felt on the feeler gauge.

    c. Hold the adjuster to prevent it from turning further and tighten the locknut securely.

    d. Recheck the clearance to make sure the adjuster did not rotate when the locknut was tightened. Readjust if necessary.

    e. Adjust the valve clearance for the remaining valves.

14. Rotate the engine two turns and recheck the clearance to make sure the adjustment is correct. Readjust if necessary.

15. Inspect the O-ring on each rocker cover. Replace if necessary.

16. Install the rocker covers (**Figure 50**) and tighten securely.

17. Install the timing hole plug (A, **Figure 46**) in the left crankcase cover.

18. Install the alternator bolt access cover (B, **Figure 46**).

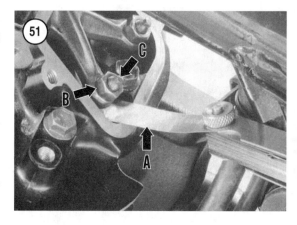

19. Install the spark plugs as described in this chapter.

20. On the rear cylinder head perform the following:

    a. Install the cylinder head cover (D, **Figure 45**) and the two retaining bolts (C).

    b. Attach the fuel hose (B, **Figure 45**) inside the retaining clamp.

    c. Connect the spark plug wire (A, **Figure 45**) to the spark plug.

21. On the front cylinder head repeat Step 20 (except the fuel hose).

22. Install the fuel tank as described in Chapter Eight or Chapter Nine.

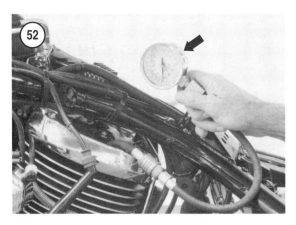

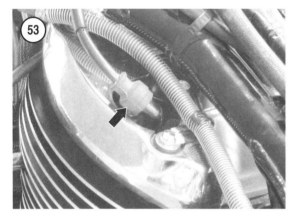

mum pressure is usually reached within 4-7 seconds. Record the pressure reading for that cylinder. The recommended cylinder compression and the maximum allowable difference between cylinders is in **Table 4**.

6. Remove the compression gauge from that cylinder.

7. Repeat Steps 4-6 for the remaining cylinder and record the reading.

8. Install the spark plugs.

9. Compression between cylinders should not vary by more than 10 percent. If the compression between cylinders differs by more than 10 percent, the low-reading cylinder has a valve or ring problem. To determine which, pour about a teaspoon of engine oil into the spark plug hole of the low-reading cylinder and repeat the procedure.

    a. If the compression increases significantly, the piston rings are probably worn.

    b. If the compression does not increase, the valves are leaking.

10. Install the spark plugs.

SPARK PLUGS

A spark plug can be used to help determine the operating condition of its cylinder when properly read. As each spark plug is removed, note its condition and refer to *Reading* in this section.

Removal/Installation

1. Remove the fuel tank as described in Chapter Eight or Chapter Nine.

CAUTION
Whenever the spark plug is removed, debris around it can fall into the plug hole, causing serious engine damage. Remove all loose debris that could fall into the spark plug openings.

2. Blow away all loose dirt and wipe off the top surface of the cylinder head cover.

3. Carefully disconnect the spark plug cap (**Figure 53**) from the spark plug. The plug cap forms a tight seal on the cylinder head cover as well as the spark plug. Grasp the plug cap and twist it from side-to-side to break the seal loose. Carefully pull the plug cap up and off the spark plug. If it is stuck to the plug, twist it slightly to break it loose.

4. Install a spark plug socket with a rubber insert onto the spark plug. Make sure it is correctly seated on the plug. Install an open end wrench or socket

COMPRESSION TEST

A compression test is one of the quickest ways to check the internal condition of the engine, including the piston rings, pistons, and head gasket. Check the compression at each tune-up, record the readings and compare them with the readings at the next tune-up. This helps spot any developing problems.

1. Before starting the compression test, make sure the following items are correct:

    a. The cylinder head bolts are tightened to the specified torque. Refer to Chapter Four.

    b. The valves are properly adjusted as described in this chapter.

    c. The battery is fully charged as described in this chapter to ensure proper engine cranking speed.

2. Warm the engine to normal operating temperature. Turn the engine off.

3. Remove and ground both spark plugs as described in this chapter.

4. Install a compression gauge (**Figure 52**) following the manufacturer's instructions. Make sure it seals properly.

5. Open the throttle completely and turn the engine over until there is no further rise in pressure. Maxi-

handle and remove the spark plug. Label the spark plug with the cylinder number.

5. Inspect the spark plug carefully. Refer to *Reading* in this section. Look for a broken center porcelain insulator, excessively eroded electrodes and excessive carbon or oil fouling.

6. Inspect the plug cap for damage.

7. Install the spark plug using the following procedure:

   a. Set the spark plug gap as described in this section.

   b. Apply a *light* coat of antiseize compound onto the threads of the spark plug before installing it. Do not use engine oil on the plug threads.

> *CAUTION*
> *The cylinder head is aluminum. The spark plug hole threads can be easily damaged by cross-threading the spark plug.*

   c. The spark plugs are recessed into the cylinder head and cannot be started by hand. With the rubber insert socket or a length of rubber hose installed on the spark plug, screw the plug in by hand until it seats. Very little effort is required. If force is necessary, the plug is cross threaded. Unscrew it and try again. Once the plug is screwed in several revolutions, remove the hose.

   d. Hand-tighten the plug until seated, then tighten the plug to 11 N•m (97 in.-lb.). Do *not* overtighten the spark plug.

8. Install the plug cap onto the spark plug. Press the plug cap onto the spark plug, rotate the assembly slightly in both directions and make sure it is attached to the spark plug and to the sealing surface of the cylinder head cover. If the cap does not completely contact the plug, the engine may develop an ignition misfire.

9. Install the fuel tank as described in Chapter Eight or Chapter Nine.

Gap

Use a spark plug gapping tool and a wire feeler gauge for the following procedure.

1. The new spark plug may be equipped with a terminal nut (A, **Figure 54**). This nut is not used on original equipment spark plug caps.

2. Insert a wire feeler gauge between the center and side electrode of the plug (**Figure 55**). The specified gap is 0.8-0.9 mm (0.031-0.036 in.). If the gap is correct, there will be a slight drag as the wire is pulled through. If there is no drag or if the gauge will not pass through, bend the side electrode with a gaping tool (**Figure 56**) and set the gap to specification.

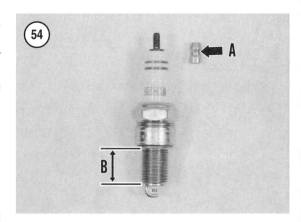

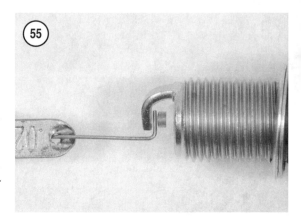

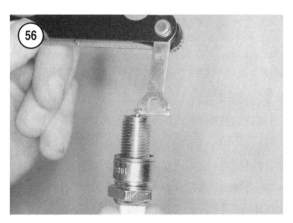

Reading

Reading the spark plugs can provide a significant amount of information regarding engine performance. Reading plugs that have been in use will give an indication of spark plug operation, air/fuel mixture composition and engine condition (oil consumption, pistons, etc.). Before checking the spark plugs, operate the motorcycle under a medium load for approximately 10 km (6 miles). Avoid prolonged idling before shutting off the engine. Remove the spark plugs as described in this section. Examine each plug and compare it to those in **Figure 57**.

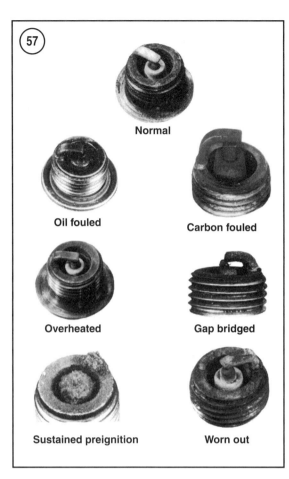

Normal

Oil fouled

Carbon fouled

Overheated

Gap bridged

Sustained preignition

Worn out

If the plugs are being read to determine if carburetor jetting is correct on 2001-2004 models, start with new plugs and operate the motorcycle at the load that corresponds to the jetting information desired. For example, if the main jet is in question, operate the motorcycle at full throttle and shut the engine off and coast to a stop.

Spark plugs are available in various heat ranges, hotter or colder than the plugs originally installed by the manufacturer. A plug with an incorrect heat range can foul, overheat and cause piston damage.

Do not change the spark plug heat range to compensate for adverse engine or carburetion conditions.

When replacing plugs, make sure the reach (B, **Figure 54**) is correct. A longer than standard plug could interfere with the piston, causing engine damage.

Refer to **Table 4** for recommended spark plugs.

Normal condition

A light tan- or gray-colored deposit on the firing tip and no abnormal gap wear or erosion indicates good engine, ignition and air/fuel mixture conditions. The plug in use is of the proper heat range. It may be serviced and returned to use.

Carbon fouled

Soft, dry, sooty deposits covering the entire firing end of the plug are evidence of incomplete combustion. Even though the firing end of the plug is dry, the plug's insulation decreases when in this condition. The carbon forms an electrical path that bypasses the electrodes resulting in a misfire condition. Carbon fouling can be caused by one or more of the following conditions:
1. Rich air/fuel mixture.
2. Spark plug heat range too cold.
3. Clogged air filter.
4. Improperly operating ignition component.
5. Ignition component failure.
6. Low engine compression.
7. Prolonged idling.

Oil fouled

An oil fouled plug has a black insulator tip, a damp oily film over the firing end and a carbon layer over the entire nose. The electrodes are not worn. Common causes for this condition are:
1. Incorrect air/fuel mixture.
2. Low idle speed or prolonged idling.
3. Ignition component failure.
4. Spark plug heat range too cold.
5. Incomplete engine break-in.
6. Worn valve guides.
7. Worn or broken piston rings.

Oil fouled spark plugs may be cleaned in an emergency, but it is better to replace them. It is important to correct the cause of fouling before the engine is returned to service.

Gap bridging

Plugs with this condition have deposits building up between the electrodes. The deposits reduce the gap and eventually close it entirely. If this condition is encountered, check for excessive carbon buildup or oil entering the combustion chamber. Make sure to locate and correct the cause of this condition.

Overheating

Badly worn electrodes and premature gap wear are signs of overheating, along with a gray or white blistered porcelain insulator surface. This condition is commonly caused by a spark plug heat range that is too hot. If the standard heat range spark plug is being used and the plug is overheated, consider the following causes:

1. Lean fuel/air mixture.
2. Improperly operating ignition component.
3. Engine lubrication system malfunction.
4. Cooling system malfunction.
5. Engine air leak.
6. Improper spark plug installation (overtightening).
7. No spark plug gasket.

Worn out

Corrosive gases formed by combustion and high voltage sparks have eroded the electrodes. A spark plug in this condition requires more voltage to fire under hard acceleration. Install a new spark plug.

Preignition

If the electrodes are melted, preignition is almost certainly the cause. Check for carburetor (2001-2004 models) or throttle body (2005-on models) mounting air leaks. Also check for advanced ignition timing or incorrect spark plug heat range. Find the cause of the preignition before returning the engine to service.

IGNITION TIMING

The ignition timing is not adjustable. However, it can be checked to make sure the ignition system is working correctly. Refer to **Table 4** for the timing specification. If the ignition timing is incorrect, refer to Chapter Two for troubleshooting.

FUEL SYSTEM ADJUSTMENT

Idle Speed Adjustment

Make sure the air filter is clean and the engine compression is within specification before adjusting the idle speed. See *Compression Test* in this chapter. Otherwise this procedure cannot be done properly.

2001-2004 models

1. Make sure the throttle cable free play is adjusted correctly. Check and adjust as described in this chapter.
2. Start the engine and let it warm approximately 2-3 minutes. Shut off the engine and make sure the carburetor choke knob (**Figure 58**) is pushed in all the way.

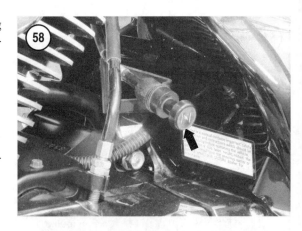

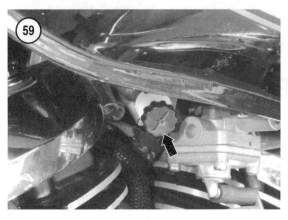

3. Connect a tachometer according to the manufacturer's instructions.
4. The idle speed knob (**Figure 59**) is located on the left, underside of the fuel tank. Turn the idle speed knob in or out to adjust the idle speed to the specification in **Table 4**.
5. Open and close the throttle a couple of times. Check for variations in idle speed, and readjust if necessary.
6. Turn off the engine.
7. Disconnect the tachometer.

2005-on models

1. Make sure the throttle cable free play is adjusted correctly. Check and adjust as described in this chapter.
2. Connect a tachometer according to the manufacturer's instructions.
3. Lift and support the fuel tank as described in Chapter Nine.
4. Start the engine and let it warm approximately 2-3 minutes.
5. The idle speed knob (A, **Figure 60**) is located on the left side of the throttle body. Turn the idle speed knob in or out to adjust the idle speed to the specifica-

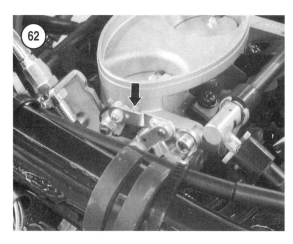

Fast Idle Speed (2005-on Models)

On 2005-on models, the ECM increases the idle speed (fast idle speed) for a specific duration depending on the ambient temperature (**Table 5**).

1. Run the engine until it reaches normal operating temperature.

2. Connect a tachometer following the manufacturer's instructions.

3. If necessary adjust normal idle speed as described in this chapter.

4. Check and adjust the throttle position (TP) sensor as described in Chapter Nine.

5. Connect a voltmeter positive lead to the blue/black TP sensor connector terminal. Connect the voltmeter negative lead to the black/brown connector terminal.

6. Start the engine and read the voltmeter with the engine at idle speed. The voltmeter should indicate approximately 1.12 volts. Turn the ignition switch off.

7. Lift and support the fuel tank as described in Chapter Nine.

8. Disconnect the white secondary throttle valve actuator connector (**Figure 61**).

9. Turn the ignition switch on.

NOTE
*The fuel tank is removed in **Figure 62** for clarity. Fuel tank removal is not necessary.*

10. Move the fast idle link to the front on the secondary throttle valve (**Figure 62**) so the secondary throttle valve is open fully.

11. Measure the TP sensor voltage as described in Step 5. Do not start the engine.

12. Subtract the voltage reading in Step 6 from the Step 10 measurement. This is the TP sensor voltage differential.

13. Refer to **Table 4** for specified voltage differential. If the TP voltage differential is not as specified, turn the fast idle screw (B, **Figure 60**) so the specified voltage differential is obtained.

14. Verify the fast idle operation. If the specified fast idle cannot be obtained, note the following possible causes and refer to Chapter Two for troubleshooting procedures:

  a. Faulty engine coolant temperature (ECT) sensor.
  b. Faulty intake air temperature (IAT) sensor.
  c. Faulty secondary throttle valve actuator (STVA).
  d. Faulty wiring or connectors.

tion in **Table 4**. Make sure the fast idle system is working correctly.

6. Open and close the throttle a couple of times. Check for variations in idle speed, and readjust if necessary.

7. Turn off the engine.

8. Disconnect the tachometer.

9. Install the fuel tank.

Idle Mixture (2001-2004 Models)

The idle mixture (pilot screw) is pre-set by the manufacturer and is not to be reset. Do not adjust the pilot screw unless the carburetor has been overhauled. Refer to Chapter Eight.

Throttle Valve Synchronization (2005-On Models)

Throttle valve synchronization ensures that each cylinder receives the same air/fuel mixture by synchronizing the vacuum in each throttle intake port.

Before synchronizing the throttle valves, make sure the air filter element is clean and the valve clearances are correct.

A vacuum gauge set which can simultaneously measure the vacuum in each cylinder is required to synchronize the throttle valves.

1. Lift and support the fuel tank as described in Chapter Nine.

2. Connect a tachometer following the manufacturer's instructions.

3. Start the engine and warm it to normal operating temperature.

4. Check and, if neccessary, adjust the idle speed as described in this section. Stop the engine.

5. Remove the fuel tank as described in Chapter Nine.

6. Using T-fittings, connect the vacuum gauge to the vacuum hose (**Figure 63**) on each side of the throttle body. Refer to **Figure 64**.

7. Reinstall the fuel tank, but support it in the raised position.

8. Synchronize the vacuum gauge following the tool manufacturer's instructions.

9. With the engine running at idle, check the gauge readings. The throttle valves are balanced if the gauge readings are the same for both cylinders.

10. Adjust the synchronization as follows:

    a. Completely close the air adjust screw (**Figure 65**) on each throttle body.

    b. Check the vacuum gauge for differences between the cylinders. Turn out the air adjust screw on the throttle body with the higher vacuum until the vacuum reading for the cylinders are the same.

    c. Snap the throttle a few times and recheck the synchronization readings. Readjust synchronization if required.

11. Check the idle speed. If necessary, adjust it as described in this chapter.

12. Stop the engine and detach the equipment.

13. Reconnect the vacuum lines. (**Figure 63**)

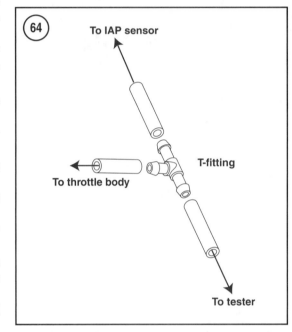

To IAP sensor

T-fitting

To throttle body

To tester

14. Lower the fuel tank (Chapter Nine).

15. Restart the engine and check the engine idle speed.

16. If necessary, adjust the throttle cable free play as described in this chapter.

Table 1 MAINTENANCE SCHEDULE

Pre-ride inspection
  Check tire pressure
  Check tire and wheel condition
  Check brake operation
  Check clutch and brake lever operation
  Check throttle operation and return
  Check steering operation
  Check and tighten axles, suspension, controls, linkage and exhaust fasteners
  Check engine oil level; add oil if necessary
  Check brake fluid level; add if necessary
  Check final drive oil level; fill as needed
  Check lights and horn operation
  Check for abnormal engine noise and leaks
  Check coolant level
  Check kill switch operation
Initial 1000 km (600 miles) or 1 month
  Change engine oil and replace oil filter
  Change final drive oil
  Check and tighten all exhaust system fasteners
  Check and tighten all chassis fasteners
  Check coolant level
Every 1000 km (600 miles) or 1 month
  Check idle speed; adjust if necessary
  Check throttle cable free play; adjust if necessary
  Check front brake pads for wear and rear pedal height
  Check front brake disc thickness; replace if necessary
  Check front brake disc for rust and corrosion; clean if necessary
  Check rear brake lining wear indicator
  Check rear brake pedal free play; adjust if necessary
  Check steering play; adjust if necessary
  Check coolant level
  Check and tighten all exhaust system fasteners
  Check and tighten all chassis fasteners
Every 6000 km (4000 miles) or 6 months
  Check air filter element for contamination; clean or replace if necessary
  Check spark plugs; replace if necessary
  Check all fuel system hoses for leaks; repair or replace if necessary
  Change engine oil
  Check idle speed; adjust if necessary
  Check throttle cable free play; adjust if necessary
  Check clutch lever free play adjustment; adjust if necessary
  Check radiator and all coolant hoses for leaks
  Check battery charge and condition
  Check front brake pads for wear
  Check front brake disc thickness; replace if necessary
  Check front brake disc for rust and corrosion; clean if necessary
  Check front brake system for leaks; repair if necessary
  Check front brake fluid level in reservoir; add fluid if necessary
  Check tire and wheel rim condition
  Lubricate all pivot points
  Check tightness of all chassis fasteners; tighten if necessary
Every 12,000 km (7500 miles) or 12 months
  All of the checks listed in 6000 km (4000 miles) or 6 months and the following:
  Replace the spark plugs
  Check front fork operation and for leaks
  Check EVAP hoses (California models)
  Check PAIR (air supply) hoses
Every 18,000 km (11,000 miles) or 18 months
  All of the checks listed in 12,000 km (7500 miles) or 12 months and the following:
  Replace air filter element
  Change engine oil and filter
Every 24,000 km (15,000 miles) or 24 months
  All of the checks listed in 12,000 km (7500 miles) or 12 months and the following:
  Check valve clearance; adjust if necessary
Every 2 years
  Replace coolant
  Replace brake fluid

(continued)

Table 1 MAINTENANCE SCHEDULE (continued)

Every 4 years*
  Replace all fuel hoses
  Replace all brake hoses
  Replace EVAP hoses (California models)

*Manufacturer's recommendation

Table 2 TIRE SPECIFICATIONS

Item	Front	Rear
Tire type	Tube	Tube
Size	130/90-16M/C (67H)	170/80-15M/C (77H)
Minimum tread depth	1.6 mm (0.06 in.)	2.0 mm (0.08 in.)
Inflation pressure (cold)*		
Touring models	225 kPa (33 psi)	225 kPa (33 psi)
All other models		
Solo	200 kPa (29 psi)	250 kPa (36 psi)
Rider and passenger	200 kPa (29 psi)	250 kPa (36 psi)

*Tire inflation pressure for original equipment tires. Aftermarket tires may require different inflation pressure. The use of tires other than those specified by the manufacturer may affect handling.

Table 3 RECOMMENDED LUBRICANTS AND FLUIDS

Brake fluid	DOT 4
Engine coolant	
Type	Ethylene glycol-based containing corrosion inhibitors for aluminum radiators
Ratio	50:50 distilled water and antifreeze
Capacity*	1.5 L (1.6 qt.)
Engine oil	
Classification	API SF/SG or SH/SJ with JASO MA
Viscosity	SAE 10W40
Capacity	
Oil change only	3.0 L (3.2 qt.)
Oil and filter change	3.4 L (3.6 qt.)
When engine completely dry	3.7 L (3.9 qt.)
Final drive oil	
Type	SAE 90, GL-5 hypoid
Capacity	200-220 ml (6.8-7.4 oz.)
Fork oil	
Viscosity	Suzuki SS-08 (#10) fork oil or equivalent
Capacity per leg	412 ml (13.9 oz.)
Fuel	
Type	Unleaded
Octane	
U.S and Canada models	87 [(R + M)/2 method] or research octane of 91 or higher
Non- U.S.and Canada models	91
Fuel tank capacity*	
2001-2004 models	17.0 L (4.5 gal.)
2005-on models	15.5 L (4.1 gal)
*Includes reserve tank	

Table 4 MAINTENANCE AND TUNE-UP SPECIFICATIONS

Battery	
Type	FTX12-BS Maintenance free (sealed)
Capacity	12 volt 10 amp hour
Brake pedal	
Free play	20-30 mm (0.8-1.2 in)
Height	75-85 mm (3.0-3.3 in.)
Clutch lever free play	10-15 mm (0.4-0.6 in.)
	(continued)

Table 4 MAINTENANCE AND TUNE-UP SPECIFICATIONS (continued)

Compression pressure (at sea level)	
Standard	1300-1700 kPa (188.5-246.5 psi)
Service limit	1100 kPa (159.5 psi)
Maximum difference between cylinders	200 kPa (28 psi)
Engine oil pressure (hot)	350-650 kPa (51-94 psi) at 3000 rpm
Fast idle TP sensor voltage differential	
2005-on models	0.064-0.096 volts
Fast idle speed	2100 rpm
Idle speed	1000-1200 rpm
Ignition timing	5° BTDC at 1100 rpm
Radiator cap release pressure	95-125 kPa (13.8-18.1 psi)
Spark plug	
Standard plug	NGK DPR7EA-9, ND X22EPR-U9
Colder plug	NGK DPR8EA-9, ND X24EPR-U9
Spark plug gap	0.8-0.9 mm (0.031-0.035 in.)
Valve clearance (cold)	
Intake	0.08-0.13 mm (0.003-0.005 in.)
Exhaust	0.17-0.22 mm (0.007-0.009 in.)
Throttle cable free play	2.0-4.0 mm (0.08-0.16 in.)
Wheel runout (front and rear)	
Axial	2.0 mm (0.08 in.)
Radial	2.0 mm (0.08 in.)

Table 5 FAST IDLE SPECIFICATIONS (2005-ON MODELS)

Ambient temperature	Fast idle rpm	Fast idle duration
-5° C (23° F)	1500-2100 rpm	Approx. 100 seconds
15° C (59° F)	1500-2100 rpm	Approx. 60 seconds
25° C (77° F)	1500-2100 rpm	Approx. 50 seconds

Table 6 MAINTENANCE AND TUNE-UP TORQUE SPECIFICATIONS

Item	N•m	in.-lb.	ft.-lb.
Engine oil drain plug	23	-	17
Final drive oil drain plug	23	–	17
Fork cap bolt	45	–	33
Fork lower clamp bolts	33	–	24
Front axle	65	–	48
Front axle pinch bolts	33	–	24
Main oil gallery plug	18	159	–
Pivot lever mounting bolt	78	–	58
Pivot link (both ends)	78	–	58
Rear axle nut	65	–	48
Shock absorber mounting bolts	50	–	37
Spark plug	18	-	13
Swing arm			
Right pivot locknut	100	–	74
Left pivot bolt	100	–	74
Right pivot bolt	9.5	84	–

CHAPTER FOUR

ENGINE TOP END

This chapter covers procedures for the cylinder head covers, rocker arms, cylinder heads, valves, cylinder blocks, pistons, piston rings and camshafts.

Refer to **Tables 1-2** for engine specifications.

CYLINDER HEAD COVER CAPS

CAUTION
The cover caps are different in order to accommodate the configuration of each cylinder head cover. Identify each cap so it can be installed in its original position.

The caps around the spark plugs (A, **Figure 1**) are secured with smaller and shorter bolts and may be removed with the engine installed in the frame. The opposite caps (B, **Figure 1**) are secured with long bolts that extend into the top of the crankcase. Because of the bolt length, these caps cannot be removed unless the engine is removed from the frame.

Removal/Installation

Right front and left rear caps

1. Remove the fuel tank as described in Chapter Eight or Chapter Nine.
2. Disconnect the spark plug wire cap from the spark plug.

3A. Right front cap—Detach the intake duct and move it aside for access to the rear mounting bolt.
3B. Left rear cap—On 2001-2004 models, detach the fuel hose from the retaining clamp.
4. Remove the cap retaining bolts, then remove each cap.
5. Install the cap and secure it with the retaining bolts while noting the following:
   a. Make sure the grommet (A, **Figure 2**) fits in each bolt hole.
   b. Install a washer (B, **Figure 2**) onto a collar (C) and install the shouldered end of the collar into the grommet.
   c. Install a washer (D, **Figure 2**) onto each bolt (E).
   d. Tighten the bolts 25 N•m (18 ft.-lb.).
6. Reverse the removal steps to complete the installation.

Left front and right rear caps

1. Remove the engine as described in Chapter Five.
2. Remove the cap retaining bolts (**Figure 3**, typical). These bolts also secure the cylinder head cover, cylinder head, and cylinder to the crankcase.
3. Install the cap and secure it with the retaining bolts while noting the following:
   a. Make sure the grommet (A, **Figure 3**) fits in each bolt hole.

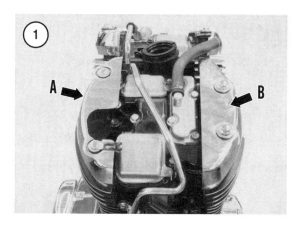

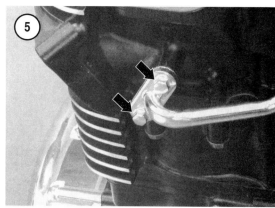

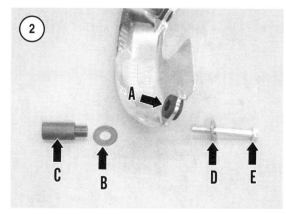

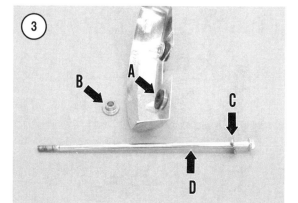

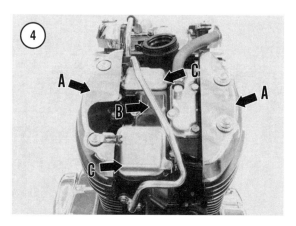

b. Install the shouldered end of the collar (B, **Figure 3**) into the grommet.

c. Install a washer (C, **Figure 3**) onto each bolt (D).

d. Tighten the bolts to 25 N•m (18 ft.-lb.).

4. Install the engine as described in Chapter Five.

CYLINDER HEAD COVERS

Removal

1. Remove the engine from the frame as described in Chapter Five.

2. Remove the spark plugs as described in Chapter Three. This will make it easier to rotate the engine in the following steps.

3. Remove the cylinder head cover caps (A, **Figure 4**) as described in this chapter.

4. Remove the PAIR pipe retaining bolts (**Figure 5**). Disconnect the pipe from the hose and remove the PAIR pipe (B, **Figure 4**).

5. Remove the timing hole plug (A, **Figure 6**) located in the left crankcase cover.

6. Remove the alternator bolt access cover (B, **Figure 6**) in the left crankcase cover.

7. Remove both rocker covers (C, **Figure 4**).

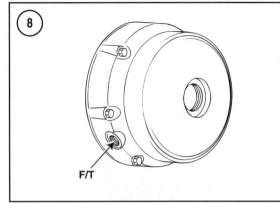

F/T

8. Use a socket to engage the flywheel retaining bolt (**Figure 7**) and rotate the crankshaft until the piston is at top dead center (TDC) on the compression stroke.

   a. When removing the cylinder head cover on the front cylinder, position the crankshaft so the FT mark (**Figure 8**) appears in the plug hole.

   b. When removing the cylinder head cover on the rear cylinder, position the crankshaft so the RT mark appears in the plug hole.

NOTE
*When the piston is at TDC on its compression stroke there will be free play in both of the rocker arms (A, **Figure 9**), indicating that both the intake and exhaust valves are closed.*

   c. With the flywheel mark in view, if both rocker arms are not loose; rotate the engine an additional 360° until both rocker arms have free play. Position the crankshaft so the appropriate mark (**Figure 8**) appears in the plug hole.

9. Loosen the cylinder head cover bolts (**Figure 10**) in a crisscross pattern in several passes. Note that there are two bolts located between the valves.

CAUTION
Do not pry off the cylinder head cover. Damage to the cylinder head cover and cylinder head may result.

10. Remove the cylinder head cover bolts (**Figure 10**), then remove the cylinder head cover. It may be necessary to tap around the perimeter of the cover with a soft-faced mallet to break the cover loose from the cylinder head. Account for the locating dowels.

Inspection

If oil is leaking from between the cylinder head cover and the cylinder head, the sealing surface of the cylinder head cover may be warped or damaged. Inspect the

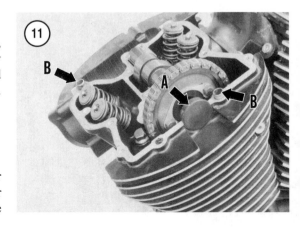

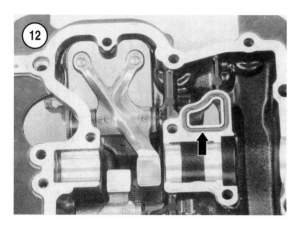

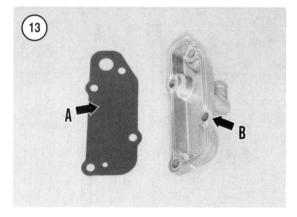

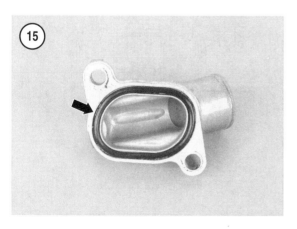

sealing surface of the cylinder head cover for scoring or other signs of damage.

1. Remove the camshaft end cap (A, **Figure 11**). The end cap may remain in the cylinder head or head cover. Replace the cap if it is damaged or deteriorated.

2. On the front cylinder head cover, remove the O-ring gasket (**Figure 12**). Note that the gasket may remain on the cylinder head.

3. Remove all the sealant residue from the cylinder head and cylinder head cover mating surfaces.

4. Thoroughly clean the cylinder head cover in solvent and dry with compressed air.

5. After the cylinder head cover has been cleaned, place the cylinder head cover gasket surface on a flat surface plate. Measure the warp by inserting a flat feeler gauge between the surface plate and the cylinder head cover at several locations around the perimeter. There should be no warp. The maximum allowable distortion is in **Table 1**. If the cylinder head cover is warped beyond the limit, replace the cylinder head cover.

6. Remove and inspect the rocker arms as described in this chapter.

7. On the rear cylinder head cover, remove the breather cover (B, **Figure 9**) and perform the following:

   a. Inspect the gasket (A, **Figure 13**) for damage or deterioration. Replace if necessary.

   b. Inspect the breather cover (B, **Figure 13**) for cracks or damage; replace if necessary.

   c. Install the gasket and cover. Tighten the retaining bolts securely.

CAUTION
*The engine coolant sensor on 2005-on models is mounted on the coolant outlet (**Figure 14**). Do not damage the sensor.*

8. On the front cylinder head cover, remove the coolant outlet (**Figure 14**) and perform the following:

   a. Inspect the outlet and cover for leaks.

   b. Install a new O-ring (**Figure 15**) onto the outlet.

   c. Install the outlet onto the cover. Tighten the bolts securely.

9. Inspect the rocker covers (A, **Figure 16**) for cracks or damage. Install a new O-ring (B, **Figure 16**). Make sure the bolt hole tabs are not cracked or warped. If these tabs are damaged it may cause an oil leak. Replace the cover(s) if necessary.

Installation

The following procedure applies to the installation of either cylinder head cover. However, the piston of the respective cylinder head cover must be at TDC on the compression stroke. Refer to Step 8 of *Removal* in this section.

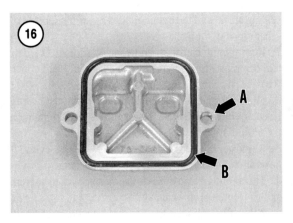

1. Make sure all sealant residue is removed from the sealing surfaces of the cylinder head and cylinder head cover.

2. On the front cylinder head cover, lubricate and install the O-ring gasket (A, **Figure 17**).

3. Apply a bead of Suzuki Bond 1216B or equivalent to the cylinder head mating surface.

4. Lubricate the contact surfaces on each rocker arm (B, **Figure 17**) and the camshaft bearing surfaces (C) in the cylinder head cover with molybdenum disulfide grease.

5. Install the camshaft rubber end cap (A, **Figure 11**) into the cylinder head recess.

6. Make sure the locating dowels (B, **Figure 11**) are in place.

7. Install the cylinder head cover and push it into position.

8. Different types of fasteners are used to secure the cylinder head cover. Refer to **Figure 18** for the location the front cylinder head cover fasteners or to **Figure 19** for the rear cylinder head cover fastener locations. Note washer and sealant locations:

    a. Allen bolt (A).

    b. Bolt and seal washer (B).

    c. Bolt with sealant applied (C).

    d. Stainless bolt (D).

9. Initially tighten the cylinder head cover bolts handtight in a crisscross pattern. Then tighten the 6 mm bolts to 10 N•m (88 in.-lb.). Tighten the 8 mm bolts to 25 N•m (18 ft.-lb.).

10. Install both rocker covers (C, **Figure 4**).

11. Install the timing hole plug (A, **Figure 6**) and the cap (B) in the left crankcase cover and tighten securely.

12. Install the spark plugs as described in Chapter Three.

13. Connect the PAIR pipe (B, **Figure 4**) to the hose and install the PAIR pipe.

14. Inspect the gasket for the PAIR pipe mounting flange and install a new gasket if necessary. Install the

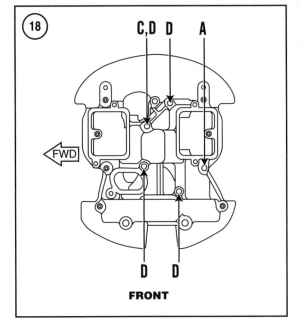

FRONT

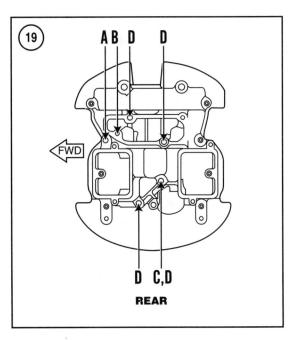

REAR

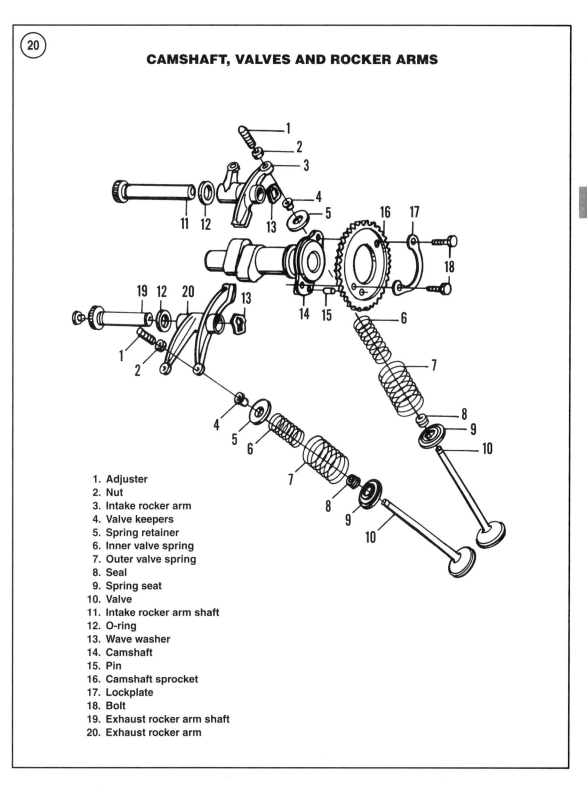

CAMSHAFT, VALVES AND ROCKER ARMS

1. Adjuster
2. Nut
3. Intake rocker arm
4. Valve keepers
5. Spring retainer
6. Inner valve spring
7. Outer valve spring
8. Seal
9. Spring seat
10. Valve
11. Intake rocker arm shaft
12. O-ring
13. Wave washer
14. Camshaft
15. Pin
16. Camshaft sprocket
17. Lockplate
18. Bolt
19. Exhaust rocker arm shaft
20. Exhaust rocker arm

PAIR pipe retaining bolts (**Figure 5**) and tighten securely.

15. Install the cylinder head cover caps as described in this chapter.

16. Install the engine into the frame as described in Chapter Five.

ROCKER ARM ASSEMBLIES

If servicing both cylinder head covers, do not intermix components between the front and rear covers. Refer to **Figure 20**.

1. Remove the rocker arm shafts (**Figure 21**) by unscrewing them from the cylinder head cover. Carefully

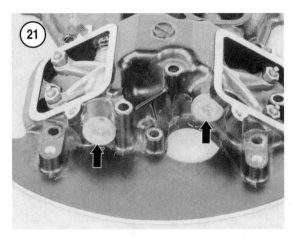

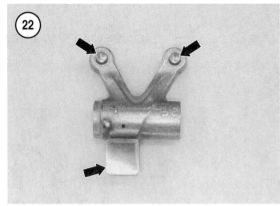

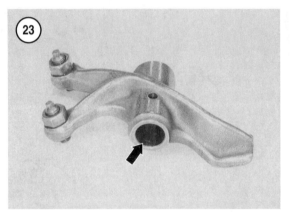

withdraw the rocker arm shaft and remove the rocker arm and wave washer.

2. Wash all parts in cleaning solvent and thoroughly dry.

3. Inspect the rocker arm pad where it contacts the cam lobe and where the adjuster contacts the valve stem (**Figure 22**). If the pad is scratched or worn unevenly, inspect the cam lobe for scoring, chipping or flat spots. Replace the rocker arm if damaged.

4. Measure the inside diameter of the rocker arm bore (**Figure 23**) and compare with the specifications in **Table 1**. Replace if excessively worn.

5. Inspect each rocker arm shaft (**Figure 24**) for signs of wear or scoring. Measure the shaft outside diameter and compare with the specification in **Table 1**. Replace if excessively worn.

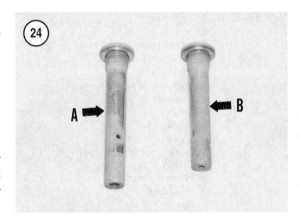

6. Coat the rocker arm shafts and rocker arm bores with molybdenum disulfide grease.

7. Install the rocker arm and shaft assemblies by reversing the removal procedure. Note the following:

    a. Make sure to reinstall the components in their original positions. The intake rocker arm shaft (A, **Figure 24**) is longer than the exhaust rocker arm shaft (B).

    b. Install the wave washers (**Figure 25**) in the positions shown in **Figure 26.**

    c. Tighten the rocker arm shafts to 27 N•m (20 ft.-lb.).

CAMSHAFTS

NOTE
*The camshafts and sprockets used in the front and rear cylinders are different. If servicing both cylinders refer to **Inspection** in this section and identify the components.*

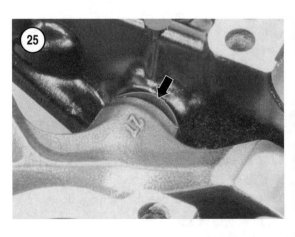

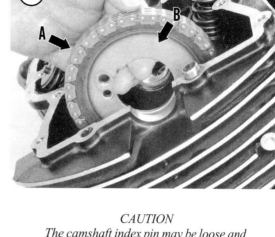

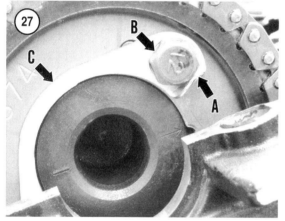

4

CAUTION
The camshaft index pin may be loose and may fall into the crankcase after removal of the lockplate.

2. Flatten the locking tabs (A, **Figure 27**) of the lockplate on the camshaft sprocket bolts (B).

3. Rotate the engine until one of the camshaft sprocket bolts is exposed. Remove that bolt.

4. Again rotate the engine until the other camshaft sprocket bolt is exposed. Remove that bolt and the lockplate (C, **Figure 27**). Discard the lockplate as a new one must be installed during installation.

5. Disengage the camshaft from the sprocket and remove the camshaft (**Figure 28**). If necessary, insert a rod (such as a drive extension) through the sprocket to hold it up after camshaft removal.

6. Disengage the drive chain (A, **Figure 29**) from the sprocket (B) and remove the sprocket.

7. Attach a piece of wire to the drive chain and tie it to the exterior of the engine. This will prevent the chain from falling into the crankcase.

CAUTION
If the crankshaft must be rotated after the camshaft is removed, pull up on the cam chain and keep it taut while rotating the crankshaft. Make certain that the drive chain is positioned correctly on the crankshaft timing sprocket. If this is not done, the drive chain may become kinked and may damage both the chain and the timing sprocket on the crankshaft.

8. Inspect the camshaft as described in this chapter.

9. The piston of the cylinder on which the camshaft is being installed must be at top dead center (TDC) when performing the following steps for correct valve timing. Hold the cam chain out and taut while rotating crankshaft to avoid damage to the chain and/or the crankcase.

Removal/Installation

The following procedure applies to the camshaft on either the front or rear cylinder. Differences between the two are noted.

1. Remove the cylinder head cover(s) as described in this chapter.

NOTE
*Although there are two timing marks (FT and RT) on the flywheel, use only the **RT** timing mark for camshaft installation on either cylinder.*

10. Use a socket to engage the alternator retaining bolt and rotate the crankshaft (**Figure 30**, typical) until the *RT* mark on the flywheel appears in the center of the plug hole (**Figure 31**). Use the *RT* mark when installing the camshaft on the front or rear cylinder.

11. A tensioner tool (Suzuki part No. 09918-53810) is needed to hold the tensioner compressed. A suitable substitute can be made from a plastic tie strap as follows:

   a. Trim the locking end of a 10-12 in. tie strap (A, **Figure 32**), to the shape of an L (B).

   b. Do not trim away too much of the plastic material as the L-shaped end must not only hold the ratchet in the compressed position, but it must also be strong enough to not break off and stay in the tensioner when the modified tie strap is withdrawn later in the procedure.

   c. Do not shorten the overall length of the tie wrap. It must be able to exit through the top of the cylinder head during assembly so it can be removed later in the installation procedure.

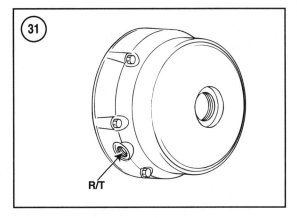

R/T

NOTE
The camshaft chain tensioner spring must remain compressed during installation of the camshaft chain and sprocket.

NOTE
The tensioner is shown removed in Step 12 for clarity. It is not necessary to remove the tensioner in this procedure.

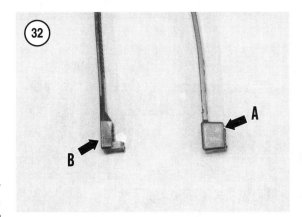

12. A camshaft tensioner assembly (**Figure 33**) automatically provides tension on the camshaft chain. The tensioner is mounted on the cylinder (A, **Figure 34**). To release the ratchet in the tensioner, push in the ratchet (A, **Figure 33**). While holding in the ratchet, push in the spring rod (B, **Figure 33**) until the spring is fully compressed. Release the ratchet and install the end of the tie strap into the gap (C, **Figure 33**) between the ratchet and tensioner body (B, **Figure 34**). This will hold the tensioner in place and keep the spring compressed.

NOTE
*Make sure the **RT** (rear cylinder) timing mark remains centered in the timing plug hole (**Figure 31**). This is necessary for proper camshaft timing.*

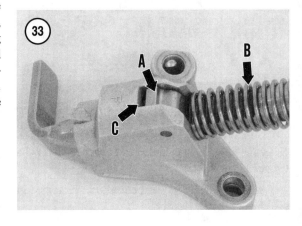

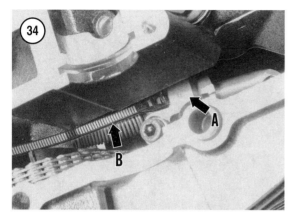

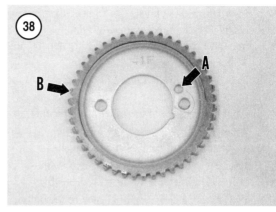

4

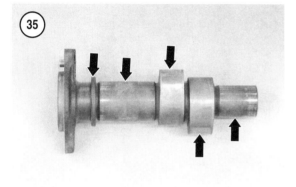

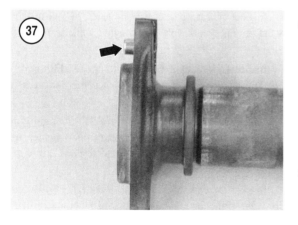

13. Install the camshaft sprocket (B, **Figure 29**) into the timing chain (A).

14. Lubricate the camshaft lobes, bearing journals and thrust flange with engine oil (**Figure 35**).

15. Install the camshaft (**Figure 28**) and position the camshaft so the timing marks (**Figure 36**) align with the top surface of the cylinder head. The arrow timing mark must point toward the front.

NOTE
When installing the camshaft sprocket onto the camshaft in Step 16, do not disturb the camshaft and misalign the timing marks. It may be necessary to reposition the sprocket in the timing chain so the camshaft pin and sprocket hole align.

16. Note the position of the index pin on the camshaft (**Figure 37**). Fit the camshaft sprocket onto the camshaft so the index hole in the sprocket (A, **Figure 38**) aligns with the index pin on the camshaft. If necessary, reposition the sprocket in the timing chain.

CAUTION
Correct camshaft installation is critical. Recheck the installation several times to make sure the alignment is correct.

17. Make sure the timing marks (A, **Figure 36**) are still aligned properly. Check all timing marks as follows:

   a. Refer to Step 10 and make sure the *T* mark is still properly aligned. Readjust if necessary.

   b. Make sure the index marks on the camshaft are perfectly aligned with the top surface of the cylinder head.

   c. Readjust if any timing marks are not aligned correctly.

18. When all timing marks are aligned correctly, perform the following:

   a. Apply threadlock to one of the cam sprocket bolts.

b. Install the new lockplate (B, **Figure 36**) so it covers the camshaft index pin and install the bolt (C) into the exposed bolt hole. Do *not* tighten the bolt at this time.

c. Rotate the crankshaft one full turn to expose the other bolt hole.

d. Apply threadlock to the other cam sprocket bolt and install it.

e. Tighten this bolt to 15 N•m (133 in.-lb.).

f. Rotate the engine one full turn to expose the other bolt and tighten it to 15 N•m (133 in.-lb.).

g. Fold over the locking tab on each of the bolts.

19. Make one final check to make sure alignment is correct. The *RT* timing mark must be centered in the plug hole when the timing marks on the camshaft are aligned with the top surface of the cylinder head.

> *CAUTION*
> *After removing the tie strap from the tensioner in Step 20, inspect the tie strap end to be sure all of it came out of the tensioner.*

20. Carefully pull the tie strap out of the camshaft drive chain tensioner.

21. Install the cylinder head cover(s) as described in this chapter.

Inspection

1. If servicing the camshafts and sprockets in both cylinders, identify the components as follows:

a. The camshafts are identified by a *F* or *R* embossed on the sprocket end of the camshaft (**Figure 39**).

b. The camshaft sprockets may also be identified by the number stamped on the sprocket (front: 41F, rear: 374), number of teeth (front: 46, rear: 42), and size (front sprocket has a larger diameter).

2. Inspect the camshaft bearing journals (A, **Figure 40**) for wear.

3. Measure all camshaft bearing journals and compare to the dimensions specified in **Table 1**.

4. Inspect the camshaft lobes (B, **Figure 40**) for wear. Even though the camshaft lobe surface appears to be satisfactory, with no visible signs of wear, measure the camshaft lobe height with a micrometer (**Figure 41**). Compare to the dimensions listed in **Table 1**. If wear exceeds the service limit, replace the camshaft.

5. Support the camshaft at its ends in V-blocks. Rotate the camshaft and measure camshaft runout at its end. Compare the measurement with the specification listed in **Table 1**.

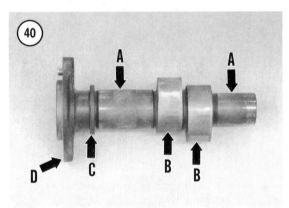

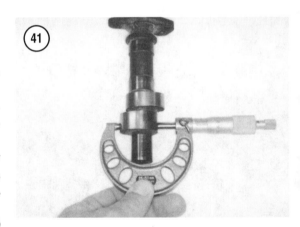

6. Inspect the camshaft thrust flange (C, **Figure 40**) for wear or damage. If worn or damaged, replace the camshaft.

7. Inspect the sprocket mounting flange (D, **Figure 40**) for cracks, warp or damage. Replace the camshaft if necessary.

8. Make sure the index pin (**Figure 37**) fits tightly in the camshaft. If the pin is loose, determine whether the camshaft, pin or both are worn and replace the worn part(s).

9. Inspect the camshaft sprocket teeth (B, **Figure 38**) for wear. If the teeth are damaged, inspect the camshaft

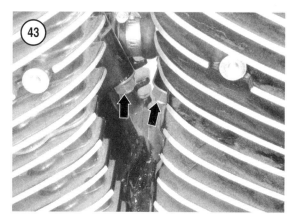

5. Initially tighten the cylinder head cover bolts handtight in a crisscross pattern. Then tighten the 6 mm bolts to 10 N•m (88 in.-lb.). Tighten the 8 mm bolts to 25 N•m (18 ft.-lb.).

6. Loosen the cylinder head cover bolts in a crisscross pattern, then remove the bolts.

7. Carefully pull the cylinder head cover straight up and off of the camshaft and cylinder head.

8. Measure the width of the flattened Plastigage material at the widest point, according to the manufacturer's instructions (**Figure 42**, typical).

> *CAUTION*
> *Be sure to remove all traces of Plastigage material from the bearing journals in the cylinder head and cylinder head cover. If any material is left in the engine, it can plug an oil control orifice and cause severe engine damage.*

9. Remove all Plastigage material from the camshaft.

10. If the oil clearance is greater than specified in **Table 1**, and the camshaft bearing journal outside diameter dimensions are within the specifications as described under *Inspection* in this chapter, replace the cylinder head and cylinder head cover.

drive chain (Chapter Five) for damage also. If either part is damaged, replace them as a set.

Journal oil clearance measurement

This procedure requires the use of Plastigage. The camshaft must be installed into the cylinder head. Before installing the camshaft, remove all gasket residue from the cylinder head and cylinder head cover mating surfaces. Wipe all oil residue from the camshaft bearing journals and bearing surfaces in the cylinder head and cylinder head cover.

1. Install the camshaft into the cylinder head with the lobes facing up. Do not attach the drive sprocket to the camshaft.

2. Make sure the locating dowels are in place in the cylinder head.

3. Place a strip of Plastigage material on top of each camshaft bearing journal, parallel to the camshaft.

> *CAUTION*
> *Do not rotate the camshaft with the Plastigage material in place.*

4. Install the cylinder head cover and push it into position.

CYLINDER HEAD AND CYLINDER

Two procedures are available to service the cylinder heads and cylinders. Each cylinder head is secured to the cylinder by a nut (**Figure 43**) located in the valley between the cylinders. Access to the nut is limited and requires removing the cylinder head and cylinder as a unit, unless a tool is fabricated to remove and tighten the nut. If the nut can be turned, the cylinder head and cylinder may be serviced separately. Refer to *Cylinder Head* in this chapter for a description of the tool.

Extra care is needed to install the cylinder head and cylinder as a unit onto the piston, as opposed to just installing the cylinder. Also, if using the cylinder head/cylinder unit procedure, the front cylinder head/cylinder unit must be removed before the rear cylinder head and cylinder are accessible.

After considering the preferred method for removing the cylinder head retaining nut, follow the appropriate procedure for cylinder head and cylinder removal and installation.

The following procedure describes removal of the cylinder head and cylinder from the crankcase as a unit assembly. The cylinder head and cylinder are separated after removal.

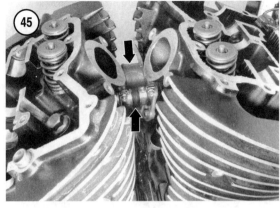

Removal

1. Remove the camshaft(s) as described in this chapter.

2A. On 2001-2004 models, remove the bolts securing the intake manifold (**Figure 44**) and remove it.

2B. On 2005-on models, loosen the clamp screw and remove the intake tube on each cylinder head.

3. Loosen the screws of the clamp bands on the coolant hoses (**Figure 45**). Move the clamps from the fittings of the cylinders and back onto the hoses.

4. To remove the front cylinder head and cylinder as a unit, proceed as follows:

   a. Using a crisscross pattern, loosen and remove the bolts (**Figure 46**) securing the cylinder head and cylinder to the crankcase.

CAUTION
Hitting or prying against the cooling fins may damage them.

   b. Loosen the cylinder head and cylinder by tapping around the perimeter base of the cylinder with a soft-faced mallet. If necessary, gently pry the cylinder from the crankcase with a broad-tipped screwdriver.

   c. Untie the wire or remove the tool holding up the camshaft chain.

   d. Carefully lift the cylinder head and cylinder assembly, then remove them from the piston and the crankcase. Disengage the short coolant hoses from the fittings of the other cylinder and cylinder head. Guide the camshaft chain through the opening in the cylinder head and cylinder and secure it to the exterior of the engine. This will prevent the camshaft chain from falling down into the crankcase. Set the cylinder head and cylinder (**Figure 47**) aside for further disassembly.

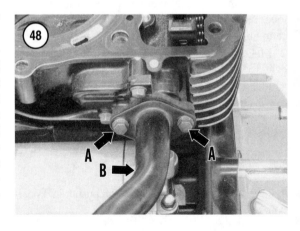

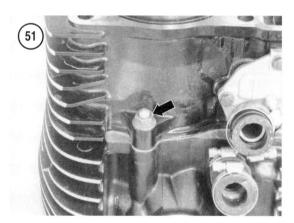

e. Remove the cylinder base gasket and discard it. Do not lose the locating dowels.

f. Stuff a clean shop cloth into the opening in the crankcase opening to keep out debris.

5. To remove the rear cylinder head and cylinder as a unit, perform the following:

a. Remove the bolts (A, **Figure 48**, typical) securing the metal coolant inlet pipe to the rear cylinder and separate the metal coolant pipe (B) from the cylinder.

b. Repeat Step 4.

Disassembly

1. If not previously removed, remove the cam chain tensioner spring retaining tool (B, **Figure 34**).

2A. On the front cylinder head and cylinder, remove the bolts (**Figure 49**) at the front and the nut (**Figure 50**) at the rear.

2B. On the rear cylinder head and cylinder, remove the nut at the front (**Figure 51**) and the nut at the rear (**Figure 52**).

CAUTION
Hitting or prying against the cooling fins may damage them.

3. Loosen the cylinder head from the cylinder by tapping around the perimeter of the cylinder head with a rubber or soft-faced mallet. If necessary, gently pry the cylinder head from the cylinder with a broad-tipped screwdriver.

4. Carefully remove the cylinder head (A, **Figure 53**) from the cylinder (B).

5. Remove the cylinder head gasket. Do not lose the locating dowels.

6. Remove the camshaft chain guide from the cylinder.

7. Remove the bolts (A, **Figure 54**) securing the camshaft chain tensioner (B) and remove the tensioner from the cylinder.

8. Inspect the cylinder head, cylinder and camshaft chain tensioner as described in this section.

Assembly

A special tool is required to hold the camshaft chain tensioner spring in the compressed position. Refer to *Camshafts* in this chapter.

> *NOTE*
> *The camshaft chain tensioners are unique and must be installed in the correct cylinder. They are marked **F** (front) (**Figure 55**) or **R** (rear).*

1. Install the correct camshaft chain tensioner (B, **Figure 54**) into the cylinder. Install the bolts (A, **Figure 54**) and tighten securely.

> *NOTE*
> *The camshaft chain tensioner spring must be compressed during installation of the camshaft chain guide.*

2. Refer to *Camshafts* and install the tensioner tool or tie strap required to hold the tensioner in the compressed position.

> *NOTE*
> *The front and rear cylinder head gaskets have a different hole pattern. Make sure to install the correct gasket on the correct cylinder.*

> *NOTE*
> *The camshaft chain guides are unique and must be installed in the correct cylinder. The front cylinder chain guide (A, **Figure 56**) is longer than the rear cylinder guide (B).*

3. If removed, install the two locating dowels (**Figure 57**) into the cylinder.

4. Install the camshaft chain guide (A, **Figure 58**) into the cylinder. Make sure it seats in the locator notch at the top of the cylinder (B, **Figure 58**).

5. Install a new cylinder head gasket (**Figure 59**). Make sure all of the gasket holes match the holes in the cylinder.

> *CAUTION*
> *If the cylinder head and cylinder do not fit together completely, do not pull them together with the bolts and nuts in the next step. Separate the two parts and*

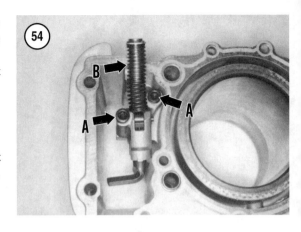

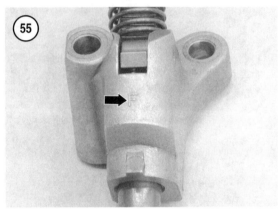

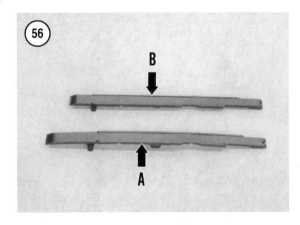

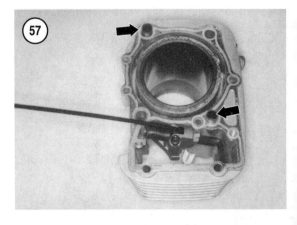

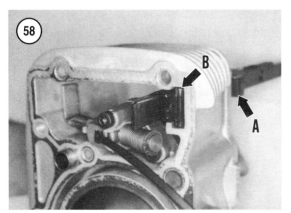

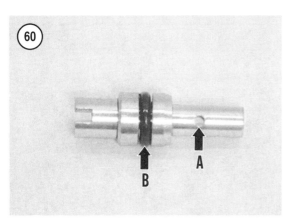

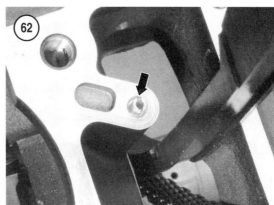

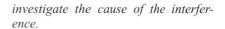

4

investigate the cause of the interfer-ence.

6. Carefully install the cylinder head (A, **Figure 53**) onto the cylinder (B). Guide the plastic tie strap up through the camshaft chain opening in the cylinder head. Push the two parts together until tight.

7A. On the front cylinder head and cylinder, install the bolts (**Figure 49**) at the front and the nut (**Figure 50**) at the rear. Tighten the bolts and nut to 25 N•m (18 ft.-lb.).

7B. On the rear cylinder head and cylinder, install the nut at the front (**Figure 51**) and the nut (**Figure 52**) at the rear. Tighten the nuts to 25 N•m (18 ft.-lb.).

Installation

1. If used, remove the shop cloth from the opening in the crankcase.

2. Apply a liberal coat of clean engine oil to the cylinder wall, especially at the lower end where the piston will be entering.

3. Apply clean engine oil to the piston and piston rings. This makes it easier to guide the piston into the cylinder bore.

4. Make sure both top surfaces of the crankcase and the bottom surface of the both cylinders are clean prior to installing a new base gasket.

5. If the oil control orifice was removed, make sure the oil hole (A, **Figure 60**) is open and that the O-ring (B) is installed. Install the oil control orifice (**Figure 61**, typical) into the crankcase, pushing it down until it bottoms in the front cylinder crankcase opening (**Figure 62**) or rear cylinder crankcase opening (**Figure 63**).

6. Install the rear cylinder head/cylinder unit as described in the following steps:

    a. Install the locating dowels (A, **Figure 64**) and a new cylinder base gasket (B).

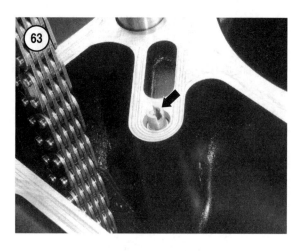

NOTE
*A piston holding tool (C, **Figure 64**) will help secure the piston when installing the cylinder. Refer to **Figure 65** for dimensions when making a tool. A soft material such as wood should be used.*

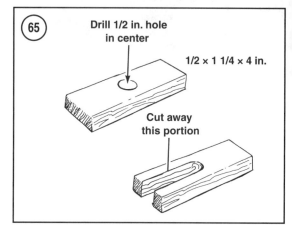

Drill 1/2 in. hole
in center

1/2 × 1 1/4 × 4 in.

Cut away
this portion

b. Make sure the end gaps of the piston rings are staggered around the circumference. Lubricate the piston rings and the inside of the cylinder bore with assembly oil or clean engine oil.

CAUTION
The following step requires the aid of an assistant. The cylinder head and cylinder assembly are long and heavy. Trying to hold the cylinder head and cylinder assembly by yourself, while guiding it onto the piston, could cause damage to the piston and/or piston rings.

c. Move the cylinder head and cylinder assembly into position on the crankcase.

d. Install the cylinder head and cylinder assembly. Guide the chain and camshaft tensioner assembly guide into the camshaft chain slot in the cylinder head and cylinder assembly. Make sure the camshaft tensioner guide indexes correctly into the tensioner assembly in the cylinder.

e. Carefully feed the camshaft chain and wire up through the opening in the cylinder head and cylinder and tie it to the exterior of the assembly.

f. Start the cylinder down over the piston while compressing each piston ring as it enters the cylinder.

g. Slide the cylinder head and cylinder assembly down until it bottoms on the crankcase.

h. Look down into the camshaft chain cavity and make sure the camshaft chain, camshaft tensioner assembly guide and the chain guide are all positioned correctly and that the camshaft chain is not binding.

NOTE
*Make sure the tensioner arm (A, **Figure 66**) is behind the chain guide (B). The cylinder head is removed for clarity.*

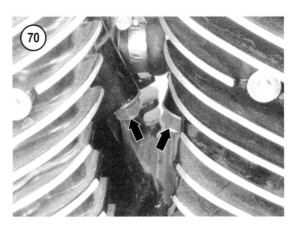

j. Replace both sections of coolant hose.

7. Repeat the preceding steps to install the front cylinder head and cylinder head assembly. The procedure is the same except the short sections of the coolant hoses must be attached to the fittings on both the cylinder head and cylinder during installation.

8. Apply a light coat of rubber lube, or equivalent, to the inner surface of the coolant hoses, to make installation easier. Tighten the hose clamps securely, but do not overtighten as the clamp may cut into the hose.

9. After installing the rear cylinder head and cylinder, connect the metal coolant pipe (B, **Figure 48**) to the cylinder.

10A. On 2001-2004 models, make sure the O-ring (**Figure 68**) is in place in the intake manifold. Install the intake manifold (**Figure 44**) and tighten the bolts securely.

10B. On 2005-on models, note that the top of each intake tube is marked *F* or *R* to indicate front or rear cylinder head location. Install the intake tube so the arrow points toward the cylinder head (**Figure 69**). Tighten the clamp screw securely.

11. Install the camshafts as described in this chapter.

Inspection

Refer to *Cylinder Head* and *Cylinder* in this chapter.

i. Install the bolts securing the cylinder head and cylinder to the crankcase. Install the long bolts near the intake port (A, **Figure 67**) and the short bolts near the exhaust port (B). Using a crisscross pattern, tighten the bolts initially to 25 N•m (18 ft.-lb.). Tighten the bolts in a crisscross pattern to a final torque of 38 N•m (28 ft.-lb.).

NOTE
Make sure hose clamps are installed onto the coolant hoses prior to installing the other cylinder head and cylinder assembly.

CYLINDER HEAD

Two procedures are available to service the cylinder heads and cylinders. Each cylinder head is secured to the cylinder by a nut (**Figure 70**) located in the valley area between the cylinders. Access to the nut is limited, which requires removing the cylinder head and cylinder as a unit, unless a tool is fabricated to remove and tighten the nut. If the nut can be turned, the cylinder head and cylinder may be serviced separately.

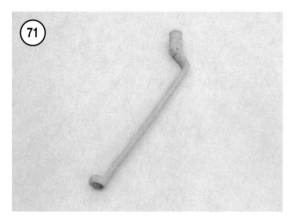

Extra care is needed to install the cylinder head and cylinder as a unit onto the piston, as opposed to just installing the cylinder onto the piston. Also, if using the cylinder head/cylinder unit procedure, the front cylinder head/cylinder unit must be removed before the rear cylinder head and cylinder are accessible.

After considering the preferred method for removing the cylinder head retaining nut, follow the appropriate procedure for cylinder head and cylinder removal and installation.

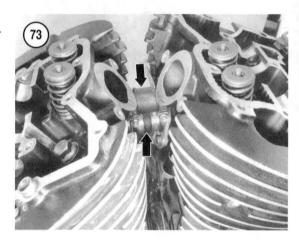

Tool Fabrication

Removal of the inner cylinder head retaining nuts (**Figure 70**) without removing the opposite cylinder requires fabrication of a tool; no manufactured tool is available. The tool shown in **Figure 71** was constructed using an offset 12-mm wrench, which was heated and bent to the desired shape. A socket was welded to one end so a 3/8-inch drive could be attached.

When constructing the tool, make sure it properly engages the nut. Also calculate the amount of offset when using a torque wrench with the tool. Refer to Chapter One.

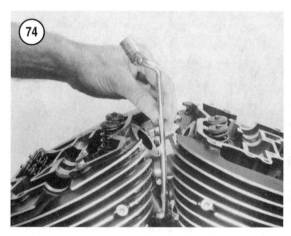

Removal

1. Remove the camshaft as described in this chapter.
2A. On 2001-2004 models, remove the bolts securing the intake manifold (**Figure 72**) and remove it.
2B. On 2005-on models, loosen the clamp screw and remove the intake tube on each cylinder head.
3. Loosen the screws of the clamp bands on the coolant hoses connecting both cylinder heads (**Figure 73**). Move the clamps from the fittings of the cylinder heads and back onto the hoses.
4A. On the front cylinder head, use the special tool (**Figure 74**) to remove the nut on the rear of the cylin-

der (A, **Figure 75**). Remove the two bolts on the front of the cylinder (**Figure 76**).

4B. On the rear cylinder head, use the special tool to remove the nut on the front of the cylinder (B, **Figure 75**). Remove the nut on the rear of the cylinder (**Figure 77**).

5. Using a crisscross pattern, loosen and remove the bolts (A and B, **Figure 78**) securing the cylinder head and cylinder to the crankcase.

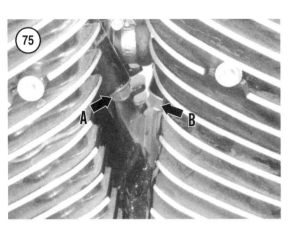

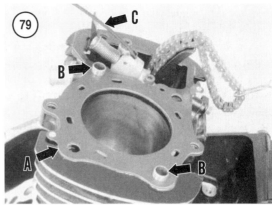

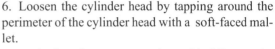

4

CAUTION
Hitting or prying against the cooling fins may damage them.

6. Loosen the cylinder head by tapping around the perimeter of the cylinder head with a soft-faced mallet.

7. Untie the wire or remove the tool holding up the camshaft chain.

8. Carefully lift the cylinder head off the cylinder. Guide the chain through the opening in the cylinder head and secure it to the exterior of the engine. This prevents the drive chain from falling into the crankcase.

9. Remove the cylinder head gasket (A, **Figure 79**) and discard it. Do not lose the locating dowels (B).

10. Place a clean shop cloth into the cam chain opening in the cylinder to prevent the entry of debris.

11. Inspect the cylinder head as described in this section.

Installation

1. Remove the clean shop cloth from the cam chain opening in the cylinder.

2. Install the cylinder head locating dowels (B, **Figure 79**).

3. Install the head gasket (A, **Figure 79**).

4. Install the cylinder head onto the cylinder while connecting the coolant hoses. Carefully guide the camshaft chain up through the camshaft chain cavity on the side of the cylinder head while moving the cylinder head into position. Also guide the cam chain tensioner spring retention tool (C, **Figure 79**) up through the cylinder head.

5. Secure the camshaft chain to the exterior of the engine.

6. Install the cylinder head bolts. Install the short bolts near the intake port (A, **Figure 78**) and the long bolts near the exhaust port (B). Using a criss-

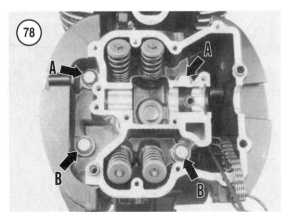

cross pattern, tighten the bolts first to 25 N•m (18 ft.-lb.), then to a final torque of 38 N•m (28 ft.-lb.).

7A. On the front cylinder head, use the special tool (**Figure 74**) to install the nut on the rear of the cylinder. Tighten the nut to 25 N•m (18 ft.-lb.). Install the two bolts on the front of the cylinder (**Figure 76**) and tighten to 25 N•m (18 ft.-lb.).

7B. On the rear cylinder head, use the tool (**Figure 74**) to install the nut on the front of the cylinder. Install the nut on the rear of the cylinder (**Figure 77**) and tighten both nuts to 25 N•m (18 ft.-lb.).

8A. On 2001-2004 models, make sure the O-ring (**Figure 68**) is in place in the intake manifold. Install the intake manifold. Tighten the bolts (**Figure 72**) securely.

8B. On 2005-on models, note that the top of each intake tube is marked *F* or *R* to indicate front or rear cylinder head location. Install the intake tube so the arrow points toward the cylinder head (**Figure 69**). Tighten the clamp screw securely.

9. Install the camshaft as described in this chapter.

Inspection

Refer to *Cylinder* in this chapter for cylinder inspection. Also refer to *Valves and Valve Components* in this chapter.

1. Remove all traces of gasket material from the cylinder head upper and lower mating surfaces. Do not scratch the gasket surface.

2. Without removing the valves, remove all carbon deposits from the combustion chamber (A, **Figure 80**) and valve ports using a wire brush.

3. Examine the spark plug threads (B, **Figure 80**) in the cylinder head for damage. If damage is minor or if the threads are dirty or clogged with carbon, use a spark plug thread tap to clean the threads following the manufacturer's instructions. If thread damage is severe, refer further service to a dealer or machine shop.

4. After the carbon is removed from the combustion chamber and the valve ports and the spark plug thread hole is repaired, clean the entire head in cleaning solvent. Dry with compressed air.

5. Clean away all carbon from the piston crown. Do not remove the carbon ridge at the top of the cylinder bore.

6. Check for cracks in the combustion chamber and exhaust port (A, **Figure 81**). Replace a cracked head.

7. Inspect the camshaft bearing area (**Figure 82**) in the cylinder head for damage, wear or burrs. Clean up if damage is minimal; replace cylinder head if necessary.

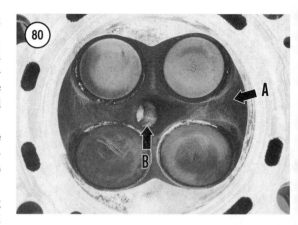

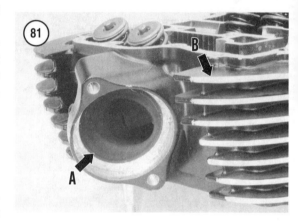

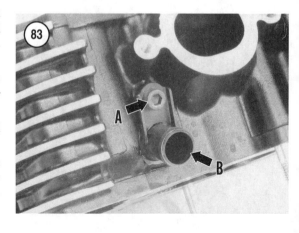

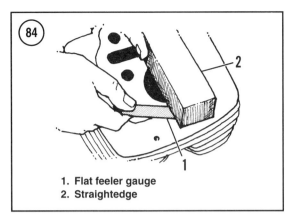

84

1. Flat feeler gauge
2. Straightedge

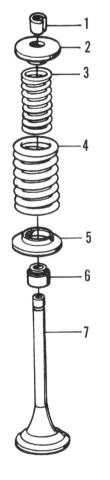

85

VALVE ASSEMBLY

1. Keepers
2. Spring retainer
3. Inner valve spring
4. Outer valve spring
5. Spring seat
6. Oil seal
7. Valve

8. Inspect the cooling fins (B, **Figure 81**) for cracks or damage.

9. Inspect the coolant hose fitting for signs of leaks. Remove the bolt (A, **Figure 83**, typical) securing the fitting (B) and remove it. Install a new O-ring seal and apply clean engine oil to the O-ring. Reinstall the fitting and tighten the bolts securely.

10. Inspect the section of coolant hose for cracks, hardness or deterioration. Replace if necessary.

11. Inspect the threads of the stud(s) for damage. Clean up with an appropriate metric die if necessary. Make sure the stud is tightly secured into the cylinder head.

12. After the head has been thoroughly cleaned, place a straightedge across the cylinder head/cylinder gasket surface (**Figure 84**) and measure at several points. Measure the warp by inserting a flat feeler gauge between the straightedge and the cylinder head at each location. If warp exceeds the service limit in **Table 1**, replace the cylinder head.

13. Inspect the valve and valve guides as described in this chapter.

14. Repeat for the other cylinder head.

VALVES AND VALVE COMPONENTS

Due to the number of special tools required for valve service, it is general practice to remove the cylinder head and refer valve service to a dealership or machine shop.

The following procedures describe how to check for valve component wear and to determine what type of service is required.

Refer to **Figure 85**.

Valve Removal

1. Remove the cylinder head as described in this chapter.

CAUTION
To avoid loss of spring tension, do not compress the springs any more than necessary to remove the keepers.

2. Compress the valve springs with a valve compressor tool (**Figure 86**, typical). Remove the valve keepers (**Figure 87**) and release the compression. Remove the valve compressor tool.

3. Remove the valve spring retainer and valve springs.

4. Prior to removing the valve, remove any burrs from the valve stem (**Figure 88**). Otherwise the valve guide will be damaged.

5. Remove the valve.

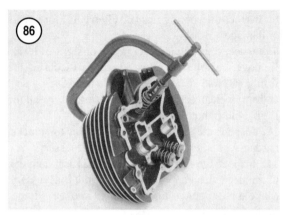

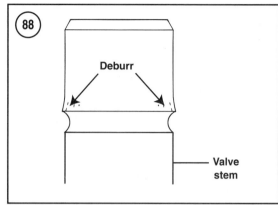

Deburr

Valve stem

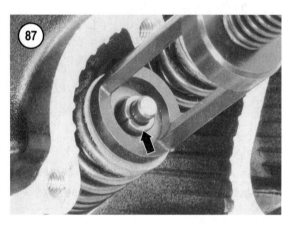

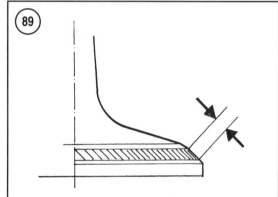

6. Remove the oil seal and spring seat from the valve guide.

7. Identify all parts as they are disassembled so that they will be installed in their original locations.

8. Repeat Steps 2-6 for the remainder of valves requiring service.

Valve Inspection

Refer to **Table 1** for specifications and replace components not within specification.

1. Clean the valves with a soft wire brush and solvent.

2. Inspect the contact surface of each valve (**Figure 89**) for burning or pitting. Unevenness of the contact surface is an indication that the valve is not serviceable. Replace the valve if the contact surface is defective.

3. Inspect the valve stem for wear and roughness and measure the runout of the valve stem as shown in **Figure 90**.

4. Measure the valve stem for wear (**Figure 91**).

5. Measure the valve face for wear (**Figure 92**).

6. Remove all carbon and varnish from each valve guide with a stiff spiral wire brush.

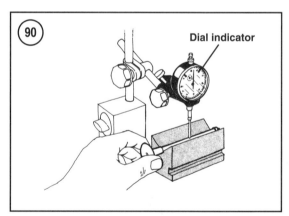

Dial indicator

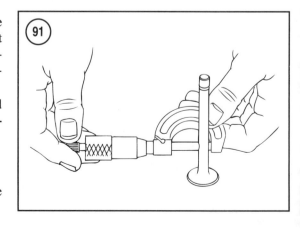

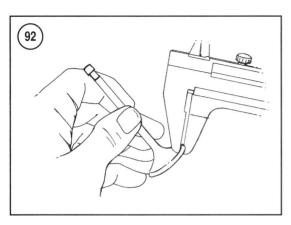

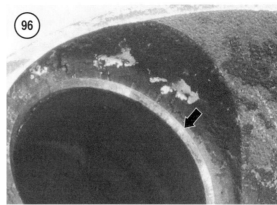

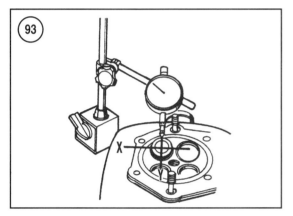

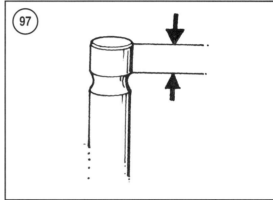

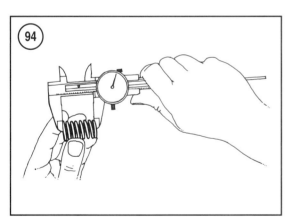

7. Insert each valve in its guide. Hold the valve with the head just slightly off the valve seat and rock it sideways in two directions (X and Y, **Figure 93**). If the stem-to-guide clearance exceeds the limit, measure the valve stem. If the valve stem is worn, replace the valve. If the valve stem is within tolerances, replace the valve guide.

8. Measure each valve spring free length (**Figure 94**). Make sure the valve is straight (**Figure 95**). Replace defective springs in pairs (inner and outer).

9. Check the valve spring retainer and valve keepers. If they are in good condition they may be reused; replace as necessary.

10. Inspect the valve seats (**Figure 96**) in the cylinder head. If worn or burned, they must be reconditioned as described in this section.

11. Inspect the valve stem end for pitting and wear. If pitted or worn, the end may be resurfaced, unless the length (**Figure 97**) is less than specification. Replace the valve(s) if the end length is less than specified.

Valve Installation

1. Install the valve spring seat (A, **Figure 98**). Take care not to confuse the valve spring retainer

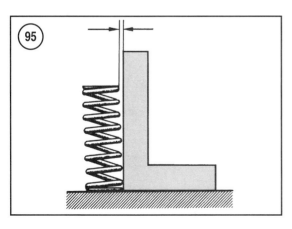

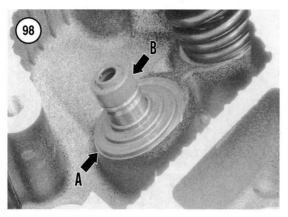

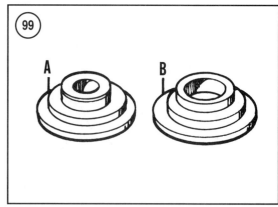

(A, **Figure 99**) with the spring seat (B). The inner diameters are different.

2. Install a new seal on each valve guide (B, **Figure 98**) and push it down until it bottoms.

3. Coat the valve stems with clean engine oil. To avoid damage to the valve stem seal, turn the valve slowly while inserting the valve into the cylinder head. Push in the valve until it bottoms.

4. One end of each valve spring has more closely-wound coils (**Figure 100**). This end of the springs faces toward the cylinder head.

5. Install the inner valve spring (A, **Figure 101**) and the outer valve spring (B).

6. Install the valve spring retainer on top of the valve springs (**Figure 102**).

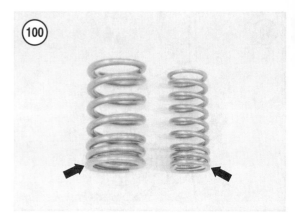

CAUTION
To avoid loss of spring tension, do not compress the springs any more than necessary to install the keepers.

7. Compress the valve springs with a compressor tool (**Figure 86**, typical) and install the valve keepers. Make sure the keepers fit snugly into the rounded groove in the valve stem.

8. Remove the compressor tool.

9. After all springs have been installed, gently tap the end of the valve stem with a soft aluminum or brass drift and hammer. This will ensure that the keepers are properly seated.

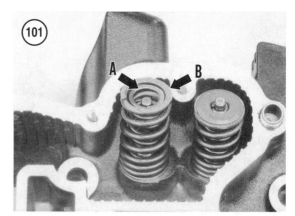

10. Repeat for all valve assemblies and for the other cylinder head if necessary.

11. Install the cylinder head(s) as described in this chapter.

Valve Guide Replacement

When valve guides are worn so that there is excessive valve stem-to-guide clearance, the guides must be replaced.

1. If still installed, remove the intake manifold or coolant fitting on the cylinder head as described in this chapter.

CAUTION
Do not heat the cylinder head with a torch. Never bring a flame into contact with the cylinder head. Direct flame can warp the cylinder head.

2. The valve guides (**Figure 103**) are installed with a slight interference fit. Place the cylinder head in a heated oven (or on a hot plate). Heat the cylinder head to a temperature between 100-150° C (212-300° F).

3. Use heavy gloves or kitchen pot holders to remove the cylinder head from the oven. Place it onto wooden blocks with the combustion chamber facing up.

4. Drive out the old valve guide with a hammer and valve guide remover (Suzuki part No. 09916-44910).

5. Remove and discard the valve guide. Never reinstall a valve guide that has been removed as it is no longer true nor within tolerances.

6. Insert a 10.5 mm valve guide reamer (A, **Figure 104**) (Suzuki part No. 09916-34580) and handle (B (part No. 09916- 34542) into the valve guide hole in the cylinder head. Rotate the reamer clockwise. Continue to rotate the reamer and work it down through the entire length of the valve guide hole in the cylinder head.

7. While rotating the reamer clockwise, withdraw the reamer from the valve guide hole in the cylinder head. Remove the reamer and handle.

CAUTION
Failure to apply clean engine oil to both the valve guide and the valve guide hole in the cylinder head will damage the cylinder head and/or valve guide.

8. Apply clean engine oil to the new valve guide and the valve guide hole in the cylinder head.

9. From the spring side of the head, drive in the new valve guide with the valve guide attachment (A, **Figure 105**) (Suzuki part No. 09916-44920) and valve guide remover (B) (part No. 09916-44910).

10. After installation, ream the new valve guide as follows:

   a. Use the 5.5 mm valve guide reamer (A, **Figure 106**) (Suzuki part No. 09916-34550) and handle (B) (09916-34542) to ream the guide.

   b. Apply cutting oil to both the new valve guide and the valve guide reamer.

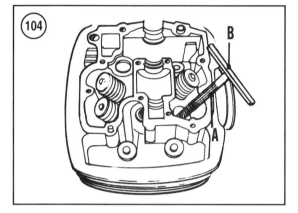

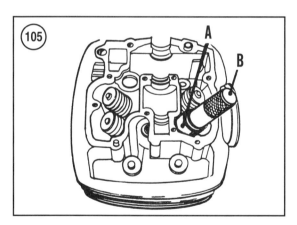

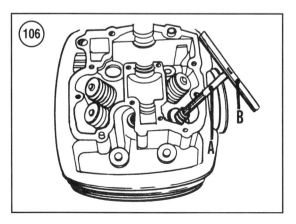

CAUTION
Always rotate the valve guide reamer clockwise. If the reamer is rotated counterclockwise, the valve guide will be damaged.

c. Rotate the reamer clockwise. Continue to rotate the reamer and work it down through the entire length of the new valve guide. Apply additional cutting oil during this procedure.

d. Rotate the reamer clockwise until the reamer has traveled all the way through the new valve guide.

e. While rotating the reamer clockwise, withdraw the reamer from the valve guide. Remove the reamer.

11. If necessary, repeat Steps 2-10 for any other valve guides.

12. Thoroughly clean the cylinder head and valve guides with solvent to wash out all metal particles. Dry with compressed air.

13. Reface the valve seats as described in this chapter.

Valve Seat Inspection

NOTE
Because of the close operating tolerances within the valve assembly, the valve stem and guide must be within tolerance; otherwise, the inspection results will be inaccurate.

1. Remove the valves as described in this chapter.

2. The most accurate method for checking the valve seal is to use Prussian Blue, or machinist's dye, available from auto parts stores or tool shops. To check the valve seal with machinist's dye, perform the following:

a. Thoroughly clean all carbon deposits from the valve face with solvent or detergent, then thoroughly dry.

b. Spread a thin layer of machinist's dye evenly on the valve face.

c. Moisten the end of a suction cup valve tool (**Figure 107**) and attach it to the valve. Insert the valve into the guide.

d. Using the suction cup tool, tap the valve up and down in the cylinder head. Do not rotate the valve or a false indication will result.

e. Remove the valve and examine the impression left by the machinist's dye. If the impression left in the dye (on the valve or in the cylinder head) is not even and continuous and the valve seat width (**Figure 108**) is not within specified

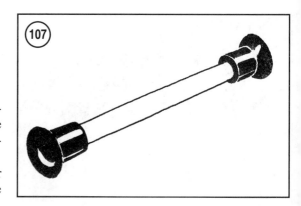

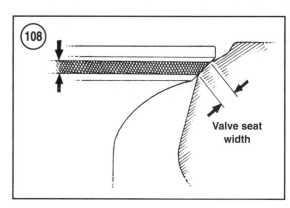

Valve seat width

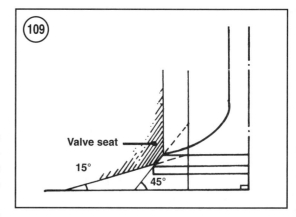

Valve seat

15°

45°

tolerance listed in **Table 1**, the cylinder head valve seat must be reconditioned.

3. Closely examine the valve seat (**Figure 96**) in the cylinder head. It should be smooth and even with a polished seating surface.

4. If the valve seat is okay, install the valves as described in this chapter.

5. If the valve seat is not correct, recondition the valve seat as described in this chapter.

Valve Seat Reconditioning

A valve cutter set (Suzuki part No. 09916-2111) is required to recondition the valve seats (valve seat

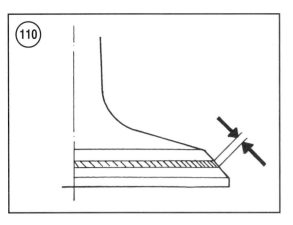

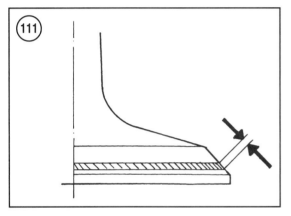

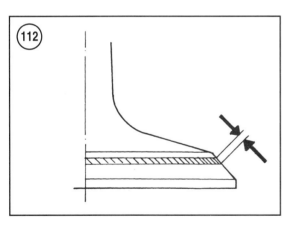

cutter [N-128], T handle [N-503], adapter [N-503-1] and solid pilot [N-100-5.22]). If these tools or their equivalents are unavailable, have a dealership or machine shop perform the procedure.

The valve seat for both the intake valves and exhaust valves are machined to the same angles. The valve contact surface is cut to 45° angle and the area above the contact surface (closest to the combustion chamber) is cut to a 15° angle (**Figure 109**).

1. Carefully rotate and insert the solid pilot into the valve guide. Make sure the pilot is correctly seated.

2. Use the 45° angle side of the cutter, install the cutter and the T-handle onto the solid pilot.

> *CAUTION*
> *Measure the valve seat contact area in the cylinder head after each cut to make sure the contact area is correct and to prevent removing too much material. If too much material is removed, the cylinder head must be replaced.*

3. Using the 45° cutter, descale and clean the valve seat with one or two turns.

4. If the seat is still pitted or burned, turn the 45° cutter additional turns until the surface is clean.

5. Remove the valve cutter, T-handle and solid pilot from the cylinder head.

6. Inspect the valve seat-to-valve face impression as follows:

    a. Spread a thin layer of machinist's dye evenly on the valve face.

    b. Moisten the end of a suction cup valve tool (**Figure 107**) and attach it to the valve. Insert the valve into the guide.

    c. Using the suction cup tool, tap the valve up and down in the cylinder head. Do not rotate the valve or a false indication will result.

    d. Remove the valve and examine the impression left by the machinist's dye.

    e. Measure the contact width as shown in **Figure 110**. Refer to **Table 1** for the seat width.

7. If the contact area is too high (**Figure 111**) on the valve, or if it is too wide, use the 15° side of the cutter and remove a portion of the top area of the valve seat material to lower and narrow the contact area.

8. If the contact area is too low (**Figure 112**) on the valve, or too narrow, use the 45° cutter and remove a portion of the lower area of the valve seat material to raise and widen the contact area.

9. After the desired valve seat position and width is obtained, use the 45° side of the cutter and T-handle to remove any burrs.

> *CAUTION*
> *Do not use any valve lapping compound after the final cut has been made.*

10. Make sure the finish has a smooth and velvety surface; it should not be shiny or highly polished. The final seating will take place when the engine is first run.

11. Repeat Steps 1-10 for all remaining valve seats.

12. Thoroughly clean the cylinder head and all valve components in solvent or detergent and hot water.

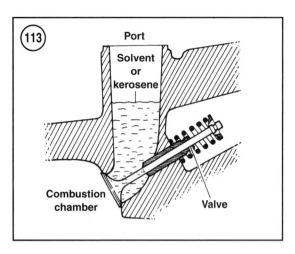

13. Install the valve assemblies as described in this chapter and fill the ports with solvent to check for leaks (**Figure 113**). If any leaks are present, the valve seats must be inspected for debris or burrs that may be preventing a proper seal.

14. If the cylinder head and valve components were cleaned in detergent and hot water, apply a light coat of engine oil to all bare metal steel surfaces to prevent rust.

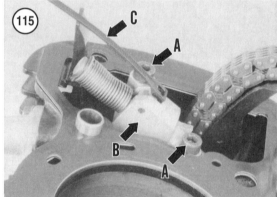

CAMSHAFT CHAIN TENSIONER

Removal/Inspection/Installation

NOTE
The camshaft chain tensioners are unique and must be installed in the correct cylinder. They are marked either **F** *(front) (**Figure 114**) or* **R** *(rear).*

1. Remove the cylinder head as described in this chapter.

2. Remove the tensioner mounting bolts (A, **Figure 115**) and remove the tensioner (B).

3. If still installed, remove the tensioner spring holding tool (C, **Figure 115**).

4. Inspect all parts of the camshaft chain tensioner (**Figure 116**) for wear or damage.

5. Make sure the ratchet operates correctly.

6. If any part of the tensioner body or rack is worn or damaged, replace the entire assembly. Replacement parts are not available.

7. After installing the tensioner, tighten the bolts securely.

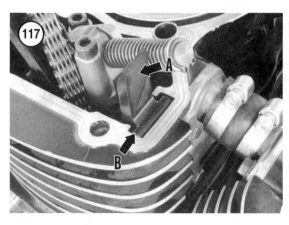

CYLINDER

Two procedures are available to service the cylinder heads and cylinders. The cylinder may be re-

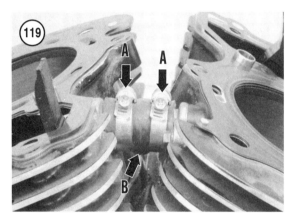

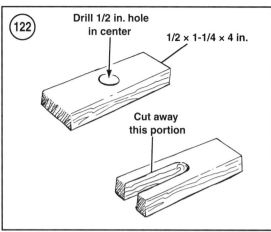

moved as a unit with the cylinder head, or remain on the crankcase after removal of the cylinder head. Refer to *Cylinder Head and Cylinder* and *Cylinder Head* in this chapter.

The following procedure applies to a cylinder that remains on the crankcase after the cylinder head has been removed.

Removal

1. Remove the camshaft chain guide (A, **Figure 117**).
2. Remove the camshaft chain tensioner as described in this chapter.
3. On the rear cylinder, remove the bolts (A, **Figure 118**) securing the metal coolant inlet pipe to the rear cylinder and separate the metal coolant pipe (B) from the cylinder.
4. Loosen the screws (A, **Figure 119**) of the clamp bands on the coolant hose (B) connecting both cylinders. Move the clamps from the fittings of the cylinders and back onto the hose.
5. Untie the wire or remove the tool holding up the camshaft chain.
6. Carefully lift the cylinder and remove it from the piston and the crankcase. Disengage the short coolant hose from the fitting of the other cylinder. Guide the camshaft chain through the opening in the cylinder and secure it to the exterior of the engine. This prevents the camshaft chain from falling down into the crankcase. Set the cylinder (**Figure 120**) aside for inspection.
7. Remove the cylinder base gasket and discard it. Account for the locating dowels.
8. Install a piston holding fixture under the piston (**Figure 121**, typical) to protect the piston skirt from damage. This fixture may be purchased or constructed of wood. See **Figure 122** for basic dimensions.

9. Stuff a clean shop cloth into the crankcase opening to keep out debris.

Installation

1. If used, remove the shop cloth from the crankcase opening.

2. Apply a liberal coat of clean engine oil to the cylinder wall, especially at the lower end where the piston will enter.

3. Also apply clean engine oil to the piston and piston rings. This makes it easier to guide the piston into the cylinder bore.

4. Make sure the piston ring end gaps are staggered evenly around the piston circumference.

5. Check that the top surface of the crankcase and the bottom surface of the cylinder are clean prior to installing a new base gasket.

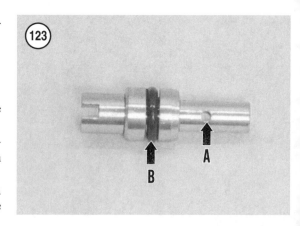

6. If the oil control orifice was removed, make sure the oil hole (A, **Figure 123**) is open and the O-ring (B) is installed. Install the oil control orifice (**Figure 124**, typical) into the crankcase, pushing it down until it bottoms in the front cylinder crankcase opening (**Figure 125**) or rear cylinder crankcase opening (**Figure 126**).

7. Install the locating dowels (A, **Figure 127**) and a new cylinder base gasket (B). Secure the piston with a piston holding fixture (C, **Figure 127**).

8. Start the cylinder down over the piston. Compress each piston ring with your fingers as it enters the cylinder.

9. Push the cylinder down past the piston rings.

10. Carefully feed the cam chain and wire up through the opening in the cylinder and tie it to the engine.

> *NOTE*
> *Install a new coolant hose (B, **Figure** 119) with its clamps between the cylinders.*

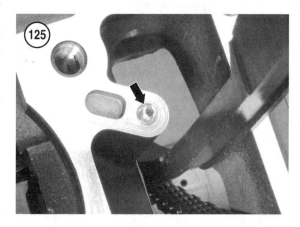

11. Slide the cylinder down until it bottoms on the piston holding fixture.

12. Remove the piston holding fixture and push the cylinder down into place onto the crankcase until it bottoms.

13. Install the cylinder head as described in this chapter.

14. On the rear cylinder, connect the metal coolant inlet pipe (B, **Figure 118**) to the rear cylinder and install the bolts (A). Tighten the bolts securely.

> *NOTE*
> *The camshaft chain guides are unique and must be installed in the correct cylinder. The front cylinder chain guide*

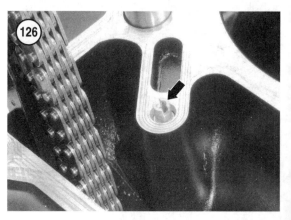

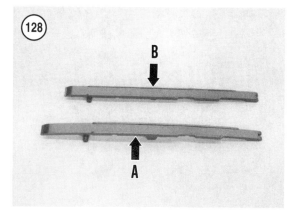

(A, **Figure 128**) is longer than the rear cylinder guide (B).

15. Install the camshaft chain guide (A, **Figure 117**) so it fits into the notch (B) in the top of the cylinder.

16. Refer to *Break-In* (Chapter Five) if the cylinder was rebored, honed or a new piston or piston rings were installed.

Inspection

1. Remove any old cylinder head gasket material with solvent. Use a gasket removal tool to gently scrape off all gasket residue. Do not damage the sealing surface or leaks may result.

2. After the cylinder has been thoroughly cleaned, place a straightedge across the cylinder-to-cylinder head gasket surface at several points. Measure warp by attempting to insert a feeler gauge between the straightedge and cylinder at each location (**Figure 129**, typical). Compare any distortion to the service limit in **Table 1**. Replace the cylinder if the gasket surface is warped beyond the service limit.

3. Thoroughly check the bore surface (**Figure 130**) for scratches or gouges. If damaged, the bore will require boring and reconditioning.

4. Determine piston-to-cylinder clearance as described in *Pistons and Piston Rings* in this chapter.

5. If the cylinder requires service, such as boring, remove all dowel pins from the cylinder prior to taking it to a dealer or machine shop for service.

6. After the cylinders have been serviced, perform the following:

> *CAUTION*
> *Use hot soapy water to clean the cylinder walls. Solvent and kerosene cannot wash fine grit out of cylinder crevices. Any grit left in the cylinders will cause premature wear to the new rings.*

   a. Wash each cylinder bore in hot soapy water.

   b. Wash out any debris from the cooling cores surrounding each cylinder.

   c. After washing the cylinder walls, wipe the cylinder wall with a clean white cloth. It should not show any traces of debris. If the rag shows any traces of debris or dirt, the wall is not thoroughly cleaned and must be rewashed.

   d. After the cylinder is cleaned, lubricate the cylinder walls with clean engine oil to prevent rust.

7. Inspect the short coolant hose fitting for leaks. Remove the bolts (A, **Figure 131** or A, **Figure 132**) securing the fitting (B) and remove it. Make sure the

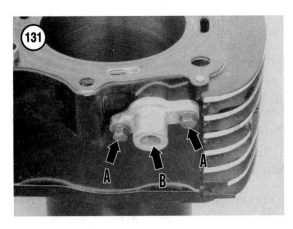

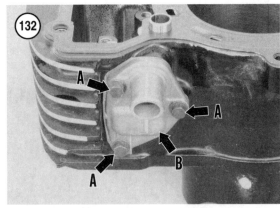

openings in the cylinder are clear. Install a new
O-ring seal and apply clean engine oil to the O-ring.
Reinstall the fitting and tighten the bolts securely.

8. On the rear cylinder, remove the coolant passage
cover mounting bolts (A, **Figure 133**), then remove
the cover (B). Make sure the openings in the cylinder
are open. Replace the O-rings on the outside and inside of the cover. Apply fresh engine oil to the O-rings.
Reinstall the fitting and tighten the bolts securely.

9. Inspect the coolant hose for cracks, hardness or
deterioration. Replace if necessary.

10. Repeat for the remaining cylinder.

PISTONS AND PISTON RINGS

Piston Removal/Installation

CAUTION
*If it is necessary to rotate the crankshaft,
pull up on the cam chains so they cannot
bind internally. Protect the pistons so
they will not be damaged when retracting
into the crankcase.*

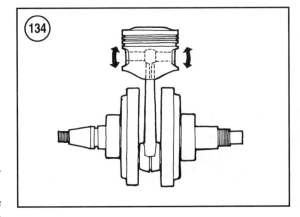

1. Remove the cylinder head and cylinder assemblies as described in this chapter.

2. Stuff clean shop cloths into the cylinder bore
crankcase opening to prevent objects from falling
into the crankcase.

3. Lightly mark the top of the piston with an *F* (front)
or *R* (rear) so it can be installed into the correct cylinder.

4. If necessary, remove the piston rings as described
in this section.

5. Before removing the piston, hold the rod tightly
and rock the piston as shown in **Figure 134**. Any
rocking motion (do not confuse with the normal sliding motion) indicates wear on the piston pin, piston
pin bore or connecting rod small-end bore (more
likely a combination of these). Mark the piston and
pin so that they will be reassembled into the same set.

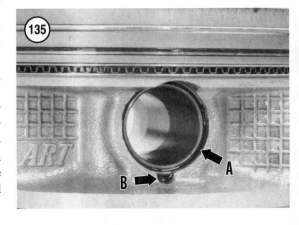

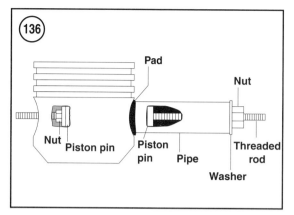

Pad

Nut

Nut

Piston pin

Piston pin

Pipe

Washer

Threaded rod

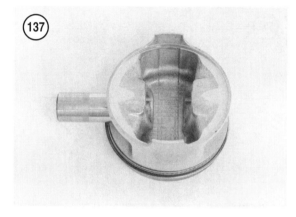

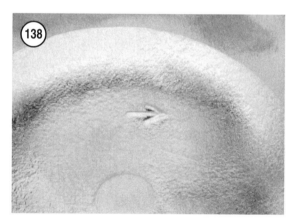

6. Remove the clips (A, **Figure 135**) from each side of the piston pin bore with a small screwdriver, scribe or needlenose pliers. Hold your finger over one edge of the clip when removing it to prevent the clip from springing out.

7. Use a proper size wooden dowel or socket extension and push out the piston pin. Do not attempt to drive out the pin. This could damage the piston pin, piston, connecting rod or crankshaft bearing.

8. If the piston pin is difficult to remove, use a home-made tool as shown in **Figure 136**.

9. Lift the piston from the connecting rod and inspect it as described in this chapter.

10. If the piston is going to be left off for some time, place a piece of foam insulation tube over the end of the rod to protect it.

11. Apply clean engine oil to the inside surface of the connecting rod piston pin bore.

12. Lubricate the piston pin with clean engine oil and install it in the piston until its end extends slightly beyond the inside of the boss (**Figure 137**).

13. Install the piston onto the connecting rod so the arrow mark on the crown (**Figure 138**) points toward the exhaust valve side of the cylinder.

14. Align the piston pin with the hole in the connecting rod. Push the piston pin through the connecting rod and into the other side of the piston until it is even with the piston pin clip grooves. If the pin will not slide easily, use the homemade tool (**Figure 136**), minus the pipe, to pull the pin into position.

> *CAUTION*
> *In the next step, install the clips so the gap does not align with the cutout in the piston (B, **Figure 135**).*

15. Install new piston pin clips (A, **Figure 135**) in both ends of the piston pin boss. Make sure they are seated in the grooves in the piston.

16. Check the installation by rocking the piston back and forth around the pin axis and from side to side along the axis. It should rotate freely back and forth but not from side to side.

17. If necessary, install the piston rings as described in this section.

18. Repeat Steps 1-17 for the remaining piston.

Piston Inspection

> *CAUTION*
> *Do not clean the piston with a wire brush.*

1. Carefully clean the carbon from the piston crown (**Figure 139**) with a chemical remover or with a soft

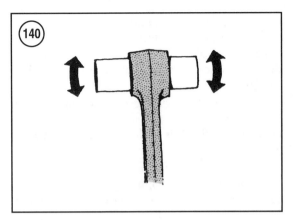

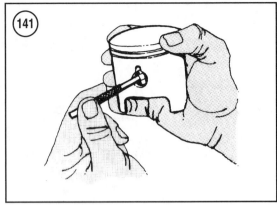

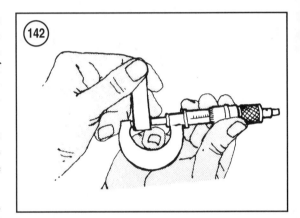

scraper. Do not remove or damage the carbon ridge around the circumference of the piston above the top ring. If the piston, rings and cylinder are found to be dimensionally correct and can be reused, removal of the carbon ring from the top of the piston or the carbon ridge from the top of the cylinder will cause excessive oil consumption.

2. Examine each ring groove for burrs, dented edges and wide wear. Pay particular attention to the top compression ring groove as it usually wears more than the other grooves.

3. If damage or wear indicates piston replacement, select a new piston as described in *Piston Clearance Measurement* in this section.

4. Lubricate the piston pin and install it in the connecting rod. Slowly rotate the piston pin and check for radial and axial play (**Figure 140**). If any play exists, the piston pin should be replaced, provided the rod bore is in good condition.

5. Measure the inside diameter of the piston pin bore (**Figure 141**). Measure the outside diameter of the piston pin (**Figure 142**). Compare the measurements with the specifications in **Table 1**. Replace the piston and piston pin as a set if either or both are worn.

6. Check the piston skirt for galling and abrasion which may have been caused by piston seizure. If light galling is present, smooth the affected area with No. 400 emery paper and oil or a fine oilstone. However, if galling is severe or if the piston is deeply scored, replace it.

7. If damage or wear indicate piston replacement, select a new piston as described in *Piston Clearance Measurement* in this section.

Piston Clearance Measurement

1. Make sure the piston and cylinder walls are clean and dry.

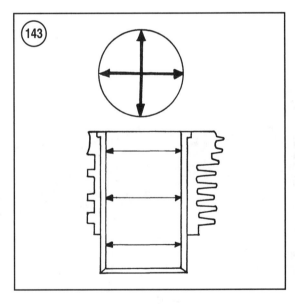

2. Measure the cylinder bore with a cylinder gauge or inside micrometer at the points shown in **Figure 143**.

3. Measure in two axes—in line with the piston-pin and at 90° to the pin. If the taper or out-of-round is 0.05 mm (0.002 in.) or greater, the cylinder must be rebored to the next oversize and a new piston and rings installed.

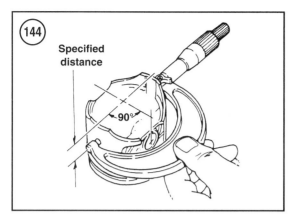

Specified distance

90°

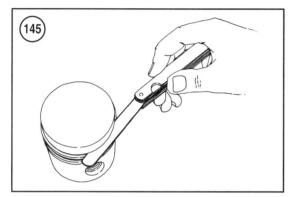

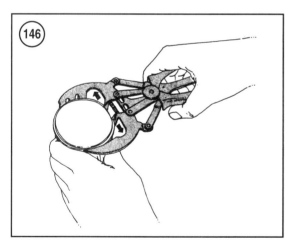

CAUTION
To maintain proper engine balance, bore both cylinders and install new pistons in pairs.

NOTE
Obtain the new pistons before the cylinders are rebored so that the pistons can be measured. Slight manufacturing tolerances must be taken into account to determine the actual size and working clearance. The piston-to-cylinder service limit is in Table 1.

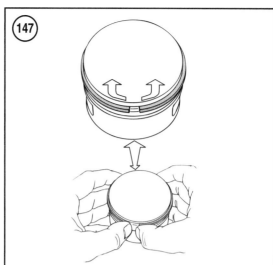

4. Measure the outside diameter of the piston across the skirt (**Figure 144**) at right angles to the piston pin. Measure at a distance 15 mm (0.60 in.) from the bottom of the piston skirt.

5. Subtract the dimension of the piston from the cylinder dimension and compare to the dimension in **Table 1**. If clearance is excessive, replace the piston and bore the cylinder to the next oversize. Purchase the new piston first, measure its diameter and add the specified clearance to determine the proper cylinder bore diameter.

Piston Ring

Removal

WARNING
Piston ring edges are very sharp.

1. Measure the side clearance of each ring in its groove with a flat feeler gauge (**Figure 145**) and compare to the specification in **Table 1**. If the clearance is greater than specified, the rings must be replaced. If the clearance is still excessive with the new rings, the piston must also be replaced.

2. Remove the old rings with a ring expander tool (**Figure 146**) or by spreading the ends with your thumbs just enough to slide the ring up over the piston (**Figure 147**). Repeat for the remaining rings.

3. Use a broken piston ring to carefully remove all carbon buildup from the ring grooves (**Figure 148**).

4. Inspect the grooves carefully for burrs, nicks or broken and cracked lands. Recondition or replace the piston if necessary.

5. To check the end gap of the top two rings, insert one ring at a time into the cylinder bore. Push it in about 20 mm (0.75 in.) with the crown of the piston to

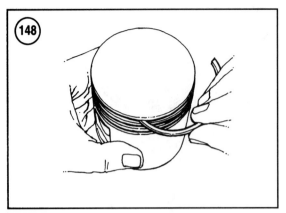

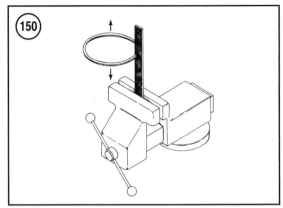

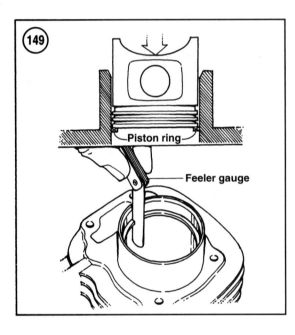

Piston ring

Feeler gauge

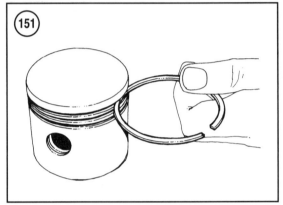

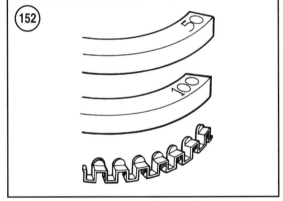

ensure that the ring is square in the cylinder bore. Measure the gap with a flat feeler gauge (**Figure 149**) and compare to the specification in **Table 1**. If the gap is greater than specified, replace the rings. When installing new rings, measure their end gap in the same manner as for old ones. If the gap is less than specified, secure a small file in a vise, grip the ends of the piston ring and enlarge the gap (**Figure 150**).

6. Rotate the top two rings around their piston grooves as shown in **Figure 151** to check for binding. Minor binding is probably caused by debris or nicks. Small nicks may be smoothed with a fine-cut file.

Installation

1. If new rings will be installed, deglaze or hone the cylinder to seat the new rings. Refer honing service to a dealership or machine shop. After honing, measure the ring end gap for each compression ring.

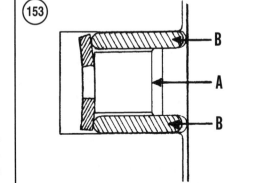

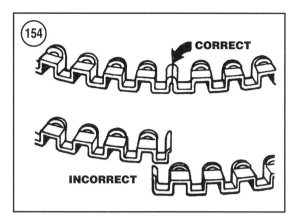

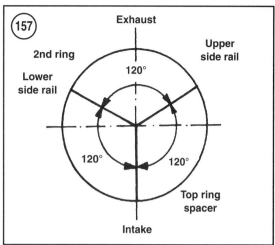

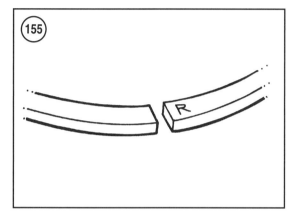

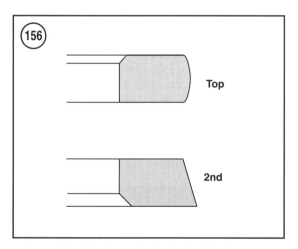

rect. Standard size rings have no color, 0.5 mm oversize rings are red, and 1.0 mm oversize rings are yellow.

4. Install the oil ring spacer first (A, **Figure 153**) then both side rails (B). New Suzuki oil ring side rails do not have top and bottom designations and can be installed either way. Make sure the ends of the expander spacer butt together (**Figure 154**). They should not overlap. If reassembling used parts, install the ring rails in their original positions.

NOTE
*Position the top and second ring with the R (**Figure 155**) or RN mark facing toward the piston crown.*

5. Install the second compression ring (with the slight side taper), then the top piston ring (**Figure 156**). Install the rings using a piston ring tool or by carefully spreading the ends with your thumbs. Make sure the marks on the piston rings (**Figure 155**) are toward the top of the piston.

6. Make sure the rings are seated completely in their grooves all the way around the piston and that the end gaps are staggered around the piston as shown in **Figure 157**.

7. If new rings were installed, measure the side clearance of each ring in its groove with a flat feeler gauge (**Figure 145**) and compare to the specification in **Table 1**.

8. Refer to *Break-In* in Chapter Five if a new piston or new piston rings were installed or if the cylinder has been bored or honed.

2. When installing oversized compression rings, check the ring number (**Figure 152**) to ensure that the correct rings are installed. The ring oversize number should be the same as the piston oversize number.

3. A paint mark on the oil ring spacer identifies oversized oil rings. When installing an oversized oil ring assembly, check the color to make sure the size is cor-

Tables 1-2 are on the following pages.

Table 1 ENGINE SERVICE SPECIFICATIONS

Item	Specifications	Service limit
Bore and stroke	83.0 × 74.4 mm (3.27 × 2.93 in.)	
Displacement	805 cc (49.1 cu. in.)	
Compression ratio	9.4 to 1	
Compression pressure (at sea level)	1300-1700 kPa (188-246 psi)	
Cylinder		
Bore	83.000-83.015 mm (3.2677-3.2683 in.)	83.085 mm (3.2711 in.)
Out of round	–	0.05 mm (0.002 in.)
Piston-to-cylinder clearance	0.045-0.055 mm (0.0018-0.0022 in.)	
Piston diameter	82.950-82.965 mm (3.2657-3.2663 in.)	82.880 mm (3.2630 in.)
Piston pin bore diameter	20.002-20.008 mm (0.7875-0.7877 in.)	20.030 mm (0.7886 in.)
Piston pin diameter	19.992-20.000 mm (0.7871-0.7874 in.)	19.980 mm (0.7866 in.)
Piston rings		
Number of rings		
Compression	2	
Oil control	1	
Ring free end gap		
Top	Approx. 9.6 mm (0.38 in.)	7.7 mm (0.30 in.)
Second	Approx. 11.8 mm (0.46 in.)	9.4 mm (0.37 in.)
Ring end gap (in cylinder bore)		
Top and second	0.20-0.35 mm (0.008-0.014 in.)	0.70 mm (0.028 in.)
Ring side clearance		
Top	–	0.180 mm (0.0071 in.)
Second	–	0.150 mm (0.0059 in.)
Ring thickness		
Top	0.97-0.99 mm (0.038-0.039 in.)	–
Second	1.17-1.19 mm (0.046-0.047 in.)	–
Connecting rod		
Small end inner diameter	20.010-20.018 mm (0.7878-0.7881 in.)	20.040 mm (0.7890 in.)
Camshaft		
Cam lobe height		
Front cylinder		
Intake	35.95-35.99 mm (1.415-1.417 in.)	35.65 mm (1.404 in.)
Exhaust	36.92-36.96 mm (1.454-1.455 in.)	36.62 mm (1.442 in.)
Rear cylinder		
Intake	35.50-35.54 mm (1.398-1.399 in.)	35.20 mm (1.386 in.)
Exhaust	36.52-36.62 mm (1.438-1.442 in.)	36.28 mm (1.428 in.)
Cam journal holder inner diameter		
Front cylinder		
Left end	25.012-25.025 mm (0.9847-0.9852 in.)	–
Right end	20.012-20.025 mm (0.7879-0.7884 in.)	–
Rear cylinder		
Left end	20.012-20.025 mm (0.7879-0.7884 in.)	–
Right end	25.012-25.025 mm (0.9847-0.9852 in.)	–

(continued)

Table 1 ENGINE SERVICE SPECIFICATIONS (continued)

Item	Specifications	Service limit
Cam journal outer diameter		
Front cylinder		
Left end	24.959-24.980 mm (0.9826-0.9835 in.)	–
Right end	19.959-19.980 mm (0.7858-0.7866 in.)	–
Rear cylinder		
Left end	19.959-19.980 mm (0.7858-0.7866 in.)	–
Right end	24.959-24.980 mm (0.9826-0.9835 in.)	–
Cam journal oil clearance	0.032-0.066 mm (0.0013-0.0026 in.)	0.150 mm (0.0059 in.)
Camshaft runout	–	0.10 mm (0.004 in.)
Valves		
Valve clearance (cold)		
Intake	0.08-0.13 mm (0.003-0.005 in.)	–
Exhaust	0.17-0.22 mm (0.007-0.009 in.)	–
Valve stem outer diameter		
Intake	5.475-5.490 mm (0.2156-0.2161 in.)	–
Exhaust	5.455-5.470 mm (0.2148-0.2154 in.)	–
Valve guide inner diameter		
Intake and exhaust	5.500-5.512 mm (0.2165-0.2170 in.)	–
Valve stem-to-guide clearance		
Intake	0.010-0.037 mm (0.0004-0.0014 in.)	–
Exhaust	0.030-0.057 mm (0.0012-0.0022 in.)	
Valve seat width		
Intake and exhaust	0.9-1.1 mm (0.035-0.043 in.)	–
Valve stem runout	–	0.05 mm (0.002 in.)
Valve head thickness	–	0.5 mm (0.02 in.)
Valve stem end length	–	3.1 mm (0.12 in.)
Valve head radial runout	–	0.03 mm (0.001 in.)
Valve springs free length		
Inner spring	–	38.3 mm (1.51 in.)
Outer spring	–	40.1 mm (1.58 in.)
Rocker arm assembly		
Rocker arm bore inner diameter	12.000-12.018 mm (0.4724-0.4731 in.)	–
Rocker arm shaft outer diameter	11.966-11.984 mm (0.4711-0.4718 in.)	–
Cylinder head and cover warp	–	0.05 mm (0.002 in.)

Table 2 ENGINE TORQUE SPECIFICATIONS

Item	N•m	in.-lb.	ft.-lb.
Camshaft sprocket bolt*	15	133	–
Camshaft tensioner mounting bolt	10	88	–
Cylinder head cover bolt			
6 mm	10	88	–
8 mm	25	–	18
Cylinder head cover cap bolts	25	–	18
Cylinder head M8 bolt and nut	25	–	18
Cylinder head M10 bolt			
Initial	25	–	18
Final	38	–	28
Rocker arm shaft	27	–	20

*Apply threadlock.

CHAPTER FIVE

ENGINE LOWER END

This chapter covers lower end engine components, including engine removal and installation. Specifications are in **Tables 1-7** at the end of this chapter.

ENGINE

Removal/Installation

1. Drain the engine oil and cooling system as described in Chapter Three.
2. Remove the seats and side covers as described in Chapter Sixteen.
3. Remove the fuel tank as described in Chapter Eight or Chapter Nine.
4. Remove the frame head covers as described in Chapter Sixteen.
5. Disconnect the wire lead from the battery negative terminal as described in Chapter Three.
6. Remove the radiator as described in Chapter Eleven.
7. Remove the coolant reservoir as described in Chapter Eleven.
8. Disconnect the coolant hoses from the engine. Refer to Chapter Eleven.
9. Remove the PAIR valve as described in Chapter Eight or Chapter Nine.
10. Remove the airbox and mounting bracket as described in Chapter Eight or Chapter Nine.
11A. On 2001-2004 models, remove the carburetor assembly as described in Chapter Eight.

11B. On 2005-on models, remove the throttle body as described in Chapter Nine.
12. Remove the exhaust system as described in Chapter Eight or Chapter Nine.
13. Remove the the secondary drive gear cover (**Figure 1**).
14. Push the rubber boot (**Figure 2**) away from the engine and onto the swing arm.
15. On 2005-on models, disconnect the connector from the engine coolant sensor (**Figure 3**).
16. At the lower clutch cable adjuster, loosen the locknuts (A, **Figure 4**) and rotate the adjuster (B) to increase the cable free play.
17. Remove the clutch release mounting bolts (A, **Figure 5**), then remove the release assembly (B).
18. Remove the clutch push rod (**Figure 6**).
19. Disconnect the spark plug lead (**Figure 7**) from each spark plug. Move the lead out of the way.
20. Refer to Chapter Ten and disconnect the following electrical wires from the engine:
    a. Starter.
    b. Alternator stator and the pulse generator.
    c. Neutral switch.
    d. Sidestand switch.
    e. Ground.
21. Remove the bolt (**Figure 8**) securing the gearshift lever and detach the lever from the gearshift shaft. Do not attempt to disconnect the shift linkage; it will be removed with the footpeg assembly.

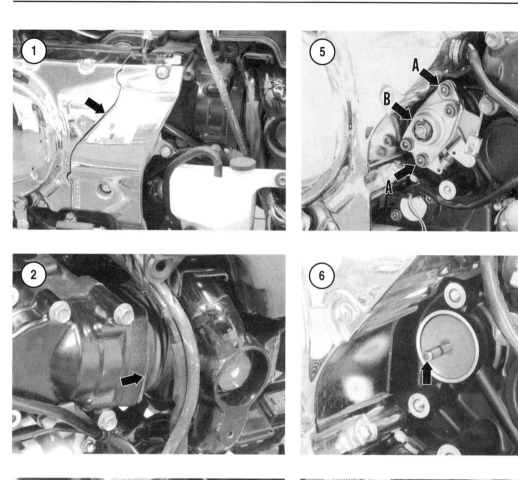

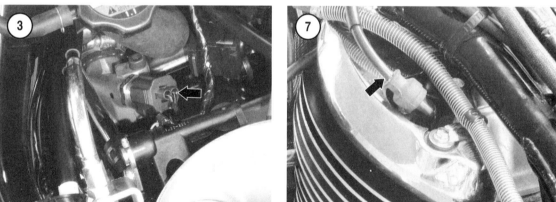

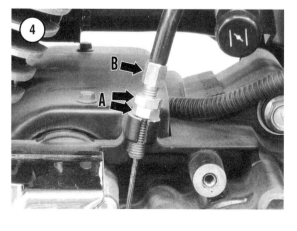

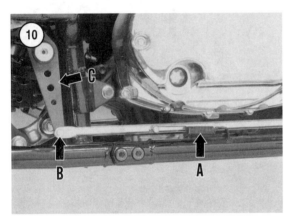

22. Remove the left footpeg assembly as described in Chapter Sixteen.

23. Remove the right, lower side cover (**Figure 9**).

24. Disconnect the rear brake rod spring (A, **Figure 10**).

25. Disconnect the rear brake rod end (B, **Figure 10**) from the pivot lever (C).

26. Disconnect the cooling fan connector (**Figure 11**).

27. Remove the right-side cooling fan mounting bolt (**Figure 12**).

NOTE
The cooling fan will be loose in the frame after removing the mounting bolts, but it cannot be removed until the subframe is removed or spread outward.

28. Remove the left-side cooling fan mounting bolts (**Figure 13**).

29. Disconnect the rear brake switch connector (A, **Figure 14**).

30. Remove the front engine mounting bolt (B, **Figure 14**).

31. Remove the front two bolts on the subframe crossmember (**Figure 15**).

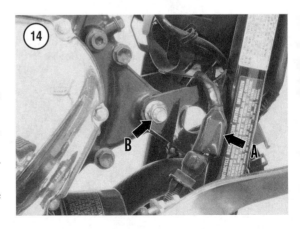

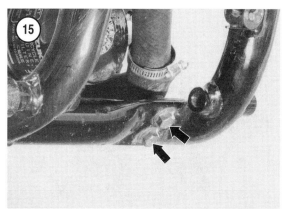

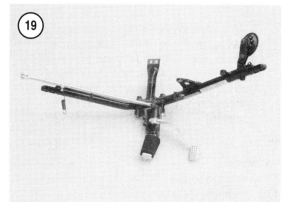

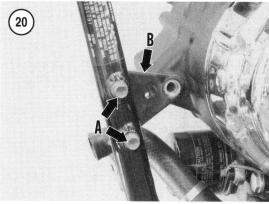

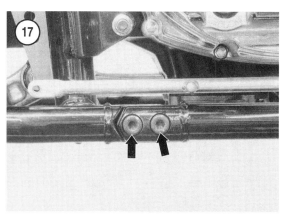

32. Loosen the front upper Allen bolts (**Figure 16**) and the lower Allen bolts (**Figure 17**) and nuts securing the subframe to the frame.

33. Remove the cooling fan (**Figure 18**). Loosen or remove the subframe bolts sufficiently so the upper tube of the subframe can be moved outward to allow passage of the fan.

34. Remove the Allen bolts, then remove the subframe assembly (**Figure 19**) from the engine and frame.

35. Remove the front mounting bracket bolts (A, **Figure 20**) and the bracket (B).

36. Place wood block(s) and a suitable jack under the engine to support it securely.

> *CAUTION*
> *The following steps require an assistant to safely remove the engine assembly from the frame.*

> *CAUTION*
> *To preserve the finish of engine parts and the frame, cover or apply protective material, such as foam tubing or carpet and duct tape, to all parts that may be damaged during engine removal.*

NOTE
After engine removal the engine may be placed on a workbench or in an engine stand. A universal automotive engine stand can be modified using fabricated metal bracing to support the engine using the rear engine mount holes (Figure 21).

37. Remove the rear, upper through bolt (**Figure 22**) and locknut.

38. Remove the rear, lower through bolt (**Figure 23**), spacer and locknut.

39. Slowly move the engine forward to disengage the engine output shaft from the driveshaft universal joint (**Figure 24**). If necessary, use a screwdriver and disengage the driveshaft universal joint from the output shaft.

40. Slightly lower the engine on the jack and continue to move the engine forward and toward the right side to clear the remaining frame members.

41. Take the engine to a workbench or engine stand for further disassembly.

42. Install by reversing the following removal steps while noting the following:

   a. Install new locknuts on the engine through bolts.

   b. Apply a light coat of molybdenum disulfide grease to the splines of the output shaft and the universal joint prior to engaging them.

   c. Tighten the engine mounting throughbolts to 79 N•m (58 ft.-lb.).

   d. Tighten the subframe Allen bolts to 50 N•m (37 ft.-lb.).

   e. Tighten the subframe lower crossmember bolts to 25 N•m (18 ft.-lb.).

   f. Tighten the engine mounting bracket bolts to 23 N•m (17 ft.-lb.)

   g. Lubricate the clutch pushrod and release mechanism with grease.

   h. Adjust the clutch cable as described in Chapter Three.

   i. Fill the engine with the recommended type and quantity of oil as described in Chapter Three.

   j. Refill the cooling system as described in Chapter Three.

   k. Start the engine and check for leaks.

OIL PUMP

Removal/Installation

The oil pump can be removed with the engine in the frame; the following figures show the engine removed for clarity.

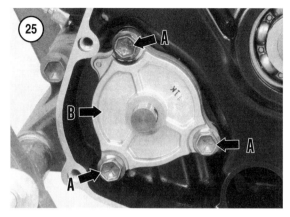

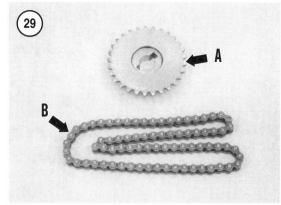

1. Remove the clutch assembly as described in Chapter Six. During clutch removal, the oil pump driven gear is removed.

2. Remove the bolts (A, **Figure 25**) securing the oil pump to the crankcase and remove the oil pump (B).

3. Using needlenose pliers, reach into the crankcase and turn the water pump shaft so the drive tang is vertical (**Figure 26**).

4. Rotate the oil pump drive shaft so the drive slot (A, **Figure 27**) will be vertical when the oil pump is installed into the crankcase.

5. Install the oil pump into the crankcase and align the oil pump drive shaft with the water pump shaft. If necessary, slightly rotate the oil pump shaft as needed for correct alignment.

6. Push the oil pump in until it bottoms.

7. Temporarily install the driven gear. Hold the oil pump in place on the crankcase and rotate the oil pump shaft to make sure it rotates freely with no binding. Remove the driven gear.

8. Install the bolts (A, **Figure 25**) and tighten to 11 N•m (97 in.-lb.).

Inspection

There are no replacement parts for the oil pump except for the driven gear and drive chain. Do not disassemble the oil pump.

1. Make sure the screw (A, **Figure 28**) securing the oil pump together is tight.

2. Inspect the oil pump body and cover for cracks (B, **Figure 27**). If worn or damaged, replace the oil pump assembly.

3. Inspect the driveshaft (A, **Figure 27**) for wear or damage. If necessary, replace the oil pump assembly.

4. Inspect the oil pump mounting bosses (B, **Figure 28**) for fractures or damage. If damaged, replace the oil pump assembly.

5. Inspect the teeth on the driven gear (A, **Figure 29**). Replace the driven gear if the teeth are damaged

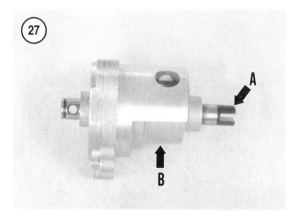

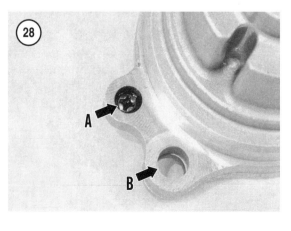

or any are missing. If the gear is damaged, inspect the drive chain (B, **Figure 29**) as it may also be damaged. Replace the chain if necessary.

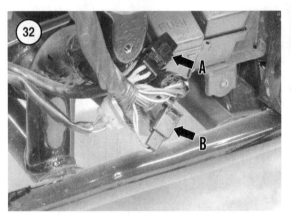

STARTER CLUTCH AND GEARS

Removal

The starter clutch and gears can be removed with the engine in the frame. For clarity, the figures show the engine removed and partially disassembled.

1. If the engine is in the frame, perform the following:
    a. Remove the left frame cover bolts, then remove the cover (**Figure 30**).
    b. Remove the secondary drive cover bolts, then remove the cover (**Figure 31**).
    c. Disconnect the alternator three-wire electrical connector (A, **Figure 32**).
    d. On 2001-2004 models, disconnect the pickup coil two-wire connector (B, **Figure 32**).
    e. On 2005-on models, disconnect the crankshaft position sensor 2-pin connector (B, **Figure 32**).

2. Remove the bolts securing the alternator cover (**Figure 33**) to the crankcase.

NOTE
Note the path of the wiring harness when withdrawing it in Step 3.

3. Remove the alternator cover. If the engine is in the frame, carefully withdraw the wiring harness from the frame. Do not lose the two locating dowels.

4. Remove the starter driven gear shaft (A, **Figure 34**) and gear (B).

5. Extract the idler shaft (A, **Figure 35**), then remove the starter idler gear (B).

6. Remove the alternator rotor as described in Chapter Ten.

7. Remove the drive key (**Figure 36**).

8. Remove the starter driven gear (**Figure 37**).

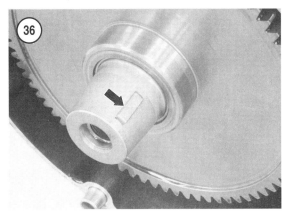

9. Inspect all components as described in this section.

10. Install by reversing the preceding removal steps. Note the following:

    a. If removed, install the two locating dowels (A, **Figure 38**).

    b. Install a new gasket (B, **Figure 38**).

    c. Install a new gasket washer onto each of the indicated alternator cover bolts (**Figure 39**).

Disassembly/Inspection/Assembly

Refer to **Figure 40**.

1. Inspect the gears (**Figure 41**) and shafts for wear or damage. Replace if necessary.

2. Set the alternator rotor and starter driven gear on the workbench with the rotor facing down.

3. Inspect the one-way clutch as follows:

    a. Attempt to rotate the starter driven gear (**Figure 42**) clockwise; it should *not* rotate.

    b. Rotate the starter driven gear (**Figure 42**) counterclockwise; it should rotate.

    c. If the one-way clutch fails either of these tests, replace the one-way clutch. The starter driven gear, starter clutch holder and one-way clutch are only available as an assembly.

4. Rotate the starter driven gear (**Figure 42**) counterclockwise and pull it up at the same time. Remove the gear from the backside of the rotor.

5. Inspect the starter driven gear for wear, chipped or missing teeth (A, **Figure 43**). Replace the gear if necessary.

6. Inspect the starter driven gear bushing (B, **Figure 43**) for wear or damage. The bushing is not available separately from the gear.

7. Inspect the starter driven gear outer surface (C, **Figure 43**) where it rides on the one-way clutch. If the surface is damaged, replace the gear.

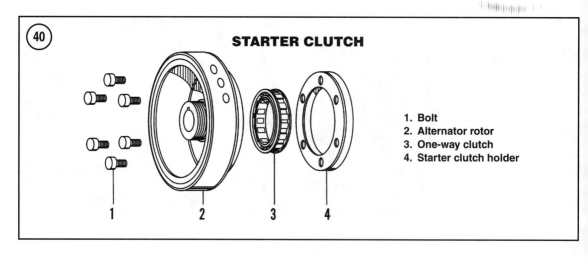

STARTER CLUTCH

1. Bolt
2. Alternator rotor
3. One-way clutch
4. Starter clutch holder

8. Inspect the rollers (A, **Figure 44**) of the one-way clutch for burrs, wear or damage. If necessary, remove the one-way clutch as follows:

   a. Use a wrench on the hex portion (A, **Figure 45**, typical) of the rotor or a strap-type wrench (B). Hold the rotor stationary while loosening the Allen bolts in the next step.

CAUTION
The Allen bolts have a locking agent applied to them during installation. Use the correct size wrench to loosen the screws, otherwise, the screw heads will be damaged.

   b. Loosen, then remove the Allen bolts (C, **Figure 45**) securing the starter clutch holder and one-way clutch to the backside of the rotor.
   c. Remove the starter clutch holder (B, **Figure 44**) and the one-way clutch from the backside of the rotor.
   d. If removed, install the one-way clutch so the flanged side fits into the notch on the starter clutch holder. Install the starter clutch holder (B, **Figure 44**) so the stepped side is toward the rotor and align the bolt holes.
   e. Apply Threadlocker Super 1303 to the Allen bolt threads prior to installation, then install the bolts (C, **Figure 45**). Use the same tool set up used for loosening the bolts and tighten the bolts to 26 N•m (19 ft.-lb.).

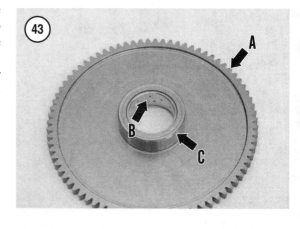

9. To install the starter driven gear onto the alternator rotor, rotate the starter driven gear (**Figure 42**) counterclockwise and push it down at the same time.

PRIMARY DRIVE GEAR

Removal/Installation

1. Remove the clutch as described in Chapter Six.

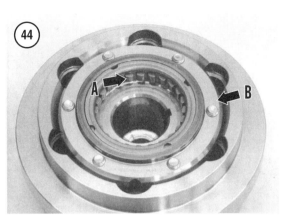

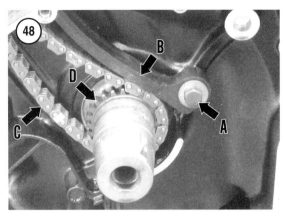

5

CAUTION
The primary drive gear bolt has left-hand threads. Turn the wrench clockwise to loosen it and counter-clockwise to tighten it.

2. Hold the primary drive gear using a pin-type spanner wrench (A, **Figure 46**).

3. Remove the bolt and the primary drive gear (B, **Figure 46**).

4. Inspect the primary drive gear. If damaged, also inspect the driven gear on the clutch outer housing.

5. Reverse the removal steps to install the primary drive gear. Tighten the bolt (left-hand threads) to 95 N•m (70 ft.-lb.).

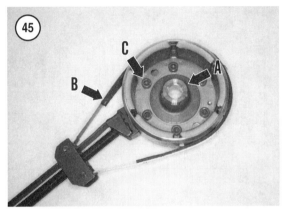

CAMSHAFT DRIVE CHAINS AND DRIVE SPROCKETS

Each camshaft is driven by a chain that attaches to a sprocket on the crankshaft. The drive sprocket for the front cylinder is located behind the alternator rotor. The drive sprocket for the rear cylinder is located behind the primary drive gear.

Removal/Installation

1. Remove the cylinder head as described in Chapter Four.

2. To remove the camshaft chain and sprocket on the front cylinder, proceed as follows:

   a. Remove the alternator rotor as described in Chapter Ten.

   b. Remove the chain guide (**Figure 47**).

   c. Remove the bolt (A, **Figure 48**) and washer securing the camshaft chain guide (B). Remove the guide and the washer behind it. There is a washer on each side of the chain guide. Account for the collar in the mounting hole in the chain guide.

d. Disengage the camshaft chain (C, **Figure 48**) from the camshaft chain sprocket and remove the chain.

3. To remove the camshaft chain and sprocket on the rear cylinder, proceed as follows:

a. Remove the primary drive gear as described in this chapter.

b. Remove the chain guide (**Figure 49**).

c. Remove the bolt (A, **Figure 50**) and washer securing the camshaft chain guide (B). Remove the guide and the washer behind it. There is a washer on each side of the chain guide. Account for the collar in the mounting hole in the chain guide.

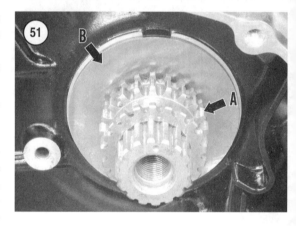

d. Disengage the camshaft chain (C, **Figure 50**) from the camshaft chain sprocket and remove the chain.

e. Remove the rear cylinder camshaft chain sprocket (A, **Figure 51**) from the crankshaft.

f. Remove the outer thrust washer (B, **Figure 51**).

4. Inspect all components as described in this section.

NOTE
The camshaft chain guides are unique and must be installed in the correct location. The front cylinder chain guide (A, Figure 52) is longer than the rear cylinder guide (B). The movable front and rear cylinder chain guides are different. The front cylinder chain guide, shown in Figure 53, is straighter than the rear cylinder chain guide.

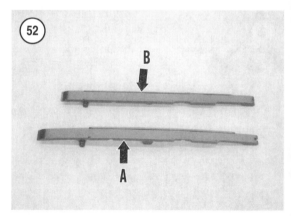

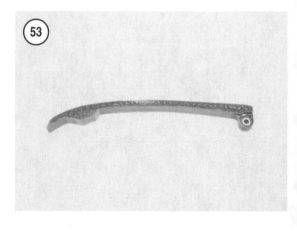

5. Install the rear cylinder, noting the following:

a. Install the outer thrust washer (**Figure 54**) with the beveled side toward the crankshaft surface.

b. Install the camshaft chain sprocket so the mark on the sprocket (A, **Figure 55**) and end of the crankshaft (B) are visible and aligned.

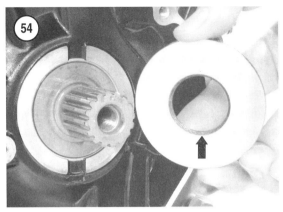

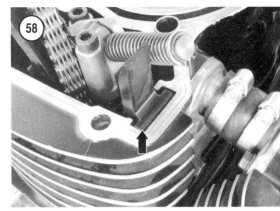

5

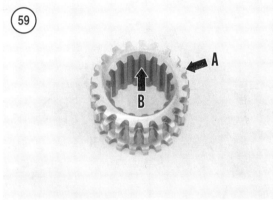

6. Install the camshaft chain onto the camshaft chain sprocket and make sure it is properly meshed.

7. Make sure the collar is in place in the cam chain guide mounting hole.

> *NOTE*
> *When installing a movable chain guide and the chain tensioner is installed, make sure the chain guide (A, **Figure 56**) fits inside the tensioner arm (B).*

8. Install the camshaft chain guide (B, **Figure 48** or B, **Figure 50**). Place a washer between the tensioner guide and the crankcase surface, then install the bolt and washer (A, **Figure 48** or A, **Figure 50**). Tighten the bolt to 10 N•m (88 in.-lb.).

9. Install the chain guide. Make sure it fits into the pocket at the bottom (**Figure 57**, typical) and in the notch in the top of the cylinder (**Figure 58**, typical).

Inspection

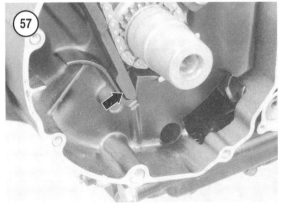

1. Inspect the rear cylinder camshaft chain sprocket (A, **Figure 59**) for chipped or missing teeth, wear or damage. Check the inner splines (B, **Figure 59**) for

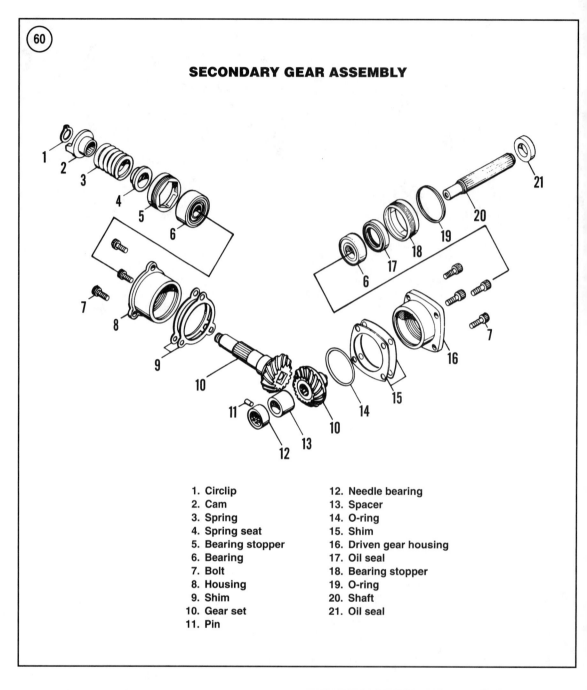

SECONDARY GEAR ASSEMBLY

1. Circlip
2. Cam
3. Spring
4. Spring seat
5. Bearing stopper
6. Bearing
7. Bolt
8. Housing
9. Shim
10. Gear set
11. Pin
12. Needle bearing
13. Spacer
14. O-ring
15. Shim
16. Driven gear housing
17. Oil seal
18. Bearing stopper
19. O-ring
20. Shaft
21. Oil seal

wear or damage, and replace the sprocket if necessary.

2. Inspect the sprocket teeth on the crankshaft for the front cylinder camshaft chain (D, **Figure 48**). Replace the crankshaft if the teeth are damaged or excessively worn.

3. Inspect the camshaft chain tensioner guides for deterioration, cracks or damage, and replace if necessary.

4. Inspect the camshaft chain for wear or damage to the links and pins. Replace if necessary. If the chain is

damaged, also inspect the sprocket at each end and replace if damaged.

SECONDARY GEAR ASSEMBLY

Removal

Refer to **Figure 60**.

1. Remove the engine as described in this chapter.

2. Install the universal joint (**Figure 61**) onto the output shaft of the secondary gear housing. This will keep the internal gears from rotating during nut removal in the following step.

3. Hold the universal joint using a suitable wrench and loosen the nut (**Figure 62**) securing the secondary gear.

4. Remove the nut and washer and the universal joint.

5. Loosen in a crisscross pattern, then remove the secondary gear housing bolts (**Figure 63**).

6. Remove the bolts (**Figure 64**) securing the secondary gearcase and remove the gearcase. Note the washer on bolt (A, **Figure 64**).

7. Remove the secondary bevel gear assembly and bearing (A, **Figure 65**).

8. Separate the crankcase as described in this chapter.

9. Remove the secondary reduction gear (**Figure 66**) from the transmission shaft.

10. Remove the Allen bolts (A, **Figure 67**) securing the secondary bevel drive gear and remove the assembly (B) from the crankcase. Also remove the shims located between the assembly and the crankcase mounting surface. Note the number of shims as the same number must be reinstalled to maintain the correct gear lash between the two bevel gears during assembly.

11. Inspect the components as described in this chapter.

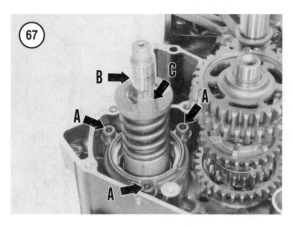

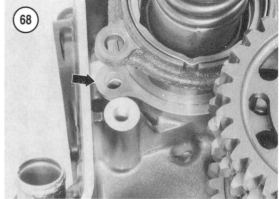

Installation

NOTE
*If the gear assemblies or crankcase are replaced, refer to **Gear Position Adjustment** in this section.*

1. Apply a light coat of engine oil to the secondary bevel drive gear receptacle in the crankcase.

2. Make sure to install the same number of shims (**Figure 68**) between the assembly and the crankcase mounting surface as noted during removal.

3. Install the secondary bevel drive gear assembly (B, **Figure 67**), then install the secondary reduction gear (**Figure 66**) onto the gear assembly to assist in installation.

4. Slowly push the secondary bevel drive gear assembly into the bore in the crankcase. Align the mounting bolt holes in the shims and assembly with the holes in the crankcase. After the bolt holes are aligned, remove the secondary reduction gear (**Figure 66**).

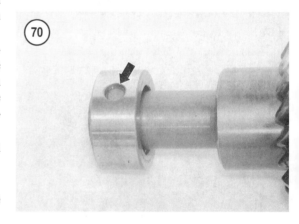

5. Install the Allen bolts (A, **Figure 67**) and tighten to 23 N•m (17 ft.-lb.).

6. Assemble the crankcase as described in this chapter.

7. Make sure the shaft bearing locating pin (**Figure 69**) is in place in the crankcase.

8. Position the secondary bevel gear assembly bearing so the hole in the bearing case (**Figure 70**) indexes properly with the locating pin (**Figure 69**) and install the secondary bevel gear assembly and bearing. Make sure the bearing has seated properly onto the locating pin.

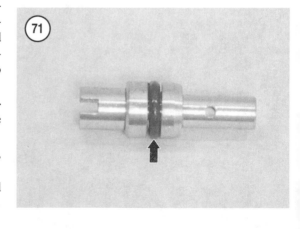

9. If removed, make sure the small O-ring seal (**Figure 71**) is in place, then install the oil control orifice (**Figure 72**). Push it down until it seats completely.

10. If removed, install the case locating dowels (B, **Figure 65**) in the crankcase.

11. Apply a light coat of gasket sealer (Suzuki Bond No. 1207) to the secondary gearcase sealing surfaces.

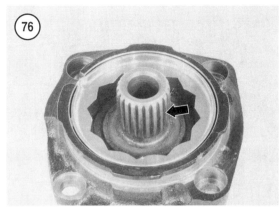

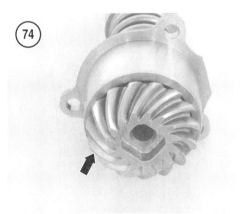

12. Position the driven gear housing so the notch (**Figure 73**) is facing down.

13. Install the gearcase and bolts (**Figure 64**). Install the washer on the bolt (A, **Figure 64**). Tighten the bolts in two stages; initially to 15 N•m (133 in.-lb.) and finally to 22 N•m (16 ft.-lb.).

14. Apply red Loctite (No. 271) to the secondary gear housing bolts prior to installation.

15. Install the secondary gear housing bolts (**Figure 63**) and tighten to 23 N•m (17 ft.-lb.).

16. Install the universal joint onto the output shaft of the secondary gear housing. This will keep the internal gears from rotating while tightening the nut in the following step.

17. Install the washer and nut (**Figure 62**).

18. Hold the universal joint using a suitable wrench and tighten the nut securing the secondary gear. Tighten the nut to 105 N•m (77 ft.-lb.).

NOTE
Make sure the transmission is in neutral.

19. Rotate the universal joint and make sure there is no binding within the secondary gear assembly. If the assembly will not rotate properly, correct the problem at this time. Remove the universal joint.

20. Install the engine into the frame as described in this chapter.

Inspection

Special tools are required to disassemble the driven shaft assembly. Refer this job to a dealer or machine shop.

1. Inspect for chipped or missing teeth on the drive gear (**Figure 74**) and the driven gear (**Figure 75**). If either gear is damaged both the drive and driven gears must be replaced as a set.

2. Inspect the driven gear assembly splines (**Figure 76**) for wear or damage. If damaged, both the drive and driven gears must be replaced as a set. Also

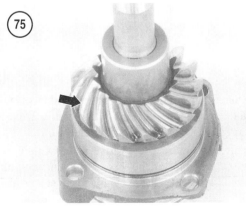

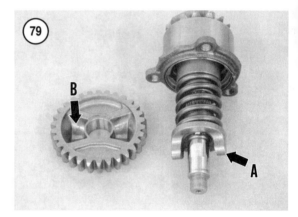

check the inner splines of the universal joint as they may also be damaged.

3. Inspect the driven gear shaft small roller bearing (**Figure 77**). Make sure it rotates freely with no binding. Replace the bearing if necessary.

4. Inspect the spring (A, **Figure 78**) for wear, cracks or damage and replace if necessary.

5. Install the secondary reduction gear (B, **Figure 78**) onto the drive gear shaft and check for proper engagement. Check the cams (A, **Figure 79**) and ramps (B) for wear, cracks or burrs. Replace if necessary.

6. Inspect the secondary reduction gear for chipped or missing teeth (A, **Figure 80**). Inspect the inner and outer bearing surfaces of the bushing (B, **Figure 80**) for wear. Insert the bushing into the gear and check for looseness or excessive wear. Replace if necessary.

7. Inspect the drive gear assembly shims (**Figure 81**) for wear or damage. Replace if necessary and replace with shims of the exact same thickness. Five different shim thicknesses are available.

8. Move the universal joint (**Figure 82**) back and forth and in and out. Check for looseness or stiffness, and replace if necessary.

9. Inspect the universal joint inner splines for wear or damage. If the splines are damaged, also inspect the outer splines on the drive shaft. Replace the universal joint if damaged.

Gear Position Adjustment

Gear position must be checked and, if necessary, adjusted if the gear assemblies or crankcase are replaced.

Refer to **Figure 60** when performing this procedure.

NOTE
Unless noted otherwise, install the original shims. Even though shim ad-

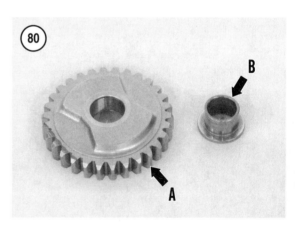

justments may be required, the original shims provide a good starting point.

Gear backlash measurement

1. Be sure to install the same number of shims (**Figure 68**) between the assembly and the crankcase mounting surface as noted during removal.

2. Install the secondary bevel drive gear assembly (B, **Figure 67**), then install the secondary reduction gear (**Figure 66**) onto the gear assembly to assist in installation.

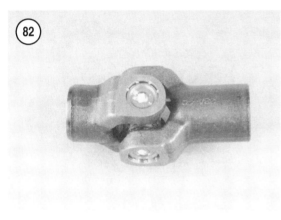

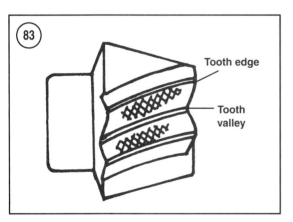

Tooth edge

Tooth valley

3. Slowly push the secondary bevel drive gear assembly into the bore in the crankcase. Align the mounting bolt holes in the shims and assembly with the holes in the crankcase. After bolt hole alignment is achieved, remove the secondary reduction gear (**Figure 66**).

4. Install the Allen bolts (A, **Figure 67**) and tighten to 23 N•m (17 ft.-lb.).

5. Make sure the shaft bearing locating pin (**Figure 69**) is in place in the crankcase.

6. Position the secondary bevel gear assembly bearing so the hole in the bearing case (**Figure 70**) indexes properly with the locating pin (**Figure 69**) and

install the secondary bevel gear assembly and bearing. Make sure the bearing has seated properly onto the locating pin.

7. If removed, install the case locating dowels (B, **Figure 65**) in the crankcase.

8. Position the driven gear housing so the notch (**Figure 73**) is facing down.

9. Install the gearcase and bolts (**Figure 64**). Install the washer on the bolt (A). Tighten the bolts in two stages; initially to 15 N•m (133 in.-lb.) and finally to 22 N•m (16 ft.-lb.).

10. Install the secondary gear housing bolts (**Figure 63**) and tighten to 23 N•m (17 ft.-lb.).

11. Install a dial indicator so the indicator end contacts a lobe (C, **Figure 67**) on the drive gear cam. Make sure the indicator is square with the lobe surface.

12. Hold the secondary driven bevel gear shaft. Pull up on the drive gear shaft to remove bearing play and rotate it in both directions while noting the dial indicator measurement. Specified backlash is in **Table 1**.

13. Install shims (15, **Figure 60**) as needed to obtain the specified backlash in **Table 1**.

Gear mesh position

1. Apply Prussian Blue or other gear marking compound onto the secondary drive and driven gear teeth.

2. Install the shims and the gear assemblies as described in *Gear Backlash Measurement* in this section.

3. Rotate the secondary driven gear shaft several rotations so a pattern is evident on the gear teeth. Hold the secondary drive gear shaft slightly to improve the impression on the gear teeth.

4. Note the gear pattern on the secondary drive gear teeth. Refer to the typical gear pattern in **Figure 83**. If the contact pattern is closer to the tooth edge, install a thinner shim. If the contact pattern is closer to the tooth valley, install a thicker shim. Refer to **Table 3** for a listing of available shims.

5. After obtaining a satisfactory gear contact pattern, recheck the gear backlash (**Table 1**).

CRANKCASE

Crankcase Disassembly

1. Remove the engine as described in this chapter.

2. Remove the following exterior assemblies from the crankcase assembly:

    a. Cylinder head and cylinder assemblies (Chapter Four).

    b. Alternator (Chapter Ten).

    c. Starter clutch assembly (this chapter).

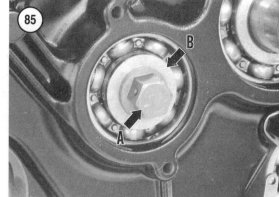

d. Camshaft chain, guides and drive sprocket (this chapter).
e. Oil pump (this chapter).
f. External shift mechanism (Chapter Six).
g. Clutch (Chapter Six).
h. Water pump (Chapter Eleven).
i. Starter (Chapter Ten).
j. Gear position sensor/neutral switch (Chapter Ten).
k. Oil pressure switch (Chapter Ten).

3. Shift the transmission into gear.

4. Install the universal joint (**Figure 84**) onto the output shaft of the secondary gear housing. This prevents transmission shaft rotation during bolt removal in the following step.

> *CAUTION*
> *The mainshaft bolt has left-hand threads. Turn the wrench clockwise to loosen it and counterclockwise to tighten it.*

5. Hold the universal joint and loosen the bolt (A, **Figure 85**) securing the transmission mainshaft to the crankcase.

6. Remove the bolt and washer (B, **Figure 85**) from the end of the shaft.

7. Remove the secondary gear assembly from the exterior of the crankcase as described in this chapter.

8. Starting on the right side, loosen all crankcase bolts 1/2 turn in a crisscross pattern, then remove the bolts. Make sure all bolts are removed. Do not lose the washer under the bolts indicated in (**Figure 86**).

9. Turn the crankcase so the left side faces up.

10. On the left side, loosen all bolts 1/2 turn in a crisscross pattern. Remove all bolts.

11. Turn the crankcase back over so the right side is facing up.

> *CAUTION*
> *Prying the crankcase halves apart may damage the gasket surfaces. The surfaces cannot be repaired and the*

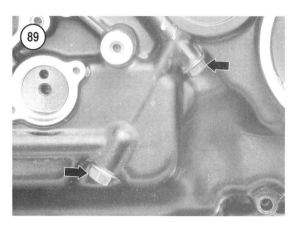

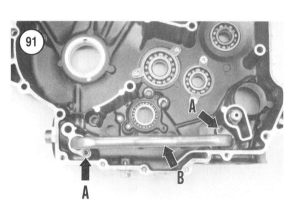

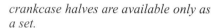

crankcase halves are available only as a set.

12. Separate the crankcase halves with a separation tool (**Figure 87**).

13. After removing the right crankcase, the transmission and crankshaft assemblies should remain in the left crankcase. Check the right crankcase to make sure no transmission shims are stuck to the bearings. If found, reinstall them in their original positions.

14. Remove the two dowel pins from the left crankcase.

15. Remove the small O-ring from the left crankcase.

16. Remove the secondary bevel drive gear assembly as described in this chapter.

17. Remove the transmission and internal shift assemblies as described in Chapter Seven.

18. Remove the crankshaft assembly as described in this chapter.

Crankcase Inspection

1. Remove all old gasket residue material from both crankcase mating surfaces. When using a gasket scraper, do not gouge the sealing surfaces, as oil and air leaks will result.

2. Remove all oil gallery plugs and sealing washers. Refer to **Figure 88**, **Figure 89** and **Figure 90**.

3. Remove the bolts (A, **Figure 91**) and remove the oil pipe (B) and O-rings from the right crankcase.

4. Remove the oil pressure relief valve (**Figure 92**) from the right crankcase.

5. Remove the clutch pushrod oil seal (**Figure 93**) from the left crankcase.

6. To service the oil sump filter, proceed as follows:

    a. Remove the oil sump cover bolts (A, **Figure 94**), then remove the cover (B).

    b. Remove the filter retaining screws (A, **Figure 95**), then remove the filter (B).

   c. Remove the O-ring in the cover (**Figure 96**).

   d. Clean the filter and cover with solvent.

   e. After cleaning the right crankcase (Step 7), re-assemble the filter and cover. Install a new O-ring in the cover.

7. Thoroughly clean the inside and outside of both crankcase halves with solvent. Dry with compressed air. When drying the bearings, do not allow the air jet to spin the bearings. Lubricate the bearings with engine oil to prevent rust.

8. Check all bolts and threaded holes for stripping, cross-threading or deposit buildup. Threaded holes should be blown out with compressed air, as dirt buildup in the bottom of a hole may prevent the bolt from being tightened properly. Replace damaged bolts and washers.

9. Inspect machined surfaces for burrs, cracks or other damage. Repair minor damage with a fine-cut file or oilstone.

10. Make sure all oil passages in both crankcase halves are clean.

11. Inspect the threads for the oil filter. Clean with a wire brush if necessary. If the threads are damaged, chase them with a metric thread die.

12. Inspect the crankcase bearings as described in this section.

13. Make sure the oil control orifice oil hole (A, **Figure 97**) is clear. Clean it with a piece of wire and compressed air.

14. Inspect the O-ring (B, **Figure 97**) for deterioration or hardness and replace if necessary.

15. Install all items removed during this inspection process.

16. Install new O-rings (**Figure 98**) onto the oil pipe prior to installation. Tighten the bolts securely.

Crankcase Bearings Inspection

1. Because of the number of bearings used in the crankcase, make sure to identify each bearing and note its location before removing it. Use the bearing markings to help identify them.

2. Clean the crankcase halves with solvent and dry with compressed air. Lubricate the bearings with engine oil.

3. Rotate the inner race of each bearing and check for play or roughness. Replace the bearing(s) if it is noisy or if it does not spin smoothly. Refer to Chapter One for general bearing replacement procedures.

4. Inspect the crankshaft main bearings (A, **Figure 99**) for wear or damage. Make sure the lock tab (B, **Figure 99**) is locked in place and the bearing is tight in the crankcase bore. Measure the bearing inside dimension as described in *Crankshaft Bearing and Oil*

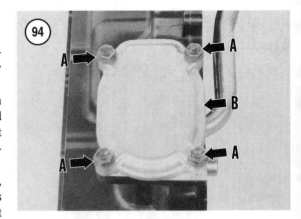

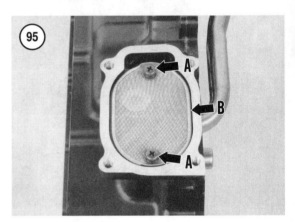

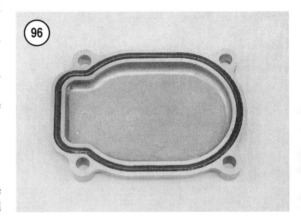

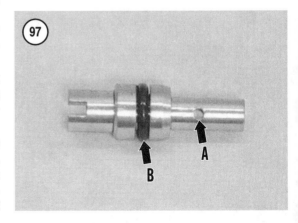

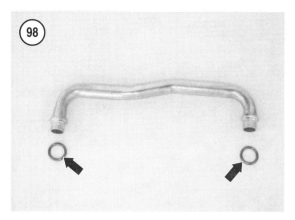

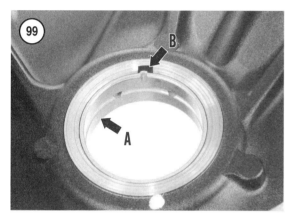

Clearance Measurement in this chapter. If the bearings are damaged or worn, replace them.

Crankcase Bearings Replacement

Crankshaft main bearings

Special tools and a hydraulic press are necessary to remove and install the crankshaft main bearings. After the new bearings are installed, they must be honed.

To avoid damage to the crankcase, entrust this procedure to a dealership or machine shop.

Other bearings

1. On bearings equipped with retainers, perform the following:

> *CAUTION*
> *The bearing retainer screws had a locking agent applied to the threads during installation and may be difficult to remove. To avoid damage or rounding off the screw head, use the recommended tool in this procedure.*

   a. Use an impact driver with the appropriate size bit and loosen the screws securing the bearing retainers. Refer to **Figure 100** and **Figure 101**.

   b. Remove the screws and retainers.

   c. Heat the crankcase to approximately 95-125° C (205-257° F) in an oven or on a hot plate. Do not attempt bearing removal by heating the crankcase with a torch as the localized heat may warp the crankcase.

   d. Use a pair of work gloves to remove the case from the oven. Place it on wood blocks.

   e. Drive out the bearing with a drift placed on the outside bearing race. A socket the same size as the bearing also works well for removal.

2. Perform Steps 1c-1e for the secondary gear shaft bearing and remove the bearing.

3. To remove bearings located in a blind hole, use a blind bearing puller (Chapter One).

4. Before installing new bearings, clean the bearing housing and oil passages with solvent. Dry thoroughly with compressed air.

5. Install new crankcase bearings as described in Chapter One. Lubricate the bearing races with clean engine oil.

6. On bearings secured by a retainer, apply red Loctite (No. 271) to the screw threads prior to installation, then install the retainer.

Crankcase Assembly

1. Coat all rotating parts with engine oil.

2. Place the left crankcase on wood blocks.

3. Install the crankshaft as described in this chapter. Make sure the connecting rods are positioned correctly in the cylinder openings (**Figure 102**).

> *NOTE*
> *Make sure the transmission shafts seat fully in the bearings. A tight fit between a shaft and bearing can prevent proper transmission operation after the crankcase is assembled.*

4. Install the shift drum, shift forks and transmission assemblies as described in Chapter Seven.

5. Install the small O-ring (**Figure 103**) into the left crankcase. Apply clean engine oil to the O-ring.

6. If removed, install the two dowel pins (**Figure 104**) into the left crankcase.

7. Apply engine oil to the transmission shafts and crankshaft bearing surfaces.

8. Clean all crankcase mating surfaces with aerosol electrical contact cleaner.

9. Make sure both crankcase sealing surfaces are perfectly clean and dry.

> *CAUTION*
> *Do not allow gasket sealer to enter the oil hole or oil groove of the main bearings.*

10. Apply a thin coat of gasket sealer (Suzuki Bond No. 1207) to the sealing surfaces of the left half.

> *CAUTION*
> *Because of the spring in the secondary drive gear assembly, there may be a gap between the crankcase halves (**Figure 105**). The gap shown is a normal gap distance, but if the gap is larger than shown, investigate the cause. The crankcase halves should fit together without force. Do not attempt to pull them together with the crankcase bolts. If the transmission shafts were disassembled, make sure a gear is not installed backwards. Do not try to force the case halves together.*

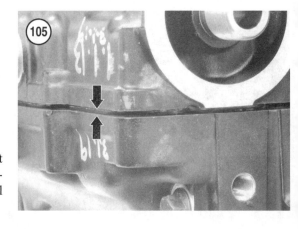

11. Align the right crankcase bearings with the left crankcase assembly. Join both halves and tap together lightly with a plastic mallet. Do not use a metal hammer.

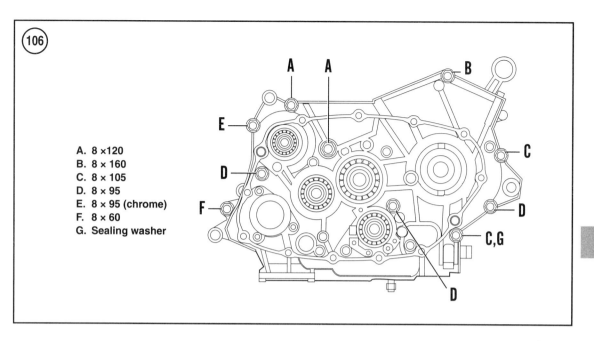

A. 8 ×120
B. 8 × 160
C. 8 × 105
D. 8 × 95
E. 8 × 95 (chrome)
F. 8 × 60
G. Sealing washer

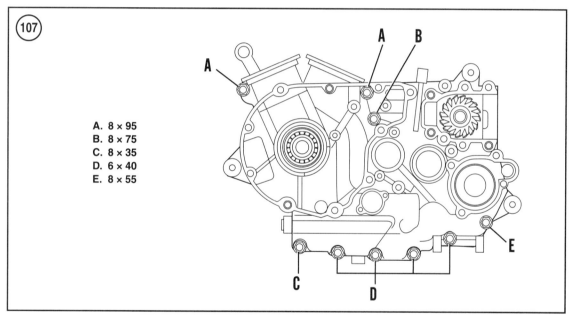

A. 8 × 95
B. 8 × 75
C. 8 × 35
D. 6 × 40
E. 8 × 55

NOTE
Install a sealing washer on the bolts identified in **Figure 106**.

12. Install the bolts in the right crankcase. Note the bolt length and location in **Figure 106**. Tighten in a crisscross pattern in the following stages:
    a. Tighten all 8 mm bolts to 15 N•m (133 in.-lb.).
    b. Tighten all 8 mm bolts to 22 N•m (16 ft.-lb.).
    c. Tighten all 6 mm bolts to 11 N•m (97 in.-lb.).
13. Install the bolts in the left crankcase. Note the bolt length and location in **Figure 107**. Tighten in a crisscross pattern in the following stages:
    a. Tighten all 8 mm bolts to 15 N•m (133 in.-lb.).

b. Tighten all 8 mm bolts to 22 N•m (16 ft.-lb.).
c. Tighten all 6 mm bolts to 11 N•m (97 in.-lb.).

14. Install the secondary gear assembly as described in this chapter.

15. Shift the transmission into gear.

16. Install the universal joint onto the output shaft of the secondary gear housing. This will prevent the internal gears from rotating during nut installation.

CAUTION
The mainshaft bolt has left-hand threads. Turn the wrench counterclockwise to tighten it.

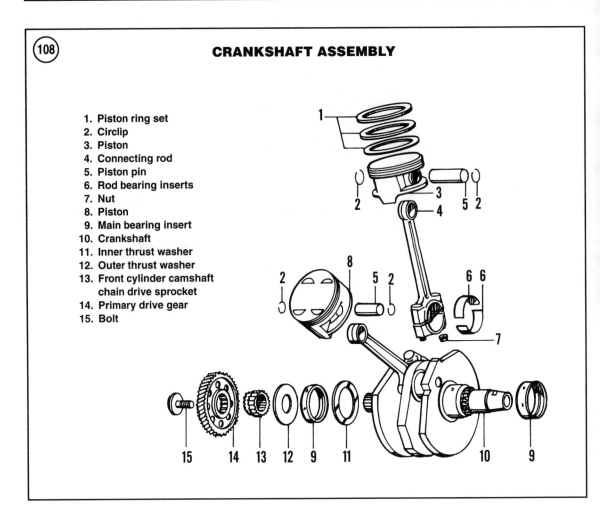

(108) CRANKSHAFT ASSEMBLY

1. Piston ring set
2. Circlip
3. Piston
4. Connecting rod
5. Piston pin
6. Rod bearing inserts
7. Nut
8. Piston
9. Main bearing insert
10. Crankshaft
11. Inner thrust washer
12. Outer thrust washer
13. Front cylinder camshaft chain drive sprocket
14. Primary drive gear
15. Bolt

17. Install the washer (B, **Figure 85**) and bolt (A) into the end of the transmission mainshaft.

18. Hold the universal joint and tighten the transmission bolt (A, **Figure 85**) to 65 N•m (48 ft.-lb.).

19. Remove the universal joint.

20. Install the following exterior assemblies onto the crankcase assembly:

   a. Oil pressure switch (Chapter Ten).

   b. Gear position sensor/neutral switch (Chapter Ten).

   c. Camshaft chain, guides and drive sprocket (this chapter).

   d. Starter (Chapter Ten).

   e. Water pump (Chapter Eleven).

   f. Clutch (Chapter Six).

   g. External shift mechanism (Chapter Six).

   h. Oil pump (this chapter).

   i. Starter clutch assembly (this chapter).

   j. Alternator (Chapter Ten).

   k. Cylinder head and cylinder assemblies (Chapter Four).

21. Install the engine as described in this chapter.

(109)

CRANKSHAFT AND CONNECTING RODS

Removal/Installation

Refer to **Figure 108**.

1. Split the crankcase as described in this chapter.

2. Remove the crankshaft assembly (**Figure 109**) from the left crankcase.

3. Remove the inner thrust washer (**Figure 110**) from the right end of the crankshaft.

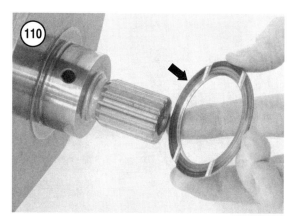

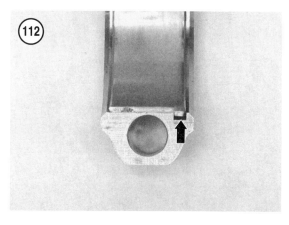

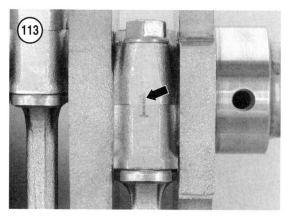

4. Remove the connecting rod cap bolt nuts (**Figure 111**) and separate the rods from the crankshaft.

> *NOTE*
> *The rear cylinder connecting rod is located nearer the tapered end (flywheel location) of the crankshaft.*

5. Mark each rod and cap as a set. Also mark them *F* (front) or *R* (rear) to indicate from which cylinder they were removed.

6. Mark each bearing insert so that it can be reinstalled in its original position, if it is reused.

7. Install the bearing inserts into each connecting rod and cap. Make sure the tabs (**Figure 112**) are locked in place correctly.

> *CAUTION*
> *If the old bearings are reused, be sure they are installed in their original positions.*

8. Lubricate the bearings and crankpins with a 1:1 mixture of engine oil and molybdenum disulfide grease.

9. Position the connecting rod and cap with the ID code number (**Figure 113**) facing the rear of the engine.

10. Install the caps and tighten the nuts to 25 N•m (18 ft.-lb.) initially, then finally to 51 N•m (38 ft.-lb.).

11. Install the inner thrust washer (**Figure 110**) onto the crankshaft so the oil grooves face in toward the crankshaft.

> *NOTE*
> *When installing the crankshaft, align the front and rear connecting rods with their respective cylinder position. Continue to check this alignment until the crankshaft is completely installed.*

12. Position the crankshaft with the flywheel (tapered) end pointing down and install the crankshaft assembly (**Figure 109**) into the left crankcase.

13. Inspect the crankshaft side thrust clearance as described in this section.

14. Assemble the crankcase as described in this chapter.

Crankshaft Side Thrust Clearance

Whenever the crankshaft is removed from the crankcase, the side thrust clearance must be checked. Adjust the side thrust clearance by replacing the inner thrust washer with one of a different thickness.

1. Install the inner thrust washer (**Figure 110**) onto the crankshaft so the oil grooves face toward the crankshaft.

> *NOTE*
> *When installing the crankshaft, align the front and rear connecting rods with their respective cylinder position in the crankcase. Continue to check this alignment until the crankshaft is completely installed.*

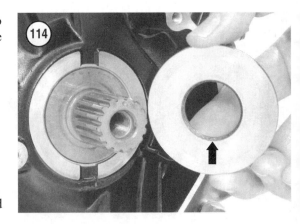

2. Position the right crankcase over the splined (right) end of the crankshaft.

3. Install the outer thrust washer onto the crankshaft with the beveled side (**Figure 114**) toward the crankcase.

4. Align the mark on the rear cylinder camshaft chain sprocket (A, **Figure 115**) with the alignment mark on the end of the crankshaft, and install the sprocket (B) onto the crankshaft. Push it down until it stops against the outer thrust washer.

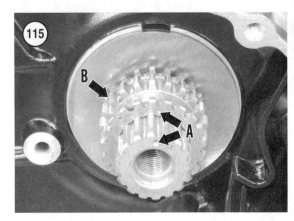

> *CAUTION*
> *The primary drive gear bolt has left-hand threads. Turn the wrench counterclockwise to tighten it and clockwise to loosen it.*

5. Install the primary drive gear (A, **Figure 116**) and bolt (B). Hold the primary drive gear using a pin-type spanner wrench (**Figure 117**) and tighten the bolt to 95 N•m (70 ft.-lb.).

6. Insert a flat feeler gauge (**Figure 118**) between the outer thrust washer and the crankcase surface. The specified thrust clearance is in **Table 1**. If the thrust clearance is incorrect, perform the following:

  a. Reverse Steps 1-6 and remove the crankshaft from the right crankcase half.

  b. Remove and measure the inner thrust washer (**Figure 119**) thickness with a Vernier caliper or micrometer.

  c. The inner thrust washers are available from a dealership in increments of 0.025 mm (0.0010 in.). The thrust washer thickness and part numbers are in **Table 2**. Select a new inner thrust washer that will provide the specified thrust clearance in **Table 1**.

  d. Install the new inner thrust washer and repeat this procedure to make sure the thrust clearance is now within specification.

  e. Remove all components from the right crankcase, then assemble as described in this chapter.

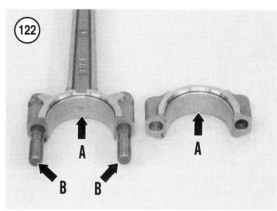

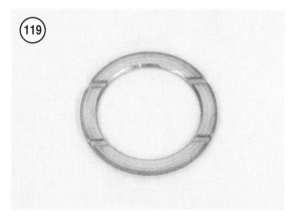

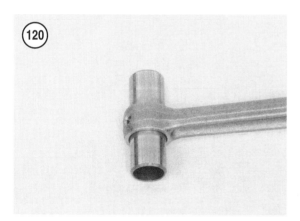

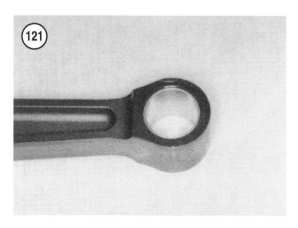

Connecting Rod Inspection

1. Check each rod and cap for damage such as cracks and burrs.

2. Inspect the connecting rod small end for wear or scoring.

3. Insert the piston pin into the connecting rod (**Figure 120**) and rotate it. Check for looseness or roughness. Replace the defective part.

4. Measure the inside diameter of the connecting rod small end (**Figure 121**). Compare to the dimension in **Table 1**. If the dimension is greater than specified, replace the connecting rod assembly.

5. Have a machine shop inspect the rods for twisting and bending.

6. Examine the bearing inserts (A, **Figure 122**) for wear, scoring or burning. They may be reused if they are in good condition. Before discarding any bearing insert, check the back and note if it is stamped with a number indicating that it is undersize. A previous owner may have fitted the engine with undersize bearings.

7. Inspect the connecting rod studs (B, **Figure 122**) for wear or damaged threads. If damaged, replace the connecting rod and stud.

8. Check bearing clearance as described in this section.

Connecting Rod Bearing and Oil Clearance Measurement

> *CAUTION*
> *If the old bearings are to be reused, make sure they are installed in their original locations.*

1. Clean the bearing inserts and crankpins. Install the bearing inserts (A, **Figure 122**) in the rod and cap.

2. Place a piece of Plastigage on one crankpin parallel to the crankshaft.

3. Install the rod, cap and nuts. Tighten the nuts to 25 N•m (18 ft.-lb.) initially, then finally to 51 N•m (38 ft.-lb.).

> *CAUTION*
> *Do not rotate the crankshaft while Plastigage is in place.*

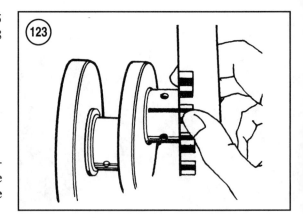

4. Remove the nuts and the rod cap.

5. Measure the width of the flattened Plastigage according to the manufacturer's instructions (**Figure 123**). Correct bearing clearance is specified in **Table 1**. Remove the Plastigage strip.

6. If the bearing clearance is greater than specified, use the following steps for new bearing selection.

7. The connecting rods and caps are marked with an ID code number *1, 2* or *3* (**Figure 124**) indicating the inside diameter of the bore in the connecting rod.

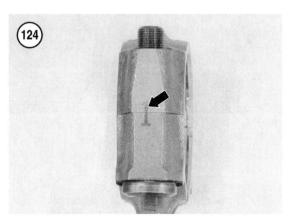

8. The crankshaft center counterbalance is stamped with a crankpin OD code number (**Figure 125**). The number following the *L* applies to the left (flywheel side) crankpin, while the number preceding the *R* applies to the right (clutch side) crankpin.

9. Select new bearings by cross-referencing the connecting rod ID code in the vertical column with the crankpin OD code number in the horizontal column. Where the columns intersect, the new bearing color is indicated. Refer to **Table 5** for the bearing color and **Table 6** for the bearing color and thickness.

10. After new bearings have been installed, recheck the clearance with Plastigage. If the clearance is out of specification, either the connecting rod or the crankshaft is worn beyond the service limit. Take the crankshaft and connecting rods to a dealership for further service.

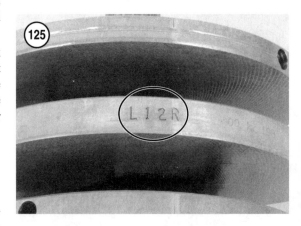

Connecting Rod Side Clearance Measurement

1. With both connecting rods attached to the crankshaft, insert a flat feeler gauge between the counterweight and the connecting rod big end (**Figure 126**).

2. The specified side clearance is in **Table 1**.

3. If the clearance is out of specification, perform the following:

    a. Measure the connecting big end width (**Figure 127**) and compare to the dimension in **Table 1**. If the width is less than specified, replace the connecting rod assembly.

    b. Measure the crankpin width (**Figure 128**) and compare to the dimension in **Table 1**.

    c. If the width is greater than specified, replace the crankshaft.

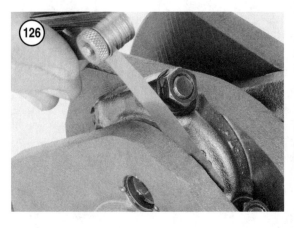

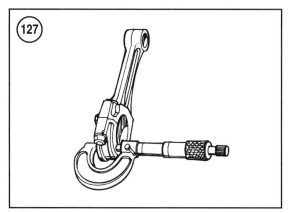

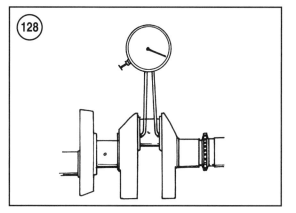

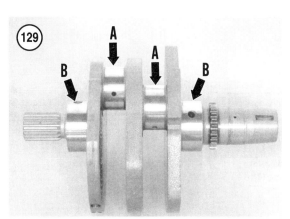

5

Crankshaft Inspection

1. Clean the crankshaft thoroughly with solvent. Clean the oil holes, flush thoroughly and dry with compressed air. Lightly oil all surfaces to prevent rust.

2. Inspect the connecting rod journals (A, **Figure 129**) and the main bearing journals (B) for scratches, ridges, scoring or nicks.

3. Measure the diameter of the main bearing journals and check for out-of-roundness and taper.

4. Inspect the camshaft chain sprocket (A, **Figure 130**) on the left end. If it is worn or damaged, replace the crankshaft.

5. Inspect the taper (B, **Figure 130**) where the alternator rotor contacts the crankshaft. If it is worn or damaged, replace the crankshaft.

6. Inspect the splines (**Figure 131**) on the right end for wear or damage. Minor damage can be cleaned up with a fine-cut file, but if damage is severe replace the crankshaft.

Crankshaft Bearing and Oil Clearance Measurement

NOTE
Removal and installation of the main bearings requires a hydraulic press and special tools. Entrust this procedure to a dealership or machine shop.

1. Clean the bearing inserts in the crankcase and the main bearing journals.

2. Measure the main journal diameter at two places.

3. Measure the main journal insert inside diameter (**Figure 132**) at two places.

4. To determine oil clearance, subtract the crankshaft diameter (Step 2) from the main journal insert diameter (Step 3).

5. The oil clearance specification is in **Table 1**. If the clearance is out of specifications, either the crankshaft or the bearing insert is worn beyond the service limit.

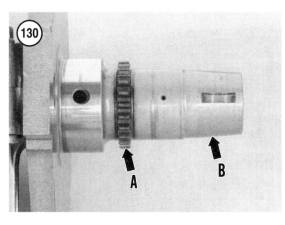

BREAK-IN

The performance and service life of the engine depends greatly on a careful and sensible break-in. For the first 1000 km (600 miles), use no more than one-half throttle and vary the speed as much as possible within the one-half throttle limit. Prolonged, steady running at one speed, no matter how moderate, is to be avoided, as is hard acceleration.

After the 1000 km (600 miles) service interval, three- quarter throttle may be used. After the motorcycle has covered at least 1000 miles, full throttle may be used.

During engine break-in, oil consumption will be higher than normal. It is therefore important to frequently check and correct oil level. At no time during the break-in or later should the oil level be allowed to drop below the lower line on the oil level window. If the

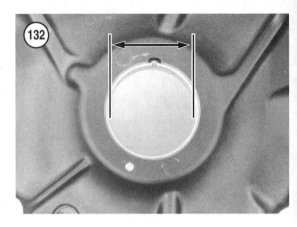

oil level is low, the oil will become overheated, resulting in insufficient lubrication and increased wear.

Change the oil and filter after the first 1000 km (600 miles).

Table 1 ENGINE SERVICE SPECIFICATIONS

Item	Specifications	Service limit
Connecting rod		
Big end width	21.95-22.00 mm (0.864-0.866 in.)	–
Big end oil clearance	0.024-0.042 mm (0.0009-0.0017 in.)	0.080 mm (0.0031 in.)
Big end side clearance	0.10-0.20 mm (0.004-0.008 in.)	0.30 mm (0.012 in.)
Small end inner diameter	20.010-20.018 mm (0.7878-0.7881 in.)	20.040 mm (0.7890 in.)
Crankshaft		
Crankpin outside diameter	40.982-41.000 mm (1.6135-1.6142 in.)	–
Crankpin width	22.10-22.15mm (0.870-0.872 in.)	
Crankshaft thrust clearance		
at primary drive gear	0.05-0.10 mm (0.002-0.004 in.)	–
Main bearing journal diameter	47.965-47.980 mm (1.8884-1.8890 in.)	–
Main bearing oil clearance	0.020-0.050 mm (0.0008-0.0020 in.)	0.080 mm (0.0031 in.)
Runout	–	0.05 mm (0.002 in.)
Secondary gear backlash	0.05-0.32 mm (0.002-0.013 in.)	–

Table 2 SECONDARY DRIVEN BEVEL GEAR SHIMS*

Part No.	Thickness
24945-05A00-0A0	0.30 mm (0.012 in.)
24945-05A00-0B0	0.35 mm (0.014 in.)
24945-05A00-0C0	0.40 mm (0.016 in.)
24945-05A00-0D0	0.50 mm (0.020 in.)
24945-05A00-0E0	0.60 mm (0.024 in.)
*A shim set is available. Verify part number and thickness of individual shims.	

Table 3 SECONDARY DRIVE BEVEL GEAR SHIMS*

Part No.	Thickness
24935-38A01-030	0.30 mm (0.012 in.)
24935-38A01-035	0.35 mm (0.014 in.)
24935-38A01-040	0.40 mm (0.016 in.)
24935-38A01-050	0.50 mm (0.020 in.)
24935-38A01-060	0.60 mm (0.024 in.)
*A shim set is available. Verify part number and thickness of individual shims.	

Table 4 CRANKSHAFT SIDE CLEARANCE THRUST WASHER THICKNESS

Part No.	Thrust washer thickness
09160-48001	1.925-1.950 mm (0.0758-0.0768 in.)
09160-48002	1.950-1.975 mm (0.0768-0.0778 in.)
09160-48003	1.975-2.000 mm (0.0778-0.0787 in.)
09160-48004	2.000-2.025 mm (0.0787-0.0797 in.)
09160-48005	2.025-2.050 mm (0.0797-0.0807 in.)
09160-48006	2.050-2.075 mm (0.0807-0.0817 in.)
09160-48007	2.075-2.100 mm (0.0817-0.0827 in.)
09160-48008	2.100-2.125 mm (0.0827-0.0837 in.)
09160-48009	2.125-2.150 mm (0.0837-0.0847 in.)
09160-48010	2.150-2.175 mm (0.0847-0.0857 in.)

Table 5 CONNECTING ROD BEARING SELECTION

Connecting rod inner diameter code number	Crankpin outer diameter code number		
	1	2	3
1	Green	Black	Brown
2	Black	Brown	Yellow
3	Brown	Yellow	Blue

Table 6 CONNECTING ROD BEARING INSERT COLOR AND THICKNESS

Color	Thickness
Green	1.485-1.488 mm (0.0585-0.0586 in.)
Black	1.488-1.491 mm (0.0586-0.0587 in.)
Brown	1.491-1.494 mm (0.0587-0.0588 in.)
Yellow	1.494-1.497 mm (0.0588-0.0589 in.)
Blue	1.497-1.500 mm (0.0589-0.0590 in.)

Table 7 ENGINE TORQUE SPECIFICATIONS

Item	N•m	in.-lb.	ft.-lb.
Camshaft chain tensioner guide bolt	10	88	–
Connecting rod cap nuts			
Initial	25	–	18
Final	51	–	38
Crankcase bolts			
6 mm	11	97	–
8 mm			
Initial	15	133	–
Final	22	–	16
Engine mounting bolts and nuts			
Engine mounting bracket	23	–	17
Subframe Allen bolts and nuts	50	–	37
Subframe lower crossmember bolts	25	–	18
Throughbolts and nuts	79	–	58
Oil pump mounting bolts	11	97	–
Primary drive gear bolt	95	–	70
Secondary drive gear nut	105	–	77
Secondary gear bevel gear assembly			
Allen bolts	23	–	17
Case bolts			
Initial	15	133	–
Final	22	–	16
Secondary gear housing bolts	23	–	17
Starter clutch assembly Allen bolts*	26	–	19
Transmission mainshaft bolt	65	–	48

*Apply threadlock (ThreeBond 1303 or equivalent)

CHAPTER SIX

CLUTCH AND EXTERNAL SHIFT MECHANISM

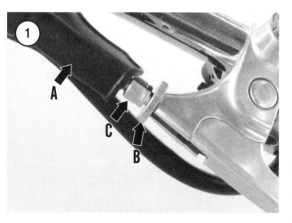

This chapter covers the clutch, clutch release mechanism and external shift mechanism. Specifications are in **Table 1** and **Table 2** at the end of this chapter.

The clutch is a wet (operates in the engine oil) multi-plate design. The clutch assembly is located on the right side of the engine. The clutch hub is attached to the transmission main shaft. The outer clutch housing is driven by the primary drive gear on the crankshaft.

Clutch release is accomplished via a pushrod/push piece assembly operating on the pressure plate. The pushrods pass through the transmission mainshaft and are activated by the clutch cable pulling on the

clutch lifter mechanism mounted in the crankcase. This system requires routine adjustment (Chapter Three) to compensate for cable stretch.

CLUTCH CABLE

Replacement

1. Slide the rubber boot (A, **Figure 1**) off the clutch hand lever adjuster.

2. At the clutch hand lever, loosen the large jam nut (B, **Figure 1**) and turn the adjuster (C) all the way in toward the clutch lever holder to allow maximum cable slack. Disconnect the cable from the clutch lever.

3. Remove the frame side cover (**Figure 2**).

4. Remove the secondary drive cover (**Figure 3**).

5. Loosen the jam nuts (A, **Figure 4**) on the lower cable housing.

6. Rotate the adjuster (B, **Figure 4**) to increase cable slack.

7. Disconnect the clutch cable end from the clutch release arm (**Figure 5**).

8. Tie a piece of heavy string onto the lower end of the old cable. Cut the string to a length that is longer than the new clutch cable.

9. Tie the other end of the string to the frame or engine component.

NOTE
It may be necessary to detach the cable clamps to extract or install the cable.

10. Remove the old clutch cable by pulling it from the top (upper cable end). Continue until the cable is removed from the frame, leaving the attached piece of string in its mounting position.

11. Untie the string from the old cable and discard the old cable.

12. Lubricate the new clutch cable as described in Chapter Three.

13. Tie the string onto the bottom end of the new clutch cable.

14. Slowly pull the string and cable to install the cable along the path of the original clutch cable. Continue until the clutch cable is correctly routed through the engine and frame. Untie and remove the string.

15. Visually check the entire length of the clutch cable as it runs through the frame and engine. Make sure there are no kinks or sharp bends. Straighten out if necessary.

16. Connect the upper cable end to the clutch lever.

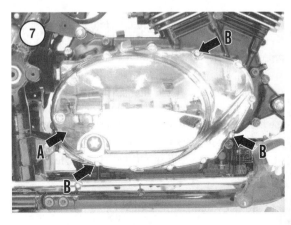

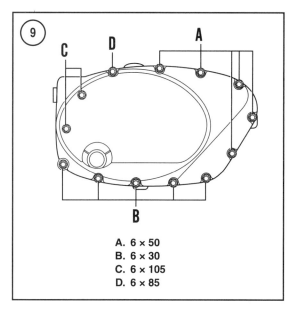

A. 6 × 50
B. 6 × 30
C. 6 × 105
D. 6 × 85

17. Reattach the lower end of the clutch cable as shown in **Figure 5**. Be sure to bend up the locking tab so the cable end is secured in the swivel fitting.
18. Adjust the clutch cable as described in Chapter Three.

CLUTCH COVER

Removal/Installation

1. Drain the engine oil as described in Chapter Three.
2. Remove the exhaust system as described in Chapter Eight or Chapter Nine.
3. Remove the frame side cover (**Figure 6**).
4. Following a crisscross pattern, loosen and then remove the bolts securing the clutch cover (A, **Figure 7**).
5. Remove the clutch cover and gasket.
6. Remove the two dowel pins (**Figure 8**) if they are loose.
7. Remove all gasket sealer residue from the crankcase and cover mating surfaces.

8. Install the two dowel pins (**Figure 8**).
9. Install a new gasket.
10. Install the clutch cover. Push the cover against the crankcase until it bottoms.
11. Note the bolt lengths in **Figure 9** and install the bolts. Three of the bolts use washers (B, **Figure 7**).

CLUTCH

Removal

Refer to **Figure 10**.
1. Remove the clutch cover as described in this chapter.
2. Following a crisscross pattern, loosen the clutch bolts (**Figure 11**) in stages.
3. Remove the bolts and washers.
4. Remove the clutch springs (A, **Figure 12**) and the pressure plate (B).
5. Remove the friction plates, steel plates, judder spring and judder spring seat.
6. Remove the thrust washer, bearing and clutch push piece (**Figure 13**).
7. If necessary, remove the clutch pushrod (**Figure 14**) from the input shaft.

CAUTION
Do not clamp the clutch holder too tight as it may damage the grooves in the clutch hub.

8. To prevent the clutch hub from turning, attach a clutch holder tool (**Figure 15**).
9. Loosen, then remove the clutch locknut (A, **Figure 16**) and washer (B).
10. Remove the clutch holder tool.
11. Remove the clutch hub (**Figure 17**).
12. Remove the thrust washer (**Figure 18**).
13. Remove the circlip (**Figure 19**) securing the oil pump driven gear.

NOTE
If the oil pump is not going to be serviced, secure a piece of duct tape over the oil pump shaft locating pin and washer to keep them in place.

14. Remove the clutch outer housing (A, **Figure 20**), oil pump drive chain (B) and oil pump driven gear (C) as an assembly.
15. Remove the needle bearing (**Figure 21**), bushing (**Figure 22**), washer (**Figure 23**) and spacer (**Figure 24**) from the transmission shaft.
16. Inspect all components as described in this section.

6

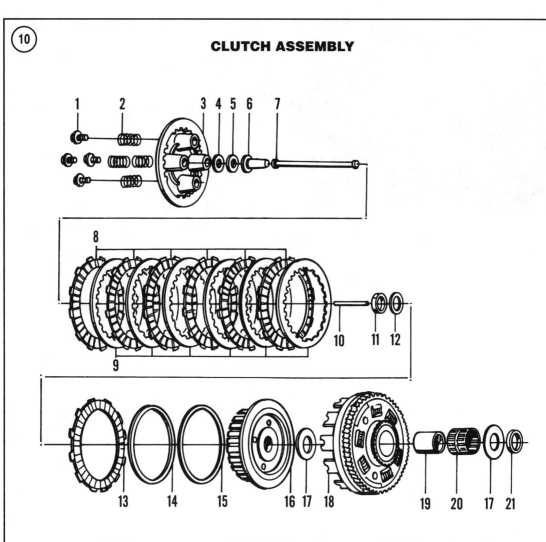

CLUTCH ASSEMBLY

1. Bolt
2. Spring
3. Pressure plate
4. Washer
5. Thrust bearing
6. Push piece
7. Pushrod (right)
8. No. 1 friction plates
9. Steel clutch plates
10. Pushrod (left)
11. Clutch nut
12. Belleville washer
13. No. 2 friction plate
14. Judder spring
15. Judder spring seat
16. Clutch hub
17. Washer
18. Outer housing
19. Bushing
20. Needle bearing
21. Spacer

Inspection

Refer to **Table 1** for clutch specifications.

1. Clean all clutch parts in petroleum-based solvent, such as a commercial solvent or kerosene, and thoroughly dry with compressed air.

2. Measure the free length of each clutch spring (**Figure 25**). Compare to the specification in **Table 1**. Replace any springs not within specification.

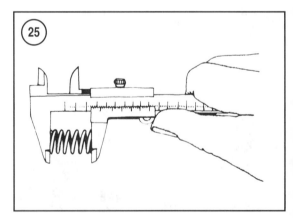

> *NOTE*
> *If any of the friction plates, steel plates or clutch springs require replacement, consider replacing all of them as a set to retain maximum clutch performance.*

> *NOTE*
> *The thickness of the No. 2 inner narrow friction plate (13, **Figure 10**) is different from all other No. 1 friction plates. Make sure to measure and record its thickness separately.*

3. Measure the thickness of each friction plate at several places around the plate as shown in **Figure 26**. Compare to the specifications in **Table 1**. Replace any friction plate not within specification.

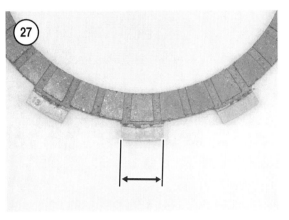

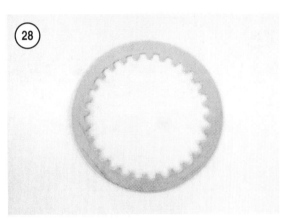

4. Measure the tab width of all tabs on each friction plate as shown in **Figure 27**. Compare to the specifications listed in **Table 1**. Replace any friction plate not within specification.

5. Check the steel clutch plates (**Figure 28**) for surface damage from heat or lack of oil. Replace any damaged plates.

6. Check the steel clutch plates for warp with a flat feeler gauge on a surface such as a piece of plate glass (**Figure 29**). Compare to the specifications in **Table 1**. Replace any plate that is warp beyond the service limit.

7. Inspect the slots (**Figure 30**) in the clutch outer housing for cracks, nicks or galling where they contact the friction plate tabs. If severe damage is evident, replace the housing.

8. Inspect the driven gear teeth (A, **Figure 31**) and oil pump drive chain sprocket teeth (B) on the clutch outer housing. Remove any small nicks with an oilstone. If damage is severe, replace the clutch outer housing.

9. Inspect the damper springs (**Figure 32**). If they are sagged or broken, replace the housing.

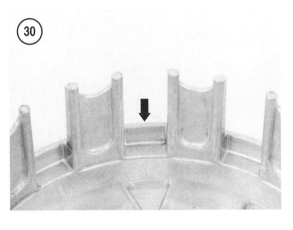

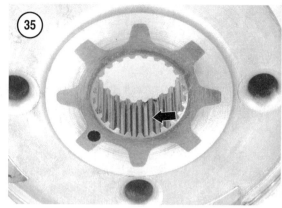

10. Inspect the outer grooves (**Figure 33**) and studs (**Figure 34**) in the clutch hub. If either show signs of wear or galling, replace the clutch hub.

11. Inspect the inner splines (**Figure 35**) in the clutch hub for damage. Remove any small nicks with an oilstone. If damage is severe, replace the clutch hub.

12. Inspect the spring cups (**Figure 36**) in the clutch pressure plate for wear or damage. Replace the clutch pressure plate if necessary.

13. Check the inner surface (C, **Figure 31**) of the clutch outer housing, where the needle bearing rides, for signs of wear or damage. Replace the clutch outer housing if necessary.

14. Check the needle bearing (A, **Figure 37**). Make sure it rotates smoothly with no signs of wear or damage. Replace if necessary.

15. Check the inner and outer surfaces of the bushing (B, **Figure 37**) for signs of wear or damage. Replace if necessary.

16. Install the bushing into the needle bearing and rotate the bushing (**Figure 38**) and check for wear. Replace either part as needed.

17. Check the push piece (**Figure 39**) for wear or damage. Replace if necessary.

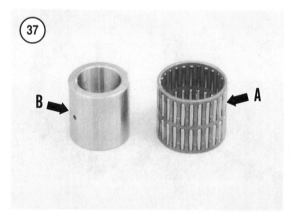

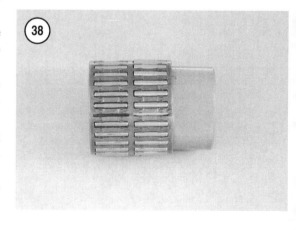

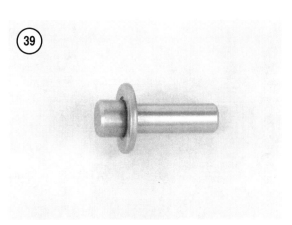

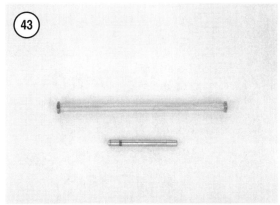

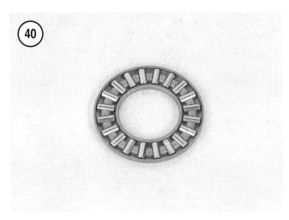

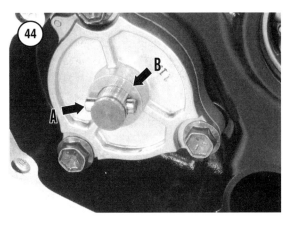

6

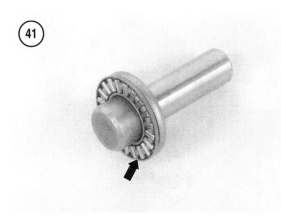

18. Check the push piece bearing (**Figure 40**). Make sure it rotates smoothly with no signs of wear or damage. Replace if necessary.

19. Install the bearing (**Figure 41**) and washer (**Figure 42**) onto the push piece and rotate them by hand. All parts should rotate smoothly. Replace any worn part.

20. Inspect the clutch right push rod and left push rod for bending (**Figure 43**). Roll them on a surface plate or piece of plate glass. Specifications for the push rods are not provided, but if either rod is bent or deformed it must be replaced.

Assembly/Installation

Refer to **Figure 10**.

1. Install the spacer (**Figure 24**), washer (**Figure 23**), and bushing (**Figure 22**) onto the transmission shaft.

2. Apply clean engine oil to the needle bearing and install the needle bearing (**Figure 21**).

3. Make sure the locating pin (A, **Figure 44**) and washer (B) are still in place on the oil pump driveshaft. If used, remove the duct tape holding the oil pump shaft locating pin and washer in place.

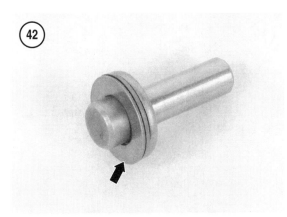

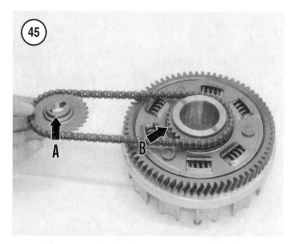

4. Assemble the oil pump driven gear, chain and clutch outer housing. Make sure the shoulder on the oil pump driven gear (A, **Figure 45**) is on the same side as the clutch chain sprocket (B).

5. Hold this assembly together and install it onto the transmission shaft as well as the oil pump driveshaft. Push the clutch outer housing down until it stops.

6. Make sure the oil pump driven gear is properly meshed with the locating pin (**Figure 46**) on the oil pump driveshaft.

7. Install the circlip (A, **Figure 19**) securing the oil pump driven gear and make sure it is properly seated.

8. Install the thrust washer (**Figure 18**).

9. Install the clutch hub (**Figure 17**).

10. Install the washer (B, **Figure 16**) so the concave side faces in.

11. Use the same special tool (**Figure 15**) set-up used in Step 8 of *Removal* in this section to hold the clutch hub.

12. Install the clutch nut (A, **Figure 16**) and tighten to 60 N•m (44 ft.-lb.).

13. Remove the special tool from the clutch hub.

14. Install the spring seat (**Figure 47**) onto the clutch hub.

15. Install the judder spring (**Figure 48**) so the concave side faces out.

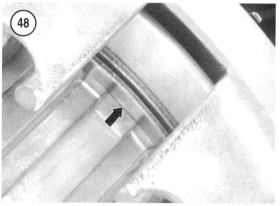

NOTE
Lubricate the contact surfaces of the friction plates and steel plates with clean engine oil prior to assembly.

16. Identify the friction plates. There is one plate (A, **Figure 49**) with a larger inner diameter (friction plate No. 2) and six plates (friction plate No. 1) with a smaller inner diameter (B).

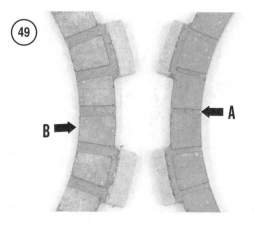

50

54

51

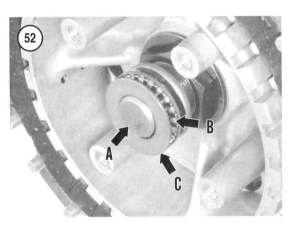

52

6

17. Install friction plate No. 2 onto the clutch hub. Friction plate No. 2 must surround the judder spring and spring seat (**Figure 50**).

18. Install a steel plate next to friction plate No. 2.

19. Install a No. 1 friction plate, then continue to install a steel plate, a friction plate and alternate them until all are installed. The last item installed is a friction plate (**Figure 51**).

20. If removed, install the right clutch pushrod (**Figure 14**) into the transmission shaft. Push it in until it bottoms against the left pushrod in the transmission shaft.

21. Install the push piece (A, **Figure 52**) into the transmission shaft.

22. Apply a light coat of clean engine oil to both sides of the washer and thrust bearing.

23. Install the thrust bearing (B, **Figure 52**) onto the push piece, then install the washer (C).

24. Install the clutch pressure plate (A, **Figure 53**).

25. Install the springs (B, **Figure 53**), washers and bolts (**Figure 54**).

26. To prevent clutch rotation when performing the next step, the following methods may be used.

   a. Place a small gear in mesh with the clutch and primary drive gears.

   b. Place a soft copper washer (copper penny) or shop cloth into mesh with the gears. This will prevent the primary drive gear from turning in the next step.

27. Using a crisscross pattern, tighten the clutch bolts (**Figure 54**) to 10 N•m (88 in.-lb.).

28. Install the clutch cover as described in this chapter.

CLUTCH RELEASE MECHANISM

Remove/Install

1. Slide the rubber boot (A, **Figure 55**) off the clutch hand lever adjuster.

53

52

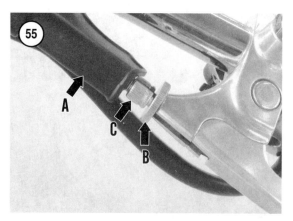

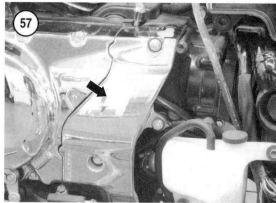

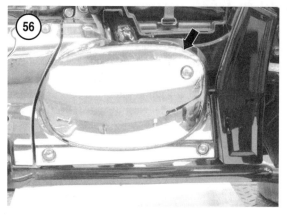

2. At the clutch hand lever, loosen the large jam nut (B, **Figure 55**) and turn the adjuster (C) all the way in toward the clutch lever holder to allow maximum cable slack. Disconnect the cable from the clutch lever.

3. Remove the side frame cover (**Figure 56**).

4. Remove the secondary drive cover (**Figure 57**).

5. Loosen the jam nuts (A, **Figure 58**) on the lower cable housing.

6. Rotate the adjuster (B, **Figure 58**) to increase cable slack.

7. Disconnect the clutch cable end from the clutch release arm (A, **Figure 59**).

8. Detach the return spring (B, **Figure 59**) from the spring bracket (C).

9. Remove the mounting bolts (D, **Figure 59**), then remove the clutch release assembly (E).

10. Operate the release mechanism and check for binding or other signs of faulty operation. Inspect the mechanism for damage. Replace if necessary.

11. Install by reversing the removal procedure. Note the following:

    a. Apply lithium multipurpose grease to the spiral splines before assembly.

    b. Loosen the stud and nut (**Figure 60**) several turns before assembly.

    c. Tighten the mounting bolts securely.

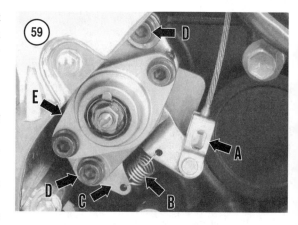

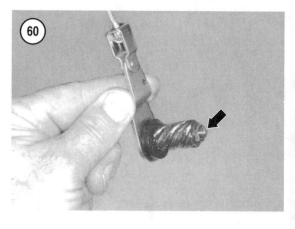

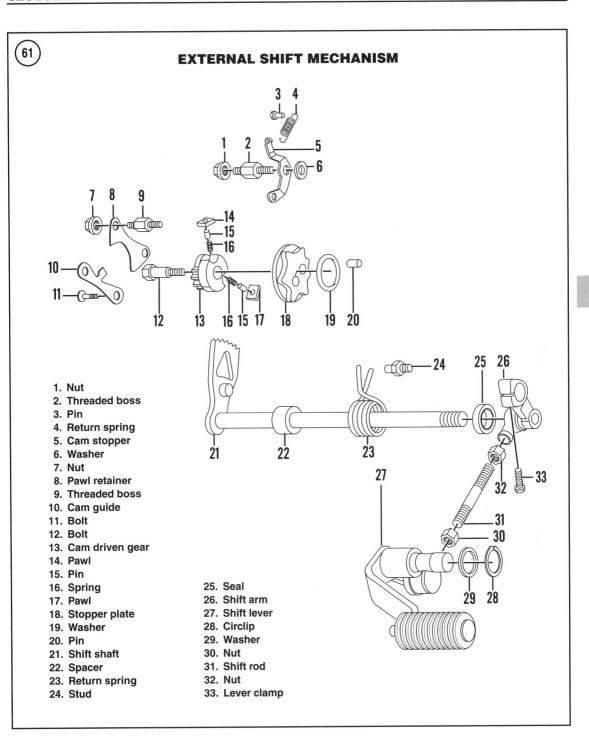

61 **EXTERNAL SHIFT MECHANISM**

1. Nut
2. Threaded boss
3. Pin
4. Return spring
5. Cam stopper
6. Washer
7. Nut
8. Pawl retainer
9. Threaded boss
10. Cam guide
11. Bolt
12. Bolt
13. Cam driven gear
14. Pawl
15. Pin
16. Spring
17. Pawl
18. Stopper plate
19. Washer
20. Pin
21. Shift shaft
22. Spacer
23. Return spring
24. Stud
25. Seal
26. Shift arm
27. Shift lever
28. Circlip
29. Washer
30. Nut
31. Shift rod
32. Nut
33. Lever clamp

d. Adjust the clutch as described in Chapter Three.

EXTERNAL SHIFT MECHANISM

The external shift mechanism is located on the same side of the crankcase as the clutch assembly. To service the internal shift mechanism (shift drum and shift forks), refer to Chapter Seven.

Removal

In this procedure the engine is shown removed and partially disassembled for clarity. It is not necessary to remove the engine from the frame for this procedure.

Refer to **Figure 61**.

1. Remove the gear shift lever clamp bolt (A, **Figure 62**), then separate the shift lever (B) from the shift shaft.

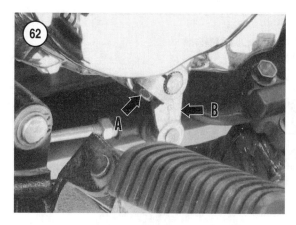

2. Remove the clutch assembly as described in this chapter.

> *CAUTION*
> *If the shift shaft is difficult to remove in Step 3, make sure it is not bent. Do not attempt to straighten the shaft as this may damage the crankcase. If necessary, use a hacksaw to cut the shaft as close to the crankcase as possible.*

3. Withdraw the shift shaft (**Figure 63**) from the crankcase.

4. Remove the bolt (**Figure 64**) securing the cam driven gear assembly.

5. Remove the nuts (A, **Figure 65**) securing the pawl retainer (B) and remove the pawl retainer.

6. Remove the screws securing the cam guide (A, **Figure 66**) and remove the cam guide.

7. Unhook the spring (B, **Figure 66**) from the stopper arm.

8. Remove the cam driven gear assembly (**Figure 67**) from the end of the shift drum. Do not lose the pawls, springs and pins in the assembly. Store these small parts in a reclosable plastic bag to avoid misplacing any parts.

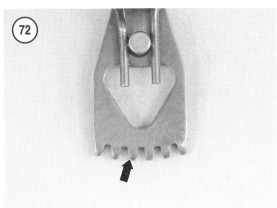

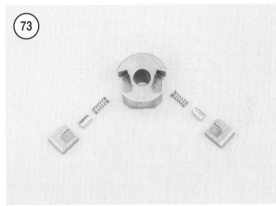

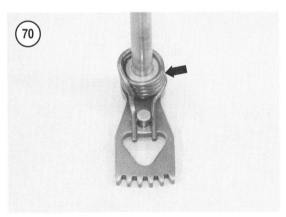

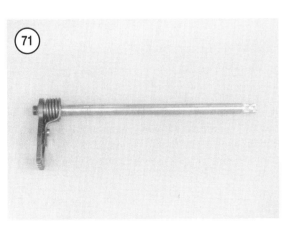

9. Remove the washer (**Figure 68**) from the end of the shift drum.

10. If necessary, remove the threaded boss (A, **Figure 69**), stopper arm (B) and washer.

Inspection

1. Inspect the return spring (**Figure 70**) on the shift shaft assembly. Replace the spring if it is broken or weak.

2. Inspect the gearshift shaft assembly (**Figure 71**) for bending, wear or other damage; replace if necessary.

3. Inspect the gear teeth (**Figure 72**) on the shift shaft assembly. Replace the shaft assembly if the teeth are broken or damaged.

4. Disassemble the cam driven gear assembly (**Figure 73**) and inspect the pawls, springs and pins for wear or damage. Replace any worn or damaged parts.

5. Inspect the ramps (**Figure 74**) on the backside of the stopper plate for wear or damage. Replace the stopper plate if necessary.

6. Inspect the cam driven gear receptacle (**Figure 75**) in the stopper plate for wear or damage. Replace the stopper plate if necessary.

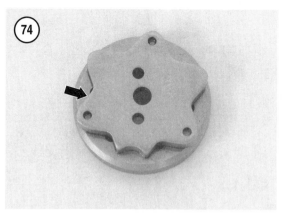

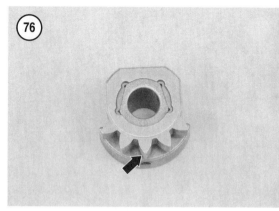

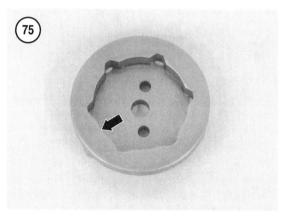

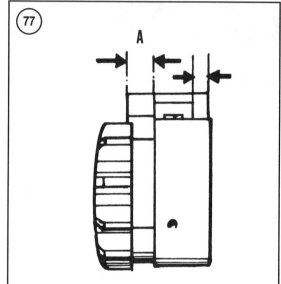

7. Inspect the gear teeth (**Figure 76**) on the cam driven gear. If broken or damaged the cam driven gear must be replaced.

8. Assemble the cam driven gear assembly as follows:

   a. Install the springs into the cam gear body.

   b. Position the pawl pins with the rounded end facing out and install them onto the springs.

   c. Install the pawls onto the pins and into the cam gear body.

   d. The pin grooves in the pawls are offset. When the pawls are installed correctly the wider shoulder (A, **Figure 77**) must face out.

   e. Hold the pawls in place and place the assembly into an aerosol spray paint can top.

Installation

1. Install the washer, stopper arm (B, **Figure 69**) and threaded boss (A). Apply threadlocker to the threads and tighten it securely.

2. Compress the spring-loaded shift pawls. Install the cam gear assembly into the receptacle of the cam driven gear (**Figure 78**).

3. Install the washer (**Figure 68**) into the end of the shift drum.

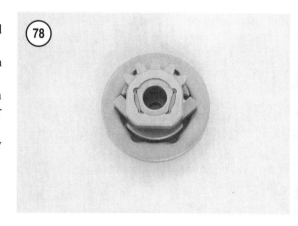

4. Align the locating holes (A, **Figure 79**) on the backside of the cam driven gear assembly with the locating pins (B) on the end of the shift drum. Install the cam driven gear assembly (**Figure 67**) onto the end of the shift drum.

5. Hook the spring (B, **Figure 66**) onto the stopper arm.

6. Install the cam guide (A, **Figure 66**) and screws. Apply threadlocker to the screw threads prior to installation. Tighten the screws securely.

7. Install the pawl retainer (B, **Figure 65**) and the nuts (A). Apply threadlocker to the threaded studs prior to installing the nuts. Tighten the nuts securely.

8. Install the bolt (**Figure 64**) securing the cam gear assembly. Apply threadlocker to the bolt threads prior to installing the bolt. Tighten the bolt securely.

9. Apply clean engine oil to the shift shaft and install the shift shaft (**Figure 63**) into the crankcase. Align the center of the cam gear with the center of the shift shaft gear (**Figure 80**), then push the shaft assembly all the way in.

10. Install the clutch assembly as described in Chapter Five.

11. Align the split on the gearshift lever joint with the alignment mark on the gearshift lever (B, **Figure 62**) and install the lever onto the gearshift shaft. Tighten the clamping bolt (A, **Figure 62**) securely.

Table 1 CLUTCH SERVICE SPECIFICATIONS

Item	Standard	Service limit
Friction disc thickness		
No. 1	2.92-3.08 mm	2.62 mm
	(0.115-0.121 in.)	(0.103 in.)
No. 2	3.42-3.58 mm	3.12 mm
	(0.135-0.141 in.)	(0.123 in.)
Friction disc tab width	15.9-16.0 mm	15.1 mm
	(0.626-0.630 in.)	(0.60 in.)
Clutch plate warp	–	0.1 mm (0.004 in.)
Clutch spring free length	49.2 mm (1.94 in.)	56.0 mm (2.20 in.)
Number of clutch plates		
Friction plates No. 1	6	
Friction plate No. 2	1	
Steel plates	6	

Table 2 CLUTCH AND GEARSHIFT MECHANISM TORQUE SPECIFICATIONS

Item	N•m	in.-lb.	ft.-lb.
Clutch nut	60	–	44
Clutch spring bolts	10	88	–

CHAPTER SEVEN

TRANSMISSION AND INTERNAL SHIFT MECHANISM

This chapter covers the transmission and internal shift mechanism. Specifications are in **Table 1** and **Table 2** at the end of this chapter.

When the clutch is engaged, the main shaft is driven by the clutch hub, which is driven by the primary crankshaft drive gear/clutch outer housing. Power transfers from the main shaft through the selected gear combination to the countershaft, which drives the engine drive sprocket.

To access the transmission and internal shift mechanism, it is necessary to remove the engine and disassemble the crankcase as described in Chapter Five.

NOTE
Suzuki terminology for the transmission shafts is different than most manufacturers. Suzuki refers to the input (main) shaft as the countershaft and the output shaft as the driveshaft. Most manufacturers, if they do not use the input/output shaft terms, refer to the input shaft as the mainshaft and the output shaft as the countershaft. Notice that this is opposite of Suzuki's parts information and keep this in mind when ordering replacement parts. In this manual, the input shaft is termed the main-shaft and the output shaft is called the countershaft.

INTERNAL SHIFT MECHANISM

Removal/Disassembly

Refer to **Figure 1.**
1. Remove the engine as described in Chapter Five.

NOTE
The neutral switch wire is part of a wire loom which contains wires for the oil pressure switch and sidestand switch.

2. Disconnect the oil pressure switch connector.
3. Remove the plastic tie strap that secures the wire loom to the neutral switch body.
4. Remove the screws (A, **Figure 2**) securing the gear position sensor/neutral switch (B) and remove the neutral switch assembly.

NOTE
The O-ring around the gear position sensor/neutral switch may remain in the cavity in the crankcase. If so, remove the O-ring.

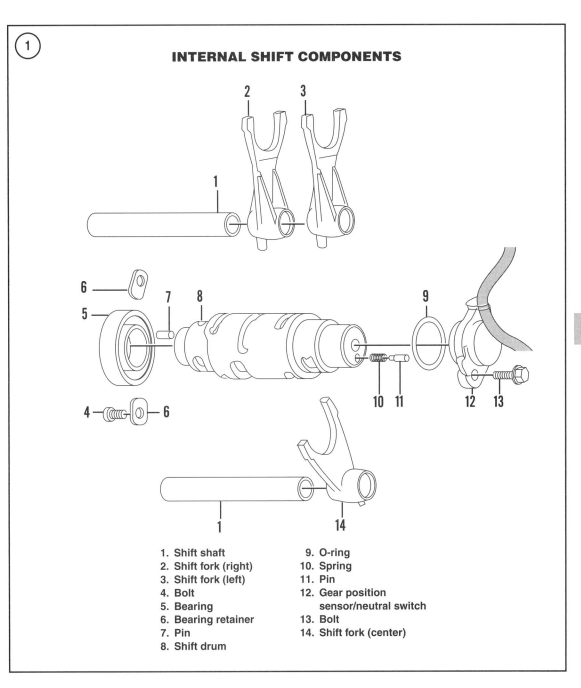

INTERNAL SHIFT COMPONENTS

1. Shift shaft
2. Shift fork (right)
3. Shift fork (left)
4. Bolt
5. Bearing
6. Bearing retainer
7. Pin
8. Shift drum
9. O-ring
10. Spring
11. Pin
12. Gear position sensor/neutral switch
13. Bolt
14. Shift fork (center)

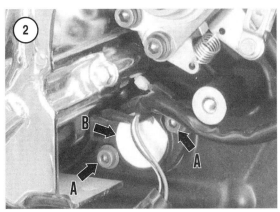

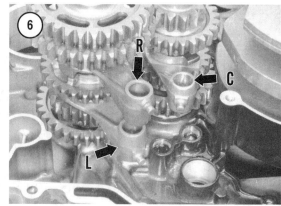

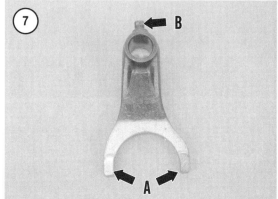

5. Remove the switch contact plunger (**Figure 3**) and spring from the end of the shift drum.

6. Split the crankcase as described in Chapter Five.

7. Hold onto the shift forks and withdraw both shift fork shafts (**Figure 4**) one at a time.

8. Move the shift forks away from the shift drum.

9. Remove the shift drum (**Figure 5**).

10. Mark the shift forks (**Figure 6**) *R*, *C* and *L* (right, center and left) so they can be reinstalled in the correct position.

11. Remove all three shift forks.

12. Thoroughly clean all parts in solvent and dry with compressed air.

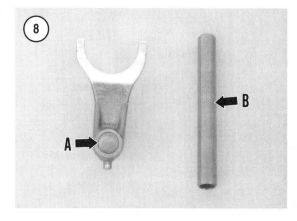

Inspection

1. Inspect each shift fork for cracks or signs of wear. Arc-shaped wear or burn marks on the fingers of the shift forks (A, **Figure 7**) indicate that the fork is contacting the gear. If the fork fingers are excessively worn, the fork must be replaced.

2. Check the bore of each shift fork (A, **Figure 8**) and the shift fork shaft (B) for burrs, wear or pitting. Replace any worn parts.

3. Install each shift fork onto the shaft (**Figure 9**) and make sure it moves freely on the shaft with no binding.

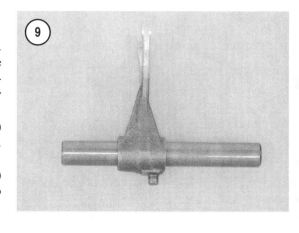

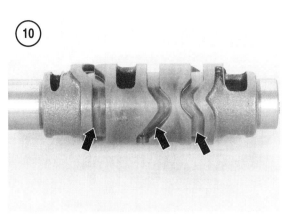

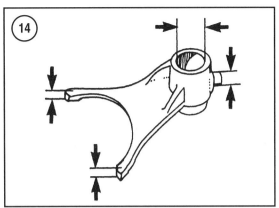

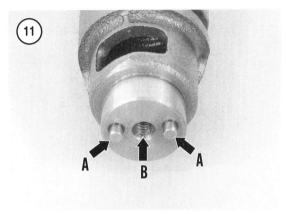

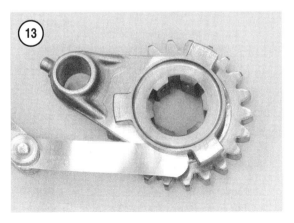

4. Check the cam follower pins (B, **Figure 7**) on each shift fork for wear or damage. The pin should ride easily along the corresponding groove in the shift drum. Replace the shift fork(s) as necessary.

5. Roll the shift shaft on a flat surface, such as a piece of plate glass, and check for any bends. If the shaft is bent, replace it.

6. Check the grooves in the shift drum (**Figure 10**) for wear or roughness. If any of the groove profiles have excessive wear or damage, replace the shift drum.

7. Inspect the cam gear locating pins (A, **Figure 11**) and threaded hole (B) in the end of the shift drum for wear or damage. Replace the shift drum if necessary.

8. Check the gear position sensor/neutral switch contact plunger and spring for wear or damage. If the spring has sagged, replace it.

9. Check the shift drum bearing (**Figure 12**). Make sure it operates smoothly with no signs of wear or damage. If damaged, replace as described in Chapter Five.

10. Inspect the shift fork-to-gear clearance as follows:

    a. Install each shift fork into its respective gear. Use a flat feeler gauge and measure the clearance between the fork and the gear as shown in **Figure 13**. Compare to the specifications in **Table 2**.

    b. If the clearance is greater than the specification, measure the width of the shift fork fingers (**Figure 14**). Replace the shift fork(s) if worn beyond the service limit in **Table 2**.

    c. If the shift fork finger width is within tolerance, measure the shift fork groove width in the gears. Compare to the specification in **Table 2**. Replace the gear(s) if the groove is worn beyond specification.

Assembly/Installation

1. Apply a light coat of clean engine oil to the shift fork shafts, the inside bores of the shift forks, the shift drum bearing surfaces and to the bearings in the crankcase.

2. Install all three shift forks (A, **Figure 15**) into their respective gears. Note the orientation of the shift fork pins (B, **Figure 15**).

3. Move the shift forks out to allow room for the installation of the shift drum.

NOTE
After installing the shift drum, make sure it rotates smoothly with no binding.

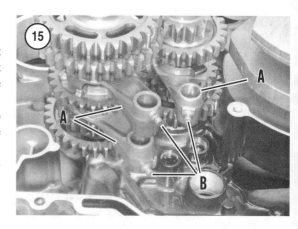

4. Install the shift drum (**Figure 5**) and push it down until it stops.

5. Move the shift forks into place in the shift drum. Make sure the guide pin on each fork is indexed into its respective groove (**Figure 16**) in the shift drum.

6. Install the shift shaft all the way through the *L* and *R* shift forks. Push it down until it bottoms.

7. Install the other shift shaft all the way through the *C* shift fork. Push it down until it bottoms.

8. Make sure the shift fork guide pins are correctly meshed with the grooves in the shift drum (**Figure 16**).

9. Assemble the crankcase as described in Chapter Five.

10. Install the gear position sensor/neutral switch contact spring and plunger (A, **Figure 17**) into the end of the shift drum. Make sure they are completely seated.

11. Apply a light coat of clean engine oil to the gear position sensor/neutral switch O-ring and install it into the groove (B, **Figure 17**) in the crankcase. Make sure it is seated correctly.

12. Install the gear position sensor/neutral switch (B, **Figure 2**), the electrical wire clamp and screws (A). Tighten the screws securely.

13. Install the engine as described in Chapter Five.

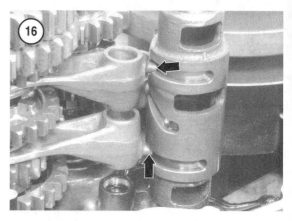

TRANSMISSION

Removal/Installation

1. Remove the internal shift mechanism as described in this chapter.

2. Remove the reduction gear (A, **Figure 18**) and bushing from the secondary bevel drive gear assembly.

NOTE
Prior to performing Step 3, make sure the bolt and washer were removed from the right end of the mainshaft during crankcase disassembly.

NOTE
Due to the extremely tight fit of the countershaft in the bearing, it may be necessary to gently pry underneath the lower gear to dislodge the countershaft from the bearing.

3. Remove the countershaft assembly (A, **Figure 19**) and mainshaft assembly (B) from the left crankcase as shown in **Figure 20**.

4. Inspect the transmission shaft assemblies as described in *Preliminary Inspection* in this section.

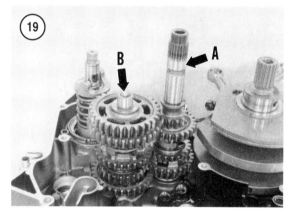

NOTE
Prior to installation, coat all bearing surfaces with assembly oil.

5. To install the transmission, assemble the countershaft and mainshaft assemblies so all gears are meshed (**Figure 20**).

6. Install the transmission into the left crankshaft (**Figure 19**). It may be necessary to gently tap the inner end of the countershaft (A, **Figure 19**) so it will pass through the bearing in the crankcase .

7. Install the reduction gear (A, **Figure 18**) and bushing onto the secondary bevel drive gear assembly.

NOTE
To determine if the countershaft is fully bottomed in the bearing, note the height of the upper gear on the countershaft versus the height of the reduction gear. The countershaft gear must be below the reduction gear (B, Figure 18).

8. After both transmission assemblies are installed, perform the following:
   a. Shift both shafts into neutral. Hold onto the mainshaft and rotate the countershaft. The countershaft should rotate freely. If it does not, shift the gear that is engaged so that both shafts are in neutral.
   b. Rotate both shaft assemblies by hand. Make sure there is no binding.

9. Reassemble the crankcase as described in Chapter Five.

Preliminary Inspection

1. Clean and inspect the assemblies prior to disassembling them. Place the assembled shaft into a large can or plastic bucket and thoroughly clean the assembly with a petroleum-based solvent, such as kerosene, and a stiff brush. Dry the assembly with compressed air or let it sit on rags to drip dry. Do this for both shaft assemblies.

2. Inspect the components for excessive wear. Check the gear teeth for chips, burrs or pitting. Smooth out minor damage with an oilstone. Replace any components with damage that cannot be repaired.

NOTE
Replace defective gears and their mating gear on the other shaft as well, even though it may not show as much wear or damage.

3. Carefully check the engagement dogs. If any are chipped, worn, rounded or missing, replace the damaged gear.

4. Rotate the transmission bearings (**Figure 21**) by hand. Check for roughness, noise and radial play. Replace any bearing that is suspect.

5. If the transmission shafts are satisfactory and do not need to be disassembled, apply assembly oil or engine oil to all components and reinstall them into the crankcase as described in this section.

NOTE
If disassembling a used, high-mileage transmission for the first time, pay particular attention to any additional shims not shown in the illustrations or photo-

7

graphs. To compensate for wear, additional shims may have been installed during a previous repair. If the transmission is being reassembled with the old parts, install these shims in their original locations because the shims will have a wear pattern. If new parts are being used, discard the additional shims.

Transmission Service

1. Parts with two different sides, such as gears, snap rings and shift forks, can be installed backward. To maintain the correct alignment and position of the parts during disassembly, store each part in order and in a divided container, such as an egg tray.

2. The snap rings are a tight fit on the transmission shafts and will bend and twist during removal. Install new snap rings during transmission assembly.

3. To avoid bending and twisting the new snap rings during installation, use the following installation technique:

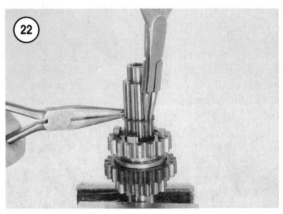

   a. Open the new snap ring with a pair of snap ring pliers while holding the back of the snap ring with a pair of pliers (**Figure 22**).

   b. Slide the snap ring down the shaft and seat it in the correct transmission groove. Make sure the snap ring seats in the groove completely.

4. When installing snap rings, align the snap ring opening with the shaft groove as shown in **Figure 23**.

5. Snap rings and flat washers have one sharp edge and one rounded edge (**Figure 24**). Install the snap rings with the sharp edge facing away from the gear producing the thrust.

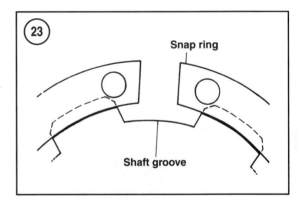

Mainshaft Disassembly/Inspection

Refer to **Figure 25**.

1. Clean the mainshaft assembly as described in *Preliminary Inspection* in this section.

2. Slide off the reduction gear.

3. Slide off the first gear and first gear bushing.

4. Slide off the splined washer and remove the circlip.

5. Slide off the fourth gear.

6. Remove the circlip and slide off the splined washer.

7. Slide off the third gear and third gear bushing.

8. From the other end of the shaft, remove the washer.

9. Slide off the second gear and second gear bushing.

10. Slide off the fifth gear.

11. Slide off the splined lockwasher.

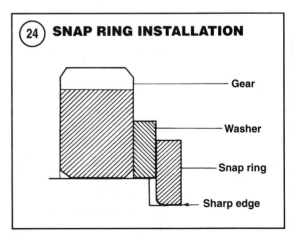

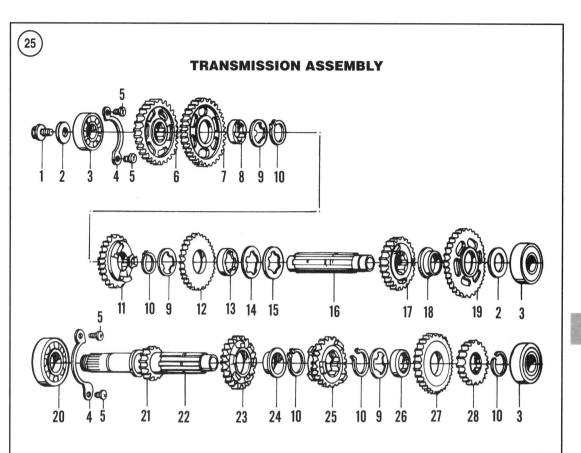

TRANSMISSION ASSEMBLY

1. Bolt
2. Washer
3. Bearing
4. Bearing retainer
5. Bolt
6. Reduction gear
7. Mainshaft first gear
8. Mainshaft first gear bushing
9. Splined washer
10. Snap rings
11. Mainshaft fourth gear
12. Mainshaft third gear
13. Mainshaft third gear bushing
14. Splined washer
15. Splined lockwasher
16. Mainshaft
17. Mainshaft fifth gear
18. Mainshaft second gear bushing
19. Mainshaft second gear
20. Bearing
21. Countershaft first gear
22. Countershaft
23. Countershaft fourth gear
24. Countershaft fourth gear bushing
25. Countershaft third gear
26. Countershaft fifth gear bushing
27. Countershaft fifth gear
28. Countershaft second gear

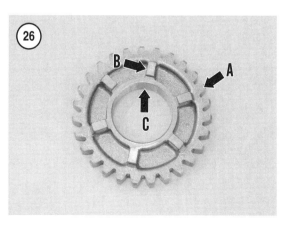

12. Rotate the splined washer in either direction to disengage the tangs from the grooves on the transmission shaft. Slide off the splined washer.

13. Check each gear for excessive wear, burrs, pitting, or chipped or missing teeth (A, **Figure 26**). Make sure the dogs (B, **Figure 26**) on the gears are in good condition.

14. Check each gear bushing (A, **Figure 27**) for excessive wear, pitting or damage. Replace if necessary.

15. Check the gear bushing inner splines (B, **Figure 27**) for excessive wear or damage. Replace if necessary.

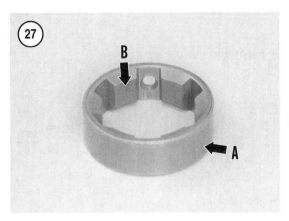

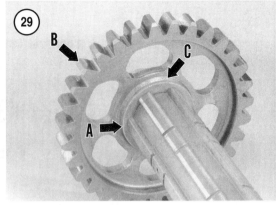

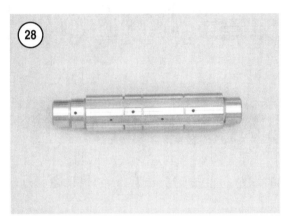

16. On gears with bushings, inspect the inner surface of the gear (C, **Figure 26**) where the bushing rides for wear, pitting or damage.

17. Inspect the splined lockwasher and splined washer for wear, cracks or damage. Replace if necessary.

18. Inspect the snap rings and splined washers for bending wear or damage. Replace if necessary.

19. Inspect the shift fork-to-gear clearance as described in *Internal Shift Mechanism* in this chapter.

NOTE
If gear replacement is necessary, it is a good idea to replace the mating gear on the countershaft even though it may not show as much wear or damage.

20. Make sure all gears and bushings slide smoothly on the mainshaft splines.

NOTE
Replace snap rings every time the transmission is disassembled to ensure proper gear alignment. Do not expand a snap ring more than necessary to slide it over the shaft.

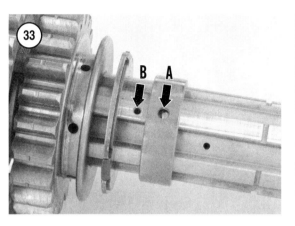

7

21. Inspect the splines and snap ring grooves (**Figure 28**) on the mainshaft. If any are damaged, replace the shaft.

Mainshaft Assembly

1. Apply a light coat of clean engine oil to all sliding surfaces.

2. Install the bushing (A, **Figure 29**) and second gear (B) onto the mainshaft. The raised hub of the gear must contact the flange of the bushing (C, **Figure 29**).

3. Install the fifth gear (**Figure 30**) so the dogs face the second gear.

4. Install the splined washer (**Figure 31**). Rotate the splined washer in either direction to engage the tangs into the mainshaft groove.

5. Install the splined lockwasher (**Figure 32**). Push it on so the tangs fit into the notches on the splined washer and lock the washer into place. Make sure the splined washer and splined lockwasher fit properly in the shaft groove.

6. Align the oil hole in the third gear bushing (A, **Figure 33**) with the transmission shaft oil hole (B) and slide on the bushing. This alignment is necessary for proper gear lubrication.

7. Slide on the third gear (**Figure 34**) so the dogs are inward.

8. Install the splined washer (**Figure 35**) and install the snap ring (**Figure 36**). Make sure the snap ring is seated correctly in the mainshaft groove.

9. Install the fourth gear with the shift fork groove going on first (**Figure 37**).

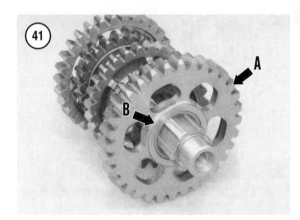

10. Install the snap ring (**Figure 38**) and slide on the splined washer (**Figure 39**).

11. Align the oil hole in the first gear bushing (A, **Figure 40**) with the transmission shaft oil hole (B) and slide on the bushing. This alignment is necessary for proper gear lubrication.

12. Install the first gear (A, **Figure 41**) so the side with the extended hub (B) is toward the end of the shaft.

13. Install the washer (A, **Figure 42**) against the second gear (B) and bushing.

14. Refer to **Figure 43** for correct placement of all gears. Make sure all snap rings are correctly seated in the mainshaft grooves.

15. Make sure each gear engages the adjoining gear properly, where applicable.

Countershaft Disassembly/Inspection

Refer to **Figure 25**.

1. Clean the countershaft assembly as described in *Preliminary Inspection* in this section.

2. Remove the snap ring and slide off the second gear.

3. Slide off the fifth gear and the fifth gear bushing.

4. Slide off the splined washer and remove the snap ring.

5. Slide off the third gear.

6. Remove the snap ring.

7. Slide off the fourth gear and fourth gear bushing.

8. Check each gear for excessive wear, burrs, pitting, chipped teeth or missing teeth (A, **Figure 26**). Make sure the dogs (B, **Figure 26**) on the gears are in good condition.

9. Check each gear bushing (A, **Figure 27**) for excessive wear, pitting or damage.

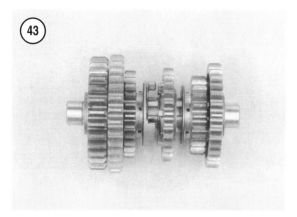

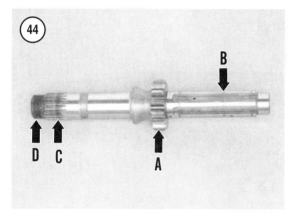

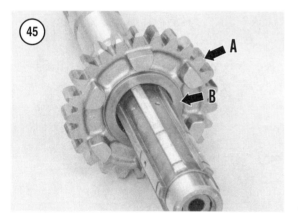

NOTE
If gear replacement is necessary, it is a good idea to replace the mating gear on the mainshaft even though it may not show as much wear or damage.

NOTE
*The first gear (A, **Figure 44**) is part of the countershaft. If the gear is defective, the countershaft must be replaced.*

15. Make sure that all gears slide smoothly on the countershaft splines.

NOTE
Replace snap rings every time the transmission is disassembled to ensure proper gear alignment. Do not expand a snap ring more than necessary to slide it over the shaft.

16. Inspect the splines and snap ring grooves (B, **Figure 44**) of the countershaft. If any are damaged, the shaft must be replaced.
17. Inspect the clutch hub splines (C, **Figure 44**) and clutch nut threads (D) of the countershaft. If any splines are damaged, the shaft must be replaced. If the threads have burrs or have minor damage, clean with a proper sized metric thread die.

Countershaft Assembly

1. Apply a light coat of clean engine oil to all sliding surfaces.
2. Slide on the fourth gear (A, **Figure 45**).
3. Position the fourth gear bushing with the flange side going on last. Slide on the bushing (B, **Figure 45**) and push it all the way into fourth gear.
4. Install the snap ring (**Figure 46**). Make sure the snap ring is correctly seated in the countershaft groove.

10. Inspect the inner splines of the bushing (B, **Figure 27**) for wear or damage. Replace if necessary.

11. On gears with bushings, inspect the inner surface of the gear (C, **Figure 26**), where the bushing rides, for wear, pitting or damage.

12. Inspect the snap rings and splined washers for bending wear or damage. Replace if necessary.

13. Inspect the splined washer for wear, cracks or damage. Replace if necessary.

14. Inspect the shift fork-to-gear clearance as described in *Internal Shift Mechanism* in this chapter.

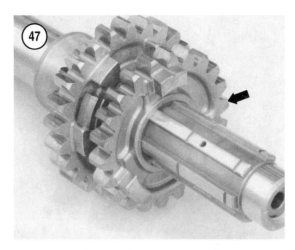

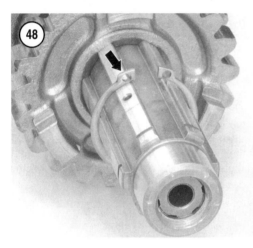

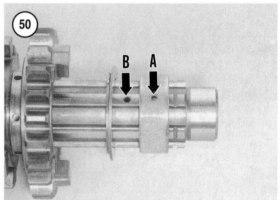

5. Position the third gear with the shift dog side going on last and slide the third gear on (**Figure 47**).

6. Install the snap ring (**Figure 48**) and the splined washer (**Figure 49**).

7. Align the oil hole in the fifth gear bushing (A, **Figure 50**) with the transmission shaft oil hole (B) and slide on the bushing. This alignment is necessary for proper gear lubrication.

8. Install the fifth gear with the shift dog side going on first (**Figure 51**).

9. Slide on the second gear (A, **Figure 52**) and install the snap ring. Make sure the snap ring (B, **Figure 52**) is correctly seated in the countershaft groove.

10. Refer to **Figure 53** for correct placement of all gears. Make sure all snap rings are correctly seated in the countershaft grooves.

11. After both transmission shafts have been assembled, mesh the two assemblies together in the correct position (**Figure 54**). Check that each gear engages properly with the adjoining gear properly, where applicable.

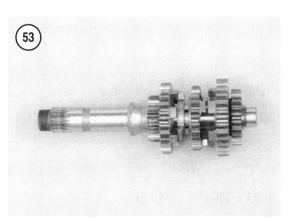

7

Table 1 TRANSMISSION SPECIFICATIONS

Transmission gear ratios	
First gear	2.461 (32/13)
Second gear	1.631 (31/19)
Third gear	1.227 (27/22)
Fourth gear	1.000 (25/25)
Fifth gear	0.814 (22/27)
Primary reduction ratio	1.690 (71/42)
Secondary reduction ratio	1.133 (17/15)

Table 2 INTERNAL SHIFT MECHANISM SERVICE SPECIFICATIONS

Item	Standard	Service limit
Shift fork-to-gear clearance	0.1-0.3 mm (0.004-0.012 in.)	0.50 mm (0.020 in.)
Shift fork groove width		
4th and 5th gears	5.50-5.60 mm (0.217-0.220 in.)	–
3rd gear	4.50-4.60 mm (0.177-0.181 in.)	–
Shift fork thickness		
4th and 5th gear (right and left)	5.30-5.40 mm (0.209-0.213 in.)	–
3rd gear (center)	4.30-4.40 mm (0.169-0.173 in.)	–

FUEL, EMISSION CONTROL AND EXHAUST SYSTEMS (2001-2004 MODELS)

This chapter covers the fuel and emission systems. Air filter service is covered in Chapter Three. Carburetor specifications are in **Tables 1-4** at the end of this chapter.

Refer to *Safety* in Chapter One before working on the fuel system.

The fuel system on 2001-2004 models consists of the fuel tank, vacuum fuel valve, carburetor, a diaphragm fuel pump and the air box.

The emission system components vary depending on the model. A crankcase breather system and a PAIR (air supply) system are used on all models. California models are equipped with an evaporative emissions control system.

CARBURETOR

Operation

The carburetor atomizes fuel and mixes it in correct proportions with air that is drawn in through the air intake. At the primary throttle opening (idle), a small amount of fuel is siphoned through the pilot jet by the incoming air. As the throttle is opened further, the air stream begins to siphon fuel through the main jet and needle jet. As the tapered needle is lifted, it occupies progressively less area of the needle jet and thus increases the effective flow capacity of the jet. At full throttle, the carburetor venturi are fully open and the needle is lifted far enough to permit the main jet to flow at full capacity.

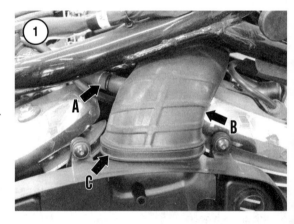

The choke circuit is a starter jet system in which the choke lever on the left handlebar opens an enrichment valve. In the open position, the slow jet discharges a stream of fuel into the carburetor venturi, enriching the mixture.

Removal/Installation

1. Disconnect the negative battery cable as described in Chapter Three.
2. Remove the air filter as described in Chapter Three.
3. Disconnect the breather hose (A, **Figure 1**) from the air intake duct (B). Loosen the clamp screw (C, **Figure 1**).
4. Loosen the air intake duct clamp screw at the carburetor (A, **Figure 2**) and detach the duct (B) from the carburetor. Either move the duct aside or remove it.

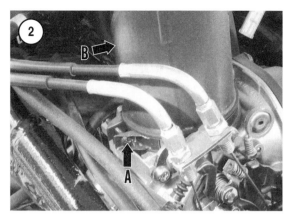

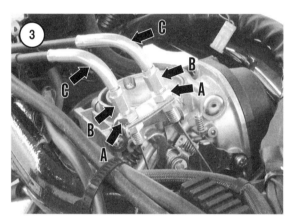

8

5. Label each throttle cable so it can be installed in its original location.

6. Loosen the jam nut (A, **Figure 3**) on each throttle cable. Rotate the adjusters (B, **Figure 3**) to increase cable slack. Detach each throttle cable (C, **Figure 3**) from the mounting bracket, then the carburetor pulley.

7. Detach the vent hose (A, **Figure 4**) from the carburetor.

8. Disconnect the throttle position (TP) sensor connector (B, **Figure 4**).

9. On non-U.S. models, disconnect the carburetor heater wire.

10. Loosen the clamp screw on the rubber intake manifold (**Figure 5**).

NOTE
Lift up, but do not remove, the carburetor assembly in Step 11 for access to the starter fitting and overflow hose.

11. Lift the carburetor off the intake manifold.

12. Unscrew the starter fitting nut (**Figure 6**) and separate the starter fitting assembly from the carburetor.

13. Loosen the clamp (**Figure 7**) and detach the overflow hose from the carburetor.

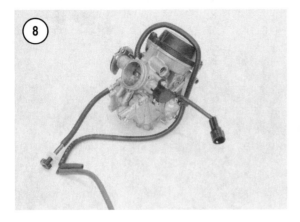

NOTE
*The idle speed control cable will re-
main attached to the carburetor and
come out with it.*

14. Remove the carburetor.

15. Cover the intake manifold with a clean lint-free cloth to prevent the entry of debris.

16. If the carburetor assembly is not going to be serviced, store it as follows:

    a. Attach a fuel line to the drain outlet on the float bowl.

    b. Hold the carburetor assembly in its normal position.

    c. Open the drain screw and drain the fuel from the float bowl into a suitable container. Dispose of the fuel properly.

    d. Carefully and slowly shake the carburetor assembly to drain out as much fuel as possible.

    e. Close the drain screw and remove the fuel hose from the float bowl fitting.

    f. Store the carburetor assembly in a clean plastic bag to avoid moisture and debris contamination.

    g. Place the carburetor assembly, right side up, in a sturdy cardboard box. Set the box in a safe place away from ignition sources.

17. Install by reversing the preceding removal steps. Note the following:

    a. Position the throttle cable adjuster on each cable in its original location. Tighten the jam nuts (A, **Figure 3**) to secure each adjuster to the mounting bracket.

    b. Adjust the throttle cables as described in Chapter Three.

Disassembly/Assembly

Refer to **Figure 9**.

CARBURETOR

1. Screw
2. Top cover
3. O-ring
4. Spring
5. Jet needle stopper
6. O-ring
7. Spring
8. Washer
9. E-ring
10. Washer
11. Jet needle
12. Washer
13. Diaphragm
14. Ring
15. Piston valve
16. Funnel
17. Screw
18. Spring
19. Screw
20. Bracket
21. Screw
22. Packing
23. Lever
24. Ring
25. Spring
26. Spring
27. Lever
28. Packing
29. E-ring
30. Spring
31. Idle speed cable
32. Cap
33. Boot
34. Holder
35. Accelerator pump
36. O-ring
37. Spring
38. Jet holder
39. Main jet
40. Pilot air jet
41. Pilot jet
42. Screen
43. O-ring
44. Fuel valve seat
45. Fuel valve
46. O-ring
47. Washer
48. Spring
49. Pilot screw
50. Plug
51. Screw
52. Pin
53. Float pivot pin

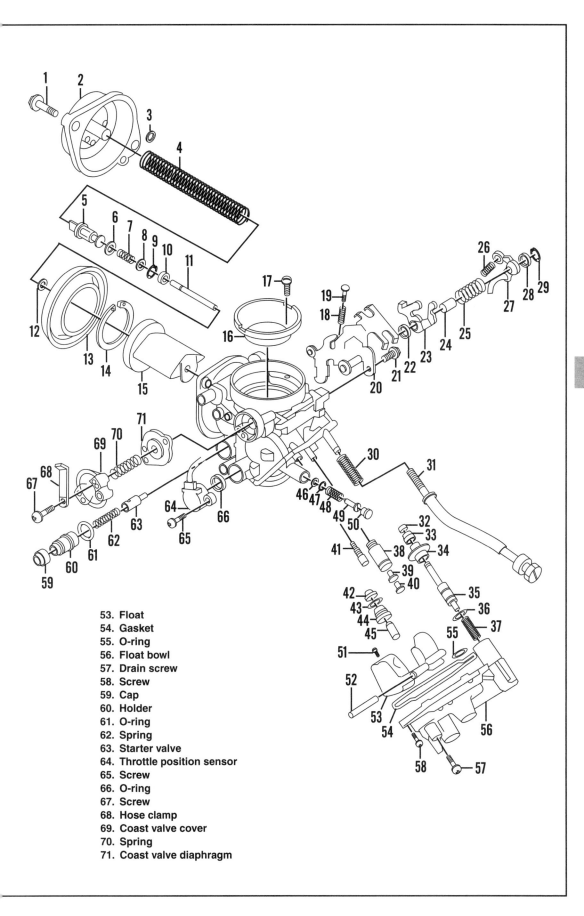

53. Float
54. Gasket
55. O-ring
56. Float bowl
57. Drain screw
58. Screw
59. Cap
60. Holder
61. O-ring
62. Spring
63. Starter valve
64. Throttle position sensor
65. Screw
66. O-ring
67. Screw
68. Hose clamp
69. Coast valve cover
70. Spring
71. Coast valve diaphragm

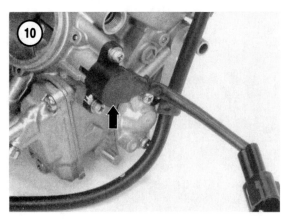

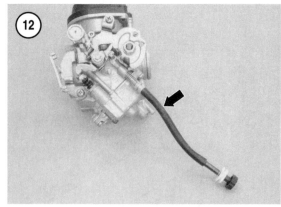

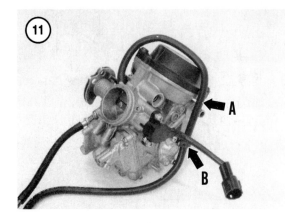

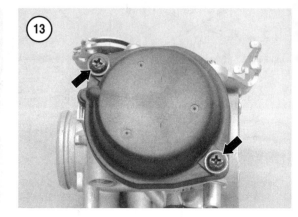

NOTE
*The throttle position (TP) sensor (**Fig-**
ure 10) is preset by the manufacturer.
Do not remove it. If removal is necessary, make alignment marks on the carburetor body and sensor so the sensor
can be installed in the **exact** same position.*

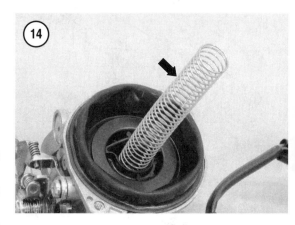

1. Remove the carburetor assembly as described in
this section.

2. Detach the vent hose (A, **Figure 11**) from the
clamp (B), then disconnect and remove the vent hose.

3. Unscrew the idle speed cable (**Figure 12**) from the
carburetor.

4. Remove the two top cover screws and the top
cover (**Figure 13**).

5. Remove the spring (**Figure 14**) from the piston
valve/diaphragm assembly.

6. Remove the piston valve/diaphragm (**Figure 15**).
Note the O-ring (**Figure 16**) that is attached to the diaphragm rim.

7. Remove the float bowl screws (A, **Figure 17**),
then remove the float bowl (B).

8. Remove the float bowl O-ring (A, **Figure 18**) and
accelerator pump passage O-ring (B).

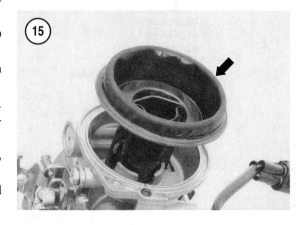

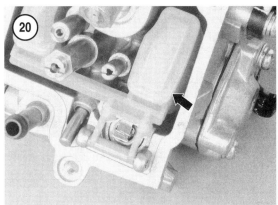

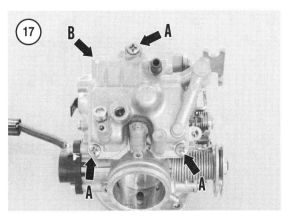

8

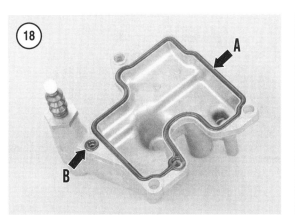

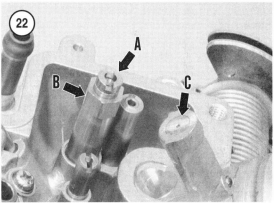

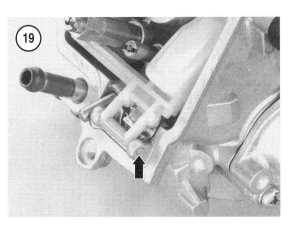

9. Use needlenose pliers and carefully remove the float pivot pin (**Figure 19**) from the float and carburetor body.

10. Carefully pull straight up and remove the float assembly (**Figure 20**). Remove the fuel valve (**Figure 21**) hanging from the float tang.

11. Unscrew and remove the main jet (A, **Figure 22**) and the main jet holder (B).

12. Unscrew and remove the pilot jet (**Figure 23**).

13. Remove the fuel valve seat retaining screw (A, **Figure 24**), then remove the fuel valve seat (B).

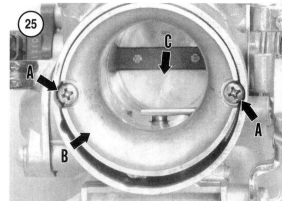

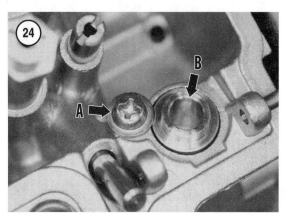

14A. On U.S. (including California) and Canadian models, the pilot screw assembly is located under a plug (C, **Figure 22**) that should not to be removed. If removal is necessary, refer to *Pilot Screw* in this chapter.

14B. On all other models, turn the pilot screw in until it *lightly seats* while counting and recording the number of turns. Reinstall the pilot screw to this same position during assembly. Unscrew and remove the pilot screw, spring, washer and O-ring.

15. To remove the pilot air jet, proceed as follows:
   a. Remove the screws (A, **Figure 25**) securing the funnel (B).
   b. Remove the funnel.
   c. Unscrew and remove the pilot air jets (**Figure 26**).

16. To disassemble the piston valve/diaphragm, perform the following:
   a. Using thin needlenose pliers, remove the stopper assembly (**Figure 27**) above the jet needle.
   b. Carefully remove the jet needle (**Figure 28**) from the piston valve.

17. Remove the coast valve cover retaining screws (A, **Figure 29**). Note the location of the hose clamp (B, **Figure 29**).

18. Remove the cover (A, **Figure 30**) and diaphragm (B).

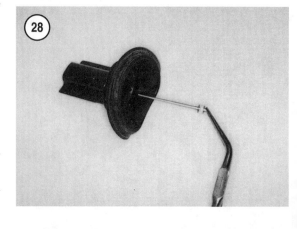

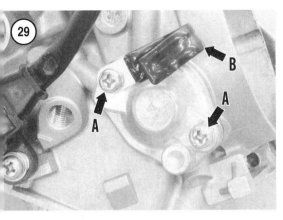

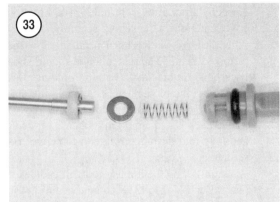

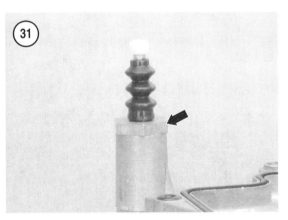

19. Unscrew and remove the accelerator pump assembly (**Figure 31**). Remove the spring inside the bore in the float bowl.

NOTE
*Further disassembly is neither necessary nor recommended. Do not remove the throttle shaft and throttle valve assemblies (C, **Figure 25**). If these parts are damaged, replace the carburetor as these items are not available separately.*

20. Clean and inspect all parts as described in this section.

21. Assemble the carburetor by reversing the disassembly steps. Note the following:

    a. Make sure the washer and E-ring (**Figure 32**) are in place and installed on the jet needle. Note the parts sequence for the jet needle and stopper assemblies in **Figure 33**.

    b. Position the jet needle stopper assembly with the spring end going in first (**Figure 27**). Push the stopper assembly down until it bottoms.

    c. Install the piston valve/diaphragm into the body, and seat it in the carburetor body. Make sure the small O-ring (**Figure 34**) is positioned

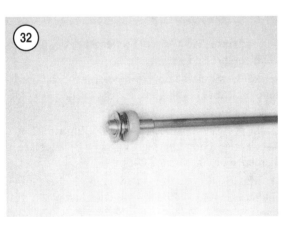

correctly around the vent hole. Install the top cover and tighten the screws securely.

d. After the top cover has been installed, move the piston valve up. The piston valve should slide back down immediately with no binding. If it binds or if the movement is sluggish, the diaphragm may have seated incorrectly or may be folded over. The diaphragm rubber is very soft and may fold during spring and top cover installation.

e. When installing the funnel, apply threadlocker (ThreeBond No. 1342 or an equivalent) to the funnel screws.

f. Install the coasting valve diaphragm so the pin (A, **Figure 35**) enters the hole (B) in the carburetor body.

g. Install the coast valve cover and diaphragm so the air holes (C, **Figure 30**) in the carburetor body, diaphragm and cover are aligned.

h. Install the accelerator pump spring (A, **Figure 36**) into the float bowl bore, then install the pump assembly (B). The piston pin (C, **Figure 36**) must fit inside the spring. Make sure to install a *new* O-ring (D, **Figure 36**).

i. Check and adjust the float height as described in this chapter.

j. After the assembly and installation are completed, adjust the carburetor as described in this chapter and in Chapter Three.

Cleaning and Inspection

> *CAUTION*
> *The carburetor body is equipped with plastic parts that cannot be removed. Do not dip the carburetor body, O-rings, float assembly, needle valve or piston valve/diaphragm into carburetor cleaner or other harsh solutions which can damage these parts.*

> *CAUTION*
> *If compressed air is not available, allow the parts to air dry or use a clean lint-free cloth. Do **not** use a paper towel to dry carburetor parts. Small paper particles could plug openings in the carburetor housing or jets.*

> *CAUTION*
> *Do **not** use wire or drill bits to clean jets. Even minor damage to the jet can alter the air/fuel mixture.*

1. Initially clean all parts in a mild petroleum-based cleaning solution. Wash the parts in hot soap and wa-

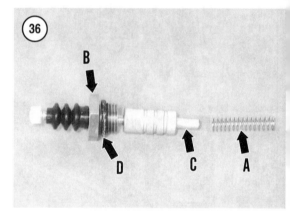

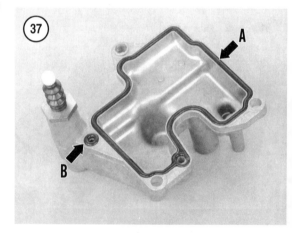

ter, and rinse them with cold water. Blow dry the parts with compressed air.

2. Allow the carburetors to dry thoroughly before assembly. Blow out the jets and the needle jet holder with compressed air.

3. Inspect the float bowl O-ring (A, **Figure 37**) and accelerator pump passage O-ring (B). Replace a hardened or deteriorated O-ring.

4. Make sure the drain screw is in good condition and does not leak. Replace the drain screw if necessary.

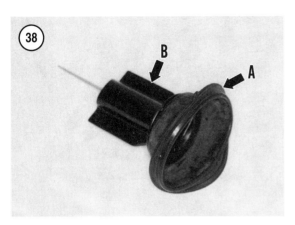

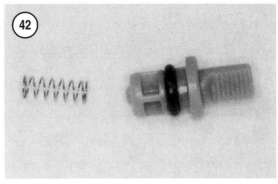

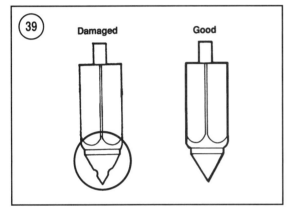

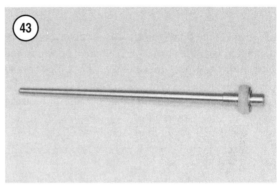

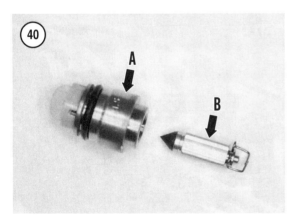

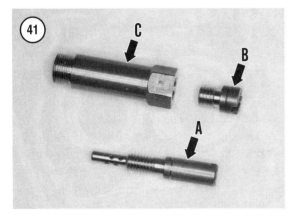

8

5. Inspect the piston valve/diaphragm (A, **Figure 38**) for cracks, deterioration or other damage. Check the piston valve sides (B, **Figure 38**) for excessive wear. Install the piston valve into the carburetor body and move it up and down in the bore. The piston valve should move smoothly with no binding or excessive play. If there is excessive play, replace the piston valve and/or carburetor body.

6. Inspect the fuel valve tapered end for steps, uneven wear or other damage (**Figure 39**). Replace if damaged.

7. Inspect the fuel valve seat (A, **Figure 40**) for steps, uneven wear or other damage. Inspect the O-ring on the fuel valve for hardness or deterioration. Replace the O-ring if necessary. Insert the fuel valve (B, **Figure 40**) and slowly move it back and forth to check for smooth operation. If either part is worn or damaged, replace both for maximum performance.

8. Inspect the pilot jet (A, **Figure 41**), main jet (B) and main jet holder (C). Make sure all holes are open and no part is worn or damaged. Replace worn parts.

9. Inspect the jet needle stopper assembly (**Figure 42**) for deterioration or damage. Inspect the O-ring for deterioration, and replace it if necessary.

10. Inspect the jet needle tapered end (**Figure 43**) for steps, uneven wear or other damage. Replace if damaged.

11. If removed, inspect the pilot screw O-ring. Replace a hardened or deteriorated O-ring.

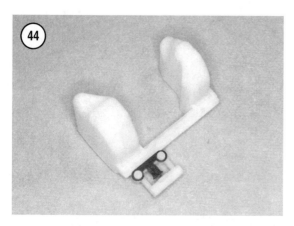

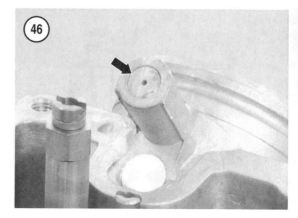

12. Inspect the float (**Figure 44**) for deterioration or damage. Place the float in a container of water and push it down. If the float sinks or if bubbles appear (indicating a leak), replace the float.

13. Make sure all openings in the carburetor housing are clear. Clean them out if they are plugged in any way, and then apply compressed air to all openings.

14. Check the top cover for cracks or damage, and replace it if necessary.

15. Make sure the throttle plate screws (A, **Figure 45**) are tight. Tighten if necessary.

16. Inspect the carburetor body for internal or external damage. If damaged, replace the carburetor assembly as the body cannot be replaced separately.

17. Move the throttle pulley (B, **Figure 45**) back and forth from stop-to-stop. The throttle lever should move smoothly and return under spring tension. If it does not move freely or if it sticks in any position, replace the carburetor housing.

18. Inspect the accelerator assembly. Replace a hardened or deteriorated O-ring (D, **Figure 36**). Inspect the accelerator pump passage O-ring on the float bowl (B, **Figure 37**). Replace a hardened or deteriorated O-ring.

PILOT SCREW

Removal/Installation
(U.S.A., California and Canada Models)

The pilot screw on these models is sealed. A plug (**Figure 46**) prevents routine adjustment. The pilot screws do not require adjustment unless the carburetors are overhauled, the pilot screws are incorrectly adjusted, or if the pilot screws require replacement. The following procedure describes how to remove and install the pilot screws.

1. Remove the float bowl.

CAUTION
Cover the carburetor to prevent debris from entering the carburetor.

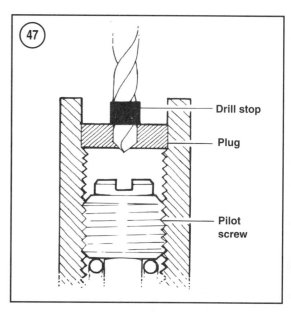

2. Set a stop 6 mm (0.23 in.) from the end of a 1/8 inch drill bit. See **Figure 47**.

3. Carefully drill a hole in the plug (**Figure 46**). Do not drill too deeply. The pilot screw will be difficult to remove if the head is damaged.

4. Screw a sheet metal screw into the plug and pull the plug from the bore.

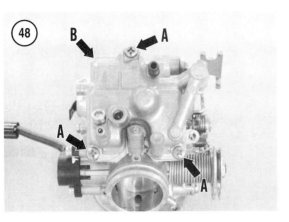

8. Inspect the O-ring and the end of the pilot screw. Replace the screw and/or O-ring if damaged or worn.

9. Install the pilot screw in the same position as noted during removal or to the specification listed in **Table 1** or **Table 2**.

10. Install a new plug by tapping it into place with a punch.

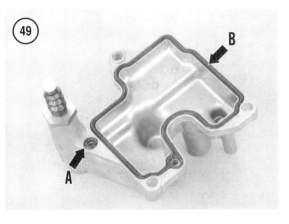

CARBURETOR FLOAT HEIGHT

Inspection/Adjustment

The needle valve and float maintain a constant fuel level in the carburetor float bowl. The carburetor assembly has to be removed and partially disassembled for this adjustment.

1. Remove the carburetor assembly as described in this chapter.

2. Remove the screws (A, **Figure 48**) securing the float bowl (B) and remove the float bowl. Do not lose the accelerator pump passage O-ring (A, **Figure 49**).

3. Hold the carburetor assembly so the float bowl mating surface is at a 45° angle to the workbench with the float arm just contacting the needle valve.

4. Measure the distance from the float bowl mating surface to the top of the float (A, **Figure 50**). The float height should be within the range specified in **Table 1** or **Table 2**.

5. If the float height is incorrect, adjust it as follows:

   a. Push out, then extract the float pivot pin (**Figure 51**) from the float and carburetor body.

   b. Carefully pull straight up and remove the float assembly. Do not lose the fuel valve (**Figure 52**) hanging on the float tang.

NOTE
Decreasing the float height raises the fuel level. Increasing the float height lowers the fuel level.

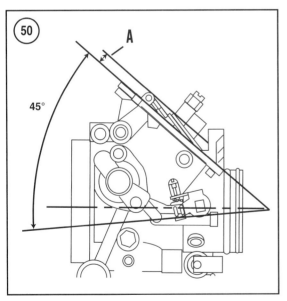

5. Screw the pilot screw in until it *lightly seats* while counting the number of turns. Record this number so the pilot screw can be reinstalled to the same position.

6. Remove the pilot screw, spring, washer and O-ring from the carburetor body.

7. Repeat for the other carburetor. Make sure to keep each carburetor's parts separate.

   c. Carefully bend the float tang (**Figure 53**).

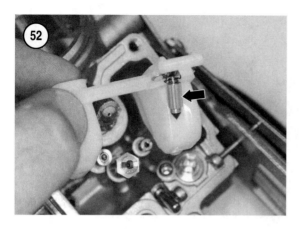

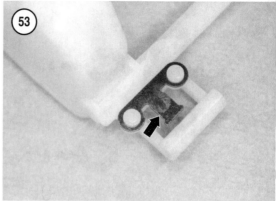

d. Install the fuel valve onto the float tang and carefully install the float assembly straight down and into place on the carburetor body.

e. Install the float pivot pin (**Figure 51**) and push it in until it is seated correctly.

6. Make sure the O-ring gasket is in place and correctly seats in the float bowl.

7. Install the float bowl and screws.

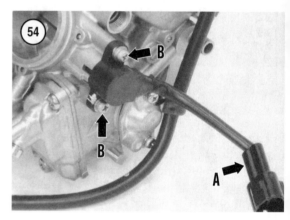

THROTTLE POSITION (TP) SENSOR

Inspection/Adjustment

1. Remove the carburetor as described in this chapter.

2. With the throttle lever fully closed, measure the resistance between the two terminals of the connector (A, **Figure 54**) as shown in **Figure 55**. If the measured value does not match the specification in **Table 3**, check for improper installation or a faulty sensor.

3. With the throttle lever in the wide open position, measure the wide open resistance across the two terminals shown in **Figure 56**. The measured value should be within the range in **Table 3**. If not, relocate the sensor as follows:

a. Loosen the TP sensor screws (B, **Figure 54**)

b. Slightly rotate the sensor. Repeat Step 3.

c. Tighten the TP sensor screws.

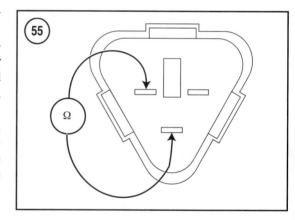

CARBURETOR HEATER (U.K. MODELS)

Removal/Installation

1. Remove the airbox as described in this chapter.

2. Disconnect the electrical lead from the carburetor heater on the bottom of the float bowl.

3. Unscrew and remove the carburetor heater.

4. Installation is the reverse of removal. Note the following:

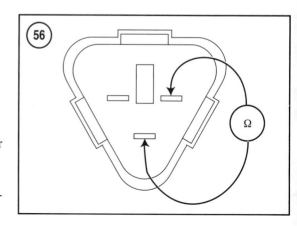

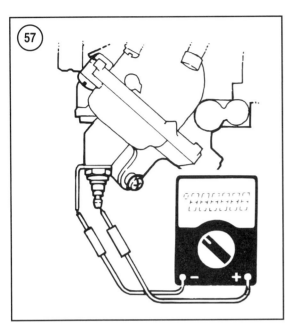

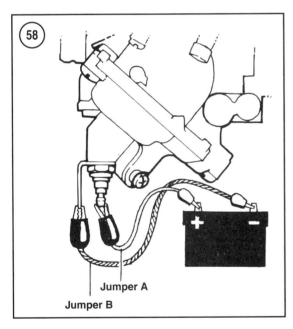

Jumper A

Jumper B

a. Apply thermo grease (Suzuki part No. 99000-59029) to the tip of the carburetor heater.

b. Tighten the carburetor heater to 3.0 N•m (27 in.-lb.).

Heater Inspection

1. Remove the airbox as described in this chapter.

2. Disconnect the electrical lead from the carburetor heater on the bottom of the float bowl.

3. Check the resistance of the heater coil as follows:

a. Connect the negative test lead of an ohmmeter to the spade connector on the heater, and connect the positive test lead to the heater body as shown in **Figure 57**.

b. Replace the heater if the resistance is outside the range specified in **Table 3**.

> *WARNING*
> *Electrical arcing may occur when connecting the jumpers in the following test. Connect the jumpers in the described order so any arcing takes place away from the carburetors.*

4. Refer to **Figure 58**. Use a battery to check the carburetor heater operation as follows:

a. Connect one end of jumper A to the battery positive terminal, and then connect the other end of jumper A to the carburetor body.

b. Connect one end of jumper B to the spade connector on the carburetor heater, and then connect the other end of jumper B to the battery negative terminal.

> *WARNING*
> *Do not touch the carburetor heater directly. It is hot.*

c. After 5 minutes, check the temperature of the float bowl by hand. It should be warm. Replace the carburetor heater if the float bowl does not heat up.

d. Disconnect the jumper B from the negative battery terminal and then from the carburetor heater. Then disconnect jumper A.

Thermoswitch Inspection

1. Unplug the thermoswitch connector from the wiring harness.

2. Remove the thermoswitch and immerse it in a pan of ice.

3. After the switch has remained in the ice for approximately 5 minutes, check the continuity between the two terminals in the thermoswitch connector **Figure 59**.

4. The chilled switch should have continuity (zero or very low resistance). Replace the switch if it is has no continuity (infinite or very high resistance).

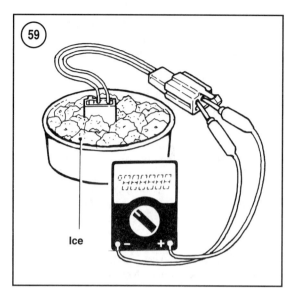

Ice

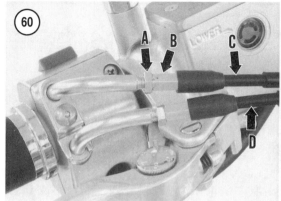

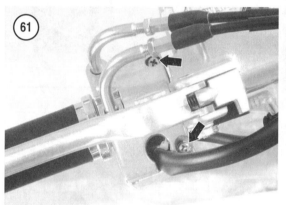

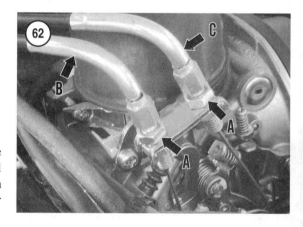

THROTTLE CABLE

Removal/Installation

> *WARNING*
> *An improperly adjusted or incorrectly routed throttle cable can cause the throttle to hang open. This could cause a crash. Do not ride the motorcycle until throttle cable operation is correct.*

> *NOTE*
> *There are two throttle cables: the pull cable (to accelerate) and the return cable (to decelerate). Label the cables before removing them to ensure correct installation.*

1. Remove the fuel tank as described in this chapter.

2. At the throttle grip, loosen the throttle cable locknut (A, **Figure 60**) and turn the adjuster (B) all the way into the switch assembly to allow maximum slack in the pull cable (C). Repeat this procedure for the return cable (D, **Figure 60**).

3. Remove the screws securing the right switch assembly together and separate the assembly halves (**Figure 61**).

4. Disconnect the throttle pull cable and the return cable from the throttle grip pulley.

5. At the carburetor loosen both jam nuts (A, **Figure 62**) securing the throttle cables to the mounting bracket.

6. Disconnect the pull cable (B, **Figure 62**) from the throttle pulley on the carburetor, then disconnect the return cable (C). Disconnect each throttle cable from the bracket on the carburetor assembly.

7. Disconnect the throttle cable from any clips and/or cable ties that secure it to the frame.

8. Note how the cable is routed through the frame, and then remove it.

9. Lubricate the new cable as described in Chapter Three. Route the new cable along the same path noted in Step 8.

10. Reverse Steps 1-7 to install the new cables. Note the following:

   a. Connect the throttle return cable, then the pull cable onto the throttle grip and switch housing.

   b. Align the locating pin (A, **Figure 63**) with the hole in the handlebar (B) and install the switch onto the handlebar. Tighten the screws securely.

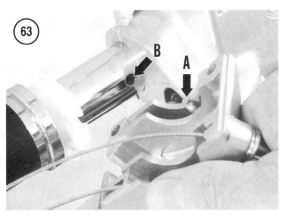

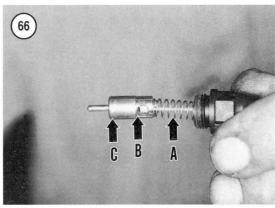

e. At the carburetor assembly, rotate the adjuster on each cable so the adjuster is at a midpoint position. Tighten the jam nuts securing each throttle cable to the mounting bracket.

f. Adjust the throttle cables as described in Chapter Three.

g. Start the engine and let it idle. Turn the handlebar from side to side and listen to the engine speed. Make sure the idle speed does not increase. If it does, the throttle cables are adjusted incorrectly or the throttle cable(s) is improperly routed. Find and correct the source of the problem before riding.

STARTER (CHOKE) CABLE

Removal/Installation

1. Remove the fuel tank as described in this chapter.

2. Partially remove the carburetor assembly to gain access to the starter cable as described in this chapter.

3. Lift up the carburetor assembly, then unscrew the starter fitting (**Figure 64**) and separate the starter fitting assembly from the carburetor.

4. Unscrew the actuating knob retaining nut (**Figure 65**), then detach the cable from the mounting bracket.

5. Disconnect the starter cable from any clips and/or cable ties securing it to the frame.

6. Note the path the starter cable follows through the frame. The new cable must be routed along the same path.

7. To disconnect the starter choke plunger assembly from the cable perform the following:

   a. Hold onto the cable end and compress the spring (A, **Figure 66**) with one hand.

   b. Unhook the cable end (B, **Figure 66**) from the plunger and remove the plunger (C).

   c. Remove the spring (**Figure 67**) from the end of the cable.

c. Connect the throttle pull cable (B, **Figure 62**) onto the rear receptacle in the throttle pulley on the carburetor, then install the return cable (C) into the front receptacle in the throttle pulley on the carburetor.

d. Operate the throttle lever and make sure the carburetor throttle linkage is operating correctly with no binding. If operation is incorrect or there is binding, make sure the cables are attached correctly and there are no tight bends in either cable.

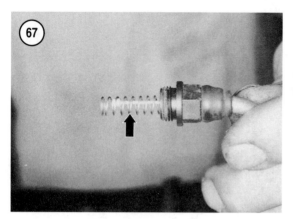

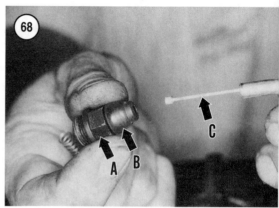

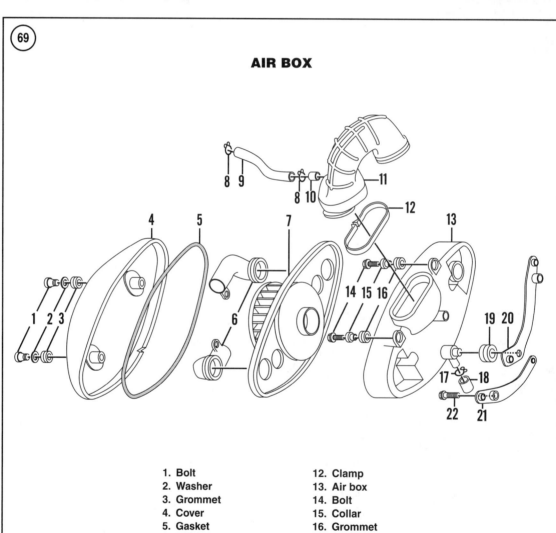

AIR BOX

1. Bolt
2. Washer
3. Grommet
4. Cover
5. Gasket
6. Intake tube
7. Air filter plate
8. Clamp
9. Breather hose
10. Tube
11. Intake duct
12. Clamp
13. Air box
14. Bolt
15. Collar
16. Grommet
17. Clamp
18. Drain cap
19. Grommet
20. Left mounting bracket
21. Right mounting bracket
22. Bolt

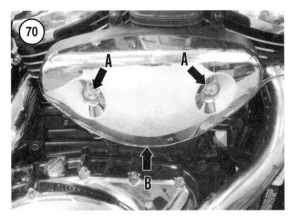

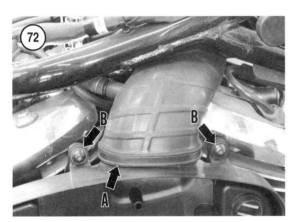

d. Remove the starter holder (A, **Figure 68**) and cap (B) from the starter cable (C).

8. Lubricate the new cable as described in Chapter Three.

9. Reverse Steps 1-7 to install the new cable. Operate the choke knob and make sure the cable operates correctly without binding. If the operation is incorrect or there is binding, carefully check that the cable is attached correctly and that there are no tight bends in the cable.

AIR BOX

The air box is located on the right side of the engine cylinders.

Removal/Installation

Refer to **Figure 69**.

1. Remove the air box cover retaining bolts (A, **Figure 70**).

> *NOTE*
> *The air filter plate assembly may remain in the cover during removal in Step 2.*

2. Remove the air box cover (B, **Figure 70**).

> *NOTE*
> *The fuel tank has been removed in the following illustrations for clarity. It is not necessary to remove the fuel tank.*

3. Remove the air filter plate (**Figure 71**).

4. Loosen the intake duct clamp (A, **Figure 72**).

5. Remove the air box mounting bolts (B, **Figure 72**).

6. Pull out the air box to release the lower mounting prong from the grommet on the mounting bracket.

7. On the backside of the air box, detach the PAIR hose from the air box (**Figure 73**) and remove the air box.

8. Inspect the air box for cracks or other damage. If any damage is noted, replace the air box to avoid the possibility of unfiltered air entering the engine.

9. Refer to Chapter Three and inspect the air filter plate as described.

10. Remove the drain plug and clean out all residue from the plug and air box. Reinstall the drain plug.

11. Make sure the air box mounting brackets (**Figure 74**) are securely attached to the cylinders.

12. Install by reversing the removal steps. Make sure all hoses are securely connected to prevent air leaks.

8

FUEL TANK

Fuel Tank Removal/Installation

> *WARNING*
> *Some fuel may spill from the fuel tank hose when performing this procedure. Because gasoline is extremely flammable and explosive, perform this procedure away from all open flames (including appliance pilot lights) and sparks. Do not smoke or allow someone who is smoking in the work area. Always work in a well-ventilated area. Wipe up any spills immediately. Refer to* **Safety** *in Chapter One.*

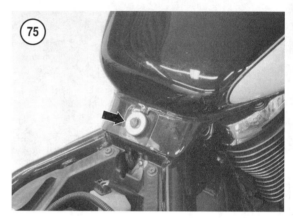

1. Remove the front seat as described in Chapter Sixteen.
2. Disconnect the negative battery cable as described in Chapter Three.
3. Refer to Chapter Ten and remove the speedometer as described.
4. Remove the fuel tank retaining bolt and washer (**Figure 75**).
5. Raise the fuel tank sufficiently for access to the fuel gauge electrical connector (**Figure 76**), then disconnect the connector.
6. Disconnect the fuel hose (A, **Figure 77**) and the vacuum hose (B) from the fuel valve (C).

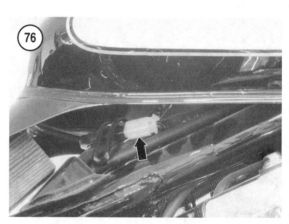

> *NOTE*
> *To drain fuel from the tank prior to removal, connect a hose to the fuel hose fitting (A,* **Figure 77***) on the fuel valve and route the hose to a suitable container. Connect a hand-held vacuum pump to the vacuum hose fitting (B,* **Figure 77***). Apply just enough vacuum to open the fuel valve so fuel will flow.*

7. Remove the idle speed control bracket retaining bolt (**Figure 78**) and separate the bracket from the fuel tank.
8. Carefully move the fuel tank rearward to disengage the front mounting cushions, then lift up the fuel tank and remove it from the frame. After the fuel tank has been inspected and serviced (if necessary), wrap the tank in a blanket or soft towels to protect the finish. Store the wrapped tank in a cardboard box, in an area where it will not be damaged.
9. Plug the end of the fuel lines and vacuum lines with golf tees to prevent the entry of debris and loss of fuel from the hose.
10. Inspect the fuel tank as described in this section.
11. Install by reversing the removal steps. Note the following:

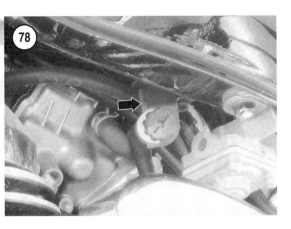

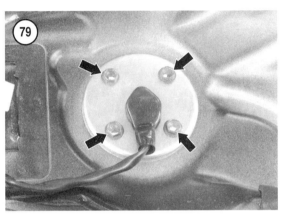

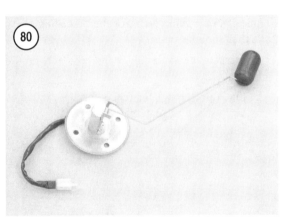

a. After installation is complete, check for fuel leaks at all hose connections after installation is completed.

b. Tighten the fuel tank mounting bolt securely.

Fuel Tank Inspection

1. Inspect the rear rubber grommet on the mounting bracket for deterioration. Replace the grommet if necessary.

2. Inspect the rubber cushions for damage or deterioration and replace if necessary.

3. Inspect the filler cap gaskets.

4. Inspect the entire fuel tank for leaks or damage. Repair or replace the fuel tank if any fuel leaks are found.

Fuel Level Sender Removal/Installation

1. Remove the fuel tank as described in this section.

2. Set the fuel tank on soft, non-scratching cloth to protect the fuel tank finish.

3. Remove the sender mounting bolts (**Figure 79**) and remove the fuel level sender (**Figure 80**) from the fuel tank.

4. Inspect the O-ring gasket (**Figure 81**) and replace if necessary.

5. Refer to *Speedometer* in Chapter Ten for testing procedure.

6. Install by reversing the removal steps. Note the following:

a. Install the sender so the triangle mark stamped on the tope fo the sender faces toward the front of the tank.

b. Tighten the mounting bolts to 10 N•m (88 in.-lb.).

c. After the fuel tank is installed, fill the tank and check for leaks.

FUEL VALVE

Removal/Installation

1. Remove the fuel tank as described in this chapter. If not already drained, drain the tank and store the fuel in a can approved for gasoline storage. Place the container in a safe place.

2. Place several old blankets or soft towels on the work bench to protect the fuel tank.

3. Turn the fuel tank upside down on the workbench.

4. Remove the bolts and washers (**Figure 82**) securing the fuel valve to the fuel tank.

5. Remove the valve and the O-ring. Discard the O-ring. Install a new O-ring during assembly.

6. Fit a new O-ring onto the valve and install the valve onto the fuel tank. Tighten the bolts securely.

7. Install the fuel tank as described in this chapter.

8. Check for fuel leaks at all hose connections after installation is completed.

Testing

1. Remove the fuel valve as described in this section.

2. Clean the fuel valve to remove any gasoline in the fuel valve. Allow the fuel valve to dry.

3. Connect a hand-operated vacuum pump to the vacuum fitting on the fuel valve.

4. While operating the pump to create vacuum, direct low-pressure air through the fuel outlet of the fuel valve. Air should exit the fuel inlet of the fuel valve.

5. If the fuel valve does not function properly, replace the fuel valve.

FUEL PUMP

All models are equipped with a diaphragm fuel pump (A, **Figure 83**) mounted on the center of the frame. Pressure pulses in the crankcase operate the fuel pump. Fuel from the fuel tank is routed to the fuel pump, which directs fuel to the carburetors. A relief valve inside the fuel pump stops output flow when the fuel level in the carburetor float bowl forces the fuel valve to close.

Removal/Installation

> *WARNING*
> *Some fuel may spill from the hoses and fuel pump when performing this procedure. Because gasoline is extremely flammable and explosive, perform this procedure away from all open flames (including appliance pilot lights) and sparks. Do not smoke or allow someone who is smoking in the work area. Always work in a well-ventilated area. Wipe up any spills immediately. Refer to Safety in Chapter One.*

1. Remove the battery box.

2. Detach the inlet fuel hose (B, **Figure 83**), outlet fuel hose (C) and vacuum hose (D) from the fuel pump. Plug the hoses to prevent fuel leaks or contamination.

3. Remove the bolts holding the fuel pump to the frame and remove the fuel pump.

4. Replace the hose clamps as necessary.

5. Installation is the reverse of the preceding steps. Note the following:

    a. Tighten the mounting bolts to 10 N•m (88 in.-lb.).

    b. Fuel flow through the fuel pump is indicated by arrows on the pump inlet and outlet.

Testing

1. Remove the battery box.

2. Detach the outlet fuel hose (C, **Figure 83**) from the fuel pump.

3. Connect a suitable hose to the outlet on the fuel pump and route the hose into a container.

4. Shift the transmission into neutral.

5. Operate the starter for a few seconds and check for fuel flowing from the fuel pump.

6. If no fuel flows from the fuel pump, check the fuel valve as described in this chapter.

7. Make sure the crankcase vacuum hose to the fuel pump is not leaking.

8. If the fuel valve and crankcase hose operate correctly, replace the fuel pump.

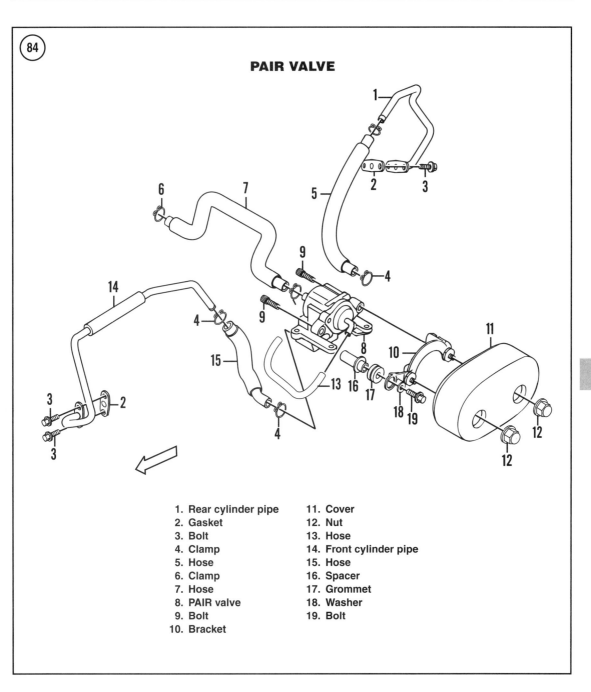

PAIR VALVE

1. Rear cylinder pipe
2. Gasket
3. Bolt
4. Clamp
5. Hose
6. Clamp
7. Hose
8. PAIR valve
9. Bolt
10. Bracket
11. Cover
12. Nut
13. Hose
14. Front cylinder pipe
15. Hose
16. Spacer
17. Grommet
18. Washer
19. Bolt

PAIR (AIR SUPPLY) SYSTEM

All models are equipped with a PAIR system that lowers emissions output by introducing air into the exhaust ports. The introduction of air raises the exhaust temperature, which consumes some of the unburned fuel in the exhaust.

The PAIR system consists of a control valve, reed valves and the vacuum and outlet hoses.

The system uses the momentary pressure variations created by the exhaust gas pulses to introduce additional air into the exhaust ports. During deceleration the control valve shuts off the airflow to the ex-haust. This prevents exhaust backfire due to the rich mixture conditions on deceleration.

Removal/Installation

Refer to **Figure 84**.

1. Remove the PAIR cover (**Figure 85**).

2. Remove the control valve mounting bracket fasteners (**Figure 86**).

3. Pull out the control valve assembly and disconnect the hoses (**Figure 87**) from the control valve.

4. Remove the control valve.

5. Reverse the removal steps to install the control valve while noting the following:

  a. The upper hose (A, **Figure 87**) connects to the air box.

  b. The left, lower hose (B, **Figure 87**) connects to the front cylinder PAIR pipe.

  c. The right, lower hose (C, **Figure 87**) connects to the rear cylinder PAIR pipe.

Inspection

1. Inspect the reed valve as follows:

  a. Remove the cover screws from the reed valve and remove the cover (**Figure 88**).

  b. Remove the reed valve from the reed-valve body.

  c. Inspect the reed valve for carbon deposits. Replace the control valve if there are deposits or the reeds are damaged.

2. Inspect the control valve as follows:

  a. Blow air into the inlet port on the bottom of the control valve (**Figure 89**).

  b. Air should flow from the two control-valve outlet ports. Replace the control valve if it does not.

  c. Connect a vacuum pump to the vacuum fitting on the top of the control valve. See **Figure 90**.

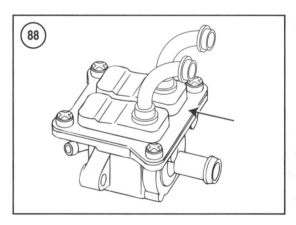

> *CAUTION*
> *The control valve could be damaged if excessive vacuum is applied. Do not exceed the specified vacuum.*

  d. Slowly apply 540 mm Hg (21.2 in. Hg) of vacuum to the control valve.

  e. Blow into the control valve inlet port. Air should not flow from the outlet ports when the applied vacuum is within the specified range. If it does, replace the control valve.

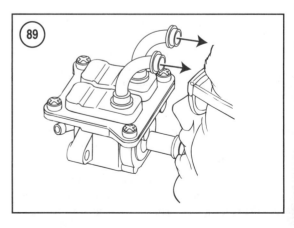

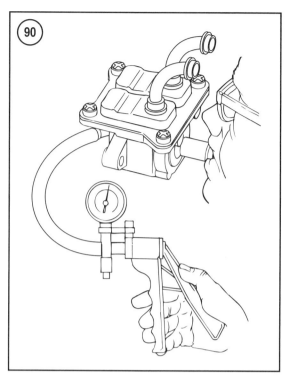

CRANKCASE BREATHER SYSTEM

All models are equipped with a closed crankcase breather system. This system routes crankcase vapors into the air intake duct, then they are drawn into the engine and burned. A breather hose is connected between the rear cylinder and the intake duct.

Inspection and Cleaning

Inspect the breather hose connected to the intake duct (**Figure 91**). Replace the hose if it is cracked or deteriorated. Make sure the hose clamps are in place and tight.

EVAPORATIVE EMISSION CONTROL SYSTEM (CALIFORNIA MODELS)

Fuel vapor from the fuel tank is routed into a charcoal canister. This vapor is stored when the engine is not running. When the engine is running these vapors are drawn through a purge control valve and into the carburetor to be burned. Refer to **Figure 92** for the location of hoses and system components.

Make sure the hoses are correctly routed and attached to the various components. Inspect the hoses and replace any if necessary. The charcoal canister and purge control valve are located on the right, rear frame downtube.

On most models, the hoses and fittings are color coded with labels or bands. If these labels or bands are deteriorated or missing, mark the hose and the fitting. Without clear identifying marks, reconnecting the hoses correctly can be difficult.

Due to the various manufacturing changes made during the years, always refer to the emission control label located on the inside of the right steering head cover.

Purge Control Valve Testing

1. Connect a hand-operated vacuum pump to the vacuum fitting as shown in **Figure 93**.

CAUTION
The control valve could be damaged if excessive vacuum is applied. Do not exceed the specified vacuum.

2. Slowly apply vacuum to the control valve until the vacuum equals 20 mm Hg (0.78 in. Hg).

3. Blow into the control valve inlet fitting (A, **Figure 93**). Air should flow from the fitting (B, **Figure 93**). If it does not, replace the control valve.

4. Plug the control valve inlet fitting (B, **Figure 93**). Blow into the control valve inlet port. Air should *not* flow from the fitting (C, **Figure 93**) when the specified vacuum is applied. If it does, replace the control valve.

5. Disconnect the vacuum pump.

6. Blow air into control valve outlet fitting (A, **Figure 94**). Air should flow from the fitting (B, **Figure 94**). If it does not, replace the control valve.

7. Plug the fitting (B, **Figure 94**) and blow into the control valve fitting (A). Air should not flow from the fitting (C, **Figure 94**). If it does, replace the control valve.

8

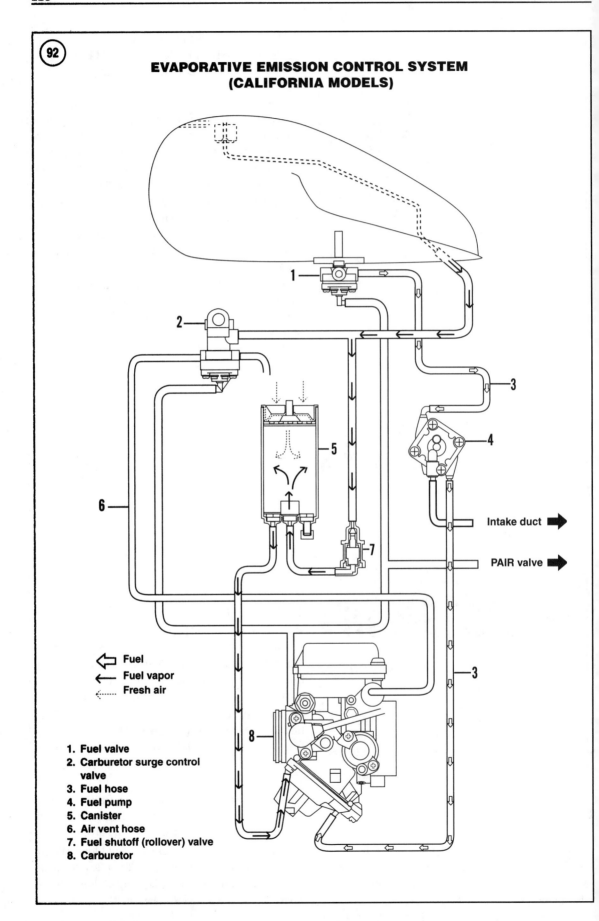

⑨②

EVAPORATIVE EMISSION CONTROL SYSTEM
(CALIFORNIA MODELS)

⇦ Fuel
← Fuel vapor
⋯ Fresh air

Intake duct ➡

PAIR valve ➡

1. Fuel valve
2. Carburetor surge control
   valve
3. Fuel hose
4. Fuel pump
5. Canister
6. Air vent hose
7. Fuel shutoff (rollover) valve
8. Carburetor

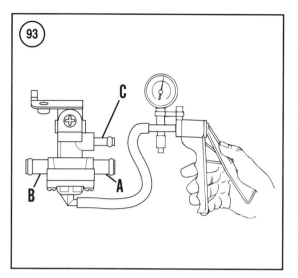

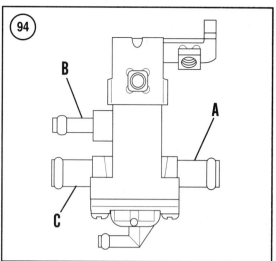

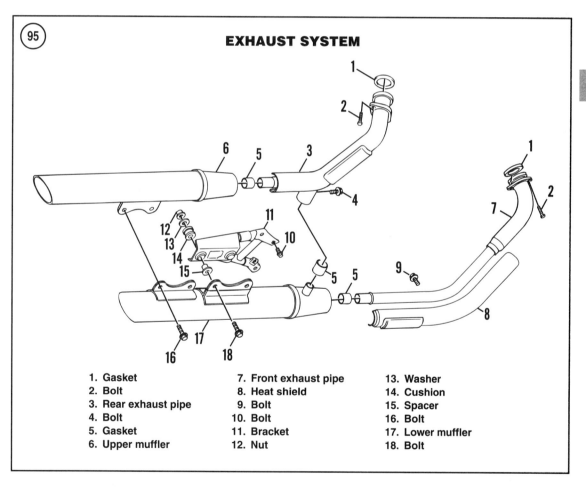

EXHAUST SYSTEM

1. Gasket	7. Front exhaust pipe	13. Washer
2. Bolt	8. Heat shield	14. Cushion
3. Rear exhaust pipe	9. Bolt	15. Spacer
4. Bolt	10. Bolt	16. Bolt
5. Gasket	11. Bracket	17. Lower muffler
6. Upper muffler	12. Nut	18. Bolt

EXHAUST SYSTEM

Check the exhaust system for deep dents and fractures. Repair or replace damaged parts immediately. Check the muffler frame mounting flanges for fractures and loose bolts. Check the cylinder head mounting flanges for tightness.

Removal/Installation

Refer to **Figure 95**.

1. Loosen the upper muffler clamping bolt (**Figure 96**).

2. Remove the upper muffler mounting bolts (**Figure 97**), then remove the upper muffler.

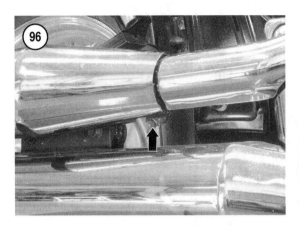

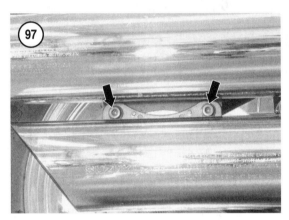

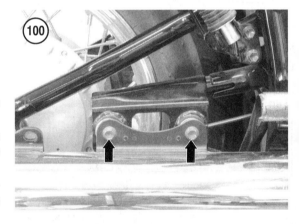

NOTE
Due to the exhaust system configura-
tion, it is easiest to remove and install
the rear cylinder exhaust pipe and
lower muffler as an assembly.

3. Loosen the lower muffler clamping bolt (**Figure 98**).

4. On the rear cylinder, remove the bolts (A, **Figure 99**) securing the exhaust pipe clamp ring (B) to the cylinder head.

5. Remove the lower muffler mounting bolts (**Figure 100**), then remove the rear cylinder exhaust pipe and lower muffler as an assembly.

6. On the front cylinder, remove the bolts (A, **Figure 101**) securing the exhaust pipe clamp ring (B) to the cylinder head.

7. Remove the exhaust pipe from the front cylinder head.

8. If necessary, loosen the pipe clamp and separate the rear cylinder exhaust pipe from the lower muffler.

9. Inspect the gaskets at all joints; replace as necessary.

10. Install a new gasket in each exhaust port (**Figure 102**).

11. Reverse the removal procedure to install the exhaust system. Note the following:

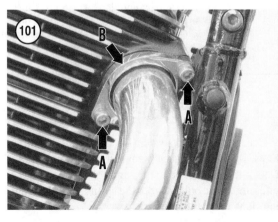

a. Install the exhaust pipe cylinder head bolts, but tighten only fingertight until the rest of the exhaust system is installed.

b. Install the complete exhaust system, but do not tighten it at this time. Make sure the exhaust pipes are correctly seated in the exhaust ports.

c. Tighten the exhaust pipe cylinder head bolts first to minimize exhaust leaks at the cylinder head. Tighten the bolts securely.

d. Tighten the rest of the exhaust system bolts securely.

e. After installation is complete, start the engine and make sure there are no exhaust leaks.

Table 1 CARBURETOR SPECIFICATIONS (U.S., CALIFORNIA AND CANADA)

Model No.	Mikuni BDSR34
Identification No.	41F2*
Bore size	34 mm
Float height	6.5-7.5 mm (0.26-0.30 in.)
Idle speed	1000-1200 rpm
Jet needle	5E23
Main jet No.	132.5
Needle jet	P-0M
Pilot jet No.	27.5
Pilot screw opening	Preset (3 turns out)
Throttle valve	95
Throttle cable free play	2.0-4.0 mm (0.08-0.16 in.)
*Identification number on California model is 41F3.	

Table 2 CARBURETOR SPECIFICATIONS (UK AND EUROPE)

Model No.	Mikuni BDSR34
Identification No.	41F1
Bore size	34 mm
Float height	6.5-7.5 mm (0.26-0.30 in.)
Idle speed	1000-1200 rpm
Jet needle	5E22-3
Main jet No.	132.5
Needle jet	P-0M
Pilot jet No.	27.5
Pilot screw opening	Preset (3 turns out)
Throttle valve	95
Throttle cable free play	2.0-4.0 mm (0.08-0.16 in.)

Table 3 FUEL SYSTEM TEST SPECIFICATIONS

Item	Specification
Carburetor heater coil resistance	approx. 4.5-13 ohms
Throttle position sensor	
Fully-closed resistance	approx. 5k ohms
Wide-open resistance	3.09k-4.63k ohms

8

Table 4 FUEL SYSTEM TORQUE SPECIFICATIONS

Item	N•m	in.-lb.	ft.-lb.
Carburetor heater	3	27	–
Fuel level sender mounting bolts	10	88	–
Fuel pump mounting bolts	10	88	–

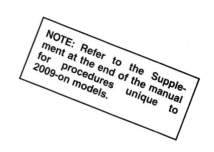

NOTE: Refer to the Supplement at the end of the manual for procedures unique to 2009-on models.

FUEL, EMISSION CONTROL AND
EXHAUST SYSTEMS (2005-ON MODELS)

9

This chapter covers the fuel, emission and exhaust systems used on 2005-on models. Air filter service is covered in Chapter Three. Refer to Chapter Two for troubleshooting procedures.

Refer to *Safety* in Chapter One prior to working on the fuel system.

The fuel system consists of the fuel tank, fuel pump, fuel pump relay, fuel injectors, throttle body, ECM and electrical components.

The emission system components vary depending on the model. A crankcase breather system and a PAIR (air supply) system is used on all models. California models are equipped with an evaporative emissions control system.

Specifications are in **Tables 1-3** at the end of this chapter.

ELECTRONIC FUEL INJECTION (EFI)

The EFI system consists of a fuel delivery system and electronic control system. Refer to **Figure 1** and **Figure 2**.

Components in the fuel delivery system include the fuel tank, fuel pump, fuel pump relay, throttle body and fuel injectors. The fuel pump is in the fuel tank and directs fuel to the fuel injectors at a regulated pressure of 300 kPa (43.5 psi). The fuel injectors are mounted on the throttle body, which is attached to both cylinder heads.

The electronic control system consists of the electronic control module (ECM) and sensors. The electronic control system determines the output of the fuel injectors, as well as controlling ignition timing.

Electronic Control Module (ECM) and Sensors

The ECM (**Figure 3**) is mounted behind the right side cover. The ECM contains a program map that determines the optimum fuel injection and ignition timing based on input from eight sensors.

The sensors (**Figure 1** and **Figure 2**) and their locations and functions are as follows:

1. The throttle position (TP) sensor, located on the throttle body and attached directly to the throttle shaft, indicates throttle angle. The ECM determines the air volume entering the engine based on the throttle angle.

2. The crankshaft position (CKP) sensor, located in the generator cover, is an inductive type sensor. The ECM determines the engine speed by how fast the machined teeth on the flywheel pass by the sensor.

3. The engine coolant temperature (ECT) sensor is located on the front cylinder head cover. The ECM

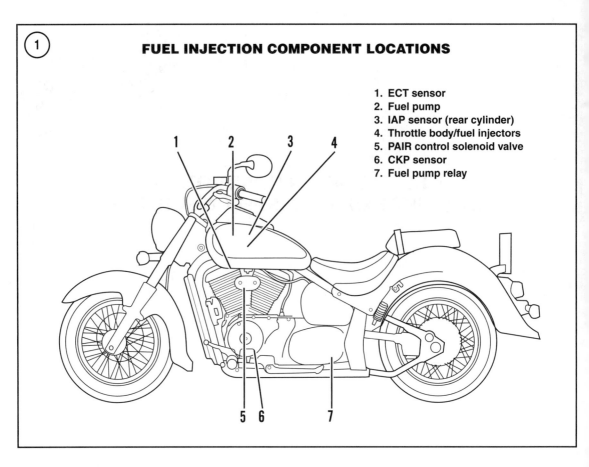

FUEL INJECTION COMPONENT LOCATIONS

1. ECT sensor
2. Fuel pump
3. IAP sensor (rear cylinder)
4. Throttle body/fuel injectors
5. PAIR control solenoid valve
6. CKP sensor
7. Fuel pump relay

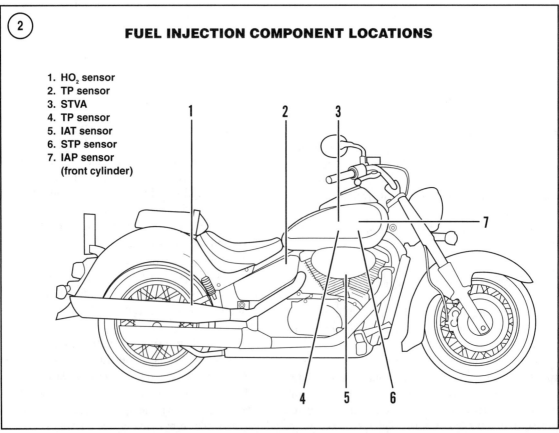

FUEL INJECTION COMPONENT LOCATIONS

1. HO$_2$ sensor
2. TP sensor
3. STVA
4. TP sensor
5. IAT sensor
6. STP sensor
7. IAP sensor
   (front cylinder)

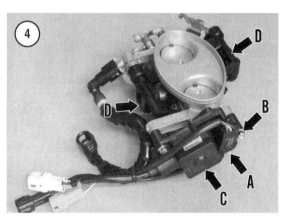

adjusts the injector opening time based on input from this sensor.

4. The intake air temperature (IAT) sensor is located on the backside of the air box. The ECM determines the air density and adjusts the injector opening time based on input from this sensor.

5. The intake air pressure (IAP) sensors are attached to the intake duct, one for each cylinder. Each IAP sensor monitors intake manifold pressure (vacuum) and sends this information to the ECM.

6. The tip-over (TO) sensor, located under the seat, interrupts the ignition and shuts off the engine if the motorcycle's lean angle is greater than 65° from vertical.

7. The secondary throttle position (STP) sensor, located on the throttle body and attached directly to the throttle shaft of the secondary throttle valves, indicates secondary throttle angle.

8. On U.K., EU, Australia Models, the heated oxygen (HO_2) sensor on the muffler provides the ECM with exhaust gas mixture information. The sensor decreases voltage output if it detects a large amount of oxygen in the exhaust gas, which indicates a lean air/fuel mixture. The heater element improves sensor performance.

Fuel Supply System

Fuel pump and filters

The fuel pump and filter assembly is located inside the fuel tank. This assembly is attached to a mounting plate on the bottom of the fuel tank. A fuel regulator attached to the fuel pump mounting bracket maintains fuel pressure.

A mesh-type inlet screen on the fuel pump prevents solid material in the fuel tank from entering the fuel pump. A filter at the outlet of the fuel pump prevents contaminants from entering the fuel lines and fuel injectors.

Fuel line

The fuel line is attached to the fuel tank tubing with quick-disconnect fittings.

The fuel supply line pressure is 300 kPa (43 psi). A check valve is located on the fuel line where it attaches to the fuel tank.

Fuel injectors

The pintle-type fuel injectors consist of a solenoid plunger, needle valve and housing. The injectors have a fixed orifice size and operate at a constant pressure.

Throttle Body

The throttle body sits atop the intake manifold between the cylinder heads. The throttle body contains the throttle-grip controlled primary throttle valves and the ECM-controlled secondary throttle valves. The secondary throttle valve actuator (SVTA) rotates the secondary throttle valve shaft as directed by the ECM. Using air/fuel maps, the ECM sets the secondary throttle valve position to optimize air flow through the throttle body bores.

Mounted on the throttle body are the throttle position sensor (A, **Figure 4**), secondary throttle position sensor (B), secondary throttle valve actuator (C) and fuel injectors (D).

FUEL DELIVERY SYSTEM TESTS

WARNING
Before disconnecting the fuel fittings, turn the ignition switch off and allow the system to internally release fuel pressure.

Some fuel may spill from the fuel hoses when performing this procedure. Because gasoline is extremely flammable and explosive, perform this procedure away from all open flames (including appliance pilot lights) and sparks. Do not allow smoking in the work area. Always work in a well-ventilated area. Wipe up any spills immediately.

The following tests evaluate the performance of the fuel delivery system components (fuel pump, pressure regulator and filters).

Fuel Pressure Test

Tools

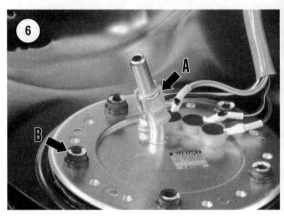

The following tools, or equivalents, are needed to perform this test:

1. Fuel pressure gauge adapter (Suzuki part No. 09940-40211).

2. Fuel pressure gauge hose attachment (Suzuki part No. 09940-40220).

3. Oil pressure gauge (Suzuki part No. 09915-77331).

4. Oil pressure gauge hose (Suzuki part No. 09915-74521).

Test procedure

1. Raise and support the fuel tank as described in this chapter.

NOTE
To disengage the hose end from the fuel pump pipe in Step 2, press in on the upper tabs of the coupler.

2. Disconnect the fuel hose (A, **Figure 5**) from the output pipe on the fuel pump. Be prepared to catch residual gasoline.

NOTE
*The plastic coupler (A, **Figure 6**) may remain on the tank pipe. Carefully remove the coupler and insert it into the fuel hose end.*

3. Use the adapters to install the gauge inline between the fuel pump and the throttle body. Follow the manufacturer's instructions. See **Figure 7**.

4. Turn the ignition switch on, and read the fuel pressure. It should equal approximately 300 kPa (43.5 psi).

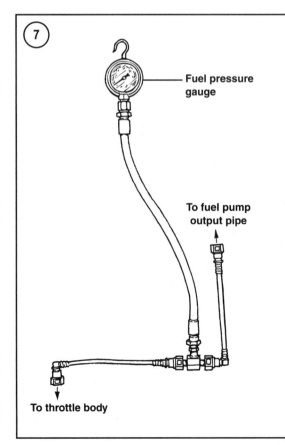

Fuel pressure gauge

To fuel pump output pipe

To throttle body

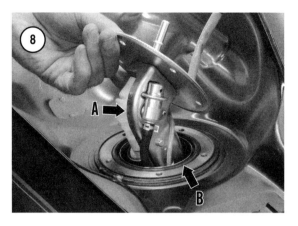

5. If fuel pressure is less than specified, check for a leak in the fuel system, a clogged fuel filter, faulty pressure regulator or faulty fuel pump.

6. If fuel pressure exceeds specification, the fuel pump check valve or the pressure regulator is faulty. The check valve is an integral part of the fuel pump and cannot be replaced separately. If the pressure regulator is faulty, replace the fuel pump mounting plate assembly.

Fuel Pump Operation Test

1. Turn the ignition switch on and listen for operation of the fuel pump.

2. If no sound is heard, test the fuel pump relay and the tip over sensor as described in this chapter. If both of these components are within specification, replace the fuel pump.

Fuel Pump Discharge Test

A graduated cylinder or similar graduated container with a capacity of at least 1.5 liters (0.5 gal.) is needed for this test.

1. Raise and support the fuel tank as described in this chapter.

2. Disconnect the fuel pump connector (B, **Figure 5**).

NOTE
To disengage the hose end from the fuel pump pipe in Step 2, press in on the upper tabs of the coupler.

3. Disconnect the fuel hose (A, **Figure 5**) from the output pipe on the fuel pump. Be prepared to catch residual gasoline.

NOTE
*The plastic coupler (A, **Figure 6**) may remain on the tank pipe. Carefully re-*

move the coupler and insert it into the fuel hose end.

4. Connect a suitable hose to the fuel pump output pipe and feed the opposite end of the hose into a graduated cylinder.

5. Apply battery voltage directly to the fuel pump for 30 seconds as follows:

   a. Use a jumper to connect the battery positive terminal to the yellow/red wire in the pump end of the fuel pump connector. Connect the negative battery terminal to the black/white terminal in the pump end of the connector.

   b. Keep the jumpers connected to the terminals for 30 seconds, and then disconnect them from the connector and from the battery terminal.

6. Measure the amount of fuel in the graduated cylinder. It should equal the fuel pump output volume specified in **Table 1**. The fuel pump is faulty or the fuel filters are obstructed if the volume is significantly less than specified.

FUEL PUMP

The fuel pump is located inside the fuel tank and operates whenever the ignition switch is on. The pressure regulator, which is an integral part of the fuel pump plate assembly, maintains fuel line pressure at 300 kPa (43 psi). The pressure regulator bypasses fuel back into the fuel tank internally, so there is no fuel return line.

Removal/Installation

1. Remove the fuel tank as described in this chapter. Drain the fuel into a suitable container.

2. Set the fuel tank on towels or a blanket on the workbench.

3. Loosen the fuel pump mounting plate bolts (B, **Figure 6**) in a crisscross pattern in several passes and remove the bolts.

4. Pull the fuel pump assembly (A, **Figure 8**) from the tank. Remove and discard the fuel pump O-ring (B, **Figure 8**).

5. Install the fuel pump by reversing the removal steps. Note the following:

   a. Apply Suzuki Super Grease A to a new O-ring, and fit the O-ring into the channel in the tank (B, **Figure 8**).

   b. Apply threadlock (Suzuki Thread Lock 1342, or equivalent) to the threads of the fuel pump bolts and install the bolts (B, **Figure 6**).

   c. Evenly tighten the bolts in a crisscross pattern to 10 N•m (88 in.-lb.).

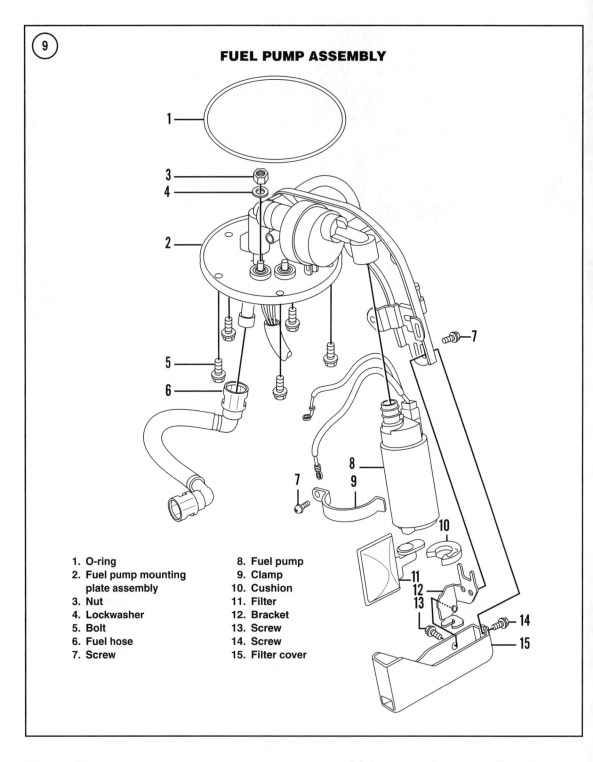

FUEL PUMP ASSEMBLY

9

1. O-ring
2. Fuel pump mounting
   plate assembly
3. Nut
4. Lockwasher
5. Bolt
6. Fuel hose
7. Screw
8. Fuel pump
9. Clamp
10. Cushion
11. Filter
12. Bracket
13. Screw
14. Screw
15. Filter cover

Disassembly

Refer to **Figure 9**.

1. Remove the fuel pump as described in this section.

CAUTION
Clean the filter pump and plate assembly before disassembly. Do not allow

debris to enter the pump or line openings.

2. Remove the intake filter cover mounting screws (A, **Figure 10** and **Figure 11**), then remove the filter cover (B, **Figure 10**).

3. Disconnect the pump electrical connector (**Figure 12**) from the pump.

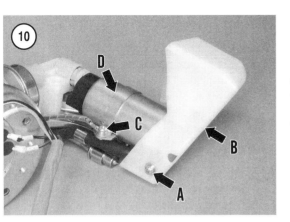

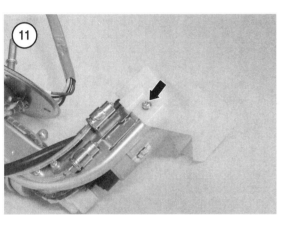

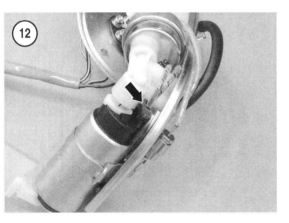

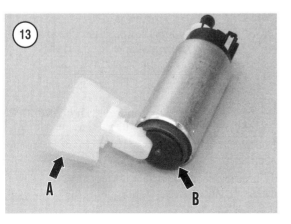

NOTE
Note the pump ground wire terminal se-
cured by the clamp screw in Step 4.

4. Remove the clamp screw (C, **Figure 10**). Remove the pump clamp (D, **Figure 10**).

5. Separate the fuel pump from the mounting bracket.

6. If necessary, remove the intake filter (A, **Figure 13**) and rubber cushion (B).

NOTE
Further disassembly is not recom-
mended. The pump plate assembly is
only available as a unit assembly.

Inspection

1. If not previously cleaned, clean the fuel pump and plate assembly, but do not allow debris to enter pump or line openings.

2. Clean the filter element (A, **Figure 13**). Replace the element if it remains obstructed.

Assembly

1. If removed, install the intake filter (A, **Figure 13**) and rubber cushion (B).

2. Install the fuel pump onto the mounting bracket.

3. Install the pump clamp (D, **Figure 10**). Place the black pump ground wire on the clamp screw, then install the screw (C, **Figure 10**) and tighten securely.

4. Attach the wire connector to the pump (**Figure 12**). Tighten the nut securely.

5. Install the filter cover (B, **Figure 10**) and mounting screws. Tighten the screws securely.

6. Install the fuel pump and plate assembly as described in this section.

FUEL PUMP RELAY

Removal/Installation

1. Disconnect the negative battery terminal cable as described in Chapter Three.

2. Remove the secondary gearcase cover (**Figure 14**).

3. Pull the relay (**Figure 15**) out of the connector.

4. Installation is the reverse of removal.

Test

1. Remove the relay from the motorcycle as described in this section.

2. Check the continuity between the A and B terminals on the relay (**Figure 16**). The relay should not have continuity.

3. Use jumpers to connect the positive terminal of a 12-volt battery to the C terminal on the relay (**Figure 16**); connect the negative battery terminal to the D relay terminal.

4. Check the continuity between the A and B relay terminals. The relay should have continuity while voltage is applied.

5. Replace the relay if it fails either portion of this test.

FUEL PRESSURE REGULATOR

The pressure regulator is part of the fuel pump mounting plate assembly. Refer to *Fuel Pump* in this chapter when servicing the pressure regulator.

THROTTLE CABLE

Removal/Installation

> *WARNING*
> *An improperly adjusted or incorrectly routed throttle cable can cause the throttle to hang open. This could cause a crash. Do not ride the motorcycle until throttle cable operation is correct.*

> *NOTE*
> *There are two throttle cables: the pull cable (to accelerate) and the return cable (to decelerate). Identify and label the cables to ensure correct reinstallation.*

1. Remove the fuel tank as described in this chapter.

2. At the throttle grip, loosen the throttle cable locknut (A, **Figure 17**) and turn the adjuster (B) all the way into the switch assembly to allow maximum slack in the pull cable (C). Repeat this procedure for the return cable (D, **Figure 17**).

3. Remove the screws securing the right switch assembly together and separate the assembly halves (**Figure 18**).

4. Disconnect the throttle pull cable and the return cable from the throttle grip pulley.

5. At the throttle body loosen both jam nuts (A, **Figure 19**) securing each throttle cable to the mounting bracket.

6. Disconnect the pull cable (B, **Figure 19**) from the throttle pulley on the throttle body, then disconnect the return cable (C). Disconnect each throttle cable from the bracket on the throttle body.

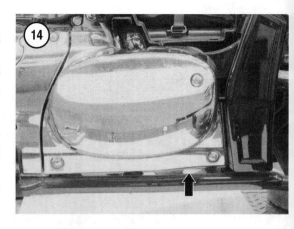

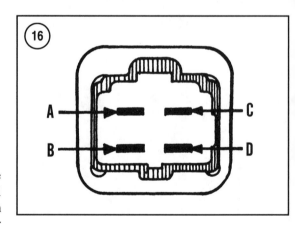

> *CAUTION*
> *Do not allow the throttle valve in the throttle body to snap shut. Doing so may damage the throttle valve or throttle body.*

7. Disconnect the throttle cable from any clips and/or cable ties that secure it to the frame.

8. Note how the cable is routed through the frame, and then remove it.

9. Lubricate the new cable as described in Chapter Three. Route the new cable along the same path noted in Step 8.

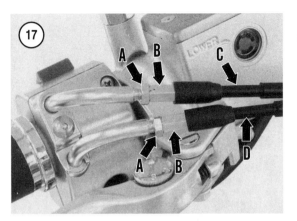

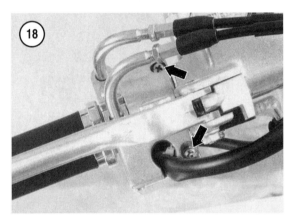

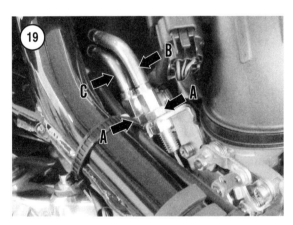

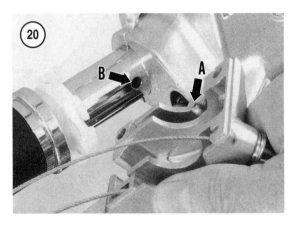

10. Reverse Steps 1-7 to install the new cables. Note the following:

   a. Connect the throttle return cable, then the pull cable onto the throttle grip and switch housing.

   b. Align the locating pin (A, **Figure 20**) with the hole in the handlebar (B) and install the switch onto the handlebar. Tighten the screws securely.

   c. Connect the throttle pull cable (B, **Figure 19**) into the rear receptacle in the throttle pulley on the throttle body, then install the return cable (C) into the front receptacle in the throttle pulley on the throttle body.

   d. Operate the throttle lever and make sure the throttle body throttle linkage is operating correctly with no binding. If operation is incorrect or there is binding, make sure the cables are attached correctly and there are no tight bends in either cable.

   e. At the throttle body assembly, rotate the adjuster on each cable in either direction so the adjuster is at a midpoint position. Tighten the jam nuts securing each throttle cable to the mounting bracket.

   f. Adjust the throttle cables as described in Chapter Three.

   g. Start the engine and let it idle. Turn the handlebar from side to side and listen to the engine speed. Make sure the idle speed does not increase. If it does, the throttle cables are adjusted incorrectly or the throttle cable(s) is improperly routed. Find and correct the source of the problem before riding.

AIR BOX

The air box is located on the right side of the engine cylinders.

Removal/Installation

Refer to **Figure 21**.

1. Remove the air box cover retaining bolts (A, **Figure 22**).

NOTE
The air filter plate assembly may remain in the cover during removal in Step 2.

2. Remove the air box cover (B, **Figure 22**).

3. Remove the air filter plate (**Figure 23**).

4. Remove the air box mounting bolts (A, **Figure 24**).

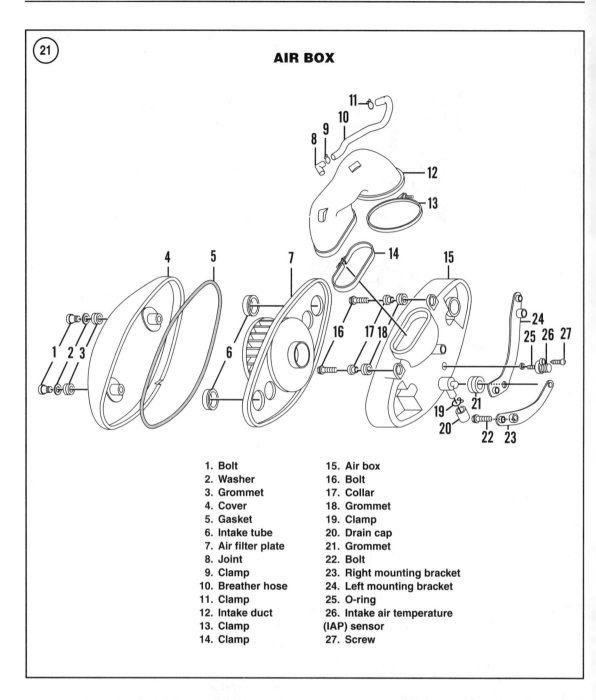

AIR BOX

1. Bolt
2. Washer
3. Grommet
4. Cover
5. Gasket
6. Intake tube
7. Air filter plate
8. Joint
9. Clamp
10. Breather hose
11. Clamp
12. Intake duct
13. Clamp
14. Clamp
15. Air box
16. Bolt
17. Collar
18. Grommet
19. Clamp
20. Drain cap
21. Grommet
22. Bolt
23. Right mounting bracket
24. Left mounting bracket
25. O-ring
26. Intake air temperature (IAP) sensor
27. Screw

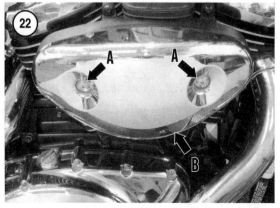

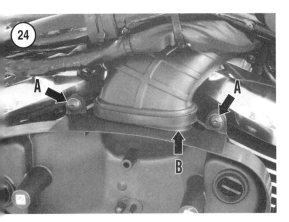

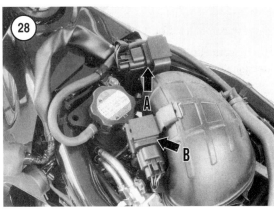

5. Pull out the air box to release the lower mounting prong from the grommet on the mounting bracket.

6. Pull out the air box. Loosen the intake duct clamp screw on the backside of the clamp (B, **Figure 24**).

7. On the backside of the air box, detach the PAIR hose from the air box (A, **Figure 25**).

8. Disconnect the intake air temperature (IAP) sensor connector (B, **Figure 25**) and remove the air box.

9. Inspect the air box for cracks or other damage. If any damage is noted, replace the air box to avoid the possibility of unfiltered air entering the engine.

10. Refer to Chapter Three and inspect the air filter plate as described.

11. Remove the drain plug and clean the plug and air box. Reinstall the drain plug.

12. Be sure the air box mounting brackets (**Figure 26**) are securely attached to the cylinders.

13. Install by reversing the preceding removal steps. Make sure all hoses are securely connected to prevent air leaks.

THROTTLE BODY

Removal/Installation

1. Remove the fuel tank as described in this chapter.

2. Remove the air box as described in this chapter.

3. Detach the breather hose from the air intake duct (**Figure 27**).

4. Remove the front cylinder intake air pressure (IAP) sensor (A, **Figure 28**) and rear cylinder IAP sensor (B) from the mounting slots on the air intake duct.

5. Loosen the clamp screw that secures the air intake duct to the throttle body (**Figure 29**).

6. Remove the air intake duct.

7. Disconnect the black throttle position sensor connector (A, **Figure 30**).

8. Disconnect the green secondary throttle position sensor connector (B, **Figure 30**).

9. Disconnect the white secondary throttle valve actuator sensor connector (C, **Figure 30**).

10. Disconnect the connector from the top of each fuel injector (**Figure 31** and **Figure 32**).

> *NOTE*
> *The throttle body is removed in Step 11 with the hoses and throttle cables still connected, which allows better access for disconnection.*

11. Loosen the intake manifold clamp screw (**Figure 33**). Lift out the throttle body.

12. On California models, disconnect the EVAP canister hoses from the throttle body.

13. Disconnect each IAP sensor vacuum hose from its fitting on the throttle body (**Figure 34**).

> *CAUTION*
> *Do not allow the throttle valve in the throttle body to snap shut. Doing so may damage the throttle valve or throttle body.*

14. Refer to *Throttle Cables* in this chapter and disconnect the throttle cables from the throttle body.

15. Remove the throttle body.

16. Install the throttle body by reversing the removal steps. Note the following:

   a. The throttle position and secondary throttle position sensor connectors have the same configuration, but different colors. The throttle position connector is black. The secondary throttle position connector is green.

   b. After installing the throttle cables, operate the throttle lever and make sure the throttle body throttle linkage is operating correctly with no binding. If operation is incorrect or there is binding, make sure the cables are attached correctly and there are no tight bends in either cable.

   c. At the throttle body assembly, rotate the adjuster on each cable in either direction so the adjuster is at a midpoint position. Tighten the jam nuts securing each throttle cable to the mounting bracket.

   d. Adjust the throttle cables as described in Chapter Three.

   e. Note that the throttle body clamps consist of a long screw (A, **Figure 35**) with a spacer (B) between the clamps. Tighten the screw securely.

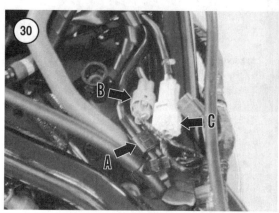

Disassembly

> *WARNING*
> *Some fuel may spill from the throttle body when performing this procedure. Because gasoline is extremely flammable and explosive, perform this procedure away from all open flames (including appliance pilot lights) and sparks. Do not allow anyone to smoke in the work area. Always work in a well-ventilated area. Wipe up any spills immediately.*

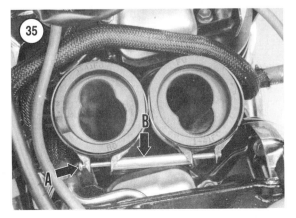

NOTE
To disengage the hose end from the throttle body pipe in Step 1, press in on the upper tabs of the coupler.

Refer to **Figure 36**.

1. Detach the fuel supply hose (**Figure 37**) from the throttle body.

NOTE
*The plastic coupler (**Figure 38**) may remain on the throttle body pipe. Carefully remove the coupler and insert it into the fuel hose end.*

2. Remove the retaining screws (A, **Figure 39**), then remove the fuel transfer hose (B).

3. Remove the retaining screws (A, **Figure 40**), then remove the fuel delivery pipe (B) and the attached fuel injector. Remove the pipe and fuel injector on each side of the throttle body.

4. Separate the fuel injector (A, **Figure 41**) from the fuel delivery pipe (B).

5. Remove the throttle position and secondary throttle position sensors as described in this chapter.

CAUTION
*Do not remove the secondary throttle valve actuator (**Figure 42**) from the throttle body.*

6. Remove the mounting screw (**Figure 43**), then separate the metal and plastic components of the fuel delivery pipes.

NOTE
Further disassembly is not necessary or recommended. Do not remove the primary or secondary throttle shaft and throttle valve assemblies. If these parts are damaged, replace the throttle body as these items are not available separately.

Inspection

CAUTION
Do not use wires to clean passages in the throttle body.

1. Clean the throttle body using a spray-type carburetor cleaner. Dry the throttle body and all passages with compressed air.

2. Inspect the throttle body for cracks or other damage that could admit unfiltered air.

3. Manually operate the throttle valves and the secondary throttle valves. They must move smoothly.

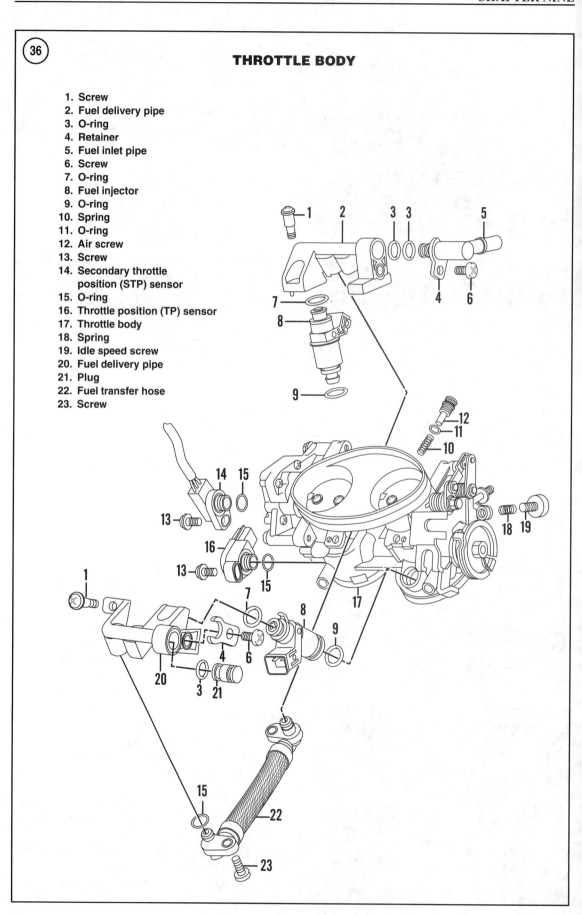

36

THROTTLE BODY

1. Screw
2. Fuel delivery pipe
3. O-ring
4. Retainer
5. Fuel inlet pipe
6. Screw
7. O-ring
8. Fuel injector
9. O-ring
10. Spring
11. O-ring
12. Air screw
13. Screw
14. Secondary throttle
    position (STP) sensor
15. O-ring
16. Throttle position (TP) sensor
17. Throttle body
18. Spring
19. Idle speed screw
20. Fuel delivery pipe
21. Plug
22. Fuel transfer hose
23. Screw

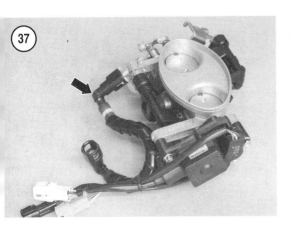

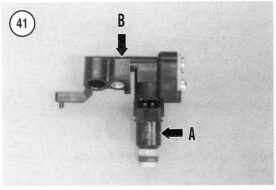

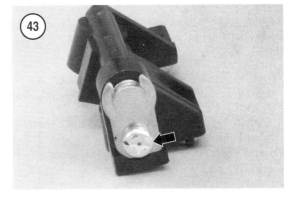

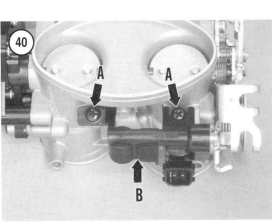

4. Check the operation of the throttle wheel and the fast idle cam assembly. Each must operate smoothly.

5. Inspect the hoses for cracks or other signs of damage. Replace any hose that is becoming brittle.

6. Check the fuel injectors as described in this chapter.

7. Replace any part that is worn or damaged.

Assembly

NOTE
Lubricate all O-rings with engine oil prior to installation.

Refer to **Figure 36**.

1. Install a new O-ring onto the metal plug and two O-rings onto the fuel inlet pipe. Insert the metal plug or fuel inlet pipe into the plastic portion of the fuel delivery pipe. Install the mounting screw (**Figure 43**) and tighten securely.

2. Install the throttle position (TP) and secondary throttle position (STP) sensors as described in this chapter.

3. Install the upper and lower O-rings onto the fuel injectors. The upper O-ring (A, **Figure 44**) has a round cross-section. The lower O-ring (B, **Figure 44**) has a square cross-section.

4. Make sure the mounting bores for the fuel injectors in the throttle body are clean.

NOTE
Do not turn the fuel injector during installation in Step 5.

5. Install each fuel injector into the fuel delivery pipe so the tang on the injector (A, **Figure 45**) fits into the slot (B) on the fuel delivery pipe.

6. Install the fuel injector and fuel delivery pipe (B, **Figure 40**) on each side, making sure the fuel injector fits properly in the throttle body. Tighten the retaining screws (A, **Figure 40**) to 3.5 N•m (31 in.-lb.).

7. Install the fuel transfer hose (B, **Figure 39**). Tighten the retaining screws securely.

8. Reattach the fuel supply hose (**Figure 37**) to the throttle body pipe.

FUEL INJECTORS

A multi-hole fuel injector for each cylinder is mounted on the throttle body. The ECM controls the opening time of the injector. The fuel injectors are not serviceable.

NOTE
Lubricate all O-rings with engine oil prior to installation.

Removal/Installation

1. Remove the throttle body as described in this chapter.

2. Remove the retaining screws (A, **Figure 39**), then remove the fuel transfer hose (B).

3. Remove the retaining screws (A, **Figure 40**), then remove the fuel delivery pipe (B) and the attached fuel injector. Remove the pipe and fuel injector on each side of the throttle body.

4. Separate the fuel injector (A, **Figure 41**) from the fuel delivery pipe (B).

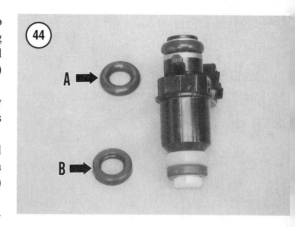

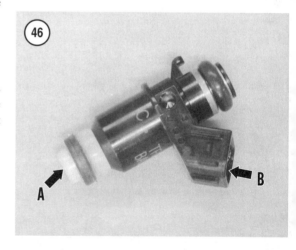

5. Install the upper and lower O-rings onto the fuel injectors. The upper O-ring (A, **Figure 44**) has a round cross-section. The lower O-ring (B, **Figure 44**) has a square cross-section.

6. Make sure the mounting bores for the fuel injectors in the throttle body are clean.

NOTE
Do not turn the fuel injector during installation in Step 7.

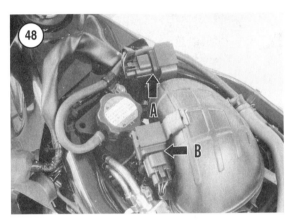

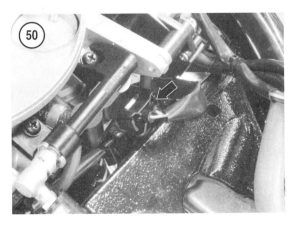

7. Install each fuel injector into the fuel delivery pipe so the tang on the injector (A, **Figure 45**) fits into the slot (B) on the fuel delivery pipe.

8. Install the fuel injector and fuel delivery pipe (B, **Figure 40**) on each side, making sure the fuel injector fits properly in the throttle body. Tighten the retaining screws (A) to 3.5 N•m (31 in.-lb.).

9. Install the fuel transfer hose (B, **Figure 39**). Tighten the retaining screws securely.

Inspection

1. Visually inspect the fuel injectors for damage. Inspect the injector nozzle (A, **Figure 46**) for carbon buildup or damage.

2. Check for corroded or damaged fuel injector connector terminals (B, **Figure 46**) and the wiring connector.

3. Make sure the mounting bores for the fuel injectors in the throttle body are clean.

Resistance Test

1. Turn the ignition switch off.

2. Remove the fuel tank as described in this chapter.

3. Remove the air box as described in this chapter.

4. Detach the breather hose from the air intake duct (**Figure 47**).

5. Remove the front cylinder intake air pressure (IAP) sensor (A, **Figure 48**) and rear cylinder IAP sensor (B) from the mounting brackets on the air intake duct.

6. Loosen the clamp screw that secures the air intake duct to the throttle body (**Figure 49**).

7. Remove the air intake duct.

8. Disconnect the connector (**Figure 50**) from the fuel injector.

9. Use an ohmmeter to measure the resistance between the two terminals in the fuel injector (**Figure 51**). The resistance should be within the range specified in **Table 2**.

10. Repeat this test for the remaining fuel injector.

Continuity Test

1. Perform Steps 1-8 of the *Resistance Test* in this section.

2. Check the continuity between each injector terminal (**Figure 51**) and ground. No continuity (infinity) should be indicated.

3. Repeat this test for the remaining fuel injector.

Voltage Test

1. Perform Steps 1-8 of the injector *Resistance Test* in this section.

2. Connect a voltmeter positive test probe to the yellow/red wire in the injector connector; connect the negative test probe to a good ground.

> *NOTE*
> *Injector voltage will be present for only three seconds after the ignition switch is turned on. If necessary, turn the switch off and then back on.*

3. Turn the ignition switch on and measure the voltage. It should equal battery voltage.

4. Repeat this test for each remaining fuel injector.

CRANKSHAFT POSITION (CKP) SENSOR

Refer to Chapter Ten.

THROTTLE POSITION (TP) SENSOR

Removal/Installation

1. Disconnect the negative battery cable (Chapter Three).

2. Remove the fuel tank as described in this chapter.

3. Remove the air box as described in this chapter.

4. Detach the breather hose from the air intake duct (**Figure 47**).

5. Remove the front cylinder intake air pressure (IAP) sensor (A, **Figure 48**) and rear cylinder IAP sensor (B) from the mounting brackets on the air intake duct.

6. Loosen the clamp screw (**Figure 49**) that secures the air intake duct to the throttle body.

7. Remove the air intake duct.

8. Disconnect the black throttle position (TP) sensor connector (**Figure 52**).

9. Make an index line across the TP sensor and throttle body so the sensor can be reinstalled in the same position during assembly.

10. Use a Torx wrench to remove the mounting screw (A, **Figure 53**), and pull the sensor (B) from the throttle shaft. Note how the sensor engages the throttle shaft.

11. Installation is the reverse of removal. Note the following:

    a. Apply Suzuki Super Grease A to the end of the throttle shaft.

    b. With the throttle valves fully closed, align the end of the throttle shaft with the slot in the sensor, and slide the sensor onto the shaft.

    c. Position the sensor so the index mark on the sensor aligns with the mark on the throttle body.

    d. Install the mounting screw and tighten it to 3.5 N•m (31 in.-lb.).

Adjustment

The Suzuki mode select switch (part No. 09930-82720) (**Figure 54**) is needed to perform this adjustment.

> *CAUTION*
> *Do not attempt this procedure without the mode select switch. Shorting the*

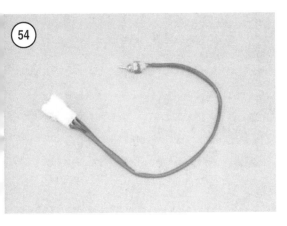

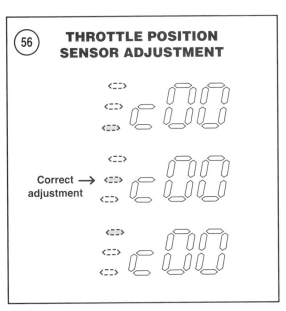

THROTTLE POSITION SENSOR ADJUSTMENT

Correct → adjustment

terminals in the dealer mode connector could damage the ECM.

1. Start the engine and run it until it reaches normal operating temperature. Check the idle speed. If necessary, adjust the idle to specification as described in Chapter Three.

2. Stop the engine.

3. Remove the right side cover as described in Chapter Sixteen.

4. Connect the mode select switch (**Figure 54**) to the dealer mode connector (**Figure 55**).

5. Turn the mode select switch to on.

6. The malfunction code cOO should appear in the meter display. The dash before the code indicates the state of the TP sensor adjustment. The dash should be in the middle position as shown in **Figure 56**. If the dash is in the upper or lower position, adjust the sensor as follows:

    a. Perform steps 3-7 of *Removal/Installation* in this section.

    b. Loosen the sensor screw (A, **Figure 53**).

    c. Rotate the sensor until the dash moves to the center position.

    d. Tighten the screw to 3.5 N•m (31 in.-lb.).

Continuity Test

1. Lift and support the fuel tank as described in this chapter.

2. Disconnect the black throttle position sensor connector (**Figure 52**).

3. Check the continuity between the yellow wire terminal in the sensor end of the connector and a good ground.

4. Reverse the test probes, and check the continuity in the opposite direction.

5. Both readings should indicate no continuity (infinity).

Resistance Test

1. Perform Steps 1-2 of the *Continuity Test* in this section.

2. Connect an ohmmeter to the yellow wire terminal in the sensor end of the connector and the black wire terminal in the sensor end of the connector.

3. Read the resistance when the throttle is fully closed and fully open. Record each reading.

4. The fully open and fully closed resistance should be within the range specified in **Table 2**.

5. Connect an ohmmeter to the blue wire terminal in the sensor end of the connector and the black wire terminal in the sensor end of the connector.

6. Read the resistance and compare with the signal resistance specified in **Table 2**.

Input Voltage Test

1. Perform Steps 1-2 of the *Continuity Test* in this section.

2. Connect a voltmeter positive test probe to the red terminal in the harness end of the sensor connector; connect the voltmeter negative probe to ground.

3. Turn the ignition switch on, and measure the input voltage. It should be within the range specified in **Table 2**.

4. Connect the voltmeter positive test probe to the red terminal in the harness end of the sensor connector; connect the negative test probe to the black/brown terminal in the harness end of the connector.

5. The input voltage should be within the range specified in **Table 2**.

Output Voltage Test

1. Remove the fuel tank as described in this chapter.

2. Make sure the sensor connector is connected to its harness mate.

3. Using a needle probe to back probe the harness connector, connect a voltmeter positive test probe to the blue/black harness wire and the negative test probe to the black/brown harness wire.

4. Turn the ignition switch on.

5. Measure the output voltage when the throttle is fully closed and fully opened. Each measurement should be within the range specified in **Table 2**.

SECONDARY THROTTLE POSITION (STP) SENSOR

Removal/Installation

> *NOTE*
> *Due to the limited space between the motorcycle frame and the sensor, a right-angle Torx wrench (Suzuki part No. 09930-11950 or equivalent) is needed to perform this procedure.*

1. Disconnect the negative battery cable (Chapter Three).

2. Remove the fuel tank as described in this chapter.

3. Remove the air box as described in this chapter.

4. Detach the breather hose from the air intake duct (**Figure 47**).

5. Remove the front cylinder intake air pressure (IAP) sensor (A, **Figure 48**) and rear cylinder IAP sensor (B) from the mounting brackets on the air intake duct.

6. Loosen the clamp screw (**Figure 49**) that secures the air intake duct to the throttle body.

7. Remove the air intake duct.

8. Disconnect the green secondary throttle position sensor connector (**Figure 57**).

9. Make an index line across the STP sensor and throttle body so the sensor can be reinstalled in the same position during assembly.

10. Use the Torx wrench to remove the mounting screw (A, **Figure 58**), pull the sensor (B) from the throttle shaft, and remove the sensor. Note how the sensor engages the throttle shaft.

11. Installation is the reverse of removal. Note the following:

   a. Apply Suzuki Super Grease A to the end of the throttle shaft.

   b. With the secondary throttle valves fully open, align the end of the throttle shaft with the slot in the sensor, and slide the sensor onto the shaft.

   c. Position the sensor so the index mark on the sensor aligns with the mark on the throttle body.

   d. Install the mounting screw and tighten it to 3.5 N•m (31 in.-lb.).

Adjustment

1. Disconnect the negative battery cable (Chapter Three).

2. Remove the fuel tank as described in this chapter.

3. Measure the resistance as follows:

a. Disconnect the green secondary throttle position sensor connector (**Figure 57**).

b. Connect an ohmmeter positive test lead to the yellow terminal in the sensor end of the connector; connect the negative test lead to the black terminal in the sensor end of the connector.

c. Manually move the secondary throttle valve link (**Figure 59**) to the rear to the fully closed position.

d. Measure the resistance. It should equal the fully closed resistance specified in **Table 2**.

e. If the measured resistance is out of specification, loosen the sensor mounting screw (A, **Figure 58**), and rotate the sensor (B) until the resistance is within specification.

f. Tighten the mounting screw to 3.5 N•m (31 in.-lb.).

Continuity Test

1. Lift and support the fuel tank as described in this chapter.

2. Disconnect the green secondary throttle position sensor connector (**Figure 57**).

3. Check the continuity between the yellow wire terminal in the sensor end of the connector and a good ground.

4. Reverse the test probes, and check the continuity in the opposite direction.

5. Both readings should indicate no continuity (infinity).

Resistance Test

1. Perform Steps 1-2 of the *Continuity Test* in this section.

2. Connect an ohmmeter to the yellow wire terminal in the sensor end of the connector and the black wire terminal in the sensor end of the connector.

3. Manually move the secondary throttle valve link (**Figure 59**). Read the resistance when the throttle is fully closed and fully open. Record each reading.

4. The fully open and fully closed resistance should be within the range specified in **Table 2**.

5. Connect an ohmmeter to the blue and black wire terminals in the sensor end of the connector.

6. Compare the reading with the Vcc resistance specification in **Table 2**.

Input Voltage Test

1. Perform Steps 1-2 of the *Continuity Test* in this section.

2. Connect a voltmeter positive test probe to the red terminal in the harness end of the sensor connector; connect the voltmeter negative probe to ground.

3. Turn the ignition switch on, and measure the input voltage. It should be within the range specified in **Table 2**.

4. Connect the voltmeter positive test probe to the red terminal in the harness end of the sensor connector; connect the negative test probe to the black/brown terminal in the harness end of the connector.

5. The input voltage should be within the range specified in **Table 2**.

Output Voltage Test

1. Remove the fuel tank as described in this chapter.

2. Make sure the sensor connector is connected to its harness mate.

3. Using a needle probe to back probe the harness connector, connect a voltmeter positive test probe to the yellow/white harness wire and the negative test probe to the black/brown harness wire.

4. Disconnect the white secondary throttle valve actuator connector (**Figure 60**).

5. Turn the ignition switch on.

6. Manually move the secondary throttle valve link (**Figure 59**). Measure the output voltage when the throttle is fully closed and fully opened. Each measurement should be within the range specified in **Table 2**.

SECONDARY THROTTLE VALVE ACTUATOR (STVA)

Operational Test

1. Disconnect the negative battery cable (Chapter Three).

2. Remove the fuel tank as described in this chapter.

3. Remove the air box as described in this chapter.

4. Detach the breather hose from the air intake duct (**Figure 47**).

5. Remove the front cylinder intake air pressure (IAP) sensor (A, **Figure 48**) and rear cylinder IAP sensor (B) from the mounting brackets on the air intake duct.

6. Loosen the clamp screw (**Figure 49**) that secures the air intake duct to the throttle body.

7. Remove the air intake duct.

8. Turn the ignition switch on, and watch the movement of the secondary throttle valves. Each should move to the fully closed position, to its fully opened position, and then to its operating position. See **Figure 61**. The operating position is approximately 95 percent open.

Continuity Test

1. Perform Steps 1-7 of the *Operational Test* in this section.

2. Disconnect the white secondary throttle valve actuator connector (**Figure 60**).

3. Check the continuity between the wire terminals in the sensor end of the connector and a good ground.

4. The tester should indicate no continuity (infinity).

Resistance Test

1. Perform Steps 1-2 of the *Continuity Test* in this section.

2. Connect the ohmmeter positive test probe to the pink terminal in the sensor end of the connector; connect the negative test probe to the black terminal in the sensor end of the connector. The resistance should equal the value in **Table 2**.

3. Connect the ohmmeter positive test probe to the white/black terminal in the sensor end of the connector; connect the negative test probe to the green ter-

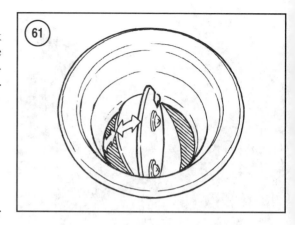

minal in the sensor end of the connector. The resistance should equal the value in **Table 2**.

FAST IDLE SPEED

The fuel system includes a fast idle system that adjusts the throttle valve position during engine warm-up. When operated, a fast idle cam opens and closes the throttle valves. The fast idle cam is automatically controlled by the secondary throttle valve actuator (STVA). During operation, the ECM monitors engine coolant temperature and ambient air temperature, then signals the STVA to set throttle valve position at fast idle if the engine is cold.

The fast idle speed is adjustable using the adjustment screw on the cam (**Figure 62**). Refer to *Fuel System Adjustments* in Chapter Three.

INTAKE AIR PRESSURE (IAP) SENSORS

Two IAP sensors, one for each cylinder, are located on the air intake duct.

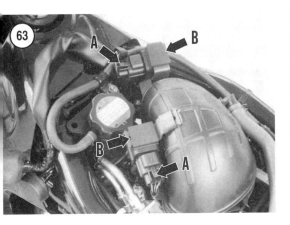

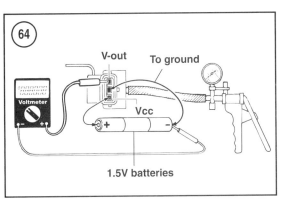

Removal/Installation

1. Disconnect the negative battery cable (Chapter Three).
2. Remove the fuel tank as described in this chapter.
3. Disconnect the connector (A, **Figure 63**) from the IAP sensor (B).
4. Remove the sensor holder from the bracket, then remove the sensor from the holder.
5. Installation is the reverse of removal.

Input Voltage Test

1. Remove the fuel tank as described in this chapter.
2. Disconnect the connector (A, **Figure 63**) from the IAP sensor.
3. Connect a voltmeter positive test probe to the red terminal in the harness connector; connect the negative test probe to ground.
4. Turn the ignition switch on, and measure the voltage. It should be within the input voltage range specified in **Table 2**.
5. Turn the ignition switch off.
6. Connect the voltmeter's positive test probe to the red terminal in the harness connector; connect the negative test probe to the black/brown terminal in the harness connector.

7. Turn the ignition switch on, and measure the voltage. It should be within the input voltage range specified in **Table 2**.
8. Repeat the test for the remaining IAP sensor, if necessary.

Output Voltage Test

NOTE
*Test results may vary due to changes in altitude and atmospheric pressure. Refer also to the **Vacuum Test** in this section.*

1. Run the engine until it reaches normal operating temperature, then shut off the engine.
2. Lift and support the fuel tank as described in this chapter.
3. Make sure the connector is securely mated to the IAP sensor.
4. Using a back probe pin to back probe the harness connector, connect a voltmeter positive test probe to the green/black wire terminal (front cylinder in 2005-2008 models, rear cylinder in 2009-on models) or the green/white wire terminal (front cylinder in 2005-2008 models, rear cylinder in 2009-on models) in the IAP sensor connector
5. Connect the negative test probe to the black/brown terminal.
6. Start the engine and let it run at idle speed.
7. Measure the voltage. It should equal the output voltage value specified in **Table 2**.

Vacuum Test

1. Remove the IAP sensor as described in this section.
2. Make sure the sensor air passage is clear, and connect a vacuum pump and gauge to the air passage (**Figure 64**).
3. Connect three new 1.5 volt batteries in series as shown in **Figure 64**. Measure the total voltage of the batteries. The voltage must be 4.5-5.5 volts.
4. Connect the battery positive terminal to the Vcc terminal in the sensor; connect the battery negative terminal to the ground terminal in the sensor.
5. Connect the voltmeter positive test probe to the V-out terminal in the sensor; connect the negative test probe to the negative end of the batteries.
6. Use the vacuum pump to apply vacuum to the sensor. The voltage reading should be within the V-out voltage range specified in **Table 2**.

9

ENGINE COOLANT TEMPERATURE (ECT) SENSOR

Removal/Installation

1. Disconnect the negative battery cable (Chapter Three).
2. Remove the fuel tank as described in this chapter.
3. Drain the coolant as described in Chapter Three.
4. Disconnect the connector (A, **Figure 65**) from the ECT sensor (B).
5. Unscrew the sensor from the cylinder head. Watch for the sealing washer installed with the sensor.
6. Installation is the reverse of removal. Include the sealing washer, and tighten the coolant sensor to 18 N•m (159 in.-lb.)

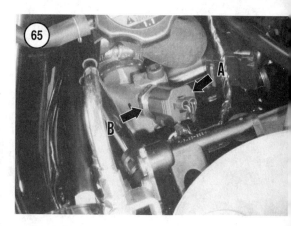

Resistance Test

1. Remove the fuel tank as described in this chapter.
2. Disconnect the connector (A, **Figure 65**) from the ECT sensor (B).

> *NOTE*
> *The motorcycle must be at room temperature (approximately 20°C [68° F]) when performing this test.*

3. Connect the ohmmeter positive test probe to the black/blue terminal in the sensor; connect the negative test probe to the black/brown terminal.
4. Measure the resistance. It should be within the range specified in **Table 2**.
5. If necessary, remove the sensor and test at various temperatures as follows:

> *NOTE*
> *The thermometer and the sensor must not touch the container sides or bottom. If either does, the test readings will be inaccurate.*

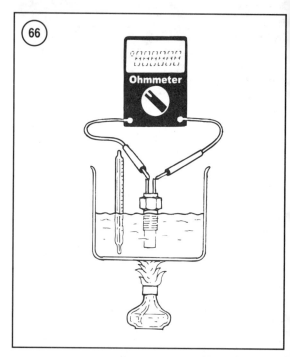

a. Fill a beaker or pan with water, and place it on a stove or hot plate.
b. Place a thermometer in the pan of water. Use a thermometer rated higher than the test temperature.
c. Mount the sensor so that the temperature sensing tip and the threaded portion of the body are submerged as shown in **Figure 66**.
d. Attach an ohmmeter to the sensor terminals as shown in **Figure 66**.
e. Gradually heat the water to the temperature range in **Table 2**. Note the resistance of the sensor when the water temperature reaches the specified values.

f. Replace the sensor if any reading equals infinity or is considerably different than the specified resistance at a given temperature.

Voltage Test

1. Remove the fuel tank as described in this chapter.
2. Disconnect the connector (A, **Figure 65**) from the ECT sensor (B).
3. Connect the voltmeter positive test probe to the black/blue terminal in the connector; connect the negative test probe to a good ground.
4. Turn on the ignition switch and measure the voltage. It should be within the range specified in **Table 2**.
5. Connect the voltmeter positive test probe to the black/blue terminal in the connector; connect the

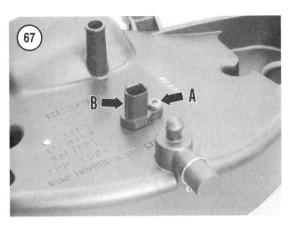

negative test probe to the black/brown terminal in the connector.

6. Turn on the ignition switch. The voltage should be within the specified range.

INTAKE AIR TEMPERATURE (IAT) SENSOR

Removal/Installation

1. Remove the air box as described in this chapter.
2. Remove the sensor mounting screw (A, **Figure 67**), then remove the sensor (B). Discard the O-ring on the sensor.
3. Installation is the reverse of removal. Install a new O-ring onto the sensor.

Resistance Test

1. Turn the ignition switch off, and perform Step 1 and Step 2 under *Removal/Installation* in this section.
2. Connect the ohmmeter positive test probe to the dark green terminal in the sensor; connect the negative test probe to the black/brown terminal.
3. Measure the resistance. It should be within specification (**Table 2**).
4. If further testing is necessary, remove the IAT sensor as described in this section, and proceed as follows:

NOTE
The thermometer and the sensor must not touch the container sides or bottom. If either does, it will result in a false reading.

  a. Fill a beaker or pan with water, and place it on a stove or hot plate.
  b. Place a thermometer in the pan of water. Use a thermometer rated higher than the test temperature.

  c. Mount the IAT sensor so the temperature sensing tip and the mounting portion of the body are submerged as shown in **Figure 66**.
  d. Attach an ohmmeter to the sensor terminals as shown in **Figure 66**.
  e. Gradually heat the water to the temperature range in **Table 2**. Note the resistance of the sensor when the water temperature reaches the specified values.
  f. Replace the IAT sensor if any reading is considerably different than the specified resistance at a given temperature.

Voltage Test

1. Turn the ignition switch off, and perform Step 1 and Step 2 under *Removal/Installation* in this section.
2. Connect the voltmeter positive test probe to the dark green terminal in the connector; connect the negative test probe to a good ground.
3. Turn on the ignition switch and measure the voltage. It should be within the range specified in **Table 2**.
4. Connect the voltmeter positive test probe to the dark green terminal in the connector; connect the negative test probe to the black/brown terminal.
5. Turn the ignition switch on. The voltage should be within the specified range.

HEATED OXYGEN (HO₂) SENSOR

A heated oxygen sensor is used on U.K., EU and Australian models.

Removal/Installation

1. Remove the right side cover as described in Chapter Sixteen.
2. Disconnect the sensor connector.
3. Unscrew the sensor from the rear cylinder muffler.
4. Reverse the removal steps to install the sensor. Tighten the sensor to 48 N•m (35 ft.-lb.).

Test

1. Remove the right side cover as described in Chapter Sixteen.
2. Use a needle probe to back probe the harness connector, then connect a voltmeter positive test probe to the white/black wire terminal in the sensor connector.

3. Connect the negative test probe to ground.

NOTE
Voltage will only be detected for a few seconds in Step 4 after the ignition switch is turned on.

4. Turn the ignition switch to on. The voltage reading should indicate battery voltage for the heater circuit.

5. Run the engine until it reaches normal operating temperature.

6. Use a needle probe to back probe the harness connector, then connect a voltmeter positive test probe to the white/blue wire terminal in the oxygen sensor connector.

7. Using a needle probe to back probe the harness connector, connect a voltmeter negative test probe to the black/brown wire terminal in the oxygen sensor connector.

8. Run the engine at idle and observe the voltage reading.

9. Disconnect the PAIR solenoid valve inlet hose, then block the valve inlet.

10. Run the engine at 5000 rpm and observe the voltage reading.

11. The voltage readings should be within the ranges specified in **Table 2**.

12. Disconnect the HO$_2$ sensor connector. Measure the resistance between the sensor terminals. The tester should indicate the reading in **Table 2**.

TIP-OVER (TO) SENSOR

Whenever the TO sensor is activated, the ECM cuts off power to the fuel pump, ignition system and fuel injection circuits.

Removal/Installation

1. Remove the right side cover as described in Chapter Sixteen.

2. Remove the fuel tank as described in this chapter.

3. Disconnect the TO sensor connector (**Figure 68**).

4. Remove the sensor from the mounting bracket on the frame.

5. Installation is the reverse of removal. Make sure the arrow on the sensor points upward.

Resistance Test

1. Remove the TO sensor as described in this section.

2. Connect the ohmmeter test probes to the red terminal and to the black/brown terminal in the sensor. Read the resistance.

3. The resistance should be within the range specified in **Table 2**.

Voltage Test

1. Remove the TO sensor as described in this section.

2. Reconnect the harness connector to the sensor. If disconnected, reconnect the electrical cable to the negative battery terminal.

3. Using a needle probe to back probe the harness connector, connect a voltmeter positive test probe to the brown/white terminal in the harness end of the connector; connect the negative test probe to the black/brown terminal.

4. Turn the ignition switch on.

5. Hold the sensor so the side marked with an arrow faces up, and read the voltage.

6. Tilt the sensor more than 65° and read the voltage.

7. Each reading should be within the range specified in **Table 2**.

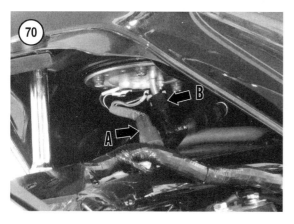

FUEL TANK

Lift Fuel Tank

The fuel tank may be lifted at the rear for access to components under the tank.

1. Remove the front seat as described in Chapter Sixteen.

2. Remove the fuel tank retaining bolt and washer (**Figure 69**).

CAUTION
Make sure to check underlying wires and hoses to prevent damage or detachment while lifting the fuel tank in Step 3.

3. Lift the fuel tank approximately 4 in. (10 cm) and position a prop under the fuel tank to support it.

Removal/Installation

WARNING
Before disconnecting the fittings, turn the ignition switch off and allow the system to internally release fuel pressure.

WARNING
*Some fuel may spill from the fuel tank hose when performing this procedure. Because gasoline is extremely flammable and explosive, perform this procedure away from all open flames (including appliance pilot lights) and sparks. Do not allow smoking in the work area. Always work in a well-ventilated area. Wipe up any spills immediately. Refer to **Safety** in Chapter One.*

1. Remove the front seat as described in Chapter Sixteen.

2. Disconnect the negative battery cable as described in Chapter Three.

3. Remove the speedometer as described in Chapter Ten.

4. Remove the fuel tank retaining bolt and washer (**Figure 69**).

5. Raise the fuel tank sufficiently for access to the fuel pump electrical connector (A, **Figure 70**), then disconnect the connector.

6. Disconnect the fuel supply hose (B, **Figure 70**) from the fuel tank pipe.

7. Move the fuel tank rearward to disengage the front mounting cushions, then lift up the fuel tank and remove it from the frame. After the fuel tank has been inspected and serviced, wrap the tank in a blanket or soft towels to protect the finish. Place the wrapped tank in a cardboard box and store it in an area where it will not be damaged.

8. Plug the end of the fuel pump pipe to prevent the entry of debris and loss of fuel.

9. Inspect the fuel tank as described in this chapter.

10. Install by reversing the preceding removal steps. Note the following:

   a. Check for fuel leaks at all hose connections after installation is completed.

   b. Tighten the fuel tank mounting bolt securely.

Inspection

1. Inspect the rear rubber grommet on the mounting bracket for deterioration. Replace the grommet if necessary.

2. Inspect the rubber cushions for damage or deterioration and replace if necessary.

3. Inspect the filler cap gaskets.

4. Inspect the entire fuel tank for leaks or damage. Repair or replace the fuel tank if any fuel leaks are found.

PAIR (AIR SUPPLY) SYSTEM

All models are equipped with the PAIR system that lowers emissions output by introducing air into the exhaust ports (**Figure 71**). The introduction of air raises the exhaust temperature, which consumes some of the unburned fuel in the exhaust.

The PAIR system consists of a control valve, reed valves, inlet and outlet hoses, and ECM (**Figure 72**). The ECM operates a solenoid valve that opens and closes the inlet air passage in the control valve. The reed valves in the control valve use the momentary pressure variations created by the exhaust gas pulses to introduce additional air into the exhaust ports.

9

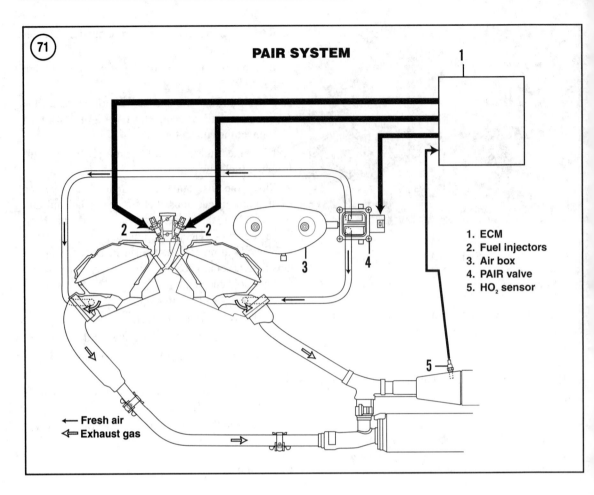

PAIR SYSTEM

1. ECM
2. Fuel injectors
3. Air box
4. PAIR valve
5. HO₂ sensor

$5. \text{HO}_2 \text{ sensor}$

← Fresh air
⇐ Exhaust gas

Removal/Installation

1. Lift and support the fuel tank as described in this chapter.
2. Remove the PAIR cover (**Figure 73**).
3. Disconnect the PAIR solenoid connector (**Figure 74**).
4. Remove the control valve mounting bracket fasteners (**Figure 75**).
5. Pull out the control valve assembly and disconnect the hoses from the control valve.
   a. The upper hose (A, **Figure 76**) connects to the air box.
   b. The left, lower hose (B, **Figure 76**) connects to the front cylinder PAIR pipe.
   c. The right, lower hose (C, **Figure 76**) connects to the rear cylinder PAIR pipe.
6. Remove the control valve.
7. Reverse the removal steps to install the control valve.

Inspection

Refer to **Figure 72**.
1. Inspect the reed valves as follows:

a. Remove the cover screws from the control valve and remove the cover.
b. Remove the reed valve from the reed valve body.
c. Inspect the reed valve for carbon deposits. Replace the control valve if there are deposits or the reeds are damaged.

2. Inspect the control valve as follows:

a. Blow air into the inlet port of the control valve (A, **Figure 76**).
b. Air should flow from the two control valve outlet ports. Replace the control valve if it does not.

3. Check the solenoid valve as follows:

a. Using a 12-volt battery, connect the positive battery wire to the black solenoid wire terminal and the negative battery wire to the black/red solenoid wire terminal.
b. Blow into the control valve inlet port. Air should not flow from the outlet ports when the battery is connected to the solenoid connector. If it does, replace the control valve. Disconnect the battery from the solenoid.

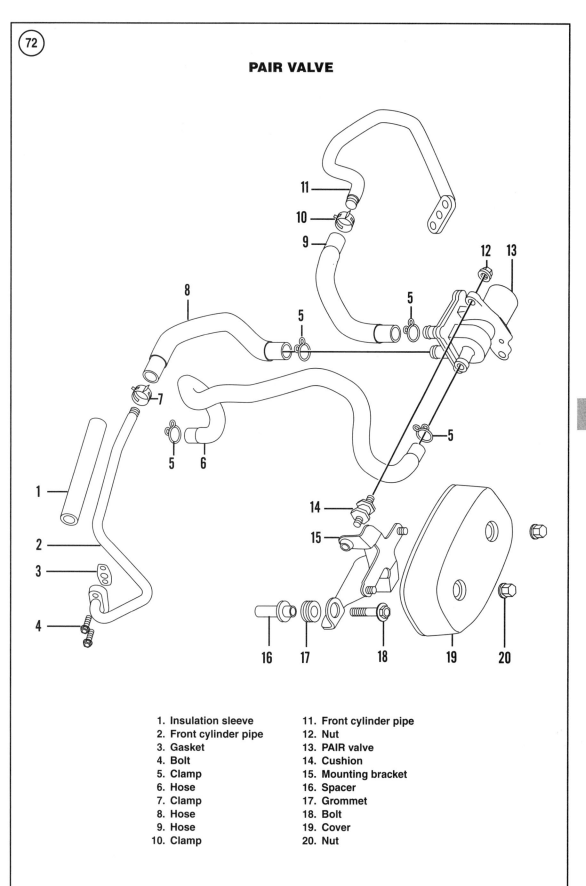

PAIR VALVE

1. Insulation sleeve
2. Front cylinder pipe
3. Gasket
4. Bolt
5. Clamp
6. Hose
7. Clamp
8. Hose
9. Hose
10. Clamp
11. Front cylinder pipe
12. Nut
13. PAIR valve
14. Cushion
15. Mounting bracket
16. Spacer
17. Grommet
18. Bolt
19. Cover
20. Nut

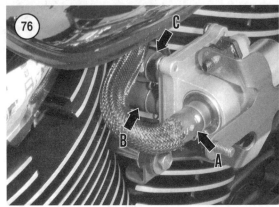

c. Connect an ohmmeter to the solenoid connector terminals. The resistance should equal the value in **Table 2**.

CRANKCASE BREATHER SYSTEM

All models are equipped with a closed crankcase breather system. This system routes crankcase vapors into the air intake duct, then they are drawn into the engine and burned. A breather hose is connected between the rear cylinder and the intake duct.

Inspection and Cleaning

Inspect the breather hose connected to the intake duct (**Figure 77**). Replace the hose if it is cracked or deteriorated. Make sure the hose clamps are in place and tight.

EVAPORATIVE EMISSION CONTROL SYSTEM (CALIFORNIA MODELS)

Fuel vapor from the fuel tank is routed into a charcoal canister. This vapor is stored when the engine is not running. When the engine is running these va-

pors are drawn into the throttle body to be burned. Refer to **Figure 78**.

Make sure the hoses are correctly routed and attached to the various components. Inspect the hoses and replace any if necessary. The charcoal canister and fuel shutoff valve are located on the right, rear frame downtube.

On most models, the hoses and fittings are color coded with labels or bands. If these labels or bands are deteriorated or missing, mark the hoses and the fittings to identify them.

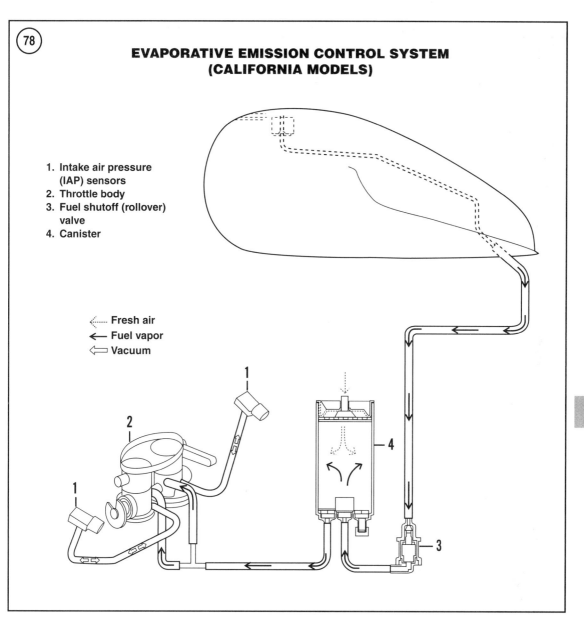

(78)

**EVAPORATIVE EMISSION CONTROL SYSTEM
(CALIFORNIA MODELS)**

1. Intake air pressure
   (IAP) sensors
2. Throttle body
3. Fuel shutoff (rollover)
   valve
4. Canister

◁······ Fresh air
◀── Fuel vapor
◁═ Vacuum

9

Due to the various manufacturing changes made during the years, always refer to the emission control label located on the inside of the right steering head cover.

EXHAUST SYSTEM

Check the exhaust system for deep dents and fractures. Repair or replace damaged parts immediately.

Check the muffler frame mounting flanges for fractures and loose bolts. Check the cylinder head mounting flanges for tightness.

Removal/Installation

1. Remove the oxygen sensor as described in this chapter, if so equipped.
2. Refer to *Exhaust System* in Chapter Eight.

Tables 1-3 are on the following pages.

Table 1 FUEL SYSTEM (EFI) SPECIFICATIONS

Item	Specification
Throttle body bore size	34 mm
Throttle body No.	
All models except California	41F0
California models	41F1
Idle speed	1000-1200 rpm
Fast idle speed	2100 rpm
Throttle cable free play	2.0-4.0 mm (0.08-0.16 in.)
Fuel pump output pressure	Approx. 300 kPa (43.5 psi)
Fuel pump output volume	Approx. 168 ml (5.7 U.S. oz.) per 10 seconds
Fuel tank capacity (total)	15.5 liters (4.1 U.S. gal.)
Fuel	
Type	Unleaded
Octane	
U.S. and Canada models	87 [(R + M)/2 method] or research octane of 91 or higher
Non- U.S.and Canada models	91

Table 2 FUEL SYSTEM (EFI) TEST SPECIFICATIONS

Item	Specification
Engine coolant temperature (ECT) sensor	
Resistance	Approx. 2.3-2.6k ohms at 20° C (68° F)
Voltage	4.5-5.5 volts
Resistance at temperature	
20° C (68° F)	Approx. 2.45k ohms
40° C (104° F)	Approx. 1.148k ohms
60° C (140° F)	Approx. 0.587k ohms
80° C (176° F)	Approx. 0.322k ohms
Fast idle speed TP sensor voltage differential	0.064-0.096 volts
Fuel injector resistance	
2005-2008 models	Approx 11.7 ohms at 20° C (68° F)
Intake air pressure (IAP) sensor	
Input voltage	4.5-5.5 volts
Output voltage	Approx. 2.6 volts at idle speed
V-out voltage	
94-100 kPa (707-760 mmHg)	3.4-4.0 volts
85-94 kPa (634-707 mmHg)	2.8-3.7 volts
76-85 kPa (567-634 mmHg)	2.6-3.4 volts
70-76 kPa (526-567 mmHg)	2.4-3.1 volts
Intake air temperature (IAT) sensor	
Resistance	Approx. 2.6k ohms at 20° C (68° F)
Voltage	4.5-5.5 volts
Resistance at temperature	
20° C (68° F)	Approx. 2.6k ohms
50° C (122° F)	Approx. 0.8k ohms
80° C (176° F)	Approx. 0.3k ohms
110° C (230° F)	Approx. 0.2k ohms
Heated oxygen (HO$_2$) sensor	
Heater voltage	Battery voltage
Voltage at idle speed	0.4 volts or less
Voltage at 5000 rpm	0.6 volts or more
Resistance	6.5-8.9 ohms
PAIR solenoid resistance	20-24 ohms at 20-30°s C (68-86° F)
Secondary throttle position (STP) sensor	
Resistance	
Fully closed	Approx 0.5k ohms
Fully open	Approx 3.9k ohms
Vcc resistance	4.6k ohms
Input voltage	4.5-5.5 volts

(continued)

Table 2 FUEL SYSTEM (EFI) TEST SPECIFICATIONS (continued)

Item	Specification
Output voltage	
Fully closed	Approx. 0.5 volts
Fully open	Approx. 3.9 volts
Secondary throttle valve actuator (STVA) resistance	Approx. 6.5 ohms
Throttle position (TP) sensor	
Input voltage	4.5-5.5 volts
Output voltage	
Fully closed	Approx. 1.1 volts
Fully open	Approx. 4.3 volts
Signal resistance	Approx 4.66k ohms
Tip-over (TO) sensor	
Resistance	19.1-19.7k ohms
Voltage	Upright: 0.4-1.4 volts
	Leaning 65°: 3.7-4.4 volts

Table 3 FUEL SYSTEM (EFI) TORQUE SPECIFICATIONS

Item	N•m	in.-lb.	ft.-lb.
Engine coolant temperature (ECT) sensor	18	159	–
Fuel delivery pipe screws	3.5	31	–
Fuel pump mounting plate bolts*	10	88	–
Heated oxygen (HO₂) sensor	48	–	35
Secondary throttle position (STVA)			
sensor screw	3.5	31	–
Throttle position (TP) sensor screw	3.5	31	–
*Apply threadlock			

9

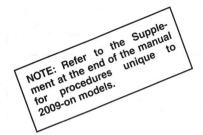
NOTE: Refer to the Supplement at the end of the manual for procedures unique to 2009-on models.

ELECTRICAL SYSTEM

This chapter covers the electrical system.

Refer to Chapter Three for battery service. Refer to **Tables 1-3** at the end of this chapter for specifications. Wiring diagrams are at the end of this manual.

PEAK VOLTAGE AND RESISTANCE TESTING

To measure peak voltage, use a tester capable of measuring peak voltage, such as the Suzuki Multi-Circuit Tester (part No. 09900-25008) or Motion Pro IgnitionMate (part No. 08-0193).

Make sure the battery of any tester being used is in good condition. The battery of an ohmmeter is the source for the current that is applied to the circuit being tested; accurate results depend on the battery having sufficient voltage.

All peak voltage specifications are minimum values. If the measured voltage meets or exceeds the specifications, the test results are acceptable.

Resistance readings will vary with temperature. The resistance increases when the temperature increases and decreases when the temperature decreases.

Specifications for resistance are based on tests usually performed at room temperature (approximately 20° C [68° F]). If a component is warm or hot let it cool to room temperature. If a component is tested at a temperature that varies from the specification test temperature, a false reading may result.

ELECTRICAL COMPONENT REPLACEMENT

Most motorcycle dealerships and parts suppliers will not accept the return of any electrical part. If the exact cause of an electrical system malfunction cannot be determined, have a dealership retest that specific system to verify the test results. This may help avert the possibility of purchasing an expensive, unreturnable part that does not fix the problem.

Consider any test results carefully before replacing a component that tests only slightly out of specification, especially resistance. A number of variables can affect test results dramatically. These include the testing meter's internal circuitry, ambient temperature and conditions under which the machine has been operated. All instructions and specifications have been checked for accuracy; however, successful test results depend to a great extent upon individual accuracy.

ELECTRICAL CONNECTORS

All models are equipped with numerous electrical components, connectors and wires. Corrosion-causing moisture can enter these electrical connectors and

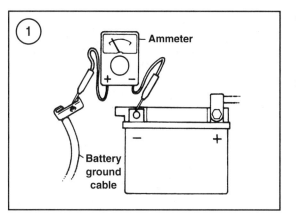

cause poor electrical connections, leading to component failure. Troubleshooting an electrical circuit with one or more corroded electrical connectors can be time-consuming and frustrating.

After cleaning both the male and female connectors, make sure they are thoroughly dry. Apply dielectric grease to the interior of one of the connectors prior to connecting the connector halves.

Do not use a substitute that may interfere with the current flow within the electrical connector. Do not use silicone sealant.

CHARGING SYSTEM

The charging system consists of the battery, alternator and a voltage regulator/rectifier. Alternating current generated by the alternator is rectified to direct current. The voltage regulator maintains the voltage to the battery and additional electrical loads at a constant voltage regardless of variations in engine speed.

Precautions

To prevent damage to the alternator and the regulator/rectifier when testing and repairing the charging system, note the following precautions:
1. Always disconnect the negative battery cable, as described in Chapter Three, before removing a component from the charging system.
2. When it is necessary to charge the battery, remove the battery from the motorcycle and recharge it as described in Chapter Three.
3. Inspect the physical condition of the battery. Look for bulges or cracks in the case, leaking electrolyte or corrosion buildup.
4. Check the wiring in the charging system for signs of chafing, deterioration or other damage.
5. Check the wiring for corroded or loose connections. Clean, tighten or reconnect as required.

Current Draw Test

Perform this test before performing the output test.
1. Disconnect the negative battery cable as described in Chapter Three.

> *CAUTION*
> *Before connecting the ammeter into the circuit in Step 2, set the meter to its highest amperage scale. This prevents a possible large current flow from damaging the meter or blowing the meter's fuse, if so equipped.*

2. Connect the ammeter between the negative battery cable and the negative battery post (**Figure 1**). Switch the ammeter from its highest to lowest amperage scale while reading the meter. If the needle swings even the slightest amount, current is draining from the system. The battery will eventually discharge.
3. If the current draw is excessive, the probable causes are:
   a. Loose, dirty or faulty electrical system connectors in the charging system wiring harness.
   b. Short circuit in the system.
   c. Damaged battery.
4. Isolate the current draw to a specific circuit by removing the fuses one at a time and observing the ammeter. If the current flow stops when a fuse is removed, that is the affected circuit. Further isolation can be achieved by disconnecting the connectors in that circuit.
5. After the current draw is repaired, disconnect the ammeter leads and reconnect the negative battery cable.

Output Test

If charging system trouble is suspected, make sure the battery is fully charged and in good condition before performing any tests. Clean and test the battery as described in Chapter Three. Make sure all electrical connectors are tight and free of corrosion.
1. Start the engine and let it reach normal operating temperature. Shut off the engine.
2. Remove the front seat as described in Chapter Sixteen.
3. Connect a portable tachometer according to the manufacturer's instructions.
4. Remove the red plastic cover from the positive battery terminal (**Figure 2**).
5. Turn the headlight dimmer switch to HI.
6. Restart the engine and let it idle.

10

7. Connect the positive test lead of a 0-25 DC voltmeter to the positive battery terminal. Connect the negative test lead to the negative battery terminal.

8. Increase engine speed to 5000 rpm. The voltage reading should be 14.0-15.5 volts. If the voltage is outside the specified range, inspect the alternator and the voltage regulator as described in this chapter. The voltage regulator/rectifier is a separate unit from the alternator and can be replaced individually.

9. If the charging voltage is too high, the voltage regulator/rectifier is probably faulty.

10. After completing the test, shut off the engine and disconnect the voltmeter and portable tachometer.

11. Install the cover (**Figure 2**) on the positive battery cable.

12. Install the front seat as described in Chapter Sixteen.

No-Load Test

1. Remove the left frame cover as described in Chapter Sixteen.

2. Remove the lower side cover (A, **Figure 3**) and left frame cover (B).

3. Disconnect the alternator three-wire (yellow wires) electrical connector (**Figure 4**).

4. Connect a portable tachometer according to the manufacturer's instructions.

> *NOTE*
> *In Step 5 connect the voltmeter test leads to the alternator end of the electrical connector disconnected in Step 3.*

5. Start the engine and let it idle.

6. Connect a 0-250 V (AC) voltmeter between each of the three terminals on the alternator end of the connector as shown in **Figure 5**.

7. Increase engine speed to 5000 rpm and check the voltage on the meter. The voltage should be greater than 70 volts.

8. Repeat this test for the remaining terminals. Take a total of three readings.

9. If the voltage in any test is less than the specified no-load voltage, shut off the engine and check the charging system wiring harness and connectors for dirty or loose-fitting terminals. Clean and repair as required. If the wiring and connectors are good, the alternator is defective and must be replaced.

10. Disconnect and remove the voltmeter and portable tachometer.

11. Reconnect the alternator connector (**Figure 4**). Make sure the connector is corrosion free and secure.

12. Install the lower side cover (A, **Figure 3**) and left frame cover (B).

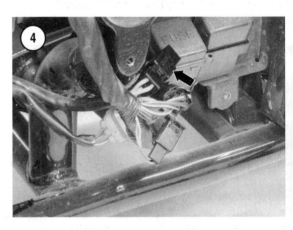

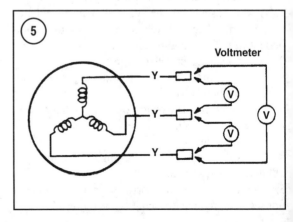

Voltmeter

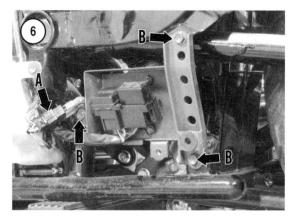

2. Remove the lower side cover (A, **Figure 3**) and the left frame cover (B).
3. Disconnect the negative battery cable (Chapter Three).
4. Disconnect the regulator/rectifier electrical connectors (A, **Figure 6**).
5. Remove the bolts (B, **Figure 6**) securing the electrical panel.
6. Remove the panel and turn it to expose the regulator/rectifier (A, **Figure 7**).
7. Remove the two mounting bolts (B, **Figure 7**) and remove the regulator/rectifier.
8. Install by reversing the preceding removal steps. Be sure the electrical connectors are tight and free of corrosion.

ALTERNATOR

Alternators generate alternating current. The electrical system, however, requires direct current in order to recharge the battery and operate the electrical equipment. The three-phase alternating current is rectified by the voltage regulator/rectifier into direct current.

Rotor Testing

The rotor is permanently magnetized and cannot be tested except by replacing it with a known good one. The rotor can become de-magnetized over time or from a sharp impact. If defective, replace the rotor.

Stator Coil Continuity Test

1. Remove the lower side cover (A, **Figure 8**) and left frame cover (B).
2. Start the engine and let it reach normal operating temperature. Shut off the engine.
3. Disconnect the alternator three-wire (yellow wires) electrical connector (A, **Figure 4**).
4. Check the continuity between each of the terminals on the alternator end of the connector as shown in **Figure 9**. If using an analog ohmmeter, be sure to zero the meter.
5. There should be continuity between all three terminals. If not, the alternator is defective and must be replaced.
6. Check for continuity between each terminal in the connector and ground. If there is continuity, one or more of the stator wires is shorted to ground. Replace the stator assembly.
7. Disconnect and remove the ohmmeter.

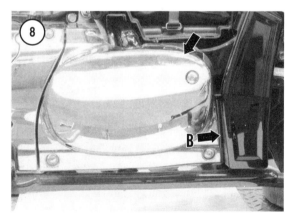

VOLTAGE REGULATOR/RECTIFIER

Testing

Special equipment is required to test the regulator/rectifier. If the regulator/rectifier is questionable, have a dealership test the unit.

Removal/Installation

1. Remove the left frame cover as described in Chapter Sixteen.

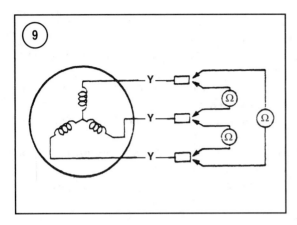

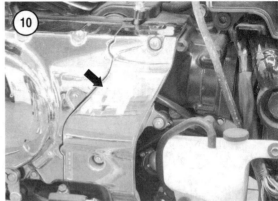

8. Reconnect the alternator electrical connector. Make sure the connector is corrosion free and tight.

9. Install the lower side cover and left frame cover.

Stator Assembly Removal/Installation

The stator assembly is located within the alternator cover.

1. Remove the lower side cover (A, **Figure 8**) and the left frame cover (B).

2. Remove the secondary drive cover (**Figure 10**).

3. Disconnect the alternator three-wire electrical connector (A, **Figure 11**) and the pickup coil two-wire connector (B).

4. Remove the alternator cover (**Figure 12**) from the crankcase.

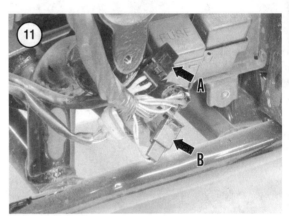

> *NOTE*
> *Note the path of the wiring harness when withdrawing it in Step 5.*

5. Remove the alternator cover while carefully withdraw the wiring harness from the frame. Do not lose the two locating dowels.

6. Place several shop cloths on the workbench to protect the alternator cover. Turn the alternator cover upside down on these cloths.

7. Remove the bolts securing the pickup coil (A, **Figure 13**) to the cover.

> *NOTE*
> *Note the location of the wiring harness holder under the pickup coil.*

8. Remove the bolts securing the wiring harness (B, **Figure 13**) to the cover.

9. Remove the bolts securing the stator assembly (C, **Figure 13**) to the cover. Carefully pull the rubber grommet (D, **Figure 13**) from the cover and remove the stator and ignition pickup coil assembly from the cover.

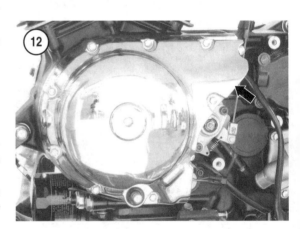

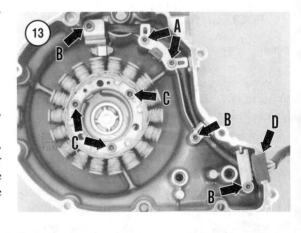

e. Install a new gasket washer on the indicated alternator cover bolts (**Figure 15**).

Rotor Removal/Installation

CAUTION
Do not attempt to remove the rotor without a puller. Doing so will damage to the engine and/or rotor. Pullers are available from part suppliers or dealerships (Suzuki part No. 09930- 33730).

1. Remove the alternator cover as described in this section.
2. Place a wrench on the hex of the rotor (A, **Figure 16**), then loosen the alternator rotor bolt (B). Do not remove the bolt, but loosen it several turns. The puller bolt will contact the rotor bolt during the pulling process.
3. Install the rotor removal tool (**Figure 17**) onto the threads of the rotor.
4. Hold the tool flats with a suitable wrench. Turn the bolt of the rotor removal tool until the rotor disengages from the crankshaft taper. Remove the rotor from the crankshaft.

CAUTION
If the rotor is difficult to remove, strike the end of the rotor removal tool (not the rotor because impact will damage it) firmly with a hammer.

CAUTION
Do not apply excessive pressure to the puller or the rotor threads may be stripped. If the rotor is difficult to remove, have a dealership perform the procedure.

5. Remove the rotor removal tool.
6. Remove the rotor bolt and washer.
7. Inspect the inside of the rotor (A, **Figure 18**) for metal debris that may have been picked up by the

10. Install by reversing the preceding removal steps while noting the following:

    a. Apply a light coat of Threadlock 1342 or equivalent to the stator mounting bolt threads before installation. Tighten the stator retaining bolts securely.

    b. Make sure the electrical connector is tight and free of corrosion.

    c. If removed, install the two locating dowels (A, **Figure 14**).

    d. Install a new gasket (B, **Figure 14**).

magnets. This debris can damage the alternator stator assembly.

8. Inspect the rotor keyway (B, **Figure 18**) for wear or damage. If damaged, replace the rotor.

9. Install by reversing the preceding removal steps while noting the following:

a. Use aerosol parts cleaner to clean all oil residue from the crankshaft taper and the matching tapered surface in the rotor. This ensures a tight fit between the rotor and the crankshaft.

b. Make sure the key is in place on the crankshaft (**Figure 19**).

c. Apply a light coat of engine oil to the mounting bolt threads before installation.

d. Make sure the washer is mounted on the rotor bolt, then tighten the alternator rotor bolt to 160 N•m (118 ft.-lb.).

ELECTRONIC IGNITION SYSTEM

The engine is equipped with an electronic ignition system. On 2001-2004 models, the system consists of a pickup coil, igniter unit, throttle position (TP) sensor, and two ignition coils and spark plugs. On 2005-on models, the igniter unit is part of the engine control module (ECM). On 2005-on models, the pickup coil is replaced with a crankshaft position (CKP) sensor.

The pickup coil (2001-2004) or CKP sensor (2005-on) portion of the system consists of external projections on the alternator rotor and the pickup coil or CKP.

The throttle position (TP) sensor is mounted on the carburetor (2001-2004) or throttle body (2005-on).

As the crankshaft rotates, the projections on the alternator rotor pass the pickup coil or CKP, which sends a signal to the igniter unit. The CPU (part of the igniter or ECM) uses this signal, input from the throttle position sensor, and a stored digital data map to determine the optimum ignition timing for the operating conditions.

The system includes an engine speed limiter. If the engine exceeds 8000 rpm, the primary current to the ignition coil/spark plug caps is interrupted.

The igniter unit or ECM also monitors the position of the gear shifter and sidestand through respective switches. The igniter or ECM stops ignition if the sidestand is down and the transmission is in any gear other than neutral, or if the transmission is shifted out of neutral with the sidestand down.

Ignition System Precautions

> *WARNING*
> *High voltage is present during ignition system operation. Do not touch ignition components, wires or test leads while the engine is running or cranking.*

> *CAUTION*
> *Do not disconnect any of the electrical connections while the engine is running.*

Troubleshooting

Refer to *Ignition System* in Chapter Two.

Pickup Coil (2001-2004 Models)

Peak voltage test

Refer to *Peak Voltage and Resistance Testing* in this chapter.

1. Remove the front seat as described in Chapter Sixteen.

2. Disconnect the igniter connector (**Figure 20**) from the igniter unit.

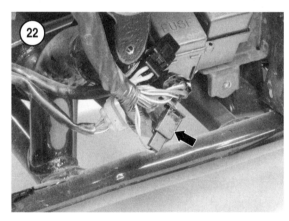

3. Connect the negative test probe to the blue/white terminal on the connector, and connect the positive test probe to the green terminal.

4. Shift the transmission into neutral and turn the ignition switch on.

5. Press the starter button and crank the engine for a few seconds and record the highest reading.

6. If the pickup coil peak voltage is less than 1.5 volts, check the peak voltage at the pickup coil coupler as follows:

   a. Remove the left frame cover as described in Chapter Sixteen.

   b. Remove the lower side cover (**Figure 21**).

   c. Disconnect the 2-pin pickup coil connector (**Figure 22**).

   d. Connect the positive test probe to the blue terminal on the pickup coil end of the connector. Connect the negative test probe to the green terminal.

   e. Shift the transmission into neutral and turn the ignition switch on.

   f. Press the starter button and crank the engine for a few seconds and record the highest reading.

7. If the peak voltage measured at the pickup coil connector is normal but the peak voltage at the igniter connector is less than 1.5 volts, replace the wiring.

8. If the peak voltage at both the pickup coil connector and the igniter connector are less than 1.5 volts, replace the pickup coil.

9. If all tests are acceptable, reconnect the electrical connector. Make sure the electrical connector is free of corrosion and is tight.

10. Install the front seat and the covers.

Resistance test

   Refer to *Peak Voltage and Resistance Test* in this chapter.

1. Remove the left frame cover as described in Chapter Sixteen.

2. Remove the lower side cover (**Figure 21**).

3. Disconnect the 2-pin pickup coil connector (**Figure 22**).

4. Check the resistance between the blue and green terminals in the pickup coil end of the connector (**Figure 22**). If the pickup coil coil resistance is outside the range of 160-300 ohms, replace the pickup coil.

5. Check the continuity between the green terminal in the pickup coil connector and ground. There should be no continuity (infinite resistance). If there is continuity, replace the pickup coil.

6. If all tests are acceptable, reconnect the electrical connector. Make sure the electrical connector is free of corrosion and is secure.

7. Install the covers.

Replacement

   The pickup coil (A, **Figure 23**) and alternator stator (B) are located inside the alternator cover. The pickup coil and stator are only available as a unit assembly. If the pickup coil is faulty, replace it by following the stator replacement procedure in this chapter.

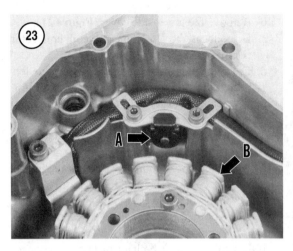

Crankshaft Position (CKP) Sensor
(2005-On Models)

Peak voltage test

Refer to *Peak Voltage and Resistance Test* in this chapter.

1. Remove the toolbox as described in Chapter Sixteen.

2. Disconnect the CKP sensor connector (**Figure 24**).

3. Connect the negative voltmeter test probe to the blue wire terminal on the connector, and connect the positive test probe to the green terminal.

4. Shift the transmission into neutral and turn the ignition switch on.

5. Press the starter button and crank the engine for a few seconds and record the highest reading.

6. If the CKP sensor peak voltage is less than 4 volts, inspect the wiring and connector terminals. If the wiring and connector are good, replace the sensor.

7. If all tests are acceptable, reconnect the electrical connector. Make sure the electrical connector is free of corrosion and is tight.

8. Install the toolbox and covers.

Resistance test

Refer to *Peak Voltage and Resistance Test* in this chapter.

1. Remove the toolbox as described in Chapter Sixteen.

2. Disconnect the CKP sensor connector (**Figure 24**).

3. Check the resistance between the blue and green wire terminals in the sensor end of the connector. If the sensor resistance is outside the range of 184-276 ohms, replace the sensor.

4. Check for continuity between each terminal in the sensor connector and ground. There should be no continuity (infinite resistance). If there is continuity, replace the sensor.

5. If all tests are acceptable, reconnect the electrical connector. Make sure the electrical connector is free of corrosion and is secure.

6. Install the toolbox and covers.

Replacement

The crankshaft position sensor (A, **Figure 23**) and alternator stator (B) are located inside the alternator cover. The sensor and stator are only available as a unit assembly. If the sensor is faulty, replace it by following the stator replacement procedure in this chapter.

Ignition Coil

The ignition coils are located on the inside of the top frame tubes above the front cylinder head (**Figure 25**).

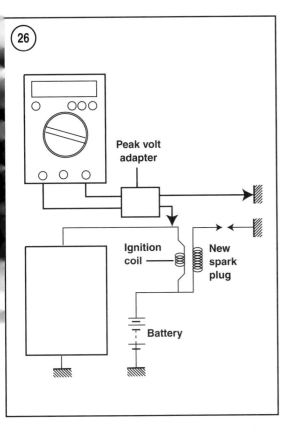

Peak volt adapter

Ignition coil — New spark plug

Battery

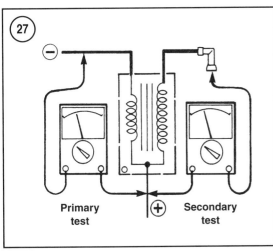

Primary test (−) (+) Secondary test

Primary peak voltage test

Refer to *Peak Voltage and Resistance Test* in this chapter.

1. Remove the fuel tank as described in Chapter Eight or Chapter Nine.

2. Remove both spark plugs as described in Chapter Three.

3. Connect a new spark plug to each plug cap.

4. Ground both spark plugs to the crankcase.

5. Check the peak voltage for the rear cylinder as follows:

a. Set the tester to voltage.

NOTE
Do not disconnect the wires from the ignition coil when performing the following test. If it is not possible to contact the coil terminal with the tester probe, pierce the wire using a needle probe.

b. Connect the positive test probe to the white wire or terminal on the ignition coil and connect the negative test probe to ground. See **Figure 26**.

c. Shift the transmission into neutral and turn the ignition switch on.

d. Press the starter button and crank the engine for a few seconds while reading the meter. Record the highest meter reading. The minimum peak voltage is 200 volts.

6. Check the peak voltage for the front cylinder by performing Step 5, except connect the positive test probe to the black/yellow wire or terminal on the ignition coil.

7. If the peak voltage reading on either ignition coil is less than specified, measure the resistance on that ignition coil.

Resistance test

Refer to *Peak Voltage and Resistance Test* in this chapter.

1. Disconnect all ignition coil wires (including the spark plug leads from the spark plugs) before testing.

2. Measure the primary coil resistance between the positive (orange/white wire) and the negative terminals (white or black/yellow wire) on the ignition coil (**Figure 27**). Specified primary coil resistance is in **Table 1**.

3. Measure the secondary coil resistance between the spark plug lead (with the spark plug cap attached) and the positive coil terminal. Specified secondary coil resistance is listed in **Table 1**.

4. If either measurement does not meet specification, replace the coil. If the coil exhibits visible damage, replace it.

5. Reconnect all ignition coil wires to the ignition coil.

6. Repeat this procedure for the other ignition coil.

Removal/installation

1. Disconnect the negative battery cable (Chapter Three).

2. Remove the fuel tank as described in Chapter Eight or Chapter Nine.

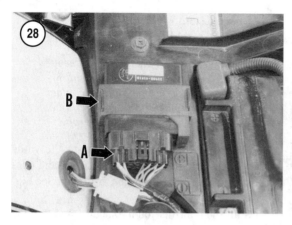

3. Disconnect all ignition coil wires, including the spark plug leads from the spark plugs.

4. Remove the screws securing the ignition coil to the frame.

5. Install by reversing the preceding removal steps. Make sure all electrical connections are corrosion-free and secure.

IGNITER (2001-2004 MODELS)

Testing

No test procedure is available. If all other ignition system components test correctly, consider the ignitor unit defective by process of elimination. However, consider that many ignition problems are caused by faulty wiring and connections. Check all wires and connections before assuming the ignitor unit is faulty.

Refer to *Electrical Component Replacement* in this chapter.

Replacement

1. Remove the rear seat as described in Chapter Sixteen.

2. Disconnect the negative battery cable (Chapter Three).

3. Disconnect the connector (A, **Figure 28**) from the igniter.

4. Remove the igniter (B, **Figure 28**) from the rubber mount.

5. Reinstall the igniter by reversing the preceding removal steps.

ELECTRONIC CONTROL MODULE (ECM) 2005-ON MODELS

The electronic control module (ECM) controls the ignition and fuel injection systems. Refer to Chapter Nine for fuel injection system components.

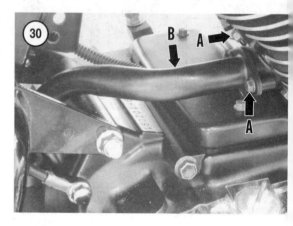

Testing

No test procedure is available. If all other ignition system components test correctly, consider the ECM faulty by process of elimination. However, consider that many electrical problems are caused by faulty wiring and connections. Check all wires and connectors before assuming the ECM is faulty.

Refer to *Electrical Component Replacement* in this chapter.

Replacement

1. Disconnect the negative battery cable (Chapter Three).

2. Remove the right side cover (Chapter Sixteen).

3. Disconnect the connectors (A, **Figure 29**) from the ECM.

4. Remove the ECM (B, **Figure 29**) from the rubber mount.

5. Reinstall the ECM by reversing the removal steps.

STARTER SYSTEM

The starting system consists of the starter, starter relay, clutch switch, sidestand switch, turn signal/

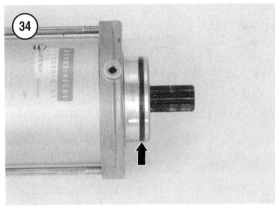

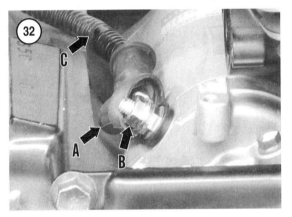

sidestand relay, gear position (GP) sensor/neutral switch, engine stop switch and the starter button.

When the starter button is pressed, it engages the starter relay and completes the circuit allowing electricity to flow from the battery to the starter. The starter rotates the engine crankshaft through the starter idler gear and the starter clutch.

CAUTION
Do not operate the starter for more than 5 seconds at a time. Let it cool approximately 10 seconds before operating it again.

Troubleshooting

Refer to Chapter Two.

Removal/Installation

1. Securely support the bike on level ground.
2. Drain the engine coolant as described in Chapter Three.
3. Disconnect the negative battery cable (Chapter Three).
4. Remove the rear cylinder exhaust pipe as described in Chapter Eight or Chapter Nine.
5. Remove the coolant pipe retaining bolts (A, **Figure 30**), then move the pipe (B) out of the way.
6. Remove the starter cover bolts (A, **Figure 31**), then remove the cover (B).
7. Pull back the rubber boot (A, **Figure 32**) from the starter electrical connector.
8. Remove the starter cable retaining nut (B, **Figure 32**) and disconnect the starter cable (C) from the starter.
9. Remove the two bolts (A, **Figure 33**) securing the starter to the crankcase.
10. Remove the starter (B, **Figure 33**).
11. Clean the starter mounting pads on the crankcase and the mounting lugs on the starter motor.
12. Inspect the O-ring (**Figure 34**) on the drive end of the starter. Replace the O-ring if necessary. Apply clean engine oil to the O-ring before installing the starter.
13. Install the starter by reversing the removal procedure. Note the following:
   a. Tighten the starter mounting bolts securely.
   b. Attach the starter cable to the starter so it can be routed through the cutout portion of the starter cover (C, **Figure 31**).
   c. Connect the negative battery cable.

10

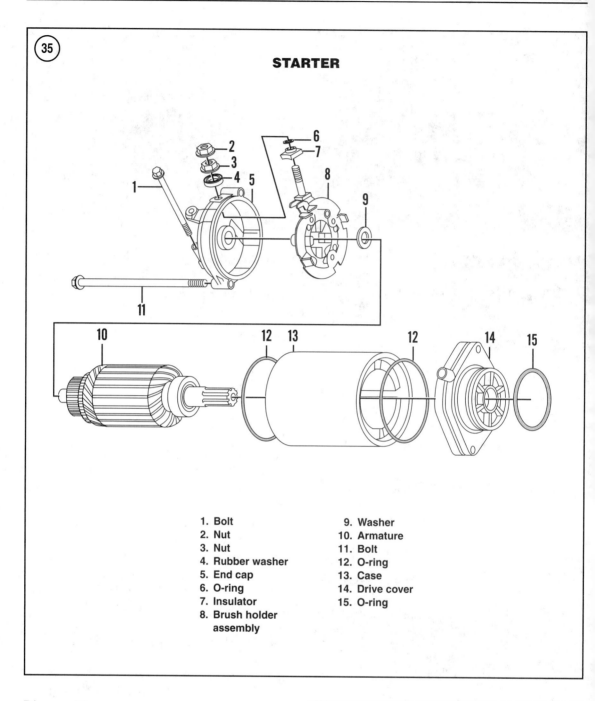

35

STARTER

1. Bolt
2. Nut
3. Nut
4. Rubber washer
5. End cap
6. O-ring
7. Insulator
8. Brush holder
   assembly
9. Washer
10. Armature
11. Bolt
12. O-ring
13. Case
14. Drive cover
15. O-ring

Disassembly

Refer to **Figure 35.**

1. Remove the case bolts and washers (A, **Figure 36**), then separate the drive cover (B) from the case.

2. Withdraw the armature (A, **Figure 37**) from the case (B). Separate the case from the end cap (C, **Figure 37**).

3. Remove the nut (A, **Figure 38**), metal washer (B), and rubber washer (C).

4. Withdraw the positive stud from the end cap and separate the end cap from the brush holder assembly (**Figure 39**).

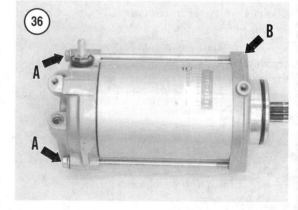

36

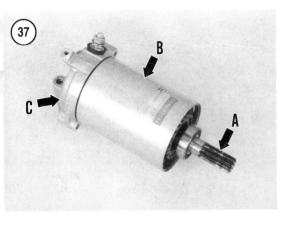

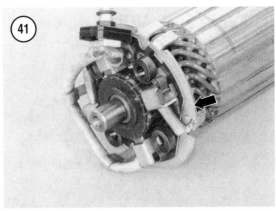

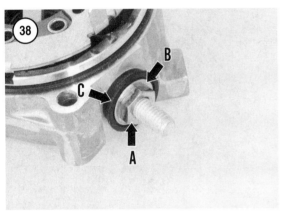

10

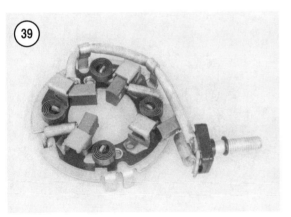

5. Remove any washers that remain on the end of the armature or in the end cap.

CAUTION
Do not immerse the armature in solvent as the coil insulation may be damaged. Wipe the windings with a cloth lightly moistened with solvent. Thoroughly dry before assembly.

6. Clean all grease, dirt and carbon from all components.

7. Inspect the starter components as described in this section.

Assembly

1. If removed, install the O-ring seal into both the drive cover and end cap (**Figure 40**).

2. Push all four brushes into their holders and carefully install the brush holder assembly (**Figure 41**) onto the armature. Push it down until it stops.

3. Install the washers (**Figure 42**) onto the end of the armature.

4. Install the insulator (A, **Figure 43**) and O-ring (B) onto the positive stud. Make sure the insulator fits properly on the stud base.

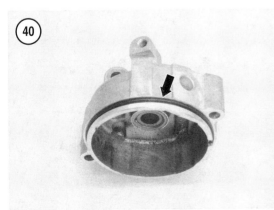

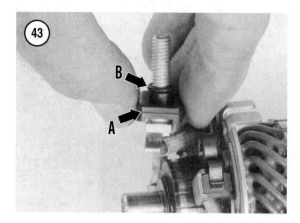

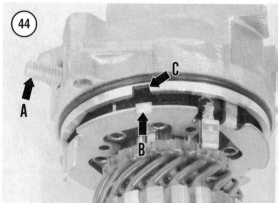

5. Install the positive stud of the brush holder into the end cap (A, **Figure 44**) and install the end cap onto the brush holder. Position the tab on the brush holder (B, **Figure 44**) into the notch in the end cap (C).

6. Install the rubber washer (C, **Figure 38**), metal washer (B) and nut (A) securing the positive stud in the end cap. Tighten the nut securely.

7. Note the locating tabs (A, **Figure 45**) on the brush holder. The tabs must align with the raised boss in the case (B, **Figure 45**) during installation.

8. Install the case onto the armature coil assembly and end cap.

9. Install the drive cover onto the case.

10. Align the case screw holes in the drive cover and end cap and push the drive cover and end cap onto the case until they bottom.

11. Apply a small amount of threadlock (ThreeBond 1344 or equivalent) to the case bolt threads prior to installation.

12. Install the case screws and washers (A, **Figure 36**) and tighten securely.

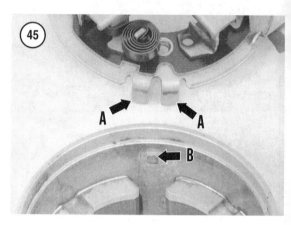

Inspection

The only starter parts available separately are the positive stud components, the O-rings and the case bolts. Individual brushes are not available separately, only as part of the brush holder assembly. If any other part of the starter is faulty, replace the starter as an assembly.

1. Inspect each brush for abnormal wear. Replace as necessary.

2. Inspect the commutator (A, **Figure 46**). The mica in a good commutator is below the surface of the copper bars. On a worn commutator, the mica and copper bars may be worn to the same level (**Figure 47**). If necessary, have the commutator serviced by a dealership or electrical repair shop.

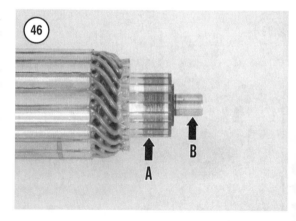

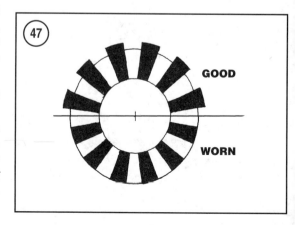

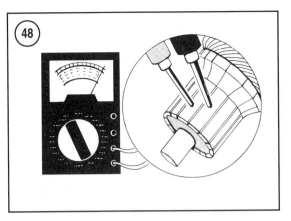

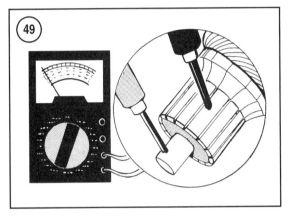

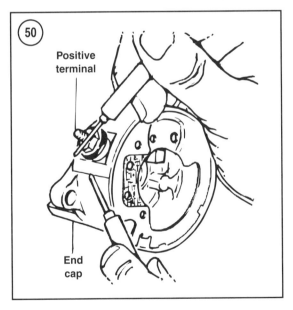

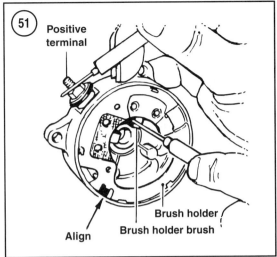

Positive terminal

Brush holder
Brush holder brush
Align

10

5. Inspect the commutator copper bars (A, **Figure 46**) for discoloration. If a pair of bars are discolored, grounded armature coils are indicated.

6. Use an ohmmeter and perform the following:

   a. Check for continuity between the commutator bars (**Figure 48**); there should be continuity between pairs of bars.

   b. Check for continuity between the commutator bars and the shaft (**Figure 49**); there should be no continuity (infinite resistance).

   c. If the unit fails either of these tests, replace the starter. The armature cannot be replaced individually.

7. Use an ohmmeter and perform the following:

   a. Check for continuity between the positive terminal and the end cap (**Figure 50**); there should be no continuity.

   b. Check for continuity between the positive terminal and the positive brushes (**Figure 51**); there should be continuity.

8. Inspect the seal (**Figure 52**) in the drive cover for wear, hardness or damage.

3. Inspect the entire length of the armature for straightness or heat damage. Rotate the ball bearing and check for roughness or binding.

4. Inspect the armature shaft where it rides in the bushing (B, **Figure 46**). Check for wear, burrs or other damage. If worn or damaged, replace starter.

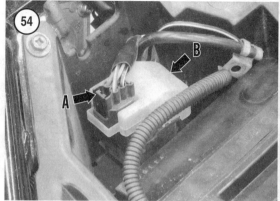

9. Inspect the bushing (**Figure 53**) in the end cap for wear or damage. If it is damaged, replace the starter.

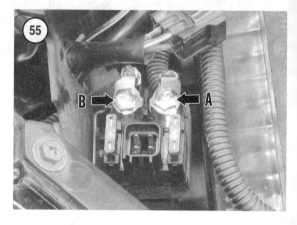

10. Inspect the magnets in the case. They should not be loose, chipped, or damaged. If they have picked up any small metal particles, remove the particles prior to reassembly.

11. Inspect the brush holder and springs for wear or damage. Replace if necessary.

12. Inspect the end cover and drive cover for wear or damage. If either is damaged, replace the starter.

13. Check the bolts for thread damage; if necessary, clean up with the appropriate size metric die. Inspect the O-rings for hardness, deterioration or damage. Replace as necessary.

STARTER RELAY

Testing

1. Remove the front seat as described in Chapter Sixteen.

2. Disconnect the negative battery cable (Chapter Three).

3. Disconnect the starter relay primary connector (A, **Figure 54**).

4. Remove the cover (B, **Figure 54**) from the starter relay.

5. Shift the transmission into neutral.

6. Remove the nuts and washers and disconnect the battery positive cable (A, **Figure 55**) and the starter negative cable (B) from the starter relay.

7. Connect a 12-volt battery to the positive terminal and negative terminal on the relay (**Figure 56**).

8. Connect an ohmmeter to the relay terminals shown in **Figure 56**. There should be continuity, indicating the relay is operating correctly. If there is no continuity, the relay is faulty and must be replaced.

9. Disconnect the 12-volt test battery from the relay.

10. Connect an ohmmeter to the relay terminals shown in **Figure 57**. There should be indicated resis-

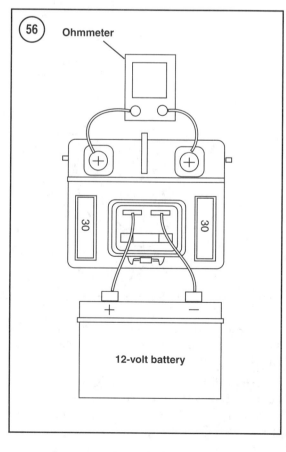

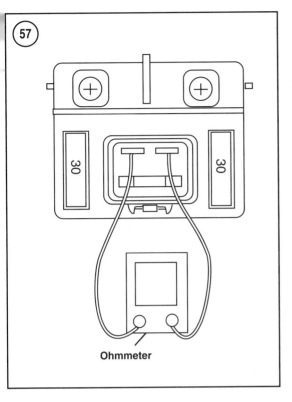

Ohmmeter

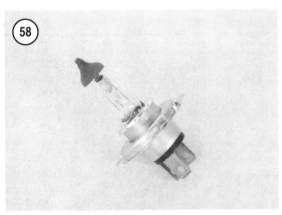

tance. Refer to the standard resistance in **Table 1**. If the resistance does not fall within these specifications, the relay is faulty and must be replaced.

11. If the relay tests correctly, reconnect all electrical wires to the relay and tighten the nuts securely. Make sure the electrical connectors are tight and the rubber boot is properly installed to keep out moisture.

12. If the relay is faulty, replace it as described in this section.

13. Reconnect the battery cables as decribed in Chapter Three.

14. Install the front seat as described in Chapter Sixteen.

Removal/Installation

1. Remove the front seat as described in Chapter Sixteen.
2. Disconnect the negative battery cable (Chapter Three).
3. Disconnect the starter relay primary connector (A, **Figure 54**).
4. Remove the cover (B, **Figure 54**) from the starter relay.
5. Disconnect the black starter lead and the red battery cable from the starter relay.
6. Remove the starter relay.
7. Install by reversing the preceding removal steps and note the following:
   a. Install both electrical cables to the relay and tighten the nuts securely.
   b. Make sure the electrical connectors are tight and the rubber boot is properly installed to keep out moisture.

LIGHTING SYSTEM

The lighting system consists of a headlight, tail-light/brake light, turn signals, indicator lights and assorted relays. Refer to **Table 2** for replacement bulb specifications.

10

Headlight Bulb Replacement

> *WARNING*
> *If the headlight has just burned out or has just been turned off, it will be hot. Do not touch the bulb. Wait for the bulb to cool before removing it.*

> *CAUTION*
> *The headlight is equipped with a quartz-halogen bulb (**Figure 58**). Do not touch the bulb glass because traces of oil on the bulb will reduce the life of the bulb. Clean any traces of oil or other chemicals from the bulb with a cloth moistened in alcohol or lacquer thinner.*

2001-2004 models

Refer to **Figure 59**.

1. Remove the screws on both sides securing the headlight assembly in the headlight housing (**Figure 60**).
2. Carefully pull the headlight lens unit out of the housing.

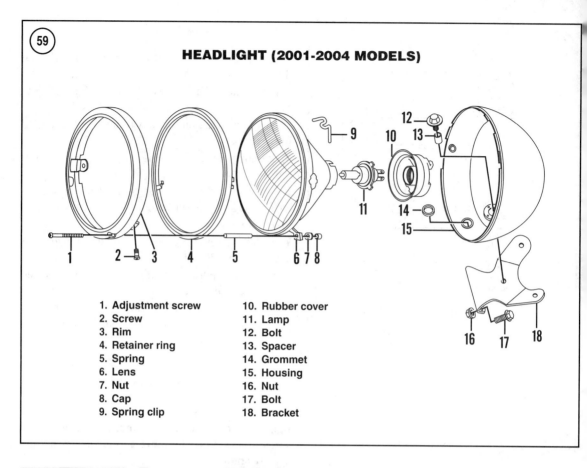

HEADLIGHT (2001-2004 MODELS)

1. Adjustment screw
2. Screw
3. Rim
4. Retainer ring
5. Spring
6. Lens
7. Nut
8. Cap
9. Spring clip
10. Rubber cover
11. Lamp
12. Bolt
13. Spacer
14. Grommet
15. Housing
16. Nut
17. Bolt
18. Bracket

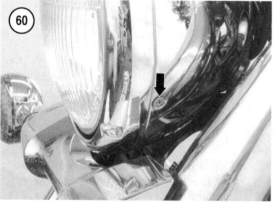

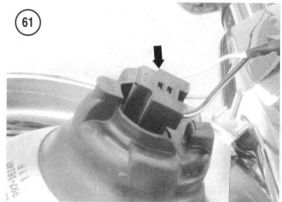

3. Disconnect the electrical connector/socket (**Figure 61**) from the headlight lens unit.

4. Remove the rubber cover (**Figure 62**).

5. Detach the bulb retaining spring (**Figure 63**).

6. Pull out the bulb (**Figure 64**).

7. Install by reversing the removal steps and note the following:

   a. Align the three tangs on the new bulb with the notches in the headlight housing and install the bulb.

   b. Install the rubber cover so the TOP mark on the cover sits at the top of the headlight assembly.

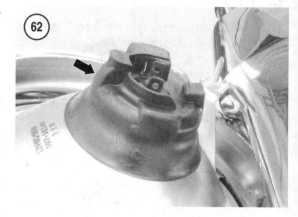

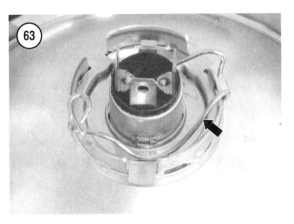

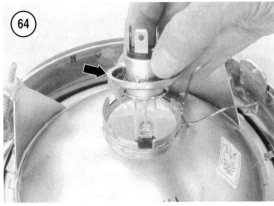

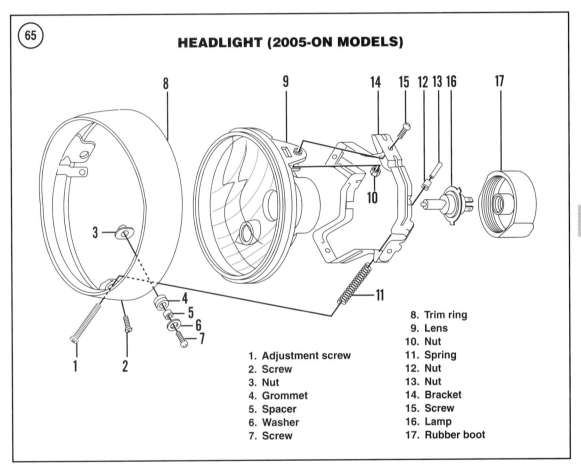

HEADLIGHT (2005-ON MODELS)

1. Adjustment screw
2. Screw
3. Nut
4. Grommet
5. Spacer
6. Washer
7. Screw
8. Trim ring
9. Lens
10. Nut
11. Spring
12. Nut
13. Nut
14. Bracket
15. Screw
16. Lamp
17. Rubber boot

Make sure the cover is correctly seated against the lens assembly and the bulb.

c. Check headlight operation.

2005-on models

Refer to **Figure 65**.

1. Remove the screws (**Figure 66**) on each side of the headlight housing.

2. Pull on the bottom of the headlight trim ring and disengage it from the headlight housing. Remove the trim ring and headlight lens unit assembly from the housing and pivot it down to gain access to the backside of the assembly.

3. Disconnect the electrical connector (A, **Figure 67**) from the backside of the bulb, then remove the headlight lens assembly.

4. Remove the rubber cover (B, **Figure 67**) from the back of the headlight lens unit.

5. Unhook the clip (A, **Figure 68**) and remove the light bulb (B).

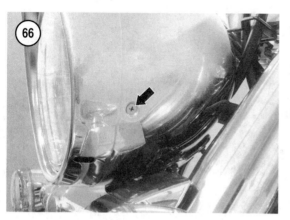

6. Install by reversing the removal steps. Note the following:

   a. Align the three tangs on the new bulb with the notches in the headlight housing and install the bulb.

   b. Install the rubber cover so the TOP mark on the cover sits at the top of the headlight assembly. Make sure the cover is correctly seated against the lens assembly and the bulb.

   c. Check headlight operation.

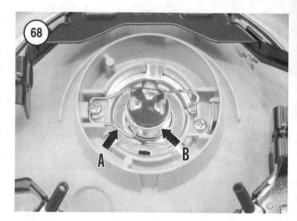

Headlight Lens and Housing Removal/Installation

2001-2004 models

Refer to **Figure 59**.

1. Remove the headlight bulb as described in this section.

2. To remove the lens from the trim ring, perform the following:

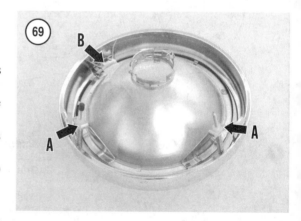

   a. Remove the aiming adjust screws and springs (A, **Figure 69**).

   b. Detach the retaining spring clip (B, **Figure 69**) securing the lens to the trim ring.

   c. Remove the lens from the trim ring.

3. To remove the headlight housing, perform the following:

   a. Remove the lens as described.

   b. Bend back the wire retaining clamps and release the wiring from the clamps.

   c. Disconnect the turn signal connectors (**Figure 70**). Refer to the wiring diagram.

   d. Remove the bolts (A, **Figure 71**) securing the headlight housing to the mounting brackets.

   e. Move the headlight housing away from the steering head area while removing the electrical connectors and harnesses. Most of the wiring passes out through the rear opening (B, **Figure 71**) in the headlight housing while the

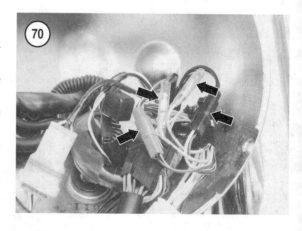

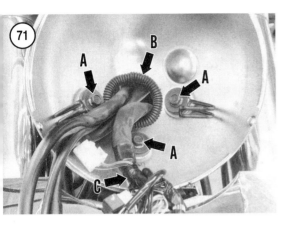

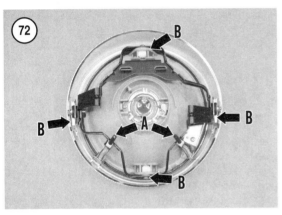

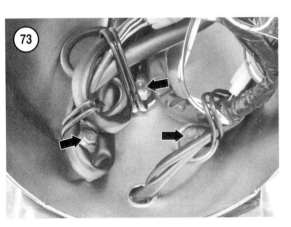

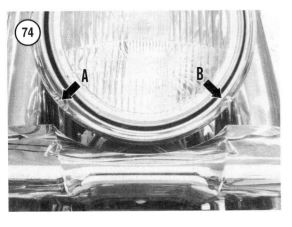

turn signal wiring passes through the lower opening (C).

   f. Remove the headlight housing. Do not lose the collar and rubber cushion in each mounting hole.

4. Install by reversing the preceding removal steps.

2005-on models

Refer to **Figure 65**.

1. Remove the headlight bulb as described in this section.

2. To remove the lens from the trim ring, perform the following:

   a. Remove the adjustment screws (A, **Figure 72**).

   b. Remove the screws, washers and spacers (B, **Figure 72**) securing the lens unit to the mounting ring and remove the mounting ring and trim ring from the lens unit.

3. To remove the headlight housing, perform the following:

   a. Remove the lens as described in Step 2.

   b. Bend back the wire retaining clamps and release the wiring from the clamps.

   c. Disconnect the turn signal connectors. Refer to the wiring diagram.

   d. Remove the bolts (**Figure 73**) securing the headlight housing to the mounting brackets.

   e. Move the headlight housing away from the steering head area while removing the electrical connectors and harnesses.

   f. Remove the headlight housing. Do not lose the collar and rubber cushion in each mounting hole.

4. Install by reversing the preceding removal steps.

Headlight Adjustment

1. On 2001-2004 models, turn the horizontal adjustment screw (A, **Figure 74**) to adjust the headlight horizontally. For vertical adjustment, turn the vertical adjustment screw (B, **Figure 74**).

2. On 2005-on models, adjust the headlight horizontally or vertically by turning the adjustment screws (**Figure 75**) through the slots in the trim ring.

Taillight/Brake Light Bulb Replacement

1. Remove the lens (**Figure 76**).

2. Push the defective bulb into the socket, turn it counterclockwise and remove it.

3. Carefully clean the lens and reflective surface on the bulb holder.

10

4. Install a new bulb.

5. Install the lens and gasket. Do not overtighten the screws or the lens may crack.

6. Check light operation.

Front and Rear Turn Signal Bulb Replacement

2001-2004 models

1. Remove the lens (**Figure 77**).

2. Push the defective bulb into the socket, turn it counterclockwise and remove it.

3. Carefully clean the lens and reflective surface on the bulb holder.

4. Install a new bulb.

5. Install the lens and gasket. Do not overtighten the screws or the lens may crack.

6. Check the turn signal light operation.

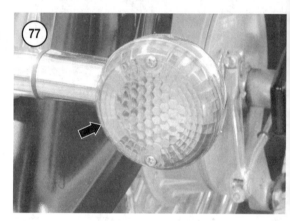

2005-on models

1. Remove the lens retaining screw (**Figure 78**).

2. Turn the lens counterclockwise and remove it.

3. Push the defective bulb into the socket, turn it counterclockwise and remove it.

4. Carefully clean the lens and reflective surface on the bulb holder.

5. Install a new bulb.

6. Install the lens and gasket.

7. Install the lens retaining screw (**Figure 78**).

8. Check the turn signal light operation.

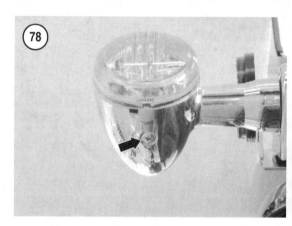

Indicator Lights

The indicator lights for high beam, turn signals, coolant temperature, oil pressure and neutral are mounted on the speedometer panel. The lights are LEDs, which are not available individually, but only as part of the speedometer panel. Refer to *Speedometer* in this chapter.

Make sure the connections and wiring are good. If so, take the speedometer to a dealership to test the indicator lights before replacing the speedometer panel.

SWITCHES

Testing

Test switches for continuity with an ohmmeter, or a test light at the switch connector plug by operating the switch in each of its operating positions and comparing the results with its switch operation diagram. For example, **Figure 79** shows a continuity diagram

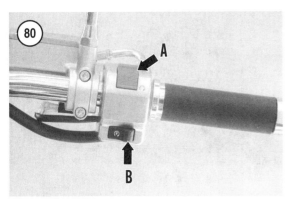

(79) **IGNITION SWITCH**

Position \ Color	R	O	Gr	Br	O/R	B/W
OFF						
ON	●――●		●――●		●――●	
P	●――――――●					
LOCK						

for a typical ignition switch. The horizontal line indicates which terminals should show continuity when the switch is in that position. In the park (P) position there should be continuity between the red and brown terminals. With the switch in the off position there should be no continuity between any of the terminals.

When testing switches, refer to the appropriate continuity diagrams in the wiring diagrams at the end of this manual and note the following:

1. First check the fuse as described in *Fuses* in this chapter.
2. Make sure the battery state of charge is acceptable (Chapter Three).

CAUTION
Do not attempt to start the engine with the battery disconnected.

3. Disconnect the switch from the circuit or disconnect the negative battery cable before performing continuity tests.
4. When separating two connectors, pull the connector housings and not the wires.
5. After isolating a defective circuit, check the connectors to make sure they are clean and properly connected. Check all wires going into a connector housing to make sure each wire is properly positioned and the wire end is not loose.
6. When reconnecting electrical connector halves, push them together until they click or snap into place.

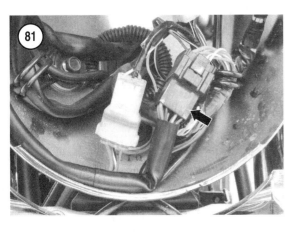

Right Handlebar Switch Housing Replacement

1. The right handlebar switch housing includes the following switches:
   a. Engine stop switch (A, **Figure 80**).
   b. Start button (B, **Figure 80**).
   c. Front brake light switch (electrical connectors only - the switch is separate).
2. Disconnect the negative battery cable (Chapter Three).
3. Remove the headlight lens unit from the headlight housing as described in this chapter.
4. Inside the headlight housing, disconnect the black connector (**Figure 81**). Pull out the wires leading to the right handlebar switch housing.
5. Remove any plastic clamps securing the wiring harness to the handlebar.
6. Disconnect the two wire connectors (**Figure 82**) from the front brake light switch.
7. At the throttle grip, loosen the throttle cable locknut (A, **Figure 83**) and turn the adjust nut (B) all the way into the switch assembly to allow maximum

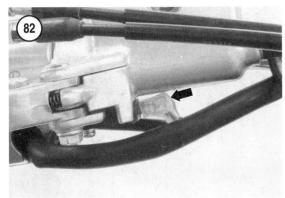

10

slack in both cables. Perform this on both the throttle opening (C, **Figure 83**) and closing (D) cables.

8. Remove the screws securing the right switch assembly together (**Figure 84**) and separate the switch assembly.

9. Disconnect the throttle opening cable, then the throttle closing cable from the throttle grip pulley.

10. Remove the switch assembly from the handlebar and frame.

11. Install by reversing the preceding removal steps. Note the following:

    a. Connect the throttle cables onto the throttle grip pulley and switch housing.

    b. Align the locating pin (A, **Figure 85**) with the hole (B) in the handlebar and install the switch onto the handlebar.

    c. Install the screws and tighten them securely.

    d. Make sure the electrical connectors are free of corrosion and secure.

    e. Check the operation of each switch mounted in the right handlebar switch housing.

    f. Operate the throttle lever and make sure the throttle linkage is operating correctly, without binding. If operation is incorrect or if there is binding, carefully check that the cable is attached correctly and there are no tight bends in the cable.

    g. Adjust the throttle cables as described in Chapter Three.

Left Handlebar Switch Housing Replacement

1. The left handlebar switch housing includes the following switches:

> *NOTE*
> *The three switches located within the left handlebar switch housing are not available separately. If one switch is damaged, replace the left switch housing assembly. The clutch switch is a separate unit and can be replaced independently.*

    a. Headlight dimmer switch (A, **Figure 86**).

    b. Turn signal switch (B, **Figure 86**).

    c. Horn button (C, **Figure 86**).

    d. Clutch switch (electrical connectors only; the switch is separate).

    e. Passing button (non-U.S.A., California and Canada models).

2. Disconnect the negative battery cable (Chapter Three).

3. Remove the headlight lens unit from the headlight housing as described in this chapter.

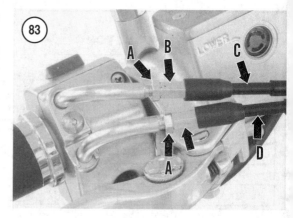

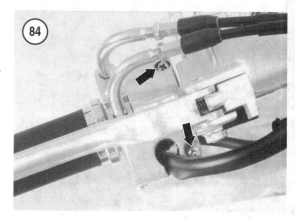

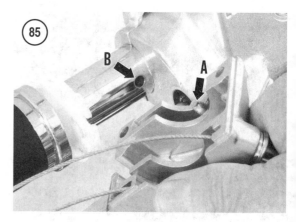

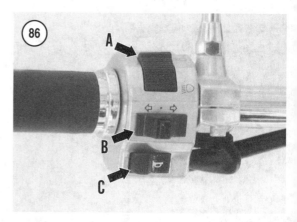

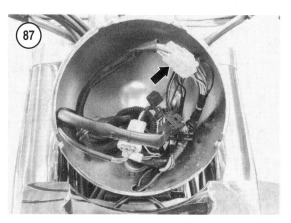

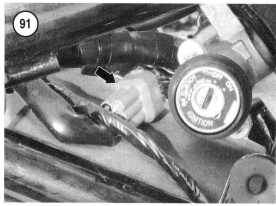

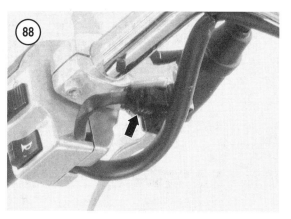

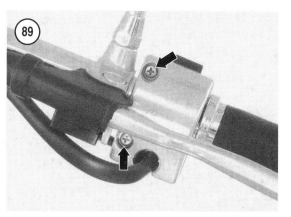

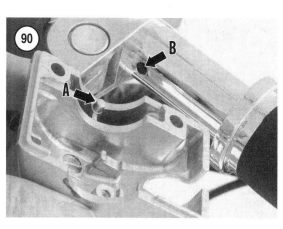

4. Inside the headlight housing, disconnect the yellow connector (**Figure 87**). Carefully pull out the wires leading to the left handlebar switch housing.

5. Remove any plastic clamps securing the wiring harness to the handlebar.

6. Disconnect the two wire connectors (**Figure 88**) from the front brake light switch.

7. Remove the screws securing the left switch assembly together (**Figure 89**) and separate the switch assembly.

8. Remove the switch assembly.

9. Install by reversing the preceding removal steps while noting the following:

   a. Align the locating pin (A, **Figure 90**) with the hole in the handlebar (B). Install the switch onto the handlebar and tighten the screws securely.

   b. Make sure the electrical connectors are free of corrosion and are tight.

   c. Check the operation of each switch.

Ignition Switch Replacement

NOTE
A tamper-resistant T-40 Torx bit is required to remove and install the ignition switch retaining bolts.

1. Disconnect the negative battery cable (Chapter Three).

2. Remove the frame head covers as described in Chapter Sixteen.

3. Disconnect the ignition switch connector (**Figure 91**).

4. Remove the Torx bolts (**Figure 92**) securing the ignition switch to the frame.

5. Install a new ignition switch. Apply threadlocking compound (ThreeBond 1303 or equivalent) to the Torx bolts and tighten them securely.

6. Reverse the preceding steps to complete installation. Make sure the electrical connector is secure and free of corrosion.

10

GP Sensor/Neutral Switch

Test

Carbureted models use a neutral switch. Fuel injected models use a gear position (GP) switch.
1. Remove the left frame side cover (Chapter Sixteen).
2. Remove the lower side cover (**Figure 93**).
3. Disconnect the white 6-pin connector (**Figure 94**).
4A. To test a neutral switch, perform the following:

CAUTION:
Make sure the ignition switch is off during this test.

a. Shift the transmission into neutral.
b. Connect an ohmmeter to the terminals in the switch side of the connector. There should be continuity between the blue and black/white terminals.
c. Shift the transmission into any gear. There should be no continuity.
4B. To test a GP sensor, perform the following:
a. Using a back probe pin to back probe the harness connector, connect a voltmeter positive test probe to the connector's pink terminal. Connect the negative test probe to a good ground.
b. Turn the ignition switch on, and measure the voltage when shifting from first gear to each of the higher gears. Voltage should equal 0.6 volts or more.
5. Replace a switch if it fails any portion of its test.

Replacement

The GP sensor/neutral switch is mounted on the left crankcase below the clutch adjuster.
1. Remove the left frame side cover as described in Chapter Sixteen.
2. Remove the lower side cover (**Figure 93**).
3. Remove the secondary drive cover (**Figure 95**).
4. Disconnect the white 6-pin electrical connector (**Figure 94**).

NOTE
The wire loom for the GP sensor/neutral switch also includes the sidestand switch and oil pressure switch wires.

5. Unscrew the oil pressure switch wire retaining nut (A, **Figure 96**) and disconnect the wire end from the switch stud.
6. Disconnect the sidestand switch connector (**Figure 97**).
7. Remove the mounting bolts and the GP sensor/neutral switch (**Figure 98**) from the crankcase.

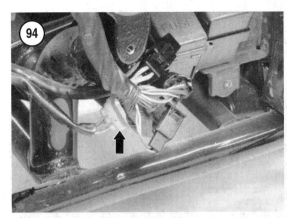

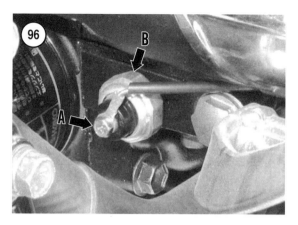

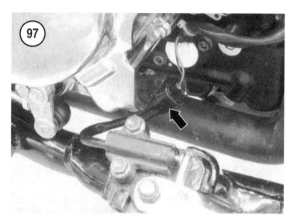

8. Remove the spring-loaded contact pins (**Figure 99**) and the O-ring.

9. Inspect the pins and springs for damage. Replace if necessary.

10. Installation is the reverse of removal. Note the following:

    a. Before installation, clean the switch contacts.

    b. Install a *new* O-ring. Lubricate the O-ring with Suzuki Super Grease A or equivalent.

    c. Install the switch and tighten the mounting screws securely.

    d. Check switch operation with the transmission in neutral.

Oil Pressure Switch

Test

When the ignition switch is turned on, the low oil pressure symbol in the speedometer display should turn on. As soon as the engine starts, the indicator light (symbol) should go out. If there is a problem within the oil pressure system or if the oil pressure drops under the normal operating pressure range, the indicator light turns on and stays on.

If the warning light is not operating correctly or does not come on when the ignition switch is in the on position (engine not running), perform the following test. The oil pressure switch (**Figure 96**) is mounted on the front bottom of the engine, next to the oil filter.

1. Check the engine oil level as described in Chapter Three. Add oil if necessary.

2. Disconnect the electrical connector (A, **Figure 96**) from the oil pressure switch (B).

3. Turn the ignition switch on.

4. Connect a jumper wire from the electrical connector to ground. The oil pressure warning light should come on.

5. If the light does not come on:

    a. Check the oil pressure warning light circuit as described in *Speedometer* in this chapter.

    b. If the indicator light and wiring are good, replace the switch as described in this section.

Replacement

The oil pressure switch (B, **Figure 96**) is mounted on the front, bottom of the engine adjacent to the oil filter.

1. Drain the engine oil as described in Chapter Three.

2. Disconnect the electrical connector (A, **Figure 96**) from the oil pressure switch.

10

3. Unscrew and remove the oil pressure switch from the crankcase.

4. Installation is the reverse of the preceding steps. Note the following:

    a. Apply a light coat of thread sealant (ThreeBond 1207 or equivalent) to the switch threads before installation.

    b. Install the switch and tighten to 14 N•m (124 in.-lb.).

Sidestand Switch

Test

The side stand switch can be tested in two ways: either use a multicircuit tester or an ohmmeter.

1. Remove the left frame side cover as described in Chapter Sixteen.

2. Remove the lower side cover (**Figure 93**).

3. Remove the secondary drive cover (**Figure 95**).

4. Disconnect the sidestand switch connector (**Figure 97**).

5. Test the diode in the sidestand switch with a multicircuit tester as follows:

    a. Set the test knob to diode test.

    b. Connect the test leads to the terminals in the switch end of the connector as shown in **Figure 100**.

    c. Move the sidestand to the up position and read the voltage on the meter.

    d. Move the sidestand to the down position and read the voltage on the meter.

    e. If the voltage is outside the range specified in **Figure 100**, replace the sidestand switch.

6. Test the continuity of the sidestand switch as follows:

    a. Connect an ohmmeter to the terminals in the switch end of the connector terminals.

    b. Move the sidestand to the up position. The meter should show continuity.

    c. Move the sidestand to the down position. The meter should show no continuity.

7. If the switch fails either of these tests, replace it.

8. Reconnect the electrical connectors and install all removed items.

Replacement

1. Remove the left frame side cover as described in Chapter Sixteen.

2. Remove the lower side cover (**Figure 93**).

3. Remove the secondary drive cover (**Figure 95**).

4. Disconnect the sidestand switch connector (A, **Figure 101**).

(100) SIDESTAND SWITCH TEST

Position \ Color	Green (+ probe)	Black/white (- probe)
UP	0.4-0.6 V	0.4-0.6 V
DOWN	1.4-1.5 V	1.4-1.5 V

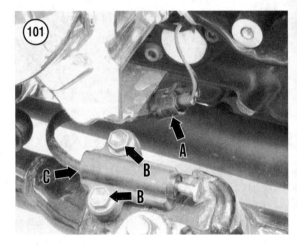

5. If necessary, move the sidestand to the down position.

6. Remove the two bolts securing the sidestand switch (B, **Figure 101**) to the sidestand and remove the switch (C).

7. Install a new switch. Apply ThreeBond 1344 to the mounting bolts and tighten them securely.

8. Move the sidestand from the lowered to the raised position and make sure the switch plunger has moved in.

9. Make sure the electrical connectors are secure and free of corrosion.

Clutch/Front Brake Lever Switches

> *WARNING*
> *Do not ride the motorcycle until the brake light and brake light switch work correctly.*

Testing

1. Disconnect the connector from the switch.

2. Connect an ohmmeter to the switch terminals.

3. Pull in the lever. There should be continuity.

4. If there is no continuity, replace the switch.

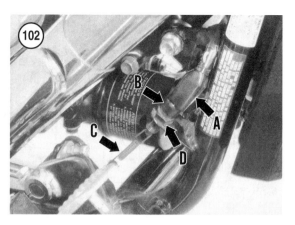

a. There must be continuity with the rear brake pedal applied and no continuity with the pedal released.

b. Replace the rear brake light switch if it fails to operate as described in the following procedure.

4. Connect the switch connector.

Removal/installation

1. Move back the boot (A, **Figure 102**) and disconnect the connector from the brake light switch (B).

2. Detach the spring (C, **Figure 102**) from the brake light switch.

3. Unscrew the brake light switch from the mounting nut (D, **Figure 102**).

4. Reverse these removal steps to install the brake light switch.

5. Refer to Chapter Three and adjust the rear brake light switch.

RELAY ASSEMBLY

The turn-signal relay, sidestand relay and diode are combined into a single component, called the relay assembly. If the turn-signal relay, sidestand relay or the diode is faulty, replace the relay assembly.

Replacement

1. Remove the left frame side cover as described in Chapter Sixteen.

2. Remove the lower side cover (**Figure 93**).

3. Remove the relay assembly (**Figure 103**) from the mounting base. Push out the tab at the end of the relay case to disengage the relay case from the mounting base latch.

4. Install the relay by reversing the removal steps.

Sidestand Test

1. Remove the relay assembly as described in this section.

2. Apply 12 volts to the relay by connecting the negative terminal of the battery to the C terminal in the relay assembly and connect the positive battery terminal to the D terminal. See **Figure 104**.

3. Use an ohmmeter to check the continuity between terminals D and E on the relay assembly. There should be continuity.

4. Replace the relay assembly if there is no continuity.

Removal/installation

1. Disconnect the connector from the switch.

2. Remove the switch mounting screw and remove the switch.

3. Install the switch and tighten the mounting screw securely.

4. Connect the connector to the switch.

5. Check operation.

Rear Brake Light Switch

WARNING
Do not ride the motorcycle until the brake light and switch work correctly.

Testing

The rear brake switch is mounted on the right, front frame downtube.

1. Move back the boot (A, **Figure 102**) and disconnect the connector from the brake switch (B).

2. Connect ohmmeter leads to the switch terminals.

3. Read the ohmmeter scale while applying and releasing the rear brake pedal. Note the following:

10

Turn Signal Test

If the turn signal light does not illuminate, first look for a defective bulb. If the bulbs are good, check the turn signal switch as described in this chapter and all electrical connections within the turn signal circuit.

If all of these components test good, replace the relay assembly.

Diode Test

1. Remove the relay assembly as described in this section.
2. Set a multicircuit tester to diode test, and measure the voltage across the diode terminals indicated in **Figure 105**. Also see **Figure 104**.
3. Replace the relay assembly if any measurement is outside the range specified in **Figure 105**.

SPEEDOMETER

The speed sensor on the front wheel provides input for the speedometer, odometer and tripmeter functions.

A panel electrical malfunction requires replacement of the entire speedometer panel. Speedometer housing parts are available individually.

If the speedometer, odometer or tripmeter does not fuction properly, inspect the speedometer sensor and the connections. If the sensor and connections are good, replace the speedometer panel.

Refer to **Figure 106** for speedometer displays.

Operation

Initial operation

1. With the battery or speedometer disconnected, the speedometer pointer will fluctuate to indicate that the computer is resetting. The pointer will end its movement at the zero position. The pointer will also move erratically if the battery or speedometer connecter is disconnected during riding.

> *NOTE*
> *If the battery or speedometer is disconnected, the clock resets to 1:00.*

2. On normal startup, the indicator lights will light for approximately three seconds then go out when the ignition switch is turned on.

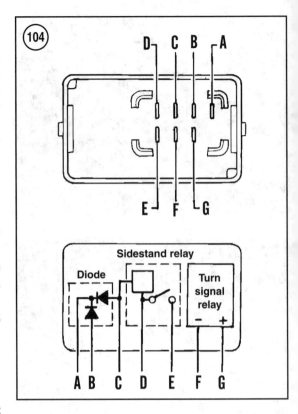

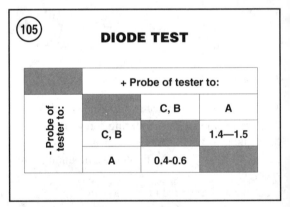

DIODE TEST

		+ Probe of tester to:	
− Probe of tester to:		C, B	A
	C, B		1.4—1.5
	A	0.4-0.6	

Running operation

1. Clock/odometer/tripmeter—Pressing the Select button changes the display to indicate the clock, odometer or tripmeter. Two tripmeters are available. Each tripmeter can be zeroed by pressing the Adjust button.
2. Clock Reset—To reset the clock time, press the Adjust button for two seconds, then press the Select button so the hour or minutes flash. While the numerals flash, push the Adjust button to change the numbers.
3. Fuel Level—On 2001-2004 models, the boxes in the graphic display indicate the fuel level. Each black box indicates fuel in the tank. When all five boxes are black the fuel tank is full. When the left-most box flickers and the remaining boxes are white, there is less than 1.5 L (0.4 gal.) in the fuel tank.

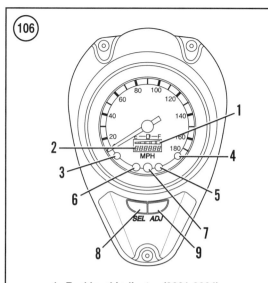

1. Fuel level indicator (2001-2004)
2. Odometer/tripmeter/clock
3. High beam indicator
4. Neutral indicator
5A. Oil pressure indicator (2001-2004)
5B. Fuel indicator (2005-on)
6A. Engine coolant temperature (ECT) indicator (2001-2004)
6B. Fuel injection indicator (2005-on)
7. Turn signal indicator
8. Select button
9. Adjust button

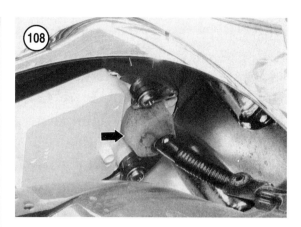

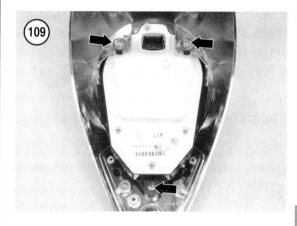

3. Carefully lift up and invert the speedometer.

4. Pull back the boot (**Figure 108**) and detach the speedometer connector.

5. Remove the speedometer.

6. Reverse the removal steps to install the speedometer.

Disassembly/Reassembly

1. Place the speedometer on a soft surface to prevent scratches to the housing.

2. Remove the speedometer sub-housing mounting screws (**Figure 109**) and separate the sub-housing from the speedometer housing.

CAUTION
Carefully separate the back assembly from the sub-housing to prevent damage to the exposed speedometer pointer.

3. Remove the sub-housing back screws (**Figure 110**) and remove the back assembly.

4. Remove the speedometer panel retaining screws (A, **Figure 111**) and separate the speedometer panel (B) from the back (C).

Removal/Installation

1. Disconnect the battery negative cable (Chapter Three).

CAUTION
Be careful not to scratch the speedometer housing or fuel tank when performing the following steps.

2. Remove the speedometer retaining bolts (**Figure 107**).

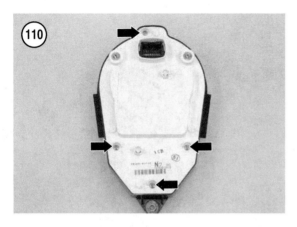

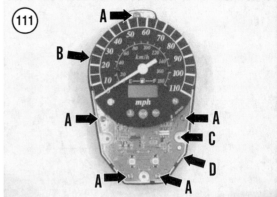

5. The speedometer panel is available only as a unit assembly. Inspect all cushions and the gasket around the rim of the back (D, **Figure 111**).

6. Reassemble by reversing the disassembly steps.

Engine Coolant Temperature Indicator Test

The light emitting diode (LED) in the speedometer panel provides engine coolant information. Check its operation as follows.

1. Remove the fuel tank as described in Chapter Eight or Chapter Nine.

2. Disconnect the engine coolant temperature (ECT) switch connector (**Figure 112**).

3. Connect a jumper between the terminals in the speedometer end of the connector.

4. Reconnect the speedometer to its connector.

5. Turn the ignition switch on. The LED in the speedometer display should turn on. If the LED fails to light, replace the speedometer panel.

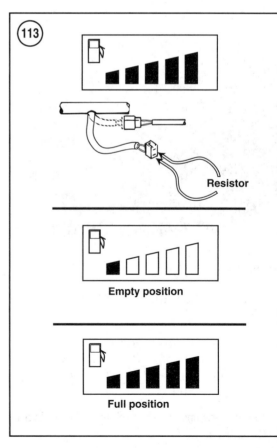

Oil Pressure Indicator Test

The light emitting diode (LED) in the speedometer panel provides oil pressure information. Check its operation as follows.

1. Disconnect the green/yellow wire (A, **Figure 96**) from the oil pressure switch (B).

2. Use a jumper wire to connect the green/yellow wire to a good engine ground.

3. Turn the ignition switch on and watch the oil pressure indicator. It should light.

4. If the indicator does not light, check the wiring and connectors between the oil pressure switch and the speedometer. If they are good, replace the speedometer panel.

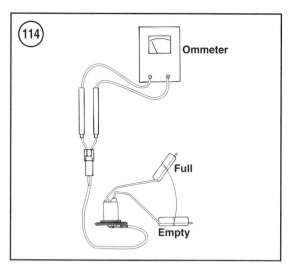

for the appropriate resistor values. Note that decreased resistance increases the number of black boxes on the speedometer display.

3. Reconnect the speedometer to its connector.

4. Turn the ignition switch on. The fuel level indicator should turn on and indicated fuel level should correspond to the resistor value specified in **Table 1**. Resistance greater than 94 ohms will cause the smallest box to flicker, which indicates a low fuel condition.

5A. If the fuel level indicator does not function as described above, replace the speedometer panel.

5B. If the fuel level indicator functions properly, check the fuel level sending unit in the fuel tank as follows:

    a. Remove the sender unit as described in Chapter Eight.

    b. Connect an ohmmeter to the fuel level gauge sending unit and move the float to both the full and empty positions (**Figure 114**).

    c. Record the ohmmeter readings in both positions and compare to the specifications in **Table 1**.

    d. If the readings are not within specification, replace the fuel level gauge sending unit.

2005-2006 models

The fuel level in the fuel tank is monitored by thermisters (**Figure 115**) attached to the fuel pump bracket. The thermisters are not available separately, but only as part of the fuel pump unit assembly. Make sure wire connections are tight. Test specifications are not available.

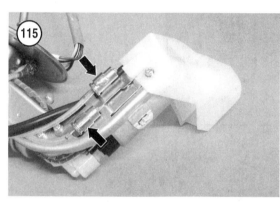

2007-2008 models

The fuel level is monitored by a fuel level sending unit using a float. The resistance of the sending unit can be tested. The fuel level indicator (meter) can be tested by installing various resistors between the yellow/black and black/white wires at the fuel level sending unit connector and observing the number of bars that illuminate on the indicator. Refer to **Table 1** for specifications.

Fuel Level Indicator Testing

2001-2004 models

The fuel level indicator display changes according to the resistance of the fuel level sender in the fuel tank. To isolate an indicator problem, perform the following tests.

1. Remove the fuel tank as described in Chapter Eight or Chapter Nine.

2. Connect a resistor to the speedometer end of the fuel tank connector (**Figure 113**). Refer to **Table 1**

Speedometer Sensor Test

1. Disconnect the negative battery cable (Chapter Three).

2. Remove the screws on both sides securing the headlight assembly in the headlight housing (**Figure 116**).

3. Carefully pull the headlight lens unit out of the housing.

4. Disconnect the electrical connector/socket (**Figure 117**) from the headlight lens unit and set the unit out of the way on a protective surface.

10

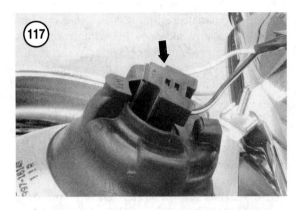

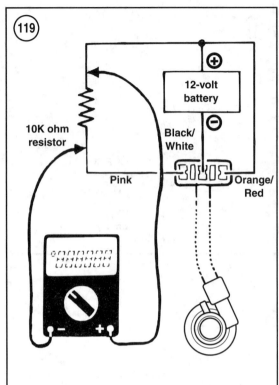

5. Inside the headlight housing, disconnect the white 3-pin connector (**Figure 118**).

6. Support the front of the motorcycle so the front wheel can be rotated.

7. Connect a 12-volt battery in series to the center connector terminal as shown in **Figure 119**.

8. Connect a 10k ohm resistor to the outer connector terminals as shown in **Figure 119**.

9. Connect a voltmeter as shown in **Figure 119**.

10. Rotate the front wheel while observing the voltmeter. The voltage reading should be between 0 and 12 volts. If otherwise, replace the speedometer sensor.

HORN

Test

1. Disconnect the negative battery cable (Chapter Three).

2. Disconnect the electrical connectors (**Figure 120**) from the horn.

3. Connect a 12 volt battery to the horn terminals. The horn should sound.

4. If it does not, replace the horn.

Removal/Installation

1. Disconnect the negative battery cable (Chapter Three).

2. Remove the radiator as described in Chapter Eleven.

3. Disconnect the electrical connector (A, **Figure 121**) from the horn.

4. Remove the bolt (B, **Figure 121**) securing the horn to the mounting bracket.

5. Remove the horn.

6. Install by reversing the removal steps. Note the following:

   a. Make sure the electrical connectors are free of corrosion and are tight.

   b. Test the horn to make sure it operates correctly.

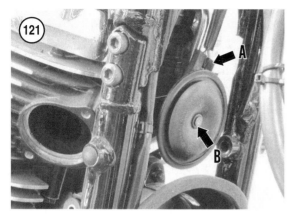

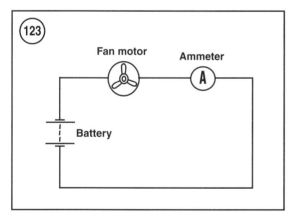

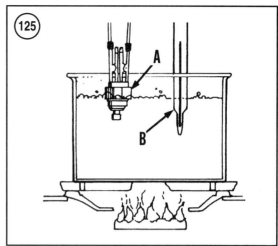

COOLING SYSTEM

Fan Test

Use an ammeter and a fully charged 12-volt battery for this test.

1. Disconnect the fan electrical connector (**Figure 122**).

2. Use jumper wires to connect the test battery to the fan connector. Also connect an ammeter in line as shown in **Figure 123**.

3. The fan should operate when power is applied. Replace the fan assembly if it does not operate.

4. With the fan running at full speed, monitor the ammeter and note the load current. Replace the cooling fan if the load current exceeds 5 amps.

Fan Switch Test

The cooling fan switch controls the radiator fan according to the engine coolant temperature using a thermostatic element in the switch. Refer also to Chapter Eleven.

1. Remove the fan switch (**Figure 124**) from the radiator as described in Chapter Eleven.

2. Fill a beaker or pan with water, and place it on a stove or hot plate.

3. Position the fan switch so that the temperature sensing tip and the threaded portion of the body are submerged as shown in A, **Figure 125**.

NOTE
The thermometer and the fan switch must not touch the container sides or bottom. If either does, it will result in a false reading.

4. Place a thermometer (B, **Figure 125**) in the pan of water.

5. If the switch has exposed terminals, attach one ohmmeter lead to the fan switch terminals as shown in A, **Figure 125**. If the switch has a nondetachable wire lead, connect the ommeter leads to the connector terminals. Check the resistance as follows:

a. Gradually heat the water.

b. When the temperature reaches 105° C (221° F), the meter should read continuity (switch on).

c. Gradually reduce the heat.

d. When the temperature lowers to approximately 100° C (212° F), the meter should not read continuity (switch off).

6. Replace the fan switch if it failed to operate as described in Step 5.

7. If the fan switch tests good, install the fan switch onto the radiator as described in Chapter Eleven.

Coolant Temperature Switch Test

1. Remove the engine coolant temperature (ECT) switch from the radiator as described in Chapter Eleven.

2. Fill a beaker or pan with water, and place it on a stove or hot plate.

NOTE
The thermometer and the switch must not touch the container sides or bottom. If either does, it will result in a false reading.

3. Position the switch so that the temperature sensing tip and the threaded portion of the body are submerged (A, **Figure 125**).

4. Place a thermometer (B, **Figure 125**) in the pan of.

5. Connect the ommeter leads to the connector terminals. Check the resistance as follows:

a. Gradually heat the water.

b. When the temperature reaches 120° C (248° F), the meter should read continuity (switch on).

c. Gradually reduce the heat.

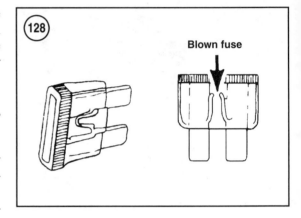

d. When the temperature lowers to approximately 113° C (235° F), the meter should not read continuity (switch off).

6. Replace the switch if it failed to operate as described in Step 5.

7. Install the switch in the radiator as described in Chapter Eleven.

FUSES

Replacement

All models are equipped with a single 30-amp main fuse that is located next to the starter relay (**Figure 126**). The remaining fuses are located in the auxiliary fuse box (**Figure 127**) behind the left, lower side cover.

If there is an electrical failure, first check for a blown fuse. A blown fuse will have a break in the element (**Figure 128**).

Whenever the fuse blows, determine the reason for the failure before replacing the fuse. Usually, the trouble is a short circuit in the wiring. This may be caused by worn-through insulation or a disconnected wire shorted to ground. Check by testing the circuit the fuse protects.

1. To replace the main fuse, perform the following:
   a. Refer to *Starter Relay* in this chapter and re-move the starter relay cover.
   b. Using needlenose pliers, pull out the fuse and visually inspect it.

   NOTE
   A spare 30A fuse may be contained in the relay housing. Always carry spare fuses.

   c. Install a new fuse and push it in all the way un-til it bottoms.
2. To remove the auxiliary fuses, perform the fol-lowing:

   a. Remove the left frame cover as described in Chapter Sixteen.
   b. Remove the lower side cover (**Figure 129**).
   c. Locate the blown fuse (**Figure 130**) and install a new one of the same amperage.
   d. There are two spare fuses (10A and 15A) lo-cated in the fuse panel.

WIRING DIAGRAMS

Wiring diagrams are located at the end of this man-ual.

10

Table 1 ELECTRICAL SYSTEM SPECIFICATIONS

Alternator	
Type	Three-phase AC
No-load voltage (engine cold)	Greater than 70 volts (AC) at 5000 rpm
Maximum output	375 watts at 5000 rpm
Regulated voltage (charging voltage)	14.0-15.5 volts at 5000 rpm
Coil resistance	0.2-1.5 ohms
Battery	
Type	FTX12-BS Maintenance free (sealed)
Capacity	12 volt 10 amp-hour
Cooling fan current (max.)	5 amps
Fuel level indicator	
Empty	More than 94 ohms
Full	Less than 17 ohms
Fuel level indicator	
Resistor	
10 ohms	5 bars
25-41 ohms	4 bars
60-81 ohms	3 bars
107-136 ohms	2 bars
172-216 ohms	1 bar
Greater than 216 ohms	flicker
Fuel level sending unit (2001-2004)	
Empty	90-100 ohms
Full	4-10 ohms
(continued)	

Table 1 ELECTRICAL SYSTEM SPECIFICATIONS(continued)

Fuel level sending unit (2007-2008)	
Float position	
Empty	Approx. 216 ohms
Full	Approx. 10 ohms
Ignition coil (2001-2004)	
Primary peak voltage (min.)	200 volts
Primary resistance	2.0-6.0 ohms
Secondary resistance	15,000-30,000 ohms
Ignition coil (2005-on)	
Primary peak voltage (min.)	200 volts
Primary resistance	2.8-4.7 ohms
Secondary resistance	24,000-36,000 ohms
Ignition system	
Type	CDI
Ignition timing	5° BTDC at 1100 rpm
Crankshaft position sensor (2005-on)	
Coil resistance	184-276 ohms
Peak voltage (min.)	4.0 volts
Pickup coil (2001-2004)	
Coil resistance	160-300 ohms
Peak voltage (min.)	1.5 volts
Starter relay resistance	3-7 ohms
Speedometer sensor voltage	0-12 volts

Table 2 BULB SPECIFICATIONS

Item	Specification
Headlight	60/55W
Position/parking light (if equipped)	4W
Taillight/brakelight	21/5W
Turn signal	
Front	21/5W
Rear	21W

Table 3 ELECTRICAL SYSTEM TORQUE SPECIFICATIONS

Item	N•m	in.-lb.	ft.-lb.
Alternator rotor bolt	160	–	118
Oil pressure switch*	14	124	–
*Apply thread sealant (Threebond 1207 or equivalent)			

COOLING SYSTEM

This chapter covers radiator and cap, thermostat, electric fan and coolant reservoir procedures. Routine maintenance is described in Chapter Three. Cooling system specifications are in **Table 1** and **Table 2** at the end of this chapter.

COOLING SYSTEM

Precautions

WARNING
Do not remove the radiator cap or any cooling system component while the engine is hot. The coolant is under pressure and can spray out, causing severe burns. The cooling system must be cool before any component is removed.

WARNING
If the engine is warm or hot, the fan may come on. Be sure the ignition is off or the battery is disconnected when working around the fan.

WARNING
Antifreeze is toxic. Do not dispose of it by flushing down a drain or pouring it onto the ground. Place old antifreeze into a suitable container and dispose of it properly. Do not store coolant where it is accessible to children or animals.

WARNING
Coolant is very slippery if spilled on concrete or a similar surface. Wipe up any spilled coolant immediately.

CAUTION
When adding coolant or refilling the system use a mixture of ethylene glycol antifreeze formulated for aluminum engines and distilled water. Do not use only distilled water (even if freezing temperatures are not expected); the antifreeze inhibits internal engine corrosion and provides lubrication for moving parts.

Temperature Warning System

A coolant temperature indicator light is located on the face of the speedometer panel. If the coolant temperature is above 120° C (248° F) when the ignition switch is on, the indicator light on the tachometer face will illuminate.

If the coolant temperature indicator light comes on, turn the engine off and allow it to cool. Determine the cause of the overheating condition before operating the motorcycle. Make sure the coolant level is between the marks on the reservoir (A, **Figure 1**). Do not add coolant to the radiator.

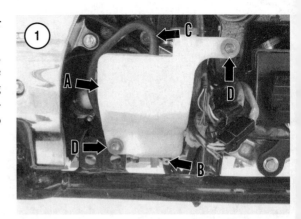

Inspection

> *CAUTION*
> *If the engine oil is contaminated with coolant, change the oil and filter after performing the coolant system repair. Refer to Chapter Three.*

1. If steam is observed at the muffler outlet, the head gasket may be damaged. If enough coolant leaks into a cylinder(s), the cylinder could hydrolock and prevent the engine from being cranked. Coolant may also be present in the engine oil. If the oil visible in the oil level gauge (located on the right crankcase cover) is foamy or milky-looking, there is coolant in the oil. If so, correct the problem before returning the motorcycle to service.

2. Check the radiator for clogged or damaged fins. If more than 15 percent of the radiator fin area is damaged, repair or replace the radiator.

3. Check all coolant hoses for cracks or damage. Replace all questionable parts. Make sure all hose clamps are tight, but not so tight that they cut the hoses. Refer to *Hoses and Hose Clamps* in this section.

4. Pressure test the cooling system as described in Chapter Three.

Hoses and Hose Clamps

After removing any cooling system component, inspect the adjoining hose(s) to determine if replacement is necessary. Hoses deteriorate over time and should be inspected carefully for conditions, which may cause them to fail. Loss of coolant will cause the engine to overheat and spray from a leaking hose can injure the rider. Observe the following when servicing hoses:

1. Make sure the cooling system is cool before removing any coolant hose or component.

2. Use original equipment replacement hoses; they are formed to a specific shape and dimension for correct fit.

3. Do not use excessive force when removing a hose from a fitting. Refer to *Service Methods* in Chapter One.

4. If the hose is difficult to install onto the fitting, soak the hose in hot water to make it more pliable. Do not use any lubricate when installing hoses.

5. Inspect the hose clamps for damage. Always use screw adjusting type hose clamps, except if otherwise specified by the manufacturer. Position the clamp head so it is accessible for future removal and it does not contact other parts.

6. With the hose correctly installed, position the clamp approximately 1/2 inch (13 mm) from the end of the hose and tighten the clamp.

COOLANT RESERVOIR

Removal/Installation

1. Remove the left frame cover as described in Chapter Sixteen.

2. Remove the lower side cover (**Figure 2**).

3. Place a suitable container under the reservoir.

4. Disconnect the lower reservoir hose (B, **Figure 1**) from the radiator, then drain the coolant in the reservoir out through the hose fitting.

5. Disconnect the reservoir vent hose (C, **Figure 1**) from the reservoir.

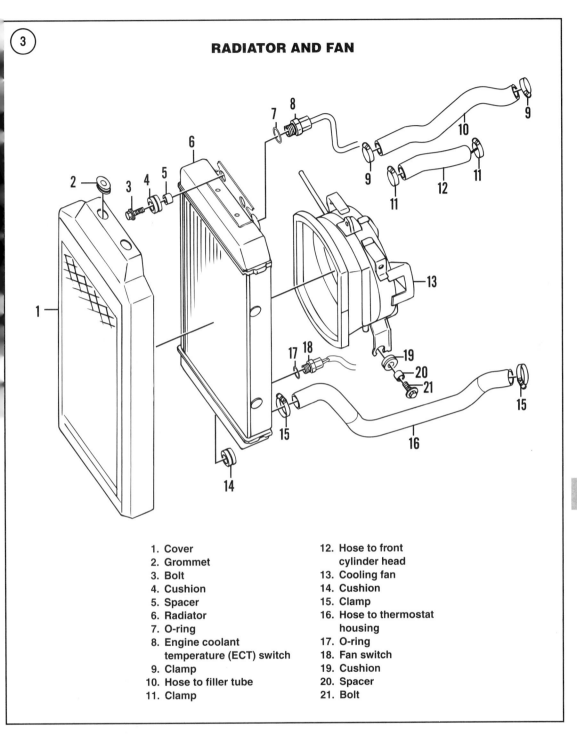

RADIATOR AND FAN

1. Cover
2. Grommet
3. Bolt
4. Cushion
5. Spacer
6. Radiator
7. O-ring
8. Engine coolant
   temperature (ECT) switch
9. Clamp
10. Hose to filler tube
11. Clamp
12. Hose to front
    cylinder head
13. Cooling fan
14. Cushion
15. Clamp
16. Hose to thermostat
    housing
17. O-ring
18. Fan switch
19. Cushion
20. Spacer
21. Bolt

6. Remove the reservoir mounting bolts (D, **Figure 1**) and remove the reservoir.

7. Remove the fill cap and drain any residual coolant from the reservoir. Dispose of the coolant properly.

8. If necessary, clean the inside of the reservoir with a liquid detergent. Thoroughly rinse the reservoir with clean water. Make sure to remove all detergent residue from the reservoir.

9. Install by reversing the removal steps.

RADIATOR

Removal/Installation

Refer to **Figure 3**.

1. Drain the cooling system as described in *Non-Scheduled Maintenance* in Chapter Three.

2. Remove the frame head covers as described in Chapter Sixteen.

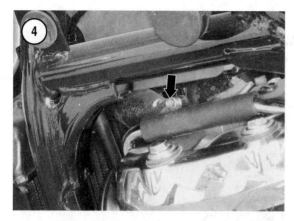

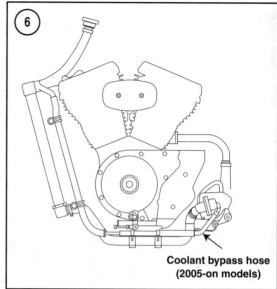

Coolant bypass hose
(2005-on models)

3. Loosen the clamp (**Figure 4**) and detach the radiator hose from the front cylinder fitting.

4. Loosen the clamp (**Figure 5**) and detach the radiator hose from the thermostat housing.

5. On 2005-on models, loosen the clamp, then detach the coolant bypass hose from the radiator (**Figure 6**).

6. Disconnect the engine coolant temperature (ECT) switch connector from the switch (**Figure 7**).

7. Disconnect the cooling fan temperature switch connector (**Figure 8**).

8. Remove the radiator cover (**Figure 9**).

9. Remove the lower radiator mounting bolt (**Figure 10**).

10. Remove the upper mounting bolts (**Figure 11**) and remove the radiator (**Figure 12**).

11. Install the radiator by reversing the removal steps.

    a. Replace any hoses if they are deteriorating or damaged in any way.

    b. Make sure the damper is in place on each radiator mount.

    c. Make sure the switch electrical connections are secure and free of corrosion.

    d. Refill the cooling system with the recommended type and quantity of coolant as described in Chapter Three.

Inspection

1. If compressed air is available, use short spurts of air directed to the *backside* of the radiator core to blow out debris.

2. Flush the exterior of the radiator with a garden hose on low pressure. Spray both the front and the

back to remove all debris. Carefully use a whisk broom or stiff paint brush to remove any stubborn dirt from the cooling fins.

> *CAUTION*
> *Do not press hard on the cooling fins or tubes.*

3. Carefully straighten out any bent cooling fins with a broad tipped screwdriver or putty knife.

4. Check for cracks or leaks at all hose fittings and side tank seams.

5. To prevent oxidation of the radiator, touch up any areas where the paint is worn off. Use a quality spray paint and apply several *light* coats. Do not apply heavy coats as this cuts down on the cooling efficiency of the radiator.

6. Inspect the rubber dampers in the radiator mounts. Replace any that are damaged.

7. Check for leaks at the switch locations.

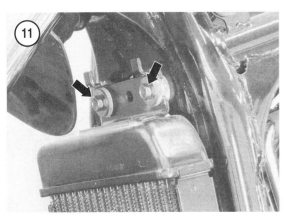

COOLING FAN

Removal/Installation

> *NOTE*
> *The exhaust system was removed for clarity. It is not necessary to remove the exhaust system to service the cooling fan.*

Refer to **Figure 3**.

1. Remove the radiator as described in this chapter.

2. Remove the right side cooling fan mounting bolt (**Figure 13**).

3. Remove the left side cooling fan mounting bolts (**Figure 14**).

4. Remove the subframe lower crossmember bolts (**Figure 15**).

11

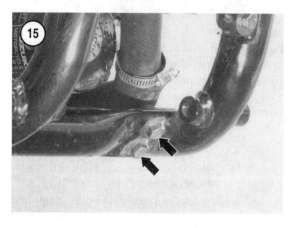

5. Remove the nut on the front engine mounting bolt (**Figure 16**).

6. Remove the upper subframe bolts (**Figure 17**).

7. Loosen the lower subframe bolts (**Figure 18**) just enough so the subframe can be moved out far enough to remove the cooling fan. Do *not* remove the bolts.

8. Disconnect the cooling fan electrical connector (**Figure 19**).

9. Move the subframe out as needed and remove the cooling fan (**Figure 20**).

10. Test the cooling fan as described in Chapter Ten.

11. Install by reversing the removal steps. Note the following:

    a. Tighten the subframe Allen bolts to 50 N•m (37 ft.-lb.).

    b. Tighten the subframe lower crossmember bolts to 25 N•m (18 ft.-lb.).

    c. Tighten the engine mounting bolt to 79 N•m (58 ft.-lb.).

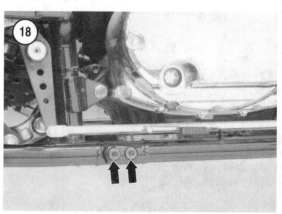

THERMOSTAT

Removal/Installation

1. Drain the cooling system as described in Chapter Three.

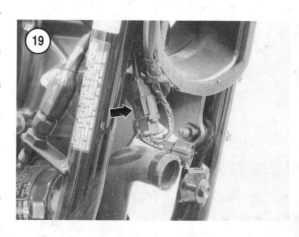

2. Remove the coolant reservoir as described in this chapter.

3. Loosen the clamp (**Figure 21**) and detach the coolant hose from the thermostat housing.

NOTE
Separate the electrical wires from the clamp on the water pump and relocate the wires to remove the water pump in Step 4.

4. Remove the water pump cover mounting bolts (A, **Figure 22**) and remove the water pump cover (B).

5. Remove the thermostat housing retaining screws (A, **Figure 23**). Remove the thermostat housing (B, **Figure 23**), then extract the thermostat (**Figure 24**).

6. If necessary, test the thermostat as described in this chapter.

7. Inspect the thermostat for damage and make sure the spring has not sagged or broken. Replace the thermostat if necessary.

8. Clean the inside of the thermostat housing of debris or old coolant residue.

9. Install by reversing the removal steps. Note the following:

   a. Inspect the water pump cover O-ring gasket (**Figure 25**) and replace if damaged.

   b. Install the thermostat so the spring end enters the water pump housing.

   c. Refill the cooling system with the recommended type and quantity of coolant as described in Chapter Three.

Test

Test the thermostat to ensure proper operation. Replace the thermostat if it remains open at normal room temperature or stays closed after the specified temperature has been reached during the test procedure.

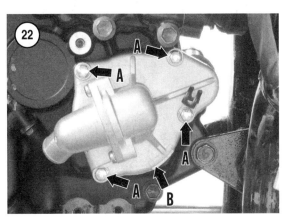

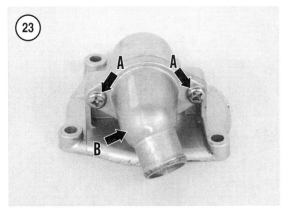

11

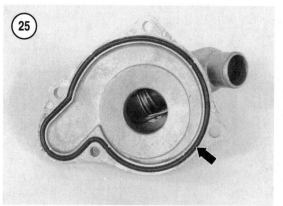

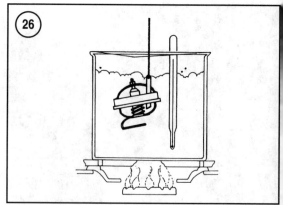

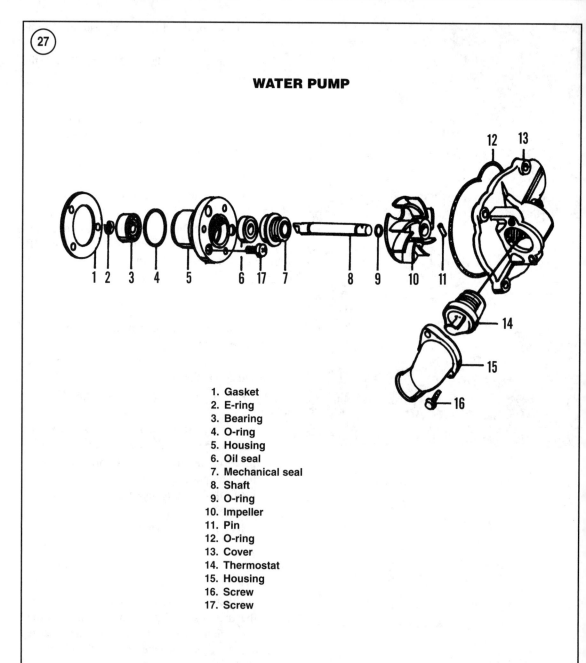

WATER PUMP

1. Gasket
2. E-ring
3. Bearing
4. O-ring
5. Housing
6. Oil seal
7. Mechanical seal
8. Shaft
9. O-ring
10. Impeller
11. Pin
12. O-ring
13. Cover
14. Thermostat
15. Housing
16. Screw
17. Screw

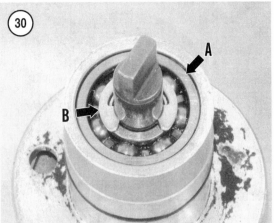

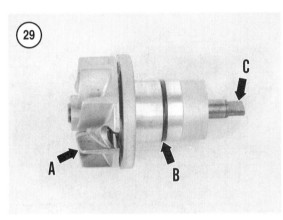

The thermometer and the thermostat must not touch the container sides or bottom. If either does, it will result in a false reading.

NOTE
Valve operation may be slow; it usually takes 3-5 minutes for the valve to open completely. If the valve fails to open, replace the thermostat (it cannot be serviced). Make sure the replacement thermometer has the same temperature rating.

Suspend the thermostat and thermometer in a pan of water (**Figure 26**). Use a thermometer rated higher than the test temperature. Gradually heat the water and continue to gently stir the water until it reaches 75° C (167° F). At this temperature the thermostat valve should open.

WATER PUMP

The water pump is mounted on the left side of the crankcase. Refer to **Figure 27**.

Removal/Installation

1. Drain the cooling system as described in Chapter Three.
2. Remove the coolant reservoir as described in this chapter.
3. Loosen the clamp (**Figure 21**) and detach the coolant hose from the thermostat housing.
4. On 2005-on models, loosen the clamp, then detach the coolant bypass hose from the water pump (**Figure 6**).
5. Separate the electrical wires from the clamp on the water pump. Relocate the wires for enough clearance to remove the water pump.
6. Remove the water pump cover mounting bolts (A, **Figure 22**) and remove the water pump cover (B).
7. Working through the cutouts in the impeller, remove the shaft housing mounting screws (**Figure 28**).
8. Extract the impeller and shaft assembly (A, **Figure 29**) from the crankcase.
9. Inspect the water pump assembly for wear or damage. Rotate the impeller and shaft to make sure the bearing (A, **Figure 30**) is not worn or damaged.
10. Inspect the impeller blades for cracks or damage; replace if necessary.
11. To install the water pump, reverse the removal procedure. Note the following:
   a. Install a new O-ring around the shaft housing (B, **Figure 29**). Lubricate the O-ring using Suzuki Super Grease A or equivalent.
   b. Install a new gasket (**Figure 31**).
   c. Install a new water pump cover O-ring gasket (**Figure 25**).
   d. Make sure the drive tang on the impeller shaft end (C, **Figure 29**) engages the drive slot in the oil pump shaft end.

11

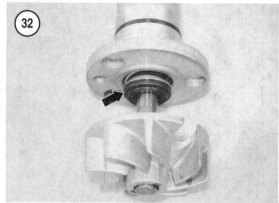

Disassembly/Inspection/Assembly

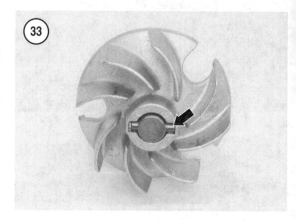

The water pump can be disassembled for replacement of the bearing, oil seal, mechanical seal and impeller. If the condition of the water pump is doubtful and most of the parts require replacement, replacement of the water pump assembly is recommended. Refer to **Figure 27**.

> *CAUTION*
> *Do not try to remove the bearing from the housing without the Suzuki special tools. If substitute tools are used, the housing may be damaged and must be replaced.*

1. Remove the E-clip (B, **Figure 30**) securing the shaft in the shaft housing.

2. Withdraw the impeller and shaft from the housing and mechanical seal (**Figure 32**).

3. If necessary, remove the impeller and pin (**Figure 33**) from the shaft.

4. If the mechanical seal is removed, also remove the oil seal in the housing behind it.

5. Remove the bearing (**Figure 34**) with a suitable bearing driver or extraction tool. Refer to Chapter One.

6. To remove the oil seal, use the same tool set-up and same procedure used for bearing removal.

7. Replace the mechanical seal as follows:

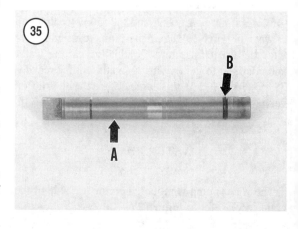

   a. Turn the housing over with the backside facing up and set it on two wood blocks.

   b. From the backside of the housing, carefully tap the mechanical seal out of the housing.

8. Inspect the shaft (A, **Figure 35**) for excessive wear and damage. Replace if necessary. Install a new O-ring (B, **Figure 35**) onto the shaft.

9. Apply clean engine oil to the outer surfaces of the new parts to be installed and to the inner surface of the housing. This makes assembly easier.

14. Install the E-clip (B, **Figure 30**) securing the shaft into the water pump housing. Make sure the E-clip is properly seated in the shaft groove.

15. Rotate the impeller and shaft and make sure it rotates without binding.

COOLING FAN SWITCH

Removal/Installation

1. Remove the radiator as described in this chapter.
2. Remove the switch (**Figure 36**).
3. If necessary, test the switch as described in Chapter Ten.
4. Install by reversing the removal steps. Note the following:
   a. Install a new O-ring. Apply a light coat of Suzuki Super Grease A or equivalent to the O-ring.
   b. Install the switch and tighten it to 17 N•m (150 in.-lb.).

ENGINE COOLANT TEMPERATURE (ECT) SWITCH

Removal/Installation

1. Remove the radiator as described in this chapter.
2. Remove the switch (**Figure 37**).
3. If necessary, test the switch as described in Chapter Ten.
4. Install by reversing the removal steps. Note the following:
   a. Install a new O-ring. Apply a light coat of Suzuki Super Grease A or equivalent to the O-ring.
   b. Install the switch and tighten it to 12 N•m (106 in.-lb.).

10. Tap the oil seal, then the bearing into the housing using a socket of the appropriate size to fit the bearing outer race. Tap the bearing in until it seats.

11. Install a new oil seal and mechanical seal. Tap them in until they are completed seated.

12. If removed, install a new O-ring onto the shaft, then install the impeller and pin.

13. Apply clean engine oil to the shaft and install the shaft and impeller into the mechanical seal (**Figure 32**) and through the bearing at the other end.

11

Table 1 COOLING SYSTEM SPECIFICATIONS

Item	Specification
Coolant capacity	1.5 L (1.6 qt.)*
Coolant type	Ethylene glycol-based, containing corrosion inhibitors for aluminum radiators
Coolant mix ratio	50:50 distilled water and antifreeze
Radiator cap release pressure	95-125 kPa (13.8-18.1 psi)
Thermostat opening	75° C (167° F)
*Includes reserve tank	

Table 2 COOLING SYSTEM TORQUE SPECIFICATIONS

Item	N•m	in.-lb.	ft.-lb.
Engine coolant temperature (ECT) switch	12	106	–
Cooling fan switch	17	150	–
Engine mounting bolts	79	–	58
Subframe Allen bolts and nuts	50	–	37
Subframe lower crossmember bolts	25	–	18

CHAPTER TWELVE

WHEELS AND TIRES

This chapter covers wheel, wheel bearing and tire procedures.

Tire and wheel specifications are in **Tables 1-3** at the end of this chapter.

WARNING
Due to the lack of a centerstand, a suitable lifting device is required to raise the motorcycle when performing some procedures in this chapter. Make sure the lift will raise and support the motorcycle safely.

NOTE
When lithium base grease is specified in the following sections, use water-resistant bearing lithium base grease.

FRONT WHEEL

Removal

Refer to **Figure 1**.

1. Support the motorcycle so the front wheel is off the ground.

2. Remove the decorative cap, then loosen the front axle pinch bolt (A, **Figure 2**).

3. Loosen, but do not remove, the axle (B, **Figure 2**).

CAUTION
Do not set the wheel down on the disc surface.

NOTE
While removing the front wheel in Step 4 disengage the speed sensor from the right side of the wheel.

4. Support or hold the front wheel, then withdraw the front axle and lower the wheel to the ground.

5. Remove the flanged spacer (**Figure 3**) from the left side of the hub.

Installation

1. Make sure the axle bearing surfaces of the fork legs and axle are free from burrs and nicks.

2. Lightly coat the axle with bearing lithium base grease and set aside until installation.

3. Install the flanged spacer into the left side of the hub (**Figure 3**).

CAUTION
If the brake disc will enter the brake caliper easily in Step 4, do not force it. Remove the brake caliper as described

12

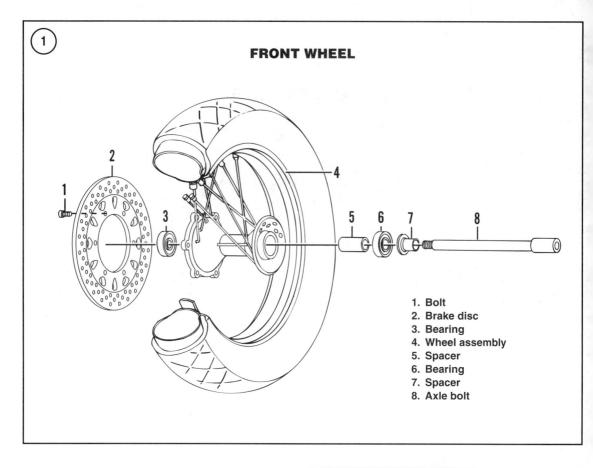

FRONT WHEEL

1. Bolt
2. Brake disc
3. Bearing
4. Wheel assembly
5. Spacer
6. Bearing
7. Spacer
8. Axle bolt

in Chapter Fifteen, install the front wheel, then reinstall the brake caliper.

4. Position the front wheel between the fork legs. Raise the wheel assembly up while installing the speed sensor on the right side of the hub. Make sure the lugs on the sensor and in the hub (**Figure 4**) mesh. Insert the brake disc between the brake pads during wheel installation.

5. Install the axle from the left side and push it through until it contacts the right fork leg.

6. Screw the axle into the right fork leg and tighten to 65 N•m (48 ft.-lb.).

7. Install the axle pinch bolt and tighten by hand.

8. Spin the front wheel and apply the front brake to reposition the brake pads in the caliper.

9. Move the motorcycle off the lift so both wheels are on the ground. Apply the front brake and pump the fork several times to seat the axle.

10. Tighten the axle pinch bolt (A, **Figure 2**) to 33 N•m (24 ft.-lb.).

11. Apply the front brake and push down hard on the handlebars several times to check for proper fork operation.

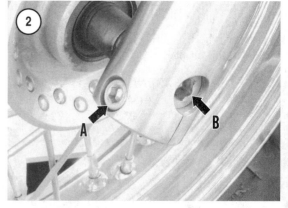

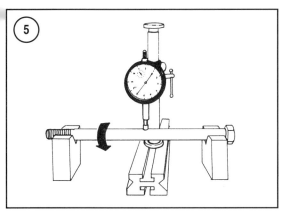

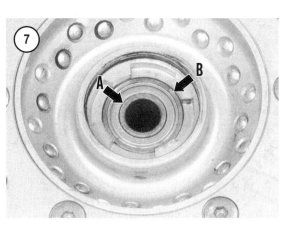

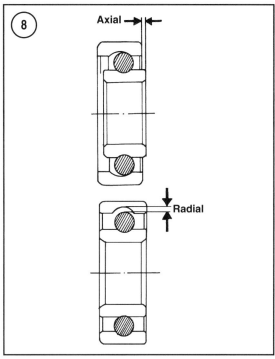

Inspection

Replace worn or damaged parts as described in this section.

1. If it is still in place, remove the flanged spacer (**Figure 3**) from the hub.

2. Clean the axle and spacer to remove all grease and dirt.

3. Remove any corrosion on the front axle and spacer with a piece of fine emery cloth.

4. Check the axle surface for any cracks or other damage.

5. Check the axle runout with a set of V-blocks and a dial indicator (**Figure 5**). If the axle is bent, replace it. Refer to **Table 1**.

6. Check the axle bolt and fork threads for damage. If damaged, repair the threads or replace the fork and axle bolt.

7. Check the disc brake bolts (**Figure 6**) for tightness. Tighten the bolts to 23 N•m (17 ft.-lb.) if necessary. To service the brake disc, refer to Chapter Fifteen.

8. Turn each bearing inner race (A, **Figure 7**) by hand. The bearing must turn smoothly. Some axial play (side to side) is normal, but radial play (up and down) must be negligible. See **Figure 8**. Inspect the bearing side seal (B, **Figure 7**). Replace the bearing if the seal is leaking or damaged. If one bearing is damaged, replace both bearings as a set. Refer to *Front Wheel Hub* in this chapter.

9. Check wheel runout as described in this chapter.

12

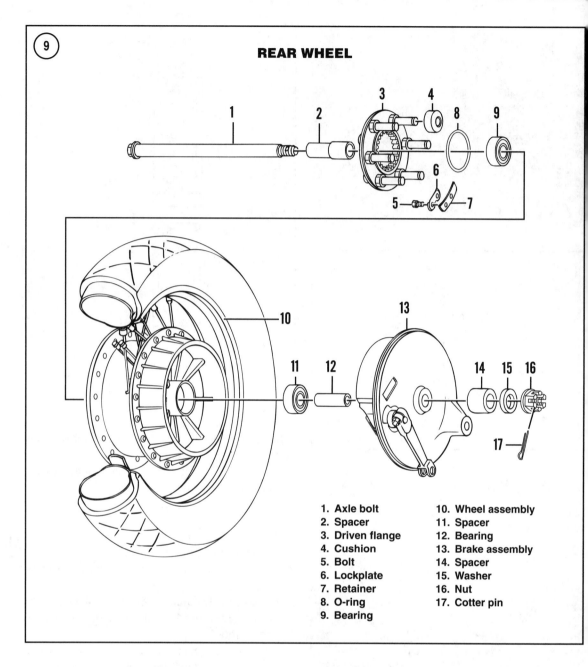

REAR WHEEL

1. Axle bolt
2. Spacer
3. Driven flange
4. Cushion
5. Bolt
6. Lockplate
7. Retainer
8. O-ring
9. Bearing
10. Wheel assembly
11. Spacer
12. Bearing
13. Brake assembly
14. Spacer
15. Washer
16. Nut
17. Cotter pin

REAR WHEEL

Removal

> **NOTE**
> *Rear wheel removal requires sufficient space between the rear fender and ground to allow wheel removal. If the lift used to raise the motorcycle does not provide the necessary clearance, refer to Chapter Sixteen and remove the rear fender.*

> **NOTE**
> *Rear wheel removal is possible without removing the exhaust system, if the tools required to access the rear axle nut are available. The following procedure includes exhaust system removal.*

Refer to **Figure 9**.

1. Support the motorcycle so the rear wheel is off the ground.

2. Remove the exhaust system as described in Chapter Eight or Chapter Nine.

3. Remove the left rear side cover (**Figure 10**) by pulling the prongs out of the grommets.

4. Remove the drive unit cover mounting bolts (A, **Figure 11**).

5. Remove the Allen bolt (B, **Figure 11**).

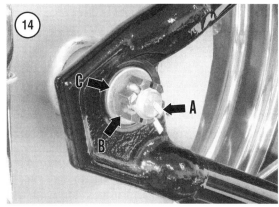

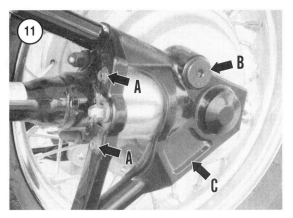

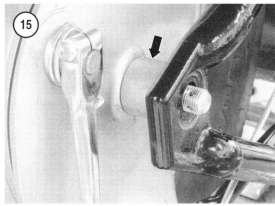

6. Remove the cover front mounting bolts (**Figure 12**).

7. Remove the drive unit cover (C, **Figure 11**).

8. Completely unscrew the rear brake adjusting nut (A, **Figure 13**).

9. Depress the brake pedal and separate the brake rod from the pivot joint (B, **Figure 13**) in the brake arm. Remove the pivot joint from the brake arm, then install the pivot joint and the adjusting nut onto the brake rod to avoid misplacing them.

10. Remove the brake torque link from the brake panel as follows:

    a. Remove the bolt, locknut and washer (C, **Figure 13**).

    b. Swing the brake torque link (D, **Figure 13**) down and out of the way.

11. Remove the cotter pin (A, **Figure 14)** from the rear axle nut. Discard the cotter pin.

12. Remove the rear axle nut (B, **Figure 14**) and washer (C).

13. Use a soft drift and carefully tap against the right end of the axle until the axle can be withdrawn from the left side. Do not lose the spacer (**Figure 15**) from the right side between the brake panel and the swing arm.

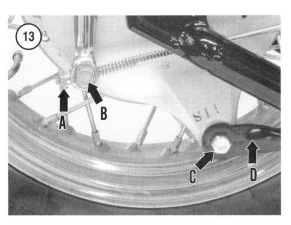

14. Slide the wheel to the right to disengage it from the hub drive splines and remove the wheel.

Installation

1. If removed, insert the spacer into the final drive unit (A, **Figure 16**), small end first.
2. Apply a light coat of lithium based NLGI No. 2 grease with molybdenum disulfide to the final driven flange splines (B, **Figure 16**).
3. Position the rear wheel so that the splines of the final driven flange and the final drive align. Slowly move the wheel back and forth and push the wheel to the left until it completely seats.
4. Position the spacer (**Figure 15**) on the right side between the brake panel and the swing arm.
5. Insert the rear axle and install the washer (C, **Figure 14**) and axle nut (B). Tighten the nut only fingertight at this time.
6. To reconnect the brake torque link (D, **Figure 13**), perform the following:
   a. Rotate the brake assembly so the brake panel arm hole and link hole align.
   b. Install the bolt, washers and nut. Tighten the bolt and nut to 25 N•m (18 ft.-lb.).
7. Tighten the rear axle nut to 65 N•m (48 ft.-lb.).
8. Install a new cotter pin and bend the ends over completely.
9. Insert the rear brake rod into the pivot in the brake arm, then install the adjusting nut (A, **Figure 13**).
10. Install the drive unit cover (C, **Figure 11**), bolt (B) and bolts (A). Install the front cover bolts (**Figure 12**). Tighten the bolts securely.
11. Install the left, rear side cover (**Figure 10**).
12. After the wheel is installed, completely rotate it several times to make sure it rotates freely and the brake works properly.
13. Adjust the rear brake free play as described in Chapter Three.

Inspection

Replace worn or damaged parts as described in this section.
1. Clean the axle and spacer to remove all grease and dirt.
2. Remove any corrosion on the front axle and spacer with a piece of fine emery cloth.
3. Check the axle surface for cracks or other damage.
4. Check the axle runout with a set of V-blocks and a dial indicator (**Figure 5**). If the axle is out of specificiation, replace it. Refer to **Table 1**.

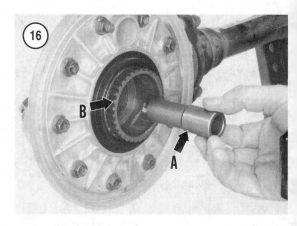

5. Turn each bearing inner race (A, **Figure 17**) by hand. The bearing must turn smoothly. Some axial play (side to side) is normal, but radial play (up and down) must be negligible. See **Figure 18**. Inspect the bearing side seal (B, **Figure 17**). Replace the bearing if the seal is leaking or damaged. If one bearing is damaged, replace both bearings as a set. Refer to *Rear Wheel Hub* in this chapter.
6. Check wheel runout as described in this chapter.

FRONT WHEEL HUB

Pre-inspection

Inspect each wheel bearing as follows:
1. Support the motorcycle with either the front or rear wheel off the ground. Make sure the axle is tightened securely.
   a. Hold the wheel along its sides (180° apart) and try to rock it back and forth. If there is any noticeable play at the axle, the wheel bearings are worn or damaged and require replacement. Have an assistant apply the front brake while rocking the wheel again. On severely worn bearings, play is detected at the bearings even though the wheel is locked in position.

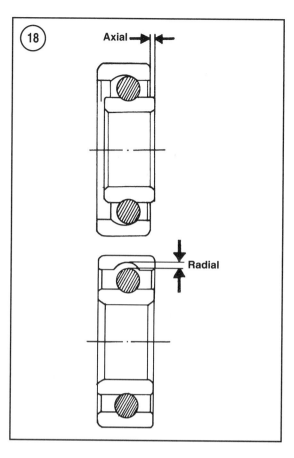

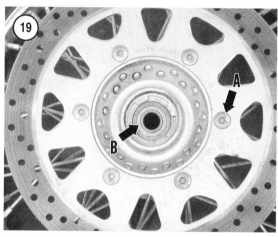

2. Remove the front wheel as described in this chapter.

3. Before removing the wheel bearings, check the tightness of the bearings in the hub by pulling the bearing up and then from side to side. The bearing should be a tight fit in the hub with no movement. If the bearing is loose and wobbles, the bearing bore in the hub may be cracked or damaged. Remove the bearings as described in this procedure and check the hub bore carefully. If any damage is found, replace the wheel. It cannot be repaired.

4. To check the ball bearings, turn each bearing inner race by hand. The bearing must turn smoothly with no roughness, catching, binding or excessive noise. Some axial play (side to side) is normal, but radial play (up and down) must be negligible (**Figure 18**). Replace all the bearings in a hub if any bearing requires replacement.

5. Check each ball bearing outer seal (B, **Figure 17**) for buckling or other damage that would allow dirt to enter the bearing.

Disassembly

1. Remove the front wheel as described in this chapter.

2. If necessary, remove the bolts (A, **Figure 19**) securing the brake disc and remove the disc.

3. Before proceeding further, inspect the wheel bearings (B, **Figure 19**) as described in this section. If they must be replaced, proceed as follows.

b. Push the front caliper in by hand to move the brake pads away from the brake disc. This makes it easier to spin the wheel when performing substep c.

c. Spin the wheel and listen for excessive wheel bearing noise. A grinding or catching noise indicates worn bearings.

d. Apply the front brake several times to reposition the brake pads in the caliper.

e. To check any questionable bearing, continue with Step 2.

NOTE
*Step 4 describes two methods of removing the wheel bearings. Step 4A requires the use of a wheel bearing remover set (**Figure 20**). Step 4B describes how to remove the bearings without special tools.*

4A. To remove the wheel bearings with a wheel bearing remover set, refer to **Figure 21** and perform the following:

    a. Select the correct size remover head and insert it into one of the bearings.

    b. From the opposite side of the hub, insert the remover shaft into the slot in the backside of the remover head. Position the hub with the remover head tool resting against a solid surface and strike the remover shaft to force it into the slit in the remover head. This wedges the remover head tool against the inner bearing race.

    c. Position the hub and strike the end of the remover shaft with a hammer to drive the bearing from the hub. Remove the bearing and tool.

    d. Remove the spacer from the hub.

    e. Repeat for the other bearing.

4B. To remove the wheel bearings without special tools:

WARNING
The hub and bearings will be hot after heating them with a torch. Wear protective gloves when handling the parts.

WARNING
Clean the hub of all chemical residue before heating it with a torch in this procedure.

    a. Heat one side of the hub with a propane torch. Work the torch in a circular motion around the hub, making sure not to hold the torch in one area. Then turn the wheel over and remove the bearing as described in the next step.

    b. Using a long drift, tilt the spacer away from one side of the bearing (**Figure 22**).

CAUTION
Do not damage the spacer when removing the bearing. If necessary, grind a clearance groove in the drift to enable it to contact the bearing while clearing the spacer.

    c. Tap the bearing out of the hub with a hammer, working in a circle around the bearing inner race.

    d. Remove the spacer from the hub.

    e. Turn the hub over and heat the opposite side.

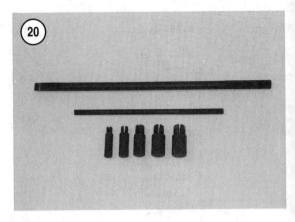

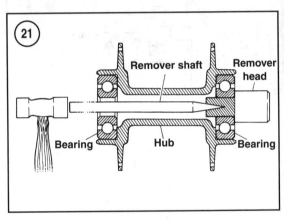

    f. Drive out the opposite bearing, using a suitable driver.

    g. Inspect the spacer for burrs or dents created during removal.

5. Clean and dry the hub and spacer.

Assembly

1. Before installing the new bearings, note the following:

    a. Install both bearings with the closed side facing out. If a bearing is sealed on both sides, install the bearing with the manufacturer's marks facing out.

    b. Install the seals with the closed side facing out.

2. Remove any dirt or debris from the hub before installing the bearings.

3. Pack the open side of each bearing with lithium base grease.

NOTE
When installing the bearings, install the right side bearing first, then the left side bearing.

4. Place the right side bearing squarely against the bore opening with its closed side facing out. Select a

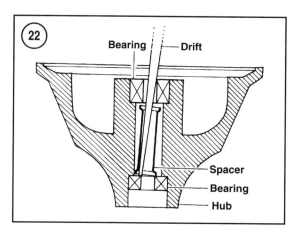

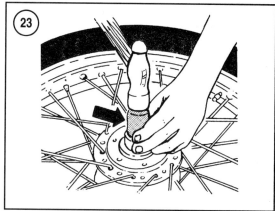

driver or socket with an outside diameter slightly smaller than the bearing's outside diameter. Drive the bearing into the bore until it bottoms (**Figure 23**).

5. Turn the wheel over and install the spacer. Center it against the first bearing's inner race.

6. Place the left side bearing squarely against the bore opening with its closed side facing out. Using the same driver, drive the bearing partway into the bearing bore, then stop and make sure the spacer is centered in the hub. If not, install the axle through the hub to align the spacer with the bearing. Remove the axle and continue installing the bearing until it bottoms in the hub.

> *CAUTION*
> *If the axle will not go into the hub, the*
> *spacer is not aligned correctly with one*
> *of the bearings.*

7. Insert the axle through the hub and turn it by hand. Check for any roughness or binding, indicating bearing damage.

Inspection

1. Check the hub mounting bore for cracks or other damage. If one bearing is a loose fit, the mounting bore is damaged. Replace the hub.

> *CAUTION*
> *The spacer operates against the wheel*
> *bearing inner races to prevent them*
> *from moving inward when the axle is*
> *tightened. If the ends of the spacer are*
> *damaged or shortened, or if it is not in-*
> *stalled in the hub, the inner bearing*
> *races move inward and bind as the axle*
> *is tightened, causing bearing damage.*

2. Inspect the spacer for cracks, corrosion or other damage. Inspect the spacer ends. If the ends appear compressed or damaged, replace the spacer. Do not

try to repair the spacer by cutting or grinding the end surfaces as this shortens the spacer.

Removing Damaged Bearings

When wheel bearings are worn or rusted, the inner race can break apart and fall out of the bearing, leaving the outer race in the hub. Because the outer race is seated against the hub shoulder, bearing removal is difficult because only a small part of the race is accessible to drive against. To remove a bearing's outer race in this situation, perform the following:

1. Heat the hub evenly with a propane torch.

2. Drive out the outer race with a drift and hammer. Grind a clearance tip on the end of the drift, if necessary, to avoid damaging the hub's mounting bore. Check this before heating the hub.

3. Apply force at opposite points around the race to prevent it from binding in the hub bore.

4. After removing the race, inspect the hub bore carefully for cracks or other damage.

REAR WHEEL HUB

Pre-inspection

Inspect each wheel bearing before removing it from the wheel hub.

> *CAUTION*
> *Remove the wheel bearings only if they*
> *require replacement. Do not remove the*
> *wheel bearings for inspection, as they*
> *may be damaged during removal.*

1. Remove the rear wheel as described in this chapter.

> *CAUTION*
> *When handling the wheel assembly in*
> *the following steps, do not lay the wheel*
> *down so it is supported by the brake*

12

disc as this could damage the disc. Support the wheel on wooden blocks.

2. Check the tightness of the bearings in the hub (A, **Figure 24**) by pulling the bearing up and then from side to side. The bearing should be a tight fit in the hub with no movement. If the bearing is loose and wobbles, the bearing bore in the hub may be cracked or damaged. Remove the bearings as described in this procedure and check the hub bore carefully. If any damage is found, replace the wheel. It cannot be repaired.

3. To check the ball bearings, turn each bearing inner race by hand. The bearing must turn smoothly with no roughness, catching, binding or excessive noise. Some axial play (side to side) is normal, but radial play (up and down) must be negligible (**Figure 18**). It is a good practice to replace all bearings in a hub if any bearing requires replacement.

4. Check each ball bearing outer seal (B, **Figure 24**) for buckling or other damage that would allow dirt to enter the bearing.

5. Inspect the splines (C, **Figure 24**) of the final driven flange. If any are damaged the flange must be replaced.

Disassembly

WARNING
Wear safety glasses while using the wheel bearing remover set.

Refer to **Figure 25**.

1. Remove the rear wheel as described in this chapter.

CAUTION
The driven flange retaining bolts removed in Step 2 are secured by threadlock. The bolts are easily sheared during removal. If the bolt feels seized, apply heat using a high-temperature heat gun to the area around the bolt hole to help loosen the bolt.

2. Straighten the locking tabs on the lockplates (A, **Figure 26**), then remove the bolts (B).

3. Remove the lockplates and retainers (C, **Figure 26**). Remove all three sets.

4. Remove the driven flange (**Figure 27**) from the hub by pulling it straight up.

5. Remove the O-ring (**Figure 28**) from the rear hub.

6. Before proceeding further, inspect the wheel bearings as described in this chapter. If they must be replaced, proceed as follows.

NOTE
*If the bearing(s) is severely damaged, refer to **Front Wheel Hub** in this chapter.*

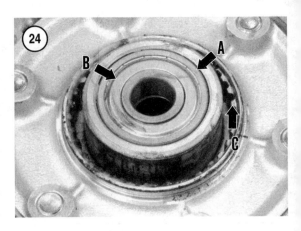

NOTE
*Step 7 describes two methods of removing the wheel bearings. Step 7A requires the use of a wheel bearing remover set (**Figure 20**). Step 7B describes how to remove the bearings without special tools.*

7A. To remove the bearings using a wheel bearing remover set, refer to **Figure 21** and perform the following:

   a. Select the correct size remover head and insert it into one of the bearings.

   b. From the opposite side of the hub, insert the remover shaft into the slot in the backside of the remover head. Position the hub with the remover head tool resting against a solid surface and strike the remover shaft to force it into the slit in the remover head. This wedges the remover head tool against the inner bearing race.

   c. Position the hub and strike the end of the remover shaft with a hammer to drive the bearing from the hub. Remove the bearing and tool.

   d. Remove the spacer from the hub.

   e. Repeat for the other bearing.

7B. If the special tools are not used, perform the following:

   a. To remove the right and left bearings and spacer, insert an aluminum or brass drift into one side of the hub.

   b. Push the inner spacer over to one side and place the drift on the inner race of the lower bearing.

   c. Tap the bearing out of the hub with a hammer, working around the perimeter of the inner race. Remove the bearing spacer and tool.

   d. Repeat for the other bearing.

8. Clean the inside and the outside of the hub with solvent. Dry with compressed air.

9. Clean the inside and the outside of the final driven flange with solvent. Dry with compressed air.

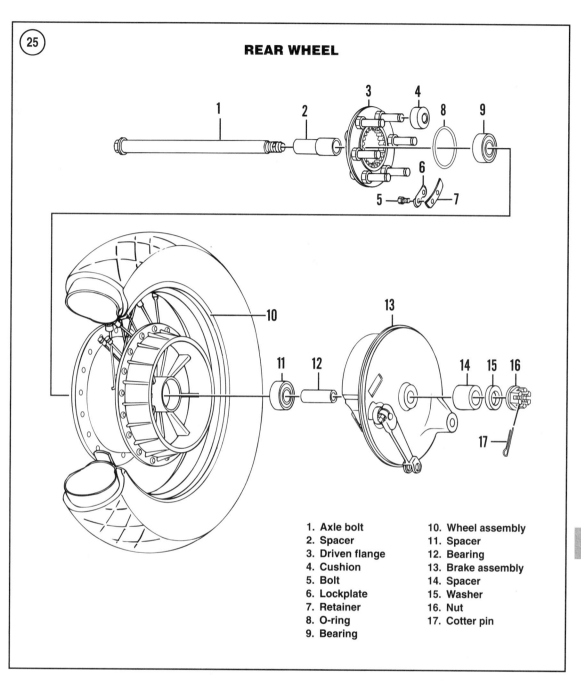

REAR WHEEL

1. Axle bolt
2. Spacer
3. Driven flange
4. Cushion
5. Bolt
6. Lockplate
7. Retainer
8. O-ring
9. Bearing
10. Wheel assembly
11. Spacer
12. Bearing
13. Brake assembly
14. Spacer
15. Washer
16. Nut
17. Cotter pin

12

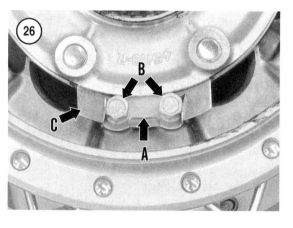

Assembly

1. On unsealed bearings, pack the bearings with a good quality bearing grease. Work the grease in between the balls thoroughly. Turn the bearing by hand a couple of times to make sure the grease is distributed evenly inside the bearing.

2. Make sure all debris is out of the hub before installing the bearings.

NOTE
Install non-sealed bearings with the single sealed side facing outward.

3. Tap the right bearing squarely into place. Strike the outer race only. Use a socket that matches the outer race diameter (**Figure 23**). Do not tap on the inner race or the bearing might be damaged. Make sure the bearing is completely seated.

4. Turn the wheel over (left side up) on the workbench and install the spacer.

5. Use the same tool setup and drive in the left side bearing until there is a slight clearance between the inner race and the spacer.

6. Make sure the holes for the retainer bolts (B, **Figure 26**) are clean and free of debris. If necessary, clean the holes with a thread restorer tool.

7. Install a new O-ring seal into the groove in the hub (**Figure 28**). Coat the O-ring with multipurpose grease.

8. Install the driven flange into the rear hub. Push it down until it is completely seated in the rear hub.

9. Install the retainers into the locking ring in the driven flange.

10. Install new lockplates (A, **Figure 26**).

CAUTION
If the bolts installed in Step 11 attempt to seize, stop turning immediately and remove the bolt. Inspect the hole for debris, corrosion or old threadlocking residue. The bolts are easily sheared.

11. Use a small amount of threadlocking compound (ThreeBond TB 1303 or equivalent) to the bolt threads prior to installation, then install the bolts (B, **Figure 26**).

12. Tighten the bolts to 10 N•m (88 in.-lb.).

13. Bend up the locking tab against a flat on each bolt.

14. Install the rear wheel as described in this chapter.

Inspection

1. Check the hub mounting bore for cracks or other damage. If one bearing is a loose fit, the mounting bore is damaged. Replace the hub.

CAUTION
The spacer operates against the wheel bearing inner races to prevent them from moving inward when the axle is tightened. If the ends of the spacer are damaged or shortened, or if it is not installed in the hub, the inner bearing races move inward and bind as the axle is tightened, causing bearing damage.

2. Inspect the spacer for cracks, corrosion or other damage. Inspect the spacer ends. If the ends appear compressed or damaged, replace the spacer. Do not try to repair the spacer by cutting or grinding the end surfaces as this shortens the spacer.

3. Inspect each rubber cushion (**Figure 29**) for wear or deterioration. Replace if necessary.

4. Inspect the driven flange as follows:

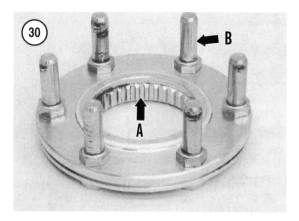

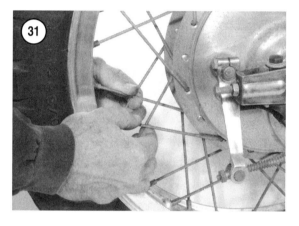

a. Inspect the inner splines (A, **Figure 30**) for wear or missing teeth.

b. Inspect the studs (B, **Figure 30**) for cracks or damage.

c. Inspect the driven flange for cracks or warp.

d. Replace the driven flange if any of these areas are damaged.

WHEEL SERVICE

Component Condition

Inspect the wheels regularly for lateral (side-to-side) and radial (up-and-down) runout, even spoke tension and visible rim damage. When a wheel has a noticeable wobble, it is out of true. This is usually caused by loose spokes, but it can be caused by a damaged hub or rim.

Truing a wheel corrects the lateral and radial runout to bring the wheel back into specification (**Table 1**). The condition of the individual wheel components affects the ability to successfully true the wheel. Note the following:

1. Spoke condition—Do not true a wheel with bent or damaged spokes. Doing so places an excessive amount of tension on the spokes, hub and rim.

Overtightening the spoke may damage the spoke nipple hole in the hub or rim. It can also cause the spokes to be drawn through the rim and possibly puncture the tube. Inspect for and replace damaged spokes.

2. Nipple condition—When truing the wheels the nipples must turn freely on the spoke. However, corroded and rusted spoke threads are common and difficult to adjust. Spray a penetrating liquid onto the nipple and allow sufficient time for it to penetrate before trying to turn the nipples. Turn the spoke wrench in both directions and continue to apply penetrating liquid. If the spoke wrench rounds off the nipple, it is necessary to remove the tire from the rim and cut the spoke(s) out of the wheel.

3. Rim condition—Minor rim runout can be corrected by truing the wheel. However, do not correct rim damage by overtightening the spokes. Inspect the rims for cracks, flat spots or dents. Check the spoke holes for cracks or elongation. Replace damaged rims and hubs.

4. Before checking the runout and truing the wheel, note the following:

a. Make sure the wheel bearings are in good condition.

b. Check each spoke hole on both sides of the hub for cracks.

c. Check runout by mounting a pointer against the fork or swing arm and slowly rotating the wheel. A truing stand can also be used.

d. Use the correct size spoke wrench. Using the wrong type of tool or incorrect size spoke wrench may round off the spoke nipples, making adjustment difficult.

Tightening Loose Spokes

This section describes steps for checking and tightening loose spokes without affecting the wheel runout. When many spokes are loose and the wheel is running out of true, refer to the *Wheel Truing Procedure* in this section.

1. Support the wheel so it can turn freely.

2. Spokes can be checked for looseness in one of two ways:

a. Hand check: Grasp and squeeze two spokes where they cross (**Figure 31**). Loose spokes can be flexed by hand. Tight spokes feel stiff with little noticeable movement. Tighten the spokes until the tension between the different spoke groups feels the same.

b. Spoke tone: Tapping a spoke causes it to vibrate and produce sound waves. Loose and tight spokes produce different sounds or tones. A tight spoke rings. A loose spoke has a soft or

12

dull ring. Tap each spoke with a spoke wrench or screwdriver (**Figure 32**) to identify loose spokes.

3. Check the spokes using one of the methods described in Step 2. If there are loose spokes, spin the wheel and note the following:

    a. If the wheel is running true, continue with Step 4 to tighten the loose spokes.

    b. If the wheel is running out of true, go to *Wheel Truing Procedure* in this section to measure runout and to true the wheel.

4. Use tape and divide the rim into four equally spaced sections. Number the sections as shown in **Figure 33**.

> *CAUTION*
> *If the spokes are hard to turn, spray penetrating oil into the top of the nipple. Wipe excess oil from the rim.*

5. Start by tightening the loose spokes in Section 1, then in sections 2, 3 and 4. Do not turn each spoke more than 1/4 to 1/2 turn at a time. Doing so overtightens the spokes and brings the wheel out of true. Work slowly while checking spoke tightness. Continue until all the spokes are tightened evenly.

6. When all of the spokes are tightened evenly, spin the wheel. If there is any noticeable runout, true the wheel as described in *Wheel Truing Procedure* in this section.

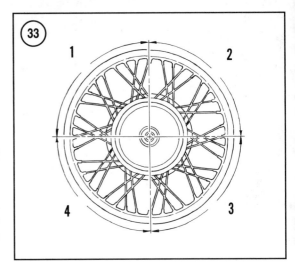

Wheel Truing Procedure

Table 1 lists axial (side-to-side) and radial (up-and-down) runout specifications.

1. Clean the rim, spokes and nipples.

2. Position a pointer against the rim as shown in **Figure 34**. If the tire is mounted on the rim, position the pointer as shown in **Figure 35**.

> *NOTE*
> *It is normal for the rim to jump at the point where the rim was welded together. Also small cuts and dings in the rim affect the runout reading, especially when using a dial indicator.*

3. Spin the wheel slowly and check the axial and radial runout. If the rim is out of adjustment, continue with Step 4.

4. Spray penetrating oil into the top of each nipple. Wipe excess oil from the rim.

> *NOTE*
> *If the runout is minimal, the tire can be left on the rim. However, if the runout is*

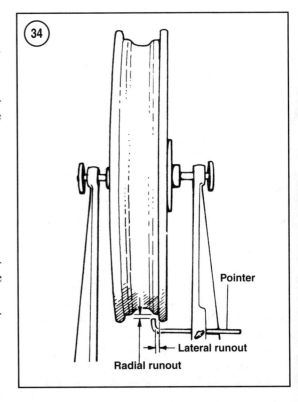

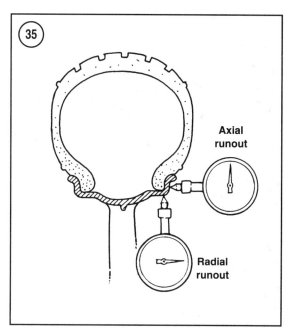

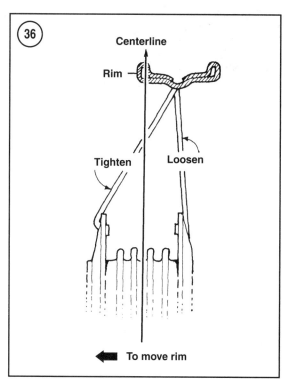

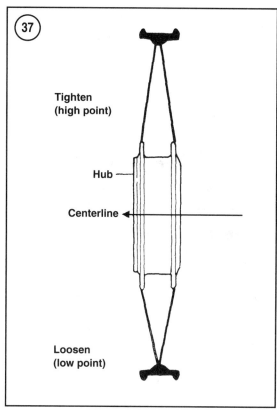

right side of the hub. Always loosen and tighten the spokes in equal number of turns.

> *NOTE*
> *Determining the number of spokes to loosen and tighten depends on how far the runout is out of adjustment. Loosen two or three spokes, then tighten the opposite two or three spokes. If the runout is excessive and affects a greater area along the rim, loosen and tighten a greater number of spokes.*

6. Radial runout adjustment: If the up and down runout is out of specification, the hub is not centered in the rim. Draw the high point of the rim toward the centerline of the wheel by tightening the spokes in the area of the high point and loosening the spokes on the side opposite the high point (**Figure 37**). Tighten the spokes in equal amounts to prevent distortion.

> *NOTE*
> *Alternate between checking and adjusting axial and radial runout. Remember, changing spoke tension on one side of the rim affects the tension on the other side of the rim.*

7. After truing the wheel, seat each spoke in the hub by tapping it with a flat nose punch and hammer. Then

excessive or if the rim must be centered with the hub (Step 5), remove the tire from the rim.

5. Lateral runout adjustment: If the side-to-side runout is out of specification, adjust the wheel. For example, to pull the rim to the left side (**Figure 36**), tighten the spokes on the left side of the hub (at the runout point) and loosen the adjacent spokes on the

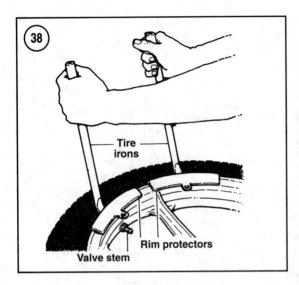

recheck the spoke tension and wheel runout. Readjust if necessary as described in *Tightening Loose Spokes* in this section.

8. Check the ends of the spokes where they are threaded in the nipples. Grind off any ends that protrude through the nipples to prevent them from puncturing the tube.

TIRES

Safety

Tire wear and performance are greatly affected by tire pressure. Have a good tire gauge on hand and check the pressure frequently. Refer to Chapter Three.

Allow a sensible break-in period for new tires. New tires have significantly less adhesion ability. Do not subject a new tire to hard corner, hard acceleration or hard braking for the first 160 km (100 miles). Scuff in the new tires in a parking lot, without having to ride in traffic.

Removal

CAUTION
It is easier to replace tires when the wheel is mounted on a raised platform. A popular item used by many home mechanics is a metal drum. Before placing the wheel on a drum, cover the drum edge with a length of garden hose, split lengthwise and secured in place with plastic ties. When changing the front tire at ground level, support the wheel on two wooden blocks to prevent the brake disc from contacting the floor.

CAUTION
Use rim protectors (Figure 38) or insert scraps of leather between the tire iron and the rim to protect the rim from damage.

NOTE
Warming the tire makes it softer and more pliable. Place the tire and wheel assembly in the sun or in a completely closed automobile. Place the new tire in the same location.

1. Remove the valve core and deflate the tire.

2. Press the entire bead on both sides of the tire into the center of the rim. If necessary, step on the sidewall, and not the rim, to break the bead. Make sure the beads are free on both sides of the rim.

3. Lubricate the beads on both sides of the tire with soapy water or a tire lubricant.

4. Insert the first tire iron under the bead on the opposite side of the valve stem. Force the bead into the center of the rim, and then pry the bead over the rim with the tire iron (**Figure 39**).

CAUTION
If it is difficult to pry the bead over the rim with the second tire iron, stop and

tube on top of the tire, facing in its original position, to help locate the object in the tire. Remove the object and check the tire for damage.

NOTE
Cracks in the inner tire liner can pinch and damage the tube. If the tube is leaking air, but there are no objects in the tire, spread the tire and check the inner liner for cracks.

2. Run a rag through the inside of the tire to locate any protruding objects. Do not use your hands.

WARNING
If there is any doubt about the condition of the tire, replace it. Do not take a chance on a tire failure at any speed.

3. If any one of the following is observed, replace the tire:
  a. A noticeable puncture or split.
  b. A scratch or split on the sidewall or along the inner liner.
  c. Any ply separation.
  d. Tread separation or abnormal wear pattern.
  e. Tread depth of less than the minimum value specified in **Table 2**. The minimum depth for aftermarket tires may vary. Refer to the tire manufacturer's information.
  f. Scratches on either sealing bead.
  g. The cord is cut in any place.
  h. Flat spots in the tread from skidding.
  i. Any abnormality in the inner liner.

4. If the tire can be reused, clean and dry the inside of the tire with compressed air.
5. Remove the rim strap from the center of the rim. Replace if damaged.
6. Use a brush to clean dirt, rust and rubber from the inside of the rim.
7. Inspect the spokes (**Figure 43**) for rust and corrosion. Then check for any spoke ends that protrude

make sure the bottom bead was broken from the rim. Excessive force splits and tears the tire bead and causes permanent tire damage.

5. Insert a second tire iron next to the first to hold the bead over the rim (**Figure 40**). While holding the tire with one tire iron, work around the tire with the second tire iron, prying the tire over the rim and working in small bites of one to two inches at a time. Be careful not to pinch the inner tube with the tire irons.

CAUTION
If the tube is being removed to fix a flat, identify the tube's installed position in the tire immediately after removing it to help locate the object in the tire.

6. When the upper bead is free of the rim, remove the inner tube from the tire (**Figure 41**).
7. Stand the tire upright and pry the second tire bead (**Figure 42**) over the rim. Then peel the tire off the rim by hand. If necessary, use a second tire iron.

Inspection

1. Inspect the tire for damage. If the tube was leaking air, pump air into it to locate the leak. Then place the

above the nipple head and into the center of the rim. Grind or file the exposed part of the spoke flush with the nipple.

8. Check the valve stem hole in the rim for any roughness or cuts that could damage the valve stem. Remove any roughness with a file.

9. Mount the wheel onto a truing stand and check runout before mounting the tire.

10. If possible, install a new tube. If not, inflate the original tube to make sure it was not punctured during tire removal. However, discard the tube if it has been previously patched or if it appears balancing liquids were introduced into the tube. Check the inner nut on the valve stem to make sure it is tight. Check the area around the valve stem for cracks and other weak spots.

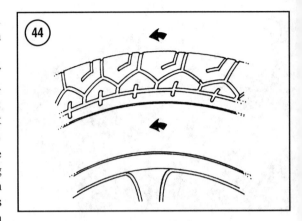

Installation

> *NOTE*
> *Installation is easier if the tire is pliable. This can be achieved by warming the tire in the sun or inside an enclosed automobile.*

1. Install the rim band around the rim by aligning the hole in the band with the hole in the rim.

2. When installing the tire on the rim, make sure the correct tire, either front or rear, is installed on the correct wheel. Also install the tire with the direction arrow facing the normal direction of wheel rotation (**Figure 44**).

> *WARNING*
> *Use a tire lubricant when installing the tire over the rim and when seating the beads. Use a commercial tire lubricant, if available. Plain or soapy water can also be used. Do not use Teflon and WD-40 aerosol spray lubes and other petroleum chemicals as a tire lubricant. These lubricants stay on the tire beads without drying out and can cause the tire to slip on the rim and damage the valve stem. Some chemicals also damage the rubber.*

> *NOTE*
> *These tires use an angled valve stem (A, **Figure 45**) that must face toward the left side of the wheel when installed. When installing the rear tire, begin by positioning the wheel with the brake drum side facing up.*

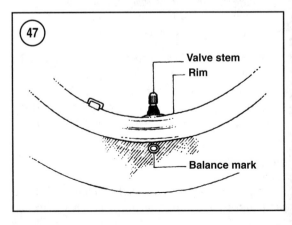

3. Sprinkle the tube with talcum powder and install it into the tire (**Figure 46**). The powder minimizes tube

chafing and helps the tube distribute itself when inflated.

NOTE
If installing the rear tube, make sure the valve stem is correctly angled with the hole in the rim.

4. Inflate the tube to shape it against the tire. Then bleed most of the air from the tube. Too much air makes tire installation difficult and too little air increases the chance of pinching the tube.

5. Most tires are marked with a colored spot near the bead that indicates a lighter point on the tire. Align this spot with the valve stem hole in the rim (**Figure 47**).

6. Lubricate the lower bead. Then start pushing the lower bead over the rim while inserting the air valve through the hole in the rim (**Figure 48**). Install the nut (B, **Figure 45**) onto the valve stem to prevent the stem from sliding back into the tire.

7. Continue to push the lower bead over the rim by hand-fitting it as much as possible. The last part of the bead is the most difficult to install. If necessary, grasp the spokes to steady the wheel and push the front part of the tire toward the inside of the rim with your knees. This may provide additional room at the back of the bead to help with its installation. If it is necessary to use a tire lever, use it carefully to avoid pinching the tube or tearing the tire bead.

8. When the lower bead is installed over the rim, turn the wheel over and check that the tube is not pinched between the bead and rim. If so, carefully push the tube back into the center of the tire by hand.

9. Turn the wheel back over and lift the upper bead to check the tube. Make sure the tube is laying evenly around the tire. If necessary, inflate the tube to remove any wrinkles, then bleed most of the air from the tube.

10. Turn the tire so the air valve is angled as shown in A, **Figure 45**. Make sure the tire balance mark identified in Step 5 aligns with the valve stem hole in the rim (**Figure 47**).

CAUTION
Do not use excessive force on the tire irons to install the upper tire bead. Instead, use your knees to push the front part of the tire (the part closest to you) toward the inside of the rim and to keep the lower bead positioned in the center of the rim. Forcing the tire irons between the upper bead and rim because the lower bead is not properly positioned can damage the rim, cut the tire bead and pinch the tube.

NOTE
Properly aligning the tire weight mark with the valve stem hole helps to reduce the amount of weight required to balance the tire.

11. Lubricate the upper tire bead, and then start installation opposite the valve stem (**Figure 49**). If necessary, relubricate the bead. Use the tire irons to pry the remaining section of bead over the rim (**Figure 50**). Remember to keep the lower bead positioned in the center of the rim when installing the upper bead.

12. When both beads are installed over the rim, perform the following:

12

a. Check the bead for uniform fit on both sides of the tire.

b. Check both sides of the tire for any part of the tube that is pinched between the tire bead and rim. Lift the tire and carefully push the tube back into the tire.

c. Turn the tire so the air valve is straight up and the tire weight mark (**Figure 47**) aligns with the valve stem hole.

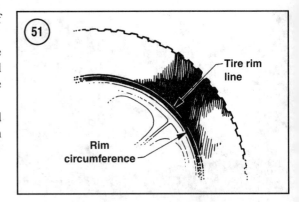

WARNING
When inflating the tire and seating the tire beads in the next step, never exceed 300 kPa (43.5 psi) inflation pressure. If the tire does not seat at the recommended pressure, do not continue by overinflating the tire. Doing so could cause the tire to burst and cause injury. Deflate the tire and repeat the procedure. Wear safety glasses and stand as far away from the tire as possible. Never stand directly over a tire while inflating it.

13. Lubricate both beads. Use a clamp-on air chuck and inflate the tire to seat the beads on the rim. Do not exceed 300 kPa (43.5 psi).

14. After inflating the tire, make sure the beads are fully seated and the rim lines are the same distance from the rim all the way around the tire (**Figure 51**). If not, deflate the tire and repeat the procedure.

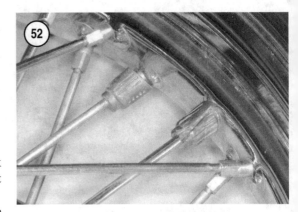

15. When the beads are correctly seated, deflate the tire (but do not break the tire beads). Inflate the tire again to help stretch the tube and seat it fully against the tire. Set the tire to the required tire pressure listed in **Table 2**. Tighten the outer valve stem nut (B, **Figure 45**) and the valve stem cap.

16. Balance the tire and wheel assembly as described in this chapter.

WHEEL BALANCE

A wheel that is not balanced is unsafe because it seriously affects the steering and handling of the motorcycle. Depending on the degree of unbalance and the speed of the motorcycle, anything from a mild vibration to a violent shimmy may occur, which may result in loss of control. An imbalanced wheel also causes abnormal tire wear.

Motorcycle wheels can be checked for balance either statically (single plane balance) or dynamically (dual plane balance). This section describes how to static balance the wheels using a wheel balancing stand.

Balance weights are used to balance the wheel and are attached to the spokes (**Figure 52**). Weight kits are available from motorcycle dealerships.

The wheel must be able to rotate freely when checking wheel balance. Because excessively worn or damaged wheel bearings affect the accuracy of this procedure, check the wheel bearings as described in this chapter. Also confirm that the tire balance mark is aligned with the valve stem (**Figure 47**).

NOTE
Leave the brake disc mounted on the front wheel when checking and adjusting wheel balance.

1. Remove the wheel as described in this chapter.

2. Clean the seals and inspect the wheel bearings as described in this chapter.

3. Clean the tire, rim and spokes. Remove any stones or pebbles stuck in the tire tread.

4A. Mount the front wheel (with brake disc attached) on a balance stand (**Figure 53**).

4B. Mount the rear wheel (with driven flange assembly and sprocket) on a balance stand (**Figure 53**).

NOTE
To check the original balance of the wheel, leave the original weights attached to the spokes.

5. Spin the wheel by hand and let it coast to a stop. Mark the tire at its bottom point with chalk.

6. Spin the wheel several more times. If the same spot on the tire stops at the bottom each time, the wheel is out of balance. This is the heaviest part of the tire.

7. Attach a test weight to the wheel at the point opposite the heaviest spot and spin the wheel again.

8. Experiment with different weights until the wheel, when spun, comes to rest at a different position each time. When a wheel is correctly balanced, the weight of the tire and wheel assembly is distributed equally around the wheel.

9. Remove the test weight and install the correct size weight or weights to the rim. Crimp the weight tightly against the spoke and nipple (**Figure 52**).

NOTE
Do not exceed 60 grams (2.1 oz.) on the front wheel or 70 grams (2.5 oz.) on the rear wheel. If a wheel requires an excessive amount of weight, make sure the weight mark on the tire aligns with the valve stem.

10. Record the weight, number and position of the weights in the maintenance log at the end of the manual. Then, if the motorcycle experiences a handling or vibration problem in the future, check for any missing balance weights as previously recorded.

11. Install the wheel as described in this chapter.

Table 1 WHEEL SPECIFICATIONS

Item	New	Service limit
Front axle runout (max.)	–	0.25 mm (0.010 in.)
Rear axle runout (max.)	–	0.25 mm (0.010 in.)
Wheel rim axial runout (max.)	–	2.0 mm (0.08 in.)
Wheel rim radial runout (max.)	–	2.0 mm (0.08 in.)

Table 2 TIRE SPECIFICATIONS

Item	Front	Rear
Tire type	Tube	Tube
Size	130/90-16M/C (67H)	170/80-15M/C (77H)
Minimum tread depth	1.6 mm (0.06 in.)	2.0 mm (0.08 in.)
Inflation pressure (cold)*		
Touring models	225 kPa (33 psi)	225 kPa (33 psi)
All other models		
Solo	200 kPa (29 psi)	250 kPa (36 psi)
Rider and passenger	200 kPa (29 psi)	250 kPa (36 psi)

*Tire inflation pressure for original equipment tires. Aftermarket tires may require different inflation pressure. The use of tires other than those specified by the manufacturer may affect handling.

Table 3 WHEEL REMOVAL TORQUE SPECIFICATIONS

Item	N•m	in.-lb.	ft.-lb.
Driven flange retaining bolts*	10	88	–
Front axle	65	–	48
Front axle pinch bolt	33	–	24
Front brake disc mounting bolt	23	–	17
Rear axle	65	–	48
Rear brake torque link bolt	25	–	18

*Apply threadlock (ThreeBond 1303 or equivalent)

12

CHAPTER THIRTEEN

FRONT SUSPENSION AND STEERING

This chapter covers the front fork and steering components. Front wheel removal, front hub service, tire changing, tire repair and wheel balancing are covered in Chapter Twelve. Front suspension specifications are in **Table 1** and **Table 2** at the end of this chapter.

> *NOTE*
> *On touring models, remove the windshield as needed to perform the procedures in this chapter.*

BALANCER WEIGHTS

A balancer weight (anti-vibration) is located in each handlebar end. The weights must be removed for access to the handlebar grips.

Removal/Installation

Refer to **Figure 1**.

> *NOTE*
> *If the bolt is removed, the retaining nut will fall loose into the handlebar.*

1. Loosen the balancer weight mounting bolt (**Figure 2**) and pull out the weight assembly. If the weight assembly will not pull out, remove the bolt and individual components.
2. Remove the weight (**Figure 3**).

3. Look inside the handlebar for burrs or nicks that may be snagging the expander. Use a file or die grinder to remove the burrs or nicks. Remove the expander and nut.
4. To install the weight assembly, assemble the components on the mounting bolt (**Figure 4**), then insert the assembly into the handlebar. Tighten the bolt securely.

HANDLEBAR

Removal

> *CAUTION*
> *Cover the front fender and front wheel with a heavy cloth or plastic tarp to protect them from accidental brake fluid spills. Brake fluid can damage painted and plastic surfaces. Immediately wash the surface using soapy water and rinse completely.*

> *CAUTION*
> *It is not necessary to remove the fuel tank, but removal will prevent possible damage to it.*

1. Remove the fuel tank as described in Chapter Eight or Chapter Nine.
2. Remove the rear view mirrors.
3. Refer to Chapter Ten and remove the left and right handlebar switch assemblies.

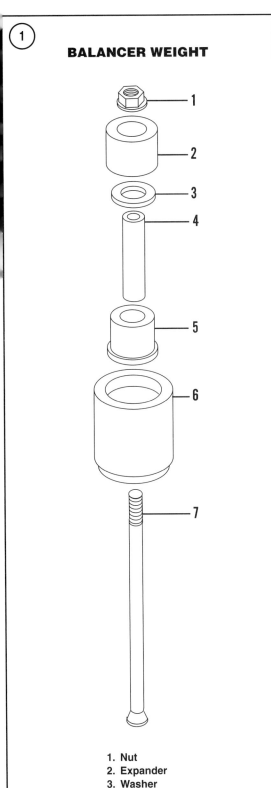

BALANCER WEIGHT

1. Nut
2. Expander
3. Washer
4. Spacer
5. Weight
6. End cap
7. Bolt

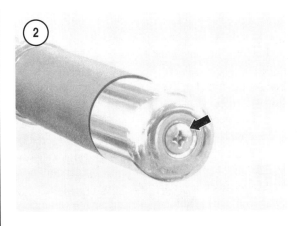

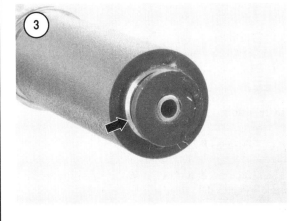

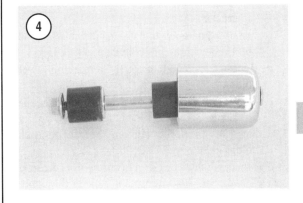

NOTE
It is not necessary to disconnect the brake line from the master cylinder when performing Step 4.

4. Refer to Chapter Fifteen and remove the front brake master cylinder from the handlebar. Lay it over the front fender. Keep the reservoir in the upright position to minimize the loss of brake fluid and to keep air from entering the brake system.

5. Disconnect the clutch cable from the clutch control lever (Chapter Six).

6. Remove the trim caps from the top of the handlebar upper holder Allen bolts.

13

7. Remove the handlebar upper holder bolts (A, **Figure 5**) and the handlebar upper holders (B).

8. Remove the handlebar.

9. If necessary, remove the balancer weight assemblies as described in this chapter and remove the following:

    a. Left hand grip.

    b. Clutch lever.

    c. Right throttle grip.

10. To remove the handlebar lower holders, refer to **Figure 6** and perform the following:

    a. Remove the holder mounting bolt nut under the upper steering bracket, then remove the bolt.

    b. Remove the handlebar lower holder.

    c. If necessary, remove the washer and rubber cushion.

    d. Repeat the procedure for the remaining lower holder.

Installation

1. If removed, refer to **Figure 6** and install the handlebar lower holder as follows:

    a. If removed, install the washer and rubber cushion into the upper steering bracket.

    b. Install the rubber washer, washer, handlebar lower holder and bolt on top of the upper steering bracket.

    c. Install the damper, rubber cushion, washer and nut. Fighter-tighten the nut at this time.

    d. Repeat the procedure for the remaining lower holder.

    e. Temporarily install the handlebar onto the holders and position the holders so the handlebar seats properly. Tighten the nut on each holder to 70 N•m (52 ft.-lb.).

2. The knurling must be clean to ensure a secure grip on the handlebar. Also, thoroughly clean the upper and lower handlebar holders. Make sure the knurled area of the handlebar and the handlebar holders are completely clean to prevent handlebar slip.

3. Install the handlebar onto the lower holders, then install the upper holders, washers and bolts. Install the upper holder so the punch mark is toward the front (C, **Figure 5**). Do not tighten the bolts at this time.

4. Position the handlebar so the punch mark on the handlebar aligns with the gap between the holders as shown in **Figure 7**.

5. Tighten the front holder bolts to 12 N•m (106 in.-lb.). Install the rear holder bolts fingertight. There must be a gap at the rear of the upper and lower holders (**Figure 8**). Tighten the front holder bolts to 23

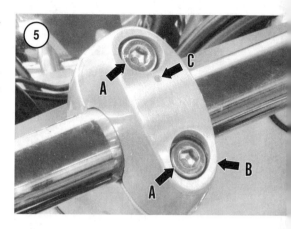

N•m (17 ft.-lb.), then tighten the rear holder bolts to 23 N•m (17 ft.-lb.).

6. Install the trim caps.

7. If removed, install the clutch lever assembly onto the left handlebar. Align the lever body gap with the punch mark on the handlebar (**Figure 9**). Tighten the clamping bolt to 10 N•m (88 in.-lb.).

8. If removed, install the left hand grip as described in this chapter.

9. If removed, lubricate and install the right hand throttle grip assembly. Rotate the throttle grip several times and make sure the grip moves freely from the full open to the full closed position with no binding.

10. Install the rear view mirrors, adjust and tighten securely.

11. Install the fuel tank as described in Chapter Eight or Chapter Nine.

12. After all assemblies are installed, test each one to make sure it operates correctly with no binding. Correct any problem at this time.

13. Adjust the clutch as described in Chapter Three.

Inspection

Check the handlebar bolt holes and the entire mounting bracket for cracks or damage. Replace a bent or damaged handlebar immediately. If the bike has been involved in a crash, thoroughly examine the handlebar, the steering stem and front fork for any signs of damage or misalignment. Correct any problem before operating the motorcycle.

HANDLEBAR LEFT HAND GRIP REPLACEMENT

NOTE
The right hand grip is part of the throttle grip assembly and cannot be replaced separately.

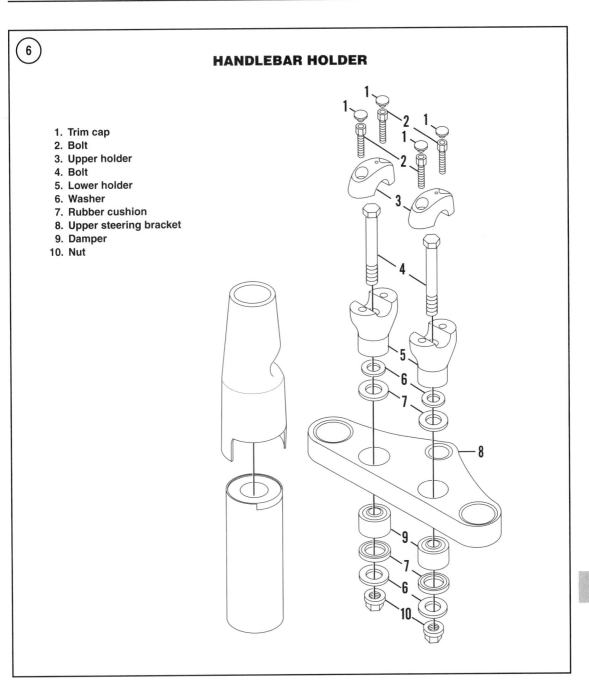

6

HANDLEBAR HOLDER

1. Trim cap
2. Bolt
3. Upper holder
4. Bolt
5. Lower holder
6. Washer
7. Rubber cushion
8. Upper steering bracket
9. Damper
10. Nut

13

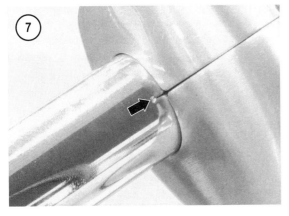

7

8

1. Remove the balancer assembly (**Figure 2**) from the end of the left handlebar as described in this chapter.

2. Slide a thin screwdriver between the left hand grip and handlebar. Spray electrical contact cleaner into the opening under the grip.

3. Pull the screwdriver out and quickly twist the grip to break its bond with the handlebar, then slide the grip off.

4. Clean the handlebar of all rubber or sealer residue.

5. Install the new grip following the manufacturer's directions. Apply an adhesive (ThreeBond Griplock, or equivalent) between the grip and handlebar. When applying an adhesive, follow the manufacturer's directions regarding drying time before operating the bike.

6. Install the balancer assembly onto the left end of the handlebar.

STEERING STEM AND HEAD

Disassembly

Refer to **Figure 10**:

1. Remove the fuel tank as described in Chapter Eight or Chapter Nine.

2. Remove the front brake master cylinder as described in Chapter Fifteen.

3. Remove the handlebar as described in this chapter.

4. Remove the horn as described in Chapter Ten.

5. Remove the front fork as described in this chapter.

6. Remove the upper fork covers (**Figure 11**).

7. Remove the headlight housing as described in Chapter Ten.

8. Remove the air guide mounting bolts (A, **Figure 12**) and air guide (B).

9. Remove the steering stem cover retaining screw (**Figure 13**). Then pull the cover (**Figure 14**) loose from the mounting grommets.

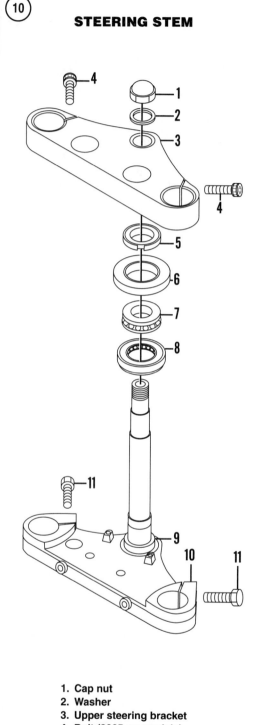

STEERING STEM

1. Cap nut
2. Washer
3. Upper steering bracket
4. Bolt (2005-on models)
5. Stem nut
6. Seal
7. Bearing assembly
8. Bearing assemblyy
9. Lower bearing race and seal
10. Steering stem
11. Bolt

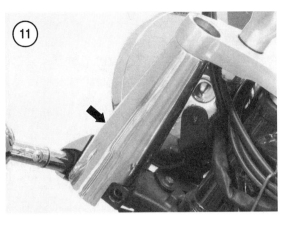

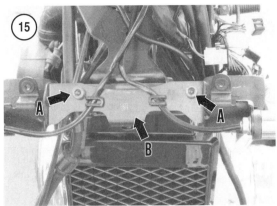

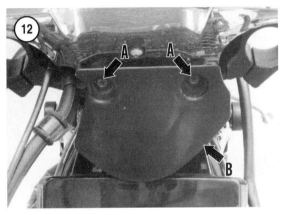

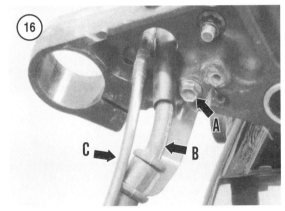

13

10. Remove the turn signal bracket mounting bolts (A, **Figure 15**), then remove the bracket (B).

11. Remove the brake hose guide retaining bolt (A, **Figure 16**), then withdraw the front brake hose (B) and speedometer sensor cable (C) from the steering stem bracket.

12. Remove the headlight mounting bracket bolts, then remove the bracket (**Figure 17**).

13. Remove the steering stem cap nut (A, **Figure 18**), washer (B) and remove the upper steering bracket assembly (C).

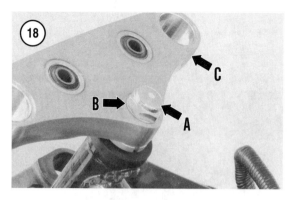

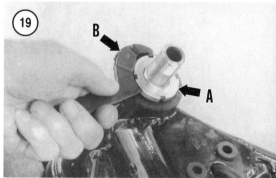

14A. Loosen the steering stem nut (A, **Figure 19**) using a spanner wrench (B, **Figure 19** [Suzuki part No. 09940-14991 or equivalent]) or a fabricated tool (**Figure 20**) made from a piece of tubing or pipe.

14B. The steering stem nut can also be loosened by carefully tapping it loose with a screwdriver or punch and hammer.

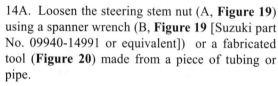

CAUTION
Support the weight of the steering stem assembly while removing the steering stem nut or the assembly will drop out of the steering head.

15. Hold onto the steering stem and remove the nut (A, **Figure 19**).

16. Lower the steering stem out of the frame. Both bearings are caged ball bearings with no loose parts.

17. Lift off the dust seal (**Figure 21**).

18. Remove the upper bearing race (**Figure 22**) and bearing (**Figure 23**) from the steering head.

CAUTION
Do not attempt to remove the lower bearing race from the steering stem unless bearing replacment is necessary. The bearing race is pressed on the steering stem and will be damaged during removal.

Inspection

1. Clean the upper and lower bearings in a bearing degreaser. Make certain the bearing degreaser is compatible with the rubber covers on each bearing. Hold onto the bearing so it does not spin and thoroughly dry both bearings with compressed air.

2. Wipe the old grease from the outer races located in the steering head, and then clean the outer races with a rag soaked in solvent. Thoroughly dry the races with a lint-free cloth.

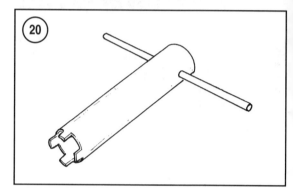

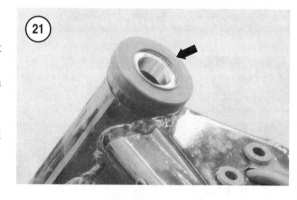

3. Check the steering stem outer races for pitting, galling and corrosion. If any race is worn or damaged, replace the race(s) and bearing as an assembly as described in this chapter.

8. Inspect the cap nut, washer and steering stem nut for wear or damage. Inspect the threads. If necessary, clean them with an appropriate size metric tap or replace the nut(s). If the threads are damaged, inspect the appropriate steering stem thread(s) for damage. If necessary, clean the threads with an appropriate size metric die.

9. Inspect the steering stem nut washer for damage. If damaged, check the underside of the steering stem nut for damage. Replace either part as necessary.

10. Inspect the steering stem and the lower bracket for cracks or other damage. Make sure the lower bracket clamping areas are free of burrs and the bolt holes are in good condition.

11. Inspect the upper steering bracket for cracks or other damage. Make sure the bracket clamping areas are free of burrs and the bolt holes are in good condition.

Installation

Refer to **Figure 10**.

1. Make sure the steering head outer races are properly seated and clean.

2. Apply an even coat of waterproof bearing grease (Suzuki Super Grease A or equivalent) to the steering head outer races, to both bearings, and to the dust seal and cap nut.

3. Install the upper bearing (**Figure 23**) and upper race (**Figure 22**) into the race in the top of the steering head.

4. Carefully slide the steering stem up into the frame (**Figure 24**). Take care not to dislodge the upper bearing.

5. Hold the steering stem in position and install the dust seal (A, **Figure 25**) on top of the upper bearing.

6. Install the steering stem nut (B, **Figure 25**). Using a suitable torque adapter (**Figure 26**), tighten the steering stem nut to 45 N•m (33 ft.-lb.).

7. Move the steering stem back and forth from lock to lock five or six times to make sure the bearings are completely seated.

4. Check the welds around the steering head for cracks and fractures. If any damage is found, have the frame repaired at a dealership, frame shop or welding service.

5. Check the balls for pitting, scratches or discoloration indicating wear or corrosion. Replace the bearing if any balls are damaged.

6. If the bearings are in good condition, pack them thoroughly with waterproof bearing grease (Suzuki Super Grease A or an equivalent). To pack the bearings, spread some grease in the palm of your hand and scrape the open side of the bearing across your palm until the bearing is packed completely full of grease. Spin the bearing a few times to determine if there are any open areas; repack if necessary.

7. Thoroughly clean all mounting parts in solvent. Dry them completely.

13

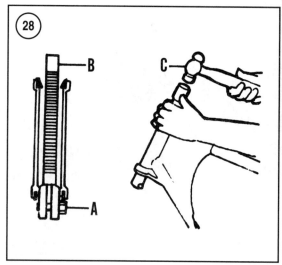

8. Back off the steering stem nut 1/4 to 1/2 turn. Make sure the steering stem moves freely.

9. Install the upper steering bracket assembly (C, **Figure 18**), washer (B) and cap nut (A). Tighten the cap nut fingertight at this time. Do not tighten the cap nut until the front forks are in place. This ensures proper alignment between the steering stem and the upper steering bracket.

10. Install the headlight mounting bracket (**Figure 17**). Tighten the bolts securely.

11. Insert the front brake hose (B, **Figure 16**) and speedometer sensor cable (C) through the steering stem bracket. Install the brake hose guide retaining bolt (A, **Figure 16**).

12. Install the turn signal bracket (B, **Figure 15**) and bolts (A).

13. Push the cover (**Figure 14**) into the mounting grommets, and install the steering stem cover retaining screw (**Figure 13**).

14. Install the air guide (B, **Figure 12**) and secure it with the mounting bolts (A).

15. Install the headlight housing as described in Chapter Ten.

16. Install the upper fork covers (**Figure 11**). Note that the right cover is indented.

17. Install the front fork as described in this chapter.

18. Check the movement of the front fork and steering stem assembly. The steering stem must turn freely from side to side, but without any free play when the fork legs are moved fore and aft.

19. Tighten the steering stem cap nut (A, **Figure 18**) to 90 N•m (66 ft.-lb.). Recheck the movement of the front end and readjust if necessary.

20. Install the horn as described in Chapter Ten.

21. Install the handlebar as described in this chapter.

22. Install the front brake master cylinder as described in Chapter Fifteen.

23. Install the fuel tank as described in Chapter Eight or Chapter Nine.

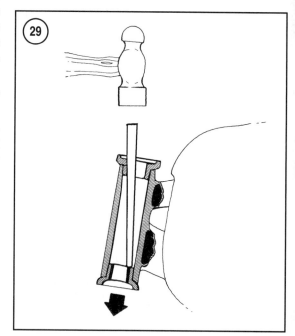

Adjustment

1. Raise the motorcycle with a jack and place wooden blocks under the frame to support the bike securely with the front wheel off the ground.

2. Grasp each fork leg at the lower end and attempt to move the fork legs back and forth. If any front end movement is detected, the steering stem nut must be adjusted.

3. Loosen the steering stem cap nut (A, **Figure 27**).

4. Turn the adjust nut (B, **Figure 27**) by gently tapping with a hammer and a punch or screwdriver. Take care not to damage the nut.

5. Tighten the steering stem cap nut to 90 N•m (66 ft.-lb.).

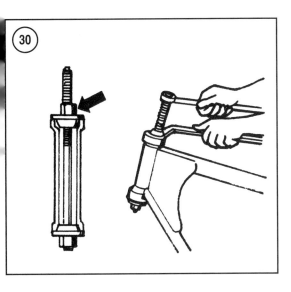

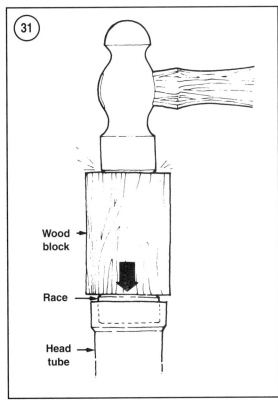

STEERING HEAD BEARING RACES

The headset and steering stem bearing races are pressed into the headset portion of the frame. Because the races are easily bent, do not remove them unless they require replacement.

Headset Bearing Race Removal/Installation

1. Remove the steering stem as described in this chapter.

2A. Use a bearing outer race remover (Suzuki part No. 09941-54911 or equivalent) to remove the headset bearing race as follows:

    a. Install the outer race remover (A, **Figure 28**) into one of the outer races.

    b. Insert the bearing remover (B, **Figure 28**) into the backside of the outer race remover.

    c. Tap on the end of the bearing remover with a hammer (C, **Figure 28**) and drive the bearing outer race out of the steering head. Remove the special tool from the outer race.

    d. Repeat for the bearing outer race at the other end of the headset.

2B. If the special tools are not used, perform the following:

    a. Insert a hardwood stick or soft punch into the head tube and carefully tap the outer race out from the inside (**Figure 29**).

    b. After it is started, work around the outer race in a crisscross pattern so that neither the race nor the head tube is damaged.

3A. Use a bearing installer (Suzuki part No. 09941-34513 or equivalent) to install the headset bearing race as follows:

    a. Position the outer races into the headset and just start them into position with a soft-faced mallet. Tap them in enough to hold them in place.

    b. Position the bearing installer (**Figure 30**) into both of the outer races.

    c. Tighten the nuts on the bearing installer and pull the outer races into place in the headset. Tighten the nuts until both bearing outer races are completely seated in the head set and are flush with the steering head surface.

    d. Remove the special tool.

3B. If the special tools are not used, perform the following:

    a. Position one of the outer races into the headset and just start it into position with a soft-faced mallet. Tap it in enough to hold it in place.

    b. Tap the outer race in slowly with a block of wood or a suitable size socket or pipe (**Figure 31**). Make sure that the race is squarely seated in the headset race bore before tapping it into place. Tap the race in until it is flush with the steering head surface.

    c. Repeat for the other outer race.

13

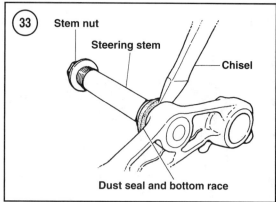

Steering Stem Lower Bearing Race Removal/Installation

Do not remove the steering stem lower bearing race and seal (**Figure 32**) unless it is going to be replaced. The lower bearing race can be difficult to remove. If it cannot be removed as described in this procedure, take the steering stem to a dealership and have them replace the bearing race.

Never reinstall a lower bearing race that has been removed as it is no longer true and will damage the rest of the bearing assembly if reused.

1. Install the steering stem bolt onto the top of the steering stem to protect the threads.

2. Use a chisel to loosen the lower bearing race from the shoulder at the base or the steering stem (**Figure 33**). Slide the lower bearing race and grease seal off the steering stem. Discard the lower bearing race and the grease seal.

3. Clean the steering stem with solvent and dry thoroughly.

4. Position the new grease seal so the outer lips face up.

5. Slide the new grease seal and the lower bearing race onto the steering stem until they stop on the raised shoulder.

6. Using a piece of pipe with the same ID as the bearing race, or a steering stem bearing race installer (Suzuki part No. 09941-74911), carefully tap on the bearing installer and drive the lower bearing race into place.

7. Remove the bearing race installer and verify that the race is seated squarely and is all the way down.

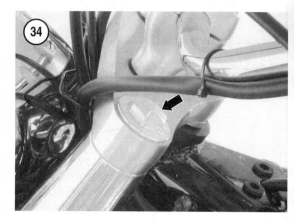

FRONT FORK

Service

To avoid mixing parts, service the fork legs individually.

Before presuming that an internal fork problem exists, drain the fork oil and refill with the proper type

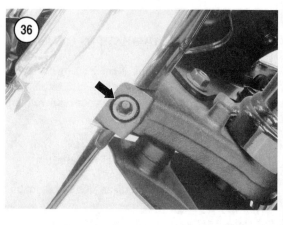

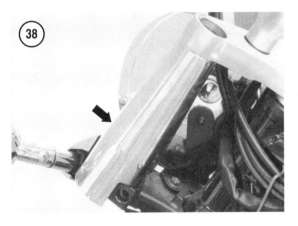

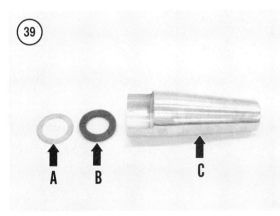

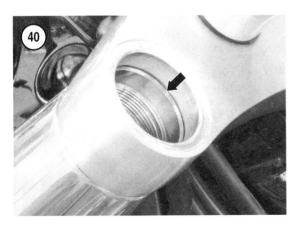

and quantity (**Table 1**). If the problem persists, such as poor damping, a tendency to bottom out or top out, follow the service procedures in this section.

Removal/Installation

1. Remove the brake caliper and brake hose from each fork leg as described in Chapter Fifteen.
2. Remove the front wheel as described in Chapter Twelve.
3. Remove the front fender as described in Chapter Sixteen.

WARNING
On 2005-on models, be careful when removing the fork cap bolt as the spring is under pressure. Protect your eyes accordingly.

4. Remove the cap bolt (**Figure 34**).

NOTE
On 2001-2004 models, the fork spring is retained by an internal spring stopper bolt. On 2005-on models, the fork spring is retained by the fork cap bolt.

NOTE
For tool accessibility when performing Step 5, it may be necessary to remove the handlebar assembly as described in this chapter.

5. On 2001-2004 models, if the fork leg is going to be disassembled, loosen the spring stopper bolt (**Figure 35**).
6. Loosen the lower fork tube clamp bolt (**Figure 36**).
7. On 2005-on models, loosen the upper fork tube clamp bolt (**Figure 37**).
8. Pull each fork leg down and out of the upper and lower steering brackets. It may be necessary to rotate the fork tube slightly while pulling it down and out.
9. If necessary, remove the upper fork covers as follows:
   a. Carefully push the fork cover (**Figure 38**) out from between the steering brackets.
   b. Remove the cushion (A, **Figure 39**) and washer (B) from the cover (C).
   c. Reverse the removal steps to install the covers. Note that the right cover is indented so it will not contact the ignition key.
10. Install by reversing the preceding removal steps. Note the following:
   a. Insert the fork until the fork tube contacts the step in the upper steering bracket (**Figure 40**).

13

FRONT FORK

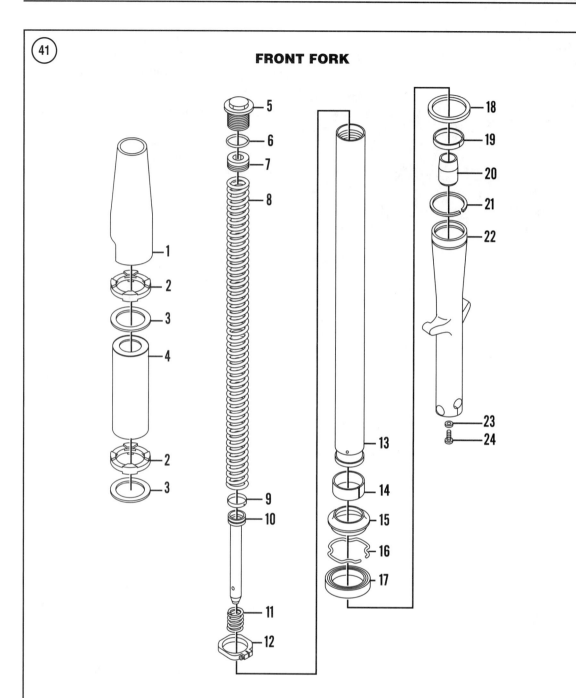

1. Upper cover
2. Cushion
3. Washer
4. Lower cover
5. Cap bolt
6. O-ring
7. Spring stopper nut
   (2001-2004)
8. Spring
9. Piston ring
10. Damper rod
11. Rebound spring
12. Cover locating ring
13. Inner tube
14. Inner tube bushing
15. Dust seal
16. Stopper ring
17. Oil seal
18. Retainer
19. Outer tube bushing
20. Oil lock piece
21. Cover guide ring
22. Slider
23. Washer
24. Allen bolt

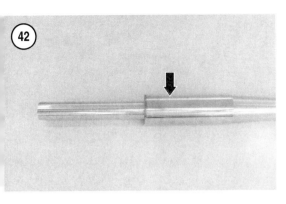

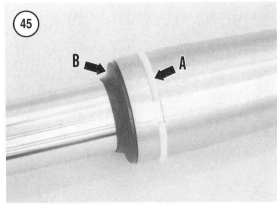

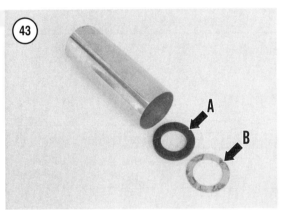

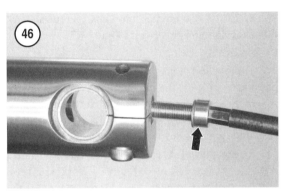

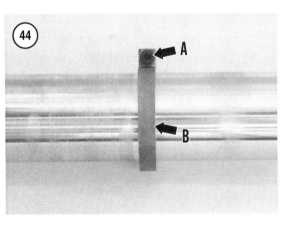

2. Remove the fork tube cover (**Figure 42**). Account for the cushion (A, **Figure 43**) and washer (B).

3. Loosen the clamp bolt (A, **Figure 44**) and remove the cover locating ring (B).

4. Remove the cover guide (A, **Figure 45**).

NOTE
When loosening the Allen bolt in the bottom of the fork tube, leave the spring stopper bolt and fork spring installed until the Allen bolt is loosened and removed. The internal spring pressure against the damper rod assembly will help hold it in place as the Allen bolt is being loosened and removed.

b. Tighten the lower fork clamp bolt (**Figure 36**) to 33 N•m (24 ft.-lb.).

c. On 2001-2004 models, if the fork legs were disassembled, tighten the spring stopper bolt (**Figure 35**) to 35 N•m (26 ft.-lb.).

d. Tighten the cap bolt (**Figure 34**) to 45 N•m (33 ft.-lb.).

e. On 2005-on models, tighten the upper fork clamp bolt (**Figure 37**) to 23 N•m (17 ft.-lb.).

5. Install the fork in a vise with soft jaws.

6. Have an assistant compress the fork tube assembly as much as possible and hold it compressed against the damper rod.

7. Loosen the Allen bolt at the base of the slider (**Figure 46**, typical) with an Allen wrench and an impact tool. Do not remove the Allen bolt at this time.

Disassembly

Refer to **Figure 41**.

1. Remove the front fork as described in this chapter.

WARNING
Be careful when removing the spring stopper bolt as the spring is under pressure. Protect your eyes accordingly.

8. On 2001-2004 models, slowly unscrew and re-move the spring stopper bolt (**Figure 47**).

9. Remove the spring.

10. Turn the fork assembly upside down over a drain pan and completely drain the fork oil. Stroke the fork several times to pump out any oil that remains. Stand the fork tube upside-down in the drain pan and allow the oil to drain for several minutes.

11. Remove the dust seal from the slider (B, **Figure 45**).

12. Remove the stopper ring (**Figure 48**) from the slider.

13. Remove the Allen bolt and washer from the base of the slider. If the Allen bolt was not loosened in Step 4, proceed as follows:

    a. Install the attachment A tool (Suzuki part No. 09940-34520) onto the T handle (Suzuki part No. 09940-34520).

    b. Insert this tool setup (A, **Figure 49**) into the fork tube and index it into the receptacle in the top of the damper rod to hold the damper rod in place.

    c. Using an Allen wrench, loosen then remove the Allen bolt and washer (B, **Figure 49**, typical) from the base of the slider.

NOTE
The oil lock piece is often stuck to the
bottom of the slider and may not come
out with the damper rod. Do not lose
the oil lock piece.

14. Turn the fork assembly upside down and slide out the damper rod assembly complete with the re-bound spring and oil lock piece.

15. Install the fork tube in a vise with soft jaws.

16. There is an interference fit between the bushing in the fork slider and bushing in the fork tube. To re-move the fork tube from the slider, pull hard on the fork tube using quick in-and-out strokes (**Figure 50**).

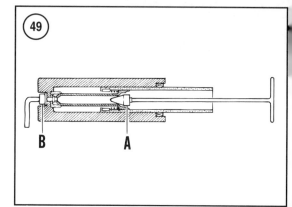

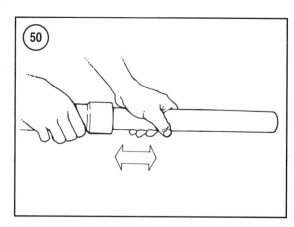

Doing so will withdraw the slider bushing, oil seal re-tainer and oil seal from the slider.

17. Withdraw the fork tube from the slider.

NOTE
Do not remove the fork tube bushing
unless it is going to be replaced. Inspect
it as described in this section.

18. Remove the oil lock piece from the slider if it did not come out in Step 11.

19. Slide off the bushing (A, **Figure 51**), oil seal re-tainer (B) and oil seal (C) from the fork tube.

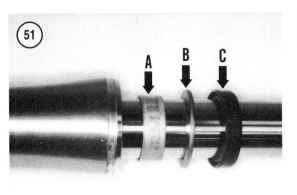

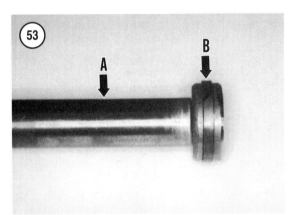

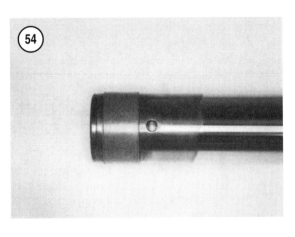

20. Inspect all parts as described in this section.

Inspection

1. Thoroughly clean all parts in solvent and dry them. Check the fork tube for signs of wear or scratches.

2. Check the damper rod for straightness (**Figure 52**). Replace a bent damper rod.

3. Make sure the oil holes in the damper rod are clear. Clean out if necessary.

4. Inspect the damper rod (A, **Figure 53**) and piston ring (B) for wear or damage. Replace if necessary.

5. Check the fork tube for straightness. If bent or severely scratched, replace it.

6. Inspect the slider for dents or exterior damage that may cause the upper fork tube to stick. Replace if necessary.

7. Inspect the brake caliper mounting bosses on the slider for cracks or other damage. If damaged, replace the slider.

8. Inspect the slider (**Figure 54**) and fork tube bushings (**Figure 55**). If either is scratched or scored, replace them. If the Teflon coating is worn off so that the copper base material is showing on approximately 3/4 of the total surface, replace the bushing. Also check for distortion on the washer and replace if necessary.

9. Inspect the fork cap bolt and spring stopper threads in the fork tube for wear or damage.

10. Inspect the fork cap bolt threads for wear or damage.

11. Inspect the spring stopper threads for wear or damage.

12. Inspect the oil seal seating area in the slider for damage or burrs. Clean up if necessary.

13. Inspect the gasket on the Allen bolt; replace if damaged.

14. Clean the threads of the Allen bolt thoroughly with cleaning solvent or spray contact cleaner.

13

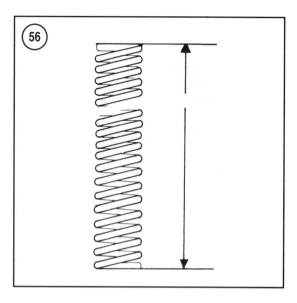

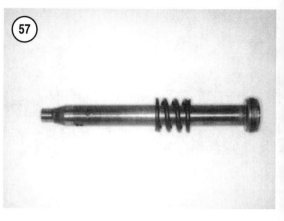

15. Measure the free length of the fork spring (not the rebound spring) as shown in **Figure 56**. If the spring free length is less than the service limit in **Table 1**, replace the spring.

16. Replace any parts that are worn or damaged.

Assembly

1. Coat all parts with fork oil (**Table 1**) prior to installation.

2. Install the rebound spring onto the damper rod (**Figure 57**) and insert this assembly into the fork tube (**Figure 58**).

3. Temporarily install the fork spring to hold the damper rod in place. Note that one end of the fork spring has coils that are close together. Install the fork spring (**Figure 59**) so the closely wound spring coils enter first.

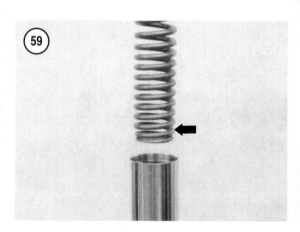

4A. On 2001-2004 models, temporarily install the spring stopper bolt and tighten securely.

4B. On 2005-on models, temporarily install the fork cap bolt and tighten securely.

5. Install the oil lock piece onto the damper rod (**Figure 60**).

6. Install the upper fork assembly into the slider.

7. Make sure the gasket washer is on the Allen bolt.

8. Apply a small amount of locking compound (Three-Bond TB1303, Loctite No. 242, or equivalent) on the damper rod Allen bolt threads prior to installation. Install the Allen bolt and tighten to 20 N•m (15 ft.-lb.).

9. Slide the bushing (A, **Figure 61**) and retainer (B) down the fork tube and rest it on top of the fork slider.

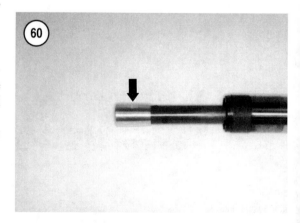

> *CAUTION*
> *Place a plastic bag over the end of the*
> *slider and coat it with fork oil. This will*

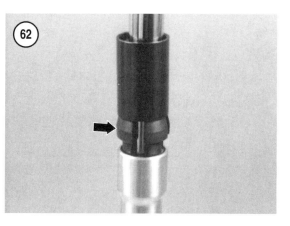

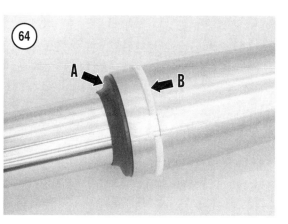

prevent damage to the dust seal and the oil seal lips when installing them over the top of the slider.

10. Install the new oil seal as follows:
   a. Coat the new seal with fork oil.
   b. Position the seal with the open groove facing up and slide the oil seal (C, **Figure 61**) down onto the fork tube.

NOTE
*A fork seal driver (**Figure 62**) is required to install the fork slider bushing and fork seal into the slider. A number of different aftermarket fork seal drivers are available that can be used for this purpose. Another method is to use a piece of pipe or metal collar with the correct dimensions to slide over the fork tube and seat against the seal. When selecting or fabricating a driver tool, it must have sufficient weight to drive the bushing and oil seal into the slider.*

   c. Slide the fork seal driver down the fork tube and seat it against the seal.
   d. Operate the driver tool to drive the fork slider bushing and fork seal into the slider. Continue until the stopper ring groove in the slider is visible above the fork seal.

11. Slide the stopper ring down the fork tube.

12. Install the stopper ring and make sure it is completely seated in the groove in the fork slider (**Figure 63**).

13. Install the dust seal (A, **Figure 64**) into the slider. Press it in until it is completely seated.

14. Unscrew the spring stopper bolt (2001-2004) or fork cap bolt (2005-on) and remove the fork spring from the fork tube.

15. Compress the fork completely.

16. Add the recommended amount of oil (**Table 1**) to the fork assembly.

17. Hold the fork assembly as vertical as possible.

18. Use an accurate ruler or an oil level gauge (Suzuki part No. 09943-74111 or equivalent), to achieve the correct oil level. Refer to **Figure 65**.

NOTE
*An oil level measuring device can be made as shown in **Figure 66**. Position the lower edge of the hose clamp at the specified oil level distance above the small diameter hole. Overfill the fork with slightly more than the required amount of oil. Position the hose clamp on the top edge of the fork tube and*

13

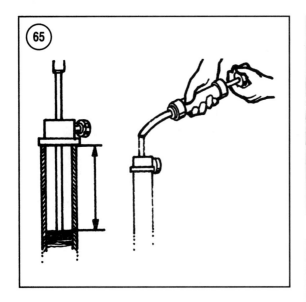

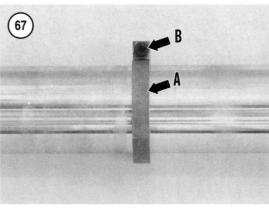

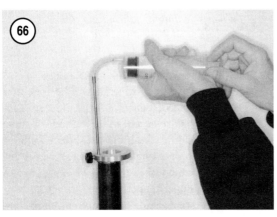

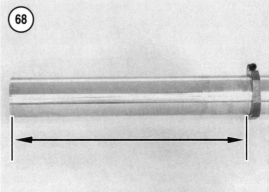

draw out the excess oil until the level reaches the small diameter hole. A precise oil level can be achieved with this device.

19. Allow the oil to settle completely and recheck the oil level measurement. Adjust the oil level if necessary.

20. Install the fork spring with the closer wound coils going in last.

21. Hold the fork assembly upright so the fork oil will not drain out.

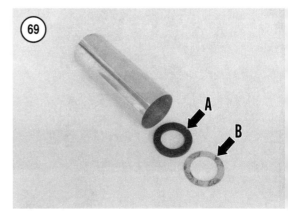

22. On 2001-2004 models, install the spring stopper bolt and tighten securely. Do not tighten to the final torque at this time.

23. Install the cover guide (B, **Figure 64**) into the groove in the slider.

24. Install the cover locating ring (A, **Figure 67**) onto the fork tube. Position the ring so it is 246.6 mm (9.70 in.) from the end of the tube (**Figure 68**). Tighten the clamp bolt (B, **Figure 67**).

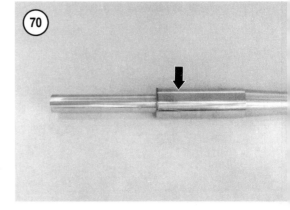

25. Install the cushion (A, **Figure 69**) and washer (B) into the fork cover, then install the cover (**Figure 70**).

26. Install the fork assemblies as described in this chapter, but do not install the fork cap bolt.

27. On 2001-2004 models, tighten the spring stopper bolt (**Figure 71**) to 35 N•m (26 ft.-lb.).

28. Inspect the O-ring seal on the fork cap bolt (**Figure 72**); replace if necessary.

29. Install the top fork cap bolt and tighten to 45 N•m (33 ft.-lb.).

30. Repeat this procedure for the other fork assembly.

Table 1 FRONT SUSPENSION SPECIFICATIONS

Item	Specification	Service limit
Front fork oil		
Viscosity	Suzuki SS-08 (#10) fork oil or equivalent	
Capacity per leg	412 mL (13.9 oz.)	
Front fork oil level	177 mm (6.97 in.)	
Front fork spring free length	–	540 mm (21.26 in.)
Front fork stroke	140 mm (5.5 in.)	–

Table 2 FRONT SUSPENSION TORQUE SPECIFICATIONS

Item	N•m	in.-lb.	ft.-lb.
Axle	65	–	48
Axle pinch bolt	33	–	24
Brake disc mounting bolt	23	–	17
Clutch lever clamp bolt	10	88	–
Fork Allen bolt[1]	20	–	15
Fork cap bolt	45	–	33
Fork lower clamp bolts	33	–	24
Fork upper clamp bolts (2005-on)	23	–	17
Fork damper rod Allen bolt	20	177	–
Fork spring stopper bolt	35	–	26
Handlebar			
Lower holder nut	70	–	52
Holder bolts			
Front			
Initial	12	106	–
Final	23	–	17
Rear	23	–	17
Steering stem cap nut	90	–	66
Steering stem nut[2]	45	–	33

1. Apply threadlock (ThreeBond 1303, Loctite No. 242, or equivalent).
2. Refer to text for complete tightening procedure.

13

CHAPTER FOURTEEN

REAR SUSPENSION AND FINAL DRIVE

This chapter covers the rear suspension and final drive. Refer to Chapter Twelve for rear wheel, rear axle and tire service information.

Rear suspension and final drive specifications are in **Tables 1-5** at the end of this chapter.

NOTE
On touring models, remove the saddlebags if necessary to perform the procedures in this chapter.

SHOCK ABSORBER

A single rear shock absorber with adjustable preload is used on all models.

Spring Preload Adjustment

Set the spring preload by turning the notched adjustment ring on the shock absorber. Rotate the adjustment ring using a suitable tool, such as the spanner tool provided in the motorcycle tool kit. The preload positions are numbered 1 (softest) through 7 (heaviest). The standard setting is position 4.

For access to the shock absorber adjustment ring, perform the following:

1. Remove the toolbox as described in Chapter Sixteen.
2. Turn the spring adjusting ring (**Figure 1**) clockwise (viewed from top) to decrease spring preload.
3. Turn the spring adjusting ring counterclockwise (viewed from top) to increase preload.

Removal

1. Remove the exhaust system as described in Chapter Eight or Chapter Nine.
2. Remove the toolbox as described in Chapter Sixteen.
3. Remove the battery as described in Chapter Three.
4. Remove the battery box retaining bolts (**Figure 2**). Removing the bolts will allow the box to move upward during shock absorber removal or installation.
5. Remove the rear side cover (A, **Figure 3**) by pulling the cover prongs out of the retaining grommets.
6. Remove the left lower side cover (B, **Figure 3**).
7. Remove the right lower side cover bolts (**Figure 4**).
8. Place a suitable jack under the motorcycle frame. Make sure the motorcycle is securely supported.
9. Raise the motorcycle so the rear wheel just touches the ground, indicating that weight is removed from the shock absorber.
10. Remove the lower shock absorber retaining bolt (A, **Figure 5**).

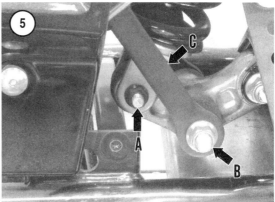

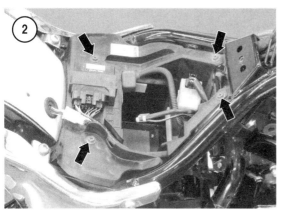

14

11. Remove the mounting hardware (B, **Figure 5**) securing the lower end of the pivot link (C).

NOTE
Do not remove the bolt in Step 12. Only withdraw it as described.

12. Withdraw the pivot link bolt (**Figure 6**) enough to release the lower end of the link (C, **Figure 5**).

13. Remove the upper shock mounting bolt (**Figure 7**).

14. Move the lower end of the pivot link (C, **Figure 5**) as needed for sufficient room to disengage the

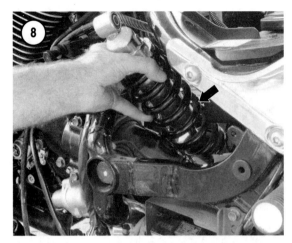

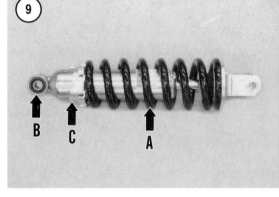

shock absorber from its mount points. Remove the shock absorber from the left side of the frame (**Figure 8**).

15. Inspect the shock absorber as described in this section.

16. Reverse the removal steps to install the shock absorber. Note the following:

    a. Tighten the shock absorber mounting bolts to 50 N•m (37 ft.-lb.).

    b. Tighten the pivot link mounting bolt to 78 N•m (58 ft.-lb.).

Inspection

No replacement parts are available for the shock absorber except for the upper bushing. Replace the shock absorber if damaged.

1. Inspect the shock absorber for oil leaks.

2. Check the spring (A, **Figure 9**) for cracks or other damage.

3. Make sure the spring preload adjust nut (B, **Figure 9**) fits properly.

4. Inspect the upper mount (B, **Figure 9**). If necessary, replace the upper bushing.

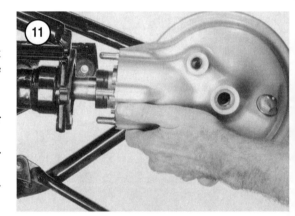

FINAL DRIVE AND DRIVESHAFT

Removal/Installation

1. Drain the oil from the final drive gearcase as described in Chapter Three.

2. Remove the rear wheel as described in Chapter Twelve.

3. Remove the final drive mounting nuts (**Figure 10**) and washers, then remove the final drive and driveshaft (**Figure 11**).

4. Locate the stopper plate (**Figure 12**) which may adhere to the final drive or to the swing arm.

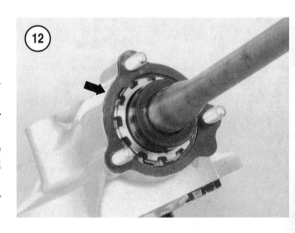

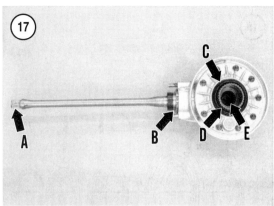

5. Reverse the removal steps to install the final drive while noting the following:

   a. Apply a lithium base grease to the driveshaft splines.

   b. Apply a thin coat of sealant (Suzuki Bond 1207B or equivalent), to both sides of the stopper plate. Install the stopper plate (**Figure 12**) onto the final drive so the tab (**Figure 13**) engages a slot on the pinion nut.

   c. Be sure the driveshaft end properly engages the splines in the universal joint in the swing arm. If the universal joint has separated from the secondary gear shaft on the engine, remove the lower right side cover (**Figure 14**). Pull back the boot (**Figure 15**) and engage the universal joint with the secondary gear shaft.

   d. Install the washers behind the retaining nuts so the concave side is toward the final drive.

   e. Tighten the final drive mounting nuts (**Figure 10**) to 40 N•m (30 ft.-lb.).

   f. Fill the gearcase with oil as described in Chapter Three.

   g. If removed, install the spacer into the final drive unit so the small end enters first (**Figure 16**).

14

NOTE
After installing the rear wheel, but before lowering the motorcycle, rotate the rear wheel with the transmission in neutral and in gear to be sure the drive train operates properly. The wheel should rotate with the transmission in neutral, but not when the transmission is in gear.

Inspection

1. Inspect the driveshaft splines (A, **Figure 17**) for excessive wear or damage.

(18)

FINAL DRIVE

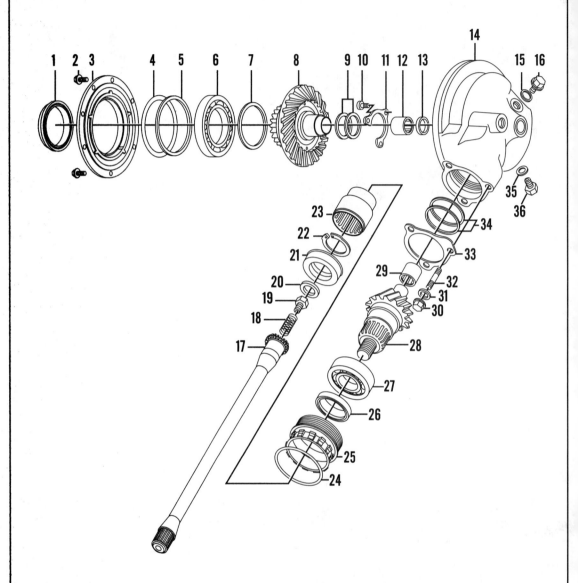

1. Oil seal
2. Bolt
3. Bearing case
4. O-ring
5. Flanged plate
6. Bearing
7. Shim
8. Ring gear
9. Shim
10. Screw
11. Bearing retainer
12. Bearing
13. Oil seal
14. Gearcase
15. O-ring
16. Oil fill bolt
17. Driveshaft
18. Spring
19. Sleeve nut
20. Washer
21. Oil seal
22. Snap ring
23. Coupling
24. O-ring
25. Bearing stopper
26. Oil seal
27. Bearing
28. Pinion gear
29. Needle bearing
30. Nut
31. Washer
32. Stud
33. Stopper plate
34. Shim
35. Washer
36. Oil drain bolt

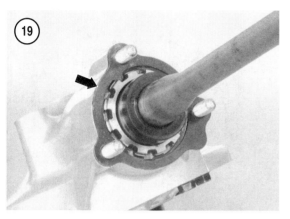

2. Check for oil leaks at the drive coupling oil seal (B, **Figure 17**) and the seal surrounding the output splines (C).

3. Inspect the output splines (D, **Figure 17**) for excessive wear or damage.

4. Check for oil in the axle shaft bore (E) and on the axle, which would indicate a faulty internal oil seal.

5. Inspect the final drive gearcase for cracks and other damage.

Tools

The final drive unit requires a number of tools for disassembly, inspection and reassembly. The price of these tools could be more than the cost of repairs performed at a dealership. The following tools are available for servicing the final drive:

1. Backlash measuring tool (Suzuki part No. 09924-34510).

2. Bearing stopper wrench (part No. 09924-62410).

3. Final drive coupling holder (part No. 09924-64510).

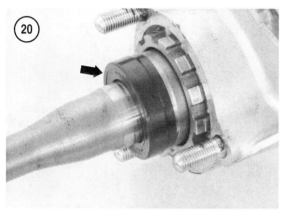

Disassembly

Refer to **Figure 18**.

1. Remove the stopper plate (**Figure 19**).

2. Remove the oil seal (**Figure 20**).

NOTE
The driveshaft is spring-loaded against the snap ring in Step 3.

3. Remove the snap ring (**Figure 21**), then remove the driveshaft and spring (**Figure 22**).

4. Remove the bearing case retaining bolts (**Figure 23**).

5. Install two 5 mm jackscrews in the threaded holes in the bearing case (A, **Figure 24**). Turn the jackscrews to separate the bearing case (B, **Figure 24**) from the gearcase. Remove the bearing case.

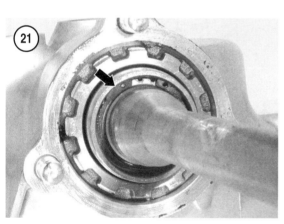

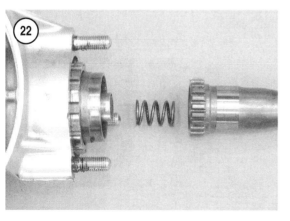

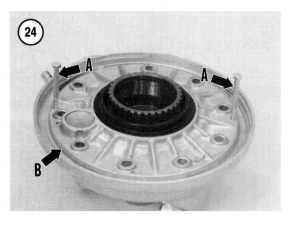

6. Note the right-side shims on the ring gear (A, **Figure 25**). Remove the shim, label it and set it aside.

7. Remove the ring gear (B, **Figure 25**).

8. Note the left-side shims on the ring gear (**Figure 26**). Remove the shim, label it and set it aside.

NOTE
The left-side shim may remain on the gearcase during disassembly.

9. Using a chisel, carefully push out the locking portion of the pinion shaft nut (**Figure 27**).

10. Use the holder to hold the coupling, then unscrew the pinion shaft nut (**Figure 28**).

11. Remove the nut (A, **Figure 29**), washer (B) and coupling (C).

12. Remove the bearing stopper (D, **Figure 29**) using the stopper wrench.

13. Remove the pinion shaft assembly. Locate the shim(s) on the pinion bearing or in the gearcase. Remove the shim(s), label it and set it aside.

Inspection

1. Clean, then inspect all components for excessive wear and damage. Remove gasket material from the mating surfaces on the bearing case and gearcase.

2. Turn the bearing (**Figure 30**) in the bearing case by hand. The bearing should turn freely and without roughness, catching or excessive noise. Replace damaged bearings as described in Chapter One. The bearing must bottom in the bearing case against the flanged plate.

NOTE
*Install the flanged plate (5, **Figure 18**) so the flanged side is away from the bearing.*

3. Remove the oil seal in the bearing case using a suitable seal removal tool. Install a new oil seal (**Figure 31**) so the closed side is out and the spring side is toward the bearing.

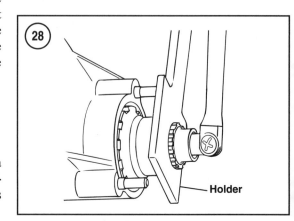

Holder

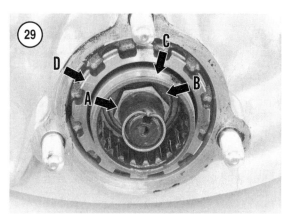

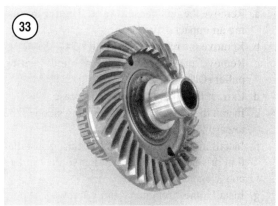

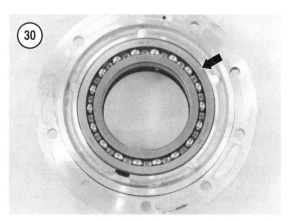

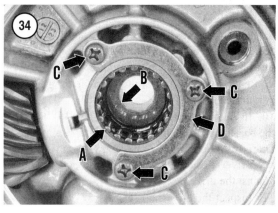

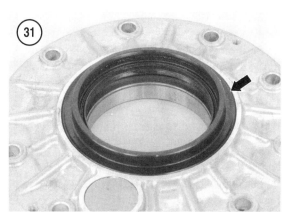

4. Remove the O-ring on the bearing case and install a new O-ring (**Figure 32**).

5. Inspect the pinion gear and bearing. Turn the bearing by hand. The bearing should turn freely and without any sign of roughness, catching or excessive noise. Replace damaged bearings as described in Chapter One. The bearing must bottom against the pinion gear shoulder.

6. Inspect the ring gear and hub (**Figure 33**). Inspect the gear teeth, splines and seal running surfaces on the hub. Replace if excessively worn or damaged.

NOTE
The roller bearing in the side of the gearcase must be removed for access to the oil seal.

7. Inspect the roller bearing (A, **Figure 34**) and oil seal (B) in the gearcase. If either is damaged, use the following replacement procedure:

CAUTION
The retainer screws identified in Step 7a are held by threadlocker. Use an impact driver to remove the screws, or the screws may be damaged.

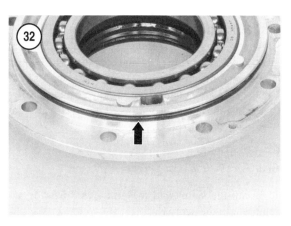

a. Remove the retainer screws (C, **Figure 34**) using an impact driver.

b. Remove the retainer (D, **Figure 34**).

c. Remove the bearing using a blind bearing puller (Chapter One).

d. Extract the oil seal from the gearcase.

e. Install the new oil seal so the spring side will be toward the bearing.

f. Install a new bearing using a bearing installation driver. Position the bearing so the marked end is against the driver.

g. Install the retainer and screws. Apply threadlocker (ThreeBond 1344 or equivalent) to the screws. Tighten the screws to 9 N•m (80 in.-lb.).

8. Replace the oil seal in the bearing stopper (**Figure 35**). Install the oil seal so the spring side is toward the threaded end of the bearing stopper.

9. Replace the O-ring around the bearing stopper (**Figure 35**).

10. Inspect the pinion bearing (**Figure 36**). Remove the bearing using a blind bearing puller tool (Chapter One). Install a new bearing using a bearing installation driver. Position the bearing so the marked end is against the driver.

11. Inspect the driveshaft (**Figure 37**) for excessive wear or damage to the splines and seal contact surface.

12. Inspect the coupling for excessive wear or damage to the splines and seal contact surface.

Preliminary Assembly

This assembly procedure describes measurement of the ring gear side clearance, gear backlash and gear position, which is required if the following components were replaced: pinion bearing (27, **Figure 18**), pinion gear (28), bearing (6), ring gear (8), gearcase (14) or bearing case (3). If only minor service was performed, such as oil seal replacement, proceed to *Final Assembly* in this section and install any original shims.

NOTE
Unless noted otherwise, install the original shims. Even though shim adjustments may be required, the original shims provide a starting point.

Ring gear side clearance

1. Install the left-side shim(s) onto the ring gear (**Figure 26**) and install the ring gear into the gearcase (B, **Figure 25**).

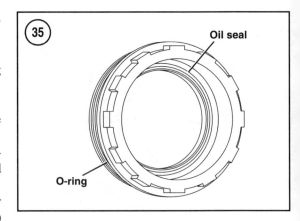

35

Oil seal

O-ring

36

2. Install the right-side shim(s) (A, **Figure 25**) onto the ring gear.

3. Position four pieces of Plastigage or soft solder on top of the shims (**Figure 38**). Use a small dab of adhesive to hold the Plastigage or soft solder in place.

NOTE
Do not rotate the gears when performing Steps 4 and 5. Do not apply sealant to the bearing case or gearcase.

4. Install the bearing case (B, **Figure 24**) and retaining bolts (**Figure 23**). Tighten the bolts to 23 N•m (17 ft.-lb.).

5. Remove the bolts and bearing case.

6. Measure the thickness of the Plastigage or soft solder, to determine the side clearance of the ring gear. The desired ring gear side clearance is 1.00 mm (0.039 in.). Install or remove right-side shim(s) (A, **Figure 25**) to obtain the desired side clearance. Refer to **Table 3** for available shims. Remove all pieces of Plastigage or soft solder.

Gear backlash measurement

1. Install the shims and the pinion and bearing assembly into the gearcase.

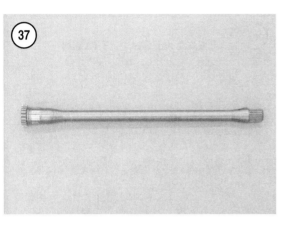

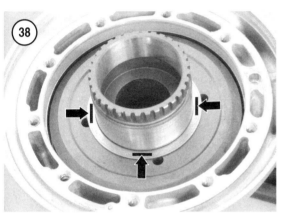

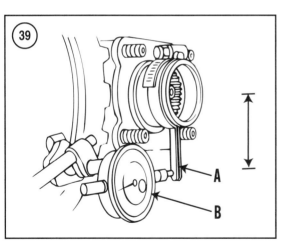

2. Install the bearing stopper (D, **Figure 29**) using the stopper wrench. Tighten the bearing stopper to 110 N•m (81 ft.-lb.).

3. Install the coupling (C, **Figure 29**), washer (B) and nut (A).

4. Use the holder to hold the coupling (**Figure 28**), then tighten the pinion shaft nut to 100 N•m (74 ft.-lb.).

5. Install the left-side shims onto the ring gear (**Figure 26**) and install the ring gear into the gearcase (B, **Figure 25**).

6. Install the right-side shims (A, **Figure 25**) onto the ring gear.

NOTE
Do not apply sealant to the bearing case or gearcase in Step 7.

7. Install the bearing case (B, **Figure 24**) and retaining bolts (**Figure 23**). Tighten the bolts to 23 N•m (17 ft.-lb.).

8. Install the backlash measuring tool onto the coupling (A, **Figure 39**, typical).

9. Position a dial indicator (B, **Figure 39**) so it contacts the tool lever at the mark on the lever.

10. Gently rotate the coupling until tooth contact occurs, then reverse direction until tooth contact occurs again. Read the dial indicator to measure the distance between the gear faces (backlash).

11. Set up the backlash measuring tools at three other locations on the coupling.

12. Average all the readings and compare the result with the desired backlash specification in **Table 1**. If the backlash is out of specification, refer to *Gear backlash adjustment* in this section.

Gear backlash adjustment

1. Remove the bearing case retaining bolts (**Figure 23**).

2. Install two 5 mm jackscrews in the threaded holes in the bearing case (A, **Figure 24**). Turn the jackscrews to separate the bearing case (B, **Figure 24**) from the gearcase. Remove the bearing case.

3. Note the right-side shim on the ring gear (A, **Figure 25**). Remove the shim, label it and set it aside.

4. Remove the ring gear (B, **Figure 25**).

5. Note the left-side shim(s) on the ring gear (**Figure 26**). Remove the shim(s), label it and set it aside.

6. Measure the combined thicknesses of the left-side and right-side shims and record the measurement. This is the total ring gear shim pack thickness.

7. Using the backlash measurement determined in *Gear backlash measurement* in this section, refer to **Table 3** and select the shims necessary to obtain the specified backlash.

8. Subtract the new left-side shim thickness from the shim pack thickness measured in Step 6. The result is the required thickness of the right-side shim(s).

9. Label and set aside the new shims for future installation.

Gear mesh position

1. Install the shims and the pinion and bearing assembly into the gearcase.

14

2. Install the bearing stopper (D, **Figure 29**) using the stopper wrench. Tighten the bearing stopper to 110 N•m (81 ft.-lb.).

3. Install the coupling (C, **Figure 29**), washer (B) and nut (A).

4. Use the holder to hold the coupling (**Figure 28**), then tighten the pinion shaft nut to 100 N•m (74 ft.-lb.).

5. Apply Prussian Blue or other gear marking compound onto the ring gear teeth.

> *NOTE*
> *Install any new shims previously selected for proper ring gear side clearance and gear backlash.*

6. Install the left-side shims onto the ring gear (**Figure 26**) and install the ring gear into the gearcase (B, **Figure 25**).

7. Install the right-side shims (A, **Figure 25**) onto the ring gear.

> *NOTE*
> *Do not apply sealant to the bearing case or gearcase in Step 8.*

8. Install the bearing case (B, **Figure 24**) and retaining bolts (**Figure 23**). Tighten the bolts to 23 N•m (17 ft.-lb.).

9. Rotate the pinion coupling several rotations so a pattern is evident on the ring gear teeth. Hold the output hub slightly to improve the impression on the gear teeth.

10. Disassemble the unit and note the gear pattern on the ring gear teeth. Refer to the typical gear patterns in **Figure 40**. If the pinion is high, install a thinner shim (34, **Figure 18**). If the pinion is low, install a thicker shim. The pinion and bearing must be removed to replace the shim. Refer to **Table 4** for available shims.

11. After obtaining a satisfactory gear contact pattern, make sure to check the gear backlash as described in this section.

Final Assembly

The following procedure describes final drive unit assembly after all inspection and adjustments have been performed as described in this section. Lubricate seals and O-rings with gear oil prior to assembly.

Refer to **Figure 18**.

1. Install the shims and the pinion and bearing assembly into the gearcase.

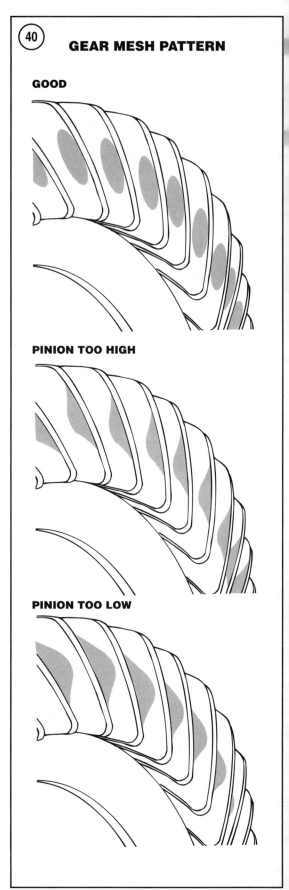

2. Install the bearing stopper (D, **Figure 29**) using the stopper wrench. Tighten the bearing stopper to 110 N•m (81 ft.-lb.).

3. Apply threadlock (Threadlock 1303 or equivalent) to the sleeve nut threads, then install the coupling (C, **Figure 29**), washer (B) and nut (A).

4. Use the holder to hold the coupling (**Figure 28**), then tighten the pinion shaft nut to 100 N•m (74 ft.-lb.).

5. Using a suitable punch, drive the rim of the nut sleeve into the notch in the end of the pinion shaft (**Figure 27**).

6. Install the left-side shims onto the ring gear (**Figure 26**) and install the ring gear into the gearcase (B, **Figure 25**).

7. Install the right-side shims (A, **Figure 25**) onto the ring gear.

8. Cut off two bolts and install them into opposite mounting bolt holes in the gearcase (**Figure 41**). The bolts will help align the bearing case with the gearcase during assembly. Make sure the bolts are long enough to permit removal.

NOTE
Do not block the breather holes when performing Step 9.

9. Apply Suzuki Bond 1216 to the mating surfaces of the bearing stopper and gearcase.

10. Install the bearing case (B, **Figure 24**) and retaining bolts (**Figure 23**). Tighten the bolts to 23 N•m (17 ft.-lb.).

11. Apply lithium based molybdenum grease to the driveshaft and coupling splines.

12. Install the spring and driveshaft into the coupling (**Figure 22**).

13. Install the snap ring (**Figure 21**).

14. Lubricate, then install a new oil seal (**Figure 20**).

15. Install the stopper plate (**Figure 19**). Be sure the tab on the stopper plate fits into a slot on the bearing stopper.

SWING ARM

Preliminary Inspection

The condition of the swing arm bearings can greatly affect the handling of the bike. Worn bearings cause wheel hop, pulling to one side under acceleration and pulling to the other side during braking. To check the condition of the swing arm bearings, perform the following steps.

1. Remove the exhaust system as described in Chapter Eight or Chapter Nine.

2. Remove the left rear side cover (A, **Figure 42**) by pulling the cover prongs out of the retaining grommets.

3. Remove the left lower side cover (B, **Figure 42**).

4. Remove the right lower side cover (**Figure 43**).

5. Remove the final drive unit as described in this chapter.

6. Remove the pivot link mounting hardware (A, **Figure 44**) and detach the links (B) from the pivot lever. Removal of the links is not required.

7. On the right side, make sure the swing arm pivot locknut (A, **Figure 45**) is tight.

14

8. On the left side, make sure the pivot bolt (**Figure 46**) is tight.

9. The swing arm is now free to move under its own weight.

NOTE
Have an assistant steady the bike when
performing Step 10 and Step 11.

10. Grasp both ends of the swing arm and attempt to move it from side to side in a horizontal arc. If more than a slight amount of movement is felt, the bearings are worn and must be replaced.

11. Grasp both ends of the swing arm and move it up and down. The swing arm should move smoothly with no binding or abnormal noise from the bearings. If there is binding or noise, the bearings are worn and must be replaced.

12. Move the swing arm and the pivot links (B, **Figure 44**) into position. Install the pivot link bolt from the left side. Install the nut (A, **Figure 44**) and tighten to 78 N•m (58 ft.-lb.).

13. Reverse the removal steps to install the removed parts.

Removal

CAUTION
Exercise care when working around the
regulator/rectifier which is mounted on
the inside of the bike frame near the
swing arm.

1. Remove the exhaust system as described in Chapter Eight or Chapter Nine.

2. Remove the left rear side cover (A, **Figure 42**) by pulling the cover prongs out of the retaining grommets.

3. Remove the left lower side cover (B, **Figure 42**).

4. Remove the right lower side cover (**Figure 43**).

5. Remove the final drive unit as described in this chapter.

6. Remove the pivot link mounting hardware (A, **Figure 44**) and detach the links (B) from the pivot lever. Removal of the links is not required.

CAUTION
Support the swing arm so it cannot fall
out after removal of the pivot bolts.

7. Loosen and remove the right pivot locknut (A, **Figure 45**).

8. Remove the right pivot bolt (B, **Figure 45**).

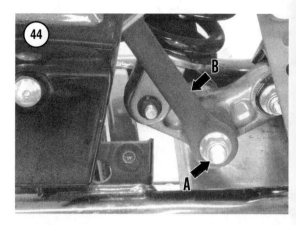

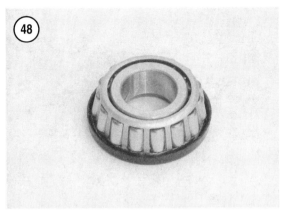

NOTE
The swing arm is equipped with tapered roller pivot bearings that may fall out when the swing arm is removed.

NOTE
The universal joint may be pulled off with the swing arm. Be prepared to catch it if it remains in the swing arm cavity.

9. Remove the left pivot bolt (**Figure 46**) and remove the rear swing arm.

NOTE
If the swing arm bearings are not going to be serviced, place a strip of duct tape over them to prevent contamination.

Inspection

1. Clean and dry the swing arm and the components.
2. Inspect the welded sections on the swing arm for cracks or other damage.
3. Remove the bearing and seal assembly (**Figure 47**). Inspect each bearing (**Figure 48**) for severe wear, pitting or other damage. If necessary, replace the bearings as described in this section.
4. Make sure the right side grease retainer plate (**Figure 49**) fits tightly in the swing arm bore.

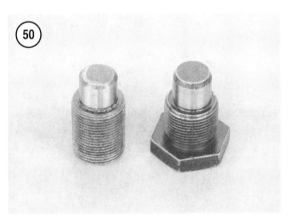

5. Inspect the pivot bolts (**Figure 50**) for excessive wear, thread damage or corrosion. Make sure the machined end on each pivot bolt is smooth. Replace if necessary.
6. Inspect the threaded holes in the frame (**Figure 51**) for corrosion or damage.
7. Replace the universal joint boot if damaged.
8. Remove the pivot links (**Figure 52**) and inspect the pivot link bearing assemblies on the swing arm as follows:

    a. Remove the spacer (**Figure 53**).

14

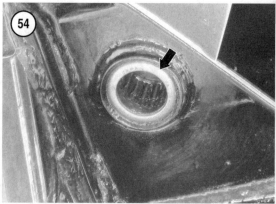

NOTE
The spacer also serves as the inner race for the bearings.

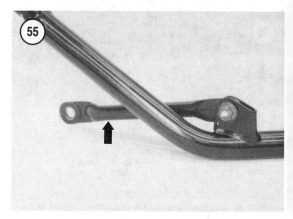

b. Use a lint-free rag to clean surface grease from the needle bearings (**Figure 54**).

c. Turn each bearing by hand. The bearing should turn smoothly without excessive play or noise. Check the rollers for wear, pitting or rust.

d. Inspect the spacer for excessive wear or damage, particularly in the areas contacted by the bearings.

e. Insert the spacer into each bearing and slowly rotate the spacer. It should turn smoothly without excessive play or noise.

f. Remove the spacer.

g. Pack each pivot bearing with waterproof bearing grease (Suzuki Super Grease A or an equivalent).

h. Install the spacer and pivot links. Tighten the pivot link bolts to 78 N•m (58 ft.-lb.).

9. Inspect the rear brake torque link (**Figure 55**). If removed, install the link retaining bolt securely.

Bearing Replacement

Replace the left and right side bearings (**Figure 47**) at the same time. Note that the dust seal is attached to the roller bearing assembly and is not available separately. The following procedure describes removal of the inner grease retainer plate and the inner bearing race.

1. Support the swing arm in a vise with soft jaws.

NOTE
Removing the grease retainer should provide a sufficient gap behind the inner bearing race to insert the jaw flanges of a blind bearing puller.

2. On the right side, use a blunt tool that matches the indented diameter of the grease retainer (**Figure 49**)

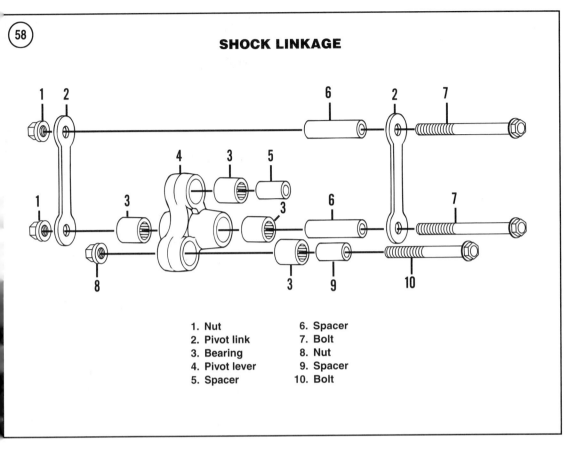

SHOCK LINKAGE

1. Nut
2. Pivot link
3. Bearing
4. Pivot lever
5. Spacer
6. Spacer
7. Bolt
8. Nut
9. Spacer
10. Bolt

and drive the grease retainer into the swing arm. Remove the grease retainer plate.

3. Using a suitable puller extract the inner bearing race (**Figure 56**) on each side.

4. On the right side, drive a new grease retainer into the swing arm so the concave side is out.

5. Drive a new inner bearing race into each side of the swing arm. Make sure the race sits squarely in the swing arm bore.

Installation

1. If removed, install the boot onto the engine so the UP mark on the boot tab is up (A, **Figure 57**).

2. If removed, install the universal joint onto the engine shaft. The long end of the universal joint must mate with the shaft.

3. Position the swing arm in the frame and install the left pivot bolt (**Figure 46**). Do not tighten the bolt.

4. Install the right pivot bolt (B, **Figure 45**), but do not tighten.

5. Tighten the left pivot bolt (**Figure 46**) to 100 N•m (74 ft.-lb.).

6. Tighten the right pivot bolt (B, **Figure 45**) to 9.5 N•m (84 in.-lb.).

7. Install the right pivot locknut (A, **Figure 45**) and tighten to 100 N•m (74 ft.-lb.).

8. Move the swing arm up and down to confirm it moves freely. If not, repeat the previous installation steps.

9. Attach the pivot links (B, **Figure 44**) to the pivot lever. Install the bolt from the left side and tighten the nut to 78 N•m (57 ft.-lb.).

10. Install the final drive unit as described in this chapter.

11. Install the right lower side cover (**Figure 43**).

12. Install the left lower side cover (B, **Figure 42**).

13. Install the left rear side cover (A, **Figure 42**).

14. Install the exhaust system as described in Chapter Eight or Chapter Nine.

SHOCK LINKAGE

Removal/Installation

Refer to **Figure 58**.

1. Remove the exhaust system as described in Chapter Eight or Chapter Nine.

2. Remove the left lower side cover (**Figure 59**).

3. Remove the lower right side cover (**Figure 60**).

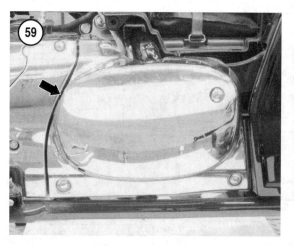

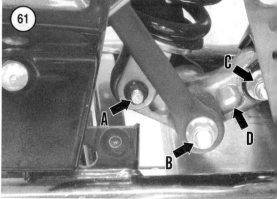

4. Support the bike securely with the rear wheel off the ground.

5. Raise the motorcycle so the rear wheel just touches the ground, indicating that weight is removed from the shock absorber.

6. Remove the lower shock absorber retaining bolt (A, **Figure 61**).

7. Remove the mounting hardware (B, **Figure 61**) securing the lower end of the pivot links.

8. Remove the pivot lever mounting bolt (C, **Figure 61**), then remove the pivot lever (D).

9. Reverse the removal steps to install the shock linkage, and note the following:

    a. Apply grease to the pivot points on the lower end of the shock absorber and to the frame mounting boss.

    b. Note that the frame mounting hole in the pivot lever is bigger than the pivot lever attachment hole.

    c. Install all bolts from the left side.

    d. Tighten the pivot lever mounting bolt to 78 N•m (58 ft.-lb.).

    e. Tighten the lower shock mounting bolt to 50 N•m (37 ft.-lb.).

    f. Tighten the pivot link mounting bolts to 78 N•m (57 ft.-lb.).

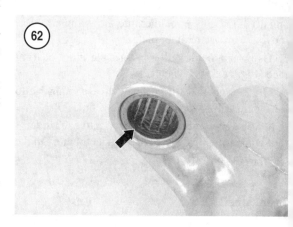

Inspection

1. Inspect the pivot lever pivot bearings as follows:

    a. Remove the spacers from the pivot lever.

    b. Use a clean lint-free rag and wipe off surface grease from the pivot needle bearings (**Figure 62**).

    c. Turn each bearing by hand. The bearing should turn smoothly without excessive play or noise. Check the rollers for wear, pitting or rust.

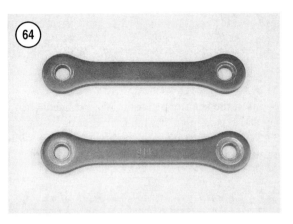

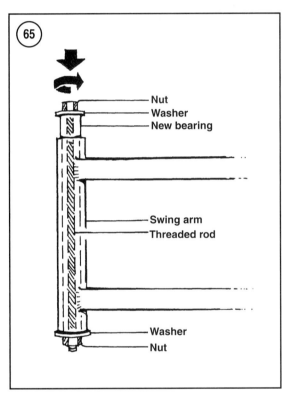

d. Reinstall the spacers (**Figure 63**) into the bearings and slowly rotate each spacer. The collars must turn smoothly without excessive play or noise.

e. Remove the spacers.

f. If the needle bearings must be replaced, refer to *Bearing Replacement* in this chapter.

2. Inspect the spacers for wear and damage. Replace each spacer as necessary.

3. Inspect the pivot lever for cracks or damage. Replace as necessary.

4. Inspect the pivot links (**Figure 64**) for bending, cracks or damage. Replace as necessary.

5. Clean the pivot bolts and nuts in solvent. Check the bolts for straightness. If a bolt is bent, it will restrict the movement of the pivot lever.

6. Before installing the spacers, coat the inner surface of the bearings with molybdenum disulfide grease.

BEARING REPLACEMENT

Swing Arm Needle Bearing

Do not remove the swing arm needle bearings unless they must be replaced. The needle bearings are pressed onto the swing arm. A blind bearing puller set is required to remove the needle bearings. The needle bearings can be installed with a homemade tool consisting of a piece of threaded rod, two thick washers, and two nuts.

NOTE
If the needle bearings are replaced, replace the spacers at the same time. The spacer serves as the inner race for the bearing.

1. If still installed, remove the spacers from the needle bearings as described in this chapter.

NOTE
In the following steps, the bearing puller grabs the inner surface of the bearing and then withdraws it from the pivot boss in the swing arm.

2. Insert the bearing puller (Suzuki part No. 09921-20220 or an equivalent blind bearing puller) through the needle bearing. Expand the puller behind the bearing.

3. Using sharp strokes of the slide hammer, withdraw the needle bearing from the pivot boss.

4. Remove the bearing puller and the bearing.

5. Repeat for the bearing on the other side.

6. Remove the special tool.

7. Thoroughly clean the inside of the pivot bore with solvent, then dry it with compressed air.

8. To make bearing installation easier, apply a light coat of grease to the exterior of the new bearings and to the inner circumference of the pivot bore.

CAUTION
Install one needle bearing at a time. Make sure the bearing is entering the pivot boss squarely, otherwise the bearing and the pivot boss may be damaged.

9. Position the bearing with the manufacturer's marks facing out.

14

10. Locate and square the new bearing in the pivot bore. Assemble the homemade tool through the pivot bore as shown in **Figure 65**.

11. Tighten the nut and pull the bearing into the pivot bore. Pull the bearing until it is flush with the outer surface of the pivot boss.

12. Remove the nut and washer adjacent to the installed bearing, then install an old bearing (or same dimension socket) on top of the installed bearing. Reassemble the tool and use the old bearing to push in the installed bearing so it is recessed 1 mm (0.039 in.).

13. Disassemble the tool and reinstall it on the opposite side, then repeat for the other bearing.

14. Remove the tool.

15. Make sure the bearings are properly seated. Turn each bearing by hand. They should turn smoothly.

16. Lubricate the new bearings with grease.

17. Repeat for the other set of bearings in the swing arm.

Pivot Lever Needle Bearing

Do not remove the pivot lever needle bearings unless they must be replaced. The needle bearings are pressed into the pivot lever. A set of blind bearing pullers is required to remove the needle bearings. The needle bearings can be installed with a homemade tool, or socket and hammer.

NOTE
If the needle bearings are replaced, replace the spacers at the same time. The spacer serves as the inner race for the bearing and should be replaced with the bearing.

1. If still installed, remove the spacers.

NOTE
In the following steps, the bearing puller grabs the inner surface of the bearing and then withdraws it from the pivot areas of the swing arm.

2. Insert the bearing puller through the needle bearing and expand it behind the front bearing.

3. Using sharp strokes of the slide hammer, withdraw the needle bearing from the front pivot hole.

NOTE
The bearings are different sizes. Mark the bearings front, center and rear as they are removed. The center two bearings are identical.

4. Remove the special tool and the bearing.

5. At the center pivot area, repeat Step 2 and Step 3 for the bearing on each side.

6. Repeat Step 2 and Step 3 for the rear bearing.

7. Thoroughly clean out the inside of the pivot bores with solvent. Dry them with compressed air.

8. To make bearing installation easier, apply a light coat of grease to the exterior of the new bearings and to the inner circumference of the pivot bores.

9. Locate and square the new bearing in the pivot bore.

10. Install the bearings with an appropriate size drift or socket that matches the outer race diameter. Tap the bearings into place so the outer end is recessed 1 mm (0.039 in.) from the side of the pivot lever.

11. Make sure the bearing is properly seated. Turn each bearing by hand. The bearing should turn smoothly.

12. Lubricate the needles of the new bearing with a waterproof bearing grease.

13. Repeat for the other bearings.

14. Before installing the spacers, coat the inner surface of the bearings with grease. Install the spacers as described in this chapter.

Table 1 REAR SUSPENSION AND FINAL DRIVE SPECIFICATIONS	
Final drive oil	
Type	SAE 90, GL-5 hypoid
Capacity	200-220 ml (6.8-7.4 oz)
Gear backlash	0.03-0.64 mm (0.001-0.025 in.)
Rear damper type	Oil damped tube
Rear suspension type	Swing arm
Rear wheel travel	105 mm (4.13 in.)
Ring gear side clearance	1.00 mm (0.039 in.)

Table 2 FINAL DRIVE RING GEAR SHIMS (RIGHT SIDE)*

Part No.	Thickness
27327-34200	0.35 mm (0.014 in.)
27327-34210	0.40 mm (0.016 in.)
27327-34220	0.50 mm (0.020 in.)
27327-34230	0.60 mm (0.024 in.)

*A shim set is available. Verify part number and thickness of individual shims.

Table 3 FINAL DRIVE RING GEAR SHIMS (LEFT SIDE)*

Part No.	Thickness
27326-34201	1.05 mm (0.041 in.)
27326-34211	1.10 mm (0.043 in.)
27326-34221	1.20 mm (0.047 in.)
27326-34231	1.25 mm (0.049 in.)
27326-34241	1.35 mm (0.053 in.)
27326-34201-140	1.40 mm (0.055 in.)
27326-34201-145	1.45 mm (0.057 in.)
27326-34201-150	1.50 mm (0.059 in.)

*A shim set is available. Verify part number and thickness of individual shims.

Table 4 FINAL DRIVE PINION GEAR SHIMS*

Part No.	Thickness
27445-38A00-030	0.30 mm (0.012 in.)
27445-38A00-035	0.35 mm (0.014 in.)
27445-38A00-040	0.40 mm (0.016 in.)
27445-38A00-050	0.50 mm (0.020 in.)
27445-38A00-060	0.60 mm (0.024 in.)

*A shim set is available. Verify part number and thickness of individual shims.

Table 5 REAR SUSPENSION TORQUE SPECIFICATIONS

Item	N•m	in.-lb.	ft.-lb.
Final drive			
Mounting nuts	40		30
Bearing retainer screws*	9	80	–
Bearing case bolts	23	–	17
Bearing stopper	110	–	81
Pinion nut	100	–	74
Pivot lever mounting bolt	78	–	58
Pivot link bolts (both sides)	78	–	58
Rear axle nut	65	–	48
Rear brake torque link bolt	25	–	18
Shock absorber mounting bolts	50	–	37
Swing arm			
Right pivot locknut	100	–	74
Left pivot bolt	100	–	74
Right pivot bolt	9.5	84	–

*Apply threadlock (ThreeBond 1344 or equivalent)

14

CHAPTER FIFTEEN

BRAKES

This chapter covers the front and rear brake systems. Brake specifications are located in **Tables 1-3** at the end of this chapter.

The brake system consists of a hydraulically actuated single disc at the front and a mechanically actuated drum at the rear.

BRAKE FLUID SELECTION

WARNING
Do not intermix silicone-based (DOT 5) brake fluid with glycol-based (DOT 4) brake fluid as it can cause brake system failure.

When adding brake fluid, use DOT 4 brake fluid from a sealed container. DOT 4 brake fluid is glycol-based and draws moisture, which greatly reduces its ability to perform correctly. Purchase brake fluid in small containers and discard any small leftover quantities. Do not store a container of brake fluid with less than 1/4 of the fluid remaining.

BRAKE SERVICE

WARNING
The proper operation of the brake system depends on a supply of clean brake fluid (DOT 4) and a clean work environment when any service is being performed. Any debris that enters the system can damage the components and cause poor brake performance.

WARNING
When working on the brake system, do not inhale brake dust. It may contain asbestos, which is a known carcinogen. Do not use compressed air to blow off brake dust. Use an aerosol brake cleaner. Wear a face mask that meets OSHA requirements. Wash hands and forearms thoroughly after completing the work. Wet down the brake dust on brake components before working on the brake system. Dispose of all brake dust and cleaning materials properly.

WARNING
Do not ride the motorcycle unless the brakes work correctly.

Consider the following when servicing the brake system:

1. The hydraulic components rarely require disassembly. Make sure it is necessary.

2. Keep the reservoir covers in place to prevent the entry of moisture and debris.

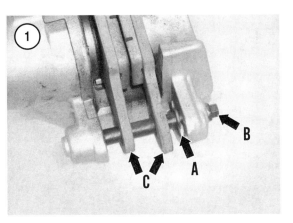

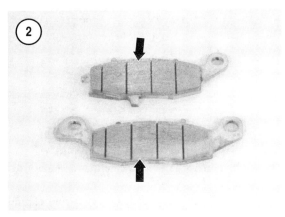

If brake fluid contacts the motorcycle, clean the area and rinse it thoroughly.

7. To help control the flow of brake fluid when filling the reservoirs, punch a small hole into the seal of a new container next to the edge of the pour spout.

8. Do not reuse brake fluid. Dispose of it properly.

9. If the hydraulic system, not including the reservoir cover, has been opened, bleed the system to remove air from the system. Refer to *Brake Bleeding* in this chapter.

FRONT BRAKE PADS

Inspection

Refer to *Periodic Maintenance* in Chapter Three.

Replacement

1. Review *Brake Service* in this chapter.

2. Place the bike on the sidestand on level ground.

3. Place a spacer between the brake lever and the throttle grip and secure it in place. That way if the brake lever is inadvertently squeezed, the pistons will not be forced out of the cylinders.

4. Remove the caliper as described in this chapter.

5. Remove the clip (A, **Figure 1**) and pin (B).

6. Remove both brake pads (C, **Figure 1**) from the caliper assembly.

7. Clean the pad recess and the end of both sets of pistons with a soft brush. Do not use solvent, a wire brush or any hard tool that would damage the cylinders or pistons.

8. Carefully remove any rust or corrosion from the disc.

9. Thoroughly clean the pad pin and clip of any corrosion or road dirt.

10. Check the friction surface (**Figure 2**) of the new pads for any debris or manufacturing residue. If necessary, clean the pads with an aerosol brake cleaner. Make sure the friction compound of the new pads is compatible with the disc material.

11. When new pads are installed in the calipers, the master cylinder brake fluid level will rise as the caliper pistons are repositioned. Perform the following:

    a. Clean all debris from the master cylinder cover and surrounding areas.

    b. Cover the area under the master cylinder to protect parts from brake fluid spills.

    c. Remove the screws securing the cover (**Figure 3**). Remove the cover and the diaphragm from the master cylinder.

    d. Temporarily install both old brake pads into the caliper and seat them against the pistons.

3. Clean parts with an aerosol brake parts cleaner or isopropyl alcohol. Never use petroleum-based solvents on internal brake system components. They will cause seals to swell and distort.

4. Do not allow brake fluid to contact plastic, painted or plated parts. It will damage the surface.

5. Before performing any procedure in which there is the possibility of brake fluid contacting the motorcycle, cover the work area with a large piece of plastic.

6. Before handling brake fluid or working on the brake system, fill a small container with soap and water and keep it close to the motorcycle while working.

15

e. Protect the caliper with a shop cloth to prevent scuffing it, then grasp the caliper and brake pad with a large pair of slip-joint pliers. Squeeze the piston back into the caliper. Repeat for each side until the pistons are completely in the caliper.

f. Constantly check the reservoir and make sure the fluid does not overflow. Draw out excess fluid if necessary.

g. The pistons should move freely. If they do not, remove and service the caliper as described in this chapter.

h. Remove the old brake pads.

12. Install the brake pad spring (A, **Figure 4**).

13. Install the brake pads (C, **Figure 1**) into the caliper, then install the pad mounting pin (B) and clip (A).

14. Carefully install the caliper assembly onto the brake disc. Be careful not to damage the leading edges of the pads during installation.

15. Remove the spacer from the front brake lever.

16. Pump the front brake lever to reposition the brake pads against the brake disc. Roll the motorcycle back and forth and continue to pump the brake lever as many times as it takes to refill the cylinders in the caliper and correctly position the brake pads against the disc.

17. Refill the master cylinder reservoir, if necessary, to maintain the correct fluid level as indicated on the side of the reservoir. Install the diaphragm and cover. Tighten the cover retaining screws securely.

18. Bed the pads in gradually for the first 2-3 days of riding by using only light pressure as much as possible. Immediate hard application glazes the new friction pads and greatly reduces their effectiveness.

FRONT BRAKE CALIPER

Review *Brake Service* in this chapter.

Removal/Installation

Refer to **Figure 5**.

1. If the caliper assembly is going to be disassembled for service, perform the following:

a. Remove the brake pads as described in this chapter.

b. Reinstall the caliper assembly onto the brake disc and fork assembly. Tighten the caliper mounting bolts only fingertight.

CAUTION
During the following procedure, do not allow the pistons to come in contact

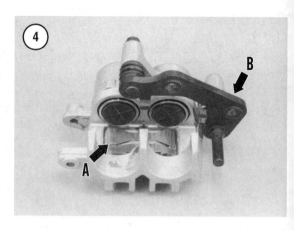

with the brake disc. If this happens the pistons may damage the disc during caliper removal.

NOTE
When performing Step 1c, compressed air may not be necessary for piston removal during caliper disassembly.

c. Slowly apply the brake lever to push the pistons part way out of the caliper assembly for ease of removal during caliper service.

2. Remove the union bolt (A, **Figure 6**) and sealing washers attaching the brake hose to the caliper assembly.

3. Place the loose end of the brake hose in a reclosable plastic bag to prevent brake fluid from contacting the wheel or fork.

4. Remove the two caliper mounting bolts (B, **Figure 6**) and lift the brake caliper off the disc.

5. If necessary, disassemble and service the caliper assembly as described in this section.

6. Install by reversing the removal steps. Note the following:

a. Install the caliper assembly onto the disc, being careful not to damage the leading edge of the brake pads.

b. Install the two caliper mounting bolts (B, **Figure 6**) and secure the brake caliper to the front fork. Tighten the caliper mounting bolts to 39 N•m (29 ft.-lb.).

c. If disconnected, connect the brake hose to the caliper. Install a new sealing washer on each side of the union bolt (A, **Figure 6**). Tighten the union bolt to 23 N•m (17 ft.-lb.).

d. Bleed the brake as described in this chapter.

Disassembly

Refer to **Figure 5**.

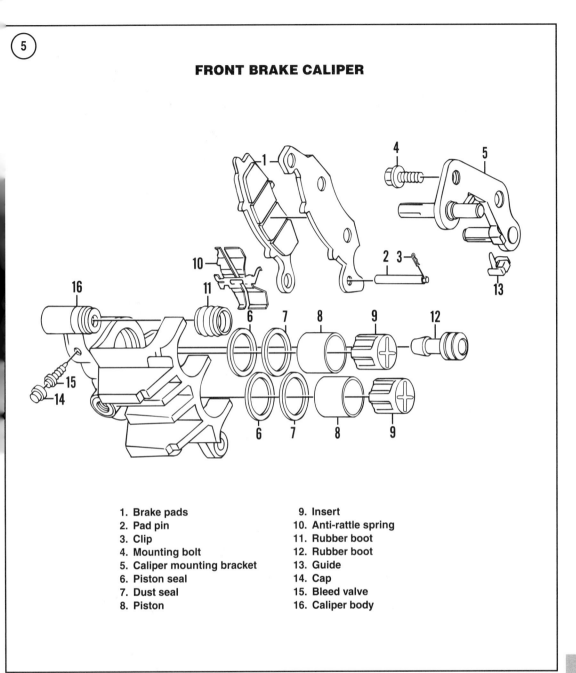

FRONT BRAKE CALIPER

1. Brake pads
2. Pad pin
3. Clip
4. Mounting bolt
5. Caliper mounting bracket
6. Piston seal
7. Dust seal
8. Piston
9. Insert
10. Anti-rattle spring
11. Rubber boot
12. Rubber boot
13. Guide
14. Cap
15. Bleed valve
16. Caliper body

15

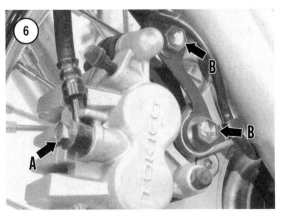

1. Remove the caliper and brake pads as described in this chapter.

2. Separate the mounting bracket (B, **Figure 4**) from the caliper.

3. When removing the pistons identify each piston so it can be reinstalled in its original cylinder.

WARNING
Use compressed air carefully. The piston can fly from the caliper at great speed and cause injury. Keep your fingers out of the way. Wear safety glasses

*and shop gloves and apply compressed
air gradually.*

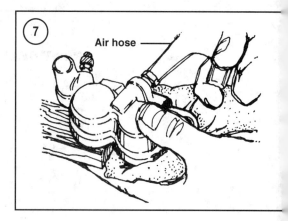

Air hose

4. Place a rag or piece of wood in the path of the pistons (**Figure 7**) and place the caliper on the workbench so that the pistons face down.

5. Blow the piston out with compressed air directed into the hydraulic fluid hole (**Figure 7**).

6. Remove the piston seals and dust seals.

7. Inspect the caliper body as described in this section.

Inspection

1. Clean the caliper and pistons with an aerosol brake cleaner or isopropyl alcohol. Thoroughly dry the parts with compressed air.

2. Make sure the fluid passageways (**Figure 8**) in the base of the piston bores are clear. Apply compressed air to the openings to make sure they are clear. Clean the passages if necessary.

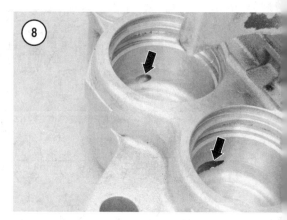

3. Inspect the piston and dust seal grooves (**Figure 9**) in the caliper body for damage. If any groove is damaged or corroded, replace the caliper assembly.

4. Inspect the union bolt threaded hole (A, **Figure 10**) in the caliper body. If worn or damaged, clean out with a metric thread tap or replace the caliper assembly.

5. Remove the bleed valve and dust cap (B, **Figure 10**). Inspect the bleed valve. Apply compressed air to the opening and make sure it is clear. If necessary, clean it out.

6. Inspect the bleed valve threaded hole in the caliper body. If worn or damaged, clean the threads with a metric tap or replace the caliper assembly.

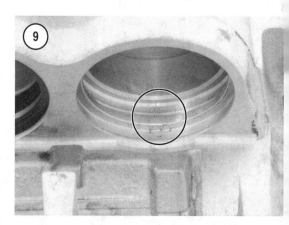

7. Install the bleed valve, and tighten it to 7.5 N•m (66 in.-lb.).

8. Remove the anti-rattle pad spring (**Figure 11**) from the caliper.

9. Inspect the caliper body (**Figure 12**) for damage and replace the caliper body if necessary.

10. Inspect the caliper cylinder bores for scratches, scoring or other damage.

11. Measure the cylinder bores' inside diameter using a bore gauge (**Figure 13**) or other suitable measuring tool. Refer to the specification in **Table 1**.

12. Inspect the pistons (A, **Figure 14**) for scratches, scoring or other damage. Each piston is equipped with a removable insert (B, **Figure 14**). The insert is only available as part of the piston assembly.

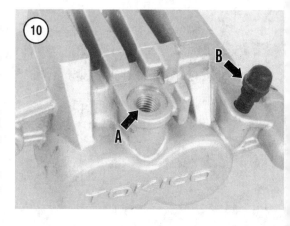

13. Measure the outside diameter of the pistons with a micrometer (**Figure 15**) or vernier caliper. Refer to the specification in **Table 1**.

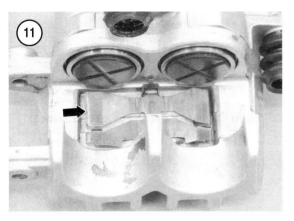

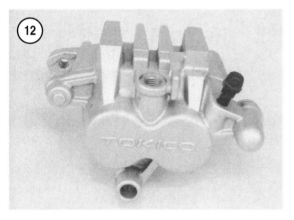

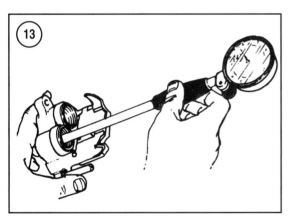

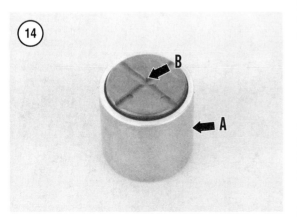

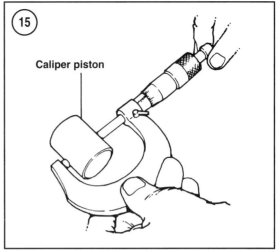

Caliper piston

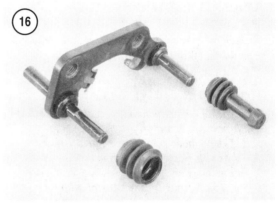

14. The piston seal helps maintain correct brake pad-to-disc clearance. If the seal is worn or damaged, the brake pads will drag, causing excessive wear and raising the brake fluid temperature. Replace the seals whenever the caliper is disassembled.

15. Inspect the mounting bracket and pins for wear or damage (**Figure 16**). Replace if necessary.

16. Inspect the brake pads for uneven wear, damage or grease contamination.

17. If there is a large difference in pad wear, the caliper is not sliding properly along the support bracket shafts causing one pad to drag against the disc. Worn caliper piston seals will also cause uneven pad wear.

Assembly

1. Install the brake pad anti-rattle spring (**Figure 11**) and make sure it is properly seated.

2. Coat the new dust seals and piston seals and piston bores with clean DOT 4 brake fluid.

3. Carefully install the new piston seals (A, **Figure 17**) into the inner grooves. Make sure the seals are properly seated in their respective grooves.

15

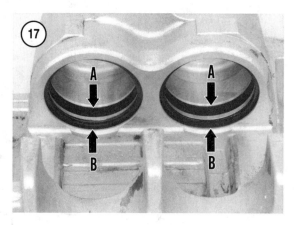

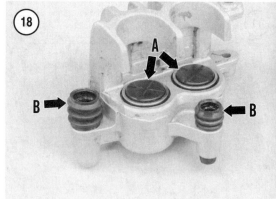

4. Carefully install the new dust seals (B, **Figure 17**) into the outer grooves. Make sure the seals are properly seated in their respective grooves.

5. Coat the pistons with clean DOT 4 brake fluid.

6. Position the pistons with the closed end facing in and install the pistons into the caliper cylinders. Push the pistons in until they bottom (A, **Figure 18**).

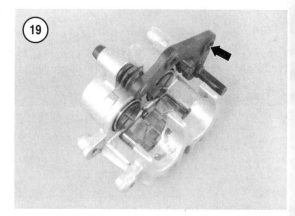

NOTE
*Prior to installing the caliper mounting bracket, apply silicone grease to the bracket pins and to the inside surfaces of the rubber boots (B, **Figure 18**) on the caliper assembly. This makes installation easier and ensures the caliper will move easily after installation on the fork slider.*

7. Install the caliper bracket boots (B, **Figure 18**).

8. Slide the caliper mounting bracket (**Figure 19**) onto the caliper assembly. Push the bracket on until it bottoms.

9. Install the caliper and brake pads as described in this chapter.

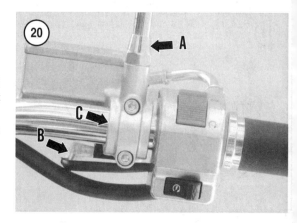

FRONT BRAKE MASTER CYLINDER

Review *Brake Service* in this Chapter.

Removal/Installation

1. Remove the rear view mirror (A, **Figure 20**) from the master cylinder clamp.

2. Disconnect the brake switch connectors (B, **Figure 20**).

3. Clean the master cylinder cover and surrouding areas of all debris.

4. Remove the screws securing the cover (**Figure 21**). Remove the cover and the diaphragm.

5. Use a shop syringe to draw all of the brake fluid out of the master cylinder reservoir.

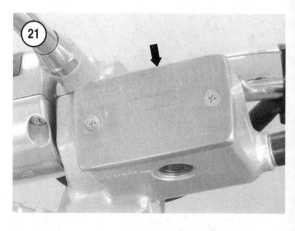

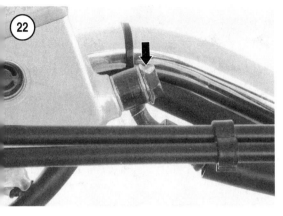

22

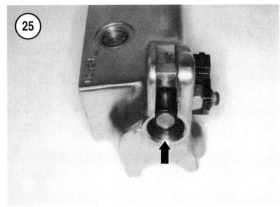

25

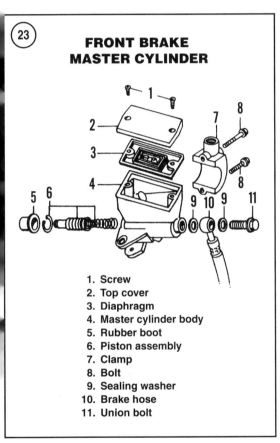

23

**FRONT BRAKE
MASTER CYLINDER**

1. Screw
2. Top cover
3. Diaphragm
4. Master cylinder body
5. Rubber boot
6. Piston assembly
7. Clamp
8. Bolt
9. Sealing washer
10. Brake hose
11. Union bolt

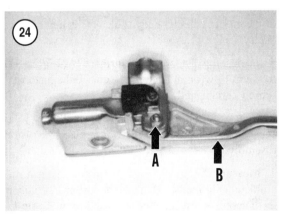

24

6. Place a shop cloth under the union bolt (**Figure 22**) to catch any spilled brake fluid.

7. Unscrew the union bolt (**Figure 22**) securing the brake hose to the master cylinder. Do not lose the sealing washer on each side of the hose fitting. Tie the loose end of the hose up to the handlebar and cover the end with a plastic bag to keep out debris.

8. Remove the bolts and clamp (C, **Figure 20**) securing the front master cylinder to the handlebar and remove the master cylinder.

9. Install by reversing the removal steps. Note the following:

    a. Position the front master cylinder onto the right handlebar and align the mating surface with the handlebar punch mark.

    b. Tighten the upper clamp mounting bolt first, then the lower bolt leaving a gap at the bottom. Tighten the bolts to 10 N•m (89 in.-lb.).

    c. Place a sealing washer on each side of the brake hose fitting (**Figure 22**) and install the union bolt. Tighten the union bolt to 23 N•m (17 ft.-lb.).

    d. Bleed the front brake as described in this chapter.

Disassembly

15

Refer to **Figure 23**.

1. Remove the master cylinder as described in this section.

2. If not already removed, remove the cover and diaphragm. Pour out any residual brake fluid and discard it. Never reuse brake fluid.

3. Remove the bolt and nut (A, **Figure 24**) securing the brake lever (B) and remove the brake lever.

4. Remove the rubber boot (**Figure 25**) from the area where the hand lever actuates the internal piston.

5. Using snap ring pliers, remove the internal snap ring (**Figure 26**) from the body.

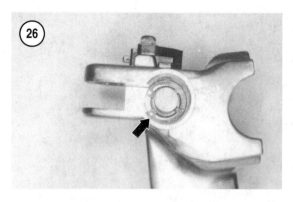

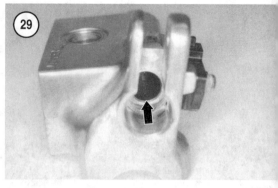

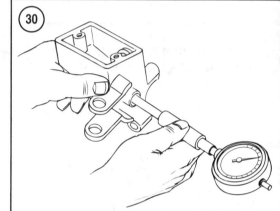

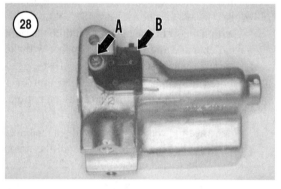

6. Remove the piston and spring assembly (**Figure 27**).

7. If necessary, remove the screw (A, **Figure 28**) securing the brake light switch to the master cylinder and remove the switch (B).

Inspection

1. Clean all parts in isopropyl alcohol or brake cleaning fluid.

2. Inspect the cylinder bore (**Figure 29**) for signs of wear and damage. Replace the master cylinder if damaged. The entire master cylinder must be replaced; the body is not available separately.

3. Measure the cylinder bore using a bore gauge (**Figure 30**). Replace the master cylinder if the bore exceeds the service limit listed in **Table 1**.

4. Make sure the passage (**Figure 31**) in the bottom of the master cylinder body is clear. Clean out if necessary.

5. Inspect the piston contact surfaces (A, **Figure 32**) for signs of wear and damage. Replace the piston assembly if damaged.

6. Check the end of the piston (**Figure 33**) for wear caused by the hand lever. If worn, replace the piston assembly.

7. Measure the diameter of the piston using a micrometer (**Figure 34**). Replace the piston assembly if its diameter is less than the service limit in **Table 1**.

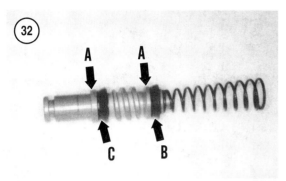

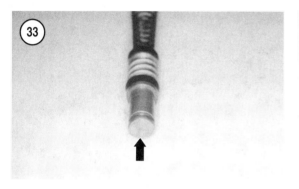

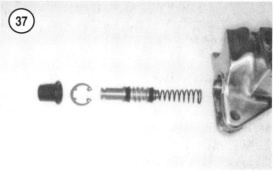

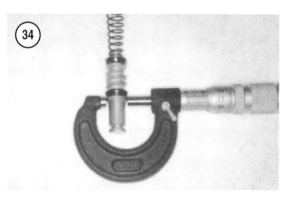

10. Inspect the pivot hole in the hand lever. If worn or elongated, replace the lever.

11. Inspect the threads in the bore (**Figure 36**) for the union bolt. If damaged, replace the master cylinder assembly.

12. Inspect the top cover and diaphragm for damage and deterioration. Replace as necessary.

Assembly

1. Soak the piston assembly in fresh DOT 4 brake fluid for at least 15 minutes to make the cups pliable. Coat the inside of the cylinder bore with fresh DOT 4 brake fluid prior to the assembly of parts.

CAUTION
When installing the piston assembly, do not allow the cups to turn inside out as they will be damaged and allow brake fluid leaks within the cylinder bore.

2. Install the spring with the tapered end facing toward the primary cup on the piston (**Figure 37**), then install the spring and the piston assembly into the cylinder bore.

3. Push the piston assembly into the bore and hold it in place. Install the snap ring (**Figure 26**) and make sure it seats correctly in the master cylinder body groove.

4. Install the rubber boot and push it all the way down until it stops.

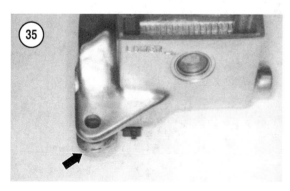

8. Replace the piston assembly if either the primary (B, **Figure 32**) or secondary cups (C) require replacement. The cups cannot be replaced separately.

9. Check the hand lever pivot lugs (**Figure 35**) on the master cylinder body for cracks or elongation. If damaged, replace the master cylinder assembly.

15

5. Install the brake lever onto the master cylinder body, then install the bolt and nut. Tighten the bolt and nut securely.

6. If removed, reinstall the brake light switch (B, **Figure 28**) and tighten the screw (A) securely.

7. Install the diaphragm and cover and screws. Do not tighten the cover screws at this time as fluid will have to be added later.

8. Install the master cylinder as described in this section.

FRONT BRAKE HOSE

Review *Brake Service* in this chapter.

Replacement

1. Remove the cap from the bleed screw (A, **Figure 38**) on the front caliper.

2. Attach a piece of hose to the bleed screw and place the loose end in a container.

3. Open the bleed screw and operate the front brake lever to pump the brake fluid out of the master cylinder, the brake hose and the caliper assembly. Operate the lever until the system is clear of brake fluid.

4. Clean the top of the master cylinder and surrounding areas of debris.

5. Remove the screws securing the cover (**Figure 39**). Remove the cover and the diaphragm.

6. Use a shop syringe to draw all of the brake fluid out of the master cylinder reservoir.

7. Unscrew the union bolt (**Figure 40**) securing the brake hose to the master cylinder. Do not lose the sealing washer on each side of the hose fitting.

8. Remove the union bolt (B, **Figure 38**) and sealing washers securing the brake hose to the brake caliper. Let any remaining brake fluid drain into the container. Dispose of the used brake fluid.

9. Cut any plastic ties securing the brake hose to electrical cables.

10. Unhook the brake hose from the retaining brackets.

11. Pull the brake hose assembly up through the lower fork bridge and the wire retainer on the upper fork bracket. Remove the brake hose from the frame.

12. Install a new hose, sealing washers and banjo bolts in the reverse order of removal. Note the following:

    a. Install new sealing washers in their correct positions.

    b. Tighten the union bolts to 23 N•m (17 ft.-lb.).

    c. Bleed the brakes as described in this chapter.

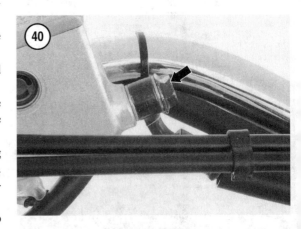

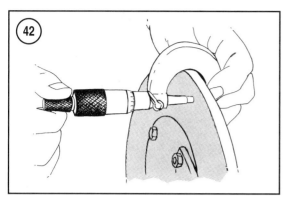

FRONT BRAKE DISC

The brake disc is separate from the wheel hub and can be removed once the wheel is removed from the bike.

Refer to Chapter Twelve for wheel removal procedures.

Inspection

It is not necessary to remove the disc from the wheel to inspect it.

The specifications for the standard and service limits are in **Table 1**. The minimum (MIN) thickness is stamped on the disc face (**Figure 41**). If the specification stamped on the disc differs from the service limit in **Table 1**, use the specification on the disc when inspecting it.

When servicing the brake disc, do not machine the disc to compensate for warp.

1. If the disc is warped and/or the pads are wearing unevenly, inspect for the following:
   a. Caliper binding on the caliper mounting bracket shafts and preventing the caliper from floating side to side on the disc.
   b. Worn or damaged brake caliper piston seals.
   c. Plugged master cylinder relief port.
   d. Worn or damaged primary cup on the master cylinder piston.

2. Measure the thickness of the disc at several locations around the disc with a vernier caliper or a micrometer (**Figure 42**). The disc must be replaced if the thickness in any area is less than that specified in **Table 1** (or the MIN dimension stamped on the disc).

3. Make sure the disc mounting bolts are tight before running this check. Check the disc runout with a dial indicator as shown in **Figure 43**.

4. Slowly rotate the wheel and watch the dial indicator. If the runout exceeds the specification in **Table 1**, replace the disc.

5. Clean the disc of any rust or corrosion, and wipe it clean with brake parts cleaner. Never use an oil-based solvent that may leave residue on the disc.

Removal/Installation

1. Remove the front wheel as described in Chapter Twelve.

> *NOTE*
> *Insert a piece of wood or vinyl tube between the pads in the brake caliper. This way, if the brake lever is inadvertently applied, the pistons will not be forced out of the cylinders. If this does happen, caliper disassembly may be required to reseat the pistons.*

2. Remove the bolts (**Figure 44**) securing the brake disc to the hub and remove the disc.

3. Install by reversing the preceding removal steps. Note the following:
   a. On a disc so marked, position the disc so the arrow on the disc points in the direction of tire rotation.

> *CAUTION*
> *The disc bolts are made from a harder material than similar bolts used on the motorcycle. When replacing the bolts,*

always use original equipment brake disc bolts.

b. Use a small amount of a locking compound (ThreeBond TB1360 or equivalent) on the brake disc bolts before installation.

c. Tighten the disc mounting bolts to 23 N•m (17 ft.-lb.).

BRAKE BLEEDING

The brake system can be bled manually or with the use of a brake bleeding tool. The manual method is described here. If there is a vacuum pump or other brake bleeding tool available, follow the instructions that came with the tool.

Review *Brake Service* in this chapter.

1. Check that all union bolts in the system are tight.

2. Remove the dust cap from the bleed valve (**Figure 45**) on the caliper assembly.

3. Connect a length of clear tubing to the bleed valve. Place the other end of the tube into a clean container. Fill the container with enough fresh brake fluid to keep the end submerged. The tube should be long enough so its loop can be higher than the bleed valve to prevent air from being drawn into the caliper during bleeding. See **Figure 46**.

4. Clean all debris from the top of the front master cylinder and surrounding areas. Remove the top cover (**Figure 47**) and diaphragm.

5. Add brake fluid to the reservoir until the fluid level is about 10 mm (3/8 in.) below the top. Loosely install the diaphragm and the cover. Leave them in place during this procedure to prevent the entry of debris.

6. Apply the front brake lever until it stops and hold it in this position.

7. Open the bleed valve with a wrench (**Figure 46**). Let the brake lever move to the limit of its travel, then close the bleed valve. Do not release the brake lever while the bleed valve is open.

8. Pump the brake lever a few times and then release it.

> *NOTE*
> *As brake fluid enters the system, the level in the reservoir drops. Add brake fluid as necessary to keep the fluid level 10 mm (3/8 in.) below the reservoir top so air will not be drawn into the system.*

9. Repeat Steps 6-8 until the brake fluid flowing from the hose is clear and free of air. If the system is difficult to bleed, tap the master cylinder or caliper with a soft mallet.

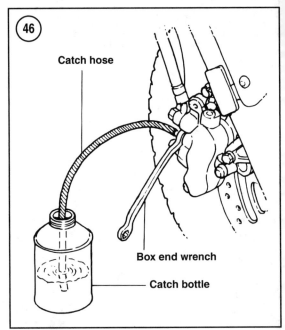

Catch hose

Box end wrench

Catch bottle

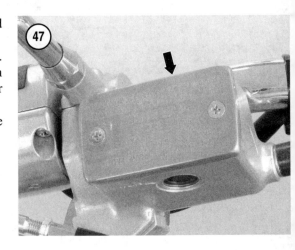

10. Test the feel of the brake lever. It should feel firm and offer the same resistance each time it is operated. If the lever feels soft, air is still trapped in the system. Repeat Steps 6-8.

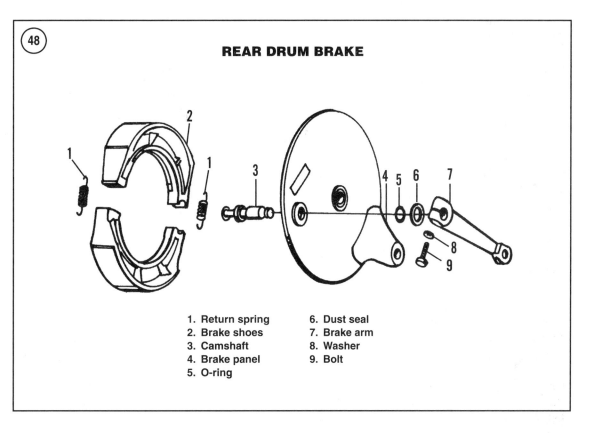

REAR DRUM BRAKE

1. Return spring
2. Brake shoes
3. Camshaft
4. Brake panel
5. O-ring
6. Dust seal
7. Brake arm
8. Washer
9. Bolt

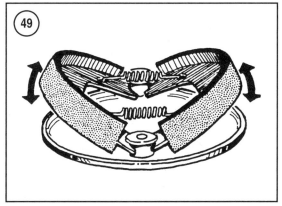

NOTE
It may be helpful to allow the bike to sit overnight. At times this will allow trapped air bubbles to release and be expelled during the next bleeding attempt.

11. When bleeding is complete, disconnect the hose from the bleed valve. Tighten the caliper bleed valve to 7.5 N•m (66 in.-lb.).

12. If necessary, add brake fluid to the master cylinder to correct the fluid level.

13. Install the diaphragm and top cover. Make sure the cover is secured in place.

14. Test ride the bike slowly at first to make sure the brakes are operating properly.

REAR DRUM BRAKE

WARNING
When working on the brake system, do not inhale brake dust. It may contain asbestos, which can cause lung injury and cancer. Wear a face mask that meets OSHA requirements for trapping asbestos particles, and wash your hands and forearms thoroughly after completing the work.

Refer to Chapter Three for adjustment.

Disassembly

Refer to **Figure 48.**
1. Remove the rear wheel as described in Chapter Twelve.
2. Pull the brake assembly straight up and out of the brake drum.
3. Carefully pull up on both brake shoes in a V-formation (**Figure 49**) and remove the brake shoes and return springs as an assembly.
4. Disconnect the return springs from the brake shoes.

15

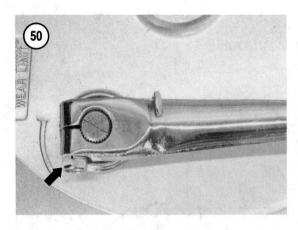

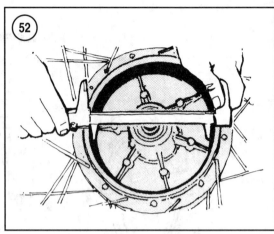

5. If necessary, remove the bolt (**Figure 50**) securing the brake arm and remove the brake arm, spring, washer and O-ring. Withdraw the camshaft from the backing plate.

Inspection

1. Thoroughly clean and dry all parts except the brake linings.
2. Check the contact surface of the drum for scoring (**Figure 51**). If there are grooves deep enough to snag a fingernail, machine the drum.
3. Measure the inside diameter of the brake drum (**Figure 52**). If the measurement is greater than the service limit in **Table 2**, either the rear hub or the rear wheel must be replaced.
4. If the drum can be turned and still stay within the maximum service limit diameter, the linings will have to be replaced and the new ones arced to conform to the new drum contour.
5. Inspect each brake shoe lining. There is no service limit for the brake shoe lining. Use the wear indicator and shoe inspection described in Chapter Three to determine whether shoe replacement is necessary.
6. Inspect the linings (**Figure 53**) for imbedded debris. Dirt can be removed with a stiff wire brush. If

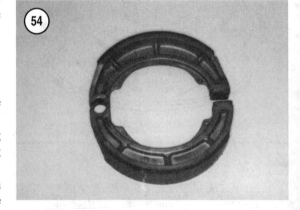

the linings are contaminated with oil or grease, replace them.

7. Inspect the brake shoe assemblies (**Figure 54**) for wear, cracks or other damage. Replace as a set if necessary.

8. Inspect the cam lobe and pivot pins (**Figure 55**) for wear or corrosion. Minor roughness can be removed with fine emery cloth.

9. Inspect the backing plate (**Figure 56**) for wear, cracks or other damage. Replace if necessary.

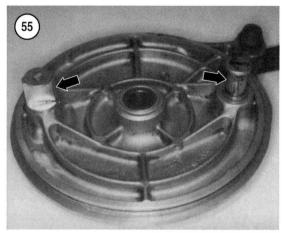

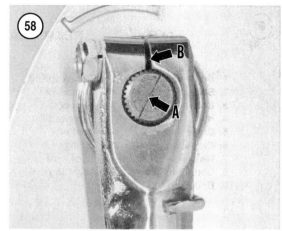

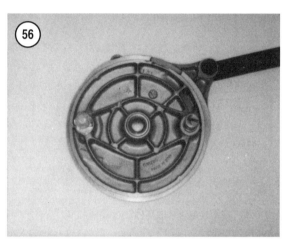

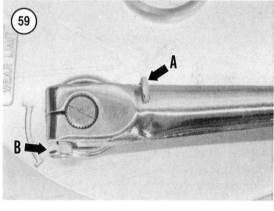

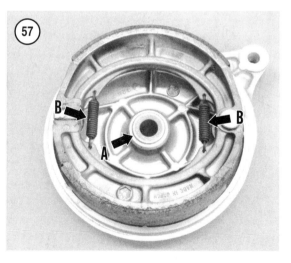

Assembly

1. If the camshaft was removed, lubricate it with a light coat of molybdenum disulfide grease. Install the cam into the backing plate from the backside.

2. From the outside of the backing plate install a new O-ring and washer onto the camshaft.

3. Install the spring and the brake arm. Note the line on the end of the camshaft (A, **Figure 58**). Install the brake arm so the end of the line is 30° offset from the gap in the end of the brake arm (B, **Figure 58**).

4. Position the outer spring end onto the brake arm as shown (A, **Figure 59**).

5. Install and tighten the bolt (B, **Figure 59**) to 10 N•m (89 in.-lb.).

6. Lubricate the camshaft and pivot post with a light coat of molybdenum disulfide grease. Avoid getting any grease on the brake backing plate where the brake linings may come in contact with it.

7. Assemble the return springs onto the brake shoes.

8. Hold the brake shoes in a V formation with the return springs attached (**Figure 49**) and snap them into place on the brake backing plate. Make sure they are firmly seated on it (**Figure 57**).

10. Inspect the rear axle bushing (A, **Figure 57**) in the backing plate for wear, scoring or other damage. Replace the backing plate if necessary; the bushing cannot be replaced.

11. Inspect the brake shoe return springs (B, **Figure 57**) for wear. If they are stretched, they will not fully retract the brake shoes. Replace as necessary.

15

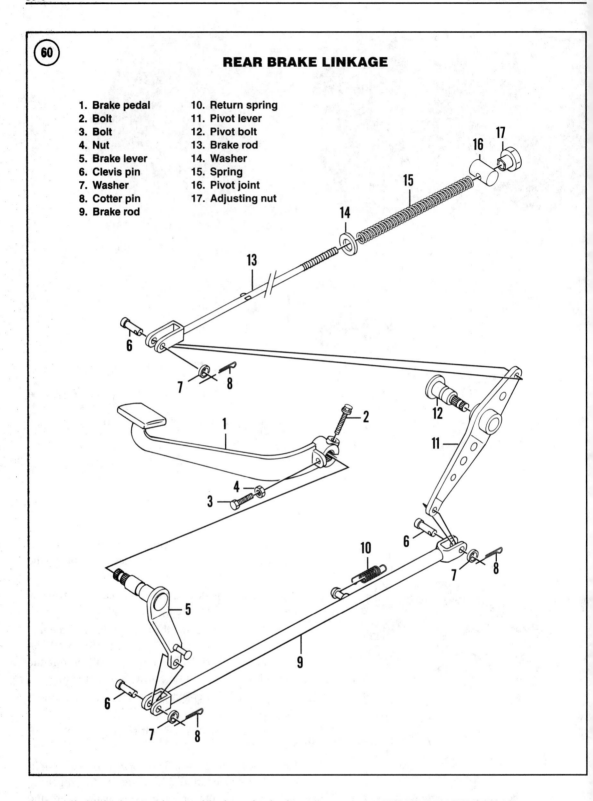

REAR BRAKE LINKAGE

1. Brake pedal
2. Bolt
3. Bolt
4. Nut
5. Brake lever
6. Clevis pin
7. Washer
8. Cotter pin
9. Brake rod
10. Return spring
11. Pivot lever
12. Pivot bolt
13. Brake rod
14. Washer
15. Spring
16. Pivot joint
17. Adjusting nut

9. Install the brake panel assembly into the brake drum.

10. Install the rear wheel as described in Chapter Twelve.

11. Adjust the rear brake as described in Chapter Three.

REAR BRAKE PEDAL

Removal/Installation

Refer to **Figure 60**.

1. Detach the rear brake switch spring (A, **Figure 61**) from the brake pedal lever.

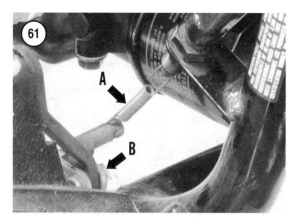

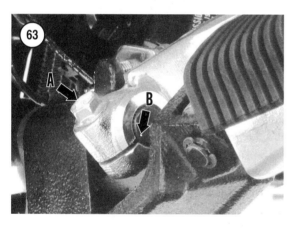

NOTE
It is necessary to lift the motorcycle for access to the return spring in Step 2. If lifting the motorcycle is not possible, remove the exhaust system as described in Chapter Eight or Chapter Nine.

2. Detach the return spring (**Figure 62**).

3. Remove the cotter pin and clevis pin (B, **Figure 61**) and disconnect the brake rod from the brake pedal lever.

4. Remove the brake pedal clamp bolt (A, **Figure 63**), then remove the brake pedal.

5. Remove the rear brake lever (**Figure 64**) from the footpeg holder.

6. Installation is the reverse of removal. Note the following:

   a. Clean and lubricate the pivot bolt surfaces with grease.

   b. Lubricate the joint pins with grease.

   c. Install a new cotter pin.

   d. Install the pedal so the gap in the pedal arm aligns with the punch mark (B, **Figure 63**) on the end of the lever shaft.

   e. Tighten the rear brake pedal clamp bolt (A, **Figure 63**) to 11 N•m (97 in.-lb.).

   f. Check the rear brake pedal height and adjust the rear brake as described in Chapter Three.

   g. Check the rear brake light operation.

15

REAR BRAKE PIVOT LEVER

Removal/Installation

Refer to **Figure 60**.

1. Remove the exhaust system as described in Chapter Eight or Chapter Nine.

2. Remove the rear side cover retaining bolt (A, **Figure 65**). Pull the cover prong out of the retaining grommet and remove the cover (B).

3. Remove the lower side cover (C, **Figure 65**).

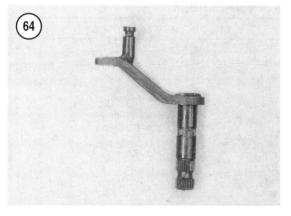

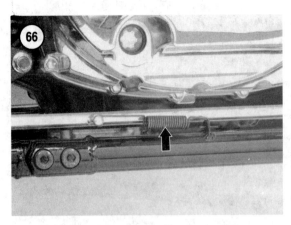

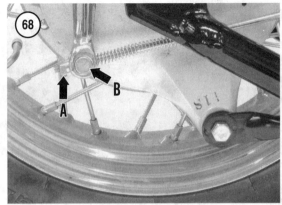

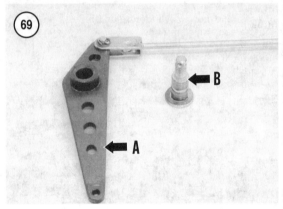

4. Detach the return spring (**Figure 66**) from the frame tube.

5. Remove the cotter pin and clevis pin (A, **Figure 67**), then detach the brake rod (B) from the pivot lever (C).

6. Remove the adjusting nut (A, **Figure 68**), then separate the brake rod from the pivot joint (B) in the brake arm. Remove the pivot joint from the brake arm, then install the pivot joint and the adjusting nut onto the brake rod to avoid misplacing them.

7. Remove the pivot lever bolt (D, **Figure 67**), then remove the lever assembly (**Figure 69**).

8. Inspect the pivot lever (A, **Figure 69**) and bolt (B) for excessive wear or damage.

9. Reverse the removal steps to install the pivot lever while noting the following:

   a. Apply grease to the pivot bolt and pivot lever bore.

   b. Tighten the pivot bolt to 29 N•m (21 ft.-lb.).

   c. Adjust the rear brake as described in Chapter Three.

Table 1 FRONT BRAKE SPECIFICATIONS

Item	New	Service limit
Brake caliper		
Cylinder bore inner diameter	30.230-30.306 mm	–
	(1.1902-1.1931 in.)	
Piston outer diameter	30.150-30.200 mm	–
	(1.1870-1.1890 in.)	
Brake disc thickness	5.0 mm (0.20 in.)	4.5 mm (0.18 in.)
Brake disc runout (max.)	–	0.3 mm (0.012 in.)
Master cylinder		
Cylinder bore inner diameter	12.700-12.743 mm	–
	(0.5000-0.5017 in.)	
Piston outer diameter	12.657-12.684 mm	–
	(0.4983-0.4994 in.)	

Table 2 REAR BRAKE SPECIFICATIONS

	New	Service limit
Rear brake drum inner diameter	–	180.7 mm (7.11 in.)

Table 3 BRAKE TORQUE SPECIFICATIONS

Item	N•m	in.-lb.	ft.-lb.
Front brake caliper bleed valve	7.5	66	–
Front brake caliper mounting bolt	39	–	29
Front brake caliper union bolt	23	–	17
Front brake disc mounting bolt[1]	23	–	17
Front brake master cylinder clamp bolt[2]	10	89	–
Front brake master cylinder union bolt	23	–	17
Rear brake arm clamp bolt	10	89	–
Rear brake pedal clamp bolt	11	97	–
Rear brake pivot bolt	29	–	21
Torque link mounting bolt			
Front	35	–	26
Rear	25	–	18

1. Apply threadlock (ThreeBond 1360 or equivalent)
2. Refer to text for tightening procedure

15

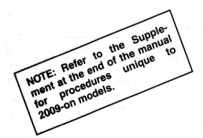
NOTE: Refer to the Supplement at the end of the manual for procedures unique to 2009-on models.

CHAPTER SIXTEEN

BODY AND FRAME

This chapter covers body panel and frame procedures. **Table 1** is at the end of the chapter.

SEATS

The rear passenger seat must be removed for access to the front seat retaining bolts.

WARNING
Verify that both seats are securely attached before riding the bike.

Removal/Installation

1. Remove the rear seat retaining bolt (A, **Figure 1**).
2. Slide the rear seat (B, **Figure 1**) rearward while removing it from the grip strap. Remove the rear seat.
3. Remove the bolts securing the front seat retaining bracket (**Figure 2**). Remove the bracket.
4. Move the front seat rearward and remove it.
5. Reverse the removal steps to install the seats while noting the following:
    a. Be sure the retaining tab on the front of the front seat fits into the recess under the fuel tank.
    b. Be sure the recess in the front of the rear seat fits around the tab on the mounting bracket.
    c. Tighten all bolts securely.

FRAME SIDE COVERS

Removal/Installation

1. On the left frame side cover, use the ignition key and turn the key lock counterclockwise (**Figure 3**).
2. On the right side frame side cover, remove the retaining bolt (**Figure 4**).
3. On both covers, pull the side cover prongs out of the retaining grommets and remove the cover.
4. Reverse the removal steps to install the side cover.

FRAME HEAD SIDE COVERS

Removal/Installation

1. Remove the fuel tank as described in Chapter Eight or Chapter Nine.

NOTE
When separating the tops of the side covers from each other disengage the interlocking tabs on the covers.

2. Pull each side cover (**Figure 5**) outward to disengage the mounting prongs from the retaining grommets.
3. Reverse the removal steps to install the frame side covers. Mesh the interlocking tabs together at the tops of the covers.

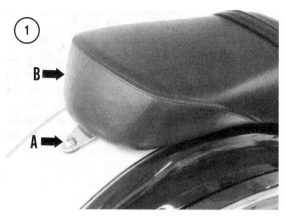

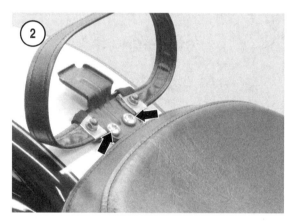

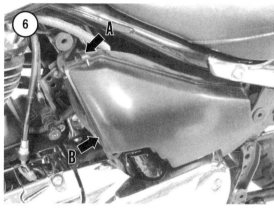

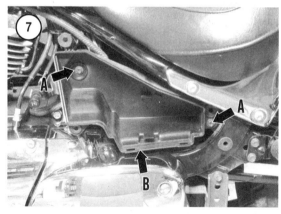

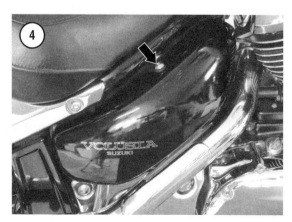

TOOLBOX

16

Removal/Installation

1. Remove the left frame side cover as described in this chapter.

2. Pull up the upper hook (A, **Figure 6**) on the toolbox cover (B), then remove the cover.

3. Remove the toolbox retaining bolts (A, **Figure 7**), then remove the toolbox (B).

4. Reverse the removal steps to install the toolbox.

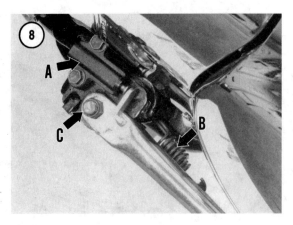

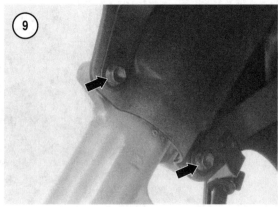

SIDESTAND

Removal/Installation

1. Securely support the motorcycle on level ground without using the sidestand.

2. Remove the sidestand switch (A, **Figure 8**) as described in Chapter Ten.

NOTE
The sidestand should be in the retracted position so there is less spring tension when detaching the spring end.

3. Disconnect the spring (B, **Figure 8**) from the sidestand bracket.

4. Remove the pivot bolt (C, **Figure 8**) from the sidestand bracket and remove the sidestand.

5. Install by reversing the removal steps. Note the following:

   a. Lubricate the pivot bolt with a waterproof bearing grease.

   b. Tighten the pivot bolt securely.

   c. Attach the long ends of the springs to the sidestand bracket.

FRONT FENDER

Removal/Installation

1. Remove the front wheel as described in Chapter Twelve.

NOTE
The lower retaining brake hose bracket is part of the fender frame.

2. Detach the front brake hose from the lower retaining bracket.

3. Remove the fender mounting bolts (**Figure 9**) on both sides and remove the fender assembly.

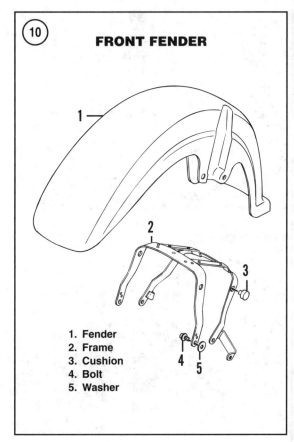

FRONT FENDER

1. Fender
2. Frame
3. Cushion
4. Bolt
5. Washer

4. If necessary, separate the frame from the fender (2, **Figure 10**).

5. Reverse the removal steps to install the front fender.

REAR FENDER

Removal/Installation

1. Remove the front seat as described in this chapter.

2. Disconnect the electrical connector (**Figure 11**).

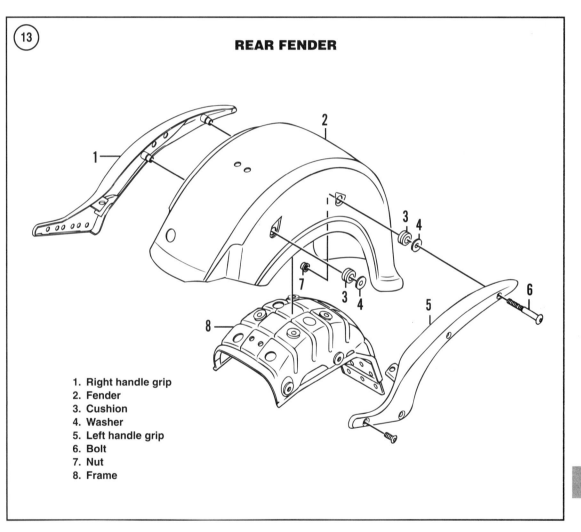

REAR FENDER

1. Right handle grip
2. Fender
3. Cushion
4. Washer
5. Left handle grip
6. Bolt
7. Nut
8. Frame

16

NOTE
The rear grip mounting bolt on each side is secured by a 12-mm nut behind the fender.

3. Remove the side handle grip mounting bolts (A, **Figure 12**) and remove the grip (B) on each side.

4. Remove the rear fender (**Figure 13**).

5. If necessary, separate the frame from the fender. (8, **Figure 10**).

6. Reverse the removal steps to install the rear fender. Note the following:

   a. Apply a small amount of threadlocking compound (ThreeBond 1303 or equivalent) to the threads of the grip mounting bolts.

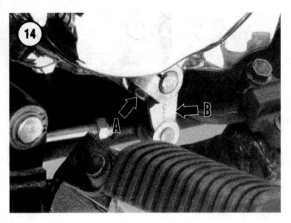

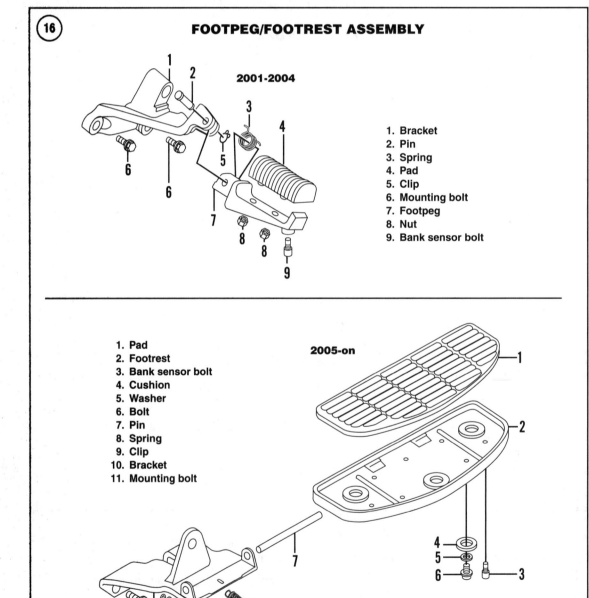

FOOTPEG/FOOTREST ASSEMBLY

2001-2004

1. Bracket
2. Pin
3. Spring
4. Pad
5. Clip
6. Mounting bolt
7. Footpeg
8. Nut
9. Bank sensor bolt

2005-on

1. Pad
2. Footrest
3. Bank sensor bolt
4. Cushion
5. Washer
6. Bolt
7. Pin
8. Spring
9. Clip
10. Bracket
11. Mounting bolt

b. Tighten the mounting bolts to 50 N•m (37 ft.-lb.).

LEFT FOOTPEG/FOOTREST

Removal/Installation

1. Remove the gearshift lever clamp bolt (A, **Figure 14**).
2. Pull the gearshift lever (B, **Figure 14**) off the shift shaft.
3. Remove the footpeg/footrest mounting bolts (**Figure 15**), then remove the assembly.
4. Disassemble the assembly as needed. Typical assemblies are shown in **Figure 16**.

5. Reverse the removal steps to install the footpeg/footrest assembly while noting the following:

   a. Align the split on the gearshift lever joint with the alignment mark on the gearshift lever and install the lever (B, **Figure 14**) onto the gearshift shaft.

   b. Tighten the clamping bolt securely.

   c. Tighten the mounting bolts (**Figure 15**) to 55 N•m (41 ft.-lb.).

   d. Adjust the gearshift pedal as described in Chapter Three.

RIGHT FOOTPEG/FOOTREST

Removal/Installation

1. Remove the rear brake pedal as described in Chapter Fifteen.

2. Remove the footpeg or footrest mounting bolts (**Figure 17**), then remove the assembly.

3. Disassemble the assembly as needed. The right footpeg or footrest assemblies are similar to the left-side units shown in **Figure 16**.

4. Reverse the removal steps to install the footpeg or footrest assembly. Tighten the mounting bolts (**Figure 17**) to 55 N•m (40 ft.-lb.).

Table 1 BODY AND FRAME TORQUE SPECIFICATIONS

	N•m	in.-lb.	ft.-lb.
Footpeg/footrest mounting bolts*	55	–	41
Rear fender side handle grip mounting bolts	50	–	37
*Apply threadlock (ThreeBond 1303 or equivalent)			

16

SUPPLEMENT

2009-ON MODEL SERVICE INFORMATION

This Supplement contains all procedures and specifications unique to the 2009-on models. If a specific procedure is not included in the Supplement, refer to that procedure in the appropriate chapter in the main body of this manual.

This Supplement is divided into sections that correspond to the chapters in the main body of this manual. **Tables 1-8** are located at the end of the appropriate sections.

CHAPTER TWO

TROUBLESHOOTING

ELECTRONIC DIAGNOSTIC SYSTEM

When troubleshooting the EFI system on 2009-on models, refer to the Malfunction Code Table (**Figure 1**), Fail-Safe Action Chart (**Figure 2**), and the Troubleshooting Chart (**Figure 3**) in this section of the Supplement.

Except for three new malfunction codes, troubleshooting problems with the ignition and fuel injection systems on 2009-on models is the same as that for earlier models. Refer to **Figures 4-6** in this section of the Supplement for malfunction codes unique to 2009-on models. Refer to *Electronic Diagnostic System* in Chapter Two of the main manual for troubleshooting procedures.

(1)

MALFUNCTION CODE TABLE

Malfunction Code	Component	Problem	Probable Cause
c00	–	No error	–
c12	Crankshaft position sensor	The ECM has not received a signal from the crankshaft position sensor within 3 seconds after receiving the start signal.	Faulty crankshaft position sensor, its wiring or connector.
c13 (front cyl.) c17 (rear cyl.)	Intake air pressure sensor	The sensor's voltage is outside the range of 0.1-4.8 volts.	Faulty intake air pressure sensor, its wiring or connector.
c14	Throttle position sensor	The sensor's voltage is outside the range of 0.1-4.8 volts.	Faulty throttle position sensor, its wiring or connector.
c15	Engine coolant temperature sensor	The sensor's voltage is outside the range of 0.1-4.6 volts.	Faulty engine coolant temperature sensor, its wiring or connector.
c21	Intake air temperature sensor	The sensor's voltage is outside the range of 0.1-4.6 volts.	Faulty intake air temperature sensor, its wiring or connector.
c23	Tip over sensor	The sensor's voltage is not within range of 0.2-4.6 volts in the 2 seconds immediately after the ignition switch has been turned on.	Faulty tip over sensor, its wiring or connector.
c24 (rear cyl.-main) c25 (front cyl.-main) c26 (rear cyl.-sub)* c27 (front cyl.-sub)*	Ignition system	The ECM does not receive a proper signal from an ignition coil.	Faulty ignition coil, its wiring or connector. Faulty power supply from the battery.

(continued)

17

① **MALFUNCTION CODE TABLE (continued)**

Malfunction Code	Related Item	Detected Failure	Probable Cause
c28	Secondary throttle valve actuator	Signal voltage from the ECM is not reaching the actuator, the ECM is not receiving a signal from the actuator, or load voltage is not reaching the actuator motor.	Faulty secondary throttle valve actuator, its wiring or connector.
c29	Secondary throttle position sensor	The sensor's voltage is outside the range of 0.1-4.8 volts.	Faulty secondary throttle position sensor, its wiring or connector.
c31	Gear position sensor	The gear position sensor's signal voltage is less than 0.6 volts for 3 or more seconds.	Faulty gear position sensor, its wiring or connector. Faulty shift cam.
c32 (rear cyl.) c33 (front cyl.)	Fuel injector	The ECM does not receive a proper signal from the fuel injector.	Faulty fuel injector, its wiring or connector. Faulty power supply to the injector.
c40	ISC valve	The circuit voltage of the drive motor is unusual.	ISC valve circuit is open or shorted to ground. The power source circuit has a break in it.
c41	Fuel pump relay	Voltage is not applied to the pump even though the fuel pump relay is energized or voltage is applied to the pump when the fuel pump relay is not energized.	Faulty fuel pump relay, wiring or connector. Faulty power source to the fuel pump relay or fuel injectors.
c42	Ignition switch	The ECM does not receive a signal from ignition switch.	Faulty ignition switch, its wiring or connector.
c44* c64*	Heated O_2 sensor	No oxygen sensor voltage is reaching the ECM. The heater does not operate.	Faulty wiring or connector. Battery voltage not supplied to the sensor.
c49	PAIR control valve	The PAIR control valve voltage is not reaching the ECM.	Faulty PAIR control valve, its wiring or connector.
c62**	EVAP purge control solenoid valve	EVAP purge control solenoid valve voltage is not reaching the ECM.	Faulty purge control solenoid valve, its wiring or connector.

*California, U.K., Europe and Australia models only.
**California models only.

② FAIL-SAFE ACTION

NOTE: The fail-safe circuit will not operate if the ECM does not receive an ignition signal from both cylinders or a fuel injector signal from both cylinders. If either condition occurs, the engine will not run.

NOTE: If the ECM does not receive complete ignition signals for one cylinder, fuel to that cylinder is cut off.

Failed Item	Fail-Safe Action	Operation Status
Crankshaft position sensor	The motorcycle stops.	Engine stops operating; cannot restart.
Intake air pressure sensor (front or rear)	Intake air pressure is set to 500 mmHg (19.69 in. Hg).	Engine continues operating; can restart.
Throttle position sensor	Throttle valve is set to 3/4 open position. Ignition timing defaults to a present value.	Engine continues operating; can restart.
Engine coolant temperature sensor	Engine coolant temperature is set to 80° C (176° F).	Engine continues operating; can restart.
Intake air temperature sensor	Intake air temperature is set to 40° C (104° F).	Engine continues operating; can restart.
Ignition signal (rear cyl.–main)	On U.S. and Canada models, fuel is cut to the rear cylinder.	On U.S. and Canada models, front cylinder continues operating; engine can restart. On California, U.K., Europe and Australia models, both cylinders continue operating; engine can restart.
Ignition signal (front cyl.–main)	On U.S. and Canada models, fuel is cut to the front cylinder.	On U.S. and Canada models, rear cylinder continues operating; can restart. On California, U.K., Europe and Australia models, both cylinders continue operating; can restart.
Ignition signal (rear cyl.–sub)*	–	The front cylinder continues operating; engine can restart.
Ignition signal (front cyl.–sub)*	–	The rear cylinder continue operating; engine can restart.
Fuel injector (rear cyl.)	–	Front cylinder continues operating; can restart.
Fuel injector (front cyl.)	–	Rear cylinder continues operating; can restart.
Secondary throttle valve actuator	Secondary throttle valve is set to the fully closed position. When the motor is disconnected or if it locks, power from the ECM is discontinued.	Engine continues operating; can restart.
Secondary throttle position sensor	Secondary throttle valve is set to the fully closed position.	Engine continues operating; can restart.
Gear position signal	Gear position signal set to fourth gear.	Engine continues operating; can restart.
Heated O_2 sensor*	Feedback compensation is inhibited. (Air/fuel ratio is set to normal.)	Engine continues operating; can restart.
PAIR control solenoid valve	ECM stops operating the PAIR control solenoid valve.	Engine continues operating; can restart.
EVAP purge control solenoid valve**	ECM stops operating the EVAP purge control solenoid valve.	Engine continues operating; can restart.

*California, U.K., Europe and Australia models only.
**California models only.

17

③ **TROUBLESHOOTING CHART**

Malfunction Code	Diagnostic Flow Chart
c00	No fault detected
c12	**Figure 18** (Chapter Two)
c13	**Figure 19** (Chapter Two)
c14	**Figure 20** (Chapter Two)
c15	**Figure 21** (Chapter Two)
c17	**Figure 22** (Chapter Two)
c21	**Figure 23** (Chapter Two)
c23	**Figure 24** (Chapter Two)
c24, c25, c26* or c27*	**Figure 25** (Chapter Two)
c28	**Figure 26** (Chapter Two)
c29	**Figure 27** (Chapter Two)
c31	**Figure 28** (Chapter Two)
c32 or c33	**Figure 29** (Chapter Two)
c40	**Figure 4** (this section of the Supplement)
c41	**Figure 30** (Chapter Two)
c42	**Figure 31** (Chapter Two)
c44 or c64	**Figure 5** (this section of the Supplement)
c49	**Figure 33** (Chapter Two)
c62**	**Figure 6** (this section of the Supplement)

*California, U.K., Europe and Australia models only.
**California models only.

④ **c40: ISC VALVE CIRCUIT MALFUNCTION**

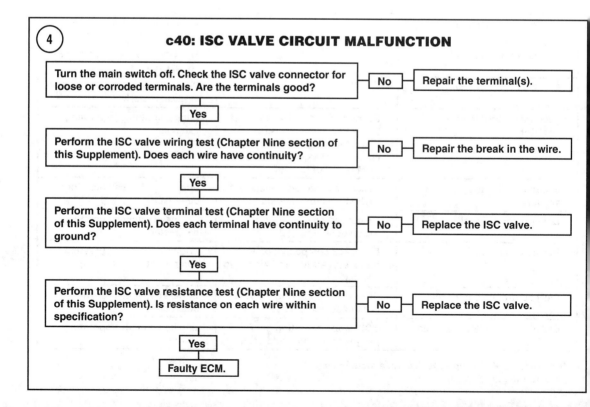

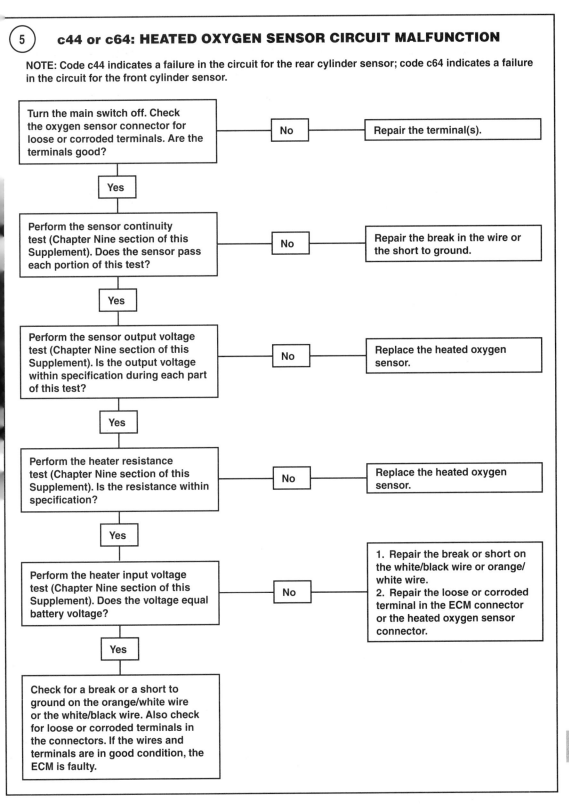

(5) **c44 or c64: HEATED OXYGEN SENSOR CIRCUIT MALFUNCTION**

NOTE: Code c44 indicates a failure in the circuit for the rear cylinder sensor; code c64 indicates a failure in the circuit for the front cylinder sensor.

Turn the main switch off. Check the oxygen sensor connector for loose or corroded terminals. Are the terminals good?

No → Repair the terminal(s).

Yes

Perform the sensor continuity test (Chapter Nine section of this Supplement). Does the sensor pass each portion of this test?

No → Repair the break in the wire or the short to ground.

Yes

Perform the sensor output voltage test (Chapter Nine section of this Supplement). Is the output voltage within specification during each part of this test?

No → Replace the heated oxygen sensor.

Yes

Perform the heater resistance test (Chapter Nine section of this Supplement). Is the resistance within specification?

No → Replace the heated oxygen sensor.

Yes

Perform the heater input voltage test (Chapter Nine section of this Supplement). Does the voltage equal battery voltage?

No → 1. Repair the break or short on the white/black wire or orange/white wire.
2. Repair the loose or corroded terminal in the ECM connector or the heated oxygen sensor connector.

Yes

Check for a break or a short to ground on the orange/white wire or the white/black wire. Also check for loose or corroded terminals in the connectors. If the wires and terminals are in good condition, the ECM is faulty.

17

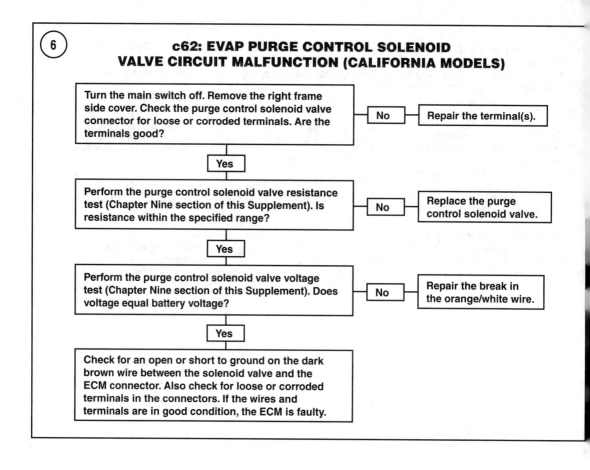

⑥

c62: EVAP PURGE CONTROL SOLENOID VALVE CIRCUIT MALFUNCTION (CALIFORNIA MODELS)

Turn the main switch off. Remove the right frame side cover. Check the purge control solenoid valve connector for loose or corroded terminals. Are the terminals good? → **No** → Repair the terminal(s).

Yes

Perform the purge control solenoid valve resistance test (Chapter Nine section of this Supplement). Is resistance within the specified range? → **No** → Replace the purge control solenoid valve.

Yes

Perform the purge control solenoid valve voltage test (Chapter Nine section of this Supplement). Does voltage equal battery voltage? → **No** → Repair the break in the orange/white wire.

Yes

Check for an open or short to ground on the dark brown wire between the solenoid valve and the ECM connector. Also check for loose or corroded terminals in the connectors. If the wires and terminals are in good condition, the ECM is faulty.

CHAPTER THREE

LUBRICATION, MAINTENANCE AND TUNE-UP

PERIODIC LUBRICATION

Engine Oil and Filter Change
(U.K., Europe and Australia Models)

The engine oil and filter change procedure is identical to the procedure for earlier models (Chapter Three) except for an engine plate that protects the bottom of the crankcase and different torque specifications.

1. Remove the engine plate from beneath the crankcase.

2. Change the engine oil and filter as described in Chapter Three.

3. Tighten the engine oil drain plug to 21 N•m (15.5 ft.-lb.).

4. Install the engine plate and tighten the fasteners securely.

Table 1 lists the recommended oil and filter change interval. This assumes that the motorcycle is operated in moderate climates and conditions. If it is operated in dusty conditions, the oil gets dirty more quickly and should be changed more frequently than recommended.

Use only high-quality detergent motor oil with an API classification of SF or SG. Use SAE 10W-40 weight oil in all models. Use a lighter viscosity oil in cool climates and a heavier viscosity oil in warm climates. Use the same brand of oil at each oil change.

PERIODIC MAINTENANCE

Air Filter Element

Remove and clean the air filter element at the interval specified in **Table 1** (this section of the

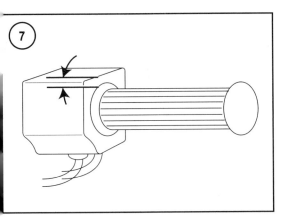

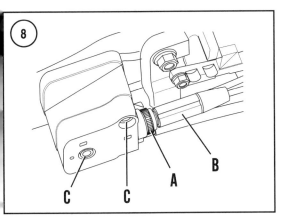

In time, throttle cable free play (**Figure 7**) increases due to cable stretch. This increase delays throttle response. Check the throttle cable free play at the interval specified in **Table 1** (this section of Supplement).

1. Securely support the motorcycle on a level surface.

2. Shift the transmission into neutral. Start the engine, and let it idle.

3. With the engine at idle speed, slowly twist the throttle. Note the amount of rotational movement of the throttle grip required to increase engine speed. This is the throttle cable free play.

4. If throttle cable free play is not within the range listed in **Table 2** (this section of Supplement), adjust the free play by performing the following:

    a. Shut off the engine.

    b. Loosen the locknut (A, **Figure 8**) on the throttle pull cable.

    c. Turn the adjuster (B, **Figure 8**) in or out until the free play is within specification.

    d. Hold the adjuster, and tighten the locknut securely.

5. Restart the engine, and check the adjustment. Repeat the procedure to readjust free play, if necessary.

Supplement). Replace the air filter element at the specified interval or if it is damaged or deteriorated.

Refer to *Air Box Removal/Inspection/Installation* in the Chapter Nine section of this Supplement.

Throttle Cable

Inspection

Inspecting the throttle cable for 2009-on models is identical to the procedure for earlier models (Chapter Three) except for the specified inspection intervals. Check the throttle cable at the interval specified in **Table 1** (this section) and adjust the free play, if necessary.

Adjustment

> *WARNING*
> *With the engine idling, move the handlebar from side to side. If the idle speed increases during this movement, check the cable adjustment and throttle cable routing through the frame. Correct any problems immediately. Do not ride the motorcycle in this unsafe condition.*

Valve Clearance
(California, U.K., Europe and Australia Models)

The valves must be adjusted when the engine is cold (below 35° C [95° F]) and when the piston for a particular cylinder is at top dead center on the compression stroke.

Checking/adjusting the valve clearance for these models is the same as the procedure in the main manual. Perform this procedure to obtain access to the rocker covers. Then refer to *Valve Clearance* in Chapter Three to check and adjust the valve clearance.

> *NOTE*
> *While it is possible to adjust the valves with the throttle body in place, the procedure is much simpler if the throttle body is removed; especially when servicing the intake valves.*

1. Remove the fuel tank, air box and throttle body as described in the Chapter Nine section of this Supplement.

2. Remove the frame head side cover from the right side (Chapter Sixteen).

3. Remove the cylinder head cover cap from the spark plug side of each cylinder by performing the following:

17

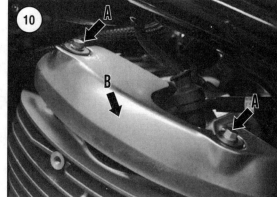

a. Working on the front cylinder, remove the upper air box bracket (**Figure 9**) so the cap will not be scratched.

b. Remove each cap bolt (A, **Figure 10**) and washer.

c. Lift the cap (B, **Figure 10**) from the cylinder head. Watch for the collar (A, **Figure 11**) and washer (B) that sit beneath each grommet (C) in the cap.

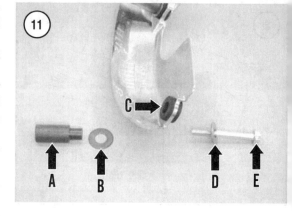

d. Repeat this process to remove the rear cylinder cap.

4. Remove the spark plugs (Chapter Three) from each cylinder so the engine can be easily turned.

5. Remove the PAIR pipe bolts (A, **Figure 12**) from the rear cylinder, and swing the PAIR pipe (B) out of the way. Watch for the gasket beneath the pipe fitting.

6. Refer to *Valve Clearance* in Chapter Three, and perform the inspection/adjustment procedure beginning at Step 5.

7. Once the valves have been checked or adjusted, reassemble the motorcycle by reversing the removal steps.

8. Install the cylinder head cover caps by as follows:

a. Make sure the grommet (C, **Figure 11**) is in place in each bolt hole.

b. Install a washer (B, **Figure 11**) onto a collar (A), and slip the shouldered end of the collar into the grommet (C).

c. Install a washer (D, **Figure 11**) onto each cap bolt (E). Install the bolts and tighten to 25 N•m (18 ft.-lb.).

d. Install the PAIR pipe bolts (A, **Figure 12**) and tighten securely.

Compression Test
(California, U.K., Europe and Australia Models)

The compression test for these models is performed the same as the test described in the main manual. Prepare these models for the test, as follows,

and then turn to *Compression Test* in Chapter Three to complete this procedure.

1. Before starting the compression test, verify the following items are within specification:

a. The cylinder head bolts are tightened properly. Refer to Chapter Four for the correct procedure and the specified torque.

b. The valves are properly adjusted.

c. The battery is fully charged to ensure proper cranking speed.

2. Warm the engine to normal operating temperature, and turn the engine off.

WARNING
Before a compression test can be performed, the fuel system must be disabled. Otherwise, fuel will enter the cylinders when the engine is turned over during the compression test, flooding the cylinders and creating explosive fuel vapors.

3. Raise and support the fuel tank. Disable the fuel system by disconnecting the 4-pin fuel pump connector (A, **Figure 13**).

4. Remove the cylinder head cover cap from the spark plug side of each cylinder as described in Step 3 of *Valve Clearance* in this section.

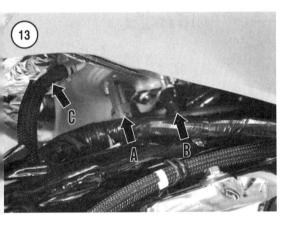

5. Remove and ground the outboard spark plug (A, **Figure 14**) from each cylinder. Disconnect the spark plug cap (B, **Figure 14**) from the remaining plug in each cylinder.

6. Refer to *Compression Test* in Chapter Three, and perform the test beginning with Step 4.

7. Once the test is completed, reassemble the motorcycle by reversing the removal steps.

8. Install the cylinder head cover caps by performing Step 8 of *Valve Clearance* in this section.

Spark Plugs

Removal/installation
(California, U.K., Europe and Australia models)

1. Remove the fuel tank and air box as described in the Chapter Nine section of this Supplement.

2. Remove the cylinder head cover cap from the spark plug side of each cylinder as described in Step 3 of *Valve Clearance* in this section.

3. Use compressed air to blow away loose dirt from each spark plug.

4. Carefully pull the spark plug cap (A, **Figure 14**) up and off the plug. If cap is stuck to the plug, twist it slightly to break it loose.

5. Label the spark plug cap (inboard or outboard and front or rear) so it can be reinstalled onto the correct spark plug.

6. Install a spark plug socket with a rubber insert onto a spark plug. Make sure the socket is correctly seated on the plug, and remove the spark plug. Repeat for the second spark plug (B, **Figure 14**) in the cylinder. Label each spark plug by cylinder (front or rear) and by location in the cylinder (inboard or outboard port). If the spark plug will be reused, it must be reinstalled into the original location.

7. Inspect each spark plug carefully. Refer to *Spark Plug Reading* in Chapter Three.

8. If the original plugs will be reused, make sure each plug is installed in the original location (inboard or outboard), and on the original cylinder (front or rear). Install the spark plugs by performing the following:

    a. Set the spark plug gap as described in *Spark Plug Gap* in Chapter Three.

    b. Apply a light coat of antiseize compound onto the threads of the spark plug. Do not use engine oil on the plug threads.

> *CAUTION*
> *The cylinder head is aluminum. The spark plug hole threads can be easily damaged by cross-threading the spark plug.*

    c. The spark plugs are recessed into the cylinder head and cannot be started by hand. Use the rubber insert socket or a length of rubber hose to turn the plug by hand until it seats. Very little effort is required. If force is needed, the plug is cross-threaded. Unscrew it and try again. Once the plug had been turned several revolutions, remove the hose.

    d. Hand-tighten the plug until it is seated, and then tighten the spark plug to 11 N•m (97 in.-lb.). Do not overtighten the spark plug.

    e. Install the plug cap onto the correct spark plug. Press the cap into the plug, rotate the assembly

17

slightly in both direction and make sure it is securely attached to the spark plug. If the cap does not completely contact the plug, the engine may develop an ignition misfire.

9. Install the cylinder head cover caps by performing Step 8 of *Valve Clearance* in this section.

Fuel System Adjustment

Throttle valve synchronization test

Throttle valve synchronization ensures that each cylinder receives the same air/fuel mixture by synchronizing the vacuum in each throttle intake port. Throttle valve synchronization can be tested with a vacuum synchronizer.

If the test reveals that the throttle valves must be synchronized, take the motorcycle to a dealership. The Suzuki Diagnostic System (SDS) tool (part No. 09904-41010) is required to adjust throttle valve synchronization.

Check the throttle valve synchronization as follows:
1. Warm up the engine. It must be at operating temperature.
2. Connect the synchronizer to the throttle body vacuum fittings by performing the following:

NOTE
The throttle body has been removed for photographic clarity.

a. Disconnect an IAP sensor vacuum hose (A, **Figure 15**) from the fitting on the throttle body. Connect a T-fitting to the IAP sensor vacuum fitting on the throttle body.
b. Connect the IAP sensor to one arm of the T-fitting, and connect the vacuum synchronizer to the other arm (**Figure 16**).

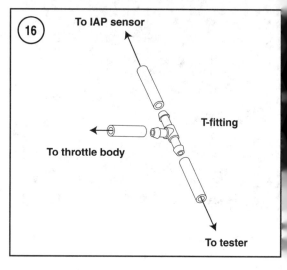

3. Repeat the process to connect the vacuum synchronizer to the remaining IAP sensor hose and vacuum fitting on the throttle body.
4. Start the engine and let it idle. Check the vacuum levels. The vacuum at each cylinder should be the same.
5. If it is not, take the motorcycle to a dealership to have the synchronization adjusted.

Table 1 MAINTENANCE SCHEDULE

Every 1000 km (600 miles) or 2 months
  Check and tighten all exhaust system fasteners
  Check the valve clearance; adjust if necessary*
  Change the engine oil and replace the oil filter
  Check the throttle cable free play; adjust if necessary*
  On California models, check the throttle valve synchronization; adjust if necessary*
  Change the final drive oil
  Check the front brake pads for wear; replace if necessary*
  Check the front brake disc thickness; replace if necessary*
  Check the front brake disc for rust or corrosion; clean if necessary*
  Check the rear brake lining wear indicator
  Check the rear brake pedal free play and height; adjust if necessary*
  Check the steering play; adjust if necessary*
  Check and tighten all chassis fasteners
                                    (continued)

Table 1 MAINTENANCE SCHEDULE (continued)

Every 6000 km (4000 miles) or 12 months
  Check the air filter element for contamination; clean or replace if necessary
  Check the spark plugs; replace if necessary
  Check all fuel system hoses for leaks; repair or replace if necessary
  Change the engine oil
  Check the throttle cable free play; adjust if necessary
  Check all radiator and coolant hoses for leaks; replace if necessary
  Check the clutch lever free play; adjust if necessary
  Check the front brake pads for wear; replace if necessary
  Check the front brake disc thickness; replace if necessary
  Check the front brake disc for rust or corrosion; clean if necessary
  Check the rear brake lining wear indicator
  Check the rear brake pedal free play and height; adjust if necessary*
  Check the front brake system for fluid leaks; replace if necessary
  Check the fluid level in the front brake reservoir; add fluid if necessary
  Check the tire and wheel condition
  Check and tighten all chassis fasteners
Every 12,000 km (7500 miles) or 24 months
  Perform all of the procedures listed in the 6000 km (4000 mile) or 12 month interval, and the following:
  Check and tighten all exhaust system fasteners*
  Check the valve clearance; adjust if necessary*
  Replace the spark plugs
  On California models, check the throttle valve synchronization; adjust if necessary*
  On California models, check the EVAP system
  Check the PAIR (air supply) system
  Check the final gear oil. Adjust the fluid level or change the oil if necessary*
  Check the steering play; adjust if necessary*
  Check the operation of the front forks and check for leaks
  Check the operation of the rear suspension*
Every 18,000 km (11,000 miles) or 36 months
  Perform all of the procedures in the 6000 km (4000 mile) or 12 month interval, and the following:
  Replace the air filter element
  Change the engine oil and replace the oil filter
Every 24,000 km (14,500 miles) or 48 months
  Perform all of the procedures listed in the 12,000 km (7500 mile) or 24 month interval, and the following:
  Replace the engine coolant
  Replace the brake fluid
Every 4 years
  Replace the EVAP hoses
  Replace the front brake hose

*Procedure is unique to 2009-on models.

Table 2 MAINTENANCE AND TUNE-UP SPECIFICATIONS

Item	Specification
Spark plug	
California, U.K., Europe and Australia models	
Standard plug	NGK DR7EA, ND X22ESR-U
Cold plug	NGK DR8EA, ND X24ESR-U
Spark plug gap	
California, U.K., Europe and Australia models	0.6-0.7 mm (0.024-0.028 in.)
Throttle cable free play	2.0-4.0 mm (0.08-0.16 in.)

Table 3 MAINTENANCE AND TUNE-UP TORQUE SPECIFICATIONS

Item	N•m	in.-lb.	ft.-lb.
Cylinder head cover cap bolt	25	–	18
Engine oil drain plug (U.K., Europe and Australia models)	21	–	15.5
Spark plug (California, U.K., Europe and Australia models)	11	97	–

17

CHAPTER NINE

FUEL, EMISSION CONTROL AND EXHAUST SYSTEMS

FUEL TANK

Removal/Installation

> *WARNING*
> *Before removing the fuel tank, turn the ignition switch off, and let the system release the fuel pressure internally.*

> *WARNING*
> *Some fuel may spill from the fuel hose when performing this procedure. Since gasoline is extremely flammable and explosive, perform this procedure away from all sparks and open flames - including appliance pilot lights. Do not allow smoking in the work area. Always work in a well-ventilated area, and immediately wipe up any spills. Refer to* ***Safety*** *in Chapter One.*

1. Remove the seats as described in Chapter Sixteen.
2. Disconnect the negative battery cable (Chapter Three).
3. Remove the speedometer as described in the Chapter Ten section of this Supplement.
4. Remove the fuel tank bolt (**Figure 17**). Lift and support the back of the tank.
5. Disconnect the 4-pin connector (A, **Figure 13**) from the fuel pump and disconnect the fuel line (B) from the fuel pump input fitting. On California models, disconnect the breather hose (C, **Figure 13**) from the fitting.
6. Pull the tank rearward until it disengages from the front mounting cushions, and lift the tank from the motorcycle.
7. Plug the fuel pump input fitting and the breather fitting (California models) so debris cannot enter the tank.
8. Inspect the fuel tank as described in Chapter Nine.
9. Installation is the reverse of removal. Check for fuel leaks after installation, and tighten the fuel tank bolt (**Figure 17**) securely.

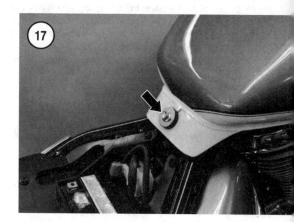

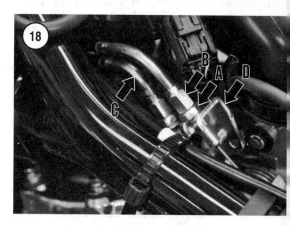

THROTTLE CABLE

Removal

> *WARNING*
> *An improperly adjusted or incorrectly routed throttle cable can cause the throttle to hang open. This could cause a crash. Do not ride the motorcycle until throttle cable operation is correct.*

> *NOTE*
> *There are two throttle cables: the pull cable (to accelerate) and the return cable (to decelerate). Identify and label each cable to ensure correct reinstallation.*

1. Remove the fuel tank as described in this section of the Supplement.

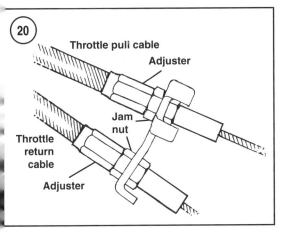

9. Note how the cable is routed through the frame, and then remove it.

Installation

1. Lubricate the new cable as described in Chapter Three. Route the new cable along the same path noted during removal.
2. Apple grease to the throttle-grip end of each cable. Connect the return cable end and pull cable end to the throttle grip pulley. Make sure each cable is properly routed in the pulley groove.
3. Align the switch locating pin with the hole in the handlebar. Then, fit the switch halves onto the handlebar, install the switch screws (C, **Figure 8**) and tighten the screws securely.
4. Apply grease to the throttle body end of the pull cable, and connect the pull cable end (A, **Figure 19**) to the throttle wheel. Set the pull cable into the throttle cable bracket (D, **Figure 18**) so a nut sits on each side of the bracket.
5. Repeat this process to install the return cable (C, **Figure 18**).
6. Turn each cable adjuster (B, **Figure 18**) in toward the throttle cable bracket (D) until the adjuster rests against the jam nut (**Figure 20**). Tighten each jam nut (A, **Figure 18**).
7. Operate the throttle and make sure the throttle linkage is operating correctly with no binding. If operation is incorrect or if binding is noticed, make sure the cables are correctly attached and that there are no tight bends in either cable.
8. Adjust the throttle pull cable as described in the Chapter Three section of this Supplement.

2. At the throttle grip, loosen the pull cable locknut (A, **Figure 8**). Turn the adjuster (B, **Figure 8**) all the way into the switch housing to create maximum slack in the pull cable.
3. Remove the switch screws (C, **Figure 8**), and separate the switch assembly halves.
4. Disconnect the ends of the pull cable and return cable from the throttle grip pulley.
5. At the throttle wheel, loosen the jam nut (A, **Figure 18**) for the pull cable. If necessary, turn the pull cable adjuster (B, **Figure 18**) in to create some slack.
6. Repeat the process to create slack for the return cable (C, **Figure 18**).

AIR BOX

Removal/Inspection/Installation

Refer to **Figure 21**.
1. Remove the air box mounting screws (**Figure 22**).
2. Loosen the clamp securing the outlet tube to the outlet port (A, **Figure 23**) on the back of the air box.
3. Pull the air box outward, and release the tang from the grommet on the mounting bracket. Separate the outlet port from the outlet tube.
4. Release the clamp, and disconnect the PAIR hose (A, **Figure 24**) from the fitting on the back of the air box.
5. Disconnect the electrical connector (B, **Figure 24**) from the intake air temperature (IAT) sensor, and remove the air box.

CAUTION
Do not allow the throttle valve in the throttle body to snap shut when disconnecting the cables. Doing so may damage the throttle valve or throttle body.

7. Disconnect the pull cable end (A, **Figure 19**) from the throttle wheel, and then disconnect the return cable end (B). Release each throttle cable from the bracket (D, **Figure 18**) on the throttle body.
8. Release the throttle cable from any clips or cable ties that secure it to the frame.

17

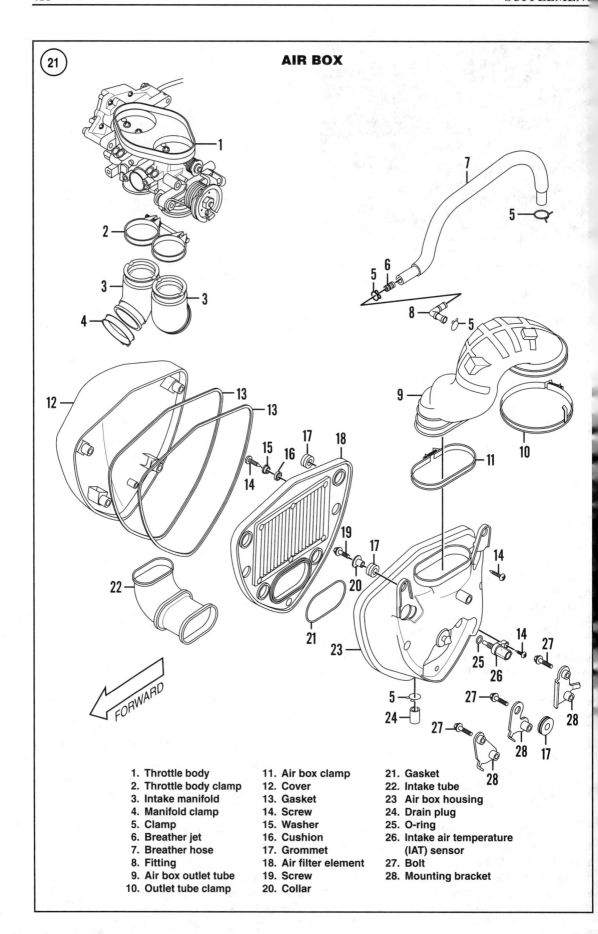

AIR BOX

FORWARD

1. Throttle body
2. Throttle body clamp
3. Intake manifold
4. Manifold clamp
5. Clamp
6. Breather jet
7. Breather hose
8. Fitting
9. Air box outlet tube
10. Outlet tube clamp
11. Air box clamp
12. Cover
13. Gasket
14. Screw
15. Washer
16. Cushion
17. Grommet
18. Air filter element
19. Screw
20. Collar
21. Gasket
22. Intake tube
23. Air box housing
24. Drain plug
25. O-ring
26. Intake air temperature (IAT) sensor
27. Bolt
28. Mounting bracket

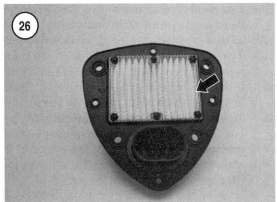

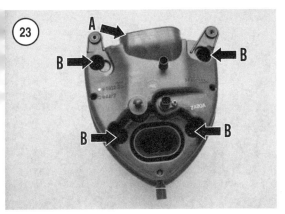

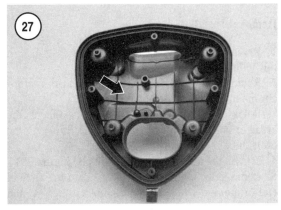

6. Remove the air box cover screws (B, **Figure 23**), and remove the cover from the air box. Watch for the cover gasket.

7. Remove the air filter screws (A, **Figure 25**) and their washers. Lift the filter element (B, **Figure 25**) from the housing.

8. Apply low-pressure compressed air to the cover side (**Figure 26**) of the air filter element. Remove all dirt and dust.

9. If the air filter is extremely dirty, or if there are any holes in the element, wipe out the interior of the air box housing (**Figure 27**) with a shop rag dampened in cleaning solvent. Remove any debris that may have passed through a broken element. Replace the filter element if damaged.

10. Inspect the air box for cracks or other damage that could admit unfiltered air. If any damage is noted, replace the air box.

11. Make sure the intake duct is in good condition.

12. Remove the drain plug (C, **Figure 25**), and clean out all residue from the plug and the air box. Reinstall the drain plug.

13. Make sure the three air-box mounting brackets (**Figure 9**, typical) are securely attached to the cylinders.

14. Install the air box by reversing the removal steps. Note the following:

17

a. Completely loosen the air box clamp (on the outlet tube) so mating the outlet port (A, **Figure 23**) to the outlet tube will not be difficult.

b. The PAIR hose (A, **Figure 24**) must be securely connected to the fitting to prevent air leaks.

c. Make sure the cover gasket is completely seated in the air-filter-element channel (D, **Figure 25**).

d. Tighten the air filer screws (A, **Figure 25**), air box cover screws (B, **Figure 23**) and air box mounting screws (**Figure 22**) securely.

e. Make sure the IAT sensor electrical connector (B, **Figure 24**) is securely fastened.

THROTTLE BODY

Removal/Installation

1. Remove the fuel tank and air box as described in this section of the Supplement.

2. Remove each IAP sensor (**Figure 28**) from it rubber mount on the air box outlet tube.

3. Release the hose clamp, and disconnect the breather hose (A, **Figure 29**) from the fitting on the outlet tube.

4. Loosen the outlet tube clamp bolt (B, **Figure 29**).

5. Remove the clamp (**Figure 30**) from the air box end of the outlet tube so the clamp will not scratch the motorcycle.

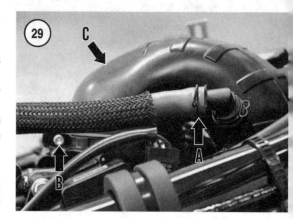

6. Lift the outlet tube (C, **Figure 29**) from the throttle body and remove it. Note how the outlet tube is routed through the motorcycle.

7. Disconnect the green, 3-pin TP sensor connector (A **Figure 31**), the white, 4-pin STV actuator connector (B) and the black, 3-pin STP sensor connector (C).

8. Disconnect each 2-pin connector from the front (**Figure 32**) and rear fuel injectors (**Figure 33**).

9. Disconnect the connector (**Figure 34**) from the ISC valve. The release tab is on the front side of the connector.

> *CAUTION*
> *Do not let the throttle valves in the throttle body slam shut when disccon-necting the cables. Doing so may damage a throttle valve or throttle body*

10. Disconnect the cables from the throttle wheel by performing Steps 5-7 of *Throttle Cable Removal* in this section of the Supplement.

11. Loosen the screw (C, **Figure 19**) securing the throttle body clamp. Then, lift the throttle body from the manifold.

12. Disconnect each IAP sensor vacuum hose (A, **Figure 15**) from the fitting on the throttle body. On California models, disconnect the EVAP hoses (B, **Figure 15**) from their fittings.

13. Remove the throttle body.

14. Install the throttle body by reversing the removal procedure. Note the following:

    a. Connect the throttle cables to the throttle wheel by performing Steps 4-8 in *Throttle Cable Installation* in this section of the Supplement.

    b. Note that the throttle body clamp mechanism consists of a long screw with a spacer between the clamps. Tighten the screw (C, **Figure 19**) securely.

    c. Tighten the outlet tube clamp bolt securely.

    d. Make sure the electrical connectors are all securely fastened.

Disassembly

> *WARNING*
> *Some fuel may spill from the throttle body during disassembly. Because gasoline is extremely flammable and explosive, perform this procedure away from sparks and all open flames – including appliance pilot lights. Do not allow any smoking within the work area. Always work in a well-ventilated area, and immediately wipe up any spills.*

Refer to **Figure 35**.

1. If necessary, remove the IAP sensor vacuum hoses (A, **Figure 36**) from their fittings. On California models, disconnect the EVAP hoses (B, **Figure 36**) from their fittings.

2. Remove the mounting screw (C, **Figure 36**), and then remove the straight plug retainer (D).

> *WARNING*
> *The straight plug (A, **Figure 37**) and the transfer pipe (B) must be pulled straight out of the transfer bore during removal so the bore surface is not scratched. If the bore is scratched, the O-rings may not seal and fuel may leak during operation.*

3. Grasp the straight plug (**Figure 38**), and pull it straight out of transfer bore in the fuel delivery pipe. Discard the O-ring.

4. Install a 5–0.8 mm bolt (**Figure 39**) into the threads in the transfer pipe within the transfer bore. Make sure the bolt is long enough so it can be turned at least 10 turns into the pipe.

5. Pull the bolt straight out of the bore, and remove the transfer pipe (**Figure 40**). Discard the O-rings.

6. Loosen and remove the fuel rail screws (A, **Figure 41**), and then remove the rear-cylinder fuel rail (B) along with the rear fuel injector. Watch for the lower O-ring (A, **Figure 42**) on the fuel injector.

7. Repeat this process to remove the front-cylinder fuel rail and injector.

8. Pull each fuel injector from the bore (A, **Figure 43**) of each fuel rail (B). Pull the injector straight out so the bore will not be scratched. Watch for upper O-ring (B, **Figure 42**) on each fuel injector.

9. If necessary, remove the throttle position sensor (A, **Figure 44**) and the secondary throttle position sensor (B) as described in Chapter Nine.

> *CAUTION*
> *Do not remove the secondary throttle valve actuator (C, **Figure 44**) from the throttle body.*

17

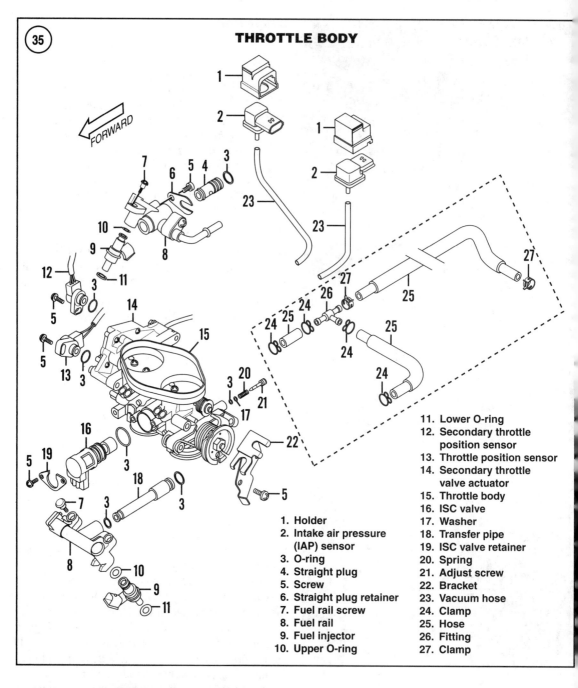

THROTTLE BODY

FORWARD

1. Holder
2. Intake air pressure (IAP) sensor
3. O-ring
4. Straight plug
5. Screw
6. Straight plug retainer
7. Fuel rail screw
8. Fuel rail
9. Fuel injector
10. Upper O-ring
11. Lower O-ring
12. Secondary throttle position sensor
13. Throttle position sensor
14. Secondary throttle valve actuator
15. Throttle body
16. ISC valve
17. Washer
18. Transfer pipe
19. ISC valve retainer
20. Spring
21. Adjust screw
22. Bracket
23. Vacuum hose
24. Clamp
25. Hose
26. Fitting
27. Clamp

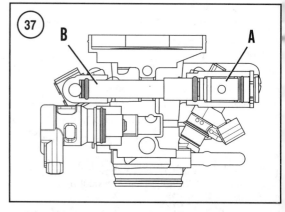

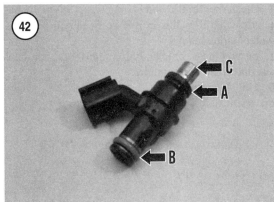

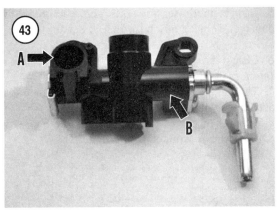

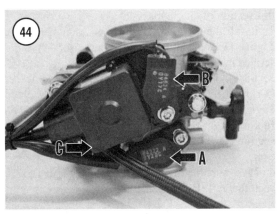

10. Do not remove the ISC valve (A, **Figure 45**) unless the Suzuki Diagnostic System (SDS) tool (part No. 09904-41010) is available. The ISC valve can not be initialized without this tool. Refer to *ISC Valve* in this section of the Supplement.

17

Inspection

> *WARNING*
> *Do not use wires to clean passages in*
> *the throttle body.*

1. Clean the throttle body using a spray-type carburetor cleaner. Dry the throttle body and all passages with compressed air.

2. Inspect the throttle body for cracks or other damage that could admit unfiltered air.

3. Manually operate the throttle valves and the secondary throttle valves. They must move smoothly.

CAUTION
*The adjusting screw (E, **Figure 36**) has been preset at the factory. Do not remove or turn the screw.*

4. Check the operation of the throttle wheel. It must move smoothly.

5. Inspect the hoses for cracks or other signs of damage. Replace any hose that is becoming brittle.

6. Check the fuel injectors as described in *Fuel Injectors* in this section of the Supplement.

7. Thoroughly clean the straight plug (A, **Figure 46**) and transfer pipe (B). Clean the inside and outside of the transfer pipe.

8. Replace any worn or damaged part(s).

Assembly

Refer to **Figure 35**.

1. If removed, install the ISC valve as described in this section of the Supplement.

2. Install the secondary throttle position sensor (B, **Figure 44**) and the throttle position sensor (A) as described in Chapter Nine.

3. Install new upper (B, **Figure 42**) and lower O-rings (A) onto the fuel injectors. Apply clean engine oil to each O-ring, and seat it in place on a fuel injector. The upper O-ring has a round cross-section; the lower O-ring has a square cross-section.

4. Make sure the fuel injector bore (A, **Figure 43**) in each fuel rail (B) is clean.

NOTE
Do not turn the fuel injector during installation.

5. Press the rear-cylinder fuel injector (A, **Figure 47**) into the bore (B) in the throttle body. Make sure the injector is completely seated in the bore.

6. Align the injector bore of the rear-cylinder fuel rail with the fuel injector, and press the fuel rail onto the injector. Make sure the fuel injector sits between the tangs (**Figure 48**) on the fuel rail.

7. Install each fuel rail screw (A, **Figure 41**), and tighten the screws to 3.5 N•m (31 in.-lb.).

8. Repeat this process to install the front-cylinder fuel injector and fuel rail.

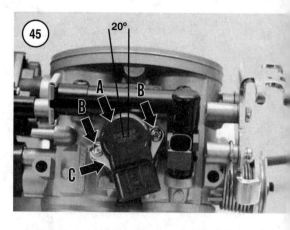

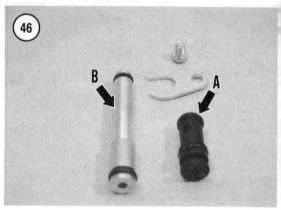

9. Install new O-rings onto the straight plug (A, **Figure 46**) and transfer pipe (B).

10. Install the transfer pipe (**Figure 40**) into the bore in the rear fuel rail. Make sure the transfer pipe (B, **Figure 37**) passes through the bore and bottoms in the port of the front fuel rail.

11. Press the straight plug (**Figure 49**) into the bore until the plug bottoms (**Figure 38**).

12. Slide the retainer (D, **Figure 36**) into the slot of the straight plug. Install and tighten the straight plug retainer screw (C, **Figure 36**) to 5 N•m (44 in.-lb.).

13. Connect the fuel hose to the fitting on the rear fuel rail.

FUEL INJECTORS

Removal/Installation

1. Remove the throttle body as described in this section of the Supplement.

2. Remove the fuel injectors by performing Steps 1-8 of *Throttle Body Disassembly* (this section of the Supplement).

3. Install the fuel injectors by performing Steps 3-12 of *Throttle Body Assembly* (this section of the Supplement).

1. Remove the throttle body as described in this section of the Supplement.

2. Remove the screws (B, **Figure 45**) and lower the ISC retainer (C) from the throttle body.

3. Pull the ISC valve (A, **Figure 45**) straight out from the bore, and then discard the O-rings. Exercise caution during removal so the bore inner surface is not scratched.

4. Once removed, have a dealership inspect the ISC valve.

Inspection

1. Visually inspect the fuel injectors for damage. Inspect the injector nozzle (C, **Figure 42**) for carbon buildup or damage.

2. Check for corroded or damaged electrical terminals in the fuel injectors and in the harness connectors.

3. Make sure the fuel injector bores (A, **Figure 43**) in the fuel rails (B) and in the throttle body (B, **Figure 47**) are clean.

ISC VALVE

Removal/Inspection

NOTE
*Do not remove the ISC valve (A, **Figure 45**) unless the Suzuki Diagnostic System (SDS) tool (part No. 09904-41010) is available. The ISC valve preset program and diagnostic trouble codes must be cleared whenever the ISC valve is removed, and the new ISC valve must be initialized upon installation. The SDS tool is needed to perform these procedures and to inspect the ISC valve.*

Installation

1. Apply oil to a new O-ring, and seat it onto the ISC valve.

2. Press the ISC valve straight into the bore in the throttle body. Position the valve so it is 20° off vertical as shown in **Figure 45**.

3. Fit the ISC retainer (C, **Figure 45**) in place, and install the two retainer screws (B). Tighten the ISC valve retainer screws to 2.1 N•m (18.5 in.-lb.).

4. If the SDS tool is not available, take the motorcycle to a dealership for ISC valve initialization and setup.

Wiring Test

1. Turn the ignition switch off.

2. Remove the fuel tank as described in this section of the Supplement.

3. Disconnect the connector (**Figure 34**) from ISC valve.

4. Disconnect the connector from the ECM.

5. Check the continuity of each wire between the ISC valve connector and the ECM connector. The blue wire connects to ECM terminal 47, the yellow wire to ECM terminal 40, green/white to ECM terminal 49, and brown to ECM terminal 38. Refer to **Figure 50** for ECM terminal locations.

6. Each wire should have continuity.

17

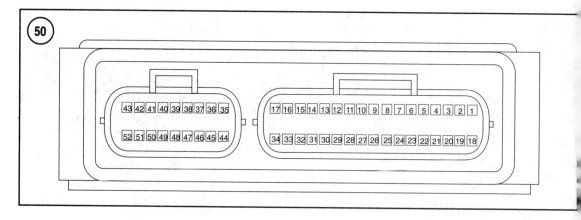

Terminal Test

1. Remove the throttle body as described in this section of the Supplement.
2. Check the continuity between each terminal in the ISC valve (A, **Figure 51**) and ground on the throttle body (B).
3. Each terminal should have continuity to ground.

Resistance Test

1. Remove the throttle body as described in this section of the Supplement.
2. Measure the resistance between the blue and yellow terminals in the ISC valve.
3. Measure the resistance between the green/white and brown terminals in the ISC valve.
4. Each resistance should equal the value listed in **Table 4**.

EVAPORATIVE EMISSION CONTROL SYSTEM (2009-ON CALIFORNIA MODELS)

Purge Control Solenoid Valve

Removal/installation

Refer to **Figure 52**.
1. Remove the right frame side cover as described in Chapter Sixteen.
2. Disconnect the electrical connector (A, **Figure 53**) from purge control solenoid valve (B).

> *CAUTION*
> *Hoses must be reinstalled on the correct fittings. Label each hose and its fitting on the purge control solenoid valve.*

3. Remove each hose (A, **Figure 54**) from the fitting on the purge control solenoid valve. Label each hose and fitting.
4. Remove the bracket bolt (B, **Figure 54**), and rotate the EVAP valve bracket outward.

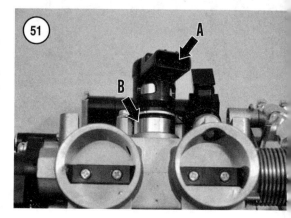

5. Remove the nut (A, **Figure 55**) from behind the bracket. Then, remove the purge control solenoid valve (B, **Figure 55**) from the bracket.
6. Install the purge control solenoid valve by reversing the removal steps.
   a. Connect each hose to the correct fitting on the purge control solenoid valve.
   b. Secure each hose in place with the clamp.
   c. Tighten the bracket bolt and the nut behind the bracket securely.

Inspection

Inspect the purge control solenoid valve by performing the following:
1. Blow through into the inlet port (A, **Figure 56**), and check for air coming out of the outlet port (B). Air should not flow from the outlet port during this portion of the test.
2. Check the air flow in the opposite direction by blowing into the outlet port. Air should not flow from the inlet port during this portion of the test. Replace the purge control solenoid valve if it fails either portion of this test.
3. Charge the purge control solenoid valve by connecting a 12 V battery to the electrical terminals (C, **Figure 56**) on the solenoid valve.

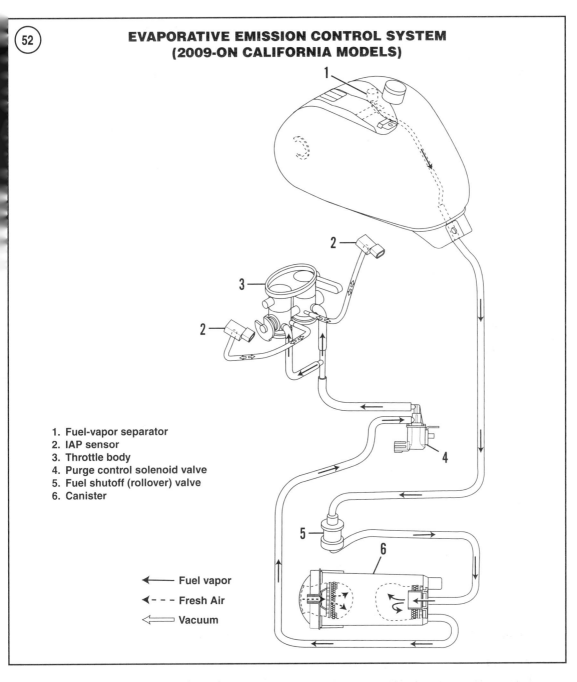

**EVAPORATIVE EMISSION CONTROL SYSTEM
(2009-ON CALIFORNIA MODELS)**

1. Fuel-vapor separator
2. IAP sensor
3. Throttle body
4. Purge control solenoid valve
5. Fuel shutoff (rollover) valve
6. Canister

← Fuel vapor
◀ - - - Fresh Air
⇐ Vacuum

17

a. Blow into the inlet port (A, **Figure 56**). Air should flow from the outlet port (B, **Figure 56**) when the solenoid is charged.

b. Replace the purge control solenoid valve if it fails this portion of the test.

4. Perform the purge control solenoid valve resistance test (this section of the Supplement). Replace the purge control solenoid valve if resistance does not equal the value listed in **Table 4**.

Resistance test

1. Remove the right frame side cover as described in Chapter Sixteen.

2. Disconnect the electrical connector (A, **Figure 53**) from purge control solenoid valve (B).

3. Check the resistance of the purge control solenoid valve by connecting an ohmmeter across the electrical terminals in the solenoid valve connector (C, **Figure 54**). The resistance should equal the value listed in **Table 4**.

Voltage test

1. Remove the right frame side cover as described in Chapter Sixteen.

2. Disconnect the electrical connector (A, **Figure 53**) from purge control solenoid valve (B).

3. Connect the positive test lead of a multimeter to the orange/white terminal in the purge control solenoid valve connector (C, **Figure 54**). Connect the negative test lead to a good ground.

4. Turn the ignition switch on, and measure the voltage. It should equal battery voltage.

Fuel Shutoff Valve

Removal/installation

The fuel shutoff valve mounts to the EVAP valve bracket, beside the purge control solenoid valve.

1. Remove the EVAP valve bracket as described in *Purge Control Solenoid Valve Removal* (this section of the Supplement).

2. Disconnect the hoses from the fuel shutoff valve (C, **Figure 55**). Label each hose and fitting on the shutoff valve.

NOTE
The fuel shutoff valve is directional. Note that the larger side of the valve sits beneath the clamp. The fuel shutoff valve must be reinstalled with this same orientation.

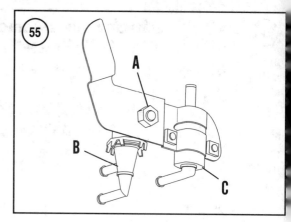

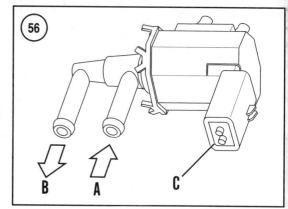

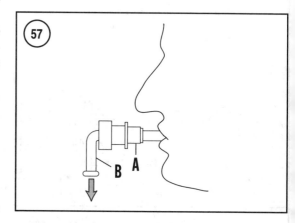

3. Remove the screws securing the valve clamp, and then remove the fuel shutoff valve (C, **Figure 55**) from the bracket.

4. Test the fuel shutoff valve by performing the following:

a. Blow into the port (A, **Figure 57**) on the smaller side of the valve. Air should flow out of the port (B, **Figure 57**) on the larger side of the valve.

b. Reverse the valve and blow into port B. Air should not flow from port A.

c. Replace the valve if it fails either portion of this test.

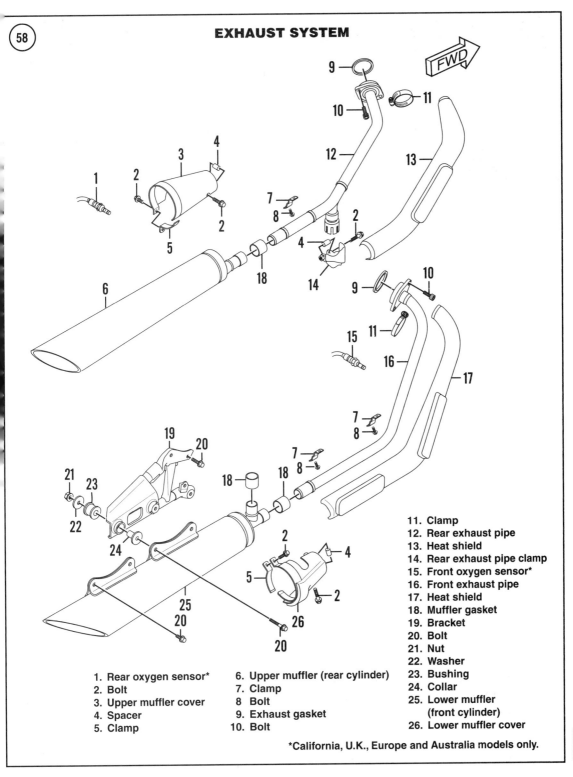

EXHAUST SYSTEM

FWD

1. Rear oxygen sensor*
2. Bolt
3. Upper muffler cover
4. Spacer
5. Clamp
6. Upper muffler (rear cylinder)
7. Clamp
8. Bolt
9. Exhaust gasket
10. Bolt
11. Clamp
12. Rear exhaust pipe
13. Heat shield
14. Rear exhaust pipe clamp
15. Front oxygen sensor*
16. Front exhaust pipe
17. Heat shield
18. Muffler gasket
19. Bracket
20. Bolt
21. Nut
22. Washer
23. Bushing
24. Collar
25. Lower muffler
   (front cylinder)
26. Lower muffler cover

*California, U.K., Europe and Australia models only.

5. Install the fuel shutoff valve by reversing the removal steps.

   a. Install the fuel shutoff valve so it is positioned as noted during removal.

   b. Secure each hose to the correct fitting on the fuel shutoff valve.

EXHAUST SYSTEM

Removal/Installation

Refer to **Figure 58**.

Remove and install the exhaust system as described in Chapter Eight. Note the following:

1. On California, U.K., Europe and Australia models, disconnect the 4-pin oxygen sensor connector for each sensor as described in *Heated Oxygen Sensor* (this section of the Supplement) during exhaust system removal.

2. During exhaust system installation, note the following:

    a. Install a new exhaust gasket into each exhaust port.

    b. Apply muffler sealant (Loctite 5920 or an equivalent) to the muffler gaskets during assembly.

    c. When joining the rear exhaust pipe onto the lower muffler, make sure the tang in the rear exhaust pipe clamp (**Figure 58**) engages a slot in the rear exhaust pipe flange.

    d. Assemble the complete exhaust system, but just install the fasteners finger-tight at this time.

    e. Evenly tighten the exhaust header bolts to 23 N•m (17 ft.-lb.).

    f. Moving from front of the exhaust system to the rear, tighten the remaining fasteners securely. Then, tighten the muffler mounting bolts to 23 N•m (17 ft.-lb.).

HEATED OXYGEN (HO₂) SENSOR (CALIFORNIA, U.K., EUROPE AND AUSTRALIA MODELS)

Two heated oxygen sensors are used on these models. The front cylinder oxygen sensor mounts in front cylinder exhaust pipe. The rear cylinder sensor mounts in the upper muffler.

Removal/Installation

1A. When replacing the front cylinder oxygen sensor, perform the following:

    a. Disconnect the sensor's 4-pin electrical connector (A, **Figure 59**), which sits beside the right motor mount.

    b. Loosen, and then remove the sensor (B, **Figure 59**) from the front exhaust pipe.

1B. When replacing the rear cylinder oxygen sensor, perform the following:

    a. Remove the right frame side cover as described in Chapter Sixteen.

    b. Disconnect the 4-pin, rear oxygen sensor connector (C, **Figure 53**). Note how the wire is routed through the motorcycle.

    c. Remove the rear muffler-cover clamp bolt (**Figure 60**). Release the clamp from the cover hook, and remove the clamp (**Figure 61**) from the cover.

    d. Remove the forward clamp bolt (**Figure 62**) from the upper muffler cover. This bolt also functions as the upper muffler clamp bolt. Watch for the spacer between the arms of the forward clamp.

    e. Rotate the upper muffler cover to expose the oxygen sensor. Loosen and then remove the sensor (**Figure 63**) from the upper muffler.

2. Installation is the reverse of removal. Tighten the oxygen sensor to 25 N•m (18.4 ft.-lb.).

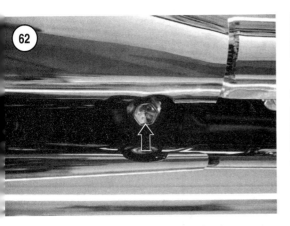

b. For the rear cylinder sensor, check for continuity on the white/blue wire between the sensor connector and the ECM connector (terminal 33).

c. For either front or rear sensor, check for continuity on the black/brown wire between the sensor connector and the ECM connector (terminal 12).

7. Continuity should exist during each portion of this test. If continuity is not found in a test, that wire has a break in it.

Sensor Continuity Test

1. Turn off the ignition switch.
2. Locate the relevant HO_2 sensor connector as described in this section, and then disconnect the 4-pin connector.
3. Perform the following continuity tests in the harness side of the connector:
   a. Check for continuity between the white/blue terminal (rear cylinder sensor) and a good ground or between the white/green terminal (front cylinder sensor) and a good ground.
   b. Check for continuity between the white/blue and black/brown terminals (rear cylinder sensor) or between the white/green and black/brown terminals (front cylinder sensor).
4. Continuity should not exist during any of these tests. If continuity is found during one or both tests, the circuit is shorted to ground.
5. Disconnect the electrical connector from the ECM and disconnect the connector for the relevant sensor.
6. Refer to **Figure 50** and perform the following continuity tests in the harness side of each connector:
   a. For the front cylinder sensor, check for continuity on the white/green wire between the sensor connector and the ECM connector (terminal 6).

Sensor Output Voltage Test

1. Securely support the motorcycle on a level surface.
2. Locate the relevant oxygen sensor connector as described in this section of the Supplement.
3. Start the engine and let it warm to operating temperature.
4. Back probe the sensor side of the relevant oxygen sensor connector, and measure the output voltage between the black and gray wires while the engine idles.
5. The voltage should be within the specification listed in **Table 4**.
6. If the voltage at idle is within specification, use a clamp to pinch off the PAIR hose (**Figure 64**) at the air box.
7. With the engine running at 5000 rpm, measure the sensor output voltage between the black and gray wires. The voltage should be within the specification listed in **Table 4**.

Heater Resistance Test

1. Turn off the ignition switch.
2. Locate the relevant oxygen sensor as described in this section of the Supplement. Then, disconnect the connector.

17

NOTE
Ambient air temperature greatly affects the resistance value of the sensor's heater. The sensor must be at ambient air temperature to yield an accurate resistance measurement.

3. Measure the resistance between both white terminals in the sensor side of the connector.
4. The resistance must be within the range in **Table 4**.

Heater Input Voltage Test

1. Locate the relevant oxygen sensor connector as described in this section of the Supplement.
2. Back probe the harness side of the oxygen sensor connector, and connect the positive test probe of a multimeter to the orange/white wire in the sensor connector.
3. Connect the negative test probe to a good ground.
4. Turn the ignition switch on, and measure the input voltage. It should equal battery voltage.

Table 4 FUEL SYSTEM (EFI) SPECIFICATIONS

Item	Specification
Fast idle speed	1800 rpm (when engine cold)
Fuel injector resistance	9.5-11.5 ohms @ 20° C (68° F)
Heated oxygen sensor	
Sensor output voltage @ idle	0.3 volts or less
Sensor output @ 5,000 rpm	0.6 volts or more
Heater resistance	6.7-9.5 volts @ 23° C (73.4° F)
ISC valve resistance	Approx. 80 ohms at 20° C (68° F)
Purge control solenoid valve resistance	Approx. 32 ohms @ 20° C (68° F)
Throttle body bore size	34 mm
Throttle body No.	
All models except California	41F2
California models	41F3
Throttle cable free play	2.0-4.0 mm (0.08-0.16 in.)

Table 5 FUEL AND EXHAUST SYSTEMS TORQUE SPECIFICATIONS

Item	N•m	in.-lb.	ft.-lb.
Exhaust header bolts	23	–	17
Fuel rail screw	3.5	31	–
Heated oxygen sensor	25	–	18.4
ISC valve retainer screw	2.1	18.5	–
Muffler mounting bolts	23	–	17
Straight plug retainer screw	5	44	–

CHAPTER TEN

ELECTRICAL SYSTEM

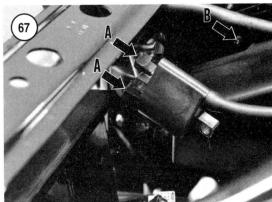

ELECTRONIC IGNITION SYSTEM

Ignition Coil

California, U.K., Europe and Australia models use two ignition coils per cylinder: a main coil and a sub coil. The front cylinder ignition coils sit inside the frame head, just above the front cylinder head. The rear cylinder ignition coils are found beneath the battery box on the left side of the frame.

Removal/installation

1. Disconnect the negative battery cable (Chapter Three).
2A. When removing a front cylinder ignition coil, perform the following:
   a. Remove the fuel tank as described in the Chapter Nine section of this Supplement.

b. Remove the frame head side covers (Chapter Sixteen).
c. Disconnect the connectors (**Figure 65**) from the ignition coil terminals, and disconnect the spark plug lead from the relevant spark plug.
d. Remove the ignition coil bolts, and then lower the ignition coil from the front ignition coil protector. Watch for the spacer behind each bolt.
2B. When removing a rear cylinder ignition coil, perform the following:
   a. Remove the battery box as described in the Chapter Sixteen section of this Supplement.
   b. Remove the ignition coil bolts (**Figure 66**), and lower the ignition coil from the rear ignition coil bracket. Watch for the spacer behind each bolt.
   c. Disconnect the connectors (A, **Figure 67**) from the ignition coil terminals, and then disconnect the spark plug lead from the relevant spark plug.
3. Install by reversing the removal procedures. Note the following:
   a. Securely fit the spacers into the holes of the front ignition coil protector (**Figure 68**) or the rear ignition coil bracket (B, **Figure 67**). Make sure a spacer is not squeezed between the frame and the protector or between the frame and bracket.
   b. Tighten the ignition coil bolts to 4.5 N•m (40 in.-lb.).
   c. Make sure all electrical connections are corrosion-free and secure.

17

Testing

Perform the ignition coil *Primary Peak Voltage Test* and the *Resistance Test* as described in Chapter Ten. Use the test terminals indicated in **Table 7** when performing these tests.

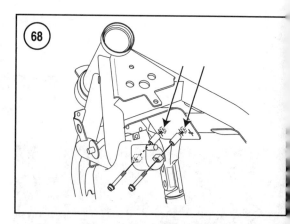

SPEEDOMETER

Removal/Installation

1. Disconnect the negative battery cable (Chapter Three).
2. Remove the speedometer bolt (**Figure 69**).
3. Slide the speedometer forward until it is released from the tank mount, and lift up the meter.
4. Disconnect the electrical connector (**Figure 70**) from the speedometer, and remove the meter.
5. If necessary, disassemble the speedometer (**Figure 71**) as described in Chapter Ten.
6. Installation is the reverse of removal. Tighten the speedometer bolt (**Figure 69**) securely.

Fuel Level Indicator Testing

1. Securely support the motorcycle on a level surface with the sidestand raised.
2. Remove the fuel tank as described in the Chapter Nine section of this Supplement.
3. Reconnect the speedometer connector (**Figure 70**) to the speedometer.
4. Connect a resistor across the yellow/black and the black/white terminals in the harness side of the 4-pin fuel pump connector (**Figure 72**). Refer to **Table 6** to select an appropriate resistor.
5. Turn the ignition switch on. After approximately 26 seconds, the fuel level indicator (**Figure 73**) should display the number of bars indicated in **Table 6**.
6. Repeat the test procedure with the remaining resistance values.
7. Replace the speedometer if the indicator does not display the correct number of bars for a given resistance.

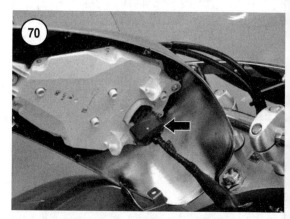

LIGHTING SYSTEM

Taillight/Brake Light Replacement

Refer to **Figure 74**.

The taillight/brake light uses LEDs which cannot be replaced. If the LEDs are burned out, replace the taillight/brake light assembly.

1. Disconnect the negative battery cable as described in Chapter Three.
2. Remove the rear wheel (Chapter Twelve).

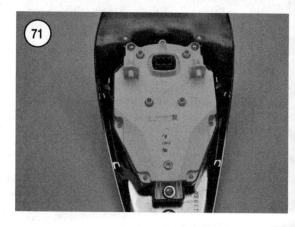

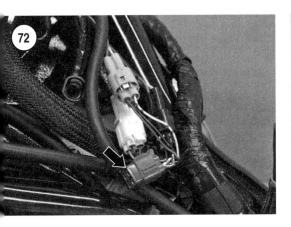

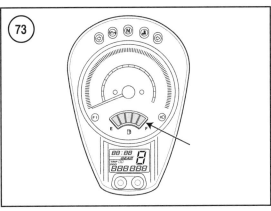

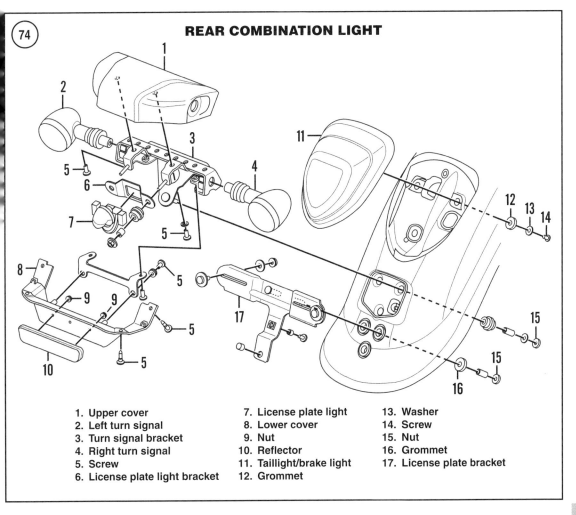

REAR COMBINATION LIGHT

1. Upper cover
2. Left turn signal
3. Turn signal bracket
4. Right turn signal
5. Screw
6. License plate light bracket
7. License plate light
8. Lower cover
9. Nut
10. Reflector
11. Taillight/brake light
12. Grommet
13. Washer
14. Screw
15. Nut
16. Grommet
17. License plate bracket

3. From beneath the rear fender, remove each tail-light/brake light screw and washer.

4. Pull the taillight/brake light assembly away from the rear fender. Disconnect the 3-pin connector from the light assembly, and remove the assembly.

5. Installation is the reverse of removal. Note the following:

    a. Make sure each grommet is securely in place in the fender. Replace a grommet as needed.

    b. Tighten the taillight/brake light screws securely.

License Plate Bulb Replacement

1. Remove the lens from the license plate light (**Figure 74**)

2. Pull the bulb from the socket, and press in the new bulb.

3. Reinstall the lens.

17

Table 6 ELECTRICAL SYSTEM SPECIFICATIONS

Item	Specification
Fuel level indicator resistance	
Five bars (tank full)	Less than 13 ohms
Four bars	21-64 ohms
Three bars	76-115
Two bars	129-187 ohms
One bar or one flickering bar	More than 203 ohms

Table 7 IGNITION COIL TEST TERMINALS

Item	Positive terminal	Negative terminal
U.S. and Canada models		
Front cylinder ignition coil	Black/yellow	Orange/white
Rear cylinder ignition coil	Black/blue	Orange/white
California, U.K., Europe and Australia models		
Front cylinder main ignition coil	Black/yellow	Orange/white
Front cylinder sub ignition coil	White	Orange/white
Rear cylinder main ignition coil	Black/blue	Orange/white
Rear cylinder sub ignition coil	Black/red	Orange/white

Table 8 ELECTRICAL SYSTEM TORQUE SPECIFICATIONS

Item	N•m	in.-lb.	ft.-lb.
Ignition coil mounting bolt	4.5	40	–

CHAPTER SIXTEEN

BODY AND FRAME

BATTERY BOX

Removal/Installation

1. Remove the battery as described in Chapter Three.

2. Disconnect the rear light sub-harness connector (A, **Figure 75**).

3. Remove the battery box screws (B, **Figure 75**).

4. Lift the battery box, and carefully move it past the starter relay, rear light sub-harness and other components. Note how all items are routed through the battery box.

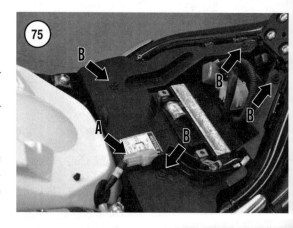

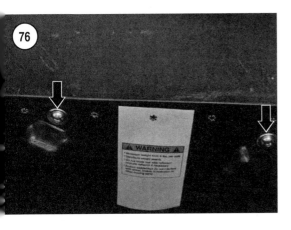

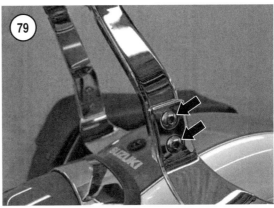

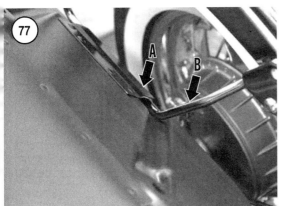

3. Lift the saddlebag until its mounting flange (A, **Figure 77**) clears the bracket (B), and remove the saddlebag.

4. If necessary, remove the bolts (A, **Figure 78**), and lower the saddlebag bracket (B) from the frame brace.

5. To remove the backrest, remove the mounting bolts (**Figure 79**) from each side. Then, lift the backrest from between the frame braces.

6. Installation is the reverse of removal. Tighten the saddlebag screws (**Figure 76**), saddlebag bracket bolts (A, **Figure 78**) and backrest mounting bolts (**Figure 79**) securely.

5. Installation is the reverse of removal. Tighten the battery box screws securely.

SADDLEBAGS AND BACKREST

Removal/Installation

1. Open the lid on the saddlebag.
2. Remove each screw (**Figure 76**) and washer. Note that the large washer sits against the leather.

WINDSHIELD

1. While an assistant holds the windshield, remove the bracket bolts (**Figure 80**) from each side.
2. Lift the windshield and vertical bracket assembly from the windshield mounting brace, and remove the windshield.
3. Installation is the reverse of removal. Tighten the windshield bracket bolts securely.

17

INDEX

18

18

T

18

WIRING
DIAGRAMS

2001-2002 U.S., CANADA AND 2001-2003 AUSTRALIA MODELS

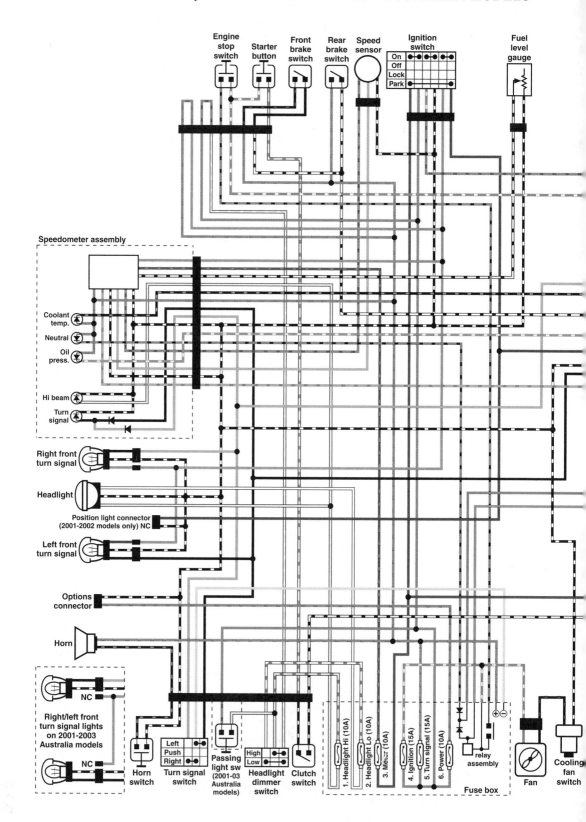

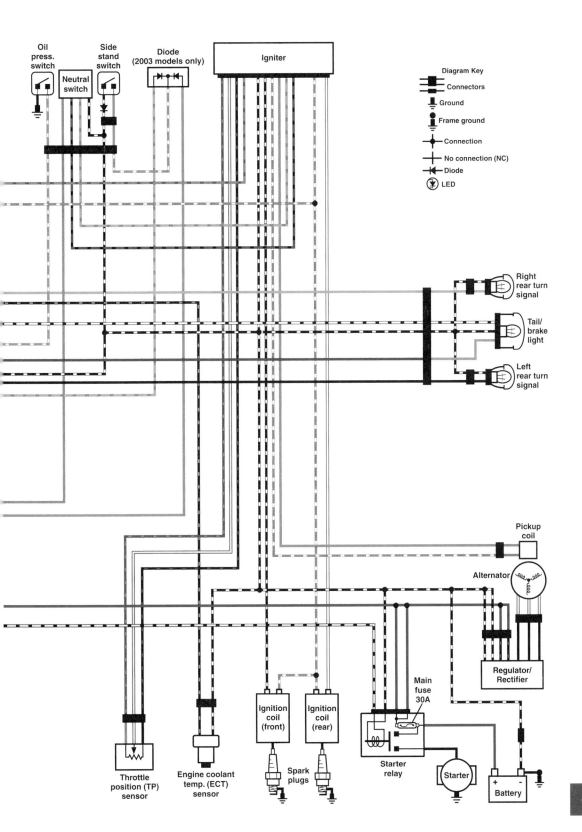

19

2001-2002 UK AND EU MODELS

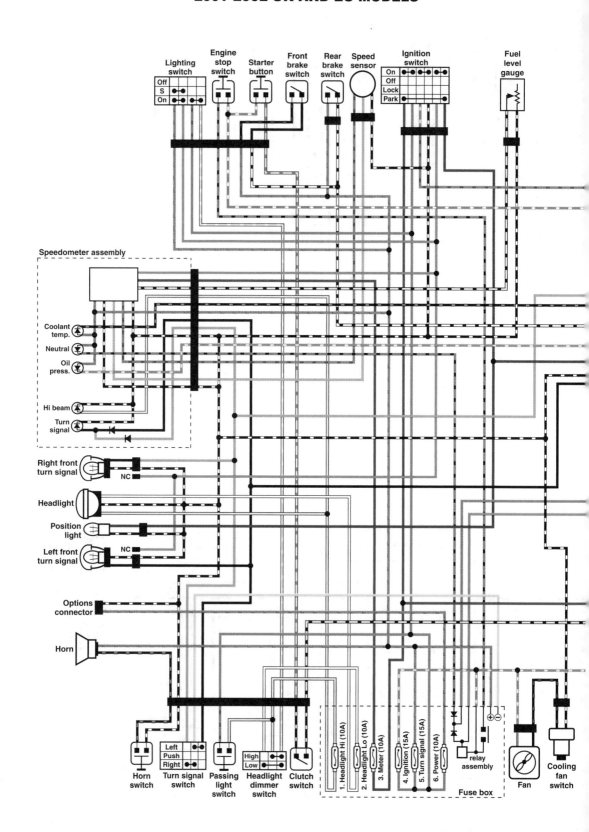

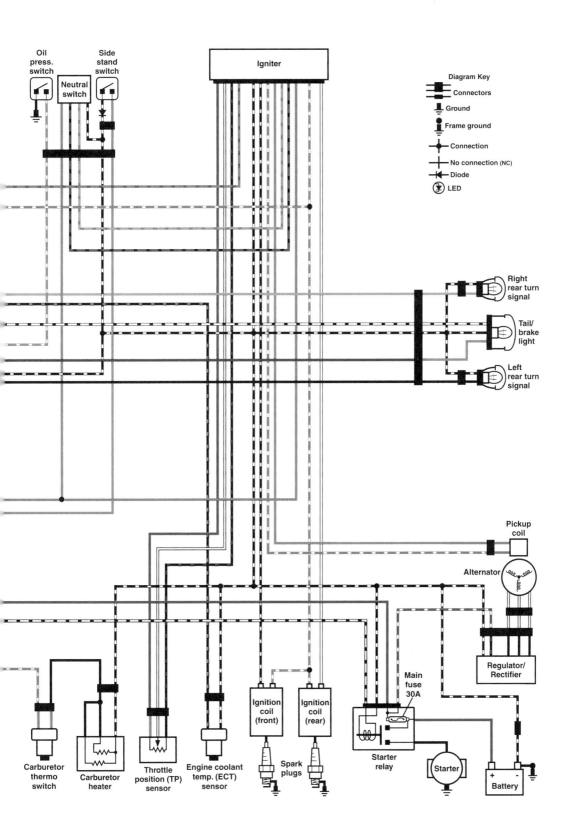

19

2003-2004 U.S. CANADA, AND 2004 AUSTRALIA MODELS

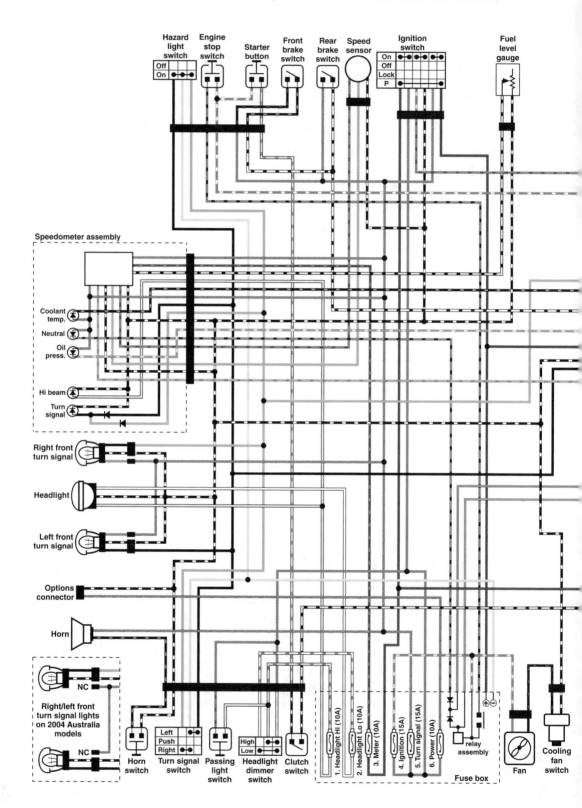

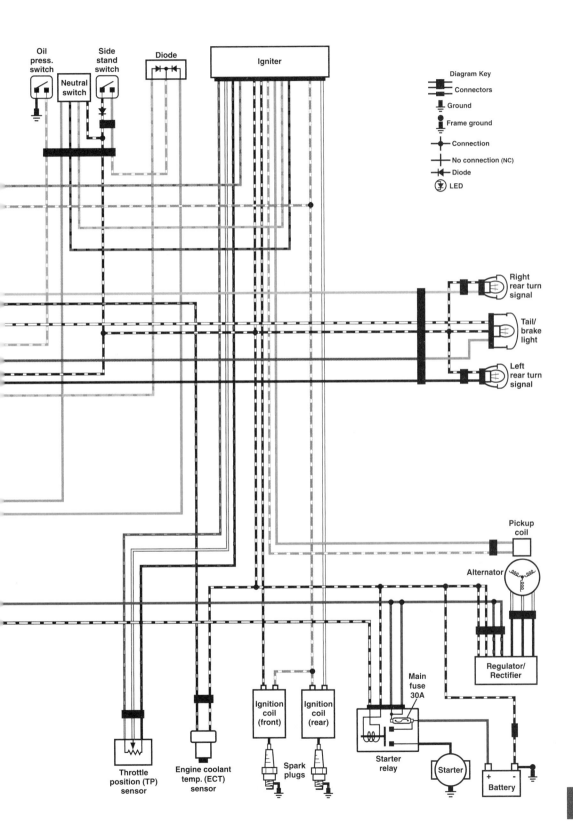

19

2003-2004 UK AND EU MODELS

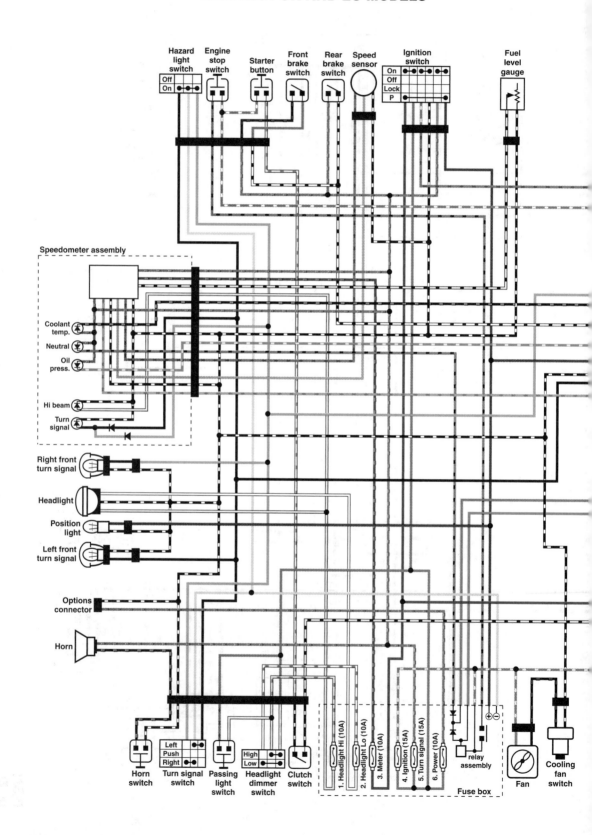

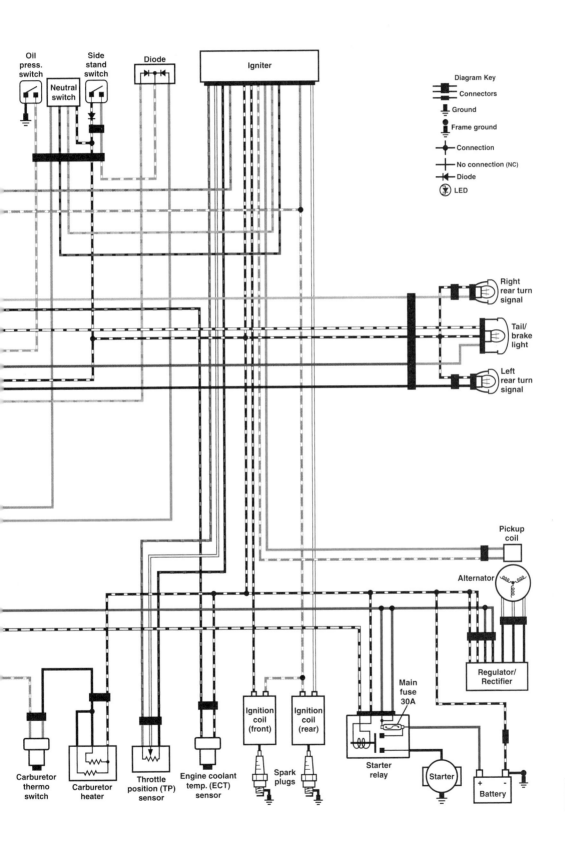

Oil press. switch

Side stand switch

Neutral switch

Diode

Igniter

Diagram Key

Connectors

Ground

Frame ground

Connection

No connection (NC)

Diode

LED

Right rear turn signal

Tail/ brake light

Left rear turn signal

Pickup coil

Alternator

Regulator/ Rectifier

Main fuse 30A

Carburetor thermo switch

Carburetor heater

Throttle position (TP) sensor

Engine coolant temp. (ECT) sensor

Ignition coil (front)

Ignition coil (rear)

Spark plugs

Starter relay

Starter

Battery

19

2005-2006 US AND CANADA MODELS

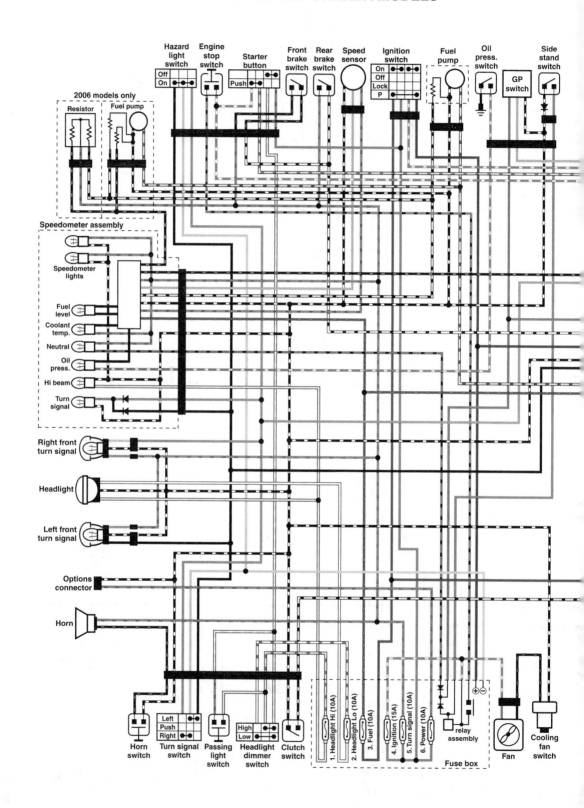

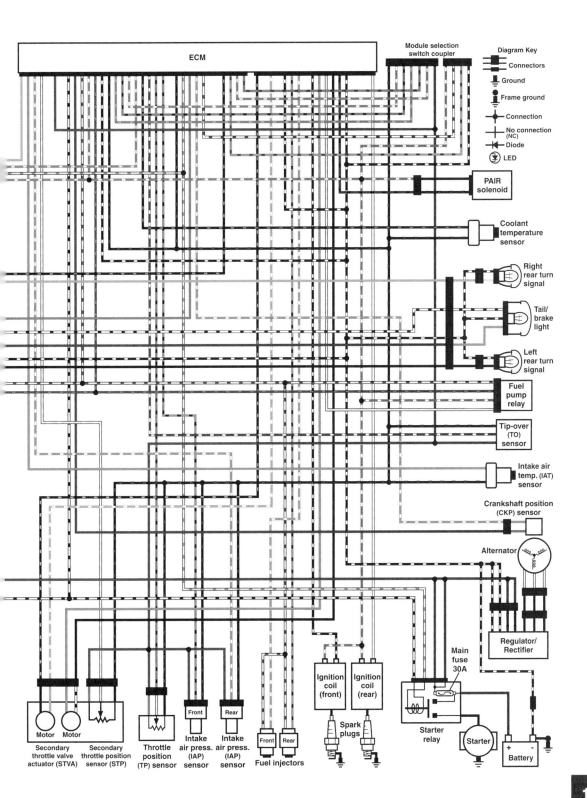

2005-2006 UK, EU AND AUSTRALIA MODELS

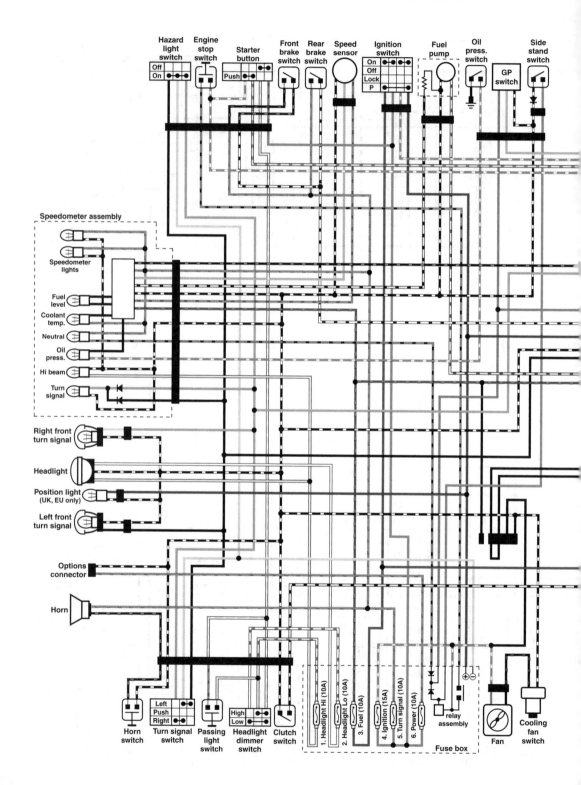

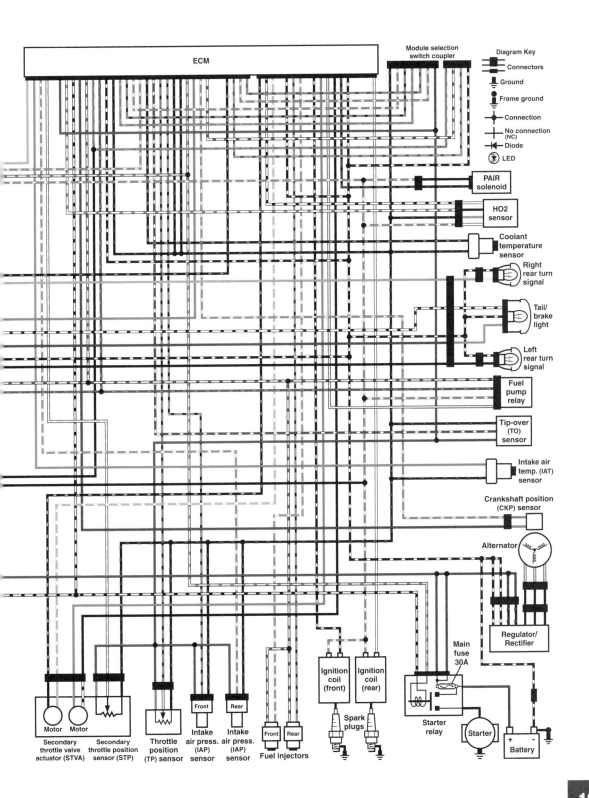

2007-2008 US AND CANADA MODELS

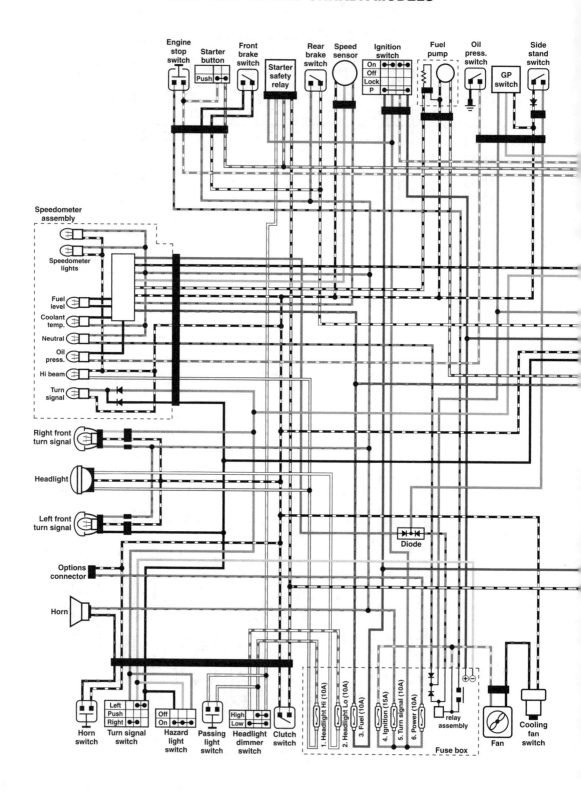

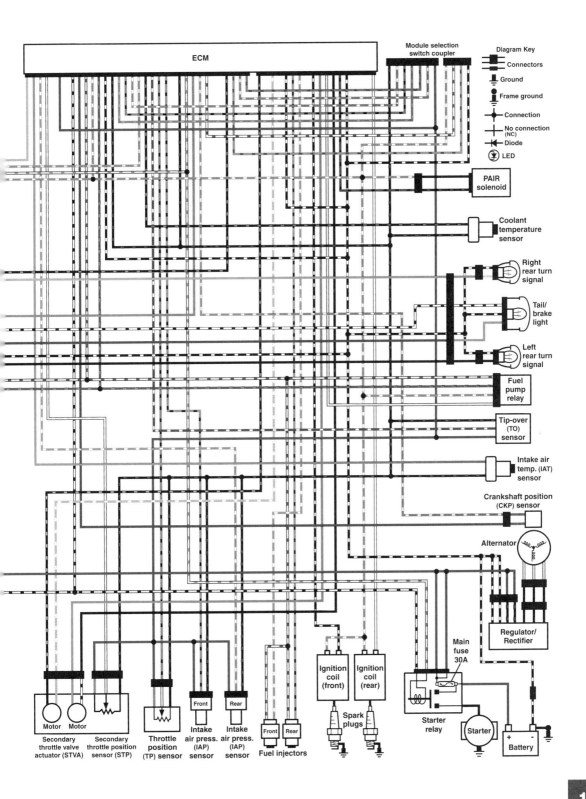

2007-2008 UK, EU AND AUSTRALIA MODELS

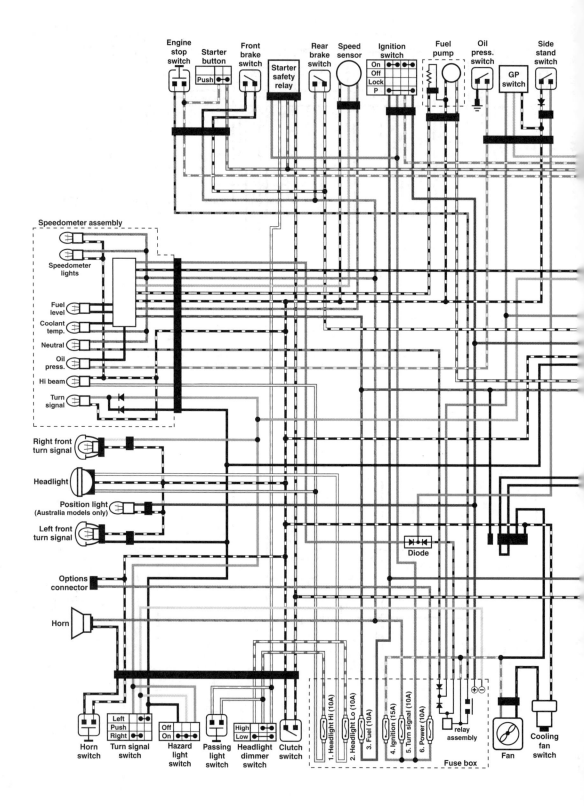

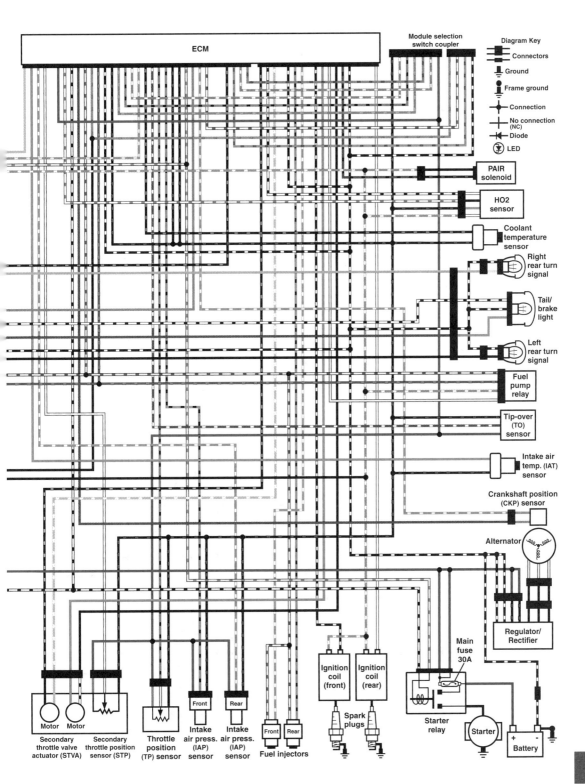

19

2009-ON VL800 (C50) U.S. AND CANADA MODELS

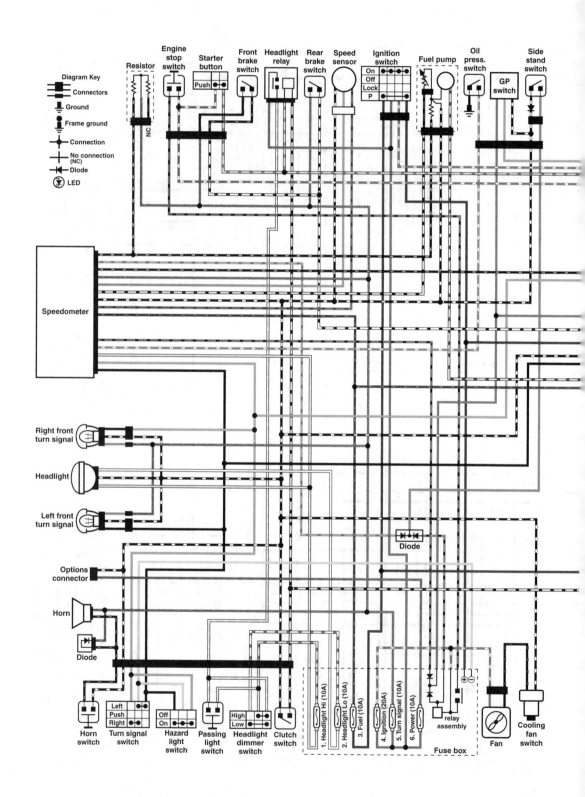

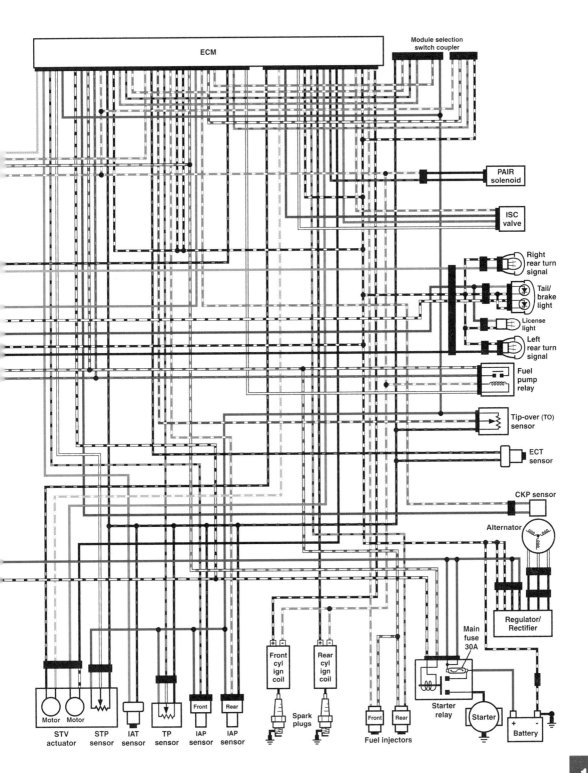

2009-ON VL800 (C50) CALIFORNIA MODELS

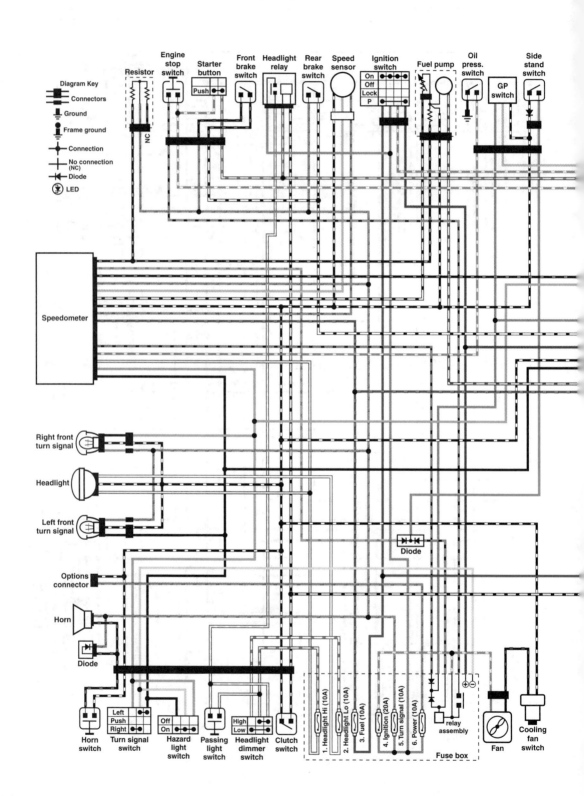

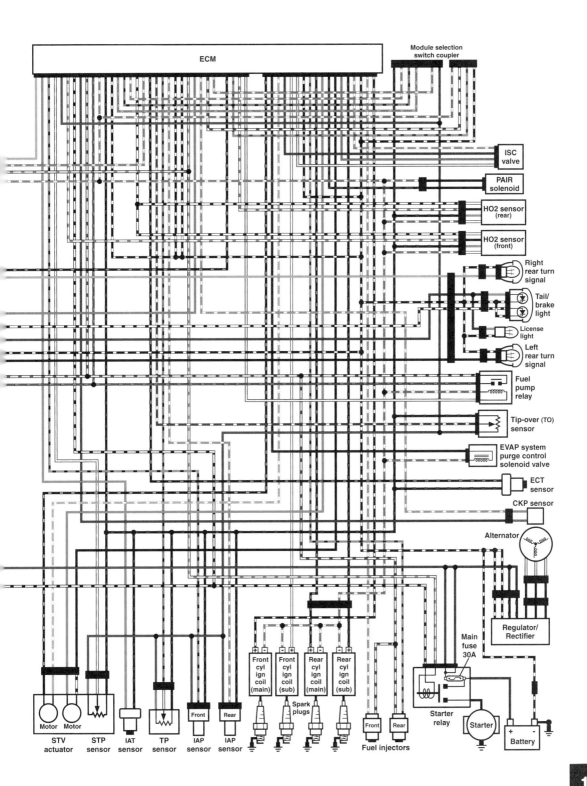

MAINTENANCE LOG

Date	Miles	Type of Service